PROFESSIONAL
VISUAL STUDIO® 2017

D1192610

Continues

PROFESSIONAL

Visual Studio® 2017

PROFESSIONAL

Visual Studio® 2017

Bruce Johnson

wrox™

A Wiley Brand

Professional Visual Studio® 2017

Published by
John Wiley & Sons, Inc.
10475 Crosspoint Boulevard
Indianapolis, IN 46256
www.wiley.com

Copyright © 2018 by John Wiley & Sons, Inc., Indianapolis, Indiana

Published simultaneously in Canada

ISBN: 978-1-119-40458-3
ISBN: 978-1-119-40460-6 (ebk)
ISBN: 978-1-119-40459-0 (ebk)

Manufactured in the United States of America

10 9 8 7 6 5 4 3 2 1

For general information on our other products and services please contact our Customer Care Department within the United States at (877) 762-2974, outside the United States at (317) 572-3993 or fax (317) 572-4002.

Wiley publishes in a variety of print and electronic formats and by print-on-demand. Some material included with standard print versions of this book may not be included in e-books or in print-on-demand. If this book refers to media such as a CD or DVD that is not included in the version you purchased, you may download this material at http://booksupport .wiley.com. For more information about Wiley products, visit www.wiley.com.

Library of Congress Control Number: 2017953997

I'd like to thank my four children, Kyle, Cameron, Gillian, and Curtis, for their love and support. All the kids are teenagers now, so they were quite happy to leave me alone to write as much as I needed. And this time around, some of them can drive. As a result, leaving me alone was even less demanding on them than it has been for past books. They are my loves and my life would be much less rich without them.

ABOUT THE AUTHOR

BRUCE JOHNSON is a partner at ObjectSharp Consulting and a 30-year veteran of the computer industry. The first third of his career was spent doing "real work," otherwise known as coding in the UNIX world. But for 20 years, he has been working on projects that are at the leading edge of Windows technology, from rich client applications to web applications and APIs, with a sprinkling of database and front-end development thrown in for good measure.

As well as having fun with building systems, Bruce has spoken hundreds of times at conferences and user groups throughout North America. He has been a Microsoft Certified Trainer (MCT) and the co-president of the Metro Toronto .NET User Group. He has also written columns and articles for numerous magazines. For all of this activity, Bruce was also a Microsoft MVP for more than ten years. At the moment, he's already working on the outline for his next book. Because why not?

ABOUT THE TECHNICAL EDITOR

JOHN MUELLER is a freelance author and technical editor. He has writing in his blood, having produced 104 books and more than 600 articles to date. The topics range from networking to artificial intelligence to database management to heads-down programming and beyond. Some of his current works include a book about machine learning, a couple of Python books, and a book about MATLAB. He has also written *AWS for Admins for Dummies*, which provides administrators with a great place to start with AWS, and *AWS for Developers for Dummies*, the counterpart for developers. His technical editing skills have helped more than 70 authors refine the content of their manuscripts. John has always been interested in development and has written about a wide variety of languages, including a highly successful C++ book. Be sure to read John's blog at http://blog .johnmuellerbooks.com. You can reach John on the Internet at John@JohnMuellerBooks.com.

CREDITS

SENIOR ACQUISITIONS EDITOR
Kenyon Brown

PROJECT EDITOR
Kelly Talbot

TECHNICAL EDITOR
John Mueller

PRODUCTION EDITOR
Athiyappan Lalith Kumar

COPY EDITOR
Kelly Talbot Editing Services

**MANAGER OF CONTENT DEVELOPMENT
AND ASSEMBLY**
Mary Beth Wakefield

PRODUCTION MANAGER
Kathleen Wisor

MARKETING MANAGER
Christie Hilbrich

EXECUTIVE EDITOR
Jim Minatel

PROJECT COORDINATOR, COVER
Brent Savage

PROOFREADER
Nancy Bell

INDEXER
Nancy Guenther

COVER DESIGNER
Wiley

COVER IMAGE
©frantic00/Shutterstock

ACKNOWLEDGMENTS

TO THE OUTSIDE, it might look like the writing of a book is an individual effort. It's not. Not even close. There is no way that this book could have come to fruition without the efforts and assistance of a number of people. The fact that the book is clear, accurate, and useful is because of the contributions of my editor, my technical editor, my copy editor, and the proofreader. And I haven't even gotten to those who are responsible for the production of the final copies. I'm incredibly grateful for everyone's help and have enjoyed working with these very talented people. It's makes the process a lot more enjoyable.

I would especially like to thank everyone at Wrox who has helped me through this process. In particular, thanks go out to Kelly Talbot. This is, if I'm not mistaken, the third or fourth book on which I have worked with Kelly. As always, his attention to detail has prevented a very large number of mistakes. But, more than that, he is not only patient, but diligent in ensuring that I meet my deadlines. Thanks also go to John Mueller, who not only made sure that the technical mistakes I made in my first draft were cleaned up before publication, but also provided some great suggestions that helped me clarify my writing. Finally, thanks to Nancy Bell, who had to slog through what I wrote and convert it to grammatically correct prose. The efforts of all of these individuals are what make the book possible and, hopefully, a success.

CONTENTS

PART II: GETTING STARTED

PART V: WEB APPLICATIONS

CHAPTER 16: ASP.NET WEB FORMS   345

CHAPTER 17: ASP.NET MVC   379

PART VIII: DATA

CHAPTER 26: VISUAL DATABASE TOOLS   551

CHAPTER 27: THE ADO.NET ENTITY FRAMEWORK   571

INTRODUCTION

AS A TOOL FOR DEVELOPERS, Visual Studio stands head and shoulders about its competition. The team responsible for developing Visual Studio has always put the productivity of people who code for a living at the top of their priority list. This version continues this tradition. Visual Studio always incorporates the latest advances in Microsoft's premier programming languages (Visual Basic and C#), as well as adding little tidbits of functionality that are a boon to coders. But at a higher level, Visual Studio 2017 embraces open-source, mobile development, and cloud computing in a variety of ways. Azure is continually introducing new features and products and Visual Studio 2017 integrates seamlessly with them. While, in theory, it is possible to create any .NET application using tools as simple as Notepad and a command-line window, the typical developer would never think to do so. Visual Studio 2017, as was the case with its predecessors, includes a host of improvements and features that are aimed at making the life of a developer easier.

Visual Studio 2017 is an enormous product no matter which way you look at it. It can be intimidating to newcomers and difficult for even experienced .NET developers to find what they need. And that's where this book comes in. *Professional Visual Studio 2017* looks at every major aspect of this developer tool, showing you how to harness each feature and offering advice about how best to utilize the various components effectively. It shows you the building blocks that make up Visual Studio 2017, breaking the user interface down into manageable chunks for you to understand. It then expands on each of these components with additional details about exactly how they work, both in isolation and in conjunction with other parts of Visual Studio 2017, along with tools that are not included in the out-of-the-box product, to make your development efforts even more efficient.

WHO THIS BOOK IS FOR

Professional Visual Studio 2017 is for developers who are new to Visual Studio as well as those programmers who have some experience but want to learn about features they may have previously overlooked.

Even if you are familiar with the way previous versions of Visual Studio worked, you may want to at least skim over Part I. These chapters deal with the basic constructs that make up the user interface. The biggest changes to the building blocks are in the installation process. It is more granular, meaning that you install only what you need and if you don't install a component initially, the installer is only a click or two away. But there are some little additions in functionality, so while you can get by without Part I, some of the changes in Visual Studio 2017 can make you a more efficient developer. And, after all, that's what you're looking to get out of this book.

If you're just starting out, you'll greatly benefit from the first part, where basic concepts are explained and you're introduced to the user interface and how to customize it to suit your own style.

WHAT THIS BOOK COVERS

Microsoft Visual Studio 2017 is arguably the most advanced integrated development environment (IDE) available for programmers today. It is based on a long history of programming languages and interfaces and has been influenced by many different variations on the theme of development environments.

Visual Studio 2017 does not represent a major departure from recent versions. Still, regardless of the type of application you're creating, there are tweaks that have been made—some small, some less so (.NET Core, for example). Familiarity with the changes helps you perform your job better. For this reason, as well as to help newcomers to Visual Studio, this book covers the breadth of the product. Along the way, you will become more familiar and comfortable with the interface.

Visual Studio 2017 comes in several versions: Community, Professional, and Enterprise. The majority of this book deals with the Professional Edition of Visual Studio 2017, but some chapters utilize features found only in the Enterprise edition. If you haven't used this edition before, read through Chapters 38 and 39 for an overview of the features it offers over and above the Professional Edition.

HOW THIS BOOK IS STRUCTURED

This book is divided into 11 parts:

- ➤ **Integrated Development Environment:** This book's first five chapters are dedicated to familiarizing you with the core aspects of Visual Studio 2017, from the IDE structure and layout to the various options and settings you can change to make the user interface synchronize with your own way of doing things.

- ➤ **Getting Started:** In this part, you learn how to take control of your projects and how to organize them in ways that work with your own style.

- ➤ **Digging Deeper:** Though the many graphical components of Visual Studio that make a programmer's job easier are discussed in many places throughout this book, you often need help when you're in the process of actually writing code. This part deals with features that support the coding of applications such as IntelliSense, code refactoring, and creating and running unit tests.

- ➤ **Desktop Applications:** Rich client applications have seen quite a transition within the .NET Framework, moving from Windows Forms applications to Windows Presentation Foundation (WPF) to Universal Windows Applications. Each of these gets its own chapter in this part.

- ➤ **Web Applications:** Web applications have seen even more transitions that Desktop applications. And just like Desktop applications, each of the three different development styles

(ASP.NET Web Forms, ASP.NET MVC, and .NET Core) gets its own chapter. And a couple of new kids on the block, Node.js and Python, are also included in this part.

➤ **Mobile Applications:** There are two different styles of mobile application development that are supported with Visual Studio 2017. Through Xamarin, it's possible to create mobile apps using familiar .NET components. And by using Apache Cordova (formerly PhoneGap), you can target mobile devices using HTML, CSS, and JavaScript.

➤ **Cloud Services:** Visual Studio 2017 supports the cloud in a wide variety of ways. The chapter on Windows Azure looks at how some of the newer features of Azure are integrated into Visual Studio. And the use of synchronization services as a data storage platform is examined, along with how to create apps for SharePoint.

➤ **Data:** A large proportion of applications use some form of data storage. Visual Studio 2017 and the .NET Framework include strong support for working with databases and other data sources. This part examines how to the Visual Database Tools, and ADO.NET Entity Framework to build applications that work with data. It also shows you how you how to take advantage of a couple of new functions within Azure to support data warehouse construction and data analytics.

➤ **Debugging:** Application debugging is one of the more challenging tasks developers have to tackle, but correct use of the Visual Studio 2017 debugging features will help you analyze the state of the application and determine the cause of any bugs. This part examines the debugging support provided by the IDE.

➤ **Build and Deployment:** In addition to discussing how to build your solutions effectively and get applications into the hands of your end users, this part also deals with the process of upgrading your projects from previous versions.

➤ **Visual Studio Editions:** The final part of the book examines the additional features only available in the Enterprise version of Visual Studio 2017. In addition, you'll also learn how Visual Studio Team Services provides an essential tool for managing software projects.

Though this breakdown of the Visual Studio feature set provides the most logical and easily understood set of topics, you may need to look for specific functions that will aid you in a particular activity. To address this need, references to appropriate chapters are provided whenever a feature is covered in more detail elsewhere in the book.

As Visual Studio has grown over the years, the size of earlier versions of this book had grown to the point where it was unwieldy. And there were even more features with Visual Studio 2017. So to avoid a book whose size would be pushing 2,000 pages, we took a number of the chapters from earlier editions of Visual Studio and put them into an online archive. These chapters contain features that have not been changed or enhanced in Visual Studio 2017. As such, the instructions found therein will apply, in general, if you're trying to use them in Visual Studio 2017. You can find the online archive on www.wrox.com.

WHAT YOU NEED TO USE THIS BOOK

To use this book effectively, you'll need only one additional item — Microsoft Visual Studio 2017 Professional Edition. With this software installed and the information found in this book, you'll be able to get a handle on how to use Visual Studio 2017 effectively in a very short period of time. In order to be able to follow along with all of the examples in the book, you'll want to be sure to install the following workloads during your Visual Studio 2017 installation (as discussed in Chapter 1):

- ➤ Universal Windows Platform

- ➤ .NET desktop development

- ➤ ASP.NET and web development

- ➤ Azure development

- ➤ Node.js development

- ➤ Data storage and processing

- ➤ Data science and analytical applications

- ➤ Mobile development with .NET

- ➤ Mobile development with Javascript

- ➤ .NET code cross-platform development

This book assumes that you are familiar with the traditional programming model, and it uses both the C# and Visual Basic (VB) languages to illustrate features within Visual Studio 2017. In addition, it is assumed that you can understand the code listings without an explanation of basic programming concepts in either language. If you're new to programming and want to learn Visual Basic, please take a look at *Beginning Visual Basic 2015* by Bryan Newsome. Similarly, if you are after a great book on C#, track down *Beginning C# 6 Programming with Visual Studio 2015* by Benjamin Perkins, Jacob Vibe Hammer, and Jon D. Reid.

Some chapters discuss additional products and tools that work in conjunction with Visual Studio. The following are all available to download either on a trial basis or for free:

- ➤ **Code Snippet Editor:** This is a third-party tool developed for creating code snippets in VB. The Snippet Editor tool is discussed in Chapter 8.

- ➤ **SQL Server 2016:** The installation of Visual Studio 2017 includes an install of SQL Server 2016 Express, enabling you to build applications that use database files. However, for more comprehensive enterprise solutions, you can use a full SQL Server 2016 instead.

- ➤ **Visual Studio 2017 Enterprise Edition:** This more advanced version of Visual Studio introduces tools for other parts of the development process such as testing and design. They are discussed in Chapters 38-39.

➤ **Team Foundation Server or Team Foundation Service:** The server product (or the cloud-based equivalent) that provides application lifecycle management throughout Visual Studio 2017. This is covered in Chapter 40.

➤ **Windows 7, Windows 8, or Windows 10:** Visual Studio 2015 is compatible with Windows 7 SP1, and 8.1, and, of course, Windows 10. It can produce applications that run on Windows XP, Windows Vista, Windows 7, Windows 8, and Windows 10.

CONVENTIONS

To help you get the most from the text and keep track of what's happening, we've used a number of conventions throughout the book.

> **WARNING** *Boxes like this one hold important, not-to-be forgotten information that is directly relevant to the surrounding text.*

> **NOTE** *Notes, tips, hints, tricks, and asides to the current discussion are offset and placed in italics like this.*

As for styles in the text:

➤ We *highlight* new terms and important words when we introduce them.

➤ We show URLs and code within the text like so: `persistence.properties`.

➤ We present code in the following way:

```
We use a monofont type for code examples.
We use bold to emphasize code that is particularly important in the present context
or to show changes from a previous code snippet.
```

SOURCE CODE

As you work through the examples in this book, you may choose either to type in all the code manually or to use the source code files that accompany the book. All the source code used in this book is available for download at `www.wrox.com`.

You can also search for the book at `www.wrox.com` by ISBN (the ISBN for this book is 978-1-119-40458-3) to find the code. And a complete list of code downloads for all current Wrox books is available at `www.wrox.com/dynamic/books/download.aspx`.

> **NOTE** *Because many books have similar titles, you may find it easiest to search by ISBN; this book's ISBN is 978-1-119-40458-3.*

Alternately, you can go to the main Wrox code download page at `www.wrox.com/dynamic/books/download.aspx` to see the code available for this book and all other Wrox books.

Most of the code on `www.wrox.com` is compressed in a .ZIP, .RAR archive, or similar archive format appropriate to the platform. Once you download the code, just decompress it with your favorite compression tool.

ERRATA

We make every effort to ensure that there are no errors in the text or in the code. However, no one is perfect, and mistakes do occur. If you find an error in one of our books, like a spelling mistake or faulty piece of code, we would be very grateful for your feedback. By sending in errata you may save another reader hours of frustration and at the same time you will be helping us provide even higher quality information.

To find the errata page for this book, go to `www.wrox.com` and locate the title using the Search box or one of the title lists. Then, on the Book Search Results page, click the Errata link. On this page you can view all errata that has been submitted for this book and posted by Wrox editors.

> **NOTE** *a complete book list including links to errata is also available at* `www.wrox.com/misc-pages/booklist.shtml`.

If you don't spot "your" error on the Errata page, click the Errata Form link and complete the form to send us the error you have found. We'll check the information and, if appropriate, post a message to the book's errata page and fix the problem in subsequent editions of the book.

P2P.WROX.COM

For author and peer discussion, join the P2P forums at `p2p.wrox.com`. The forums are a web-based system for you to post messages relating to Wrox books and related technologies and interact with other readers and technology users. The forums offer a subscription feature to email you topics of interest of your choosing when new posts are made to the forums. Wrox authors, editors, other industry experts, and your fellow readers are present on these forums.

At `http://p2p.wrox.com` you will find a number of different forums that will help you, not only as you read this book, but also as you develop your own applications. To join the forums, just follow these steps:

1. Go to `p2p.wrox.com` and click the Register link.

2. Read the terms of use and click Agree.

3. Complete the required information to join as well as any optional information you wish to provide and click Submit.

4. You will receive an e-mail with information describing how to verify your account and complete the joining process.

> **NOTE** *You can read messages in the forums without joining P2P but in order to post your own messages, you must join.*

Once you join, you can post new messages and respond to messages other users post. You can read messages at any time on the Web. If you would like to have new messages from a particular forum emailed to you, click the Subscribe to this Forum icon by the forum name in the forum listing.

For more information about how to use the Wrox P2P, be sure to read the P2P FAQs for answers to questions about how the forum software works as well as many common questions specific to P2P and Wrox books. To read the FAQs, click the FAQ link on any P2P page.

PROFESSIONAL

Visual Studio® 2017

PART I
Integrated Development Environment

1

A Quick Tour

WHAT'S IN THIS CHAPTER?

- ➤ Installing and getting started with Visual Studio 2017
- ➤ Creating and running your first application
- ➤ Debugging and deploying an application

Ever since software has been developed, there has been a need for tools to help write, compile, debug, and deploy applications. Microsoft Visual Studio 2017 is the next iteration in the continual evolution of a best-of-breed integrated development environment (IDE).

This chapter introduces the Visual Studio 2017 user experience and shows you how to work with the various menus, toolbars, and windows. It serves as a quick tour of the IDE, and as such it doesn't go into detail about what settings can be changed or how to go about customizing the layout because these topics are explored in the following chapters.

GETTING STARTED

Recent versions of Visual Studio have seen incremental improvements in the installation experience. However, Visual Studio 2017 has pretty much completely revamped the installation options and workflow. It has been designed to not only get you up and running quickly, but also to easily select only those options you need to have installed. This section walks you through the installation process and getting started with the IDE.

Installing Visual Studio 2017

The installer for Visual Studio 2017 is what Microsoft calls a "low-impact installer." The idea arose as Microsoft compared the footprint used by Visual Studio 2015 with the kinds of experiences that users were not only requesting, but also using. As surprising as it might seem, not every developer needs to have Visual Studio support for Windows Forms, ASP.NET, WPF, Universal Apps, and C++ out of the box.

Visual Studio 2015 and earlier versions were optimized so that pressing F5 to run a program would work out of the box. It wasn't expected that you would need to install any other components in order to get the large majority of .NET applications running. While this was a definite plus regarding ease of use, it made for a large (some might say bloated) footprint for Visual Studio.

In Visual Studio 2017, the installation process takes a different point of view. Instead of automatically installing "everything," you get to pick and choose the different components that you want to install. Yes, you had a little bit of that in the past, but now the number of options that you have is greatly increased. However, more options doesn't necessarily mean a better installation experience. In fact, it's probably the opposite, as you try to figure out which of a hundred different options you need to install to work on your project. To address that challenge, the Visual Studio 2017 installer uses the concept of workloads.

When you launch the Visual Studio 2017 installation process (an application of only a couple of megabytes in size), you'll see the dialog in Figure 1-1 appear relatively quickly. Naturally, this is after you have read (in great detail, of course) and accepted the licensing information and privacy statements.

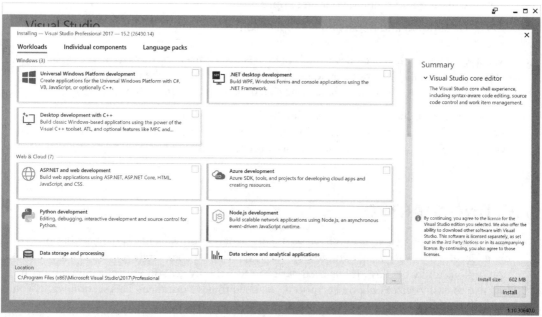

FIGURE 1-1

This is the main hub for the installer and the location where the desired components are specified. There are two modes for identifying the components. In Figure 1-1, you are looking at the workloads. The workloads have been divided into five different categories. To include a workload in the installation, simply click on it, showing a blue checkbox in the top right corner. You can add any number of the workloads as part of the installation. The available workloads are:

➤ **Universal Windows Platform development:** Used if you are creating applications for the Universal Windows Platform, regardless of your language of choice.

➤ **.NET desktop development:** Allows you to create applications, using either WPF or Windows Forms. This is also where you find the Console application template.

➤ **Desktop development with C++:** Used to build classic Windows-based applications. This option is appropriate if you expect to be using Visual C++, the Active Template Library (ATL), or Microsoft Foundation Classes (MFC).

➤ **ASP.NET and web development:** Adds the components used to build web applications, including ASP.NET, ASP.NET Core, and plain old HTML/Javascript/CSS.

➤ **Azure development:** Includes the Azure SDK, tools, and project templates that allow you to create Azure-based cloud applications.

➤ **Python development:** Includes support for cookiecutter, Python 3, and tools that are used to interact with Azure. And, optionally, you can include other distributions of Python, such as Anaconda.

➤ **Node.js development:** One of the new tools supported by Visual Studio 2017, this workload includes the components that allow you to create network applications using the Node.js platform.

➤ **Data storage and processing:** Some recent additions to the Azure platform include Azure Data Lake, Hadoop, and Azure ML (Machine Learning). This workload includes the templates and tools to develop applications for this platform, along with the Azure SQL Server database.

➤ **Data science and analytical applications:** Brings together three languages that are also found in other workloads: R, Python, and F#. These tools can be used to build a wide variety of analytics-based applications.

➤ **Office/SharePoint development:** Used to create a wide variety of Office and SharePoint applications, including Office add-ins, SharePoint solutions, and Visual Studio Tools for Office (VSTO) add-ins.

➤ **Mobile development with .NET:** One of the three technologies that Visual Studio 2017 supports for mobile development, this workload allows you to create iOS, Android, or Windows applications using Xamarin.

➤ **Mobile development with JavaScript:** Similar concept to the previous entry, but instead of using Xamarin, your applications are developed using Tools for Apache Cordova and JavaScript.

➤ **Mobile development with C++:** And the last of the three mobile development environments allows you to create iOS, Android, and Windows applications using C++.

➤ **Game development with Unity:** Unity is a broadly used and very flexible cross-platform game development environment. This workload allows you to create 2D and 3D games using the Unity framework.

➤ **Game development with C++:** Supports the creation of games using C++ along with libraries like DirectX, Unreal, or Cocos2d.

➤ **Visual Studio extension development:** Lets you create add-ons and extensions for use in Visual Studio. Included in this are code analyzers and tool windows that take advantage of the Roslyn compiler functionality.

➤ **Linux development with C++:** Windows 10 includes an option to install an Ubuntu-based Linux Bash shell. This workload includes the set of tools and libraries that allow you to create applications that run in Linux using Visual Studio.

➤ **.NET Core cross-platform development:** .NET Core is a popular approach to cross-platform development. This workload allows you to create .NET Core applications, including web applications.

WORKLOADS USED IN THIS BOOK

In order to work through the examples in the book, there are a number of workloads that need to be installed. Specifically:

➤ Universal Windows Platform

➤ .NET desktop development

➤ ASP.NET and web development

➤ Azure development

➤ Node.js development

➤ Data storage and processing

➤ Data science and analytical applications

➤ Mobile development with .NET

➤ Mobile development with Javascript

➤ .NET code cross-platform development

The second mode for choosing components is more granular. If you select the Individual Components link at the top of the installation screen, the list of components shown in Figure 1-2 appears. From here you can select any or all of the individual components that you want to install on your machine.

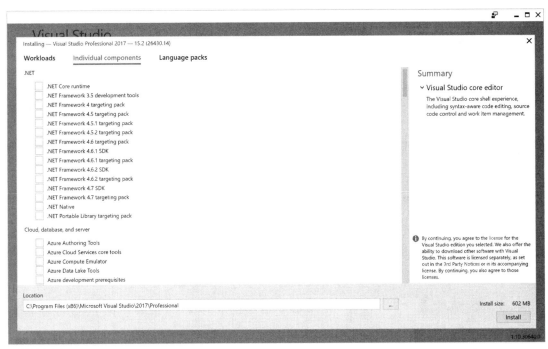

FIGURE 1-2

> **NOTE** *To see the relationship between the workloads and the more granular components that are included, simply select a workload. A list of the components that are included appears in the pane on the right side of the dialog.*

The third installation option you have for Visual Studio is to include one or more of the supported language packs. Clicking on the Language Packs link displays the list of language packs that are available (see Figure 1-3).

Once you have selected your components (either individually or as part of a workload), choose the installation location and click on Install. Now comes the longer part of the process. You'll see the progress dialog, an example of which is shown in Figure 1-4. Depending on which components you already have installed on your computer, you might be prompted to restart your computer midway through or at the end of the installation process. When all the components have been successfully installed, the original dialog changes slightly (as shown in Figure 1-5). This final dialog is also the starting point for adding features to Visual Studio in the future.

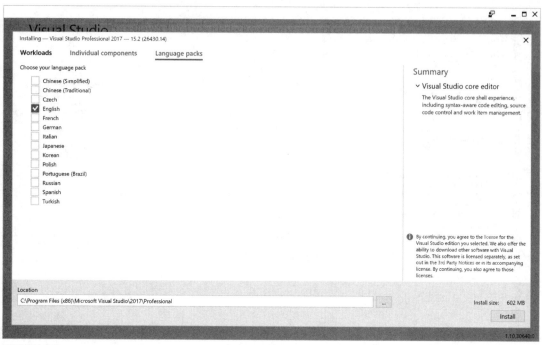

FIGURE 1-3

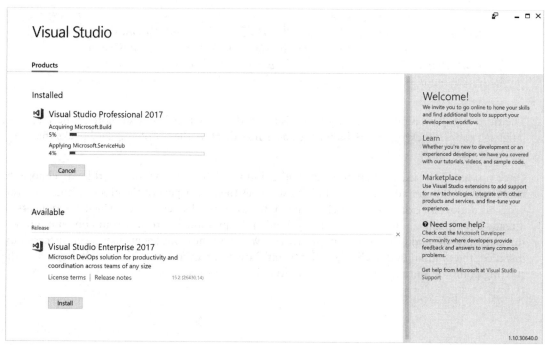

FIGURE 1-4

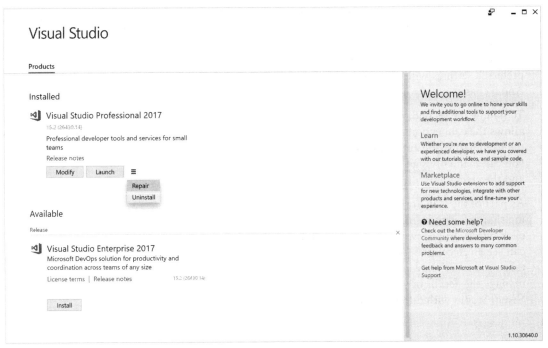

FIGURE 1-5

Running Visual Studio 2017

The first time you run Visual Studio 2017, you might be given the opportunity to sign in. If you had already signed in from within Visual Studio 2015, you won't be prompted to log in. Your credentials are remembered between the versions. However, if you're new to Visual Studio, then you'll be asked to provide a Microsoft Live account.

This behavior is part of an effort to cloud-enable Visual Studio—to connect Visual Studio settings and functionality to assets that are available across the Internet. There is no requirement for you to log in. The login page includes a Not Now, Maybe Later link. Clicking on that link skips a number of steps and lets you get to Visual Studio quickly. But there are some decent benefits that can be derived by signing in.

Is Visual Studio Really Cloud Enabled?

The quick answer is "Yes." A more accurate answer is "Yes, if you want it to be." Part of the research work behind creating this feature involved Microsoft gaining an understanding of how developers identified themselves to various online functions. In general, most developers have two or more Microsoft accounts that they use when they develop. There is a primary identity, which typically maps to the credentials used by the person while working. Then there are additional identities used to access external functions, such as Team Foundation Server, or to publish apps onto the various Microsoft stores.

To mimic how developers work with these multiple online identities, Microsoft introduces a hierarchical relationship between these identities within Visual Studio. When you sign in, the account you specify is the primary identity for the Visual Studio IDE. It should, in theory, represent you (that is you, the person). Every place you sign into Visual Studio with the same credentials, your preferred settings will follow you. This includes customizations like themes and keyboard bindings. And a change on one device will automatically flow to the other devices you are signed into.

To handle the secondary credentials, Visual Studio 2017 contains a secure credential store. This allows the connections that you have made to external services to be remembered and used without the need to provide authentication each time. Naturally, you can manually sign out from a particular connection and the credentials will be removed.

As part of the cloud enabling, you see your name (assuming that you logged in) in the top right of the IDE. If you click on the drop-down arrow (shown in Figure 1-6), you can see an Account Settings link. Clicking on that link takes you to a dialog (see Figure 1-7) in which you can manage the details of your account, including associating Visual Studio with different accounts.

FIGURE 1-6

FIGURE 1-7

Along with providing a mechanism for editing the basic contact information for the profile, the dialog includes a list of the Microsoft Live accounts that have been "remembered" on your current machine.

THE VISUAL STUDIO IDE

The first time you launch Visual Studio 2017 , you will most likely see a dialog indicating that Visual Studio is configuring the development environment. When this process is complete, Visual Studio 2017 opens, ready for you to start working, as shown in Figure 1-8.

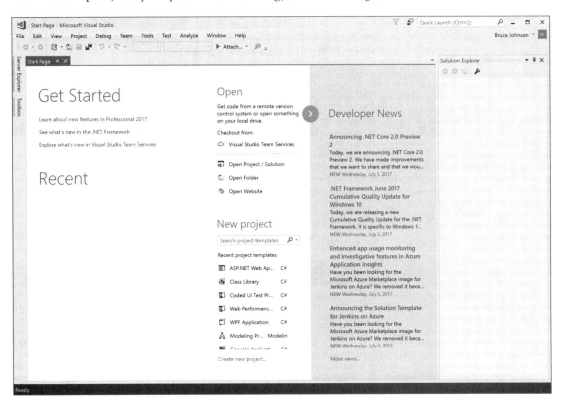

FIGURE 1-8

You'll see the Start page in the center of the screen. The bulk of the page contains links to the most common functions that you're likely to perform. For example, there is a list of Recent projects, along with links that allow you to open existing projects or create a new project. And in the latter case, the most commonly used templates are prominently on display. The previous version of the Start page included a news feed of interest to developers, and that feed is still present in Visual Studio 2017. And in the top left, there is also a Get Started section with links to information that is useful to new users of Visual Studio.

Before you launch into building your first application, you must take a step back to look at the components that make up the Visual Studio 2017 IDE. Menus and toolbars are positioned along the top of the environment, and a selection of subwindows, or panes, appears on the left, right, and bottom of the main window area. In the center is the main editor space. Whenever you open a code file, an XML document, a form, or some other file, it appears in this space for editing. With each file you open, a tab is created so that you can easily switch between opened files.

On either side of the editor space is a set of tool windows. These areas provide additional contextual information and functionality. For the general developer settings, the default layout includes the Solution Explorer and Properties on the right, and the Server Explorer and Toolbox on the left. The tool windows on the left are in their collapsed, or *unpinned*, state. If you click a tool window's title, it expands; it collapses again when it no longer has focus or you move the cursor to another area of the screen. When a tool window is expanded, you see a series of three icons at the top right of the window, similar to those shown in the top right corner of Figure 1-9.

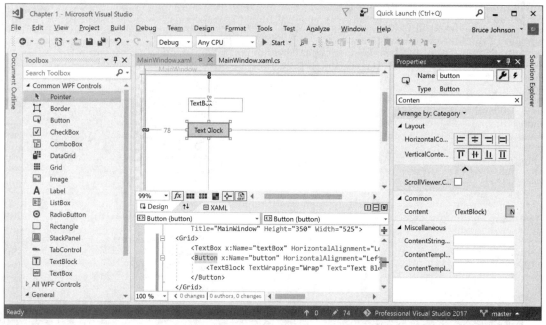

FIGURE 1-9

If you want the tool window to remain in its expanded, or *pinned*, state, you can click the middle icon, which looks like a pin. The pin rotates 90 degrees to indicate that the window is now pinned. Clicking the third icon, the X, closes the window. If later you want to reopen this or another tool window, you can select it from the View menu.

> **NOTE** *Some tool windows are not accessible via the View menu; for example, those having to do with debugging, such as threads and watch windows. In most cases these windows are available via an alternative menu item; for the debugging windows, it is the Debug menu.*

When the first icon, the down arrow, is clicked, a context menu opens. Each item in this list represents a different way to arrange the tool window. As you would imagine, the Float option enables the tool window to be placed anywhere on the screen, independent of the main IDE window. This is useful if you have multiple screens because you can move the various tool windows onto the additional screen, allowing the editor space to use the maximum screen real estate. Selecting the Dock as Tabbed Document option makes the tool window into an additional tab in the editor space. In Chapter 4, "The Visual Studio Workspace," you'll learn how to effectively manage the workspace by docking tool windows.

Developing, Building, Debugging, and Deploying Your First Application

Now that you have seen an overview of the Visual Studio 2017 IDE, this section walks you through creating a simple application that demonstrates working with some of these components. This is, of course, the mandatory "Hello World" sample that every developer needs to know, and it can be done in either Visual Basic .NET, or C#, depending on what you feel more comfortable with.

1. Start by selecting File ⇨ New ⇨ Project. This opens the New Project dialog, as shown in Figure 1-10. There is a tree on the left side of the dialog for grouping templates based on language and technology. And there is also a search box in the top-right corner. The right pane of this dialog displays additional information about the project template you have selected. Lastly, you can select the version of the .NET Framework that the application will target using the drop-down at the top of the dialog.

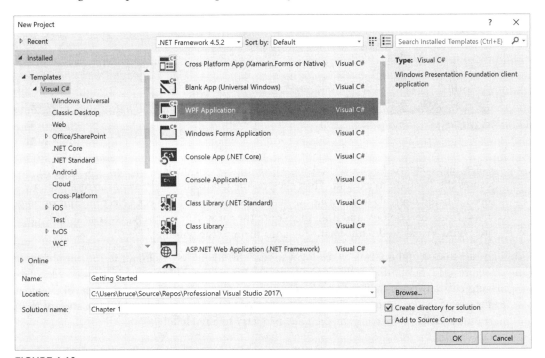

FIGURE 1-10

Select WPF Application from the Templates area (this item exists under the root Visual Basic and Visual C# nodes, or under the subnode Windows) and set the Name to **GettingStarted** before selecting OK. This creates a new WPF application project, which includes a single startup window and is contained within a Chapter 1 solution, as shown in the Solution Explorer window of Figure 1-11. This startup window has automatically opened in the visual designer, giving you an approximate graphical representation of what the window will look like when you run the application. The Properties tool window is collapsed and sits on the right side of the windows.

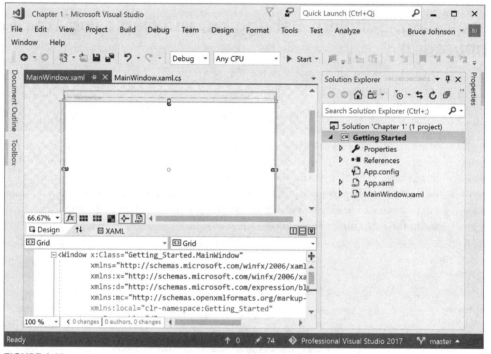

FIGURE 1-11

2. Click the collapsed Toolbox window, which appears on the left side of the screen. This causes the Toolbox to expand. Then click on the pin icon, which keeps the tool window open. To add controls to the window in the GettingStarted project, select the appropriate items from the Toolbox and drag them onto the form. Alternatively, you can double-click the item, and Visual Studio automatically adds them to the window.

3. Add a button and textbox to the form so that the layout looks similar to the one shown in Figure 1-12. Select the textbox, and select the Properties tool window. (You can press F4 to automatically open the Properties tool window.) Change the name of the control (found at the top of the Properties tool window) to **txtSayHello**. Repeat for the Button control, naming it **btnSayHello** and setting the `Content` property to **Say Hello!**

You can quickly locate a property by typing its name into the search field located beneath the Name field. In Figure 1-12 **Conten** has been entered to reduce the list of Properties so that it's easier to locate the Content property.

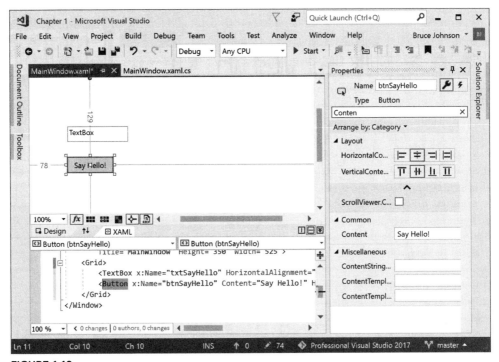

FIGURE 1-12

After you add controls to the window, the tab is updated with an asterisk (*) after the text to indicate that there are unsaved changes to that particular item. If you attempt to close this item while changes are pending, you are asked if you want to save the changes. When you build the application, any unsaved files are automatically saved as part of the build process.

> **NOTE** *One thing to be aware of is that some files, such as the solution file, are modified when you make changes within Visual Studio 2017 without your being given any indication that they have changed. If you try to exit the application or close the solution, you are still prompted to save these changes.*

4. Deselect all controls (you can click an empty spot on the screen to do this), and then double-click the button. This not only opens the code editor with the code-behind file for

this form, it also creates and wires up an event handler for the click event on the button. Figure 1-13 shows the code window after a single line has been added to echo the message to the user.

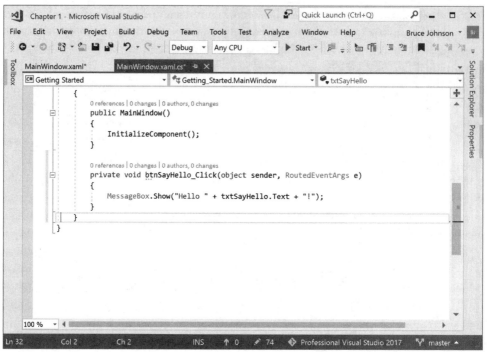

FIGURE 1-13

5. Before you build and execute your application, place the cursor somewhere on the line containing `MessageBox.Show` and press F9. This sets a breakpoint; when you run the application by pressing F5 and then click the "Say Hello!" button, the execution halts at this line. Figure 1-14 illustrates this breakpoint being reached. The data tip, which appears when the mouse hovers over the line, shows the contents of the `txtSayHello.Text` property.

The layout of Visual Studio in Figure 1-14 is significantly different from the previous screenshots because a number of tool windows are visible in the lower half of the screen, and command bars are visible at the top. Also, the status bar at the bottom of the IDE is orange, as opposed to the blue that appears when in design mode. When you stop running or debugging your application, Visual Studio returns to the previous layout. Visual Studio 2017 maintains two separate layouts: design time and run time. Menus, toolbars, and various windows have default layouts for when you edit a project, whereas a different setup is defined for when a project is executed and debugged. You can modify each of these layouts to suit your own style, and Visual Studio 2017 remembers them.

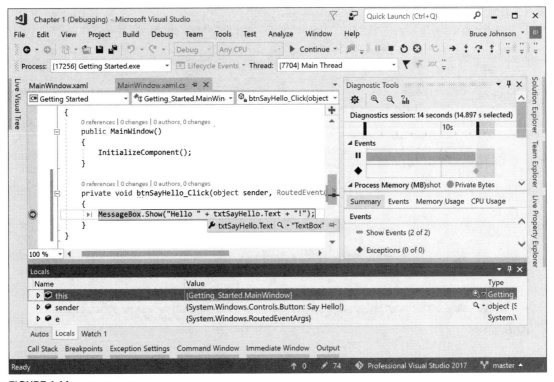

FIGURE 1-14

6. You need to deploy your application. Whether you build a rich client application using Windows Forms or WPF, or a web application using IIS, Azure, Node.js, or any of a number of other technologies, Visual Studio 2017 has the capability to publish your application. Double-click the Properties node in Solution Explorer, and select the Publish node to display the options for publishing your application, as shown in Figure 1-15.

In Figure 1-15, the publishing folder has been set to a local path (by default, the path is relative to the directory in which the project is found), but you can specify a network folder, an Internet Information Services (IIS) folder, or an FTP site instead. After you specify where you want to publish to, clicking Publish Now publishes your application to that location.

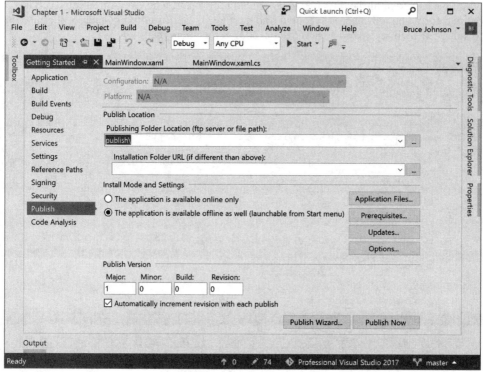

FIGURE 1-15

SUMMARY

You've seen how the various components of Visual Studio 2017 work together to build an application. The following list outlines the typical process of creating a solution:

1. Use the File menu to create a solution.

2. Use the Solution Explorer to locate the window that needs editing, and double-click the item to show it in the main workspace area.

3. Drag the necessary components onto the window from the Toolbox.

4. Select the window and each component in turn, and edit the properties in the Properties window.

5. Double-click the window or a control to access the code behind the component's graphical interface.

6. Use the main workspace area to write code and design the graphical interface, switching between the two via the tabs at the top of the area.

7. Use the toolbars to start the program.

8. If errors occur, review them in the Error List and Output windows.

9. Save the project using either toolbar or menu commands, and exit Visual Studio 2017.

In subsequent chapters, you'll learn how to customize the IDE to more closely fit your own working style. You'll also see how Visual Studio 2017 takes a lot of the guesswork out of the application development process and a number of best practices for working with Visual Studio 2017 that you can reuse as a developer.

The Solution Explorer, Toolbox, and Properties

WHAT'S IN THIS CHAPTER?

➤ Arranging files with the Solution Explorer

➤ Adding projects, items, and references to your solution

➤ Working with the Properties tool window

➤ Including your own properties in the Properties tool window

WROX.COM CODE DOWNLOADS FOR THIS CHAPTER

The wrox.com code downloads for this chapter can be found at www.wrox.com by searching for this book's ISBN number (978-1-119-40458-3). The code and any related support files are located in their own folder for this chapter.

In Chapter 1, "A Quick Tour," you briefly saw and interacted with a number of the components that make up the Visual Studio 2017 IDE. Now you get an opportunity to work with three of the most commonly used tool windows: the Solution Explorer, the Toolbox, and Properties.

Throughout this and other chapters you see references to keyboard shortcuts, such as Ctrl+S. In these cases, we assume the use of the general development settings, as shown in Chapter 1. Other profiles may have different key combinations. And, as you will see in upcoming chapters, you can use the Quick Launch area to get to commands regardless of the development settings that you use.

THE SOLUTION EXPLORER

Most of the time, when you create or open an application, or for that matter just a single file, Visual Studio 2017 uses the concept of a solution to tie everything together. Visual Studio 2017 introduces the concept of a Folder view, which is discussed further later in this chapter. For most situations (and definitely for most existing projects), the solution is the root element of a project.

Typically, a solution is made up of one or more projects, each of which can have multiple items associated with it. In the past these items were typically just files, but increasingly projects are made up of items that may consist of multiple files, or in some cases no files at all. Chapter 6, "Solutions, Projects, and Items," goes into more detail about projects, the structure of solutions, and how items are related.

The Solution Explorer tool window (Ctrl+Alt+L) provides a convenient visual representation of the solution, projects, and items, as shown in Figure 2-1. In this figure you can see three projects presented in a tree: a C# Windows Presentation Foundation (WPF) application, a C# Windows Communication Foundation (WCF) service library, and a Visual Basic (VB) class library.

Each project has an icon associated with it that typically indicates the type of project and the language it is written in. There are some exceptions to this rule: Some projects, such as SQL Server or Modeling projects, aren't tied to a specific language.

One node is particularly noticeable because the font is boldfaced. This indicates that this project is the startup project — in other words, the project that is launched when you select Debug ⇨ Start Debugging or press F5. To change the startup project, right-click the project you want to nominate and select Set as StartUp Project. You can also nominate multiple projects as startup projects via the Solution Properties dialog, which you can reach by selecting Properties from the right-click menu of the Solution node.

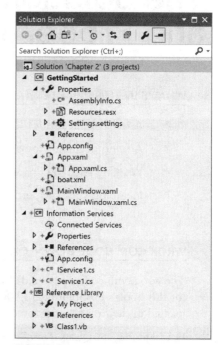

FIGURE 2-1

> **NOTE** *With certain environment settings, the Solution node is not visible when only a single project exists. A problem with this setting is that it becomes difficult to access the Solution Properties window. To get the Solution node to appear, you can either add another project to the solution or check the Always Show Solution item from the Projects and Solutions node in the Options dialog, accessible via Tools ⇨ Options.*

The toolbar across the top of the Solution Explorer gives access to a number of different functions related to the solution, from the ability to collapse all the files in the tree to creating a new instance of the Solution Explorer. For example, the Show All Files icon (see Figure 2-2) expands the solution listing to display the additional files and folders.

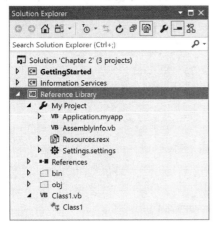

FIGURE 2-2

In this expanded view you can see all the files and folders contained under the project structure. Unfortunately, if the file system changes, the Solution Explorer does not automatically update to reflect these changes. Use the Refresh button (two buttons to the left of the Show All Files button) to make sure you see the current list of files and folders.

The Solution Explorer toolbar is contextually aware, with different buttons displayed depending on the type of node selected. This is shown in Figure 2-3. The image on the left shows the toolbar when a .XAML file is selected. It includes a View Code icon (the fourth from the right). However, when a different file is selected, as illustrated in the image on the right, the View Code icon is missing.

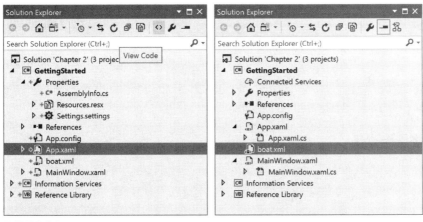

FIGURE 2-3

There is another, relatively unusual mechanism for navigating through the projects and files in a solution. To the left of each item in the tree is an icon, which when clicked shows a different context menu. Included in this menu is an option called Scope to This. When the Scope to This option is clicked, the contents of the Solution Explorer change so that the selected node in the solution becomes the top level of the tree view. Figure 2-4 shows the view when Scope to This has been clicked for the GettingStarted project.

Along with navigating down the solution using the Scope to This option, the Solution Explorer also allows for moving backward and forward through the navigation. At the top left of the Solution Explorer's toolbar, there is a left arrow that you can use to navigate up the hierarchy. So if that arrow were clicked, the full solution would be displayed, as shown in Figure 2-2. And there is also a right-facing arrow that, when clicked, navigates forward into the scoped view.

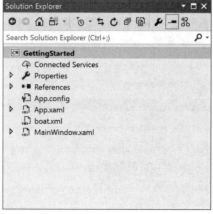

FIGURE 2-4

Visual Studio 2017 includes the ability of opening a folder instead opening a solution. While it is available for any project type, it would seem to be most relevant to web applications where there is no need to tie the elements of the project together beyond existing within a single project. While a similar idea (Web Sites) was included in earlier versions of Visual Studio (and is still available in Visual Studio 2017), increased support for build tools like Grunt and Bower has brought the feature to the forefront.

First, it is possible at any time to switch between the Solution view and the Folder view for a solution. Figure 2-5 illustrates the difference between the two views. The fourth button from the left in both views is used to toggle between views.

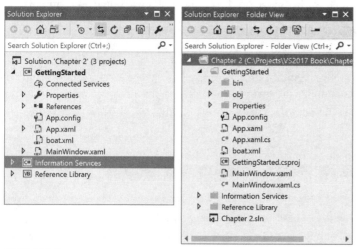

FIGURE 2-5

The Solution view is on the left and looks familiar to regular users of past version of Visual Studio. The Folder view is on the right. What previously had been a project is now a folder (assuming that is how you organized your solution in the file system). Files that had been grouped together in the Solution view (like App.xaml and App.xaml.cs) now appear as individual files in the Folder view. Artifacts like the .sln file are now visible in the solution explorer. And the context menu has changed significantly, with the Folder view having far fewer choices.

If you have been using Visual Studio for a while, it's natural to ask what purpose the Folder View serves. For most projects, the answer is "not much." However, as odd as it might sound, the folder structure that is displayed in the traditional view of the Solution Explorer is actually a virtual one. That is, the files in the file system don't need to follow the folder structure shown in the Solution Explorer. Your files can be placed in a single folder in the file system but show up within a folder structure in your project.

For most projects, this is not a big deal. Actually, it's irrelevant to the running of your application. The build process is able to figure out where the files are and compile them into the appropriate assemblies, and your application runs. However, for certain kinds of projects (and web applications, including .NET Core, are the leading culprits), the physical folder structure matters. The Folder View allows you to quickly and easily see how the files lay out physically.

The rest of this chapter concentrates on the options available in the Solution view.

In the Solution view in Visual Studio 2017, expanding any source code node reveals the properties and methods for a given class. And the context menu for the node contains options targeting the selected item. When you right-click a class (not the code file, but the actual class), the context menu includes Base Types, Derived Types, and Is Used By options. These options change the scope of the Solution Explorer to the base class, the derived classes, and the classes used by the selected class, respectively.

As you continue navigating into the properties and methods, the context menu includes Calls, Is Called By, and Is Used By. These options scope the Solution Explorer to the classes that call this class, classes that are called by this class, and classes that are used by this class, respectively.

Previewing Files

One of the more interesting features of Visual Studio 2017 is the file preview capability of Solution Explorer. One of the buttons at the top of the Solution Explorer is Preview Selected Items (shown in Figure 2-6). When it has been selected, as you navigate through the files in the Solution Explorer (to "navigate," the file must be selected either with the mouse or by using the cursor), the file appears on the Preview tab (Figure 2-6).

At this moment, the file has not been modified but is simply open to look at. You are free to navigate through the file as you would any other file. However, when you navigate to another file in the Solution Explorer, the Preview tab is replaced with the new file. In other words, it is no longer required to have a proliferation of tabs to view the contents of various files in your solution.

When you decide to stop previewing the file, it automatically moves to the tabs on the left side of your editor window. You make the choice to stop previewing either by editing the file directly (by typing, for example) or by selecting the Open option from the drop-down list on the right of the Preview tab.

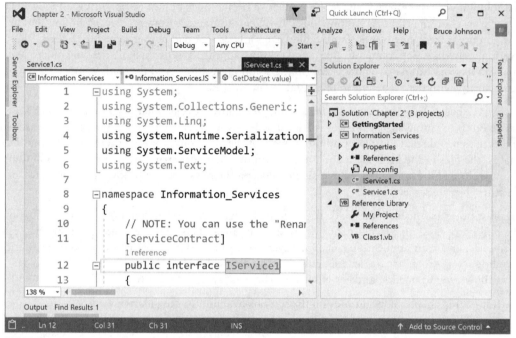

FIGURE 2-6

Common Tasks

In addition to providing a convenient way to manage projects and items, the Solution Explorer has a dynamic context menu that gives you quick access to some of the most common tasks, such as building the solution or individual projects, accessing the build configuration manager, and opening files. Figure 2-7 shows how the context menu varies depending on which item is selected in the Solution Explorer.

The first items in the left and center menus relate to building either the entire solution or the selected project. In most cases, selecting Build is the most efficient option, because it only builds projects where one or more of the contained files have changed. However, in some cases you may need to force a Rebuild, which builds all dependent projects regardless of their states. If you just want to remove all the additional files that are created during the build process, you can invoke Clean. This option can be useful if you want to package your solution to email it to someone — you wouldn't want to include all the temporary or output files that are created by the build.

For most items in the Solution Explorer, the first section of the context menu is similar to the right menu in Figure 2-7. The default Open and Open With items allow you to determine how the item will be opened. This is of particular use when you work with files that have a custom editor. A common example is a RESX file. By default, Visual Studio 2017 opens this file type using the built-in resource editor, but this prevents you from making certain changes and doesn't support all data types you might want to include. (Chapter 56, "Resource Files," in the online archive goes into how you can use your own data types in resource files.) By using the Open With menu item, you can use the XML Editor instead.

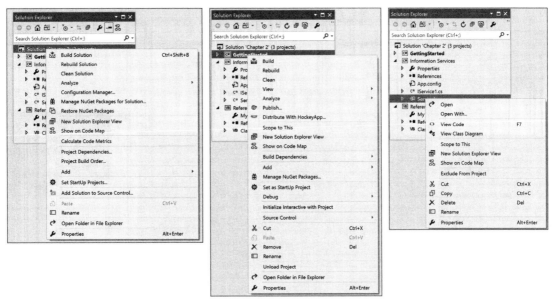

FIGURE 2-7

> **NOTE** *The context menu for the Solution, Project, and Folder nodes contains the Open Folder in File Explorer item. This enables you to open File Explorer (Windows Explorer) quickly to the location of the selected item, saving you the hassle of having to navigate to where your solution is located, and then find the appropriate subfolder.*

Adding Projects and Items

The most common activities carried out in the Solution Explorer are the addition, removal, and renaming of projects and items. To add a new project to an existing solution, select Add ➪ New Project from the context menu off the Solution node. This invokes the dialog in Figure 2-8. Project templates can be sorted and searched from this dialog, and the pane on the right side displays information about the selected project, such as the type of project and its description. As well, the light-weight installer means that a template you're looking for might be in a workload that has not already been installed. To relaunch the installer and add a desired workload, there is an Open Visual Studio Installer link that will start that process for you. Chapter 11, "Project and Item Templates," covers creating your own Project and Item templates, including setting these properties.

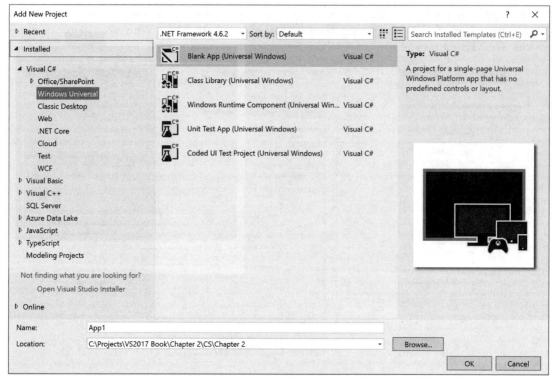

FIGURE 2-8

In the Installed templates hierarchy on the left side of the Add New Project dialog, the templates are primarily arranged by language (Azure Data Lake being the exception) and then by technology. There are also nodes for Recent templates and Online templates. The Online templates can be sorted and searched in the same way as your Installed templates.

The other thing you will notice in this dialog is the ability to select different framework versions through a dropdown at the middle top of the form. Visual Studio 2017 does not require a migration for most project types. So if you have existing projects that you don't want to have to migrate forward to a more recent version of the .NET Framework, you can still immediately take advantage of the current features in Visual Studio 2017. The framework selection is also included in the search criteria, limiting the list of available project templates to those that are compatible with the selected .NET Framework version.

NOTE *When you open your existing Visual Studio 2012, 2013, or 2015 solutions or projects in Visual Studio 2017, they will not necessarily go through the upgrade wizard. (See Chapter 34, "Upgrading with Visual Studio 2017," for more information.) To be precise, the act of opening a project in Visual Studio 2017 might cause modifications to the project, but it will still be able to be opened in earlier versions of Visual Studio (in some cases, even as far back as Visual Studio 2010). This is both important enough to warrant additional comment. What this means for developers is that they might be able to use Visual Studio 2017 to modify "legacy" projects (thus getting the benefits of using the latest version of the IDE). At the same time, projects that have been opened in Visual Studio 2017 will still open in Visual Studio 2015, 2013, or 2012. For projects that are from versions earlier than Visual Studio 2012, the upgrade wizard will be triggered. These matters are discussed further in Chapter 34.*

One of the worst and most poorly understood features in Visual Studio is the concept of a Web Site project. This is distinct from a Web Application project, which can be added via the aforementioned Add New Project dialog. To add a Web Site project, you need to select Add ⇨ New Web Site from the context menu off the Solution node. This displays a dialog similar to the one shown in Figure 2-9, where you can select the type of web project to be created. In most cases, this simply determines the type of default item that is to be created in the project.

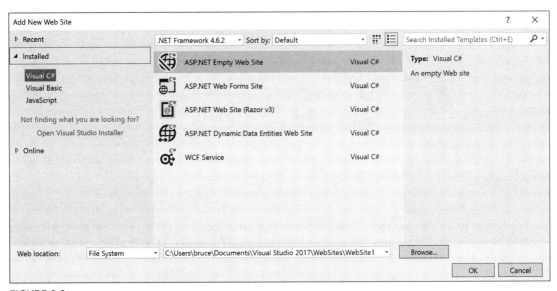

FIGURE 2-9

> **NOTE** *It is important to note that some of the web projects listed in Figure 2-9 can also be created by going through the ASP.NET Web Application options in the Add New Project dialog. However, understand that they will not generate the same results because significant differences exist between Web Site projects (created via the Add New Web Site dialog) and Web Application projects (created via the Add New Project dialog). The differences between these project types are covered in detail in Chapter 16, "ASP.NET Web Forms."*

When you have a project or two in your solution, you need to start adding items. You do this via the Add context menu item off the project node in the Solution Explorer. The first submenu, New Item, launches the Add New Item dialog, as shown in Figure 2-10.

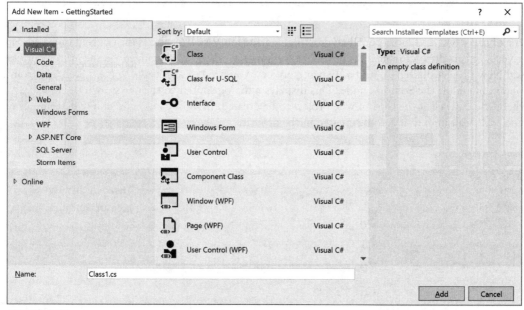

FIGURE 2-10

In addition to listing only those item templates that are relevant to the project you have selected, the Add New Item dialog enables you to search the installed templates, as well as go online to look for templates made available by third parties.

Returning to the Add context menu, you will notice a number of predefined shortcuts such as User Control and Class. The shortcuts that appear depend on the type of project to which the item is being added. These do little more than bypass the stage of locating the appropriate template within the Add New Item dialog. With just a few exceptions, the Add New Item dialog is still displayed because you need to assign a name to the item being created.

It is important to make the distinction that you are adding items rather than files to the project. Though a lot of the templates contain only a single file, some, like the Window or User Control, add multiple files to your project.

Adding References

Each new software development technology that is released promises better reuse, but few can actually deliver on this promise. One way that Visual Studio 2017 supports reusable components is via the references for a project. If you expand the References node for any project, you can observe a number of .NET Framework libraries, such as System and System.Core, which need to be included by the compiler to successfully build the project. Essentially, a reference enables the compiler to resolve type, property, field, and method names back to the assembly where they are defined. If you want to reuse a class from a third-party library, or even your own .NET assembly from another project, you need to add a reference to it via the Add Reference context menu item on the project node of the Solution Explorer.

When you launch the Reference Manager dialog, as shown in Figure 2-11, Visual Studio 2017 interrogates the local computer, the Global Assembly Cache, and your solution to present a list of known libraries that can be referenced. This includes both .NET and COM references that are separated into different lists, as well as projects and recently used references.

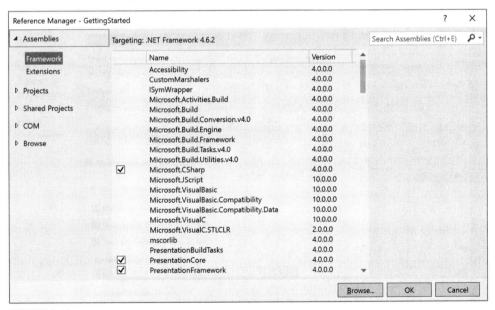

FIGURE 2-11

As in other project-based development environments going back as far as the first versions of VB, you can add references to projects contained in your solution, rather than adding the compiled binary components. The advantage to this model is that it's easier to debug into the referenced component and helps ensure you are running the latest version of all components, but for large solutions this may become unwieldy.

> **NOTE** *When you have a solution with a large number of projects (large can be relative to your computer but typically anything more than 20), you may want to consider having multiple solutions that reference subsets of the projects. Loads and builds are actually done in parallel, which helps with their speed. Still, keeping the number of projects in your solution to a minimum ensures a nice debugging experience throughout the entire application. But be warned. The segregation of projects into different solutions is not nearly as clear-cut as you might initially imagine. Not because it's difficult to do (it's actually easy), but because you'll find there are a number of different approaches that might be the "best," depending on your goals. For example, you may want to create different solutions to support build configurations (see Chapter 33, "Build Customization") that build a subset of the projects.*

Adding Service References

The other type of reference that the Solution Explorer caters to is service references. These references were once referred to as Web references, but since the advent of the WCF there is a more general Add Service Reference menu item. This invokes the Add Service Reference dialog, which you can see in Figure 2-12. In this example the drop-down feature of the Discover button has been used to look for Services in Solution.

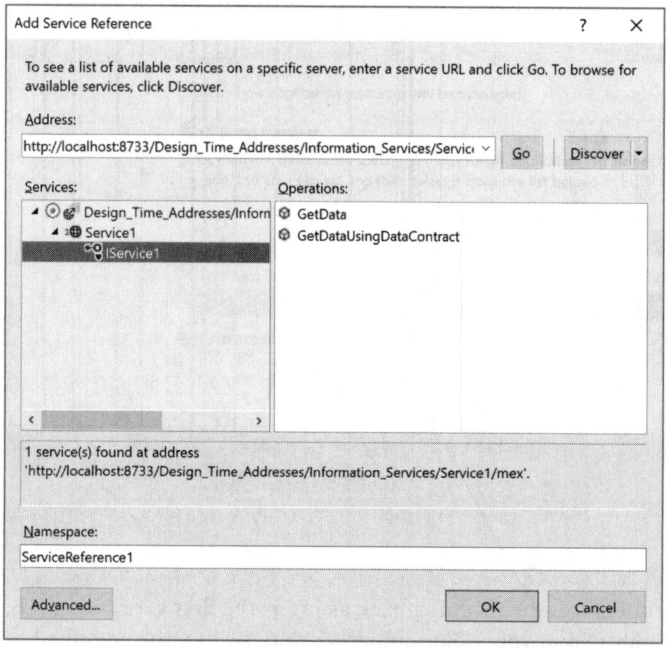

FIGURE 2-12

If any errors are thrown while Visual Studio 2017 attempts to access the service information, a hyperlink is provided that opens the Add Service Reference Error dialog. This generally gives you enough information to resolve the problem.

In the lower-left corner of Figure 2-12 is an Advanced button. The Service Reference Settings dialog that this launches enables you to customize which types are defined as part of the service reference. By default, all the types used by the service are re-created in the client application unless they are implemented in an assembly that is referenced by both the service and the application. The Data Type area of this dialog is used to change this behavior. There is also an Add Web Reference button in the lower-left corner of the Service Reference Settings dialog, which enables you to add more traditional .NET Web service references. This might be important if you have some limitations or are trying to support intersystem operability. Adding services to your application is covered in more detail in Chapter 51, "Windows Communication Foundation (WCF)" in the online archive.

Adding Connected Services

Applications today find themselves more dependent on external services to provide some common functionality. Although you are always free to browse to the website of the service provider, download the client assembly (or read through the documentation for the API), and implement that required functionality in your application, Visual Studio 2017 gives you a tool that streamlines the process and reduces complexity. That tool is invoked by using the Connected Services option in the Add context menu.

> **NOTE** *If you don't see the Connected Services option in the Add context menu, that's because the project you have selected doesn't support any of the available services.*

When Connected Services is selected, a pane that looks like the one shown in Figure 2-13 appears in your editor space.

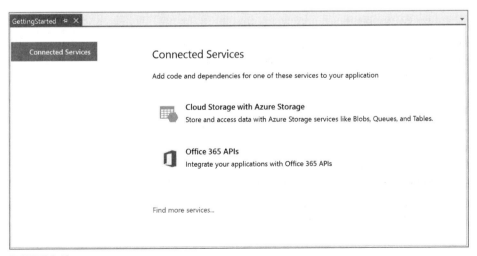

FIGURE 2-13

There are two choices available to you out of the box, as well as a relatively easy way to find more. The choices are Cloud Storage with Azure Storage and Office 365 APIs.

Once you have selected a service, separate dialogs walk through the steps necessary to add the assemblies, configurations, and supporting files to your project. The details of what you need to provide vary widely based on the type of service, so they are beyond the scope of the book. But, in general, figure that you'll need to provide credentials for an account that has access to the service (such as a Microsoft Live Account for accessing the Azure functionality).

At the bottom of Figure 2-13, there is a Find More Services link. Clicking on the link reveals the Extensions and Updates dialog, as seen in Figure 2-14.

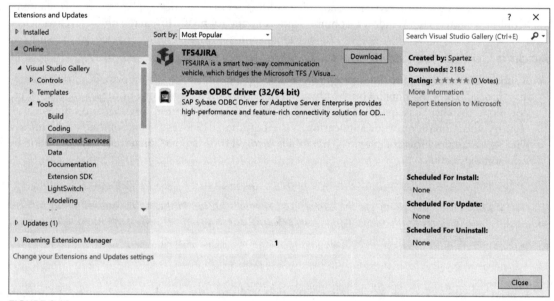

FIGURE 2-14

Although you can use the Extensions and Updates dialog to install many different tools, in this particular instance, you are immediately placed in the Connected Services section. (See the list on the left side.) If you want to use any of the other services, select the appropriate service and click on the Download or Install button that appears.

Adding Analyzers

The compiler that Visual Studio 2017 uses, a rewrite of the compiler that was used for all versions of Visual Studio up to Visual Studio 2013, enables a plethora of features and functionality to Visual Studio users. Most importantly, the source of this innovation is no longer limited to Microsoft. Third parties and open-source groups can contribute their ideas to the larger community for users.

Whether you were aware of it or not, compilation of .NET is a big part of what Visual Studio has been doing for years. All the IntelliSense that you get is the result of a compilation process that is constantly running in the background, updating the syntax tree so that, for example, as soon as you add a class to your project, IntelliSense can show the properties and methods of that class elsewhere in the solution.

The tools that have been enabled by the compiler change are known as code analyzers. They can work intimately with your code to identify problems and offer solutions.

If you want to add an analyzer to one of your projects, there are a number of options. Within the Solution Explorer, right-click on the project and select the Add ⇨ Analyzer option from the context menu. The dialog shown in Figure 2-15 is displayed.

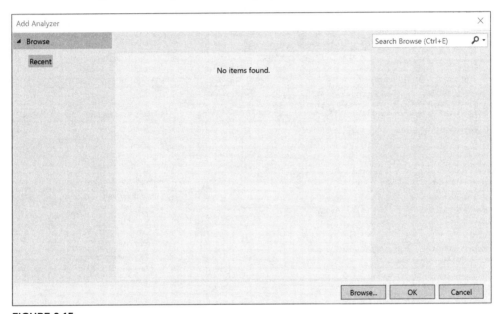

FIGURE 2-15

The dialog is not particularly compelling in terms of its functionality. If you had added an analyzer assembly to a project recently, you'll see it appear in the list of recently added analyzers that appears by default. You can also browse to the location of an analyzer assembly that has already been installed on your computer and include it in your project.

> **NOTE** *Don't be surprised by the lack of analyzers in Figure 2-15. In order to appear in this list, the analyzer would have to have been installed on your machine. And more often than not, analyzers are added to projects through NuGet. In that case they are not actually installed locally (by being copied to a project) and therefore won't appear in this dialog.*

Adding NuGet Packages

NuGet is the go-to location for packages that can be used within your application. And through different extensions, the way you add NuGet Packages to your projects has evolved into two separate workflows.

The most conveniently accessible workflow involves using a graphical interface integrated into Visual Studio 2017. In the Solution Explorer, right-click on the project to which you are adding the package and select Manage NuGet Packages from the context menu. This displays the page shown in Figure 2-16.

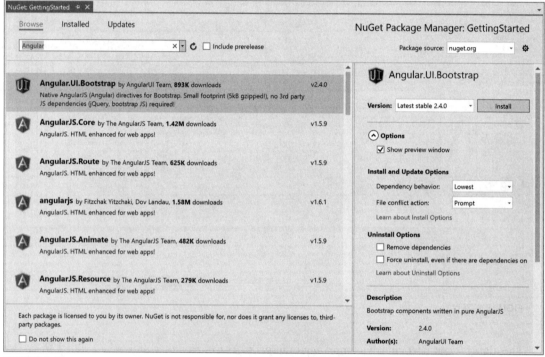

FIGURE 2-16

The purpose of the dialog is to allow you to search for the desired package. Across the top of the page are a number of controls that impact the details of the packages that are returned. The drop-down on the top right, labeled Package Source, is used to select the NuGet repository that will be searched. You can filter the packages based on whether you have already installed them previously, whether there is an updated one available, or whether you want to include any prerelease versions (for example, versions that are in beta) in the list. Finally, the text box at the top is used to specify the package that you are looking for. In Figure 2-16, all the packages that contain the word *angular* in the title or description are being shown.

Once you have identified the desired package, click on it in the left side of the page to display specific details on the right side. To install the package, click on the Install button. By default, this will install the most recent release. If the package you select has a number of different versions available, you can choose a specific version from the Version drop-down box.

When you click the Install button for a product, you will be shown a list of the files that will be added or updated to your project if you proceed. It appears in a dialog similar to the one found in Figure 2-17. Clicking OK will continue with the installation, whereas clicking Cancel will abort the installation.

The Dependency Behavior drop-down in Figure 2-16 controls whether and which dependencies are loaded. In Figure 2-17, there are nine dependencies that need to be installed, as well as two updates. To understand the basics of dependency behavior, consider that one of the updates is jQuery 2.1.1. This is the minimum version of jQuery that the installed component requires. This installation will use this version because the Lowest dependency behavior was selected. Other options include Highest (which would take the highest major version), Highest Minor (which would take the highest major and minor version), and Highest Patch (which takes even the patches associated with the most recent version). You can also simply ignore the dependencies.

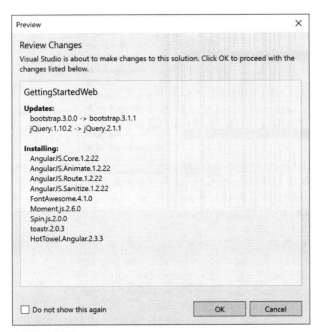

FIGURE 2-17

There is an option used to handle file conflicts. The choices are to prompt you when there are different versions of the same file being installed, to automatically overwrite the existing file with the new file, and to automatically ignore any files that already exist.

The second option you have to install NuGet packages involves going through a command window. To launch the window, which is shown in Figure 2-18, select the Tools ⇨ NuGet Package Manager ⇨ Package Manager Console menu option.

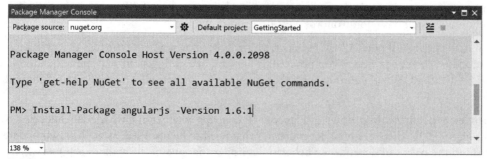

FIGURE 2-18

As soon as the command window is ready, you can enter the specific NuGet commands that are required to install the desired package. In Figure 2-18, version 1.6.1 of the angularjs package is being installed. You can easily install, update, or uninstall any package that you desire through the command line, although the details of the various commands are beyond the scope of the book.

THE TOOLBOX

One of the major advantages over many other IDEs that Microsoft has offered developers is true drag-and-drop placement of elements during the design of both web and rich client applications. These elements are available in the Toolbox (Ctrl+Alt+X), a tool window accessible via the View menu.

The Toolbox window contains all the available components for the currently active document being shown in the main workspace. These can be visual components, such as buttons and textboxes; invisible, service-oriented objects, such as timers and system event logs; or even designer elements, such as class and interface objects used in the Class Designer view.

> **NOTE** *An interesting feature of the Toolbox is that you can copy snippets of code into the Toolbox by simply selecting a region and dragging it onto the Toolbox. You can rename and reorder your code snippets, making it useful for presentations or storing chunks of code you use frequently.*

Visual Studio 2017 presents the available components in groups rather than as one big mess of controls. This default grouping enables you to more easily locate the controls you need — for example, data-related components are in their own Data group.

By default, groups are presented in List view (see the left side of Figure 2-19). Each component is represented by its own icon and the name of the component. If you prefer to guess what some of the more obscure components are, you can also display the components as a set of icons, as shown with the All WPF Controls group on the right side of Figure 2-19. You can change the view of each control group individually — right-click anywhere within the group area and toggle the List View option in the context menu.

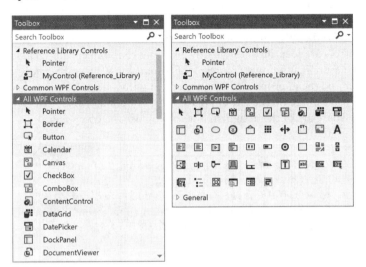

FIGURE 2-19

Regardless of how the components are presented, the way they are used in a program is usually the same: Click and drag the desired component onto the design surface of the active document, or double-click the component's entry for Visual Studio to automatically add an instance. Visual components, such as buttons and textboxes, appear in the design area where they can be repositioned, resized, and otherwise adjusted via the property grid. Nonvisual components, such as the Timer control, appear as icons with associated labels in a nonvisual area below the design area, as shown in Figure 2-20.

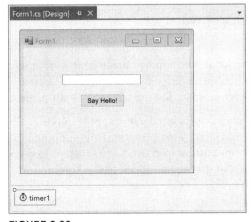

FIGURE 2-20

At the top-left side of Figure 2-19 is a group called Reference Library Controls with a single component, MyControl. Reference_Library is actually the name of a class library that is defined in the same solution, and it contains the MyControl control. When you start to build your own components or controls, instead of your having to manually create a new tab and go through the process of adding each item to the Toolbox, Visual Studio 2017 automatically interrogates all the projects in your solution. If any components or controls are identified (essentially any class that implements *System .ComponentModel.IComponent* or *System.Windows.FrameworkElement* for WPF and Silverlight), a new tab is created for that project and the appropriate items are added with a default icon and class name (in this case MyControl), as you can see on the left in Figure 2-19. For components, this is the same icon that appears in the nonvisual part of the design area when you use the component.

> **NOTE** *Visual Studio 2017 interrogates all projects in your solution, both at startup and after build activities. This can take a significant amount of time if you have a large number of projects. If this is the case, you should consider disabling this feature by setting the AutoToolboxPopulate property to false under the Windows Forms Designer node of the Options dialog (Tools ⇨ Options).*

To customize how your items appear in the Toolbox, you need to add a 16 × 16 pixel bitmap to the same project as your component or control. Then, select the newly added bitmap from within the Solution Explorer and navigate to the Properties window. Make sure the Build property on the bitmap is set to Embedded Resource. Finally, mark your control class with the `ToolboxBitmap` attribute:

VB

```
<ToolboxBitmap(GetType(MyControl), "MyControlIcon.bmp")>
Public Class MyControl
```

C#

```
[ToolboxBitmap(typeof(MyControl), "MyControlIcon.bmp")]
public class MyControl
```

This attribute uses the type reference for MyControl to locate the appropriate assembly from which to extract the `MyControlIcon.bmp` embedded resource. Other overloads of this attribute can use a file path as the only argument. In this case you don't even need to add the bitmap to your project.

Unfortunately, you can't customize the way the automatically generated items appear in the Toolbox. However, if you manually add an item to the Toolbox and select your components (as opposed to allowing Visual Studio to auto-populate it), you'll see your custom icon. And your custom icon will appear in the nonvisual space on the designer, regardless of how it was added to the Toolbox.

Arranging Components

Having Toolbox items in alphabetical order is a good default because it enables you to locate items that are unfamiliar. However, if you're using only a handful of components and are frustrated by having to continuously scroll up and down, you can create your own groups of controls and move existing object types around.

Repositioning an individual component is easy. Locate it in the Toolbox, and click and drag it to the new location. When you're happy with where it is, release the mouse button and the component moves to the new spot in the list. You can move it to a different group in the same way — just keep dragging the component up or down the Toolbox until you have located the right group. These actions work in both List and Icon views.

If you want to copy the component from one group to another, rather than move it, hold down the Ctrl key as you drag, and the process duplicates the control so that it appears in both groups.

Sometimes it's nice to have your own group to host the controls and components you use the most. To create a new group in the Toolbox, right-click anywhere in the Toolbox area and select the Add Tab command. A new blank tab will be added to the bottom of the Toolbox with a prompt for you to name it. After you name the tab, you can then add components to it by following the steps described in this section.

When you first start Visual Studio 2017, the items within each group are arranged alphabetically. However, after moving items around, you may find that they're in a bewildering state and you may decide that you simply need to start again. All you have to do is right-click anywhere within the group and choose the Sort Items Alphabetically command.

By default, controls are added to the Toolbox according to their class names. This means you end up with some names that are hard to understand, particularly if you add COM controls to your Toolbox. Visual Studio 2017 enables you to modify a component's name to something more understandable.

To change the name of a component, right-click the component's entry in the Toolbox and select the Rename Item command. An edit field appears inline in place of the original caption, enabling you to name it however you like, even with special characters.

If you've become even more confused, with components in unusual groups, and you have lost sight of where everything is, you can choose Reset Toolbox from the same right-click context menu. This restores all the groups in the Toolbox to their original states, with components sorted alphabetically and in the groups in which they started.

> **NOTE** *Remember: Selecting Reset Toolbox permanently deletes any of your own custom-made groups of commands, so be sure you want to perform this function!*

Visual Studio 2017 includes a search function for the Toolbox. At the top of the Toolbox there is a Search area. As you type characters into this area, the components in the Toolbox are filtered to match. The search is implemented so that it finds the characters that have been typed any place they exist in the name of the control. Because the search is performed across all the groups, this is a convenient way to locate controls, provided that you know all or part of the name. Figure 2-21 shows what the Toolbox might look like after "tex" has been entered into the Search area.

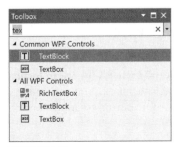

FIGURE 2-21

Adding Components

Sometimes you'll find that a particular component you need is not present in the lists displayed in the Toolbox. Most of the main .NET components (or the WPF components, if you're building an application using XAML) are already present, but some are not. For example, the WebClient class component is not displayed in the Toolbox by default. Managed applications can also use COM components in their design. When added to the Toolbox, COM objects can be used in much the same way as regular .NET or WPF components, and if coded correctly you can program against them in precisely the same way using the Properties window and referring to their methods, properties, and events in code.

To add a component to your Toolbox layout, right-click anywhere within the group of components you want to add it to and select Choose Items. After a moment (this process can take a few seconds because Visual Studio needs to interrogate the .NET cache to determine all the possible components you can choose from), you are presented with a list of .NET or WPF components, depending on the type of project. Figure 2-22 shows the list of WPF components that would be visible for a project that uses XAML. The process for loading this form can be slow, which is why developers can be thankful that Visual Studio 2017 uses a progress bar to indicate the assemblies that are being loaded.

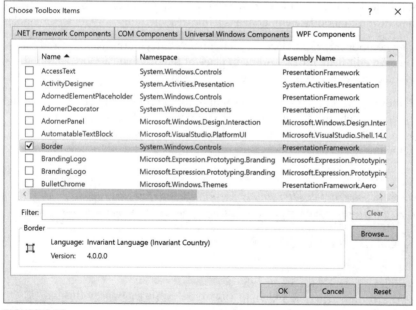

FIGURE 2-22

Scroll through the list to locate the item you want to add to the Toolbox and check the corresponding check box. You can add multiple items at the same time by selecting each of them before clicking the OK button to apply your changes. You can also remove items from the Toolbox by deselecting them from the list. Note that this removes the items from any groups to which they belong, not just from the group you are currently editing.

If you find it hard to locate the item you need, you can use the Filter box, which filters the list based on name, namespace, and assembly name. On rare occasions the item may not be listed at all. This can happen with nonstandard components, such as ones that you build yourself or that are not registered in the Global Assembly Cache (GAC). You can still add them by using the Browse button to locate the physical file on the computer. After you select and deselect the items you need, click the OK button to save them to the Toolbox layout.

COM components and Universal Windows components can be added in the same manner. Simply switch over to the relevant tab in the dialog window to view the list of available, properly registered COM components to add. Again, you can use the Browse button to locate controls that may not appear in the list.

PROPERTIES

One of the most frequently used tool windows built into Visual Studio 2017 is the Properties window (F4), as shown in Figure 2-23. The Properties window is made up of a property grid and is contextually aware, displaying only relevant properties of the currently selected item, whether that item is a node in the Solution Explorer or an element in the form design area. Each line represents a property with its name and corresponding value in two columns. The right side of Figure 2-23 shows the updated property grid for WPF applications, which includes a preview icon and search capabilities.

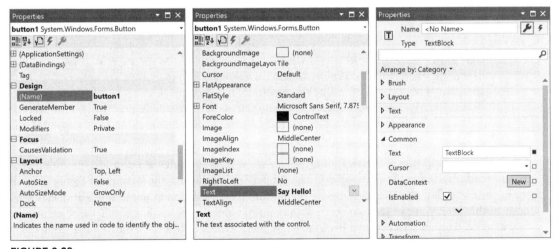

FIGURE 2-23

The Properties window is capable of grouping properties or sorting them alphabetically — you can toggle this layout using the first two buttons at the top of the Properties window. It has built-in editors for a range of system types, such as colors, fonts, anchors, and docking, which are invoked when you click into the value column of the property to be changed. When a property is selected, as shown in the center of Figure 2-23, the property name is highlighted, and a description is presented in the lower region of the property grid.

In the Properties window, read-only properties are indicated in gray and you cannot modify their values. The value Say Hello! for the Text property on the center of Figure 2-23 is boldfaced, which indicates that this is not the default value for this property. Similarly on the right side of Figure 2-23, the Text property has a filled-in black square to the right of the value, indicating the value has been specified. If you inspect the following code that is generated by the designer, you will notice that a line exists for each property that is boldfaced in the property grid — adding a line of code for every property on a control would significantly increase the time to render the form.

VB

```
Me.btnSayHello.Location = New System.Drawing.Point(12, 12)
Me.btnSayHello.Name = "btnSayHello"
Me.btnSayHello.Size = New System.Drawing.Size(100, 23)
Me.btnSayHello.TabIndex = 0
Me.btnSayHello.Text = "Say Hello!"
Me.btnSayHello.UseVisualStyleBackColor = True
```

C#

```
this.btnSayHello.Location = new System.Drawing.Point(12, 12);
this.btnSayHello.Name = "btnSayHello";
this.btnSayHello.Size = new System.Drawing.Size(100, 23);
this.btnSayHello.TabIndex = 0;
this.btnSayHello.Text = "Say Hello!";
this.btnSayHello.UseVisualStyleBackColor = true;
```

> **NOTE** *For Web and WPF applications, the properties set in the Properties window are persisted as markup in the .aspx or .xaml file, respectively. As with the Windows forms designer, only those values in the Properties window that have been set are persisted into markup.*

In addition to displaying properties for a selected item, the Properties window also provides a design experience for wiring up event handlers. The Properties window on the left side of Figure 2-24 illustrates the event view that is accessible via the lightning bolt button at the top of the Properties window. In this case, you can see that there is an event handler for the click event. To wire up another event, you can either select from a list of existing methods via a drop-down list in the value column, or you can double-click the value column. This creates a new event-handler method and wires it up to the event. If you use the first method you notice that only methods that match the event signature are listed.

Certain components, such as the DataGridView, expose a number of commands, or shortcuts, which can be executed via the Properties window. On the right side of Figure 2-24 you can see two commands for the `DataGridView`: Edit Columns and Add Column. When you click either of these command links, you are presented with a dialog for performing that action. If the commands are not immediately visible, right-click the Properties window and select Commands from the context menu.

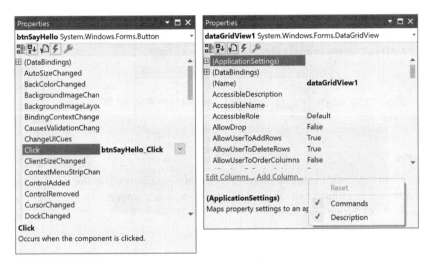

FIGURE 2-24

If the Properties window has only a small amount of screen real estate, it can be difficult to scroll through the list of properties. If you right-click in the property grid, you can uncheck the Command and Description options to hide these sections of the Properties window.

Extending the Properties Window

You have just seen how Visual Studio 2017 highlights properties that have changed by boldfacing the value. The question that you need to ask is, "How does Visual Studio 2017 know what the default value is?" The answer is that when the Properties window interrogates an object to determine what properties to display in the property grid, it looks for a number of design attributes. These attributes can be used to control which properties are displayed, the editor that is used to edit the value, and what the default value is. To show how you can use these attributes on your own components, start with adding a simple automatic property to your component:

VB

```
Public Property Description As String
```

C#

```
public string Description { get; set; }
```

The Browsable Attribute

By default, all public properties display in the property grid. However, you can explicitly control this behavior by adding the `Browsable` attribute. If you set it to `false` the property does not appear in the property grid:

VB

```
<System.ComponentModel.Browsable(False)>
Public Property Description As String
```

C#

```
[System.ComponentModel.Browsable(false)]
public string Description { get; set; }
```

DisplayName Attribute

The `DisplayName` attribute is somewhat self-explanatory; it enables you to modify the display name of the property. In our case, we can change the name of the property as it appears in the property grid from `Description` to `VS2017 Description`:

VB

```
<System.ComponentModel.DisplayName("VS2017 Description")>
Public Property Description As String
```

C#

```
[System.ComponentModel.DisplayName("VS2017 Description")]
public string Description { get; set; }
```

Description

In addition to defining the friendly or display name for the property, it is also worth providing a description, which appears in the bottom area of the Properties window when the property is selected. This ensures that users of your component understand what the property does:

VB

```
<System.ComponentModel.Description("My first custom property")>
Public Property Description As String
```

C#

```
[System.ComponentModel.Description("My first custom property")]
public string Description { get; set; }
```

Category

By default, any property you expose is placed in the Misc group when the Properties window is in grouped view. Using the `Category` attribute, you can place your property in any of the existing groups, such as Appearance or Data, or a new group if you specify a group name that does not yet exist:

VB

```
<System.ComponentModel.Category("Appearance")>
Public Property Description As String
```

C#

```
[System.ComponentModel.Category("Appearance")]
public string Description { get; set; }
```

DefaultValue

Earlier you saw how Visual Studio 2017 highlights properties that have changed from their initial or default values. The `DefaultValue` attribute is what Visual Studio 2017 looks for to determine the default value for the property:

VB

```
Private Const cDefaultDescription As String = "<enter description>"
<System.ComponentModel.DefaultValue(cDefaultDescription)>
Public Property Description As String = cDefaultDescription
```

C#

```
private const string cDefaultDescription = "<enter description>";
private string mDescription = cDefaultDescription;
[System.ComponentModel.DefaultValue(cDefaultDescription)]
public string Description
{
    get
    {
        return mDescription;
    }
    set
    {
        mDescription = value;
    }
}
```

In this case, if the value of the `Description` property is set to `"<enter description>"`, Visual Studio 2017 removes the line of code that sets this property. If you modify a property and want to return to the default value, you can right-click the property in the Properties window and select Reset from the context menu.

> **NOTE** *The* `DefaultValue` *attribute does not set the initial value of your property. It is recommended that if you specify the* `DefaultValue` *attribute you also set the initial value of your property to the same value, as done in the preceding code.*

AmbientValue

One of the features we all take for granted but that few truly understand is the concept of ambient properties. Typical examples are background and foreground colors and fonts. Unless you explicitly set these via the Properties window, they are inherited — not from their base classes, but from their parent control. A broader definition of an ambient property is a property that gets its value from another source.

Like the `DefaultValue` attribute, the `AmbientValue` attribute is used to indicate to Visual Studio 2017 when it should not add code to the designer file. Unfortunately, with ambient properties you can't hard-code a value for the designer to compare the current value to because it is contingent on the property's source value. Because of this, when you define the `AmbientValue` attribute, this tells the designer that it needs to look for a function called `ShouldSerializePropertyName`. For example, in our case, the designer would look for a method called `ShouldSerializeDescription`. This method is called to determine if the current value of the property should be persisted to the designer code file:

VB

```
Private mDescription As String = cDefaultDescription
<System.ComponentModel.AmbientValue(cDefaultDescription)>
Public Property Description As String
    Get
        If Me.mDescription = cDefaultDescription AndAlso
                            Me.Parent IsNot Nothing Then
            Return Parent.Text
        End If
        Return mDescription
    End Get
    Set(ByVal value As String)
        mDescription = value
    End Set
End Property

Private Function ShouldSerializeDescription() As Boolean
    If Me.Parent IsNot Nothing Then
        Return Not Me.Description = Me.Parent.Text
    Else
        Return Not Me.Description = cDefaultDescription
    End If
End function
```

C#

```
private string mDescription = cDefaultDescription;
[System.ComponentModel.AmbientValue(cDefaultDescription)]
```

```
public string Description{
    get{
        if (this.mDescription == cDefaultDescription &&
            this.Parent != null){
            return Parent.Text;
        }
        return mDescription;
    }
    set{
        mDescription = value;
    }
}

private bool ShouldSerializeDescription(){
    if (this.Parent != null){
        return this.Description != this.Parent.Text;
    }
    else{
        return this.Description != cDefaultDescription;
    }
}
```

When you create a control with this property, the initial value would be set to the value of the `DefaultDescription` constant, but in the designer you would see a value corresponding to the `Parent.Text` value. There would also be no line explicitly setting this property in the designer code file, as reflected in the Properties window by the value being non-boldfaced. If you change the value of this property to anything other than the `DefaultDescription` constant, you'll see that it becomes bold and a line is added to the designer code file. If you reset this property, the underlying value is set back to the value defined by `AmbientValue`, but all you'll see is that it has returned to displaying the `Parent.Text` value.

SUMMARY

In this chapter you have seen three of the most common tool windows in action. Knowing how to manipulate these windows can save you considerable time during development. However, the true power of Visual Studio 2017 is exposed when you start to incorporate the designer experience into your own components. This can be useful even if your components aren't going to be used outside your organization. Making effective use of the designer can improve not only the efficiency with which your controls are used, but also the performance of the application you are building.

3

Options and Customizations

WHAT'S IN THIS CHAPTER?

- ➤ Customizing the Visual Studio 2017 start page
- ➤ Tweaking options
- ➤ Controlling window layout

WROX.COM CODE DOWNLOADS FOR THIS CHAPTER

The wrox.com code downloads for this chapter can be found at www.wrox.com by searching for this book's ISBN number (978-1-119-40458-3). The code and any related support files are located in their own folder for this chapter.

In this chapter you'll learn how you can customize the IDE to suit your working style. You'll also learn how to manipulate tool windows, optimize the code window for maximum viewing space, and change fonts and colors to reduce developer fatigue.

As Visual Studio has grown, so too has the number of settings that you can adjust to optimize your development experience. Unfortunately, unless you've periodically spent time sifting through the Options dialog (Tools ➪ Options), it's likely that you've overlooked one or two settings that might be important or make your development life easier. Through the course of this chapter, you'll see a number of settings that, hopefully, are worth further investigation.

The ability to customize your settings is not new to Visual Studio 2017. Nor is the ability to import and export settings. However, Microsoft's push to the cloud has had an impact on Visual Studio. You can automatically synchronize your settings between the cloud and any instance of Visual Studio that you log in to.

A number of Visual Studio extensions add their own nodes to the Options dialog because this provides a one-stop shop for configuring settings within Visual Studio. Note also that some developer setting profiles, as selected in Chapter 1, "A Quick Tour," show only a reduced list of options. In this case, checking the Advanced check box shows the complete list of available options.

THE START PAGE

By default, when you open a new instance of Visual Studio 2017, you see the Start Page. You can adjust this behavior from the Environment ⇨ Startup node of the Options dialog. Other alternatives are to display the Home Page (which you can set via the Environment ⇨ Web Browser node), the last loaded solution, the open or new project dialogs, or no action at all.

The reason that most developers stick with the Start Page is that it provides a useful starting point from which to jump to any number of actions. In Figure 3-1, you can see that there is a link in the middle column for creating or opening projects and connecting to Visual Studio Team Services. On the left, there is a list of previously opened projects, allowing you to quickly open projects that you have recently been working on. Hovering the mouse over a project displays a horizontal pin on the right side. Clicking the pin changes its orientation to vertical to indicate that the project has been pinned to the Recent Projects list. You can right-click a project and, using a context menu option, remove the project from the list. If the Start Page is closed and you want to open it again, you can do so by selecting the File ⇨ Start Page menu item.

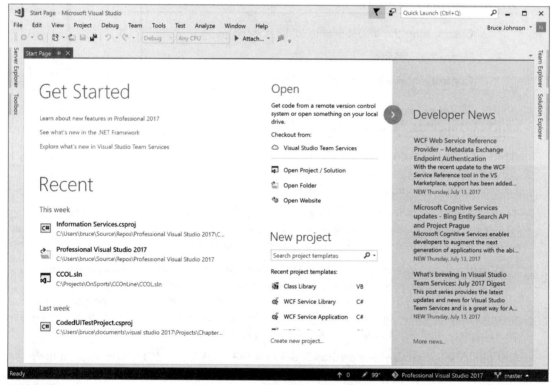

FIGURE 3-1

On the right of the Start Page is a Developer News feed. In general, the stories that you'll see here are related to the various products and tools that might be of interest to Visual Studio developers.

Customizing the Start Page

In Visual Studio 2017, the Start Page is a Windows Presentation Foundation (WPF) control hosted within the integrated development environment (IDE) shell. You can tailor the Start Page to feature information or actions relevant to you. Rather than modifying the default Start Page, Visual Studio supports user-specific or custom Start Pages. This functionality is enabled by creating a Visual Studio Extension (VSIX) package. The details related to the creation and deployment of VSIX packages are covered in Chapter 62, "Managed Extensibility Framework (MEF)" in the online archive.

WINDOW LAYOUT

If you are unfamiliar with Visual Studio, the behavior of the numerous tool windows may strike you as erratic because they seem to appear in random locations and then come and go when you move between writing code (design time) and running code (run time). Actually, Visual Studio 2017 remembers the locations of tool windows in each of these modes. This way, you can optimize the way you write and debug code separately.

The toolbars in Visual Studio that are visible by default, as well as the buttons contained within them, have been decreasing in number over the different versions. The simplification was based on a lot of user feedback (gathered through both questioning and metering) that identified the buttons that were most commonly used in the previous toolbars. The buttons that, for whatever reason, didn't make the cut can always be added manually. They are just not part of the default set. And the icons that remain are, for the most part, the ones most frequently used.

As you open different items from the Solution Explorer, you can see that the number of toolbars across the top of the screen varies depending on the type of file being opened. Each toolbar (and, indeed, each button) has a built-in association to specific file extensions so that Visual Studio knows to display the toolbar (or enable/disable a button) when a file with one of those extensions is opened. If you close a toolbar when a file is open that has a matching file extension, Visual Studio remembers this when future files with the same extension are opened.

> **NOTE** *You can reset the association between toolbars and the file extensions via the Customize dialog (Tools ⇨ Customize). On the Commands tab, select the appropriate toolbar, and click the Reset All button.*

Viewing Windows and Toolbars

After a tool window or toolbar has been closed, it can be difficult to locate it again. Luckily, the most frequently used tool windows are accessible via the View menu. Other tool windows, mainly related to debugging, are located under the Debug ⇨ Windows menu.

All the toolbars available in Visual Studio 2017 are listed under the View ⇨ Toolbars menu item. This includes toolbars from third-party extensions that you have installed. Each toolbar currently visible is marked with a check beside the appropriate menu item. You can also access the list of toolbars by right-clicking in any empty space in the toolbar area at the top of the Visual Studio window.

When a toolbar is visible, you can customize which buttons are displayed, either via View ➪ Toolbars ➪ Customize or Tools ➪ Customize. Alternatively, as shown in Figure 3-2, if you select the down arrow at the end of a toolbar, you see a list of all the buttons available on that toolbar, from which you can check the buttons you want to appear on the toolbar.

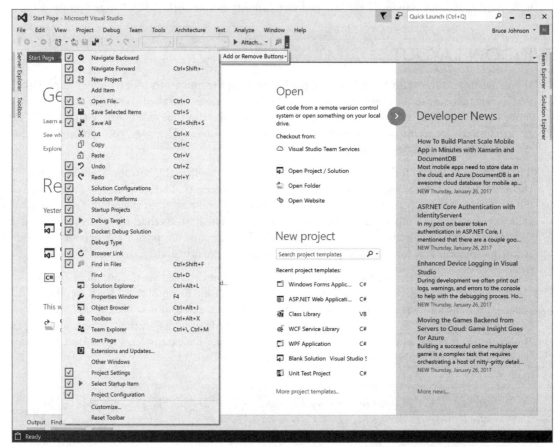

FIGURE 3-2

Docking

Each tool window has a default position, which it resumes when it is opened from the View menu. For example, by default View ➪ Toolbox opens the Toolbox docked to the left edge of Visual Studio. When a tool window is opened and is docked against an edge, it has two states, pinned and unpinned. As you saw in Chapter 1, you can toggle between these states by clicking the vertical pin to unpin the tool window or the horizontal pin to pin the tool window.

As you unpin a tool window, it disappears back against the edge of the IDE, leaving visible a tag displaying the title of the tool window. To redisplay the tool window, the default behavior requires that you click the visible tag. If you would prefer the window to appear when the mouse hovers over the tag, go into the Options dialog and locate the Environment ⇨ Tabs and Windows node. At the bottom, there is an option named Show Auto-Hidden Windows on Mouse Over. If you check this, then as you move your mouse over the tab, the hidden window becomes visible. Most developers accept the default location of tool windows, but occasionally you may want to adjust where the tool windows appear. Visual Studio 2017 has a sophisticated system for controlling the layout of tool windows. In Chapter 1 you saw how you could use the drop-down, next to the Pin and Close buttons at the top of the tool window, to make the tool window floating, dockable, or even part of the main editor space (using the Tabbed Document option).

When a tool window is dockable, you have a lot of control over where it is positioned. In Figure 3-3 you can see the Properties window, which has been dragged away from its default position at the right of the IDE. To begin dragging, you need to click either the title area at the top of the tool window or the tab at the bottom of the tool window and drag the mouse in the direction you want the window to move. If you click in the title area, you see that all tool windows in that section of the IDE will also be moved. Clicking the tab results in only the corresponding tool window moving.

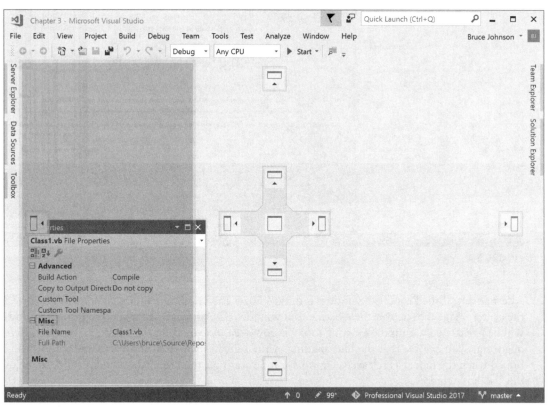

FIGURE 3-3

As you drag the tool window around Visual Studio 2017, you see that translucent icons appear at different locations around the IDE. These icons are a useful guide to help you position the tool window exactly where you want. In Figure 3-4 the Toolbox window has been pinned against the left side. Now when the Properties window is positioned over the left icon of the center image, the blue shading again appears on the inside of the existing tool window. This indicates that the Properties window will be pinned to the right of the Toolbox window and visible if this layout is chosen. If the far left icon were selected, the Properties window would again be pinned to the left of the IDE, but this time to the left of the Toolbox window.

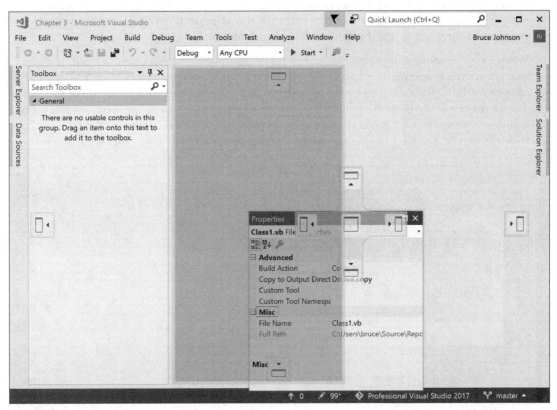

FIGURE 3-4

Alternatively, if the Properties window is dragged over the Toolbox window as shown in Figure 3-5, the center image moves over the existing tool window. This indicates that the Properties window will be positioned within the existing tool window area. As you drag the window over the different quadrants, you can see that the blue shading again indicates where the tool window will be positioned when the mouse is released. Figure 3-5 indicates that the Properties window appears below the Toolbox window.

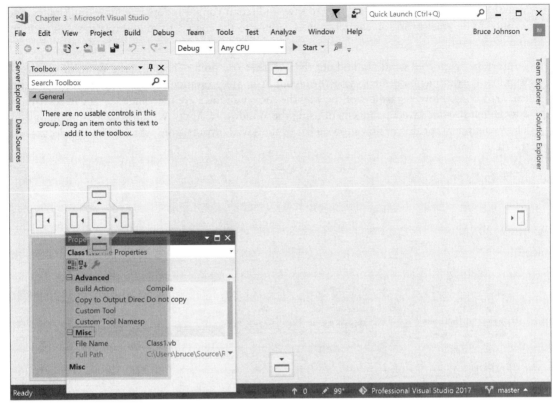

FIGURE 3-5

> **NOTE** *If you have a large screen or multiple screens, it is worth spending time laying out the tool windows you use frequently. With multiple screens, using floating tool windows means that you can position them away from the main editor space, maximizing the utility of your screen real estate. If you have a small screen, you may find that you continually have to adjust which tool windows are visible, so becoming familiar with the docking and layout options is essential.*

Saving the Window Layout

One of the more frustrating user experiences with Visual Studio occurs when you are using a laptop that is only occasionally connected to a multi-monitor environment. It's wonderful that you can position your tool windows while you are in multi-monitor mode. However, if you remove the external monitors from your laptop and launch Visual Studio, all the tool windows reposition themselves so that they are visible on your single screen. And when you plug back into the multi-monitors, you need to go through the effort of repositioning the windows.

Visual Studio 2017 includes the ability to save and recall your Window Layout — multiple window layouts, to be precise. So you can more easily adjust to the change from multiple to single monitors and back again.

To start, get your tool windows laid out the way that you prefer. Then use the Window ⇨ Save Window Layout menu option to save the layout. You are prompted for the name of the layout that you are saving. Now, regardless of the way the tools windows are rearranged, you can reset the window layout to your saved arrangement using the Window ⇨ Apply Window Layout menu option. The flyout menu for this option shows a list of the saved layouts from which you can select, as illustrated in Figure 3-6.

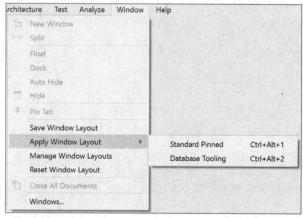

FIGURE 3-6

If you want to manage your saved window layouts, select the Window ⇨ Manage Window Layouts menu option. This launches the Manage Windows Layouts dialog (shown in Figure 3-7), which contains a list of the saved layouts and allows you to delete or rename the arrangements that have been saved.

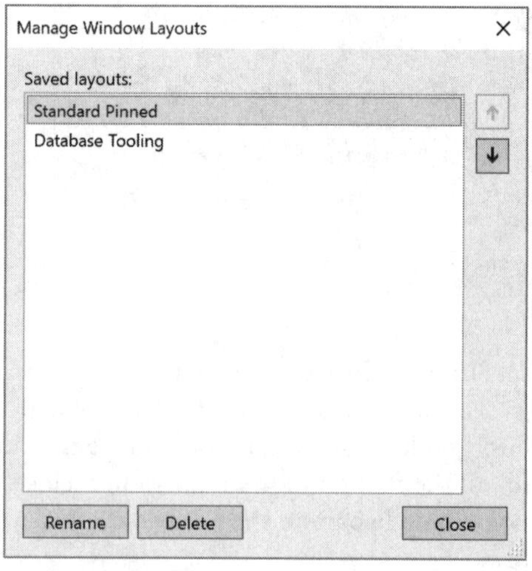

FIGURE 3-7

Finally, if you would like to reset your tool windows to their default locations, there is the Window ➪ Reset Window Layout menu option ready to assist you in this endeavor.

THE EDITOR SPACE

Like most IDEs, Visual Studio 2017 was built up around the central code-editing window. Over time, it evolved and became much more than a simple text editor. Though most developers spend considerable time writing code in the editor space, an increasing number of designers are available for performing tasks such as building forms, adjusting project settings, and editing resources. Regardless of whether you write code or do form design, you are going to spend a lot of your time within Visual Studio 2017 in the editor space. Because of this, you should know how to tweak the settings so that you can work more efficiently.

Visual Studio 2017 supports the ability to apply a theme to your IDE. There are three main themes that are available in Visual Studio 2017: Dark, Light, and Blue. For Light, the color choices are gray and black. For Dark, the color choices are black and white. Few, if any, gradients can be found. The only coloration appears in the icons used in the toolbars and as an accent in the various tool windows. The Blue theme is intended to resemble the colors that were found in Visual Studio 2012 and earlier.

The default theme is Light, which is what the vast majority of images in this book were created in. The top image in Figure 3-8 shows the Dark theme, and the bottom image is the Blue theme.

You can change the theme through the Options option on the Tools menu. You can select the color theme from the drop-down that appears in the Environment node.

Navigating Open Items

After opening multiple items in the editor space, you might notice that you run out of room across the top and can no longer see the tabs for all the items you have opened. Of course, you can go back to the Solution Explorer window and select a specific item. If the item is already open, it displays without reverting to its saved state. However, it is still inconvenient to have to find the item in the Solution Explorer.

Luckily, Visual Studio 2017 has a number of shortcuts to access the list of open items. Like most document-based applications, Visual Studio has a Windows menu. When you open an item, its title is added to the bottom section of this menu. To display an open item, just select the item from the Windows menu or click the generic Windows item, which displays a modal dialog from which you can select the item you want.

Another alternative is to use the drop-down menu at the end of the tab area of the editor space. Figure 3-9 shows the drop-down list of open items from which you can select the item you want to access.

The right side of Figure 3-9 is the same as the left side except for the drop-down icon. This menu also displays a down arrow, but this one has a line across the top. This line indicates that there are more tabs than can fit across the top of the editor space.

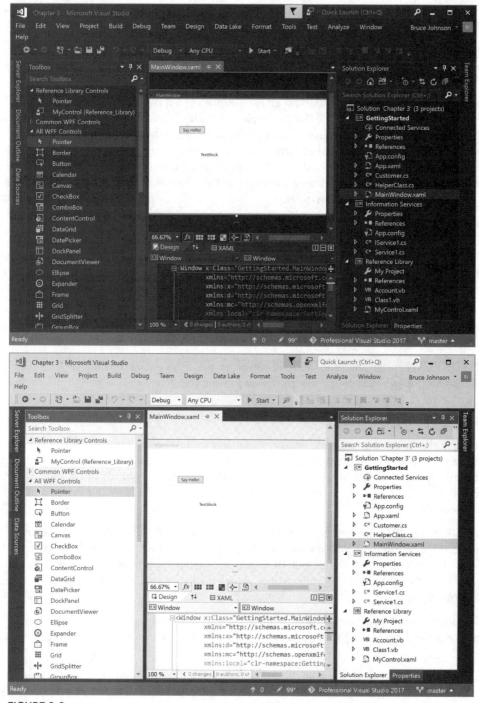

FIGURE 3-8

MainWindow.xaml
Class1.vb
IService1.cs
MainWindow.xaml
MainWindow.xaml.cs
Class1.vb
IService1.cs
MainWindow.xaml
MainWindow.xaml.cs

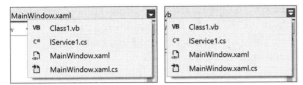

FIGURE 3-9

Another way to navigate through the open items is to press Ctrl+Tab, which displays a temporary window, as shown in Figure 3-10. It is a temporary window because when you release the Ctrl key it disappears. However, while the window is open, you can use the arrow keys or press Tab to move among the open windows.

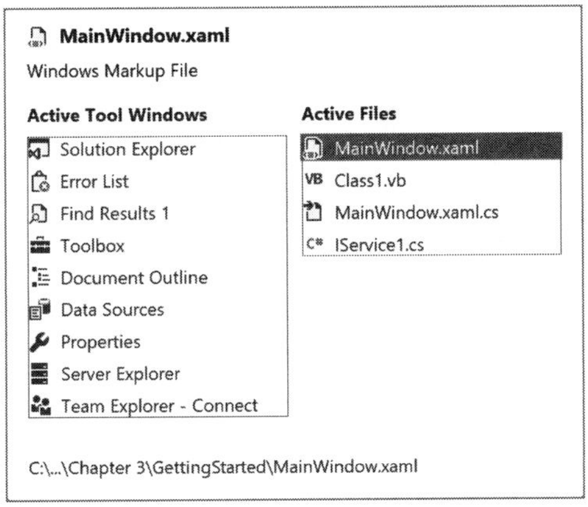
MainWindow.xaml
Windows Markup File
Active Tool Windows
Solution Explorer
Error List
Find Results 1
Toolbox
Document Outline
Data Sources
Properties
Server Explorer
Team Explorer - Connect
Active Files
MainWindow.xaml
Class1.vb
MainWindow.xaml.cs
IService1.cs
C:\...\Chapter 3\GettingStarted\MainWindow.xaml

FIGURE 3-10

The Ctrl+Tab window is divided into two sections: Active Tool Windows and Active Files (which actually also contains some items that don't correspond to a single file). As the number of either active files or active tool windows increases, the windows expand vertically until there are 15 items, at which point an additional column is formed.

> **NOTE** *If you get to the point where you see multiple columns of active files, you might consider closing some or all of the unused files. The more files Visual Studio 2017 has open, the more memory it uses and the slower it performs. Even in 2017, Visual Studio is still only a 32-bit application.*

If you right-click the tab of an open item, you will see a hidden context menu that gives you a quick way to do common tasks such as save or close the file that's associated with the tab. Several particularly useful actions are Close All Documents, Close All but This, Copy File Path and Open Containing Folder. These are self-descriptive; the first closes all open documents, the second closes all tabs other than the one you clicked to get the context menu, the third copies the full path for the select file into the clipboard, and the fourth opens the folder that contains the file in Windows Explorer. Because all the windows are dockable, there are also actions to Float or Dock as Tabbed Document, which are enabled depending on what state the tab is in.

Fonts and Colors

Some of the first things that presenters change in Visual Studio are the fonts and colors used in the editor space to make the code more readable. However, it shouldn't just be presenters who adjust these settings. Selecting fonts and colors that are easy for you to read and that aren't harsh on the eyes can make you more productive and enable you to code for longer without feeling fatigued. Figure 3-11 shows the Fonts and Colors node of the Options dialog, where you can make adjustments to the font, size, color, and styling of different display items.

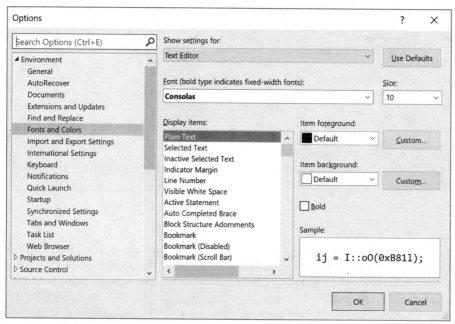

FIGURE 3-11

To adjust the appearance of a particular text item within Visual Studio 2017, you first need to select the area of the IDE that it applies to. In Figure 3-11, the Text Editor has been selected and has been used to determine which items should appear in the Display Items list. When you find the relevant item in this list, you can make adjustments to the font and colors.

> **NOTE** *Some items in the Display Items list, such as Plain Text, are reused by a number of areas within Visual Studio 2017, which can result in some unpredictable changes when you tweak fonts and colors.*

...mber that proportional fonts are usually not as effective for writing ...wn as fixed-width fonts). Fixed-width fonts are distin-...s bolded) from the variable-width types, so they are

...7 automatically colors the code based on the type of file. For ...in blue, variable names and class references in black, and ... can see that there is a line running up the left side of the ...cks are. You can click the minus sign to condense the ...tire Form1 code block.

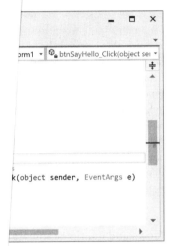

...es are shown in Figures 3-13 and 3-14. In Figure 3-13, ...e Options dialog. (See the Text Editor ⇨ All Languages ⇨

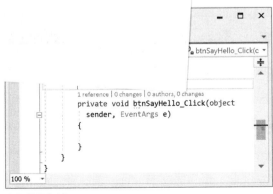

```
1 reference | 0 changes | 0 authors, 0 changes
private void btnSayHello_Click(object
    sender, EventArgs e)
{

}
```

FIGURE 3-13

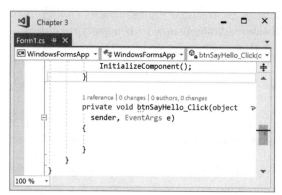

FIGURE 3-14

Unfortunately, enabling word wrapping can make it hard to work out which lines have been wrapped. Fortunately, Visual Studio 2017 has an option (immediately below the check box to enable word wrapping in the Options dialog) that can display visual glyphs at the end of each line that indicate a line has been wrapped to the next line (see Figure 3-14). There are also two other visual guides you can use. On the left, outside the code block markers, you can include line numbers. These can be enabled via the Line Numbers check box below both the Word Wrap and Visual Glyphs check boxes. The other guide is the use of dots that represent space in the code. Unlike the other visual guides, this one can be enabled via the Edit ⇨ Advanced ⇨ View White Space menu item when the code editor space has focus.

Full-Screen Mode

If you have a number of tool windows and multiple toolbars visible, you might have noticed that you quickly run out of space for actually writing code. For this reason, Visual Studio 2017 has a full-screen mode that you can access via the View ⇨ Full Screen menu item. Alternatively, you can press Shift+Alt+Enter to toggle in and out of full-screen mode. Figure 3-15 shows the top of Visual Studio 2017 in full-screen mode. As you can see, no toolbars or tool windows are visible, and the window is completely maximized, even to the exclusion of the normal Minimize, Restore, and Close buttons. And the text Full Screen appears in the menu bar. By clicking on the text, you can toggle out of full-screen mode.

FIGURE 3-15

NOTE *If you use multiple screens, full-screen mode can be particularly useful. Undock the tool windows and place them on the second monitor. When the editor window is in full-screen mode, you still have access to the tool windows, without having to toggle back and forth. If you undock a code window this will not be set to full screen.*

Tracking Changes

To enhance the experience of editing, Visual Studio 2017 uses line-level tracking to indicate which lines of code you have modified during an editing session. When you open a file to begin editing there will be no line coloring. However, when you begin to edit, you notice that a yellow (light gray for the Dark theme) mark appears next to the lines that have been modified. In Figure 3-16 you can see that the `Console.WriteLine` line has been modified since this file was last saved.

FIGURE 3-16

When the file is saved, the modified lines change to having a green (same color in the Dark theme) mark next to them. In Figure 3-17 the first `Console .WriteLine` line has changed since the file was opened, but those changes have been saved to disk. However, the second `Console.WriteLine` line has not yet been saved.

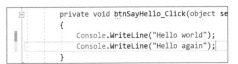

FIGURE 3-17

NOTE *If you don't find tracking changes to be useful, you can disable this feature by unchecking the Text Editor ⇨ General ⇨ Track Changes node in the Options dialog.*

OTHER OPTIONS

You can use many options that haven't yet been mentioned to tweak the way Visual Studio operates. The remainder of this chapter presents some of the more useful options that can help you be more productive.

Keyboard Shortcuts

Visual Studio 2017 ships with many ways to perform the same action. Menus, toolbars, and various tool windows provide direct access to many commands, but despite the huge number available, many more are not accessible through the graphical interface. Instead, these commands are accessed (along with most of those in the menus and toolbars) via keyboard shortcuts.

These shortcuts range from the familiar Ctrl+Shift+S to save all changes, to the obscure Ctrl+Alt+E to display the Exceptions Settings window. As you might have guessed, you can set your own keyboard shortcuts and even change the existing ones. Even better, you can filter the shortcuts to operate only in certain contexts, meaning you can use the same shortcut differently depending on what you're doing.

Figure 3-18 shows the Keyboard node in the Environment section of the Options dialog with the Visual C# 2005 keyboard mapping scheme selected. If you want to change to use a different keyboard mapping scheme, simply select it from the drop-down, and press the Reset button.

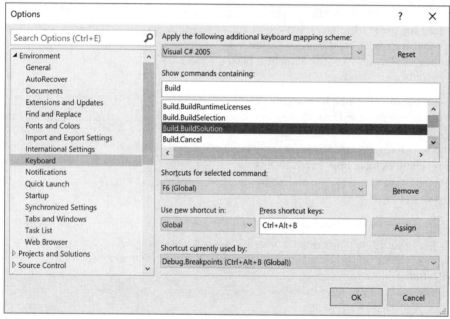

FIGURE 3-18

> **NOTE** *The keyboard mapping schemes are stored as VSK files at* `C:\Program Files\Microsoft Visual Studio 15.0\Common7\IDE` *(or* `C:\Program Files (x86)\Microsoft Visual Studio 15.0\Common7\IDE` *if you are using the 64-bit version of Windows). This is the keyboard mapping file format used in versions of Visual Studio after Visual Studio 2005. To import keyboard mappings from Visual Studio 2005, use the Import and Export Settings wizard described in the "Importing and Exporting Settings" section later in this chapter; for earlier versions, copy the appropriate VSK file into the aforementioned folder, and you can select it from the mapping scheme drop-down the next time you open the Options dialog.*

The listbox in the middle of Figure 3-18 lists every command that is available in Visual Studio 2017. Unfortunately, this list is quite extensive and the Options dialog is not resizable, which makes navigating this list difficult. To make it easier to search for commands, you can filter the command list using the Show Commands Containing textbox. In Figure 3-18 the word *Build* has been used to filter the list down to all the commands starting with or containing that word. From this list the `Build.BuildSolution` command has been selected. Because there is already a keyboard shortcut assigned to this command, the Shortcuts for Selected Command drop-down and the Remove button have been enabled. It is possible to have multiple shortcuts for the same command, so the drop-down enables you to remove individual assigned shortcuts.

> **NOTE** *Having multiple shortcuts is useful if you want to keep a default shortcut — so that other developers feel at home using your setup — but also add your own personal one.*

The remainder of this dialog enables you to assign a new shortcut to the command you have selected. Simply move to the Press Shortcut Keys textbox, and as the label suggests, press the appropriate keys. In Figure 3-18 the keyboard chord Ctrl+Alt+B has been entered, but this shortcut is already being used by another command, as shown at the bottom of the dialog window. If you click the Assign button, this keyboard shortcut will be remapped to the `Build.BuildSolution` command.

To restrict a shortcut's use to only one contextual area of Visual Studio 2017, select the context from the Use New Shortcut In drop-down list. The currently selected Global option indicates that the shortcut should be applied across the entire environment, but the list of elements in the drop-down includes a surprisingly large list of designers and editors found in Visual Studio.

Quick Launch

The continuing proliferation of commands available in Visual Studio cannot be fully addressed by programming keyboard shortcuts. Aside from the sheer number of commands, it is also possible to run out of reasonable keyboard combinations.

To alleviate this problem, Visual Studio 2017 includes a feature called Quick Launch. Opened from the top-left portion of the toolbar or by using the Ctrl+Q shortcut (and shown in Figure 3-19), visually, it looks like any other search textbox. The difference is that the scope of the search is every command that exists within Visual Studio. So regardless of whether the command is in the toolbar, on one of the menus, or not associated with either, the search box can find it.

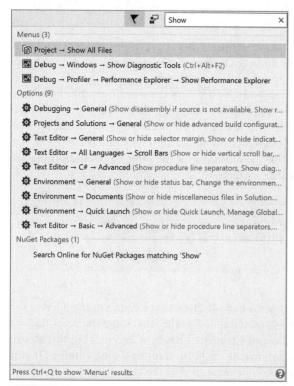

FIGURE 3-19

The search box is also a progressive one. As you type characters, the list of possible matches displays. The matches are placed in up to five different categories: Most Recently Used, Menus, Options, NuGet Packages, and Open Documents. Not all the matches are shown in each category. (The results would be too overwhelming, in some cases.) If you want to see more results from a particular category, you can use Ctrl+Q or Ctrl+Shift+Q to navigate back and forth through the categories, showing more from each category as appropriate.

You can also limit your search to the items in a specific category directory from the textbox. For example, entering the text `@mru font` would display the most recently used items that include the term "font." For the other categories, the scoping keywords are @menu, @opt, and @doc.

The default setting for Quick Launch is to not persist the search terms. After you move your cursor outside the Quick Launch area, the text area is cleared. If you want to modify this behavior so that the search terms are persisted, you can use the Quick Launch node in Tools ⇨ Options. Ensuring that the Show Search Results from Previous Search When Quick Launch Is Activated check box is checked allows your previous search terms to be preserved the next time you access Quick Launch.

Projects and Solutions

Several options relate to projects and solutions. The first of these is perhaps the most helpful — the default locations of your projects. By default, Visual Studio 2017 uses the standard Documents and Settings path common to many applications (see Figure 3-20), but this might not be where you want to keep your development work.

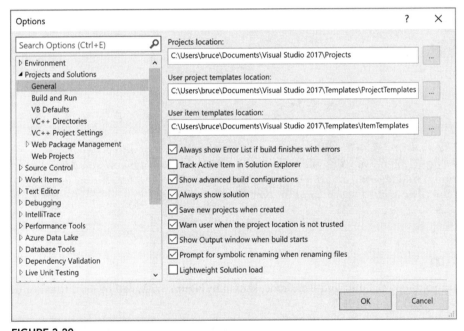

FIGURE 3-20

You can also change the location of template files at this point. If your organization uses a common network location for corporate project templates, you can change the default location in Visual Studio 2017 to point to this remote address rather than map the network drive.

You can adjust a number of other options to change how projects and solutions are managed in Visual Studio 2017. One of particular interest is Track Active Item in Solution Explorer. With this option enabled, the layout of the Solution Explorer changes as you switch among items to ensure the current item is in focus. This includes expanding (but not collapsing again) projects and folders, which can be frustrating on a large solution because you are continually having to collapse projects so that you can navigate more effectively.

Another option that relates to solutions, but doesn't appear in Figure 3-20, is to list miscellaneous files in the Solution Explorer. Say you are working on a solution and you have to inspect an XML document that isn't contained in the solution. Visual Studio 2017 will happily open the file, but you will have to reopen it every time you open the solution. Alternatively, if you enable Environment ⇨ Documents ⇨ Show Miscellaneous Files in Solution Explorer via the Options dialog, the file will be temporarily added to the solution. The miscellaneous files folder to which this file is added is shown in Figure 3-21.

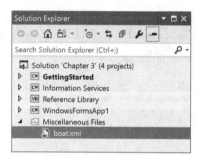

FIGURE 3-21

> **NOTE** *Visual Studio 2017 will automatically manage the list of miscellaneous files, keeping only the most recent ones, based on the number of files defined in the Options dialog. You can get Visual Studio to track up to 256 files in this list, and files will be evicted based on when they were last accessed.*

Build and Run

The Projects and Solutions ⇨ Build and Run node, shown in Figure 3-22, can be used to tailor the build behavior of Visual Studio 2017.

To reduce the amount of time it takes to build your solution, you may want to increase the maximum number of parallel builds that are performed. Visual Studio 2017 can build in parallel only those projects that are not dependent, but if you have a large number of independent projects, this might yield a noticeable benefit. Be aware that on a single-core or single-processor machine this may actually increase the time taken to build your solution.

Figure 3-22 shows that projects will Prompt to Build when they are out of date, and that if there are build errors, the solution will not launch. Both these options can increase your productivity, but be warned that they eliminate dialogs letting you know what's going on.

> **NOTE** *The last option worth noting in Figure 3-22 is the MSBuild project build output verbosity. In most cases the Visual Studio 2017 build output is sufficient for debugging build errors. However, in some cases, particularly when building ASP.NET projects, you need to increase verbosity to diagnose a build error. Visual Studio 2017 has the capability to control the log file verbosity independently of the output.*

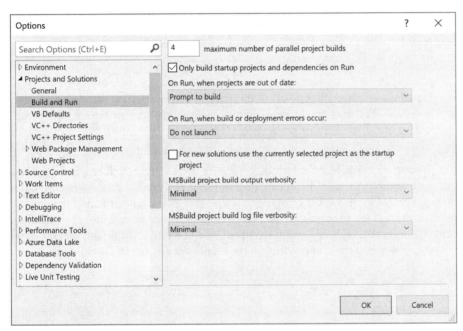

FIGURE 3-22

VB Options

VB programmers have four compiler options that can be configured at a project or a file level. You can also set the defaults on the Projects and Solutions ➪ VB Defaults node of the Options dialog.

Option Strict enforces good programming practices by making developers explicitly convert variables to their correct types, rather than letting the compiler try to guess the proper conversion method. This results in fewer runtime issues and better performance.

> **NOTE** *We advise strongly that you use Option Strict to ensure that your code is not implicitly converting variables inadvertently. If you are not using Option Strict, with all the language features included in .NET Framework, you may not be making the most effective use of the language.*

IMPORTING AND EXPORTING SETTINGS

When you have the IDE in exactly the configuration you want, you may want to back up the settings for future use. You can do this by exporting the IDE settings to a file that can then be used to restore the settings or even transfer them to a series of Visual Studio 2017 installations so that they all share the same IDE setup.

> **NOTE** *The Environment ⇨ Import and Export Settings node in the Options dialog enables you to specify a team settings file. This can be located on a network share, and Visual Studio 2017 can automatically apply new settings if the file changes.*

To export the current configuration, select Tools ⇨ Import and Export Settings to start the Import and Export Settings wizard. The first step in the wizard is to select the Export option and which settings are to be backed up during the export procedure.

As shown in Figure 3-23, a variety of grouped options can be exported. The screenshot shows the Options section expanded, revealing that the Debugging and Projects settings will be backed up along with the Test Execution and Performance Tools configurations. As the small exclamation icon indicates, some settings are not included in the export by default because they contain information that may infringe on your privacy. You need to select such sections manually if you want them to be included in the backup. After you select the settings you want to export, you can progress through the rest of the wizard, which might take a few minutes depending on the number of settings being exported.

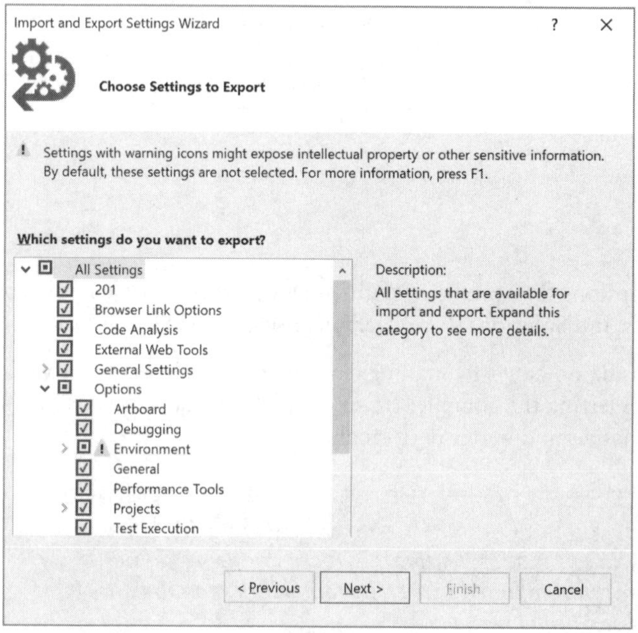

FIGURE 3-23

Importing a settings file is just as easy. The same wizard is used, but you select the Import option on the first screen. Rather than simply overwriting the current configuration, the wizard enables you to back up the current setup first.

You can then select from a list of preset configuration files — the same set of files from which you can choose when you first start Visual Studio 2017 — or browse to a settings file that you created previously. When the settings file has been chosen, you can then choose to import only certain sections of the configuration or import the whole lot.

The wizard excludes some sections by default, such as External Tools or Command Aliases, so that you don't inadvertently overwrite customized settings. Make sure you select these sections if you want to do a full restore.

> **NOTE** *If you just want to restore the configuration of Visual Studio 2017 to one of the default presets, you can choose the Reset All Settings option in the opening screen of the wizard, rather than go through the import process.*

Visual Studio provides the ability for team members to share settings. One of the reasons this facility can be so useful is the result of seemingly innocuous settings, such as the tab stops and whether tabs are converted to spaces. When different team members have different settings, merely editing a file can cause nonfunctional code changes (for example, the addition or removal of a space at the beginning of a line has no effect on the functioning on the code). However, when these code files get checked in to a source code repository, those changes have the potential to appear as conflicts.

If you are working with a team of developers on the same code base, it's a good idea to work from a common settings file. In the Environment ⇨ Import and Export Settings option of the Tools ⇨ Options menu, there is a Use Team Settings File check box, as shown in Figure 3-24.

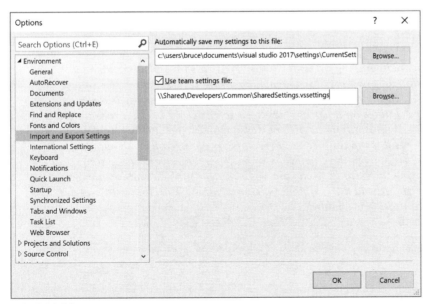

FIGURE 3-24

When this check box is selected, a path to a shared Visual Studio settings file must be specified. In case you are concerned about losing any individuality with respect to customizing Visual Studio, only those settings that are found in the shared settings file are applied. You can create your own customizations so long as they don't conflict with the shared settings.

Synchronized Settings

Like many Microsoft products, Visual Studio 2017 is increasing its awareness of all things cloud. You can sign in to Visual Studio with a Microsoft account and your Visual Studio settings will be synchronized across all of your machines. This synchronization process, although turned on by default (presuming that you have signed in), does not apply to every single setting in Visual Studio. The following settings are synchronized:

- ➤ Your development settings (that is, the set of options and keyboard bindings you selected when you launched Visual Studio for the first time)

- ➤ The Theme settings on the Environment ➪ General options page

- ➤ All of the settings on the Environment ➪ Fonts and Colors options page

- ➤ All keyboard shortcuts on the Environment ➪ Keyboard options page

- ➤ All settings on the Environment ➪ Startup options page

- ➤ All settings on the Text Editor options pages

- ➤ All user-defined command aliases

It is possible to turn synchronization off altogether, through the Environment ➪ Synchronized Settings option page (see Figure 3-25). To turn off synchronization completely, make sure that the Synchronize Settings Across Devices When Signed into Visual Studio check box is not selected. It's also possible to segregate the synchronization of the settings so that they are only shared when you are logged in to Azure Active Directory and not when you're logged in to an on-premise Active Directory domain.

> **NOTE** *If you are upgrading to Visual Studio 2017, it's possible that you will receive a slightly different message when configuring your synchronized settings. Specifically, a warning message might appear in the Options dialog box saying "Synchronized settings on this machine have been disabled because the online collection of settings is different." There is also a link to resolve the conflict. If you choose to resolve the conflict, a dialog appears giving you three options: copying the settings from the cloud to your environment (overwriting your local settings), copying the settings from your environment to the cloud (overwriting your cloud settings), and not enabling synchronization. With the first two selections, synchronization is enabled.*

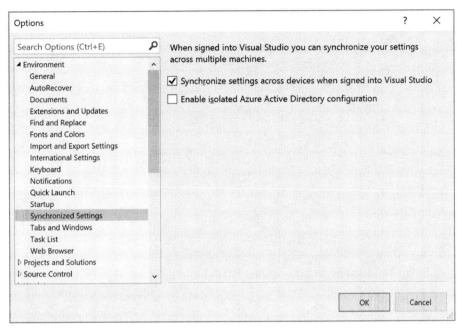

FIGURE 3-25

SUMMARY

This chapter covered only a core selection of the useful options available to you as you start to shape the Visual Studio interface to suit your own programming style; many other options are available. These numerous options enable you to adjust the way you edit your code, add controls to your forms, and even select the methods to use when debugging code.

The settings within the Visual Studio 2017 Options page also enable you to control how and where applications are created, and even to customize the keyboard shortcuts you use. What's more, the options that you modify on one instance of Visual Studio can be automatically and seamlessly synchronized across all of the different instances of Visual Studio that you use.

Throughout the remainder of this book, you can see the Options dialog revisited according to specific functionality such as compiling, debugging, and writing macros.

The Visual Studio Workspace

WHAT'S IN THIS CHAPTER?

➤ Using the code editor

➤ Exploring the core Visual Studio tool windows

➤ Navigating through your code

WROX.COM CODE DOWNLOADS FOR THIS CHAPTER

The wrox.com code downloads for this chapter can be found at www.wrox.com by searching for this book's ISBN number (978-1-119-40458-3). The code and any related support files are located in their own folder for this chapter.

So far you have seen how to get started with Visual Studio 2017 and how to customize the IDE to suit the way that you work. In this chapter, you'll learn to take advantage of some of the built-in commands, shortcuts, gestures, and supporting tool windows that can help you to write code and design forms.

THE CODE EDITOR

As a developer you're likely to spend a considerable portion of your time writing code, which means that knowing how to tweak the layout of your code and navigating it effectively are particularly important. The Windows Presentation Foundation (WPF)-based code editor provides numerous features, including navigating, formatting, using multiple monitors, creating tab groups, searching, and more.

The Code Editor Window Layout

When you open a code file for editing, you are working in the code editor window, as shown in Figure 4-1. The core of the code editor window is the code pane in which the code displays.

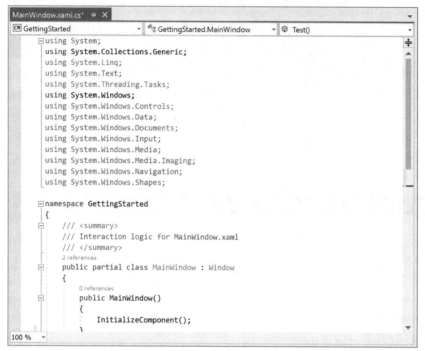

```
MainWindow.xaml.cs*  ⊸ ✕
🔧 GettingStarted              ▾  🔧 GettingStarted.MainWindow    ▾  ⊕ Test()                    ▾
      ⊟using System;                                                                          ⊹
       using System.Collections.Generic;
       using System.Linq;
       using System.Text;
       using System.Threading.Tasks;
       using System.Windows;
       using System.Windows.Controls;
       using System.Windows.Data;
       using System.Windows.Documents;
       using System.Windows.Input;
       using System.Windows.Media;
       using System.Windows.Media.Imaging;
       using System.Windows.Navigation;
       using System.Windows.Shapes;

      ⊟namespace GettingStarted
       {
      ⊟     /// <summary>
            /// Interaction logic for MainWindow.xaml
            /// </summary>
            2 references
      ⊟     public partial class MainWindow : Window
            {
                 0 references
      ⊟          public MainWindow()
                 {
                     InitializeComponent();
                 }
100 % ▾
```

FIGURE 4-1

Above the code pane are three drop-down lists that can help you navigate the code file. Known as the Navigation Bar, it can be turned on or off through the Text Editor ⇨ All Language ⇨ General node of the Options dialog (Tools ⇨ Options). Or you can turn it on and off for individual languages.

The first drop-down lists the projects in which the file can be found. This capability is present to support the shared file functionality that Visual Studio offers. The second drop-down contains the different classes defined in the code file, and the third one lists the members of the class selected in the second drop-down. These are listed in alphabetical order, making it easier to find a method or member definition within the file.

> **NOTE** *The drop-down lists do not apply to every code editor window in Visual Studio. The appearance of the editor window varies based on the type of file you are editing. For example, XML files don't have the drop-down lists. C#, Visual Basic, and JavaScript do. As well, if you use a third-party add-in such as ReSharper or CodeRush, you might have different behaviors and options available to you.*

As you modify the code in the code editor window, lines of code that you've modified since the file has been opened are marked in the left margin — yellow for unsaved changes and green for those that have been saved.

Regions

Effective class design usually results in classes that serve a single purpose and are not overly complex or lengthy. However, there will be times when you have to implement so many interfaces that your code file will become unwieldy. In this case, you have a number of options, such as partitioning the code into multiple files or using regions to condense the code, thereby making it easier to navigate.

The introduction of partial classes (where the definition of a class can be split over two or more files) means that at design time you can place code into different physical files representing a single logical class. The advantage of using separate files is that you can effectively group all methods that are related; for example, methods that implement an interface. The problem with this strategy is that navigating the code then requires continual switching between code files.

An alternative is to use named code regions to condense sections of code that are not currently in use. In Figure 4-2 you can see that two regions are defined, called `Constructor` and `Event Handlers`. Clicking the minus sign next to `#region` condenses the region into a single line and clicking the plus sign expands it again.

```
namespace GettingStarted
{
    2 references
    public partial class MainWindow : Window
    {
        #region Constructor

        0 references
        public MainWindow()
        {
            InitializeComponent();
        }

        #endregion

        Event Handlers
    }
}
```

FIGURE 4-2

> **NOTE** *You don't need to expand a region to see the code within it. Simply hover the mouse cursor over the region, and a tooltip displays the code within it.*

Outlining

In addition to regions that you have defined, you have the ability to auto-outline your code, making it easy to collapse methods, comments, and class definitions. Auto-outlining is enabled by default, but if it's not enabled you can enable it using the Edit ⇨ Outlining ⇨ Start Automatic Outlining menu item. Before you get freaked out, you won't see this menu item if automatic outlining is enabled. Instead, you'll see a Stop Outlining menu item.

Figure 4-3 shows four condensable regions. One is a defined region called `Constructor`; however, there are also three other automatic regions, outlining the class, the XML comments, and the constructor method (which has been collapsed). Automatic outlines can be condensed and expanded in the same way as regions you define manually.

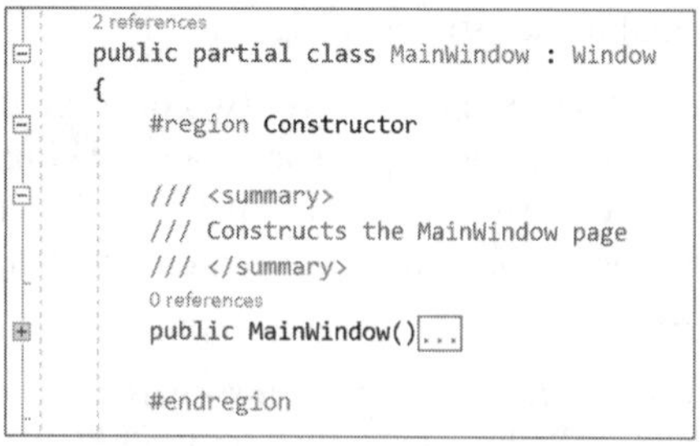

```
2 references
public partial class MainWindow : Window
{
    #region Constructor

    /// <summary>
    /// Constructs the MainWindow page
    /// </summary>
    0 references
    public MainWindow()...

    #endregion
```

FIGURE 4-3

The Edit ⇨ Outlining menu provides a number of commands to help in toggling outlining, such as collapsing the entire file to just method/property definitions (Edit ⇨ Outlining ⇨ Collapse to Definitions) and expanding it to display all collapsed code again (Edit ⇨ Outlining ⇨ Toggle All Outlining). The other way to expand and condense regions is via the keyboard shortcut Ctrl+M, Ctrl+M. This shortcut toggles between the two layouts.

> **NOTE** *One trick for C# developers is that Ctrl+] enables you to easily navigate from the beginning of a region, outline, or code block to the end and back again.*

Code Formatting

By default, Visual Studio 2017 assists you in writing readable code by automatically indenting and aligning. However, it is also configurable so that you can control how your code is arranged. Common to all languages is the ability to control what happens when you create a new line. In Figure 4-4 you can see that there is a Tabs node under the Text Editor ⇨ All Languages node of the Options dialog. Setting values here defines the default value for all languages, which you can then overwrite for an individual language using the Basic ⇨ Tabs node (for VB.NET), C# ⇨ Tabs, or other language nodes.

By default, the indenting behavior for both C# and VB.NET is smart indenting, which will, among other things, automatically add indentation as you open and close enclosures. Smart indenting is not available for all languages, in which case block indenting is used.

> **NOTE** *If you are working on a small screen, you might want to reduce the tab and indent sizes to optimize screen usage. Keeping the tab and indent sizes the same ensures that you can easily indent your code with a single tab keypress.*

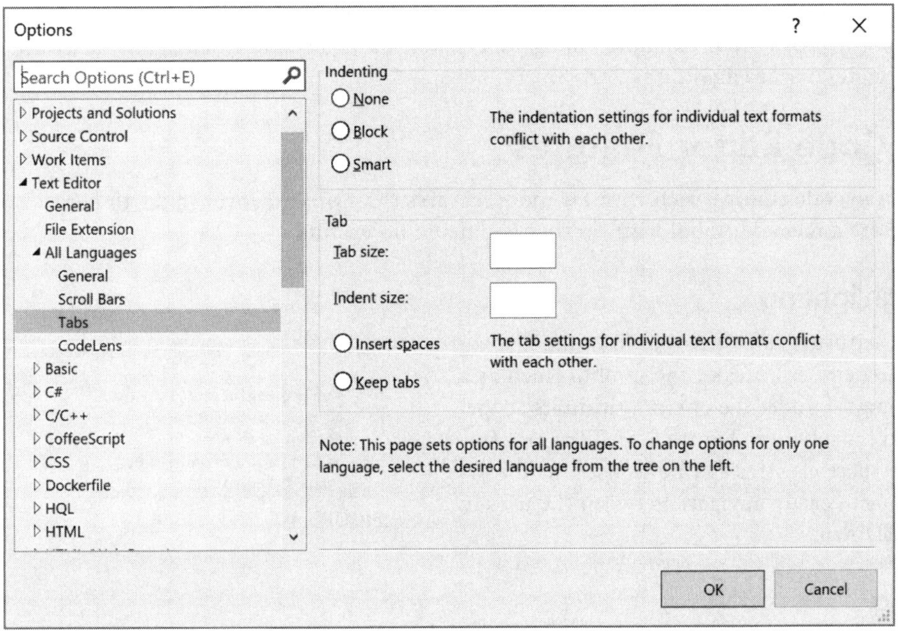

FIGURE 4-4

Visual Studio's Smart Indenting does a good job of automatically indenting code as it is written or pasted into the code editor, but occasionally you can come across code that has not been properly formatted, making it difficult to read. To have Visual Studio reformat the entire document and set the brace locations and line indentations, select Edit ⇨ Advanced ⇨ Format Document or press Ctrl+K, Ctrl+D. To reformat just the selected code block, select Edit ⇨ Advanced ⇨ Format Selection or press Ctrl+K, Ctrl+F.

When writing code, to indent an entire block of code one level without changing each line individually, simply select the block and press Tab. Each line has a tab inserted at its start. To unindent a block one level, select it and press Shift+Tab.

> **NOTE** *You may have noticed the Tabify/Untabify Selected Lines commands under the Edit ⇨ Advanced menu and wondered how these differ from the Format Selection command. These commands simply convert leading spaces in lines to tabs and vice versa, rather than recalculating the indenting as the Format Selection command does.*

Navigating Forward/Backward

As you move within and between items, Visual Studio 2017 tracks where you have been, in much the same way that a web browser tracks the sites you have visited. Using the Navigate Forward and

Navigate Backward items from the View menu, you can easily go back and forth between the various locations in the project that you have changed. The keyboard shortcut to navigate backward is Ctrl+–. To navigate forward again it is Ctrl+Shift+–.

Additional Code Editor Features

The Visual Studio code editor is rich with far more features than we can cover in depth here. However, here are a few additional features that you may find useful.

Reference Highlighting

Another great feature is reference highlighting, also known as Code Lens. All uses of the symbol (such as a method or property) under the cursor within its scope are highlighted (as shown in Figure 4-5). This makes it easy to spot where else this symbol is used within your code. You can easily navigate between the uses by Ctrl+Shift+Up/Down.

```
foreach (Account account in assignedAccounts)
{
    account.BeginEdit();
    account.DivisionId = 0;
    account.BranchId = 0;
    account.CostCentreId = 0;
    account.EndEdit();
```

FIGURE 4-5

Code Zooming

You can use Ctrl+Mouse Wheel to zoom in and out of your code (effectively making the text larger or smaller). This feature can be especially useful when presenting to a group to enable the people at the back of the audience to see the code being demonstrated. The bottom-left corner of the code editor also has a drop-down enabling you to select from some predefined zoom levels.

Word Wrap

You can turn on word wrap in the code editor from the options. Go to Tools ➪ Options, expand the Text Editor node, select the All Languages subnode, and select the Word Wrap option. You can also choose to display a return arrow glyph where text has been wrapped by selecting the Show Visual Glyphs for Word Wrap option below the Word Wrap option.

You can turn this on for the current project by selecting Edit ➪ Advanced ➪ Word Wrap.

Line Numbers

To keep track of where you are in a code file, you may find it useful to turn on line numbers in the code editor (as shown in Figure 4-6). To turn line numbers on, go to Tools ➪ Options, expand the Text Editor node, select the All Languages subnode, and select the Line Numbers option.

Visual Studio 2017 includes a code editor feature named the Heads Up Display. In Figure 4-6, notice the small bit of text above the class declaration and the method signature (2 references and 0 references, respectively, along with information about how many uncommitted changes have been made, if this code has been checked into source control). This text indicates the number of times that the class or method is referenced elsewhere in the project.

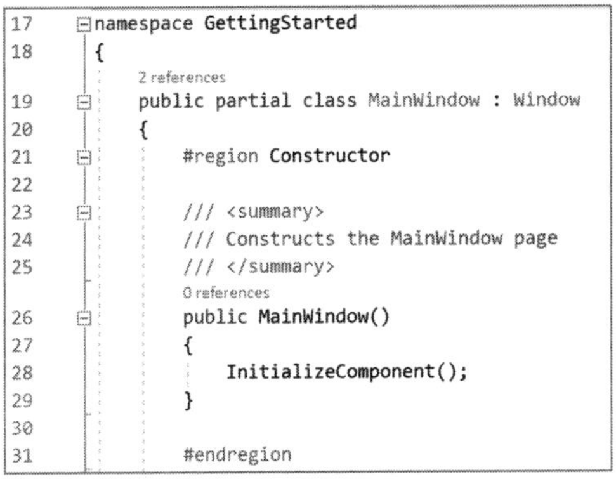

```
17   ⊟namespace GettingStarted
18    {
         2 references
19   ⊟    public partial class MainWindow : Window
20        {
21   ⊟        #region Constructor
22
23   ⊟        /// <summary>
24            /// Constructs the MainWindow page
25            /// </summary>
         0 references
26   ⊟        public MainWindow()
27            {
28                InitializeComponent();
29            }
30
31            #endregion
```

FIGURE 4-6

If you click the text, a pop-up window displays (an example is shown in Figure 4-7) that includes some useful details about the references. This includes the file names and line numbers where the references are found.

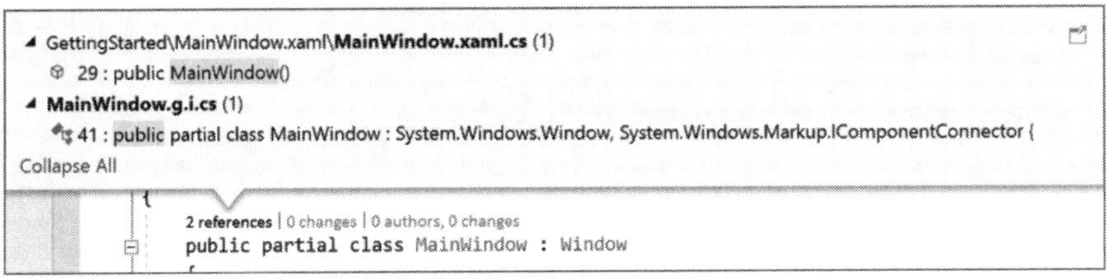

```
◢ GettingStarted\MainWindow.xaml\MainWindow.xaml.cs (1)
    ☉  29 : public MainWindow()
◢ MainWindow.g.i.cs (1)
    ⚡ 41 : public partial class MainWindow : System.Windows.Window, System.Windows.Markup.IComponentConnector {
Collapse All
```

```
                {
               2 references | 0 changes | 0 authors, 0 changes
   ⊟           public partial class MainWindow : Window
```

FIGURE 4-7

If you double-click one of the references, that file opens up in the editor window and the cursor is placed on the line that references the method or class. Just hovering your mouse over a reference causes a pop-up window to display; the window contains not just the line you're hovering over, but also the two or three lines before and after it, which enables you to see a little more detail about the reference without navigating directly to the file.

Auto Brace Complete

Auto Brace Complete is a popular feature that automatically adds the closing parenthesis, quote, brace, and bracket for you as you type code into the editor. The completions themselves are language aware, so that, for example, comments in C++ will autocomplete, yet the same keystrokes typed into a C# editor will not.

Split View

Sometimes you want to view two different parts of the same code file at the same time. Split view enables you to do this by splitting the active code editor window into two horizontal panes separated by a splitter bar. These can then be scrolled separately to display different parts of the same file simultaneously (as shown in Figure 4-8).

FIGURE 4-8

To split a code editor window, select Split from the Window menu. Alternatively, drag the handle directly above the vertical scrollbar down to position the splitter bar.

Drag the splitter bar up and down to adjust the size of each pane. To remove the splitter simply double-click the splitter bar, or select Remove Split from the Window menu.

Tear Away (Floating) Code Windows

If you have multiple monitors, a great feature is the ability to "tear off" or float code editor windows (and tool windows) and move them outside the main Visual Studio IDE window (as shown in Figure 4-9), including onto another monitor. This allows you to make use of the extra screen real estate that having multiple monitors provides by enabling multiple code editor windows to be visible at the same time over separate monitors. It is also possible to place these floating windows onto a "raft" so that they can be moved together (as shown in Figure 4-10). To tear off a window, make sure it has the focus, and then select Float from the Window menu. Alternatively, right-click the title bar of the window and select Float from the drop-down menu, or simply click and drag the tab for that window (effectively tearing it away from its docked position) and position it where you want it to be located.

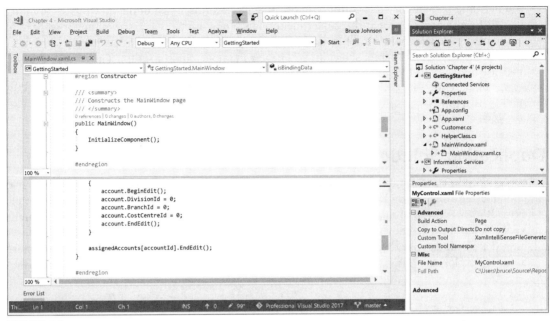

FIGURE 4-9

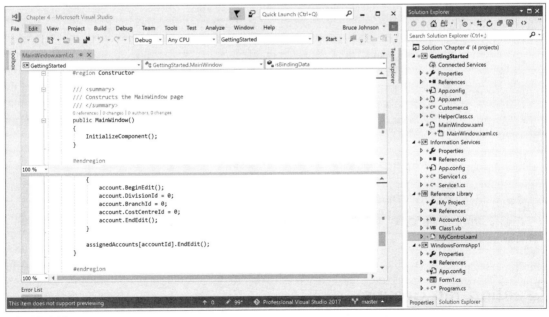

FIGURE 4-10

You may find halving the code editor window in Split view (discussed in the previous section) to view different parts of a file at the same time too much of a limited view, so you might want to use the floating code windows feature instead to open another code editor window for the same file, and place it, say, on a different screen (if you have a multiple monitor setup). The trick to doing this (because double-clicking the file again in the Solution Explorer simply activates the existing code editor window instance for that file) is to select New Window from the Window menu. This opens the file currently being viewed in another window, which you can then tear away and position as you please.

Duplicating Solution Explorer

If you work in a multi-monitor environment, a limitation in early versions of Visual Studio was that only one copy of Solution Explorer was available. In Visual Studio 2017, this limitation does not exist. Right-click one of the elements in the Solution Explorer and select New Solution Explorer View. When clicked, a new floating Solution Explorer window is created. This window can be moved around, just like the windows previously described. Figure 4-11 illustrates the newly created Solution Explorer.

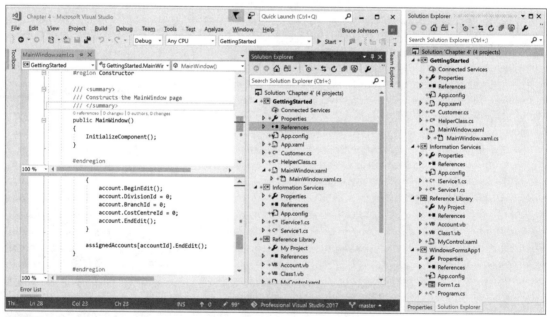

FIGURE 4-11

Creating Tab Groups

If you don't have the privilege of having more than one monitor, it is still possible to view more than one code editor window at the same time. You do this by creating tab groups and tiling these groups to display at the same time. As their name would indicate, a tab group is a group of code editor window tabs, with each tab group appearing in a separate tile. Multiple tab groups can be created, limited only by the amount of screen real estate they occupy. You can choose to tile the tab groups vertically or horizontally; you cannot use a mix of the two.

To start this process, you drag a tab below or beside an existing one and dock it to achieve the same effect. This starts a new tab group and creates a tile for it (as shown in Figure 4-12).

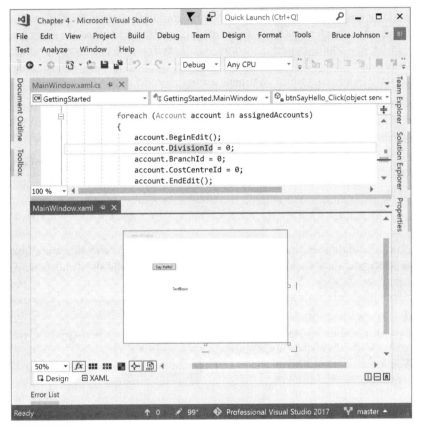

FIGURE 4-12

You can drag tabs between tab groups or move them between tab groups using Window ➪ Move to Next Tab Group and Window ➪ Move to Previous Tab Group. These options are also available from the drop-down menu when right-clicking a tab.

To restore the user interface to having a single tab group again, move the tabs from the new tab groups back into the original one again and the tiling will be removed.

Advanced Functionality

To be a truly productive developer, it can help to know various advanced features available in the code editor that are hidden away but can save you a lot of time. Here are some of the most useful commands that aren't immediately obvious within the code editor.

Commenting/Uncommenting a Code Block

Often you need to comment or uncomment a block of code, and you don't want to have to add/remove the comment characters to/from the start of each line, especially when there are many lines in the block. Of course, in C# you could wrap the block of code between a /* and */ to comment it out, but this type of comment isn't available in Visual Basic, and it can be problematic in C# when commenting out a block that already contains a comment using this style.

Visual Studio provides a means to comment/uncomment a block of code easily, by selecting the block and then selecting Edit ➪ Advanced ➪ Comment Selection to comment it out, or selecting Edit ➪ Advanced ➪ Uncomment Selection to uncomment it.

The easiest way to access these commands (you are likely to use these often) is via their shortcuts. Press Ctrl+K, Ctrl+C to comment a block of code, and Ctrl+K, Ctrl+U to uncomment it. The Text Editor toolbar is another simple means to access these commands.

Block Selection

Also known as box selection, column selection, rectangle selection, or vertical text selection, block selection is the ability to select text in a block (as shown in Figure 4-13) instead of the normal behavior of selecting lines of text (stream selection).

To select a block of text, hold down the Alt key while selecting text with the mouse, or use Shift+Alt+Arrow with the keyboard. This feature can come in handy when, for example, you have code lined up and want to remove a vertical portion of that code (such as a prefix on variable declarations).

```
private readonly string value3 = String.Empty;
private readonly string value2 = String.Empty;
private readonly string value1 = String.Empty;
private readonly string value4 = String.Empty;
private readonly string value5 = String.Empty;
```

FIGURE 4-13

Multiline Editing

Multiline editing extends the abilities of block selection. With block selection, after selecting a vertical block of text you can only delete, cut, or copy the block. With multiline editing you can type after selecting a vertical block of text, which will replace the selected text with what's being typed on each line, as shown in Figure 4-14. This can be handy for changing a group of variables from readonly to const, for example.

```
private con string value3 = String.Empty;
private con string value2 = String.Empty;
private con string value1 = String.Empty;
private con string value4 = String.Empty;
private con string value5 = String.Empty;
```

FIGURE 4-14

> **NOTE** *You can also insert text across multiple lines by creating a block with zero width and simply starting to type.*

The Clipboard Ring

Visual Studio keeps track of the last 20 snippets of text that have been copied or cut to the clipboard. To paste text that was previously copied to the clipboard but overwritten, instead of the normal Ctrl+V when pasting, use Ctrl+Shift+V. Pressing V while holding down Ctrl+Shift cycles through the entries.

Full-Screen View

You can maximize the view for editing the code by selecting View ⇨ Full Screen, or using the Shift+Alt+Enter shortcut. This effectively maximizes the code editor window, hiding the other tool windows and the toolbars. To return to the normal view, press Shift+Alt+Enter again, or click the Full-Screen toggle button that has been added to the end of the menu bar.

Go to Definition

To quickly navigate to the definition of the class, method, or member under the cursor, right-click and select Go to Definition, or simply press F12.

Find All References

You can find where a method or property is called by right-clicking its definition and selecting Find All References from the drop-down menu, or placing the cursor in the method definition and pressing Shift+F12. This activates the Find All References window (see Figure 4-15) and displays the locations throughout your solution where that method or property is referenced.

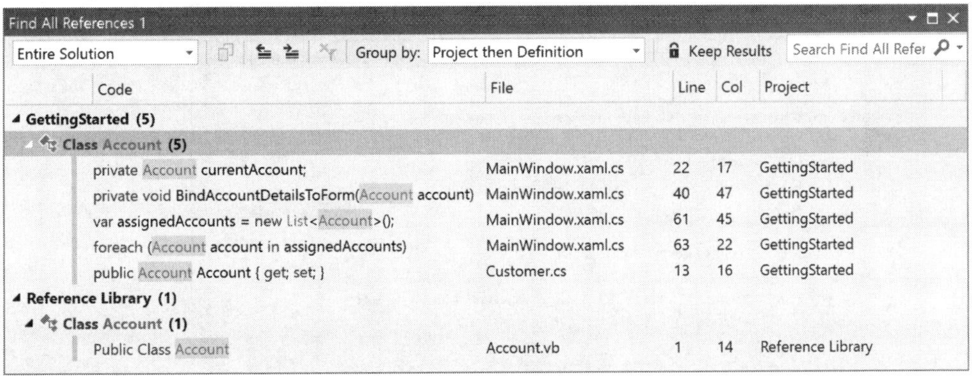

FIGURE 4-15

The Find All References window has significantly changed in Visual Studio 2017. Where the references used to be in a flat list, you now have the ability to see them in a hierarchy. And you can change the default of Project then Definition by selecting one of the choices in the Group By combo box at the top center of the window. Or you can create your own grouping by right-clicking the results and using the Grouping option in the context menu.

You can then double-click a reference in the results window to navigate to that result in the code editor window. Or, if you just need to see a glimpse of the context for the reference, you can hover over the reference and the code around the reference appears as a tooltip.

CODE NAVIGATION

Microsoft takes the view that Visual Studio is a productivity tool for developers rather than being only a place where code is edited. For this reason, there are a large number of features targeted at helping developers do common tasks faster. Visual Studio 2017 focuses on helping developers understand and discover code more effectively. This section goes over these features and how they might best be used.

Peek Definition

As you investigate code, there is frequently a need to quickly check on an invoked method. When you right-click the method and select Go to Definition from the context menu, the file containing the method opens and the method appears in the code editor. However, the file you were editing is no longer in focus. Although this is definitely not an insurmountable problem, it is an inconvenience.

The Peek Definition command enables developers to view the definition of a method without leaving their current editing context. Right-click the method as before, but select the Peek Definition option from the context menu. As shown in Figure 4-16, the method definition is visible, and a blue bar on the left side indicates the location of the method within the visible code.

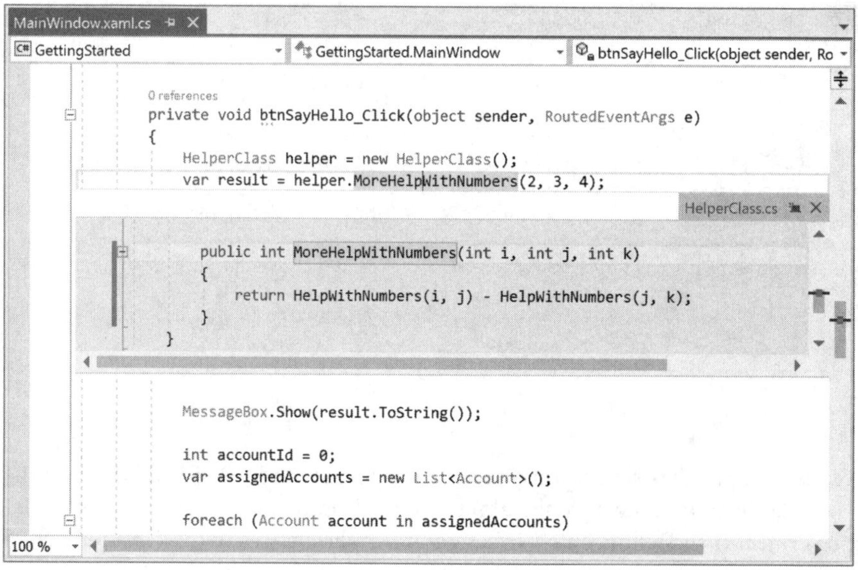

FIGURE 4-16

Aside from allowing you to view the code, Peek Definition enables you to edit the code while you peek at it. And, while you hover over a method in the peek window, you can right-click and select Peek Definition to drill down into that method. When you are more than one level deep, a collection of blue and white circles appears (see Figure 4-17). Clicking on the circles enables you to easily navigate backward and forward through the call hierarchy.

```
MainWindow.xaml.cs
[C#] GettingStarted              GettingStarted.MainWindow        btnSayHello_Click(object sender, Ro

        0 references
        private void btnSayHello_Click(object sender, RoutedEventArgs e)
        {
            HelperClass helper = new HelperClass();
            var result = helper.MoreHelpWithNumbers(2, 3, 4);
                                                            HelperClass.cs
        {
            private int HelpWithNumbers(int i, int j)
            {
                return i * j;
            }
        }


        MessageBox.Show(result.ToString());

        int accountId = 0;
        var assignedAccounts = new List<Account>();

        foreach (Account account in assignedAccounts)
100 %
```

FIGURE 4-17

Finally, if you want to promote the peeked file to the main editor window, there is a Promote to Document icon just to the right of the file name on the Peek Window tab.

Enhanced Scrollbar

The enhanced scrollbar, with its visual cues that provide information about the file that you are editing, is a very popular productivity tool. The visual cues include the location of errors and warnings, breakpoints, bookmarks, and search results. Figure 4-18 illustrates some of the different markers on the enhanced scrollbar.

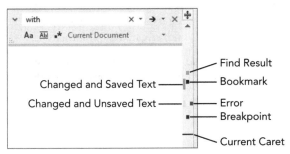

FIGURE 4-18

The scrollbar in Visual Studio 2017 includes the Map mode feature, which is turned off by default. To enable it, you go to the Text Editor ⇨ All Languages ⇨ Scroll Bars node in the Tools ⇨ Options dialog box, as shown in Figure 4-19. This particular node controls Map mode for every language. However, Map mode can be turned on or off for each language by going into the Scroll Bars node within the specific language.

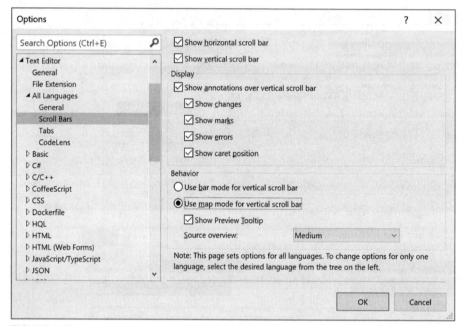

FIGURE 4-19

In the Behavior section, a radio button allows you to toggle between the Vertical Scrollbar mode and the Map mode. When Map mode is enabled, you can also configure the preview tooltip and specify the size of the source code map (which also works out to be how wide the scrollbar is). Figure 4-20 shows the toolbar with all of these functions enabled.

A subtle feature is that Map mode is used wherever the code editor scrollbar exists. This includes the scroll bar in the Peek Definition screen.

The source code map is intended to provide a high-level, visual representation of the code that is being edited. You are not supposed to be able to make out the code itself — only the shape of the code is discernible. The intent is for this shape to assist you as you navigate through the file.

You can also see a preview tip. As you move your mouse up and down along the scrollbar (not click-dragging the mouse, but just hovering), a tooltip window appears that shows a preview of the code at the point where your mouse is (see Figure 4-21).

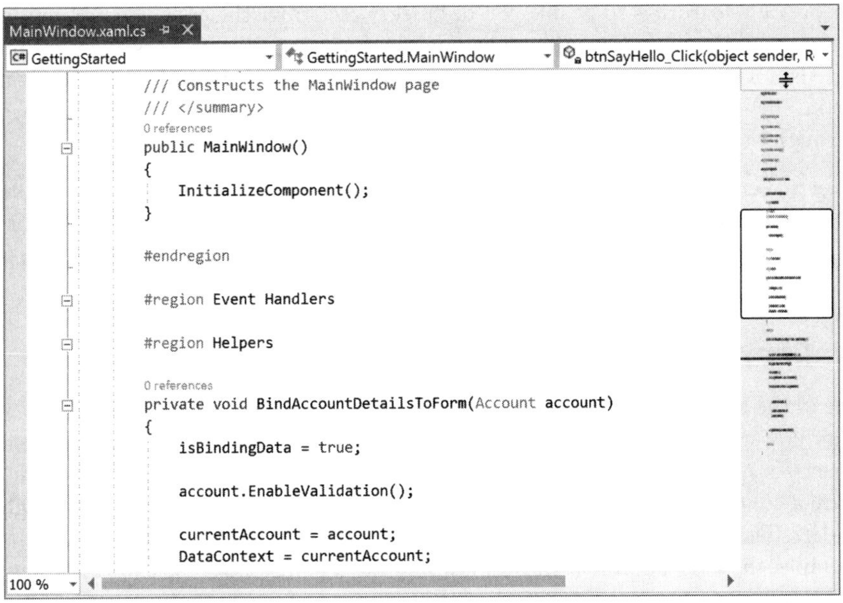

MainWindow.xaml.cs
GettingStarted
GettingStarted.MainWindow
btnSayHello_Click(object sender, R
/// Constructs the MainWindow page
/// </summary>
0 references
public MainWindow()
{
InitializeComponent();
}
#endregion
#region Event Handlers
#region Helpers
0 references
private void BindAccountDetailsToForm(Account account)
{
isBindingData = true;
account.EnableValidation();
currentAccount = account;
DataContext = currentAccount;
100 %

FIGURE 4-20

Chapter 4
MainWindow.xaml.cs
GettingStarted
GettingStarted.MainWindow
BindAccountDetailsToForm(Accour
/// Constructs the MainWindow page
/// </summary>
0 references | 0 changes | 0 authors, 0 changes
public MainWindow()
{
InitializeComponent();
}
#endregion
#region Event Handlers
#region Helpers
private void BindAccountDetail
{
isBindingData = true;
account.EnableValidation()
currentAccount = account;
DataContext = currentAccount;
{
account.BeginEdit();
account.DivisionId = 0;
account.BranchId = 0;
account.CostCentreId = 0;
account.EndEdit();
}
100 %

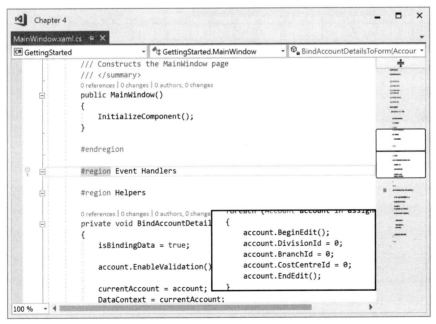

FIGURE 4-21

The idea behind the preview feature is to enable you to quickly recognize the code you are looking for without needing to scroll through the entire code window. Experientially, it works well for determining if your mouse is hovering over the part of the code you want to edit next. It is not really useful (nor is it intended to be) if you are looking for a particular variable or function. There are better ways to navigate through the code file for that purpose.

The capability to click to scroll is inherent in the preview window. As you are hovering over the different parts of your code file, you can change the view of the entire code window by clicking; for example, instead of moving the scrollbar handle up and down, you can click the position in the file you want to move to.

Structure Visualizer

On the opposite side of the code editor is the Structure Visualizer. This was a favorite feature from the Productivity Power Tools (a set of extensions to Visual Studio designed to improve the productivity of developers), and it has now been added to Visual Studio 2017. As you can see in Figure 4-22, there are a couple of faint, dotted vertical lines to the left of the code and to the right of the region expanders. There is one line for each level of contextual hierarchy in the code. For instance, in this example, the leftmost line is the namespace, the second line is the class and the third line is the method. When you hover over the line, the definition for all of the elements in the hierarchy (include any regions) appears as a tool tip. The goal of this feature is to give you an at-a-glance look at exactly where the code falls within the namespace/class/method hierarchy.

FIGURE 4-22

Navigate To

The design of the interface for Navigate To is intended to keep you "in the flow," that is, among other things, to avoid forcing your hands to leave the keyboard. When you strike the appropriate keyboard chord (Ctrl+, is the default, but if that doesn't work the Edit ➪ Navigate menu option is available), a small window appears in the top-right corner of the editor window, as shown in Figure 4-23.

As you start to type, Visual Studio uses a semantic search to display a list of matches. (In other words, instead of a straight text search, Visual Studio uses its understanding of the classes and methods in your code project as a relevancy guide.) Based on previous telemetry, the first item is the one you most commonly looked for previously, so it is automatically selected and the corresponding file appears as a preview. If you select another file (either by using the cursor or the mouse), that file is displayed in the preview tab. The Escape key closes the navigation window and puts you back to your original position.

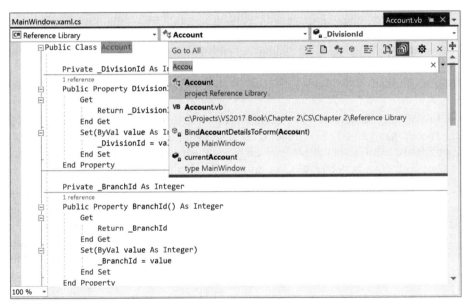

FIGURE 4-23

At the top of the NavigateTo dialog is a toolbar that allows you to perform some basic filtering on the results. For instance, you can restrict the displayed items to Files, Symbols, Members, or Types. As well, you can modify the scope of the search so that it is limited to the current document or includes not just the current solution but also external dependencies. There is also a gear icon that lets you modify some settings for the Navigate To functionality. For instance, you can make the window appear in the top center instead of the top right. And you can toggle whether the Preview window is used when you click on an item.

THE COMMAND WINDOW

As you become more familiar with Visual Studio 2017, you will spend less time looking for functionality and more time using keyboard shortcuts to navigate and perform actions within the IDE.
One of the tool windows that is often overlooked is the Command window, accessible via View ⇨
Other Windows ⇨ Command Window (Ctrl+Alt+A). From this window you can execute any existing Visual Studio command or macro, as well as any additional macros you may have recorded or
written. Figure 4-24 illustrates the use of IntelliSense to show the list of commands that can be executed from the Command window. This list includes all macros defined within the current solution.

FIGURE 4-24

A full list of the Visual Studio commands is available via the Environment ⇨ Keyboard node of the
Options dialog (Tools ⇨ Options). The commands all have a similar syntax based on the area of the
IDE that they are derived from. For example, you can open the debugging output window (Debug
⇨ Windows ⇨ Output) by typing **Debug.Output** into the Command window.

The commands fall into three rough groups. Many commands are shortcuts to either tool windows
(which are made visible if they aren't already open) or dialogs. For example, File.NewFile opens
the new file dialog. Other commands query information about the current solution or the debugger.
Using Debug.ListThreads lists the current threads, in contrast to Debug.Threads, which opens
the Threads tool window. The third type includes those commands that perform an action without
displaying a dialog. This would include most macros and a number of commands that accept arguments. (A full list of these, including the arguments they accept, is available within the MSDN documentation.) There is some overlap between these groups: For example, the Edit.Find command can
be executed with or without arguments. If this command is executed without arguments, the Find
and Replace dialog displays. Alternatively, the following command finds all instances of the string
MyVariable in the current document (/d) and places a marker in the code window border against
the relevant lines (/m):

```
>Edit.Find MyVariable /m /d
```

Although there is IntelliSense within the Command window, you may find typing a frequently used
command somewhat painful. Visual Studio 2017 has the capability to assign an alias to a particular
command. For example, the alias command can be used to assign an alias, e?, to the Find command used previously:

```
>alias e? Edit.Find MyVariable /m /d
```

With this alias defined you can easily perform this command from anywhere within the IDE: Press Ctrl+Alt+A to give the Command window focus, and then type **e?** to perform the find-and-mark command.

You will have imported a number of default aliases belonging to the environment settings when you began working with Visual Studio 2017. You can list these using the `alias` command with no arguments. Alternatively, if you want to find out what command a specific alias references, you can execute the command with the name of the alias. For example, querying the previously defined alias, e?, would look like the following:

```
>alias e?
alias e? Edit.Find SumVals /m /doc
```

Two additional switches can be used with the `alias` command. The `/delete` switch, along with an alias name, removes a previously defined alias. If you want to remove all aliases you may have defined and revert any changes to a predefined alias, you can use the `/reset` switch.

THE IMMEDIATE WINDOW

Quite often when you write code or debug your application, you want to evaluate a simple expression either to test a bit of functionality or to remind yourself of how something works. This is where the Immediate window comes in handy. This window enables you to run expressions as you type them. Figure 4-25 shows a number of statements — from basic assignment and print operations to more advanced object creation and manipulation.

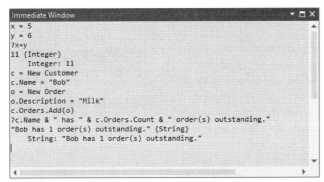

FIGURE 4-25

> **NOTE** *In Visual Basic you can't do explicit variable declaration in the Immediate window (for example, Dim x as Integer), but instead you do this implicitly via the assignment operator. The example shown in Figure 4-25 shows a new customer being created, assigned to a variable c, and then used in a series of operations. When using C#, new variables in the Immediate window must be declared explicitly before they can be assigned a value.*

The Immediate window supports a limited form of IntelliSense, and you can use the arrow keys to track back through the history of previous commands executed. Variable values can be displayed by means of the `Debug.Print` statement. Alternatively, you can use its ? alias. Neither of these is necessary in C#; simply type the variable's name into the window, and press Enter to print its value.

When you execute a command in the Immediate window while in Design mode, Visual Studio will build the solution before executing the command. If your solution doesn't compile, the expression cannot be evaluated until the compilation errors are resolved. If the command execute code has an active breakpoint, the command will break there. This can be useful if you work on a particular method that you want to test without running the entire application.

You can access the Immediate window via the Debug ⇨ Windows ⇨ Immediate menu or the Ctrl+Alt+I keyboard chord, but if you work between the Command and Immediate windows, you may want to use the predefined aliases `cmd` and `immed`, respectively.

> **NOTE** *To execute commands in the Immediate window, you need to add > as a prefix (for example, >cmd to go to the Command window); otherwise Visual Studio tries to evaluate the command as a statement. Also, you should be aware that the language used in the Immediate window is that of the active project. The examples shown in Figure 4-25 can work only if a Visual Basic project is currently active.*

THE CLASS VIEW

Although the Solution Explorer is probably the most useful tool window for navigating your solution, it can sometimes be difficult to locate particular classes and methods. The Class view tool window provides you with an alternative view of your solution that lists namespaces, classes, and methods so that you can easily navigate to them. Figure 4-26 shows a simple Windows application that contains a single form (`MainWindow`), which is selected in the class hierarchy. Note that there are two GettingStarted nodes. The first is the name of the project (not the assembly as you might expect), and the second is the namespace that `MainWindow` belongs to. If you were to expand the Project References node you would see a list of assemblies that this project references. Drilling further into each of these would yield a list of namespaces, followed by the classes contained in the assembly.

In the lower portion of Figure 4-26, you can see the list of members that are available for the class `MainWindow`. Using the right-click shortcut menu, you can filter this list based on accessibility, sort and group the list, or use it to navigate to the selected

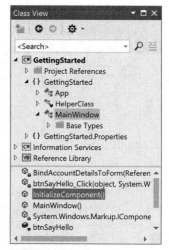

FIGURE 4-26

member. For example, clicking Go to Definition on `InitializeComponent()` would take you to the `MainWindow.xaml.cs` file.

The Class view is useful for navigating to generated members, which are usually in a file hidden in the default Solution Explorer view (such as the designer file in the previous example). It can also be a useful way to navigate to classes that have been added to an existing file — this would result in multiple classes in the same file, which is not a recommended practice. Because the file does not have a name that matches the class name, it becomes hard to navigate to that class using the Solution Explorer; hence the Class view is a good alternative.

THE ERROR LIST

The Error List window displays compile errors, warnings, and messages for your solution, as shown in Figure 4-27. You can open the Error List window by selecting View ⇨ Error List or by using the keyboard shortcut Ctrl+\, Ctrl+E. Errors appear in the list as you edit code and when you compile the project. Double-clicking an error in the list opens the file and takes you to the line of code that is in error.

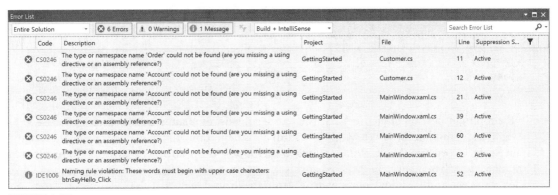

FIGURE 4-27

You can filter the entries in the list by toggling the buttons above the list to select the types of errors (Errors, Warnings, and Messages) you want to display. As well, you can filter the list by the process that generated the error or warning. More specifically, some errors are generated by Intellisense, while others are generated when you build the project. You can configure the window to show errors from one source or the other or both.

THE OBJECT BROWSER

Another way to view the classes that make up your application is via the Object Browser. Unlike most other tool windows, which appear docked to a side of Visual Studio 2017 by default, the Object Browser appears in the editor space. To view the Object Browser window, select View ⇨ Object Browser, or use the keyboard shortcut Ctrl+Alt+J (or F2, depending on your keyboard settings). As you can see in Figure 4-28, at the top of the Object Browser window is a drop-down box that defines the object browsing scope. This includes a set of predefined values, such as All Components, different versions of the .NET Framework, and My Solution, as well as a Custom Component Set. Here, My Solution is selected and a search string of started has been entered. The contents of the main window are then all the namespaces, classes, and members that match the search string.

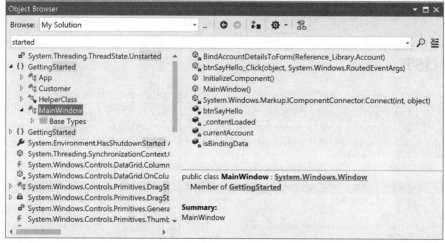

FIGURE 4-28

In the top right portion of Figure 4-28, you can see the list of members for the selected class (MainWindow), and in the lower window the full class definition, which includes its base class and namespace information. One of the options in the Browse drop-down is a Custom Component Set. To define what assemblies are included in this set, you can either click the ellipsis next to the drop-down or select Edit Custom Component Set from the drop-down itself.

SUMMARY

In this chapter you have seen a number of tool windows that can help you not only write code but also prototype and try it out. Making effective use of these windows can dramatically reduce the number of times you need to run your application to test the code you are writing. This, in turn, can improve your overall productivity and eliminate idle time spent waiting for your application to run.

5

Find and Replace and Help

WHAT'S IN THIS CHAPTER?

➤ Using Visual Studio's various Find and Replace tools

➤ Navigating Visual Studio's local help system

WROX.COM CODE DOWNLOADS FOR THIS CHAPTER

The wrox.com code downloads for this chapter can be found at www.wrox.com by searching for this book's ISBN number (978-1-119-40458-3). The code and any related support files are located in their own folder for this chapter.

To be a productive developer, you need to navigate your way around a code base and find what you need quickly. Visual Studio 2017 provides not just one but a number of search functions, each suited to particular searching tasks. The first part of this chapter discusses each of these search functions and when and where to use them.

Visual Studio 2017 is an immensely complex development environment that encompasses multiple languages based on an extensive framework of libraries and components. You can find it almost impossible to know everything about the IDE, let alone each of the languages or even the full extent of the .NET Framework. As both the .NET Framework and Visual Studio evolve, it becomes increasingly difficult to stay abreast of all the changes; moreover, it is likely that you need to know only a subset of this knowledge. Of course, you periodically need to obtain more information on a specific topic. To help you in these situations, Visual Studio 2017 comes with comprehensive documentation in the form of the MSDN Library, accessible either online, offline (as a downloadable book) or through a DVD. The second part of this chapter walks you through the methods to research documentation associated with developing projects in Visual Studio 2017.

QUICK FIND/REPLACE

The simplest means to search in Visual Studio 2017 is via the Quick Find dialog.

The find-and-replace functionality in Visual Studio 2017 is split into two broad tiers with a shared dialog and similar features: Quick Find and the associated Quick Replace are for searches that you need to perform quickly on the document or project currently open in the IDE. These two tools have limited options to filter and extend the search, but as you'll see in a moment, even those options provide a powerful search engine that goes beyond what you can find in most applications.

> **NOTE** *This search tool is best suited for when you need to do a simple text-based search/replace (as opposed to searching for a symbol).*

Quick Find

Quick Find is the term that Visual Studio 2017 uses to refer to the most basic search functionality. By default, it enables you to search for a simple word or phrase within the current document, but even Quick Find has additional options that can extend the search beyond the active module, or even incorporate regular expressions in the search criteria.

> **NOTE** *While there is an option in Quick Find to allow you to utilize regular expressions, one feature that is missing is the ability to easily select from a list of commonly used patterns. The expectation (and it is based on metrics gathered by Microsoft) is that the vast majority of quick finds don't use regular expressions. Instead, the ability to select from a list of common patterns can be found in the Find in Files functionality described later in this chapter.*

To start a Find action, press the standard keyboard shortcut Ctrl+F or select Edit ➪ Find and Replace ➪ Quick Find. Visual Studio displays the basic Find window, with the default Quick Find action selected (see Figure 5-1).

FIGURE 5-1

Type the search criteria into the Find textbox, or select from previous searches by clicking the drop-down arrow and scrolling through the list of criteria that have been used. By default, the scope of the search is restricted to the current document or window you're editing, unless you have a number of lines selected, in which case the default scope is the selection.

As you type each character into the search textbox, the editor moves to the next match for the text you entered. For example, typing f would find the first letter f, regardless of whether it is found within a word, such as in *offer*, or on its own. Typing an o would then move the cursor to the first instance of *fo*—such as *form*, and so on.

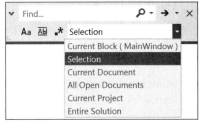

You can change the scope for the search. At the bottom of the dialog, you'll see a Scope field. This drop-down list gives you additional options based on the context of the search itself, including Current Block, Selection, Current Document, Current Project, Entire Solution, and All Open Documents (shown in Figure 5-2).

FIGURE 5-2

Find-and-replace actions always wrap around the selected scope looking for the search terms, stopping only when the find process has reached the starting point again. As Visual Studio finds each result, it highlights the match and scrolls the code window so that you can view it. If the match is already visible in the code window, Visual Studio does not scroll the code. Instead, it just highlights the new match. However, if it does need to scroll the window, it attempts to position the listing so that the match is in the middle of the code editor window.

> **NOTE** *After you perform the first Quick Find search, you no longer need the dialog to be visible. You can simply press F3 to repeat the same search.*

If you were comfortable using the Quick Find search box that was in the Standard toolbar, it is no longer part of the default configuration. You can still add it to the toolbar, but you need to do so manually.

Quick Replace

Performing a Quick Replace is similar to performing a Quick Find. You can switch between Quick Find and Quick Replace by clicking the caret to the left of the search textbox. If you want to go directly to Quick Replace, you can do so with the keyboard shortcut Ctrl+H or the menu command Edit ⇨ Find and Replace ⇨ Quick Replace. The Quick Replace options (see Figure 5-2) are the same as those for Quick Find, but with an additional field where you can specify what text should be used in the replacement.

> **NOTE** *A simple way to delete recurring values is to use the replace functionality with nothing specified in the Replacement Term text area. This enables you to find all occurrences of the search text and decide if it should be deleted.*

The Replacement Term field works in the same way as Find—you can either type a new replacement string, or with the drop-down list provided choose any you previously entered.

Find Options

Sometimes you want to specify criteria and filter the search results in different ways. Click the triangle icon next to search text. A drop-down expands to show recently used search values (see Figure 5-3).

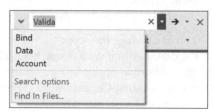

FIGURE 5-3

Also, below the search text, there are three buttons (shown in Figure 5-1). These are actually toggle buttons that enable you to refine the search to be case-sensitive (the left button) or to be an exact match (the middle button). And you can specify that you are performing a more advanced search that uses regular expressions (the right button). If you need a list of commonly used regular expressions, they are not in the Quick Find. But, as you will see shortly, these are found in the Find All Files dialog. To use regular expressions in Quick Find, you need to write them from scratch.

Find and Replace Options

You can further configure the find-and-replace functionality with its own set of options in the Tools ⇨ Options dialog. Found in the Environment group, the Find and Replace options enable you to enable/disable displaying informational and warning messages, as well as to indicate whether or not the Find What field should be automatically filled with the current selection in the editor window.

FIND/REPLACE IN FILES

The *Find in Files* and *Replace in Files* commands enable you to broaden the search beyond the current solution to whole folders and folder structures, and even to perform mass replacements on any matches for the given criteria and filters. Additional options are available to you when using these commands, and search results can be placed in one of two tool windows, so you can easily navigate them.

> **NOTE** *This search tool is best suited when you need to do a simple text-based search/replace across files that are not necessarily a part of your current solution.*

Find in Files

The powerful part of the search engine built into Visual Studio is in the Find in Files command. Rather than restrict yourself to files in the current solution, Find in Files gives you the ability to search entire folders (along with all their subfolders), looking for files that contain the search criteria.

The Find in Files dialog, as shown in Figure 5-4, can be invoked via the menu command Edit ⇨ Find. Alternatively, if you have the Quick Find dialog open, you can switch over to Find in Files mode by clicking the small drop-down arrow next to Quick Find and choosing Find in Files. You can also use the keyboard shortcut Ctrl+Shift+F to launch this dialog.

Most of the Quick Find options are still available to you, including regular expressions searching, but instead of choosing a scope from the project or solution, use the Look In field to specify where the search is to be performed. Either type the location you want to search or click the ellipsis to display the Choose Search Folders dialog, as shown in Figure 5-5.

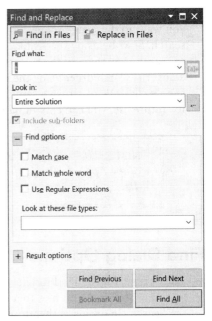

FIGURE 5-4

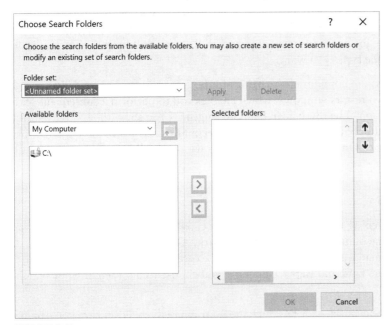

FIGURE 5-5

You can navigate through the entire filesystem, including networked drives, and add the folders you want to the search scope. This enables you to add disparate folder hierarchies to the one single search. Start by using the Available Folders list on the left to select the folders that you would like to search. Add them to the Selected Folders list by clicking the right arrow. Within this list you can adjust the search order using the up and down arrows. After you add folders to the search, you can simply click OK to return a semicolon-delimited list of folders. If you want to save this set of folders for future use, you can enter a name into the Folder Set drop-down and click Apply.

> **NOTE** *The process to save search folders is less than intuitive, but if you think of the Apply button as more of a Save button, then you can make sense of this dialog.*

Find Dialog Options

The options for the Find in Files dialog are similar to those for the Quick Find dialog. Because the search is performed on files that are not necessarily open within the IDE or are even code files, the Search Up option is therefore not present. There is an additional filter that can be used to select only specific file types to search in.

The Look at These File Types drop-down list contains several extension sets, each associated with a particular language, making it easy to search for code in Visual Basic, C#, J#, and other languages. You can type in your own extensions too, so if you work in a non-Microsoft language, or just want to use the Find in Files feature for non-development purposes, you can still limit the search results to those that correspond to the file types you want.

In addition to the Find options are configuration settings for how the results display. For searching, you can choose one of two results windows, which enables you to perform a subsequent search without losing your initial action. The results can be quite lengthy if you show the full output of the search, but if you're interested only in finding out which files contain the information you're looking for, check the Display Filenames Only option, and the results window will be populated with only one line per file.

Regular Expressions

Regular expressions take searching to another level, with the capability to do complex text matching based on the full RegEx engine built into the .NET Framework. Although this book doesn't go into great detail on the advanced matching capabilities of regular expressions, it's worth mentioning the additional help provided by the Find and Replace dialog if you choose to use them in your search terms.

Figure 5-6 shows the Expression Builder for building a regular expression. From here you can easily build your regular expressions with a menu showing the most commonly used regular expression phrases and symbols, along with English descriptions of each.

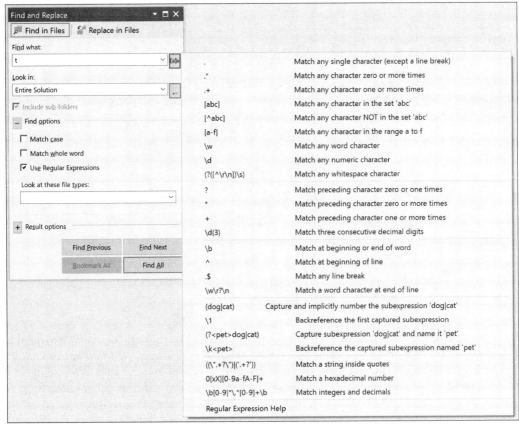

FIGURE 5-6

An example of where using regular expressions might come in handy is when reversing assignments. For example, if you have this code:

VB

```
Description = product.Description
Quantity = product.Quantity
SellPrice = product.SellPrice
```

C#

```
Description = product.Description;
Quantity = product.Quantity;
SellPrice = product.SellPrice;
```

and want to reverse the assignments like so:

VB

```
product.Description = Description
product.Quantity = Quantity
product.SellPrice = SellPrice
```

C#

```
product.Description = Description;
product.Quantity = Quantity;
product.SellPrice = SellPrice;
```

This would be a perfect use for performing a Quick Replace with regular expressions rather than modifying each line of code manually. Be sure you select Use Regular Expressions in the Find Options, and enter the following as the Find What text:

VB

```
{<.*} = {.*}
```

C#

```
{<.*} = {.*};
```

and the following as the Replace With text:

VB

```
\2 = \1
```

C#

```
\2 = \1;
```

As a brief explanation, you are searching for two groups (defined by the curly brackets) separated by an equals sign. The first group is searching for the first character of a word (<) and then any characters (.*). The second group is searching for any characters until an end-of-line character is found in the VB example or a semicolon is found in the C# example. Then when you do the replace, you are simply inserting the characters from the second group found in its place, an equals sign (surrounded by a space on each side), and then the characters from the first group found (followed by a semicolon in the C# example). If you aren't familiar with regular expressions, it may take some time to get your head around it, but it is a quick-and-easy way to perform an otherwise rather mundane manual process.

Results Window

When you perform a Find in Files action, results display in one of two Find Results windows. These appear as open tool windows docked to the bottom of the IDE workspace. For each line that contains the search criteria, the results window displays a full line of information, containing the filename and path, the line number that contained the match, and the actual line of text itself, so you can instantly see the context (see Figure 5-7).

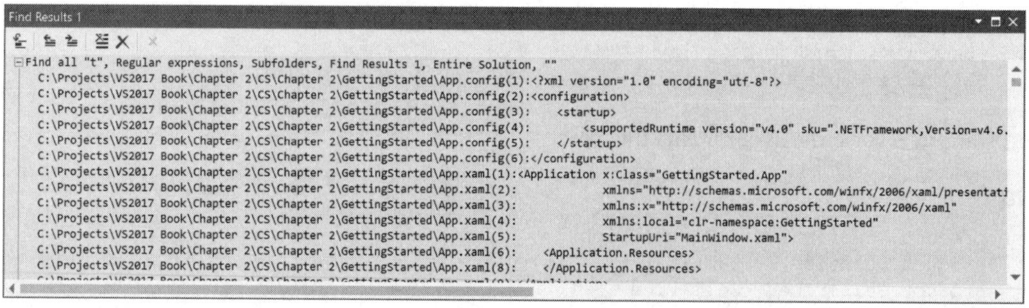

FIGURE 5-7

In the top left corner of each results window is a small toolbar, as shown in Figure 5-7 and magnified in Figure 5-8, for navigation within the results. These commands are also accessible through a context menu.

Simply double-click a specific match to navigate to that line of code.

Replace in Files

Although it's useful to search a large number of files and find a number of matches to your search criteria, even better is the Replace in Files action. Accessed via the keyboard shortcut Ctrl+Shift+H or the drop-down arrow next to Quick Replace, Replace in Files performs in much the same way as Find in Files, with all the same options.

The main difference is that you can enable an additional Results option when you're replacing files. When you perform a mass replacement action like this, it can be handy to have a final confirmation before committing changes. To have this sanity check available to you, select the Keep Modified Files Open After Replace All check box (shown at the bottom of Figure 5-9).

FIGURE 5-8

FIGURE 5-9

Note that this feature works only when you use Replace All; if you just click Replace, Visual Studio opens the file containing the next match and leaves the file open in the IDE anyway.

> **WARNING** *Important: If you leave the Keep Modified Files Open After Replace All option unchecked and perform a mass replacement on a large number of files, they will be changed permanently without your having any recourse to an undo action. Be very sure that you know what you're doing.*

Regardless of whether or not you have this option checked, after performing a Replace All action, Visual Studio reports back to you how many changes were made. If you don't want to see this dialog box, you have an option to hide the dialog with future searches.

ACCESSING HELP

You are exposed to a wide range of technologies as a developer. Not only do they evolve at a rapid pace, but you are also constantly bombarded with additional new technologies that you must get up to speed on quickly. It's impossible to know everything about these technologies, and being a developer involves constantly learning. Often, knowing how to find information on using these technologies is as important a skill as actually implementing them. Luckily, you can choose from a multitude of information sources on these technologies. The inclusion of IntelliSense into IDEs over a decade ago was one of the most useful tools to help developers write code, but it's rarely a substitute for a full-blown help system that provides all the ins and outs of a technology. Visual Studio's help system provides this support for developers.

The easiest way to get help for Visual Studio 2017 is to use the same method you would use for almost every Windows application ever created: Press the F1 key, the universal shortcut key for help. Visual Studio 2017's help system uses Microsoft Help Viewer 2. Rather than using a special "shell" to host the help and enable you to navigate around and search it, the help system runs in a browser window. To support some of the more complex features of the help system such as the search functionality (when using the offline help), there is a help listener application that runs in your system tray and serves these requests. The address in the browser's address bar points to a local web server on your machine. The online and offline help modes look and behave similarly to one another, but this chapter specifically focuses on the offline help.

> **NOTE** *You may find that you receive a Service Unavailable message when using the help system. The likely cause of this error is that the help listener is no longer running in your system tray. Simply open the help system from within Visual Studio and the help listener automatically starts again.*

The help system in Visual Studio is contextual. This means that if, for example, the cursor is currently positioned on a XAML tag in a Windows Store project and you press F1, the help window opens immediately with a mini-tutorial about what the class is and how to use it, as shown in Figure 5-10.

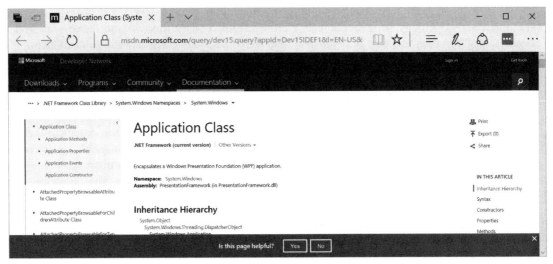

FIGURE 5-10

This is incredibly useful because more often than not if you simply press F1, the help system navigates directly to the help topic that deals with the problem you're currently researching.

However, in some situations you want to go directly to the table of contents within the help system. Visual Studio 2017 enables you to do this through the View Help menu item in its main Help menu (see Figure 5-11).

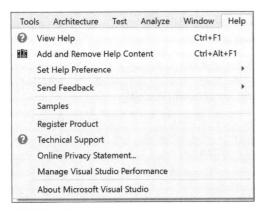

FIGURE 5-11

In addition to the several help links, you also have shortcuts to MSDN forums and for reporting a bug.

Navigating and Searching the Help System

Navigating through the help system should be familiar because it is essentially the same as navigating the MSDN documentation on the web. On the left side of the browser window, you can find links to pages in the same part of the help system as the page currently viewed. You can also find links that might be related to the current page.

In the top left of the browser window, you can find a search textbox. Enter your search query here (in much the same way you would in a search engine such as Google or Bing). This search is a full text search of the pages in the help system, and your query does not necessarily need to appear in the title of the pages. This takes you to the results, which are again provided in a manner similar to the results from a search engine. A one-line extract from the page of each result displays to help you determine if it is the article you are after, and you can click through to view the corresponding page.

Configuring the Help System

When you first start using the help system, it's a good idea to configure it to your needs. To do so, select the Help ⇨ Set Help Preferences menu. The menu provides two options: Use Online Help and Use Local Help.

The first option, Use Online Help, sets the help system to use the MSDN documentation on the web. Now pressing F1 or opening the help from the Help menu automatically navigates to the appropriate page in the documentation on MSDN online (for the current context in Visual Studio). Selecting the Use Local Help option navigates to the appropriate page in the documentation installed locally (assuming that the documentation has actually been installed on your machine).

The advantage of the online help over the offline help is that it is always up to date and won't consume space on your hard drive (assuming you don't install the help content). The disadvantage is that you must always have an active Internet connection, and at times (depending on your bandwidth) it may be slower than the offline version to access. Essentially it is a trade-off, and you must choose the most appropriate option for your work environment.

With the Use Local Help option selected, using F1 or opening help from the Help menu launches the Help Viewer. This viewer (refer to Figure 5-10) provides a user experience roughly the same as the Web documentation (navigation on the left, body of the content on the right).

The final option in the Help menu is Add and Remove Local Help Content, which enables you to remove product documentation sets from your local disk and free some disk space. The screen shows the documentation sets currently installed, and you can uninstall a documentation set by pressing the Remove hyperlink button next to its name.

SUMMARY

As you've seen in this chapter, Visual Studio 2017 comes with a number of search-and-replace tools, each suited to a particular type of search task to enable you to navigate and modify your code quickly and easily.

The help system is a powerful interface to the documentation that comes with Visual Studio 2017. The ability to switch easily between online and local documentation ensures that you can balance the speed of offline searches with the relevance of information found on the web. And the abstract paragraphs shown in all search results, regardless of their locations, help reduce the number of times you might click a false positive.

PART II
Getting Started

Solutions, Projects, and Items

➤ Creating and configuring solutions and projects

➤ Controlling how an application is compiled, debugged, and deployed

➤ Configuring the many project-related properties

➤ Including resources and settings with an application

➤ Enforcing good coding practices with the Code Analysis Tools

➤ Modifying the configuration, packaging, and deployment options for web applications

WROX.COM CODE DOWNLOADS FOR THIS CHAPTER

The wrox.com code downloads for this chapter can be found at www.wrox.com by searching for this book's ISBN number (978-1-119-40458-3). The code and any related support files are located in their own folder for this chapter.

Other than the simplest applications, such as Hello World, most applications require more than one source file. This raises a number of issues, such as how the files will be named, where they will be located, and whether they can be reused. Within Visual Studio 2017, the concept of a *solution*, containing a series of *projects*, made up of a series of *items*, is used to enable developers to track, manage, and work with their source files. The IDE has a number of built-in features that aim to simplify this process, while still allowing developers to get the most out of their applications. This chapter examines the structure of solutions and projects, looking at available project types and how they can be configured.

SOLUTION STRUCTURE

Whenever you work within Visual Studio, you have a solution open. When you edit an ad hoc file, this is a temporary solution that you can elect to discard when you complete your work. However, the solution enables you to manage the files that you're currently working with, so in most cases saving the solution means that you can return to what you were doing at a later date without having to locate and reopen the files on which you were working.

> **NOTE** *A solution should be thought of as a container of related projects. The projects within a solution do not need to be of the same language or project type. For example, a single solution could contain an ASP.NET web application written in Visual Basic, an F# library, and a C# WPF application. The solution enables you to open all these projects together in the IDE and manage the build and deployment configuration for them as a whole.*

The most common way to structure applications written within Visual Studio is to have a single solution containing a number of projects. Each project can then be made up of a series of both code files and folders. The main window in which you work with solutions and projects is the Solution Explorer, as shown in Figure 6-1.

Within a project, you use folders to organize the source code that have no application meaning associated with them (with the exception of web applications, which can have specially named folders that have specific meaning in this context). Some developers use folder names that correspond to the namespace to which the classes belong. For example, if class `Person` is found within a folder called `DataClasses` in a project called FirstProject, the fully qualified name of the class could be `FirstProject.DataClasses.Person`.

FIGURE 6-1

Solution folders are a useful way to organize the projects in a large solution. Solution folders are visible only in the Solution Explorer — a physical folder is not created on the filesystem. Actions such as Build or Unload can be performed easily on all projects in a solution folder. Solution folders can also be collapsed or hidden so that you can work more easily in the Solution Explorer. Projects that are hidden are still built when you build the solution. Because solution folders do not map to a physical folder, they can be added, renamed, or deleted at any time without causing invalid File references or source control issues.

> **NOTE** *Miscellaneous Files is a special solution folder that you can use to keep track of other files that have been opened in Visual Studio but are not part of any projects in the solution. The Miscellaneous Files solution folder is not visible by default. You can find the settings to enable it under Tools ⇨ Options ⇨ Environment ⇨ Documents.*

Because the format for the solution file has not changed since Visual Studio 2012, you can open the same solution file with all subsequent versions. As you would expect, you can open a file in Visual Studio 2017 that was originally created in Visual Studio 2013. Even better, you can use Visual Studio 2013 to open a solution file originally created in Visual Studio 2017.

In addition to tracking which files are contained within an application, solution and project files can record other information, such as how a particular file should be compiled, project settings, resources, and much more. Visual Studio 2017 includes nonmodal dialog for editing project properties, whereas solution properties still open in a separate window. As you might expect, the project properties are those properties pertaining only to the project in question, such as assembly information and references, whereas solution properties determine the overall build configurations for the application.

SOLUTION FILE FORMAT

Visual Studio 2017 actually creates two files for a solution, with extensions .suo and .sln (solution file). The first of these is a rather uninteresting binary file and hence difficult to edit. It contains user-specific information — for example, which files were open when the solution was last closed and the location of breakpoints. This file is marked as hidden, so it won't appear in the solution folder using Windows Explorer unless you enable the option to show hidden files.

> **WARNING** *Occasionally the .suo file becomes corrupted and causes unexpected behavior when building and editing applications. If Visual Studio becomes unstable for a particular solution, you should exit and delete the .suo file. It will be re-created by Visual Studio the next time the solution is opened.*

The .sln solution file contains information about the solution, such as the list of projects, build configurations, and other settings that are not project-specific. Unlike many files used by Visual Studio 2017, the solution file is not an XML document. Instead, it stores information in blocks, as shown in the following example solution file:

```
Microsoft Visual Studio Solution File, Format Version 12.00
# Visual Studio 15
```

```
VisualStudioVersion = 15.0.26014.0
MinimumVisualStudioVersion = 10.0.40219.1
Project("{FAE04EC0-301F-11D3-BF4B-00C04F79EFBC}") = "SampleWPFApp",
    "SampleWPFApp\SampleWPFApp.csproj",
    "{F745050D-7E66-46E5-BAE2-9477ECAADCAA}"
EndProject
Global
    GlobalSection(SolutionConfigurationPlatforms) = preSolution
        Debug|Any CPU = Debug|Any CPU
        Release|Any CPU = Release|Any CPU
    EndGlobalSection
    GlobalSection(ProjectConfigurationPlatforms) = postSolution
        {68F55325-0737-40A4-9695-B953F613E2B6}.Debug|Any CPU.ActiveCfg =
        Debug|Any CPU
        {68F55325-0737-40A4-9695-B953F613E2B6}.Debug|Any CPU.Build.0 =
        Debug|Any CPU
        {68F55325-0737-40A4-9695-B953F613E2B6}.Release|Any CPU.ActiveCfg =
        Release|Any CPU
        {68F55325-0737-40A4-9695-B953F613E2B6}.Release|Any CPU.Build.0 =
        Release|Any CPU
    EndGlobalSection
    GlobalSection(SolutionProperties) = preSolution
        HideSolutionNode = FALSE
    EndGlobalSection
EndGlobal
```

In this example, the solution consists of a single project, SampleWPFApp, and a `Global` section outlining settings that apply to the solution. For instance, the solution itself is visible in the Solution Explorer because the `HideSolutionNode` setting is FALSE. If you were to change this value to TRUE, the solution name would not display in Visual Studio.

Note that the Version stamp shown in the preceding code is 12.00, which is the same as the version used for Visual Studio 2012, 2013, 2015, and 2017. This is nicely consistent with the idea that the same solution file can be opened using a previous version of Visual Studio.

SOLUTION PROPERTIES

You can reach the solution Properties dialog by right-clicking the Solution node in the Solution Explorer and selecting Properties. This dialog contains two nodes to partition Common and Configuration properties, as shown in Figure 6-2.

The following sections describe the Common and Configuration properties nodes in more detail.

Common Properties

You have three options when defining the startup project for an application, and they're somewhat self-explanatory. Selecting Current Selection starts the project that has current focus in the Solution Explorer. Single Startup Project ensures that the same project starts up each time. This is the default selection because most applications have only a single startup project. You can use the drop-down list to indicate the single project that you need to start. The last option, Multiple Startup Projects, allows for multiple projects to be started in a particular order. This can be useful if you have a client/server application specified in a single solution and you want them both to be running. When running multiple projects, it is also relevant to control the order in which they start up. Use the up and down arrows next to the project list to control the order in which projects are started.

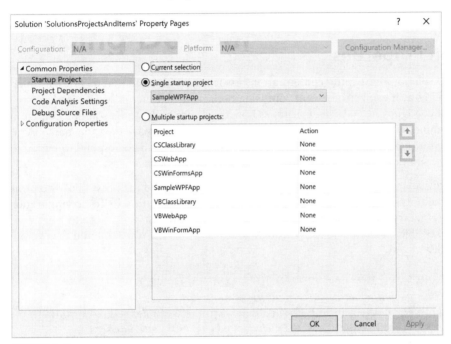

FIGURE 6-2

The Project Dependencies section is used to indicate other projects on which a specific project is dependent. For the most part, Visual Studio manages this for you as you add and remove Project references for a given project. However, sometimes you may want to create dependencies between projects to ensure that they are built in the correct order. Visual Studio uses its list of dependencies to determine the order in which projects should be built. This window prevents you from inadvertently adding circular references and from removing necessary project dependencies.

In the Debug Source Files section, you can provide a list of directories through which Visual Studio can search for source files when debugging. This is the default list that is searched before the Find Source dialog displays. You can also list source files that Visual Studio should not try to locate. If you click Cancel when prompted to locate a source file, the file will be added to this list.

The Code Analysis Settings section is available only in the Visual Studio Enterprise edition. This allows you to select the static code analysis rule set that will be run for each project. Code Analysis is discussed in more detail later in the chapter.

> **NOTE** *If you have never specified a code analysis run in Visual Studio, it's possible that the Solution Properties window won't have the Code Analysis Settings section even if you run one of the appropriate editions. To correct this, run Code Analysis directly from the menu. When the analysis finishes, this section becomes visible to you on the solution properties.*

Configuration Properties

Both projects and solutions have build configurations associated with them that determine which items are built and how. It can be somewhat confusing because there is actually no correlation between a project configuration, which determines how things are built, and a solution configuration, which determines which projects are built, other than they might have the same name. A new solution defines both Debug and Release (solution) configurations, which correspond to building all projects within the solution in Debug or Release (project) configurations.

For example, a new solution configuration called Test can be created, which consists of two projects: MyClassLibrary and MyClassLibraryTest. When you build your application in Test configuration, you want MyClassLibrary to be built in Release mode so that you're testing as close to what you would release as possible. However, to step through your test code, you want to build the test project in Debug mode.

> **NOTE** *You can switch between configurations and platforms easily via the Standard toolbar. There is a drop-down available for both the desired configuration and the platform, enabling a quick change whenever the need arises.*

When you build in Release mode, you don't want the Test solution to be built or deployed with your application. In this case, you can specify in the Test solution configuration that you want the MyClassLibrary project to be built in Release mode and that the MyClassLibraryTest project should not be built.

When you select the Configuration Properties node from the Solution Properties dialog, as shown in Figure 6-3, the Configuration and Platform drop-down boxes are enabled. The Configuration drop-down contains each of the available solution configurations (Debug and Release by default, Active, and All). Similarly, the Platform drop-down contains each of the available platforms. Whenever these drop-downs appear and are enabled, you can specify the settings on that page on a per-configuration and per-platform basis. You can also use the Configuration Manager button to add additional solution configurations and platforms.

When adding solution configurations, there is an option (checked by default) to create corresponding project configurations for existing projects (projects will be set to build with this configuration by default for this new solution configuration), and an option to base the new configuration on an existing configuration. If the Create Project Configurations option is checked and the new configuration is based on an existing configuration, the new project configuration copies the project configurations specified for the existing configuration.

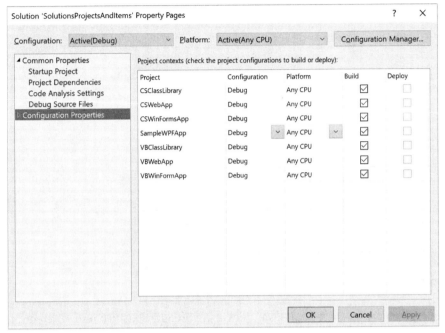

FIGURE 6-3

The other thing you can specify in the solution configuration file is the type of CPU for which you are building. This is particularly relevant if you want to deploy to 64-bit architecture machines. The options available for creating new platform configurations are limited by the types of CPU available: x86 and x64.

You can reach all these solution settings directly from the right-click context menu from the Solution node in the Solution Explorer window. Whereas the Set Startup Projects menu item opens the Solution Configuration window, the Configuration Manager, Project Dependencies, and Project Build Order items open the Configuration Manager and Project Dependencies windows. The Project Dependencies and Project Build Order menu items will be visible only if you have more than one project in your solution.

When the Project Build Order item is selected, this opens the Project Dependencies window and lists the build order, as shown in Figure 6-4. This tab reveals the order in which projects will be built, according to the dependencies. This can be useful if you maintain references to project binary assemblies rather than Project references, and it can be used to double-check that projects are built in the correct order.

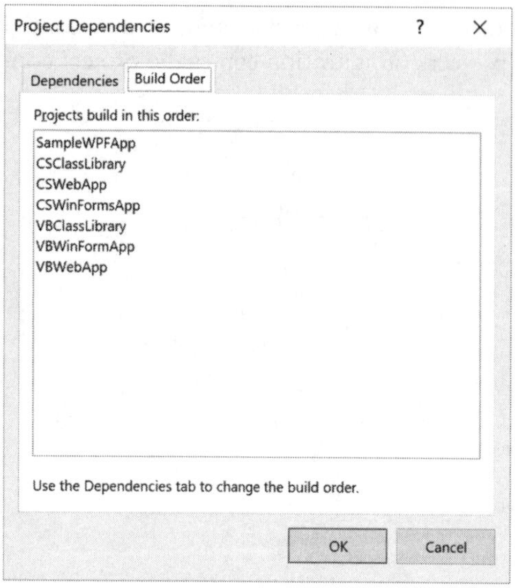

FIGURE 6-4

PROJECT TYPES

Within Visual Studio, the projects for Visual Basic and C# are broadly classified into different categories. With the exception of Web Site projects, which are discussed separately later in this chapter, each project contains a project file (`.vbproj` or `.csproj`) that conforms to the MSBuild schema. Selecting a project template creates a new project, of a specific project type, and populates it with initial classes and settings. Following are some of the more common categories of projects as they are grouped under Visual Studio:

➤ **Classic Desktop:** The Windows project category is the broadest category and includes most of the common project types that run on end-user operating systems. This includes the Windows Forms executable projects, Console application projects, and Windows Presentation Foundation (WPF) applications. These project types create an executable (`.exe`) assembly that is executed directly by an end user. The Windows category also includes several types of library assemblies that can easily be referenced by other projects. These include both class libraries and control libraries for Windows Forms and WPF applications. A class library reuses the familiar DLL extension. The Windows Service project type can also be found in this category.

➤ **Web:** The Web category includes the project types that run ASP.NET. This includes ASP.NET web applications (including MVC and Web API) and ASP.NET Core Web applications (both .NET Core and .NET Framework). Adding an ASP.NET web application starts a wizard session that enables you to create each of the different types of web projects.

➤ **Office/SharePoint:** As its name suggests, the Office/SharePoint category contains templates used to create managed code add-ins for Microsoft Office products, such as Outlook, Word, or Excel. These project types use Visual Studio Tools for Office (VSTO) and are capable of creating add-ins for most products in the Office 2013 and 2016 product suite. It also contains projects that target SharePoint, such as SharePoint Workflows or Web Parts. Visual Studio 2017 includes templates for the Office and SharePoint Add-Ins. These templates enable you to create applications that work within the App Model introduced with the 2013 versions of these products.

➤ **.NET Core:** The .NET Core category contains projects that are based on the .NET Core library. This is a version of .NET that is capable of running on Windows, Linux, and MacOS. Here you will find templates for console applications, a class library, unit test projects, and ASP.NET applications.

➤ **.NET Standard:** The .NET Standard template is used to create a library that conforms to the formal specification for .NET. Probably the easiest way to think of a .NET Standard project is as the most recent incarnation of a Portable Class Library (PCL) that can be executed on a variety of platforms.

➤ **Cloud:** This section contains templates that are related to cloud development. While you might automatically assume that this means Azure (and the Azure templates are in this category), it also includes ASP.NET templates as well. In the Azure group, there are a couple of templates that can be used to create Azure components, such as WebJobs, Mobile Apps, and Resource Groups.

➤ **Test:** The Test category includes a project type for projects that contain tests using the MSTest unit testing framework.

➤ **WCF:** This contains a number of project types for creating applications that provide Windows Communication Foundation (WCF) services.

➤ **Windows UAP:** The Windows Universal App Platform (UAP) category is new to Visual Studio 2017, although in terms of content, it is quite similar to the Windows Store category from Visual Studio 2015. There is a requirement that you be running Windows 8.1 or greater to create a Windows UAP application. If you haven't upgraded and you try to create a project, you are redirected to a page that includes a link to start the upgrade process. When you are running Windows 8.1, the templates for Windows Store applications appear under this heading.

➤ **Workflow:** This contains a number of project types for sequential and state machine workflow libraries and applications.

The Add New Project dialog box, as shown in Figure 6-5, enables you to browse and create any of these project types. The target .NET Framework version is listed in a drop-down selector in the top center of this dialog box. If a project type is not supported by the selected .NET Framework version, such as a WPF application under .NET Framework 2.0, that project type will not display. Also be aware that the exact list of categories that you see depends a great deal on the workloads that you have installed. If you expect to see a particular project template and you can't find it, it could very well be that the associated workload hasn't been installed. There is a link (labelled Open Visual Studio Installer) at the bottom of the list of categories that will launch the Visual Studio installer, allowing you to easily add the workload that you're looking for.

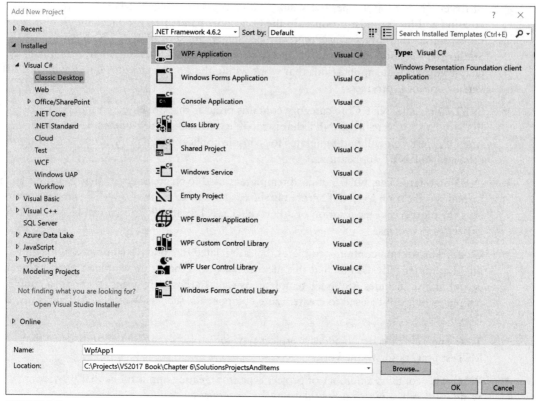

FIGURE 6-5

PROJECT FILES FORMAT

The project files (`.csproj`, `.vbproj`, or `.fsproj`) are text files in an XML document format that conforms to the MSBuild schema. The XML schema files for the latest version of MSBuild are installed with the .NET Framework, by default in `C:\WINDOWS\Microsoft.NET\Framework\v4.0.30319\MSBuild\Microsoft.Build.Core.xsd`.

> **NOTE** *To view the project file in XML format, right-click the project and select Unload Project. Then right-click the project again and select Edit <project name>. This displays the project file in the XML editor, complete with IntelliSense.*

The project file stores the build and configuration settings that have been specified for the project and details about all the files that are included in the project. In some cases, a user-specific project file is also created (.csproj.user or .vbproj.user), which stores user preferences such as startup and debugging options. The .user file is also an XML file that conforms to the MSBuild schema.

PROJECT PROPERTIES

You can reach the project properties by either right-clicking the Project node in Solution Explorer and then selecting Properties, or by double-clicking My Project (Properties in C#) just under the Project node. In contrast to solution properties, the project properties do not display in a modal dialog. Instead, they appear as an additional tab alongside your code files. This was done in part to make it easier to navigate between code files and project properties, but it also makes it possible to open project properties of multiple projects at the same time. Figure 6-6 illustrates the project settings for a Visual Basic Windows Forms project. This section walks you through the vertical tabs on the project editor for both Visual Basic and C# projects.

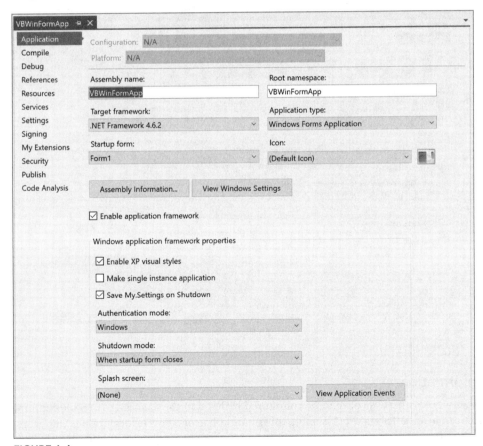

FIGURE 6-6

The project properties editor contains a series of vertical tabs that group the properties. As changes are made to properties in the tabs, a star is added to the corresponding vertical tab. This functionality is limited, however, because it does not indicate which fields within the tab have been modified.

Application

The Application tab, visible in Figure 6-6 for a Visual Basic Windows Forms project, enables the developer to set the information about the assembly that will be created when the project is compiled. These include attributes such as the output type (that is, Windows or Console Application, Class Library, Windows Service, or a Web Control Library), application icon, startup object, and the target .NET Framework version. The Application tab for C# applications, as shown in Figure 6-7, has a different format, and provides a slightly different (and reduced) set of options such as the ability to configure the application manifest directly.

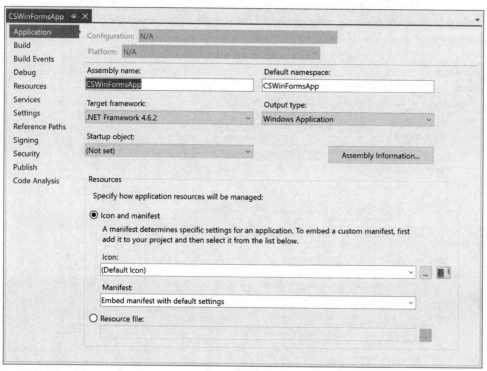

FIGURE 6-7

Assembly Information

Attributes that would otherwise have to be configured by hand in the `AssemblyInfo` file contained in the project can also be set via the Assembly Information button. This information is important because it shows up when an application is installed and when the properties of a file are viewed in

Windows Explorer. Figure 6-8 (left) shows the assembly information for a sample application and Figure 6-8 (right) shows the properties of the compiled executable.

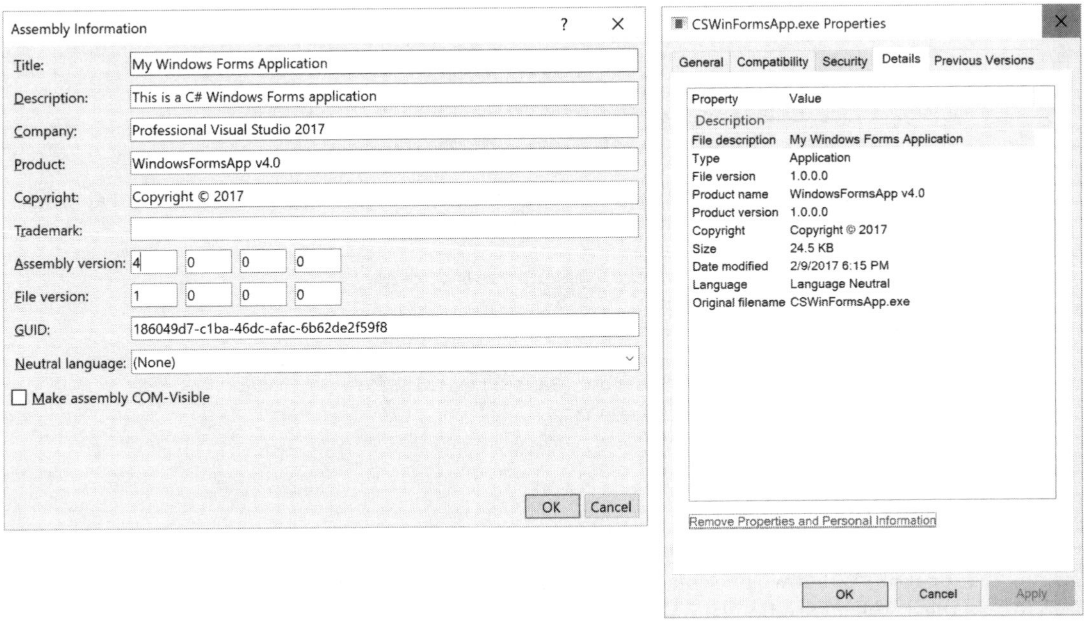

FIGURE 6-8

Each of the properties set in the Assembly Information dialog is represented by an attribute that is applied to the assembly. This means that the assembly can be queried in code to retrieve this information. In Visual Basic, the `My.Application.Info` namespace provides an easy way to retrieve this information.

User Account Control Settings

Visual Studio 2017 provides support for developing applications that work with User Account Control (UAC). This involves generating an assembly manifest file, which is an XML file that notifies the operating system if an application requires administrative privileges on startup. In Visual Basic applications, you can use the View Windows Settings button on the Application tab to generate and add an assembly manifest file for UAC to your application. The following code shows the default manifest file generated by Visual Studio:

```
<?xml version="1.0" encoding="utf-8"?>
<asmv1:assembly manifestVersion="1.0" xmlns="urn:schemas-microsoft-com:asm.v1"
        xmlns:asmv1="urn:schemas-microsoft-com:asm.v1"
        xmlns:asmv2="urn:schemas-microsoft-com:asm.v2"
        xmlns:xsi="http://www.w3.org/2001/XMLSchema-instance">
    <assemblyIdentity version="1.0.0.0" name="MyApplication.app" />
    <trustInfo xmlns="urn:schemas-microsoft-com:asm.v2">
```

```
<security>
  <requestedPrivileges xmlns="urn:schemas-microsoft-com:asm.v3">
    <!-- UAC Manifest Options
      If you want to change the Windows User Account Control level replace the
      requestedExecutionLevel node with one of the following.

    <requestedExecutionLevel  level="asInvoker" />
    <requestedExecutionLevel  level="requireAdministrator" />
    <requestedExecutionLevel  level="highestAvailable" />

      If you want to utilize File and Registry Virtualization for backward
      compatibility then delete the requestedExecutionLevel node.
    -->
    <requestedExecutionLevel level="asInvoker" />
  </requestedPrivileges>
  <applicationRequestMinimum>
    <defaultAssemblyRequest permissionSetReference="Custom" />
    <PermissionSet ID="Custom" SameSite="site" />
  </applicationRequestMinimum>
</security>
</trustInfo>
</asmv1:assembly>
```

If the UAC-requested execution level is changed from the default `asInvoker` to `require Administrator`, Windows presents a UAC prompt when the application launches. If you have UAC enabled, Visual Studio 2017 also prompts you to restart in Administrator mode if an application requiring admin rights starts in Debug mode. Figure 6-9 shows the prompt that is shown in Windows allowing you to restart Visual Studio in Administrator mode.

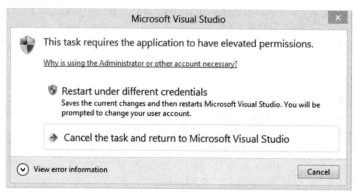

FIGURE 6-9

If you agree to the restart, Visual Studio not only restarts with administrative privileges, it also reopens your solution including all files you had opened. It even remembers the last cursor position.

Application Framework (Visual Basic Only)

Additional application settings are available for Visual Basic Windows Forms projects because they can use the Application Framework that is exclusive to Visual Basic. This extends the standard event model to provide a series of application events and settings that control the behavior of the application. You can enable the Application Framework by checking the Enable Application Framework check box. The following three check boxes control the behavior of the Application Framework:

➤ **Enable XP Visual Styles:** XP visual styles are a feature that significantly improves the look and feel of applications running on Windows XP or later, because it provides a much smoother interface through the use of rounded buttons and controls that dynamically change color as the mouse passes over them. Visual Basic applications enable XP styles by default and can be disabled from the Project Settings dialog or controlled from within code through the `EnableVisualStyles` method on the Application class.

➤ **Make Single Instance Application:** Most applications support multiple instances running concurrently. However, an application opened more than two or three times may be run only once, with successive executions simply invoking the original application. Such an application could be a document editor, whereby successive executions simply open a different document. This functionality can be easily added by marking the application as a single instance.

➤ **Save My Settings on Shutdown:** Selecting the Save My Settings on Shutdown option ensures that any changes made to user-scoped settings will be preserved, saving the settings provided prior to the application shutting down.

This section also allows you to select an authentication mode for the application. By default this is set to Windows, which uses the currently logged-on user. Selecting Application-defined allows you to use a custom authentication module.

You can also identify a form to be used as a splash screen when the application first launches and specify the shutdown behavior of the application.

Compile (Visual Basic Only)

The Compile section of the project settings, as shown in Figure 6-10, enables the developer to control how and where the project is built. For example, the output path can be modified so that it points to an alternative location. This might be important if the output is to be used elsewhere in the build process.

The Configuration drop-down selector at the top of the tab page allows different build settings for the Debug and Release build configuration.

If your dialog is missing the Configuration drop-down selector, you need to check the Show Advanced Build Configurations property in the Projects and Solutions node of the Options window, accessible from the Tools menu. Unfortunately, this property is not checked for some of the built-in setting profiles — for example, the Visual Basic Developer profile.

Some Visual Basic–specific properties can be configured in the Compile pane. Option Explicit determines whether variables that are used in code must be explicitly defined. Option Strict forces the type of variables to be defined, rather than it being late-bound. Option Compare determines whether strings are compared using binary or text comparison operators. Option Infer specifies whether to allow local type inference in variable declarations or whether the type must be explicitly stated.

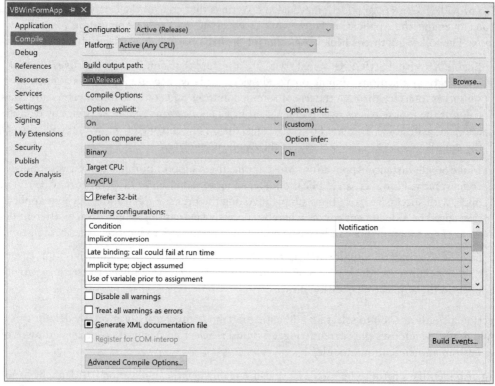

FIGURE 6-10

> **NOTE** *All of these compile options can be controlled at either the Project or File level. File-level compiler options override Project-level options.*

The Compile pane also defines a number of different compiler options that can be adjusted to improve the reliability of your code. For example, unused variables may only warrant a warning, whereas a path that doesn't return a value is more serious and should generate a build error. It is possible to either disable all these warnings or treat all of them as errors.

Visual Basic developers also have the ability to generate XML documentation. Of course, because the documentation takes time to generate, it is recommended that you disable this option for debug builds. This can speed up the debugging cycle; however, when the option is turned off, warnings are not given for missing XML documentation.

The last element of the Compile pane is the Build Events button. Click this button to view commands that can be executed prior to and after the build. Because not all builds are successful, the execution of the post-build event can depend on a successful build. C# projects have a separate Build Events tab in the project properties pages for configuring pre- and post-build events.

Build (C# and F# Only)

The Build tab, as shown in Figure 6-11, is the C# equivalent of the Visual Basic Compile tab. This tab enables the developer to specify the project's build configuration settings. For example, the Optimize code setting can be enabled, which results in assemblies that are smaller, faster, and more efficient. However, these optimizations typically increase the build time, and as such are not recommended for the Debug build.

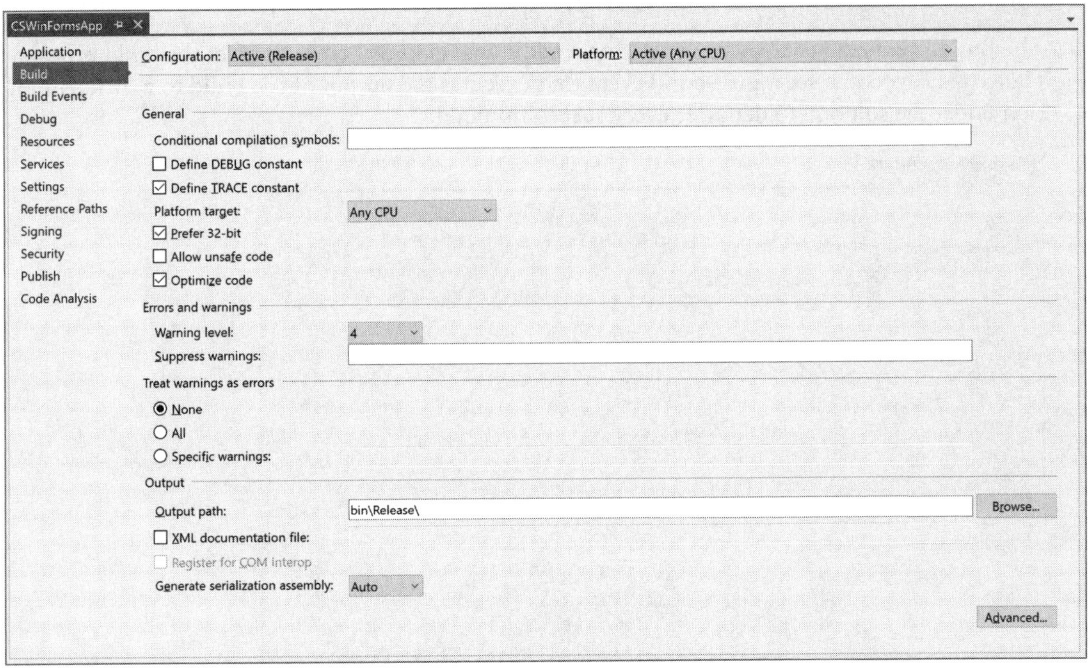

FIGURE 6-11

On the Build tab, the DEBUG and TRACE compilation constants can be enabled. Alternatively, you can easily define your own constants by specifying them in the Conditional compilation symbols textbox. The value of these constants can be queried from code at compile time. For example, the DEBUG constant can be queried as follows:

C#

```
#if(DEBUG)
    MessageBox.Show("The debug constant is defined");
#endif
```

VB

```
#If DEBUG Then
    MessageBox.Show("The debug constant is defined")
#End If
```

The compilation constants are defined on the Advanced Build Settings dialog, which can be displayed by clicking the Advanced button at the bottom right of the Build tab.

The Configuration drop-down selector at the top of the tab page allows different build settings for the Debug and Release build configuration. You can find more information on the Build options in Chapter 33, "Build Customization."

Build Events (C# and F# Only)

The Build Events tab enables you to perform additional actions before or after the build process. In Figure 6-12, you can see a post-build event that executes the output of the build to a different location under the solution folder after every successful build.

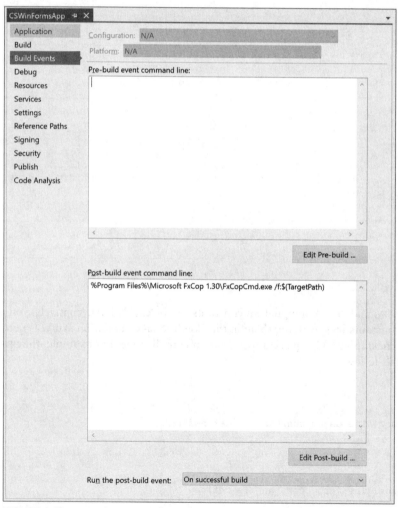

FIGURE 6-12

You can use environment variables such as `ProgramFiles` in your command lines by enclosing them with the percent character. A number of macros are also available, such as `ProjectName` and `SolutionDir`. These macros are listed when the Macros buttons on the Edit Pre-build and Edit Post-build dialog boxes are clicked and can be injected into the command wherever needed.

Debug

The Debug tab, shown in Figure 6-13, determines how the application will be executed when run from within Visual Studio 2017. This tab is not visible for web applications — instead, the Web tab is used to configure similar options.

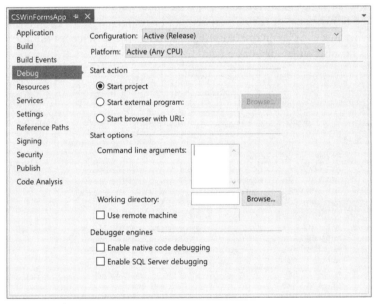

FIGURE 6-13

Start Action

When a project is set to start up, this set of radio buttons controls what actually happens when the application is run within Visual Studio. The default value is to start the project, which calls the Startup object specified on the Application tab. The other options are to either run an executable or launch a specific website.

Start Options

The options that can be specified when running an application are additional command-line arguments (generally used with an executable start action) and the initial working directory. You can also specify to start the application on a remote computer. Of course, this is possible only when debugging is enabled on the remote machine.

Debugger Engines

Debugging can be extended to include unmanaged code and SQL Server. With these options checked, it becomes possible to enlist unmanaged code and SQL Server stored procedures in the debug process. For example, you can open a stored procedure through the Server Explorer, set a breakpoint and, while debugging your application through Visual Studio, the breakpoint will be hit and execution stopped when the stored procedure is called by your application.

References (Visual Basic Only)

The References tab enables the developer to reference classes in other .NET assemblies, projects, and native DLLs. When the project or DLL has been added to the References list, a class can be accessed either by its full name, including namespace, or the namespace can be imported into a code file so that the class can be referenced by just the class name. Figure 6-14 shows the References tab for a project that has a reference to a number of framework assemblies.

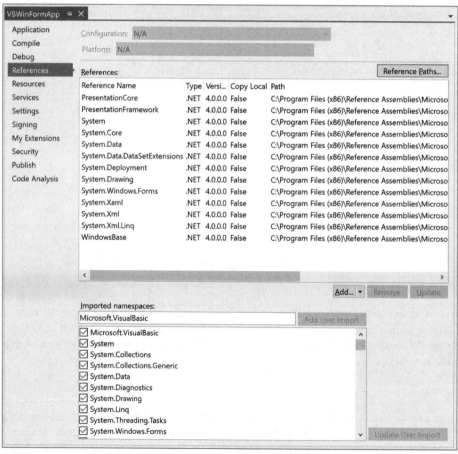

FIGURE 6-14

> **NOTE** *Having unused references in your project is not generally a problem. Although some people don't like it because it makes the solution "messy," from a performance perspective, there is no impact. Assemblies that are not used are not copied to the output directory.*

When an assembly has been added to the Reference list, any public class contained within that assembly can be referenced within the project. Where a class is embedded in a namespace (which might be a nested hierarchy), referencing a class requires the full class name. Both Visual Basic and C# provide a mechanism for importing namespaces so that classes can be referenced directly. The References section allows namespaces to be globally imported for all classes in the project, without being explicitly imported within the class file.

References to external assemblies can be either File references or Project references. File references are direct references to an individual assembly. You can create File references by using the Browse tab of the Reference Manager dialog box. Project references are references to a project within the solution. All assemblies that are output by that project are dynamically added as references. Create Project references by using the Solution tab of the Reference Manager dialog box.

> **WARNING** *You should generally not add a File reference to a project that exists in the same solution. If a project requires a reference to another project in that solution, a Project reference should be used.*

The advantage of a Project reference is that it creates a dependency between the projects in the build system. The dependent project will be built if it has changed since the last time the referencing project was built. A File reference doesn't create a build dependency, so it's possible to build the referencing project without building the dependent project. However, this can result in problems with the referencing project expecting a different version from what is included in the output.

Resources

You can add or remove Project resources via the Resources tab, as shown in Figure 6-15. In the example shown, four icons have been added to this application. Resources can be images, text, icons, files, or any other serializable class.

This interface makes working with resource files at design time easy. Chapter 56, "Resource Files," in the online archive examines in more detail how you can use resource files to store application constants and internationalize your application.

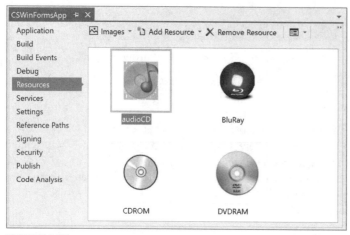

FIGURE 6-15

Services

Client application services allow Windows-based applications to use the authentication, roles, and profile services that were introduced with Microsoft ASP.NET 2.0. The client services enable multiple web- and Windows-based applications to centralize user profiles and user-administration functionality.

Figure 6-16 shows the Services tab, which is used to configure client application services for Windows applications. When enabling the services, the URL of the ASP.NET service host must be specified for each service. This will be stored in the `app.config` file. The following client services are supported:

➤ **Authentication:** This enables the user's identity to be verified using either the native Windows authentication or a custom forms-based authentication that is provided by the application.

➤ **Roles:** This obtains the roles an authenticated user has been assigned. This enables you to allow certain users access to different parts of the application. For example, additional administrative functions may be made available to admin users.

➤ **Web Settings:** This stores per-user application settings on the server, which allows them to be shared across multiple computers and applications.

Client application services utilize a provider model for web services extensibility. The service providers include offline support that uses a local cache to ensure that it can still operate even when a network connection is not available.

Client application services are discussed further in Chapter 47, "Client Application Services," in the online archive.

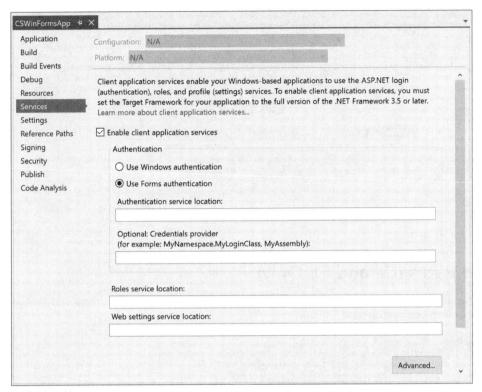

FIGURE 6-16

Settings

Project settings can be of any type and simply reflect a name/value pair whose value can be retrieved at run time. Settings can be scoped to either the application or the user, as shown in Figure 6-17. Settings are stored internally in the `Settings.settings` file and the `app.config` file. When the application is compiled, this file is renamed according to the executable generated — for example, `SampleApplication.exe.config`.

Application-scoped settings are read-only at run time and can be changed only by manually editing the config file. User settings can be dynamically changed at run time and may have a different value saved for each user who runs the application. The default values for User settings are stored in the `app.config` file, and the per-user settings are stored in a `user.config` file under the user's private data path.

Application and User settings are described in more detail in Chapter 54, "Configuration Files," in the online archive.

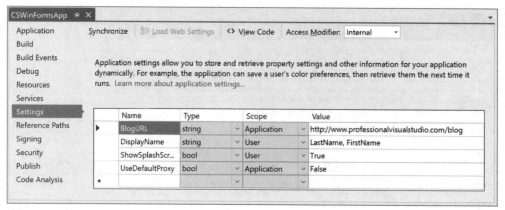

FIGURE 6-17

Reference Paths (C# and F# Only)

The Reference Paths tab, as shown in Figure 6-18, is used to specify additional directories that are searched for referenced assemblies.

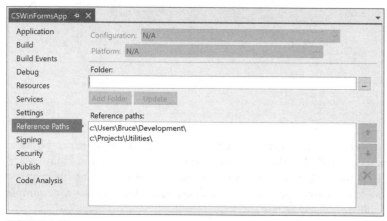

FIGURE 6-18

When an assembly reference has been added, Visual Studio resolves the reference by looking in the following directories in this order:

1. The project directory.

2. Directories specified in this Reference Paths list.

3. Directories displaying files in the Reference Manager dialog box.

4. The `obj` directory for the project. This is generally only relevant to COM interop assemblies.

Signing

Figure 6-19 shows the Signing tab, which provides developers with the capability to determine how assemblies are signed in preparation for deployment. An assembly can be signed by selecting a key file. A new key file can be created by selecting <New...> from the file selector drop-down.

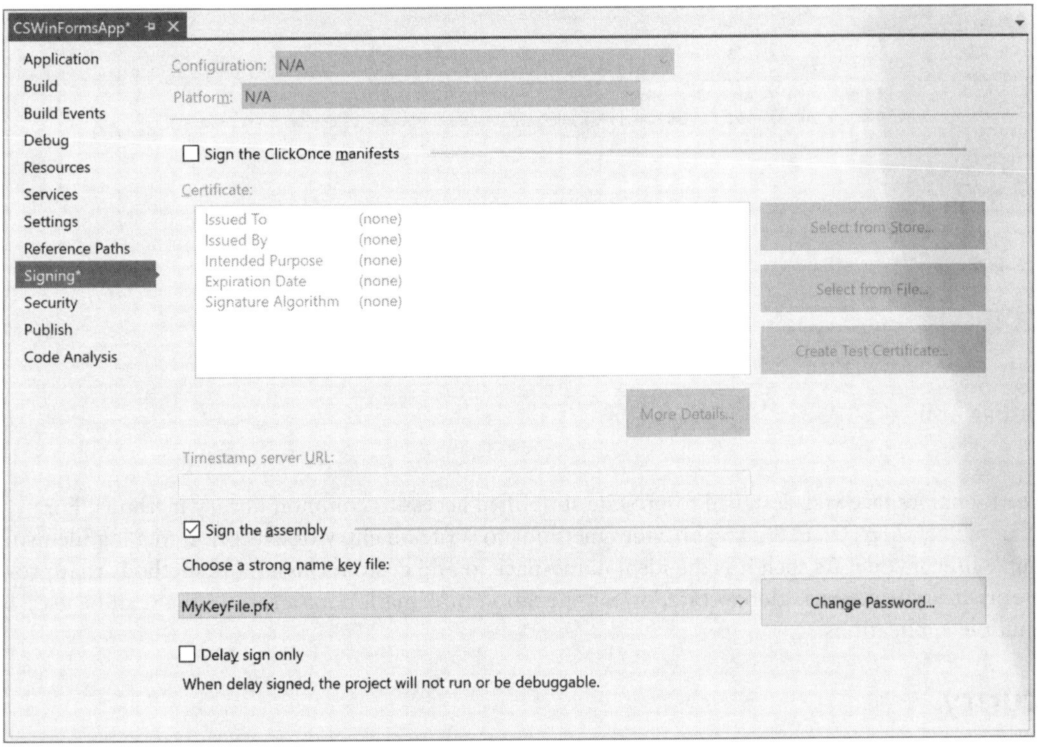

FIGURE 6-19

The ClickOnce deployment model for applications enables an application to be published to a website where a user can click once to download and install the application. Because this model is supposed to support deployment over the Internet, an organization must be able to sign the deployment package. The Signing tab provides an interface for specifying the certificate to use to sign the ClickOnce manifests.

Chapter 48, "Assembly Versioning and Signing," in the online archive provides more detail on assembly signing and Chapter 35, "Packaging and Deployment," discusses ClickOnce deployments.

My Extensions (Visual Basic Only)

The My Extensions tab, as shown in Figure 6-20, enables you to add a reference to an assembly that extends the Visual Basic My namespace, using the extension methods feature. Extension methods were initially introduced to enable LINQ to be shipped without requiring major changes to the base class library. They allow developers to add new methods to an existing class, without having to use inheritance to create a subclass or recompile the original type.

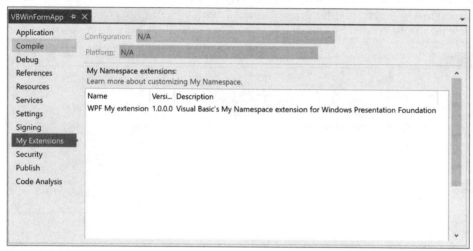

FIGURE 6-20

The My namespace was designed to provide simplified access to common library methods. For example, My.Application.Log provides methods to write an entry or exception to a log file using a single line of code. As such it is the ideal namespace to add custom classes and methods that provide useful utility functions, global state, or configuration information, or a service that can be used by multiple applications.

Security

Applications deployed using the ClickOnce deployment model may be required to run under limited or partial trust. For example, if a low-privilege user selects a ClickOnce application from a website across the Internet, the application needs to run with partial trust as defined by the Internet zone. This typically means that the application can't access the local filesystem, has limited networking capability, and can't access other local devices such as printers, databases, and computer ports.

The Security tab, illustrated in Figure 6-21, allows you to define the trust level that is required by your application to operate correctly.

Modifying the permission set that is required for a ClickOnce application may limit who can download, install, and operate the application. For the widest audience, specify that an application should run in partial-trust mode with security set to the defaults for the Internet zone. Alternatively, specifying that an application requires full trust ensures that the application has full access to all local resources but necessarily limits the audience to local administrators.

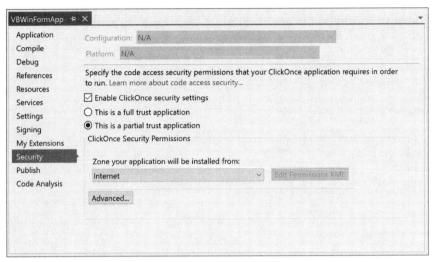

FIGURE 6-21

Publish

The ClickOnce deployment model can be divided into two phases: initially publishing the application and subsequent updates, and the download and installation of both the original application and subsequent revisions. You can deploy an existing application using the ClickOnce model using the Publish tab, as shown in Figure 6-22.

If the install mode for a ClickOnce application is set to be available offline when it is initially downloaded from the website, it will be installed on the local computer. This places the application in the Start menu and the Add/Remove Programs list. When the application is run and a connection to the original website is available, the application determines whether any updates are available. If there are updates, users are prompted to determine whether they want the updates to be installed.

The ClickOnce deployment model is explained more thoroughly in Chapter 35, "Packaging and Deployment."

Code Analysis

Most developers who have ever worked in a team have had to work with an agreed-upon set of coding standards. Organizations typically use an existing standard or create their own. Unfortunately, standards are useful only if they can be enforced, and the only way that this can be effectively done is to use a tool. In the past this had to be done using an external utility. All editions of Visual Studio 2017 (including the Community edition) have the capability to carry out static code analysis from within the IDE.

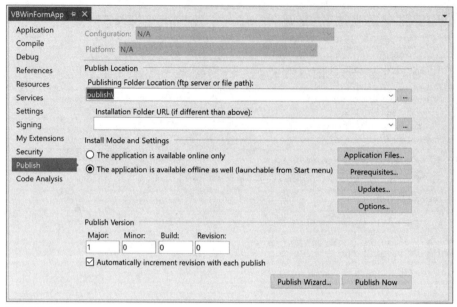

FIGURE 6-22

The Code Analysis tab, as shown in Figure 6-23, can be used to enable code analysis as part of the build process.

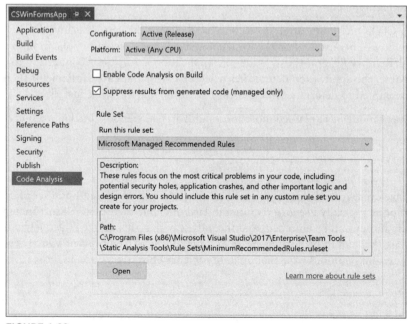

FIGURE 6-23

When the Enable Code Analysis on Build checkbox is checked, then code analysis will be performed automatically for each build. Alternatively, you can right-click a project and select Analyze ⇨ Run Code Analysis on Solution or Analyze ⇨ Run Code Analysis on the current project.

The basic unit of definition in code analysis is a rule. A rule consists of a specific criterion that needs to be met in order for the rule to pass. For instance, a rule might be something like "a variable has been declared but never used" or "the result of an expression is always null." These rules can be combined into a collection of rules known as a *ruleset*.

In the Code Analysis tab, you specify which ruleset is going to be applied to your code when code analysis is run. More than 200 built-in rules are conveniently organized into 11 rulesets. You can even create your own sets of rules (Add New Item ⇨ Code Analysis Rule Set) if the ones provided by Microsoft don't meet your needs. Beyond that, you can add custom rules if needed.

Depending on your project, you might want to exclude some particular rules. To get to the details of a particular ruleset, click on the Open button to display a pane similar to Figure 6-24.

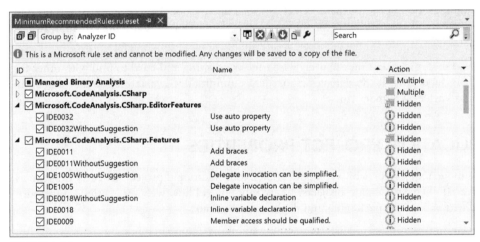

FIGURE 6-24

Unchecking the checkbox that appears to the left of a rule disables that rule. The dropdown box on the right controls what happens when a rule fails to be met, such as whether it's a warning or a build error.

When you build your application, any errors or warnings associated with code analysis appear in the Error List. Within that pane, if you right-click a warning and select Show Error Help, you have a description of the rule, the cause, the steps on how to fix violations, and suggestions on when to suppress warnings. Suppressing warnings is done with `System.Diagnostics.CodeAnalysis`
`.SuppressMessageAttribute`, which can be applied to the offending member or to the assembly as a whole. You can quickly and easily generate these attributes by selecting one of the Suppress Message menu options from the right-click menu in the Errors window.

When you first start with Code Analysis tools, you should turn on all the rules and either exclude or suppress the warnings as needed. This is an excellent way to learn best practices. After a couple of iterations, new code written will be less prone to violating a rule. If you start a new project, you might want to add a check-in policy, which prevents code with Analysis warnings from being checked in.

> **NOTE** *Never suppress a warning unless you have a good reason. Finding these violations again can be quite difficult.*

C/C++ CODE ANALYSIS TOOL

This tool is similar to the Managed Code Analysis Tool but works for unmanaged code. To activate it simply go to your C++ project's properties window, look for the Code Analysis node inside the Configuration Properties, and select Yes for Enable Code Analysis for C/C++ on Build. Every time you compile your project, the tool intercepts the process and attempts to analyze each execution path.

It can help you detect crashes that are otherwise time-consuming and hard to find with other techniques, such as debugging. It can detect memory leaks, uninitialized variables, pointer management problems, and buffer over/under runs.

WEB APPLICATION PROJECT PROPERTIES

Due to the unique requirements of web applications, four additional project property tabs are available to ASP.NET Web Application projects. These tabs control how web applications run from Visual Studio as well as the packaging and deployment options.

Web

The Web tab, shown in Figure 6-25, controls how Web Application projects are launched when executed from within Visual Studio. Visual Studio ships with a built-in web server suitable for development purposes. The Web tab enables you to configure the port and virtual path that this runs under. You may also choose to enable NTLM authentication.

> **NOTE** *The Enable Edit and Continue option allows editing of code behind and standalone class files during a debug session. Editing of the HTML in an* .aspx *or* .ascx *page is allowed regardless of this setting; however, editing inline code in an* .aspx *page or an* .ascx *file is never allowed.*

The debugging options for web applications are explored in Chapter 58, "Debugging Web Applications," in the online archive.

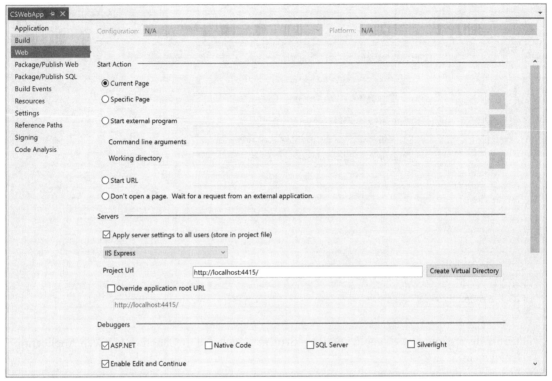

FIGURE 6-25

Package/Publish Web

Application deployment has always been a difficult challenge, especially for complex web applications. A typical web application is composed of not only a large number of source files and assemblies, but also images, stylesheets, and JavaScript files. To complicate matters further, it may be dependent on a specific configuration of the IIS web server.

Visual Studio 2017 simplifies this process by allowing you to package a Web Application project with all the necessary files and settings contained in a single compressed (.zip) file. Figure 6-26 shows the packaging and deployment options that are available to an ASP.NET web application.

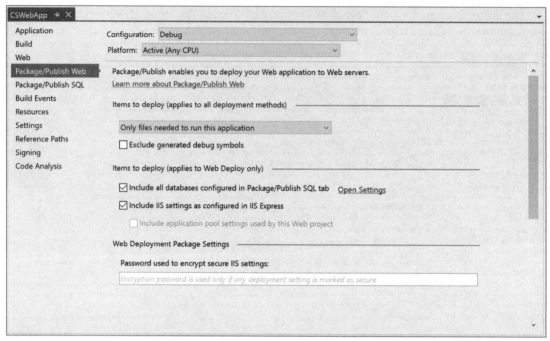

FIGURE 6-26

Further discussion on web application deployment is included in Chapter 36, "Web Application Deployment."

Package/Publish SQL

All but the simplest of web applications are backed by a database of some description. For ASP.NET web applications this is typically a SQL Server database. Visual Studio 2017 includes support for packaging one or more SQL Server databases. Although the project properties still include a sheet titled Package/Publish SQL, that page is not available by default. Instead, the configuration for SQL deployment appears as part of the Publish Web Wizard.

As illustrated in Figure 6-27, when you create a package you can specify a connection string for your source database. You can allow Visual Studio to create SQL scripts for the database schema only or schema and data. You can also provide custom SQL scripts to be executed either before or after the auto-generated script.

Chapter 36 explores the web application deployment options in more detail.

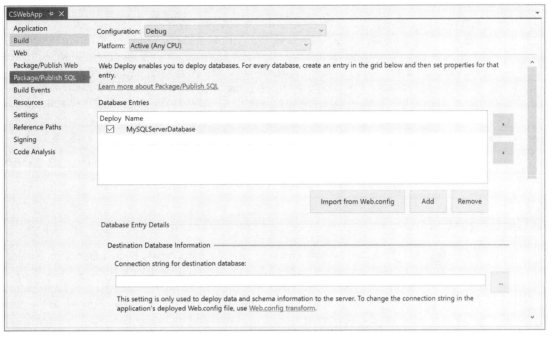

FIGURE 6-27

WEB SITE PROJECTS

The Web Site project functions quite differently from other project types. Web Site projects do not include a `.csproj` or `.vbproj` file, which means they have a number of limitations for build options, project resources, and managing references. Instead, Web Site projects use the folder structure to define the contents of the project. All files within the folder structure are implicitly part of the project.

Web Site projects provide the advantage of dynamic compilation, which allows pages to be edited without rebuilding the entire site. The file can be saved and simply reloaded in the browser. As such, they enable extremely short code and debug cycles. Microsoft first introduced Web Site projects with Visual Studio 2005; however, it was quickly inundated with customer feedback to reintroduce the Application Project model, which had been provided as an additional download. By the release of Service Pack 1, Web Application projects were back within Visual Studio as a native project type.

> **NOTE** *Since Visual Studio 2005, an ongoing debate has been raging about which is better — Web Site projects or Web Application projects. Unfortunately, there is no simple answer to this debate. Each has its own pros and cons, and the decision comes down to your requirements and your preferred development workflow. That said, the majority of web projects use the Web Application template. Unless you have a compelling reason to use a Web Site project, it is recommended that the Web Application project be your default choice.*

You can find further discussion on Web Site and Web Application projects in Chapter 16, "ASP.NET Web Forms."

NUGET PACKAGES

One of the changes that have been slowly creeping into the .NET world is the reliance on NuGet as the platform for deploying components. NuGet is an open source platform that allows .NET components, as well as native components written in C++, to be distributed easily and automatically to your development platform. And with Visual Studio 2017, that reliance grows to the point where NuGet is used to handle deploying everything up to and including the .NET Framework. Fortunately, access to NuGet is available through a couple of mechanisms within Visual Studio 2017.

As a developer of components, you bundle everything necessary to install your software into a package (kept in a .nupkg file). Included in the package are the assemblies that need to be deployed and a manifest file that describes the contents of the package and what needs to be changed in the project to support your components (changes to configuration files, references to be added, and so on).

NuGet Package Manager

There are two main ways to bring a package from NuGet into your project. Although your preference likely depends on your predilection for command line versus graphical interfaces, it is expected that the most common method involves the NuGet Package Manager integrated into the Solution Explorer. In the Solution Explorer, right-click on a project and select the Manage NuGet Packages option. The page shown in Figure 6-28 appears. A similar page can be accessed through the Tools ➪ NuGet Package Manager ➪ Manage NuGet Packages for Solution menu option.

The elements of the page are designed to help you find the packages that you need to add to your project. The search box on the right gives you the ability to search the NuGet repository. The controls on the left let you choose the repository source. The options available out-of-the-box are nuget .org, preview.nuget.org (contains preview versions of components), and Microsoft. As well, you can filter the results of your search so that only already installed packages and packages with updates are shown.

Select the package that you want to include in your project. The details of the package appear in the panel on the right side of the page. The package can be installed by clicking on the Install button. If you would like to see the changes that would be made because of installing the package, click on the Preview button.

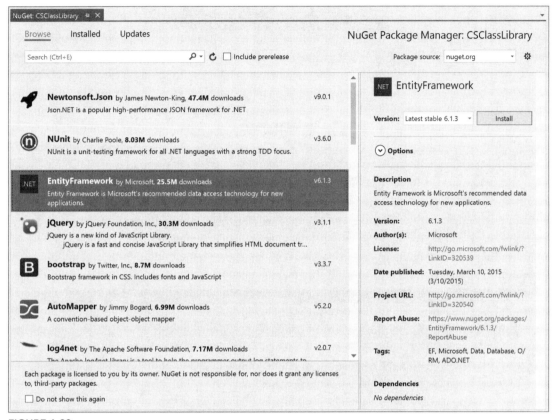

FIGURE 6-28

The last piece of functionality available on this page is initiated through the gear icon to the right of the search box. Clicking on the gear launches the Options dialog and displays the NuGet Package Manager pane, as seen in Figure 6-29.

The main function of the screen shown in Figure 6-29 is to allow you to configure the NuGet repositories that are searched by the Package Manager. You can add new repositories by clicking on the plus button in the top right of the dialog and then updating the Name and Source fields at the bottom of the page.

Package Manager Console

You access the command-line interface used to manage NuGet packages through the Tools ⇨ NuGet Package Manager ⇨ Package Manager Console menu option. The screen shown in Figure 6-30 appears.

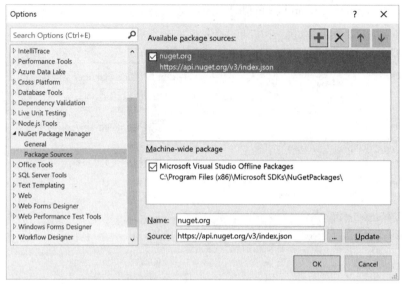

FIGURE 6-29

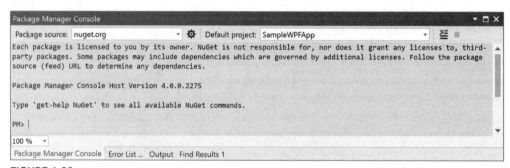

FIGURE 6-30

The challenge at this point is knowing the various commands that are available to you to help manage the packages. The most basic is `install-package`, which takes the name of the package as a parameter. A complete list of the commands is well beyond the scope of this book. As indicated in the description found in Figure 6-30, `get-help NuGet` provides a list that is a decent start.

SUMMARY

In this chapter you have seen how a solution and projects can be configured using the user interfaces provided within Visual Studio 2017. In particular, this chapter showed you how to do the following:

➤ Create and configure solutions and projects.

➤ Control how an application is compiled, debugged, and deployed.

➤   Configure the many project-related properties.

➤   Include resources and settings with an application.

➤   Enforce good coding practices with the Code Analysis Tools.

➤   Modify the configuration, packaging, and deployment options for web applications.

In subsequent chapters, many of the topics, such as building and deploying projects and the use of resource files, are examined in more detail.

IntelliSense and Bookmarks

WHAT'S IN THIS CHAPTER?

➤   Improving efficiency with contextual help

➤   Detecting and fixing simple errors

➤   Reducing keystrokes

➤   Generating code

➤   Navigating source code with bookmarks

WROX.COM CODE DOWNLOADS FOR THIS CHAPTER

The wrox.com code downloads for this chapter can be found at www.wrox.com by searching for this book's ISBN number (978-1-119-40458-3). The code and any related support files are located in their own folder for this chapter.

One of the design goals of Visual Studio has always been to improve the productivity of developers. IntelliSense is one of those functions that fit perfectly into this category. It has been around for more than a decade, and it has become so deeply embedded in the day-to-day world of coders that we pretty much take it for granted. And yet, from version to version, Microsoft is still able to find tweaks and improvements that make it even more useful. This chapter illustrates the many ways in which IntelliSense helps you write your code. Among the topics covered are detecting and repairing syntax errors, harnessing contextual information, and variable name completion. You'll also learn how to set and use bookmarks in your code for easier navigation.

INTELLISENSE EXPLAINED

IntelliSense is the general term for automated help and actions in a Microsoft application. The most commonly encountered aspects of IntelliSense are those wavy lines you see under words that are not spelled correctly in Microsoft Word, or the small visual indicators in a Microsoft Excel spreadsheet that inform you that the contents of the particular cell do not conform to what was expected.

Even these basic indicators enable you to quickly perform related actions. Right-clicking a word with red wavy underlining in Word displays a list of suggested alternatives. Other applications have similar features.

The good news is that Visual Studio has had similar functionality for a long time. In fact, the simplest IntelliSense features go back to tools such as Visual Basic 6. With each release of Visual Studio, Microsoft has refined the IntelliSense features, making them more context-sensitive and putting them in more places so that you always have the information you need right at your fingertips.

In Visual Studio 2017, the IntelliSense name is applied to a number of different features, from visual feedback for bad code and smart tags for designing forms to shortcuts that insert whole slabs of code. These features work together to provide you with deeper insight, efficiency, and control of your code. Some of Visual Studio's features, such as Suggestion mode and Generate From Usage, are designed to support the alternative style of application development known as test-driven development (TDD).

General IntelliSense

The simplest feature of IntelliSense gives you immediate feedback about bad code in your code listings. Figure 7-1 shows one such example, in which an unknown data type is used to instantiate an object. Because the data type is unknown where this code appears, Visual Studio draws a red (C# and C++) or blue (VB) wavy line underneath to indicate a problem.

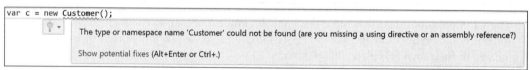

```
var c = new Customer();
```
The type or namespace name 'Customer' could not be found (are you missing a using directive or an assembly reference?)

Show potential fixes (Alt+Enter or Ctrl+.)

FIGURE 7-1

> **NOTE** *You can adjust the formatting of this color feedback in the Fonts and Colors group of Options.*

Hovering the mouse over the offending piece of code displays a tooltip to explain the problem. In this example the cursor was placed over the data type, with the resulting tooltip "The type or namespace name 'Customer' could not be found."

Visual Studio looks for this kind of error by continually compiling the code you write in the background, and checking for anything that can produce a compilation error. If you were to add the Customer class to your project, Visual Studio would automatically process this and remove the IntelliSense marker.

The idea of a smart tag associated with an error is not new. However, recent versions of Visual Studio have introduced a number of innovations that improve upon its utility. In Figure 7-1, you'll see a light bulb. This is the smart tag indicator, and it is visible (and therefore usable) in a number of different situations. When it comes to errors, the light bulb appears when Visual Studio can offer you one or more corrective courses of action. Clicking on the arrow to the right of the light bulb displays the available options, as seen in Figure 7-2.

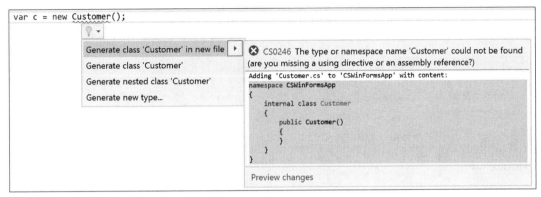

FIGURE 7-2

As you can see, Visual Studio can come up with different ways to correct the problem of a missing type. The ways are variations of "create a class of type Customer," with the difference being the location and scope of the class. As you move your mouse over the different choices, the box on the right provides an example of what the correction will look like. You can even go a step further and click on the Preview Changes link to see a more detailed description of the change, including the files that will be affected. Figure 7-3 provides an example.

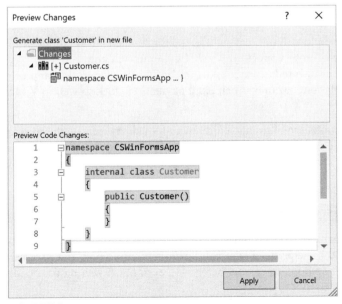

FIGURE 7-3

> **NOTE** *The traditional shortcut key used by Microsoft applications to activate an IntelliSense smart tag has been Shift+Alt+F10, but Visual Studio 2017 provides the more wrist-friendly Ctrl+. (period) shortcut for the same action.*

The smart tag technology found in Visual Studio is not solely reserved for the code window, nor does it always involve light bulbs. Visual Studio 2017 also includes smart tags on visual components when you edit a form or user control in Design view (see Figure 7-4).

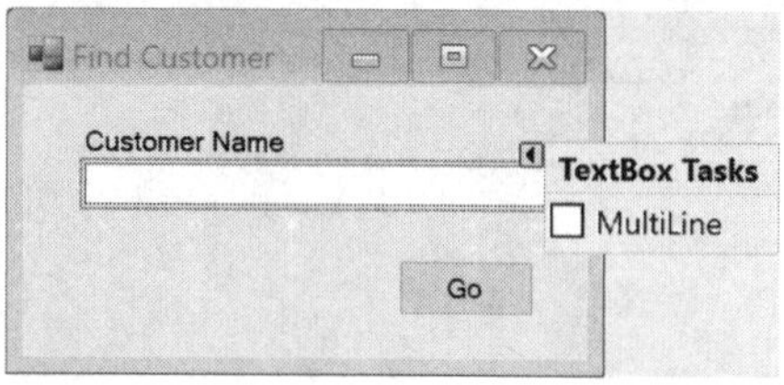

FIGURE 7-4

> **NOTE** *The keyboard shortcuts for opening smart tags also work for visual controls.*

When you select a control that has a smart tag, a small triangle appears at the top-right corner of the control. Click this button to open the smart tag Tasks list. Figure 7-4 shows the Tasks list for a standard TextBox control.

IntelliSense and C++

Visual Studio 2017 includes full IntelliSense support for C++/CLI (Common Language Infrastructure). C++ has a fair amount of IntelliSense support itself. C++ developers will appreciate how functionality such as autocompletion, parameter help, and navigation work so well in Visual Studio 2017.

All of the topics in the following sections are of as much interest to C++ developers as they are to VB and C# developers. The underlying infrastructure provides robust IntelliSense performance, and a wide array of IntelliSense features are now included. So C++ developers can rejoice and bask in the warm glow of IntelliSense.

Completing Words and Phrases

The power of IntelliSense in Visual Studio 2017 becomes apparent almost immediately. As you type, various drop-down lists are displayed to help you choose valid members, functions, and parameter types, thus reducing the potential for compilation errors before you even finish writing your code.

When you become familiar with the IntelliSense behavior, you'll notice that it can greatly reduce the amount of code you actually have to write. This can be a significant savings to developers using more verbose languages such as Visual Basic.

In Context

In Visual Studio 2017, IntelliSense appears almost as soon as you begin to type within the code window. Figure 7-5 illustrates the IntelliSense displayed during the creation of a For loop in Visual Basic. On the left side of the image, IntelliSense appeared as soon as the f was entered, and the list of available words progressively shrank as each subsequent key was pressed. As you can see, the list is made up of all the alternatives, such as statements, classes, methods, or properties, that match the letters entered (in this case those containing the word For).

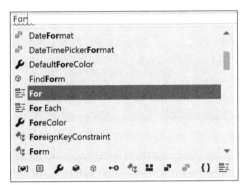
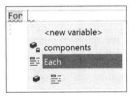

FIGURE 7-5

At the bottom of the list is a collection of icons that can be used to reduce the list of alternatives. The icons correspond to different types of items in the list and match the icon that appears to the left of each alternative. By clicking on an icon, you toggle on and off the inclusion of alternatives of that type in the list.

As you continue typing a space (after the For), the IntelliSense list contracts to show just the next possible keywords (components and Each). And there is a <new variable> item at the top of the list to indicate that it's possible for you to specify a new variable at this location.

> **NOTE** *The* <new variable> *item appears only for Visual Basic users.*

Although it can be useful that the IntelliSense list is reduced based on the letters you enter, this feature is a double-edged sword. Quite often you will be looking for a variable or member but won't quite remember what it is called. In this scenario, you might enter the first couple of letters of a guess and then use the scrollbar to locate the right alternative. Clearly, this won't work if the letters you have entered have already eliminated the alternative. To bring up the full list of alternatives, simply press the Backspace key with the IntelliSense list visible. Alternatively, Ctrl+Space lists all of the alternatives if the IntelliSense list is not visible.

IntelliSense assistance is not limited to members that begin with the characters you type. The entered characters are considered a word by IntelliSense. Then, as it looks for matches, it considers words that appear in the middle of member names. IntelliSense does this by looking for word boundaries within the member names based on Pascal casing. Figure 7-6 shows an example in C# where typing `Console.in` will find `In`, `InputEncoding`, `IsInputRedirected`, `OpenStandardInput`, `SetIn`, and `TreatControlCAsInput` but does not find `LargestWindowHeight` despite the fact that it contains the substring "in."

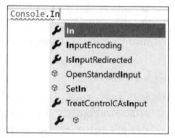

FIGURE 7-6

> **NOTE** *If you know exactly what you are looking for, you can save even more keystrokes by typing the first character of each word in uppercase. As an example, if you type* `System.Console.OSI` *then* `OpenStandardInput` *will be selected by IntelliSense.*

If you find that the IntelliSense information is obscuring other lines of code, or you simply want to hide the list, you can press Esc. Alternatively, if you simply want to view what is hidden behind the IntelliSense list without closing it completely, you can hold down the Ctrl key. This makes the IntelliSense list translucent, enabling you to read the code behind it, as shown in Figure 7-7.

```
Dim myColor = ConsoleColor.
                        Black
Dim myData As New List(Of String)(500)
                        Blue
                        Cyan
                        DarkBlue
                        DarkCyan
                        DarkGray
                        DarkGreen
                        DarkMagenta
                        DarkRed
```

FIGURE 7-7

The IntelliSense list is not just for informational purposes. You can select an item from this list and have Visual Studio actually insert the full text into the editor window for you. You have a number of ways to select an item from the list. You can double-click the wanted item with the mouse; you can use the arrow keys to change which item is highlighted and then press the Enter or Tab key to insert the text; and finally, when an item is highlighted in the list, it will automatically be selected if you enter a *commit character*. Commit characters are those that are not normally allowed within member names. Examples include parentheses, braces, mathematical symbols, and semicolons.

List Members

Because IntelliSense has been around for so long, most developers are familiar with the member list that appears when you type the name of an object and immediately follow it by a period. This indicates that you are going to refer to a member of the object, and Visual Studio automatically displays a list of members available to you for that object. If this is the first time you've accessed the member list for a particular object, Visual Studio simply shows the members in alphabetical order with the top of the list visible. However, if you've used it before, it highlights the last member you accessed to speed up the process for repetitive coding tasks.

Suggestion Mode

By default, when Visual Studio 2017 shows the IntelliSense member list, one member is selected, and as you type, the selection is moved to the item in the list that best matches the characters entered. If you press Enter, Space, or type one of the commit characters (such as an open parenthesis), the currently selected member is inserted into the editor window. This default behavior is known as *completion mode*.

In most cases completion mode provides the wanted behavior and can save you a great deal of typing, but it can be problematic for some activities. One such activity is test-driven development, where references are frequently made to members that have not yet been defined. This causes IntelliSense to select members that you didn't intend it to and insert text that you do not want.

To avoid this issue you can use the IntelliSense *suggestion mode*. When IntelliSense is in suggestion mode, one member in the list will have focus but will not be selected by default. As you type, IntelliSense moves the focus indicator to the item that most closely matches the characters you typed, but it will not automatically select it. Instead, the characters that you type are added to the top of the IntelliSense list, and if you type one of the commit characters or press Space or Enter, the exact string that you typed is inserted into the editor window.

Figure 7-8 shows an example of the problem that suggestion mode is designed to address. On the left side you can write a test for a new method called Load on the CustomerData class. The CustomerData class does not have a method called Load yet, but it does have a method called LoadAll.

FIGURE 7-8

On the right side of Figure 7-8, you can type **Load** followed by the open parenthesis character. IntelliSense incorrectly assumes that you wanted the LoadAll method and inserts it into the editor.

To avoid this behavior you can turn on suggestion mode by pressing Ctrl+Alt+Space. Currently when you type Load, it appears at the top of the IntelliSense list. When you type the open parenthesis character, you get Load as originally intended (see Figure 7-9).

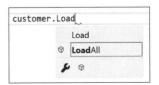

FIGURE 7-9

> **NOTE** *You can still make a selection from the IntelliSense list by using the arrow keys. Also, you can select the item that has focus in the member list by pressing the Tab key.*

> **NOTE** *IntelliSense remains in suggestion mode until you press Ctrl+Alt+Space again to revert back to completion mode.*

Stub Completion

In addition to word and phrase completion, the IntelliSense engine has another feature known as *stub completion*. This feature can be seen in Visual Basic when you create a function by writing the declaration of the function and pressing Enter. Visual Studio automatically reformats the line, adding the appropriate `ByVal` keyword for parameters that don't explicitly define their contexts, and also adding an `End Function` line to enclose the function code. Another example can be seen when editing an XML document. When you type the open tag of a new element, Visual Studio automatically puts the closing tag in for you.

Visual Studio 2017 takes stub completion an extra step by enabling you to do the same for interface and method overloading. When you add certain code constructs, such as an interface in a C# class definition, Visual Studio gives you the opportunity to automatically generate the code necessary to implement the interface. To show you how this works, the following steps outline a task in which the IntelliSense engine generates an interface implementation in a simple class:

1. Start Visual Studio 2017 and create a C# Windows Forms Application project. When the IDE has finished generating the initial code, open `Form1.cs` in the code editor.

2. At the top of the file, add a `using` statement to provide a shortcut to the `System.Collections` namespace:

   ```
   using System.Collections;
   ```

3. Add the following line of code to start a new class definition:

   ```
   public class MyCollection: IEnumerable
   ```

   After you type the `IEnumerable` keyword, Visual Studio adds a red wiggly line underneath, indicating that there is an error.

4. Hover your mouse pointer over the `IEnumerable` keyword. In a moment, a light bulb indicator, along with a message (as shown in Figure 7-10), appears.

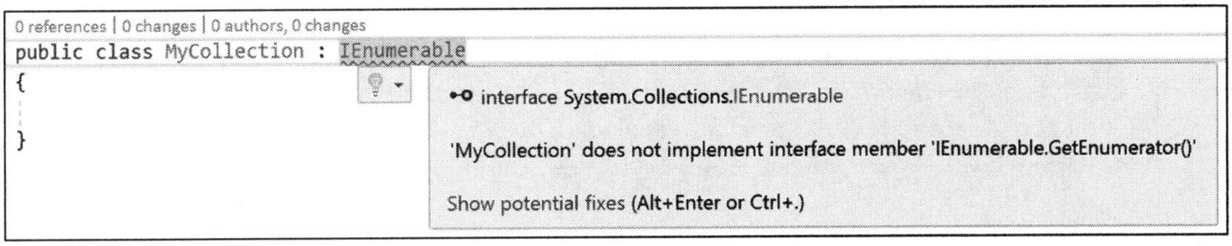

FIGURE 7-10

The information area to the right of the light bulb describes the error that Visual Studio has detected. The details of this text depend greatly on the error. For this one, it basically indicates that you have declared that a class will implement an interface (IEnumerable) but have not yet implemented all the elements required by that interface.

5. Click either the drop-down arrow to the right of the light bulb or the Show Potential Fixes link in the text area. This reveals a list (see Figure 7-11) of how Visual Studio can fix the error. If you hover over the options, the text area on the right shows in more detail the changes that would be made by selecting the fix. In addition, you can preview the change or make the change across the document, the project, or the entire solution.

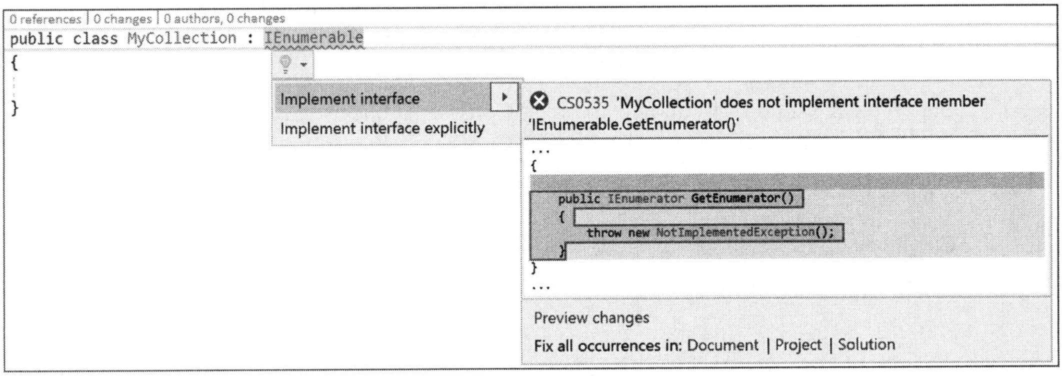

FIGURE 7-11

6. Select the Implement Interface option, and Visual Studio 2017 automatically generates the rest of the code necessary to implement the minimum interface definition.

The light bulb is not only available while hovering over the source of the error. If the cursor is positioned on a line that has an error, the light bulb appears to the left of the code line, as illustrated in Figure 7-12. Clicking on the light bulb starts the same fixing process that is described in step 5.

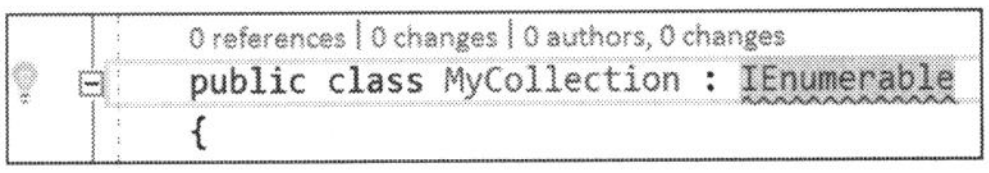

FIGURE 7-12

> **NOTE** *Though generated properties and classes can be used as they are, when a method stub is generated, the body of the method will throw a* `NotImplementedException` *if it is executed.*

Event handlers can also be automatically generated by Visual Studio 2017. The IDE does this much as it performs interface implementation. When you write the first portion of the statement (for instance, `myBase.OnClick +=`), Visual Studio gives you a suggested completion that you can select simply by pressing Tab.

Generate From Usage

Rather than generating code from a definition that already exists, sometimes it is more convenient to generate the definition of a code element from the way you have used it. This is especially true if you practice test-driven development, where you write tests for classes that have not been defined yet. It would be convenient to generate the classes from the tests themselves, and this is the purpose of the Generate From Usage feature in C# and Visual Basic.

To understand how you might use this in practice, the following steps outline the creation of a simple `Customer` class by writing some client code that uses it, and then generating the class from that usage:

1. Start Visual Studio 2017 and create a C# Console Application project. When the IDE is ready, open the `Program.cs` file.

2. Update the `Main` method with the following code:

   C#

   ```
   Customer c = new Customer
   {
     FirstName = "Joe",
     LastName = "Smith"
   };

   Console.WriteLine(c.FullName);
   c.Save();
   ```

3. You should see a red wiggly line underneath both instances of the class name `Customer`. Right-click one of them, and select Quick Actions and Refactorings from the context menu. This displays a set of data similar to what is shown in Figure 7-10. But in this case, when you click on the drop-down arrow, the options are more appropriate for creating the `Customer` class that is missing. Select the Generate class for 'Customer' in 'YourAppName' (in new file). This creates a new class in your project called `Customer`. If you open `Customer.cs`, you'll see a class declaration that includes the `FirstName` and `LastName` automatic properties. Visual Studio will then discover that `FullName` and `Save` are not members of this class.

4. For the `FullName` member that does not exist, use the light bulb functionality to add it to the `Customer` class. Look at `Customer.cs` again, and note that Visual Studio has provided an implementation for you.

5. You can do the same for the Save method by right-clicking and selecting the Generate 'Customer.Save' option from the Quick Actions and Refactorings list.

> **NOTE** *When you generate a method stub in this manner, you might notice that the method is always marked as being internal. The reason for this has to do with a "best practices" approach that Microsoft code-generator is taking. Specifically, it is giving the minimum access required for a method to be invoked from the call site. An internal method can be called from within the assembly but is not accessible from outside the assembly. This meets the security best practice of "least privilege."*

If the undefined code that you want to generate is a type, you have the option to Generate Class or Generate New Type. If you select Generate New Type, the Generate Type dialog displays (see Figure 7-13). This dialog gives you more options to configure your new type, including class, enumeration, interface, or structure; if the new type should be public, private, or internal; and where the new type should go.

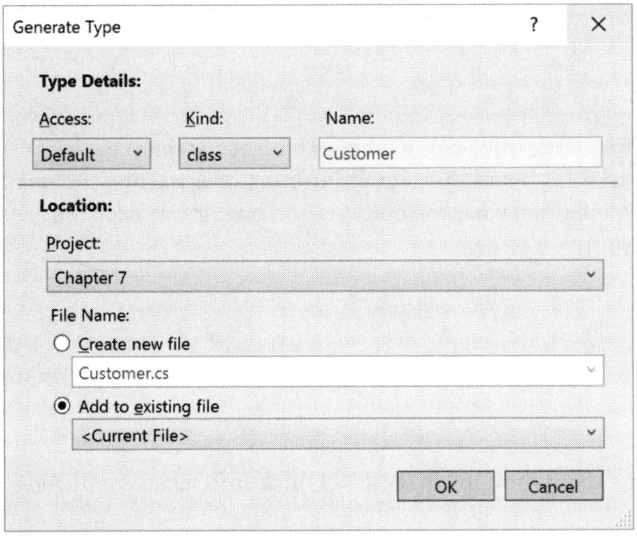

FIGURE 7-13

Parameter Information

As you create the call to a function, IntelliSense displays the parameter information as you type. The problem is that parameter information is shown only if you are actually modifying the function call. Therefore, you can see this helpful tooltip as you create or change the function call but not if you are just viewing the code. The result is that programmers sometimes inadvertently introduce changes into their code because they intentionally modify function calls so that they can view the parameter information associated with the calls. And these changes, while functionally meaningless, can cause conflicts to be detected by your source control.

Visual Studio 2017 eliminates that potential problem by providing an easily accessible command to display the information without modifying the code. The keyboard shortcut Ctrl+Shift+Space displays the information about the function call, as displayed in Figure 7-14. You can also access this information through the Edit ➪ IntelliSense ➪ Parameter Info menu command.

> **NOTE** *In Figure 7-14 the* `PrintGreeting` *method takes two parameters. The second parameter is optional and displays in square brackets with an assignment showing its default value if you don't provide one. VB programmers will be familiar with this syntax, and it has been included in C# ever since version 4.0.*

```
c.PrintGreeting("Mike");
   void Customer.PrintGreeting(string customerName, [string format = "Hello {0}"])
```

FIGURE 7-14

Quick Info

In a similar vein, sometimes you want to see the information about an object or interface without modifying the code. The Ctrl+K, Ctrl+I keyboard shortcut or hovering over the object name with the mouse displays a brief tooltip explaining what the object is and how it was declared (see Figure 7-15).

```
var backColor = frm.BackColor;
            ⚙ (field) MainForm Program.frm
```

FIGURE 7-15

You can also display this tooltip through the Edit ➪ IntelliSense ➪ Quick Info menu command.

JAVASCRIPT INTELLISENSE

If you build web applications, you can work in JavaScript to provide a richer client-side experience for your users. Unlike C# and Visual Basic, which are compiled languages, JavaScript is an interpreted language, which means that traditionally the syntax of a JavaScript program has not been verified until it is loaded into the browser. Although this can give you a lot of flexibility at run time, it requires discipline, skill, and a heavy emphasis on testing to avoid a large number of common mistakes.

In addition to this, while developing JavaScript components for use in a browser, you must keep track of a number of disparate elements. This can include the JavaScript language features, HTML DOM elements, and handwritten and third-party libraries. Luckily Visual Studio 2017 provides a full IntelliSense experience for JavaScript, which can help you to keep track of all these elements and warn you of syntax errors.

As you type JavaScript into the code editor window, Visual Studio lists keywords, functions, parameters, variables, objects, and properties just as if you were using C# or Visual Basic. This works for built-in JavaScript functions and objects as well as those you define in your own custom scripts and those found in third-party libraries. Visual Studio can also detect and highlight syntax errors in your JavaScript code.

> **NOTE** *The keyboard shortcuts for each Visual Studio 2017 install depend on the settings selected (that is, Visual Basic Developer, Visual C# Developer, and so on). All the shortcut keys in this chapter are based on using the General Developer Profile setting.*

> **NOTE** *Since Internet Explorer 3.0, Microsoft has maintained its own dialect of JavaScript called JScript. Technically, the JavaScript tools in Visual Studio 2017 are designed to work with JScript, so you sometimes see menu options and window titles containing this name. In practice, the differences between the two languages are so minor that the tools work equally well with either one.*

The JavaScript IntelliSense Context

To prevent you from accidentally referring to JavaScript elements that are not available, Visual Studio 2017 builds up an IntelliSense context based on the location of the JavaScript block that you edit. The context is made up of the following items:

- ➤ The current script block. This includes inline script blocks for `.aspx`, `.ascx`, `.master`, `.html`, and `.htm` files.

- ➤ Any script file imported into the current page via a `<script />` element or a ScriptManager control. In this case the imported script file must have the `.js` extension.

- ➤ Any script files that are referenced with a references directive (see the section "Referencing Another JavaScript File").

- ➤ Any references made to XML Web Services.

- ➤ The items in the Microsoft AJAX Library (if you work in an AJAX-enabled ASP.NET web application).

Referencing Another JavaScript File

Sometimes one JavaScript file builds upon the base functionality of another. When this happens they are usually referenced together by any page using them but have no direct reference explicitly defined. Because there is no explicit reference, Visual Studio 2017 cannot add the file with the base functionality to the JavaScript IntelliSense context, and you won't get full IntelliSense support. The exception to this is when you create JavaScript-based Windows Store applications where all the references are traversed to provide full IntelliSense context.

> **NOTE** *Visual Studio keeps track of files in the context and updates JavaScript IntelliSense whenever one of them changes. Sometimes this update may be pending and the JavaScript IntelliSense data will be out of date. You can force Visual Studio to update the JavaScript IntelliSense data by selecting Edit ⇨ IntelliSense ⇨ Update JScript IntelliSense.*

To allow Visual Studio to discover the base file and add it to the context, you can provide a reference to it by using a references directive. A references directive is a special kind of comment that provides information about the location of another file. You can use references directives to make a reference to any of the following:

➤ **Other JavaScript files:** This includes .js files and JavaScript embedded in assemblies. It does not include absolute paths, so the file you reference must be a part of the current project.

➤ **Web Service (.asmx) files:** These also must be a part of the current project, and Web Service files in Web Application projects are not supported.

➤ **Pages containing JavaScript:** One page may be referred to in this way. If any page is referenced, no other references can be made.

Following are some examples of references directives. These must appear before any other code in your JavaScript file.

JAVASCRIPT

```
// JavaScript file in current folder
/// <reference path="Toolbox.js" />

// JavaScript file in parent folder
/// <reference path="../Toolbox.js" />

// JavaScript file in a path relative to the root folder of the site
/// <reference path="~/Scripts/Toolbox.js" />

// JavaScript file embedded in Assembly
/// <reference name="Ajax.js" path="System.Web.Extensions, …" />

// Web Service file
/// <reference path="MyService.asmx" />

// Standard Page
/// <reference path="Default.aspx" />
```

> **NOTE** *A few restrictions exist on how far references directives will work. First, references directives that refer to a path outside of the current project are ignored. Second, references directives are not recursively evaluated, so only those in the file currently being edited are used to help build the context. References directives inside other files in the context are not used.*

XAML INTELLISENSE

Since the introduction of XAML, there has been support for IntelliSense in the editor window. Structurally, XAML is well-formed XML and, as such, the same capabilities exist for a XAML file as for any XML file in which Visual Studio is aware of the schema. As a result, it was fairly easy for developers to enter XAML by hand. The different elements were readily available, as were the attributes associated with each element.

Where XAML IntelliSense had issues was in the area of data binding. The data binding syntax that XAML provides is quite rich, but IntelliSense was never able to provide the hints that developers had come to expect. The reason is not hard to fathom — the data context on which data binding depends is a runtime value. And because editing is not a runtime value, it is hard to determine the properties that are exposed on the data context.

In Visual Studio 2017, IntelliSense for data binding is available, with some caveats. The requirement is that the data context for the XAML document must be defined from within the document. If you set the data context from outside the XAML document, which is a common practice if you are using a Model-View-ViewModel (MVVM) pattern, then you need to set the design-time data context within the document. This has no effect on the runtime functionality of your XAML page, yet still allows IntelliSense to get the necessary information.

Another issue is how IntelliSense handles data binding in resources, such as data templates. These data templates can be defined in an external resource dictionary, which makes it impossible for IntelliSense to determine what the active data context is. To address this, you can set the design-time data context for the template in the external resource dictionary directly. Alternatively, after the design-time data context is defined in the XAML page, you can use the Go to Definition command (F12 is the default keystroke to invoke the command) and Visual Studio automatically does the work to copy the data context.

The matching options that IntelliSense uses with XAML are mostly the same as with programming languages. In other words, they support matching based on Pascal casing (where the beginning of every word has a capital letter) or word-based substrings (where the typed characters match a word). However, XAML also includes the idea of fuzzy matching. As illustrated in Figure 7-16, the element `StackPanel` is selected even though the typed characters `StakPa` are only marginally close to the correct element.

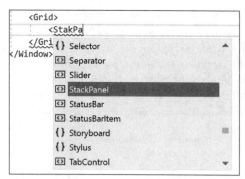

FIGURE 7-16

INTELLISENSE OPTIONS

Visual Studio 2017 sets up a number of default options for your experience with IntelliSense, but you can change many of these in the Options dialog if they don't suit your own way of doing things. Some of these items are specific to individual languages.

General Options

The first options to look at are in the Environment section under the Keyboard group. Every command available in Visual Studio has a specific entry in the keyboard mapping list (see the Options dialog shown in Figure 7-17, accessible via Tools ⇨ Options).

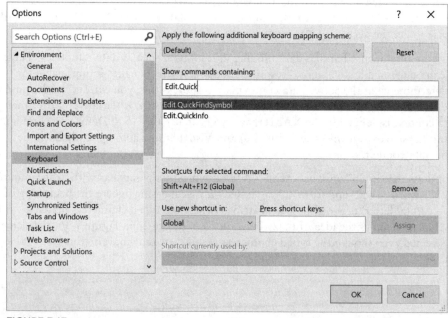

FIGURE 7-17

You can override the predefined keyboard shortcuts or add additional ones. The commands for the IntelliSense features are shown in Table 7-1.

TABLE 7-1: IntelliSense Commands

COMMAND NAME	DEFAULT SHORTCUT	COMMAND DESCRIPTION
Edit.QuickInfo	Ctrl+K, Ctrl+I	Displays the Quick Info information about the selected item
Edit.CompleteWord	Ctrl+Space	Attempts to complete a word if there is a single match, or displays a list to choose from if multiple items match
Edit.ToggleCompletionMode	Ctrl+Alt+Space	Toggles IntelliSense between suggestion and completion modes
Edit.ParameterInfo	Ctrl+Shift+Space	Displays the information about the parameter list in a function call
Edit.InsertSnippet	Ctrl+K, Ctrl+X	Invokes the Code Snippet Picker from which you can select a code snippet to insert code automatically
Edit.GenerateMethod	Ctrl+K, Ctrl+M	Generates the full method stub from a template
Edit.ImplementAbstractClassStubs	None	Generates the abstract class definitions from a stub
Edit.ImplementInterfaceStubsExplicitly	None	Generates the explicit implementation of an interface for a class definition
Edit.ImplementInterfaceStubsImplicitly	None	Generates the implicit implementation of an interface for a class definition
View.QuickActions	Ctrl+.	Displays the Quick Actions (Light Bulb) information for the current context

Use the techniques discussed in Chapter 3, "Options and Customizations," to add additional keyboard shortcuts to any of these commands.

Statement Completion

You can control how IntelliSense works on a global language scale (see Figure 7-18) or per individual language. In the General tab of the language group in the Options dialog, you'll want to change the Statement Completion options to control how member lists should be displayed, if at all.

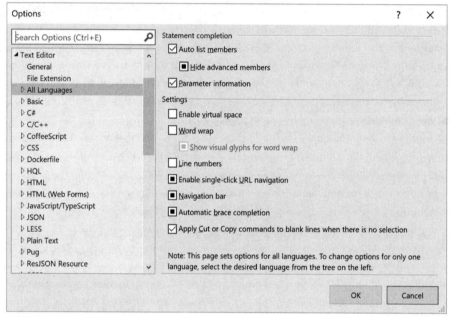

FIGURE 7-18

C#-Specific Options

Besides the general IDE and language options for IntelliSense, some languages, such as C#, provide an additional IntelliSense tab in their own sets of options. Displayed in Figure 7-19, IntelliSense for C# can be further customized to fine-tune how the IntelliSense features should be invoked and used.

First, you can turn off completion lists so that they do not appear automatically. Some developers prefer this because the member lists don't get in the way of their code listings. If the completion list is not to be automatically displayed, but instead only shown when you manually invoke it, you can choose what is to be included in the list in addition to the normal entries, including keywords and code snippet shortcuts.

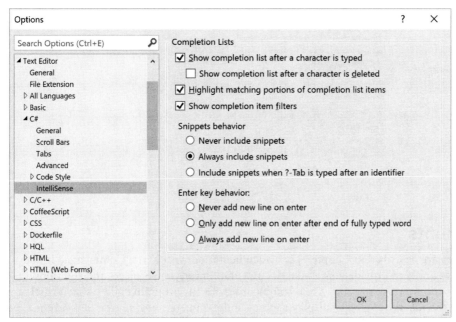

FIGURE 7-19

EXTENDED INTELLISENSE

In addition to the basic aspects of IntelliSense, Visual Studio 2017 also implements extended IDE functionality that falls into the IntelliSense feature set. These features are discussed in detail in Chapters 8, "Code Snippets and Refactoring," and Chapter 42, "Documentation with XML Comments" in the online archive, but this section provides a quick summary of what's included in IntelliSense.

Code Snippets

Code snippets are sections of code that can be automatically generated and pasted into your own code, including associated references and using statements, with variable phrases marked for easy replacement. To invoke the Code Snippets dialog, press Ctrl+K, Ctrl+X. Navigate the hierarchy of snippet folders (shown in Figure 7-20) until you find the one you need. If you know the shortcut for the snippet, you can simply type it and press Tab, and Visual Studio invokes the snippet without displaying the dialog. In Chapter 8, "Code Snippets and Refactoring," you'll see just how powerful code snippets are.

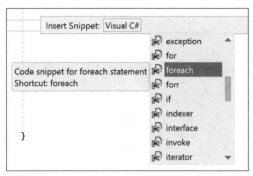

FIGURE 7-20

XML Comments

XML comments are described in Chapter 42, "Documentation with XML Comments," in the online archive as a way to provide automated documentation for your projects and solutions. However, another advantage to using XML commenting in your program code is that Visual Studio can use it in its IntelliSense engine to display tooltips and parameter information beyond the simple variable-type information you see in normal user-defined classes.

Adding Your Own IntelliSense

Visual Studio 2017 supports different levels of IntelliSense for a wide variety of languages. The range of support goes from syntax colorization (that is, keywords and operators in a language appear in a different color) to understanding syntax and context sufficiently to support Navigate To functionality. As of this writing, the following languages (aside from the "mainstream" .NET languages) are supported for only syntax colorization and autocomplete: Bat, Clojure, CoffeeScript, CSS, Docker, INI, Jade, Javadoc, JSON, LESS, LUA, Make, Markdown ++, Objective-C, PowerShell, Python, Rust, ShaderLab, SQL, and YAML. If you don't recognize all of those languages, take solace that you're not alone.

The next level of IntelliSense support includes the ability to create code snippets (as described in Chapter 8, "Code Snippets and Refactoring"). Languages that are supported (again, as of this writing) are: CMake, Go, Groovy, HTML, Java, Javadoc, JavaScript, Lua, Perl, PHP, R, Ruby, Shellscript, Swift, and XML. Keep in mind that support for Code Snippets also includes support for syntax colorization and autocomplete.

The list of languages supported for Navigate To functionality is much smaller: C++, C#, Go, Java, JavaScript, PHP, TypeScript, and Visual Basic.

You can also add your own IntelliSense schemas, normally useful for XML and HTML editing, by creating a correctly formatted XML file and installing it into the `Common7\Packages\schemas\xml` subfolder inside your Visual Studio installation directory. (The default location is `C:\Program Files\Microsoft Visual Studio 15.0`.) An example of this would be extending IntelliSense support for the XML editor to include your own schema definitions. The creation of such a schema file is beyond the scope of this book, but you can find schema files on the Internet by searching for IntelliSense Schema in Visual Studio.

BOOKMARKS AND THE BOOKMARK WINDOW

Bookmarks in Visual Studio 2017 enable you to mark places in your code modules so that you can easily return to them later. They are represented by indicators in the left margin of the code, as shown in Figure 7-21.

To toggle between bookmarked and not bookmarked on a line, use the shortcut Ctrl+K, Ctrl+K. Alternatively, you can use the Edit ⇨ Bookmarks ⇨ Toggle Bookmark menu command to do the same thing.

> **NOTE** *Remember that toggle means just that. If you use this command on a line already bookmarked, it removes the bookmark.*

Figure 7-21 shows a section of the code editor window with two bookmarks set. The top bookmark is in its normal state, represented by a dark rectangle. The lower bookmark has been disabled and is represented by a hatched gray rectangle. Disabling a bookmark enables you to keep it for later use while excluding it from the normal bookmark-navigation functions.

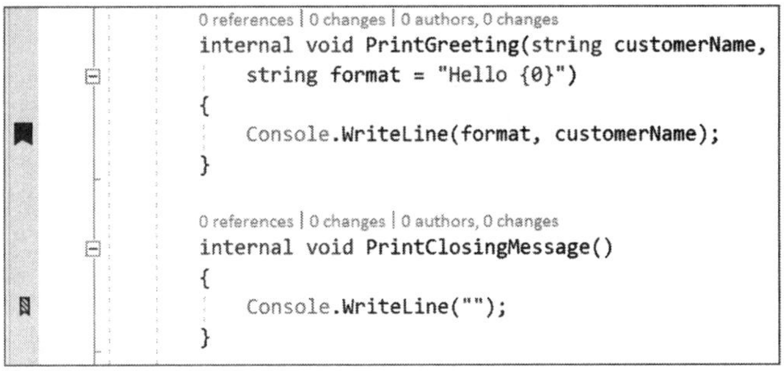

```
0 references | 0 changes | 0 authors, 0 changes
internal void PrintGreeting(string customerName,
    string format = "Hello {0}")
{
    Console.WriteLine(format, customerName);
}


0 references | 0 changes | 0 authors, 0 changes
internal void PrintClosingMessage()
{
    Console.WriteLine("");
}
```

FIGURE 7-21

To enable or disable a bookmark use the Edit ⇨ Bookmarks ⇨ Enable Bookmark toggle menu command. Use the same command to re-enable the bookmark. This seems counterintuitive because you actually want to disable an active bookmark, but for some reason the menu item isn't updated based on the cursor context.

Along with the ability to add and remove bookmarks, Visual Studio provides a Bookmarks tool window, shown in Figure 7-22. You can display this tool window by pressing Ctrl+K, Ctrl+W or via the View Bookmark Window menu item. By default, this window is docked to the bottom of the IDE and shares space with other tool windows, such as the Task List and Find Results windows.

> **NOTE** *You may want to set up a shortcut for disabling and enabling bookmarks if you plan to use them a lot in your code management. To do so, access the Keyboard Options page in the Environment group in Options and look for* `Edit.EnableBookmark`.

Figure 7-22 illustrates some useful features of bookmarks in Visual Studio 2017. The first feature is the ability it gives you to create folders that can logically group the bookmarks. In the example list, notice that a folder named Old Bookmarks contains a bookmark named Bookmark3.

Bookmark	File Location	Line Number
☑ ▪ Bookmark2	C:\Users\bruce\Source\Repos\Professional Visual Studio 2017\Chapter 7\SolutionsProjectsAndIte...	83
◢ ☑ **Old Bookmark**		
☑ ▪ Bookmark3	C:\Users\bruce\Source\Repos\Professional Visual Studio 2017\Chapter 7\SolutionsProjectsAndIte...	88

FIGURE 7-22

To create a folder of bookmarks, click the New Folder icon in the toolbar along the top of the Bookmarks window. (It's the second button from the left.) This creates an empty folder (using a default name of Folder1, followed by Folder2, and so on) with the name of the folder in focus so that you can make it more relevant. You can move bookmarks into the folder by selecting their entries in the list and dragging them into the wanted folder. Note that you cannot create a hierarchy of folders, but it's unlikely that you'll want to. Bookmarks can be renamed in the same way as folders, and for permanent bookmarks, renaming can be more useful than accepting the default names of Bookmark1, Bookmark2, and so forth. Folders are not only a convenient way of grouping bookmarks; they also provide an easy way for you to enable or disable a number of bookmarks in one go, simply by using the check box beside the folder name.

To navigate directly to a bookmark, double-click its entry in the Bookmarks tool window. Alternatively, if you want to cycle through all the enabled bookmarks defined in the project, use the Previous Bookmark (Ctrl+K, Ctrl+P) and Next Bookmark (Ctrl+K, Ctrl+N) commands. You can restrict this navigation to only the bookmarks in a particular folder by first selecting a bookmark in the folder and then using the Previous Bookmark in Folder (Ctrl+Shift+K, Ctrl+Shift+P) and Next Bookmark in Folder (Ctrl+Shift+K, Ctrl+Shift+N) commands.

The last two icons in the Bookmarks window are Toggle All Bookmarks, which can be used to disable (or re-enable) all the bookmarks defined in a project, and Delete, which can be used to delete a folder or bookmark from the list.

> **NOTE** *Deleting a folder also removes all the bookmarks contained in the folder. Visual Studio provides a confirmation dialog to safeguard against accidental loss of bookmarks. Deleting a bookmark is the same as toggling it off.*

Bookmarks can also be controlled via the Bookmarks submenu, which is found in the Edit main menu. In Visual Studio 2017, bookmarks are also retained between sessions, making permanent bookmarks a much more viable option for managing your code organization.

Task lists are customized versions of bookmarks displayed in their own tool windows. The only connection that still exists between the two is that there is an Add Task List Shortcut command still in the Bookmarks menu. Be aware that this does not add the shortcut to the Bookmarks window but instead to the Shortcuts list in the Task List window.

SUMMARY

IntelliSense functionality extends beyond the main code window. Various other windows, such as the Command and Immediate tool windows, can harness the power of IntelliSense through statement and parameter completion. Any keywords, or even variables and objects, known in the current context during a debugging session can be accessed through the IntelliSense member lists.

IntelliSense in all its forms enhances the Visual Studio experience beyond most other tools available to you. Constantly monitoring your keystrokes to give you visual feedback or automatic code completion and generation, IntelliSense enables you to be extremely effective at writing code quickly and correctly the first time. In the next chapter you'll dive into the details behind code snippets, a powerful addition to IntelliSense.

In this chapter you've also seen how you can set and navigate between bookmarks in your code. Becoming familiar with using the associated keystrokes can help you improve your coding efficiency.

Code Snippets and Refactoring

One of the advantages of using an integrated development environment (IDE) over a plain text editor is that it's designed to help you be more productive and efficient by enabling you to write code faster. Two of Visual Studio 2017's most powerful features that help increase your productivity are its support for code snippets and the refactoring tools that it provides.

Code snippets are small chunks of code that can be inserted into an application's code base and then customized to meet the application's specific requirements. They do not generate full-blown applications or whole files, unlike project and item templates. Instead, code snippets are used to insert frequently used code structures or obscure program code blocks that are not easy to remember. In the first part of this chapter, you see how using code snippets can improve your coding efficiency enormously.

This chapter also focuses on Visual Studio 2017's refactoring tools — refactoring is the process of reworking code to improve it without changing its functionality. This might entail simplifying a method, extracting a commonly used code pattern, or even optimizing a section of code to make it more efficient.

With Visual Studio 2017, C# and VB have come closer to parity in terms of the supported refactoring tools. As the built-in refactorings are discussed in this chapter, there will generally be an indication of those that are supported in C# only.

CODE SNIPPETS REVEALED

Visual Studio 2017 includes extensive code snippet support that allows a block of code along with predefined replacement variables to be inserted into a file, making it easy to customize the inserted code to suit the task at hand.

Storing Code Blocks in the Toolbox

Before looking at code snippets, this section looks at the simplest means Visual Studio provides to insert predefined blocks of text into a file. Much as it can hold controls to be inserted on a form, the Toolbox can also hold blocks of text (such as code) that can be inserted into a file. To add a block of code (or other text) to the Toolbox, simply select the text in the editor and drag it over onto the Toolbox. This creates an entry for it in the Toolbox with the first line of the code as its name. You can rename, arrange, and group these entries like any other element in the Toolbox. To insert the code block, you simply drag it from the Toolbox (as shown in Figure 8-1) to the desired location in a file. Or simply double-click the Toolbox entry to insert it at the current cursor position in the active file.

FIGURE 8-1

> **NOTE** *Many presenters use this simple feature to quickly insert large code blocks when writing code live in presentations.*

This is the simplest form of code snippet behavior in Visual Studio 2017, but with its simplicity comes limited functionality, such as the lack of ability to modify and share the snippets. Nevertheless, this method of keeping small sections of code can prove useful in some scenarios to maintain a series of code blocks for short-term use.

Code Snippets

Code snippets are a much more useful way to insert blocks of code into a file. Code snippets are defined in individual XML files, each containing a block of code that programmers may want to insert into their code. They may also include replaceable parameters, making it easy to customize the inserted snippet for the current task. They are integrated with Visual Studio's IntelliSense, making them easy to find and insert into a code file.

> **NOTE** *VB code snippets also give you the ability to add assembly references and insert* Imports *statements.*

Visual Studio 2017 ships with many predefined code snippets for the two main languages, VB and C#, along with snippets for JavaScript, HTML, XML, CSS, Testing, Office Development, C++, and SQL Server. These snippets are arranged hierarchically in a logical fashion so that you can easily locate the appropriate snippet. Rather than locate the snippet in the Toolbox, you can use menu commands or keyboard shortcuts to bring up the main list of groups.

In addition to the predefined code snippets, you can create your own code snippets and store them in this code snippet library. Because each snippet is stored in a special XML file, you can even share them with other developers.

Following are three scopes under which a snippet can be inserted:

➤ **Class Declaration:** The snippet actually generates an entire class.

➤ **Member Declaration:** This snippet scope includes code that defines members, such as methods, properties, and event handler routines. This means it should be inserted outside an existing member.

➤ **Member Body:** This scope is for snippets that are inserted into an already defined member, such as a method.

Using Snippets in C#

Insert Snippet is a special kind of IntelliSense that appears inline in the code editor. Initially, it displays the words Insert Snippet along with a drop-down list of code snippet groups from which to choose. After you select the group that contains the snippet you require (using up and down arrows, followed by the Tab key), it shows you a list of snippets, and you can simply double-click the one you need. (Alternatively, pressing Tab or Enter with the required snippet selected has the same effect.)

To insert a code snippet in C#, simply locate the position where you want to insert the generated code, and then the easiest way to bring up the Insert Snippet list is to use the keyboard shortcut combination of Ctrl+K, Ctrl+X. You have two additional methods to start the Insert Snippet process. The first is to right-click at the intended insertion point in the code window and select Insert Snippet from the context menu that is displayed. The other option is to use the Edit ➪ IntelliSense ➪ Insert Snippet menu command.

At this point, Visual Studio brings up the Insert Snippet list, as Figure 8-2 demonstrates. As you scroll through the list and hover the mouse pointer over each entry, a tooltip displays to indicate what the snippet does and a shortcut that you can use to insert it.

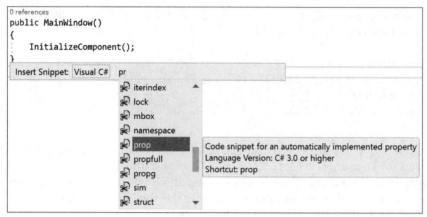

FIGURE 8-2

To use the shortcut for a code snippet, simply type it into the code editor (note that it appears in the IntelliSense list) and press the Tab key twice to insert the snippet at that position.

Figure 8-3 displays the result of selecting the Automatically Implemented Property snippet. To help you modify the code to fit your own requirements, the sections you would normally need to change (the replacement variables) are highlighted, with the first one conveniently selected.

```
namespace CSWpfApp
{
    /// <summary>
    /// Interaction logic for MainWindow.xaml
    /// </summary>
    2 references
    public partial class MainWindow : Window
    {
        0 references
        public MainWindow()
        {
            InitializeComponent();
        }

        — references
        public int MyProperty { get; set; }
    }
}
```

FIGURE 8-3

When you change the variable sections of the generated code snippet, Visual Studio 2017 helps you even further. Pressing the Tab key moves to the next highlighted value, ready for you to override the value with your own. Shift+Tab navigates backward, so you have an easy way to access the sections of code that need changing without needing to manually select the next piece to modify. Some code snippets use the same variable for multiple pieces of the code snippet logic. This means changing the value in one place results in it changing in all other instances.

To hide the highlighting of these snippet variables when you finish, you can simply continue coding, or press either Enter or Esc.

Using Snippets in VB

Code snippets in VB have additional features beyond what is available in C#, namely the ability to automatically add references to assemblies in the project and insert Imports statements into a file that the code needs to compile.

To use a code snippet, first locate where you want the generated code to be placed in the program listing, and position the cursor at that point. You don't have to worry about the associated references and Imports statements; they will be placed in the correct location. Then, as with C# snippets, you can use one of the following methods to display the Insert Snippet list:

➤ Use the keyboard chord Ctrl+K, Ctrl+X.

➤ Right-click and choose Insert Snippet from the context menu.

➤ Run the Edit ⇨ IntelliSense ⇨ Insert Snippet menu command.

VB also has an additional way to show the Insert Snippet List: Simply type ? and press Tab.

Do so, and then navigate through the hierarchy and insert a snippet named Draw a Pie Chart. Figure 8-4 demonstrates how you might navigate through the hierarchy to find the snippet and insert it into your project.

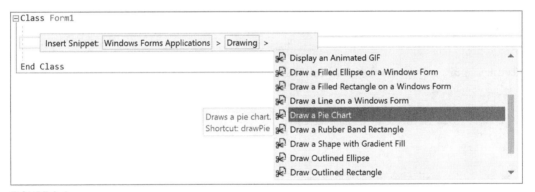

FIGURE 8-4

You might have noticed in Figure 8-4 that the tooltip text includes the words Shortcut: drawPie. This text indicates that the selected code snippet has a text shortcut that you can use to automatically invoke the code snippet behavior without navigating the code snippet hierarchy. As with C#, all you need to do is type the shortcut into the code editor and press the Tab key once for it to be inserted. In VB the shortcut isn't case-sensitive, so you can generate this example by typing drawpie and pressing Tab. Note that shortcuts don't appear in IntelliSense in VB as they do in C#.

After inserting the code snippet, if it contains replacement variables, you can enter their values and then navigate between these by pressing Tab as described for C#. To hide the highlighting of these snippet variables when you are done, you can simply continue coding, or right-click and select Hide Snippet Highlighting. If you want to highlight all the replacement variables of the code snippets inserted since the file was opened, right-click and select Show Snippet Highlighting.

Surround With Snippet

The last snippet action, available in C#, is the capability to surround an existing block of code with a code snippet. For example, to wrap an existing block with a conditional `try-catch` block, right-click and select Surround With, or select the block of code and press Ctrl+K, Ctrl+S. This displays the Surround With drop-down that contains a list of surrounding snippets that are available to wrap the selected line of code, as shown in Figure 8-5.

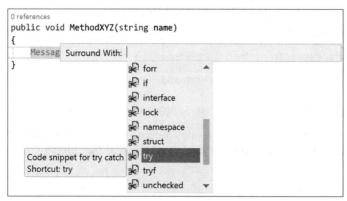

FIGURE 8-5

Selecting the `try` snippet results in the following code:

C#

```csharp
public void MethodXYZ(string name)
{
    try
    {
        MessageBox.Show(name);
    }
    catch (Exception)
    {
        throw;
    }
}
```

Code Snippets Manager

The Code Snippets Manager is the central library for the code snippets known to Visual Studio 2017. You can access it via the Tools ➪ Code Snippet Manager menu command or the keyboard shortcut chord Ctrl+K, Ctrl+B.

When it is initially displayed, the Code Snippets Manager shows the HTML snippets available, but you can change it to display the snippets for the language you are using via the Language drop-down list. Figure 8-6 shows how it looks when you're editing a C# project. The hierarchical folder structure follows the same set of folders on the PC by default, but as you add snippet files from different locations and insert them into the different groups, the new snippets slip into the appropriate folders.

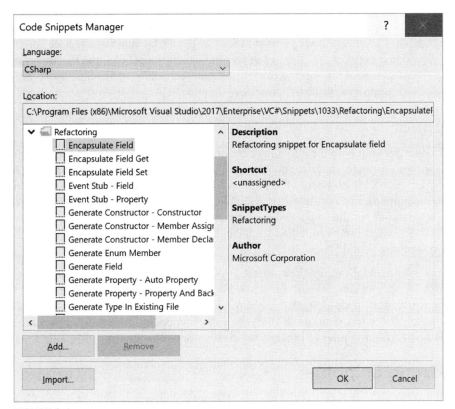

FIGURE 8-6

If you have an entire folder of snippets to add to the library, such as when you have a corporate setup and need to import the company-developed snippets, use the Add button. This brings up a dialog that you use to browse to the required folder. Folders added in this fashion appear at the root level of the tree — on the same level as the main groups of default snippets. However, you can add a folder that contains subfolders, which will be added as child nodes in the tree.

Removing a folder is just as easy — actually it's dangerously easy. Select the root node that you want to remove, and click the Remove button. Instantly, the node and all child nodes and snippets are removed from the Snippets Manager without a confirmation window. If you do this by accident, you should click the Cancel button and open the dialog again. If you've made changes you don't want to lose, you can add them back by following the steps explained in the previous walkthrough, but it can be frustrating trying to locate a default snippet folder that you inadvertently deleted from the list.

> **NOTE** *The removal of a folder is permanent. There is no undo feature available to protect you from an inadvertent mistake.*

The location for the code snippets installed with Visual Studio 2017 is deep within the installation folder. By default, the code snippet library when running on 32-bit Windows is installed in `%program-files%\Microsoft Visual Studio 15.0\VB\Snippets\1033` for VB snippets and `%programfiles%\Microsoft Visual Studio 15.0\VC#\Snippets\1033` for C#. For 64-bit Windows, replace `%pro-gramfiles%` with `%programfiles(x86)%`. You can import individual snippet files into the library using the Import button. The advantage of this method over the Add button is that you get the opportunity to specify the location of each snippet in the library structure.

Creating Snippets

Visual Studio 2017 does not ship with a code snippet creator or editor. However, Bill McCarthy's Snippet Editor allows you to create, modify, and manage your snippets (including support for VB, C#, HTML, JavaScript, and XML snippets). The Snippet Editor is an open-source project hosted on CodePlex. With the help of other MVPs, it is also available in a number of different languages. You can download the source code for the snippet editor from the Wrox download code section. This source code is the same as what can be found on CodePlex, except that a section has been added to the app.config file to support Visual Studio 2017.

Creating code snippets by manually editing the `.snippet` XML files can be a tedious and error-prone process, so the Snippet Editor makes it a much more pleasant experience. When you start the Snippet Editor, you can notice a drop-down list in the top left corner. If you select SnippetEditor .Product.Utility from the list, a tree containing all of the known snippets appears. By expanding a node you can see a set of folders similar to those in the code snippet library.

Reviewing Existing Snippets

An excellent feature of the Snippet Editor is the view it offers of the structure of any snippet file in the system. This means you can browse the default snippets installed with Visual Studio, which can provide insight into how to better build your own snippets.

Browse to the snippet you're interested in, and double-click its entry to display it in the Editor window. Figure 8-7 shows a simple snippet to Display a Windows Form. Four main panes contain all the associated information about the snippet. From top to bottom, these panes are described in Table 8-1.

TABLE 8-1: Information Panes for Snippets

PANE	FUNCTION
Properties	The main properties for the snippet, including title, shortcut, and description.
Code	Defines the code for the snippet, including all Literal and Object replacement regions.
References	If your snippet requires assembly references, this tab enables you to define them.
Imports	Similar to the References tab, this tab enables you to define any Imports statements required for your snippet to function correctly.

Browsing through these panes enables you to analyze an existing snippet for its properties and replacement variables. In Figure 8-7, there is a single replacement region with an ID of formName and a default value of Form.

To demonstrate how the Snippet Editor makes creating your own snippets straightforward, follow this next exercise to create a snippet that creates three subroutines, including a helper subroutine:

1. Start the Snippet Editor and create a new snippet. To do this, select a destination folder in the tree, right-click, and select Add New Snippet from the context menu displayed.

2. When prompted, name the snippet **Create A Button Sample** and click OK. Double-click the new entry to open it in the Editor pane.

> **NOTE** *Creating the snippet does not automatically open the new snippet in the Editor — don't overwrite the properties of another snippet by mistake!*

3. The first thing you need to do is edit the Title, Description, and Shortcut fields (see Figure 8-8):

   ➤ Title: **Create A Button Sample**

   ➤ Description: **This snippet produces the code to create a button and hook an event.**

   ➤ Shortcut: **CreateAButton**

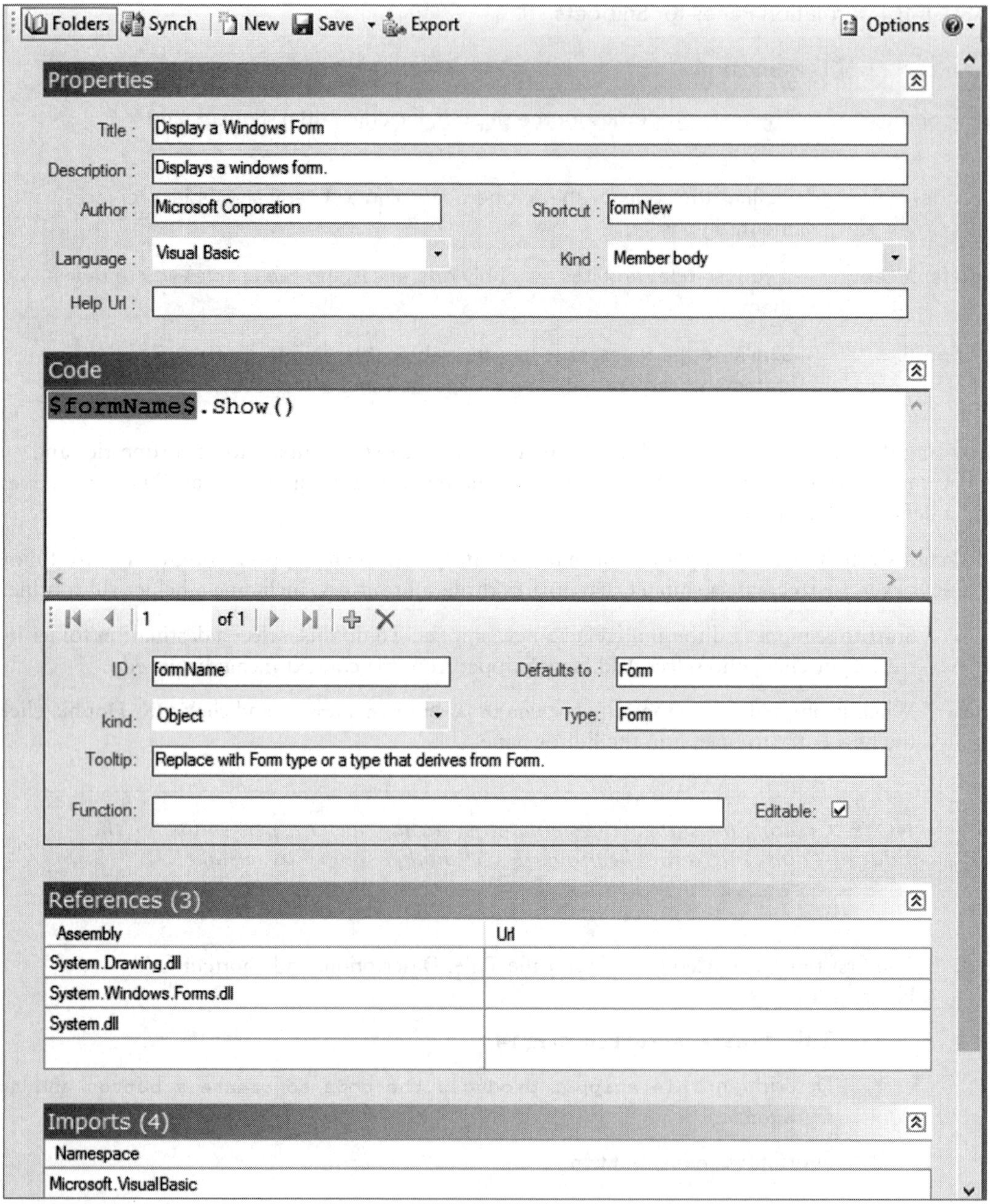
Folders
Synch
New
Save
Export
Options
Properties
Title :
Display a Windows Form
Description :
Displays a windows form.
Author :
Microsoft Corporation
Shortcut :
formNew
Language :
Visual Basic
Kind :
Member body
Help Url :
Code
$formName$.Show()
1
of 1
ID :
formName
Defaults to :
Form
kind:
Object
Type:
Form
Tooltip:
Replace with Form type or a type that derives from Form.
Function:
Editable:
References (3)
Assembly
Url
System.Drawing.dll
System.Windows.Forms.dll
System.dll
Imports (4)
Namespace
Microsoft.VisualBasic

FIGURE 8-7

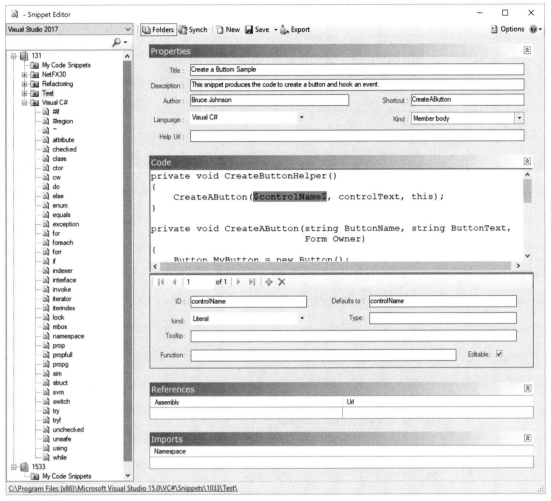

FIGURE 8-8

4. Because this snippet contains member definitions, set the Type to Member Declaration.

5. In the Editor window, insert the code necessary to create the three subroutines:

VB

```
Private Sub CreateButtonHelper
    CreateAButton(controlName, controlText, Me)
End Sub

Private Sub CreateAButton(ByVal ButtonName As String, _
                          ByVal ButtonText As String, _
                          ByVal Owner As Form)
```

```vb
        Dim MyButton As New Button

        MyButton.Name = ButtonName
        MyButton.Text = ButtonName
        Owner.Controls.Add(MyButton)

        MyButton.Top = 0
        MyButton.Left = 0
        MyButton.Text = ButtonText
        MyButton.Visible = True

        AddHandler MyButton.Click, AddressOf ButtonClickHandler
    End Sub

    Private Sub ButtonClickHandler(ByVal sender As System.Object, _
                            ByVal e As System.EventArgs)
        MessageBox.Show("The " & sender.Name & " button was clicked")
    End Sub
```

C#

```csharp
    private void CreateButtonHelper()
    {
        CreateAButton(controlName, controlText, this);
    }

    private void CreateAButton(string ButtonName, string ButtonText,
                        Form Owner)
    {
        Button MyButton = new Button();

        MyButton.Name = ButtonName;
        MyButton.Text = ButtonName;
        Owner.Controls.Add(MyButton);

        MyButton.Top = 0;
        MyButton.Left = 0;
        MyButton.Text = ButtonText;
        MyButton.Visible = true;

        MyButton.Click += MyButton_Click;
    }

    private void  MyButton_Click(object sender, EventArgs e)
    {
        MessageBox.Show("The " + sender.Name + " button was clicked");
    }
```

6. Your code differs from that shown in Figure 8-8 in that the word `controlName` does not appear highlighted. In Figure 8-8, this argument has been made a replacement region. You can do this by selecting the entire word, right-clicking, and selecting Add Replacement (or alternatively, clicking the Add button in the area below the code window).

7. Change the replacement properties like so:

➤ ID: controlName

➤ Defaults to: **"MyButton"**

➤ Tooltip: The name of the button

8. Repeat this for `controlText`:

➤ ID: controlText

➤ Defaults to: **"Click Me!"**

➤ Tooltip: The text property of the button

Your snippet is finished and ready to use. You can use Visual Studio 2017 to insert the snippet into a code window.

Distributing Code Snippets

If you have created a number of code snippets and want to share them with your friends and colleagues, the simplest approach is to send the `.snippet` files and have them use the Import feature in the Code Snippet Manager. However, if you are trying to make the process a little easier (or you have more than a few friends), you can package the snippet into a Visual Studio installer (`.vsi`) file and allow them to automatically install it into their Visual Studio instance.

For our example, consider the following snippet, which has been placed into the `SayHello.snippet` file.

```xml
<?xml version="1.0" encoding="utf-8"?>
<CodeSnippet Format="1.0.0"
    xmlns="http://schemas.microsoft.com/VisualStudio/2005/CodeSnippet">
  <Header>
    <Title>Say Hello</Title>
    <Author>Bruce Johnson</Author>
    <Description>C# snippet for being polite...because I'm Canadian,
after all</Description>
    <HelpUrl>
    </HelpUrl>
    <Shortcut>sayh</Shortcut>
  </Header>
  <Snippet>
    <Code Language="C#">
      <![CDATA[Console.WriteLine("Hello World");]]>
    </Code>
  </Snippet>
</CodeSnippet>
```

Snippets can easily be distributed using a `.vsi` file. The simple structure of a `.vsi` file makes the process very easy. First, the file itself is just a `.zip` file with the extension changed to `.vsi`. Second, in the file itself, there is a manifest (which has a `.vscontent` extension) that describes what the components of the `.vsi` file are.

So, to distribute the snippet shown above, create a file called `SayHello.vscontent`. The content of the file (which is well-formed XML) looks like the following.

```
<VSContent xmlns="http://schemas.microsoft.com/developer/vscontent/2005">
    <Content>
        <FileName>SayHello.snippet</FileName>
        <DisplayName>Polite C# Code</DisplayName>
        <Description>C# snippet for being polite </Description>
        <FileContentType>Code Snippet</FileContentType>
        <ContentVersion>2.0</ContentVersion>
        <Attributes>
            <Attribute name="lang" value="c#"/>
        </Attributes>
    </Content>
</VSContent>
```

After you have saved the snippet, add both the `.vscontent` file and the `SayHello.snippet` file to a `.zip` file. Then change the extension on that file to `.vsi` instead of `.zip`. The file is ready for you to give to your friends and colleagues; when they double-click it, the snippet will be installed into Visual Studio.

ACCESSING REFACTORING SUPPORT

There are a number of ways to invoke the refactoring tools in Visual Studio 2017, including from the right-click context menu, light bulbs, and the Edit ⇨ Refactor menu option. Regardless of your entry point, the refactoring user experience includes contextual awareness to help smooth the process. Specifically, the context menu shows only the items that apply to the currently selected code and the cursor position. In addition, you can use light bulb as the starting point for any refactoring, and it is only present when there are refactorings that apply to the current context. The full list of refactoring actions available within Visual Studio 2017 includes Rename, Extract Method, Encapsulate Field, Extract Interface, Promote Local Variable to Parameter, Remove Parameters, and Reorder Parameters. You can also use Generate Method Stub and Remove and Sort Usings, which can be loosely classified as refactoring. And two new refactoring actions have been added: Inline Temporary Variable and Inline Local.

The good news for VB developers is that Visual Studio 2017 provides support for all these refactorings. It's just one more thing you can attribute to the development of the Roslyn compiler.

REFACTORING ACTIONS

The following sections describe each of the refactoring options and provide examples of how to use built-in support for both C# and VB (when appropriate).

Extract Method

One of the best ways to start refactoring a long method is to break it up into several smaller methods. The Extract Method refactoring action is invoked by selecting the region of code you want moved out of the original method and selecting Extract Method from the quick action options or using the Refactor ⇨ Extract Method context menu option.

The mechanism for naming your new method utilizes the same interface that code snippets do. When you select Extract Method, the method is immediately removed from its current location and padded to a new method. The name of the method is set to `NewMethod`, and a call to the new method replaces the extracted code block in the original call site. The method name is highlighted, and if you change it (as you are likely to), the name of the method at the calling site is changed as well. If there are variables within the block of code to be extracted that were used earlier in the original method, they automatically appear as variables in the method signature.

For example, in the following code snippet, if you want to extract the conditional logic into a separate method, you can select the code, shown in bold, and choose Refactor ⇨ Extract Method from the right-click context menu:

C#

```
private void button1_Click(object sender, EventArgs e)
{
    string connectionString = Properties.Settings.Default.ConnectionString;
    if (connectionString == null)
    {
        connectionString = "DefaultConnectionString";
    }
    MessageBox.Show(connectionString);
    /* ... Much longer method ... */
}
```

The result of the refactor is illustrated in Figure 8-9.

At this point, the Extract Method refactor is finished, and you are now in a Rename refactor. In this case, the Rename is related to the name of the method you just extracted. Your cursor is placed in the name of the new method. As you change the name, the change is immediately reflected in both locations. Notice the area in the top right of Figure 8-9. This area controls the Rename refactor. It contains a couple of options that are described in the "Rename" section later in this chapter. But more importantly, it includes an Apply button that must be clicked to confirm the renaming of the method from `NewMethod` to whatever you entered.

Encapsulate Field

Another common task when refactoring is to encapsulate an existing class variable with a property. This is what the Encapsulate Field refactoring action does. To invoke this action, select the variable you want to encapsulate, and then choose Quick Actions and Refactorings from the context menu. This displays the list of refactoring options, as shown in Figure 8-10.

Choose the type of encapsulation you want to use. The difference, as indicated by the `and use property`, and `but still use field` text, is whether existing references to the public field will continue to use the private field or use the public property instead. The name of the created property is generated from the name of the selected variable.

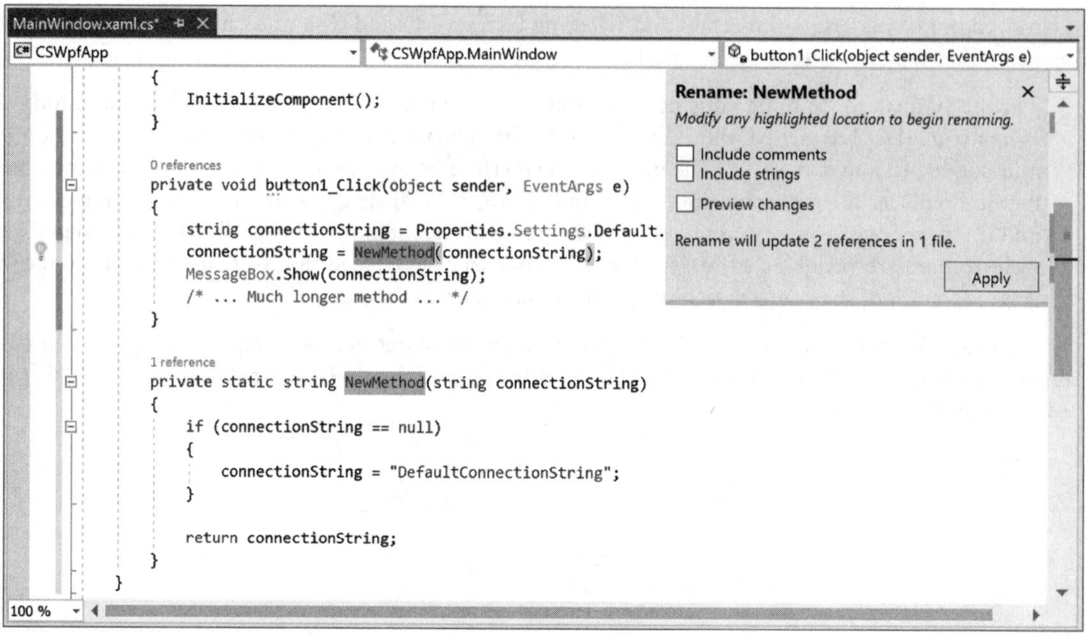

FIGURE 8-9

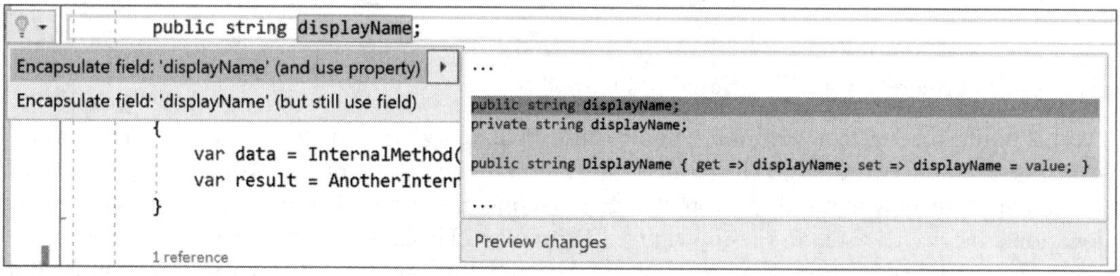

FIGURE 8-10

Extract Interface

As a project goes from prototype or early-stage development to a full implementation or growth phase, it's often necessary to extract the core methods for a class into an interface to enable other implementations or to define a boundary between disjointed systems. In the past you could do this by copying the entire method to a new file and removing the method contents, so you were just left with the interface stub. The Extract Interface refactoring action enables you to extract an interface based on any number of methods within a class. When this refactoring action is invoked on a class, the user interface in Figure 8-11 displays.

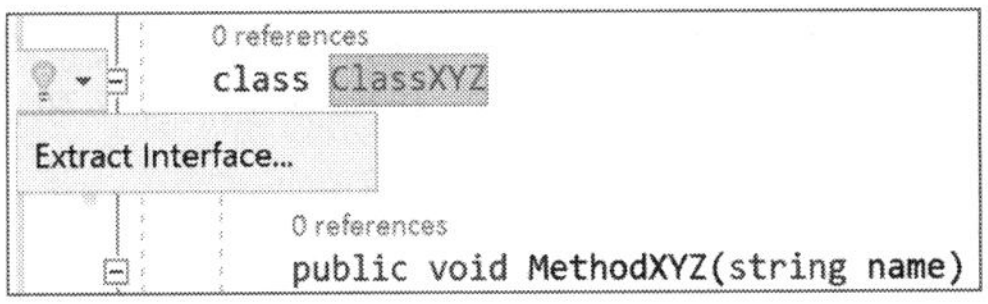

FIGURE 8-11

Choose the Extract Interface option and the dialog shown in Figure 8-12 appears. This enables you to select which methods are included in the interface. When selected, those methods are added to the new interface. The new interface is also added to the original class.

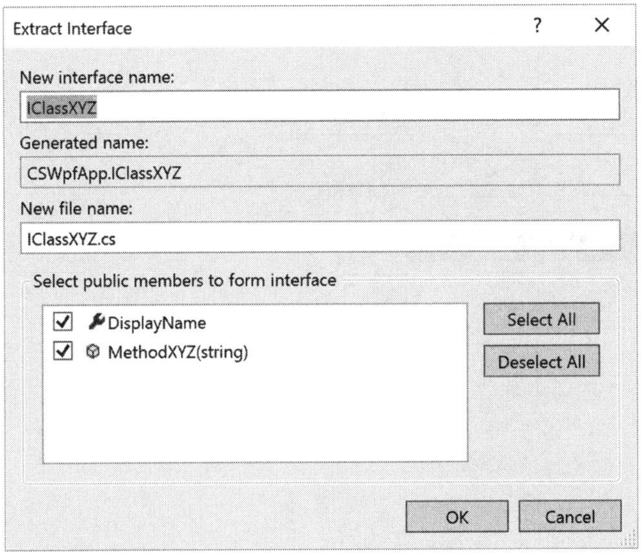

FIGURE 8-12

Change Signature

Sometimes it's necessary to completely reorder parameters or remove parameters from the method signature. This is often for cosmetic reasons, but it can also aid readability and is sometimes warranted when implementing interfaces. Or perhaps the parameter is no longer needed by the underlying functionality.

When you're modifying a method signature, one of the challenges is finding the method calls that are affected. By using the refactoring function, you can considerably reduce the searching that must be done for any compilation errors that would occur. This function is also particularly useful when there are multiple overloads for a method, and changing the signature may not generate compile errors; in such a case, runtime errors may occur due to semantic, rather than syntactical, mistakes.

To access the Change Signature functionality, select the method to be modified and choose Quick Actions and Refactorings from the context menu. That displays the interface shown in Figure 8-13.

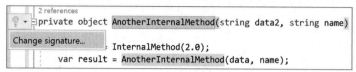

FIGURE 8-13

Selecting the Change Signature option causes the Change Signature dialog, as shown in Figure 8-14, to appear. Through this dialog, you can move parameters up and down in the list according to the order in which you want them to appear, or you can remove them completely. When you're finished, click OK to complete the refactoring.

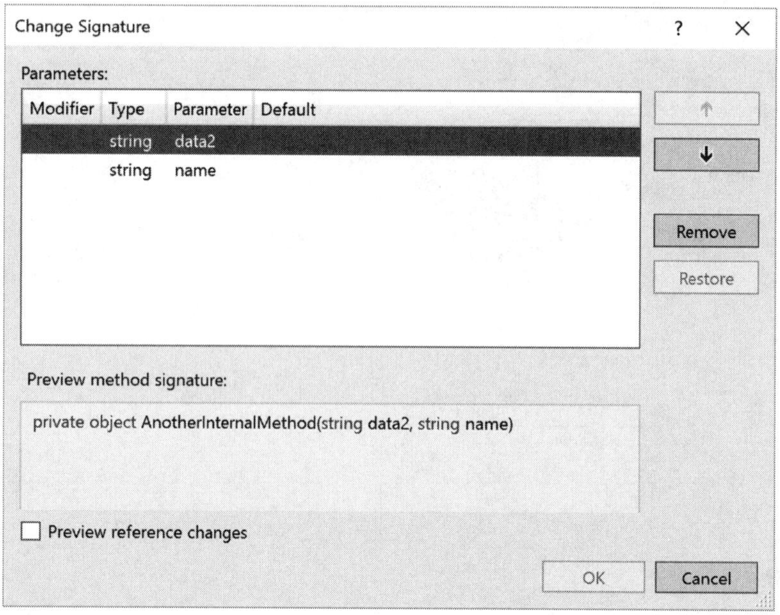

FIGURE 8-14

Inline and Explaining Variables

These two refactorings provide both sides of a common scenario. That scenario revolves around the user of temporary, local variables in a method.

The purpose of the Inline Temporary Variables refactor is best demonstrated with code. Consider the following method.

C#

```
public void MethodXYZ(string name)
{
    var data = InternalMethod(2.0);
    var result = AnotherInternalMethod(name, data);
}
```

The inlining of the temporary variable `data` results in the parameter line for `AnotherInternalMethod` containing the call to `InternalMethod` instead of using the `data` variable. The refactor is accessed through the Quick Actions and Refactorings option in the right-click context menu after selecting the variable. The interface is visible in Figure 8-15. The preview section of Figure 8-15 should give you a decent indication of what the inlining would look like.

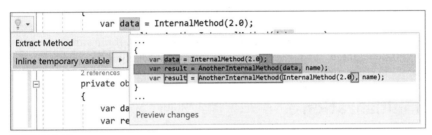

FIGURE 8-15

The `Introduce` explaining variable refactor goes the other way. In this case, you select the expression that is used in the method signature. The Quick Actions and Refactorings option in the context menu displays the interface (seen in Figure 8-16) that allows you to create an explaining variable that is placed back into the method signature.

```
var start = 1;
var data = InternalMethod(start + 2);

Introduce local for 'start + 2'          ...
                                         var start = 1;
Introduce local for all occurrences of 'start + 2'    var data = InternalMethod(start + 2);
                                         int v = start + 2;
Extract Method                           var data = InternalMethod(v);
                                         var result = AnotherInternalMethod(data, name);
Change signature...                       ...

            var data = InternalMet    Preview changes
            var result = AnotherIn
```

FIGURE 8-16

If the selected expression is a constant, then along with being able to create a local variable (as a constant), you could also refactor into a class-level constant variable.

Rename

The Rename refactor is used in a number of other refactorings and as a standalone method. To trigger the standalone version, select a variable and then choose Rename from the right-click context menu. The interface shown in Figure 8-17 appears.

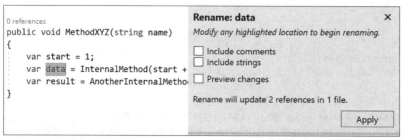

FIGURE 8-17

Now type the new name for the variable and click on the Apply button to complete the refactor. The options that appear in the right of Figure 8-17 are used to control the areas that are searched for the renaming. If you select the Include Comments option, then if the variable name appears in a string, it will be changed to the new variable name. For the Include Strings option, if the variable name is found in a string, it will be updated. And if you want to preview the changes, check the Preview Changes check box before clicking Apply.

Simplify Object Initialization

The ability to set properties of an object at the same time as the object is created has been available in .NET compilers for a number of years. As of Visual Studio 2017, there is now a compiler warning (IDE00017) that is generated if you don't use object initializers but instead have a series of property assignments immediately after instantiating an object. The goal of this refactoring is to simplify the process of fixing this warning.

With your cursor on the instantiation code, the Lightbulb or Quick Actions and Refactorings context menu includes a couple of options. If you choose Object initialization can be simplified, then you see a preview similar to what is visible in Figure 8-18. Alternatively, you can select the Suppress IDE00017 option, and the compiler directive that suppresses the warning will be inserted into your code.

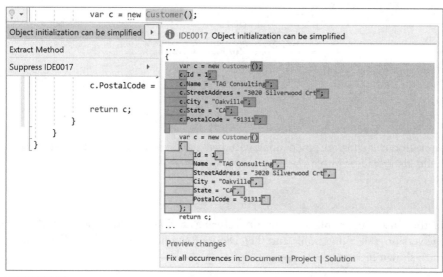

FIGURE 8-18

Inline Variable Declarations

For many, Inline Variable Declarations addresses a pet peeve in C#. If you use methods like `TryParse` that include an out parameter, it is necessary to declare the variable before using it in the method call. An example of this can be found below:

C#

```
int parsedValue
if (Int32.TryParse(stringToParse, out parsedValue))
{
    // Do stuff
}
```

With C# 7, it is now possible to declare the out parameter at the same time as it is used. And Inline Variable Declarations is used to perform a refactoring to get to the situation. With your cursor on the variable name (`parsedValue` in the example), the Lightbulb includes the Inline Variable Declarations options, shown in Figure 8-19.

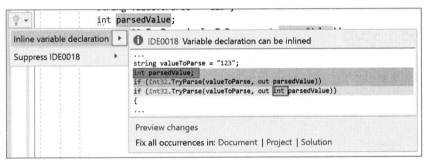

FIGURE 8-19

Use "throw" Expression

The goal of this refactoring is to reduce the amount of code surrounding null checks. As well, it takes advantage of a new C# 7 features that allow for throw expressions to be executed from within a null coalescing operator. The code being replaced is a relatively standard null check, as seen below.

C#

```
if (value == null)
{
    throw new ArgumentNullException(nameof(value));
}
name = value;
```

With your cursor on the value parameter, the option to Use 'throw' expression appears in the list of possible refactorings. When you hover your mouse over that option, an interface similar to Figure 8-20 appears.

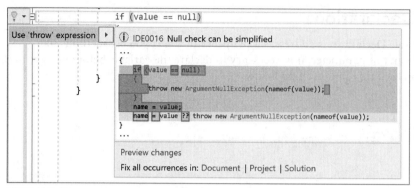

FIGURE 8-20

The suggested change is to use the null coalescing operator to either assign value to name or, in the case where value is null, throw an exception. In other words, the result is the same, but the number of lines of code has decreased.

Generate Method Stub

As you write code, you may realize that you need to call a method that you haven't written yet. For example, the following snippet illustrates a new method that you need to generate at some later stage:

VB

```
Private Sub MethodA()
    Dim InputA As String
    Dim InputB As Double
    Dim OutputC As Integer = NewMethodIJustThoughtOf(InputA, InputB)
End Sub
```

C#

```
public void MethodA()
{
    string InputA;
    double InputB;
    int OutputC = NewMethodIJustThoughtOf(InputA, InputB);
}
```

Of course, the preceding code generates a build error because this method has not been defined. Using the Generate Method Stub refactoring action (available as a Quick Actions and Refactorings from the context menu), you can generate a method stub. As you can see from the following sample, the method stub is complete with input parameters and output type:

VB

```
Private Function NewMethodIJustThoughtOf(ByVal InputA As String,
                                         ByVal InputB As Double) As Integer
    Throw New NotImplementedException
End Function
```

C#

```
private int NewMethodIJustThoughtOf(string InputA, double InputB)
{
    throw new NotImplementedException();
}
```

Remove and Sort Usings

It's good practice to maintain a sorted list of Using statements in each file (in C#), and reference only those namespaces that are actually required within that file. After a major refactoring of your code, you may find that you have a number of using directives at the top of your code file that are no longer used. Rather than going through a process of trial and error to determine what is and isn't used, you can use an operation in Visual Studio to do this for you by right-clicking in the code editor and choosing Remove and Sort Usings (shown in Figure 8-21). (In VB, the option is Remove and Sort Imports.) The using directives, using aliases, and external assembly aliases not used in the code file are removed. And the entire list is sorted. The using directives from the System namespace appear first; then the using directives from other namespaces appear in alphabetical order. If you have aliases defined for namespaces, these are moved to the bottom of the list, and if you use external assembly aliases (using the extern keyword in C#), these are moved to the top of the list.

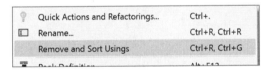

FIGURE 8-21

> **NOTE** *The default Visual Studio template code files have the* using *statements at the top of the file outside the namespace block. However, if you follow the static code analysis guidelines, these specify that using statements should be contained within the namespace block. The Remove and Sort Usings functions handle either situation based upon the current location of the* using *statements in the file and retaining that location.*

SUMMARY

Code snippets are a valuable inclusion in the Visual Studio 2017 feature set. You learned in this chapter how to use them and how to create your own, including variable substitution (and Imports and reference associations for VB snippets). With this information, you can create your own library of code snippets from functionality that you use frequently, saving you time in coding similar constructs later. This chapter also provided examples of each of the refactoring actions available within Visual Studio 2017.

Server Explorer

WHAT'S IN THIS CHAPTER?

➤ Querying hardware resources and services on local and remote computers

➤ Using the Server Explorer to easily add code to your applications that works with computer resources

WROX.COM CODE DOWNLOADS FOR THIS CHAPTER

The wrox.com code downloads for this chapter can be found at www.wrox.com by searching for this book's ISBN number (978-1-119-40458-3). The code and any related support files are located in their own folder for this chapter.

The Server Explorer is one of the few tool windows in Visual Studio that is not specific to a solution or project. It allows you to explore and query hardware resources and services on local or remote computers. You can perform various tasks and activities with these resources, including adding them to your applications.

The Server Explorer, as shown in Figure 9-1, has four types of resources to which it can connect out of the box. The first, found under the Azure node, gives you access to a few of the types of Azure components that you can create. More details about these components can be found in Chapter 23, "Windows Azure." The second type of resources is under the Data Connections node and allows you to work with all aspects of data connections, including the ability to create databases, add and modify tables, build relationships, and even execute queries. Chapter 26, "Visual Database Tools," covers the Data Connections functionality in detail. The third, under the Servers node, enables you to access hardware resources and services on a local or remote computer. This functionality is explored in detail in this chapter. Finally, you can add a connection to a SharePoint server and browse SharePoint-specific resources such as Content Types, Lists, Libraries, and Workflows. The visible connection types depend on the SDKs that you have installed.

FIGURE 9-1

SERVER CONNECTIONS

The Servers node would be better named Computers because you can use it to attach to and interrogate any computer to which you have access, regardless of whether it is a server or a desktop workstation. Each computer is listed as a separate node under the Servers node. Below each computer node is a list of the hardware, services, and other components that belong to that computer. Each of these contains a number of activities or tasks that can be performed. Several software vendors have components that extend the functionality provided by the Server Explorer.

To access Server Explorer, on the View menu, select Server Explorer. By default, the local computer appears in the Servers list. To add another computer, right-click the Servers node, and select Add Server from the context menu.

Entering a computer name or IP address initiates an attempt to connect to the machine using your credentials. If you do not have sufficient privileges, you can elect to connect using a different username by clicking the appropriate link. The link appears to be disabled, but clicking it does bring up a dialog, as shown in Figure 9-2, in which you can provide an alternative username and password.

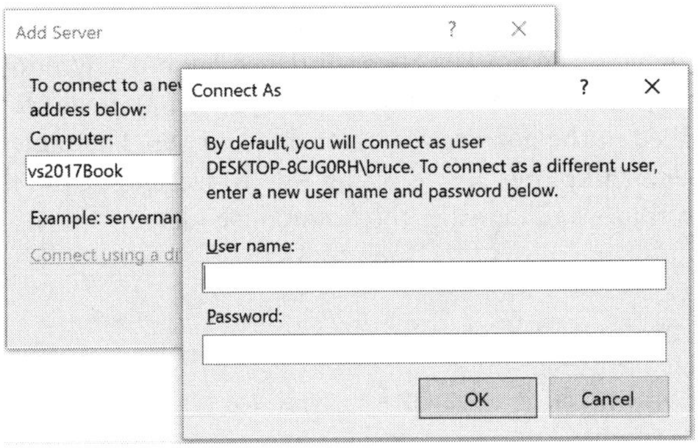

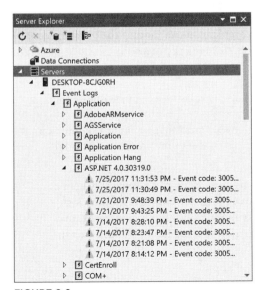

FIGURE 9-2

> **NOTE** *In order to access the resources on any server, you need to connect to that server with an account that has access to the desired resources.*

Event Logs

The Event Logs node gives you access to the machine event logs. You can launch the Event Viewer from the right-click context menu. Alternatively, as shown in Figure 9-3, you can drill into the list of event logs to view the events for a particular application. Clicking any of the events displays information about the event in the Properties window.

FIGURE 9-3

Although the Server Explorer is useful for interrogating a machine while writing your code, the true power comes with the component creation you get when you drag a resource node onto a Windows Form. For example, if you drag the Application node onto a Windows Form, you get an instance of the `System.Diagnostics.EventLog` class added to the nonvisual area of the designer. The same can be done by right-clicking the log in the Server Explorer and selecting Add to Designer from the context menu. You can then write an entry to this event log using the following code:

C#

```
this.eventLog1.Source = "My Server Explorer App";
this.eventLog1.WriteEntry("Something happened",
                    System.Diagnostics.EventLogEntryType.Information);
```

VB

```
Me.EventLog1.Source = "My Server Explorer App"
Me.EventLog1.WriteEntry("Something happened",
                    System.Diagnostics.EventLogEntryType.Information)
```

> **NOTE** *Because the preceding code creates a new Source in the Application Event Log, it requires administrative rights to execute. If you run Windows 8 with User Account Control enabled, you should create an application manifest. This is discussed in Chapter 6, "Solutions, Projects, and Items."*

After you run this code, you can view the results directly in the Server Explorer. Click the Refresh button on the Server Explorer toolbar to ensure that the new Event Source displays under the Application Event Log node.

For Visual Basic programmers, an alternative to adding an `EventLog` class to your code is to use the built-in logging provided by the `My` namespace. For example, you can modify the previous code snippet to write a log entry using the `My.Application.Log.WriteEntry` method:

VB

```
My.Application.Log.WriteEntry("Button Clicked", TraceEventType.Information)
```

You can also write exception information using the `My.Application.Log.WriteException` method, which accepts an exception and two optional parameters that provide additional information.

Using the `My` namespace to write logging information has a number of additional benefits. In the following configuration file, an `EventLogTraceListener` is specified to route log information to the event log. However, you can specify other trace listeners — for example, the `FileLogTraceListener`, which writes information to a log file by adding it to the `SharedListeners` and `Listeners` collections:

```
<?xml version="1.0" encoding="utf-8" ?>
<configuration>
    <system.diagnostics>
```

```
<sources>
    <source name="DefaultSource" switchName="DefaultSwitch">
        <listeners>
            <add name="EventLog"/>
        </listeners>
    </source>
</sources>
<switches>
    <add name="DefaultSwitch" value="Information"/>
</switches>
<sharedListeners>
    <add name="EventLog"
        type="System.Diagnostics.EventLogTraceListener"
        initializeData="ApplicationEventLog"/>
</sharedListeners>
</system.diagnostics>
</configuration>
```

This configuration also specifies a switch called `DefaultSwitch`. This switch is associated with the trace information source via the `switchName` attribute and defines the minimum event type that will be sent to the listed listeners. For example, if the value of this switch were `Critical`, events with the type Information would not be written to the event log. The possible values of this switch are shown in Table 9-1.

TABLE 9-1: Values for DefaultSwitch

DEFAULTSWITCH	EVENT TYPES WRITTEN TO LOG
Off	No events
Critical	Critical events
Error	Critical and Error events
Warning	Critical, Error, and Warning events
Information	Critical, Error, Warning, and Information events
Verbose	Critical, Error, Warning, Information, and Verbose events
ActivityTracing	Start, Stop, Suspend, Resume, and Transfer events
All	All events

Note that there are overloads for both `WriteEntry` and `WriteException` that do not require an event type to be specified. In this case the event type defaults to Information and Error, respectively.

Message Queues

The Message Queues node, expanded in Figure 9-4, gives you access to the message queues available on your computer. You can use three types of queues: private, which does not appear when a foreign computer queries your computer; public, which is visible when queried by a foreign computer; and system, which is used for unsent messages and other exception reporting.

> **NOTE** *To use the Message Queues node, you need to ensure that MSMQ is installed on your computer. You can do this via Programs and Features in the Control Panel. Select the Turn Windows Features On or Off task menu item, and then select the check box to enable the Microsoft Message Queue (MSMQ) Server feature.*

In Figure 9-4, a message queue called samplequeue has been added to the Private Queues node by selecting Create Queue from the right-click context menu. After you create a queue, you can create a properly configured instance of the `MessageQueue` class by dragging the queue onto a new Windows Form. To demonstrate the functionality of the `MessageQueue` object, add two TextBoxes and a button to the form, laid out as shown in Figure 9-5. The Send button is wired to use the `MessageQueue` object to send the message entered in the first textbox. In the `Load` event for the form, a background thread is created that continually polls the queue to retrieve messages, which can populate the second textbox:

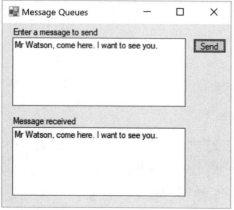

FIGURE 9-4

FIGURE 9-5

C#

```
public Form1()
{
    InitializeComponent();
    var monitorThread = new System.Threading.Thread(MonitorMessageQueue);
    monitorThread.IsBackground = true;
    monitorThread.Start();
```

```csharp
        this.button1.Click +=new EventHandler(btn_Click);
}

private void btn_Click(object sender, EventArgs e)
{
    this.messageQueue1.Send(this.textBox1.Text);
}

private void MonitorMessageQueue()
{
    var m = default(System.Messaging.Message);
    while (true)
    {
        try
        {
            m = this.messageQueue1.Receive(new TimeSpan(0, 0, 0, 0, 50));
            this.ReceiveMessage((string)m.Body);
        }
        catch (System.Messaging.MessageQueueException ex)
        {
            if (!(ex.MessageQueueErrorCode ==
                System.Messaging.MessageQueueErrorCode.IOTimeout))
            {
                throw ex;
            }
        }
        System.Threading.Thread.Sleep(10000);
    }
}

private delegate void MessageDel(string msg);
private void ReceiveMessage(string msg)
{
    if (this.InvokeRequired)
    {
        this.BeginInvoke(new MessageDel(ReceiveMessage), msg);
        return;
    }
    this.textBox2.Text = msg;
}
```

VB

```vb
    Private Sub Form_Load(ByVal sender As Object, ByVal e As System.EventArgs) _
                        Handles Me.Load
        Dim monitorThread As New Threading.Thread(AddressOf MonitorMessageQueue)
        monitorThread.IsBackground = True
        monitorThread.Start()
    End Sub

    Private Sub btn_Click(ByVal sender As System.Object, ByVal e As System.EventArgs) _
                        Handles Button1.Click
        Me.MessageQueue1.Send(Me.TextBox1.Text)
    End Sub
```

```
Private Sub MonitorMessageQueue()
    Dim m As Messaging.Message
    While True
        Try
            m = Me.MessageQueue1.Receive(New TimeSpan(0, 0, 0, 0, 50))
            Me.ReceiveMessage(m.Body)
        Catch ex As Messaging.MessageQueueException
            If Not ex.MessageQueueErrorCode = _
                    Messaging.MessageQueueErrorCode.IOTimeout Then
                Throw ex
            End If
        End Try
        Threading.Thread.Sleep(10000)
    End While
End Sub

Private Delegate Sub MessageDel(ByVal msg As String)
Private Sub ReceiveMessage(ByVal msg As String)
    If Me.InvokeRequired Then
        Me.BeginInvoke(New MessageDel(AddressOf ReceiveMessage), msg)
        Return
    End If
    Me.TextBox2.Text = msg
End Sub
```

Note in this code snippet that the background thread is never explicitly closed. Because the thread has the IsBackground property set to True, it is automatically terminated when the application exits. As with the previous example, because the message processing is done in a background thread, you need to switch threads when you update the user interface using the BeginInvoke method. Putting this all together, you get a form like the one shown in Figure 9-5.

As messages are sent to the message queue, they appear under the appropriate queue in Server Explorer. Clicking the message displays its contents in the Properties window.

Performance Counters

One of the most common things developers forget to consider when building an application is how it will be maintained and managed. For example, consider an application that was installed a year ago and has been operating without any issues. All of a sudden, requests start taking an unacceptable amount of time. It is clear that the application is not behaving correctly, but there is no way to determine the cause of the misbehavior. One strategy to identify where the performance issues are (or to see them coming before they become a problem) is to use performance counters. Windows has many built-in performance counters that you can use to monitor operating system activity, and a lot of third-party software also installs performance counters so administrators can identify any rogue behavior.

The Performance Counters node in the Server Explorer tree, expanded in Figure 9-6, has two primary functions. First, it enables you to view and retrieve information about the currently installed counters. You can also create new performance counters, as well as edit or delete existing counters. Under the Performance Counters node is a list of categories and under those is a list of counters.

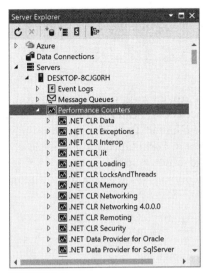

FIGURE 9-6

To edit either the category or the counters, select Edit Category from the right-click context menu for the category. To add a new category and associated counters, right-click the Performance Counters node, and select Create New Category from the context menu. Both of these operations use the dialog shown in Figure 9-7. Here, a new performance counter category has been created that will be used to track a form's open and close events.

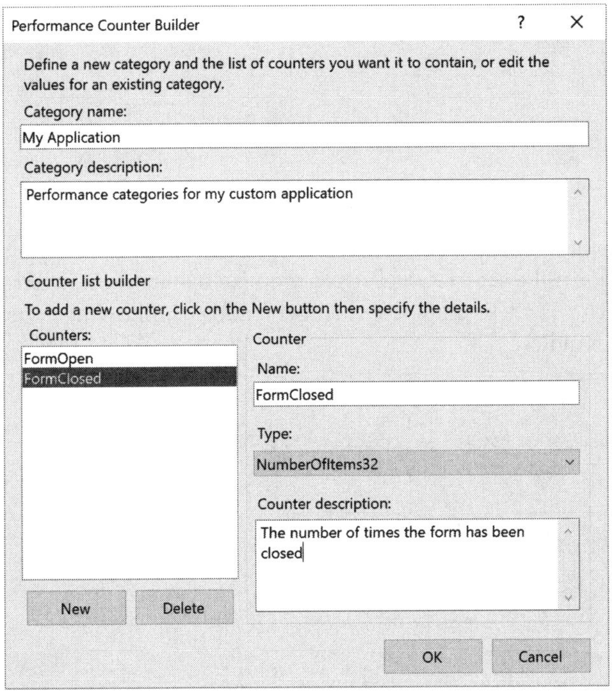

FIGURE 9-7

> **NOTE** *The ability to edit categories is limited to those categories that you created.*

The second function of the Performance Counters section is to provide an easy way for you to access performance counters via your code. By dragging a performance counter category onto a form, you gain access to the ability to read and write to that performance counter. To continue with this chapter's example, drag the new My Application performance counters, Form Open and Form Closed, onto a new Windows Form. Also add a couple of textboxes and a button so that you can display the performance counter values. Finally, rename the performance counters so they have friendly names. This should give you a form similar to the one shown in Figure 9-8.

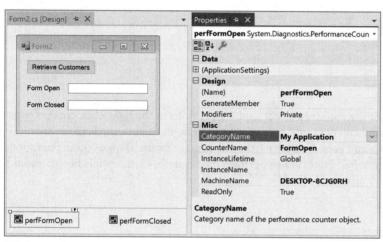

FIGURE 9-8

In the properties for the selected performance counter, you can see that the appropriate counter — in this case, Form Open — has been selected from the My Application category. There is also a MachineName property, which is the computer from which you are retrieving the counter information, and a ReadOnly property, which needs to be set to False if you want to update the counter. (By default, the ReadOnly property is set to True.) To complete this form, add the following code to the Retrieve Counters' button click event handler:

C#

```
this.textBox1.Text = this.perfFormOpen.RawValue.ToString();
this.textBox2.Text = this.perfFormClose.RawValue.ToString();
```

VB

```
Me.textBox1.Text = Me.perfFormOpen.RawValue
Me.textBox2.Text = Me.perfFormClose.RawValue
```

You also need to add code to the application to update the performance counters. For example, you might have the following code in the Form `Load` event handlers:

C#

```
this.perfFormOpen.Increment();
```

VB

```
Me.perfFormOpen.Increment()
```

When you dragged the performance counter onto the form, you may have noticed a *smart tag* (small arrow that appears near the top-right corner when a control is selected) on the performance counter component that had a single item, Add Installer. When the component is selected, you can notice the same action at the bottom of the Properties window. Clicking this action in either place adds an `Installer` class to your solution that can be used to install the performance counter as part of your installation process. Of course, for this installer to be called, the assembly it belongs to must be added as a custom action for the deployment project.

To create multiple performance counters, you can simply select each additional performance counter and click Add Installer. Visual Studio 2017 directs you back to the first installer that was created and has automatically added the second counter to the `CountersCollectionData` collection of the `PerformanceCounterInstaller` component, as shown in Figure 9-9.

You can also add counters in other categories by adding additional `PerformanceCounterInstaller` components to the design surface. You are now ready to deploy your application with the knowledge that you can use a tool such as PerfMon to monitor how your application behaves.

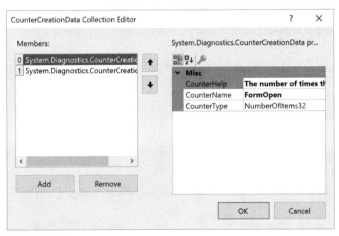

FIGURE 9-9

Services

The Services node, expanded in Figure 9-10, shows the registered services for the computer. The icon associated with each service indicates the state of that service. Possible states are Stopped,

Running, or Paused. The icons are similar to what you find on a DVD player: the triangle is running, the square is stopped, and the two rectangles is paused. Selecting a service displays additional information about the service, such as other service dependencies, in the Properties window.

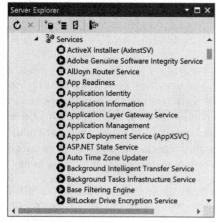

FIGURE 9-10

As with other nodes in the Server Explorer, each service can be dragged onto the design surface of a form. This generates a `ServiceController` component in the nonvisual area of the form. By default, the `ServiceName` property is set to the service that you dragged across from the Server Explorer, but this can be changed to access information and control any service. Similarly, the `MachineName` property can be changed to connect to any computer to which you have access. The following code shows how you can stop a Service using `ServiceController` component:

C#

```csharp
this.serviceController1.Refresh();
if (this.serviceController1.CanStop)
{
    if (this.serviceController1.Status ==
            System.ServiceProcess.ServiceControllerStatus.Running)
    {
        this.serviceController1.Stop();
        this.serviceController1.Refresh();
    }
}
```

VB

```vb
Me.ServiceController1.Refresh()
If Me.ServiceController1.CanStop Then
    If Me.ServiceController1.Status = _
            ServiceProcess.ServiceControllerStatus.Running Then
        Me.ServiceController1.Stop()
        Me.ServiceController1.Refresh()
    End If
End If
```

In addition to the three main states — Running, Paused, or Stopped — other transition states are ContinuePending, PausePending, StartPending, and StopPending. If you are about to start a service that may be dependent on another service that is in one of these transition states, you can call the `WaitForStatus` method to ensure that the service starts properly.

DATA CONNECTIONS

The Data Connections node enables you to connect to a database and perform a large range of administrative functions. You can connect to a wide variety of data sources including any edition of SQL Server, Microsoft Access, Oracle, or a generic ODBC data source. Figure 9-11 shows the Server Explorer connected to a SQL Server database.

The Server Explorer provides access to the Visual Database, which allows you to perform a large range of administrative functions on the connected database. You can create databases; add and modify tables, views, and stored procedures; manage indexes, execute queries, and much more. Chapter 26, "Visual Database Tools," covers aspects of the Data Connections functionality.

FIGURE 9-11

SHAREPOINT CONNECTIONS

One of the useful features of Visual Studio 2017 is the ability to connect to a Microsoft Office SharePoint Server with the Server Explorer. This feature allows you to navigate and view many of the SharePoint resources and components.

The Server Explorer provides only read-only access to SharePoint resources — you cannot, for example, create or edit a list definition. Even so, it can be useful to have ready access to this information in Visual Studio when developing a SharePoint application. As with many of the components under the Servers node, you can also drag and drop certain SharePoint resources directly onto the design surface of your SharePoint project.

SUMMARY

In this chapter, you learned how you can use Server Explorer to manage and work with computer resources and services. Chapter 26 continues the discussion on the Server Explorer, covering the Data Connections node in more detail.

PART III
Digging Deeper

10

Unit Testing

WROX.COM CODE DOWNLOADS FOR THIS CHAPTER

The wrox.com code downloads for this chapter can be found at www.wrox.com by searching for this book's ISBN number (978-1-119-40458-3). The code and any related support files are located in their own folder for this chapter.

Application testing is one of the most important parts of writing software. Research into the costs of software maintenance have revealed that a software defect can cost up to 100 times more to fix if it makes it to a production environment than if it had been caught during development (from a report by the System Sciences Institute at IBM). At the same time, a lot of testing involves repetitive, dull, and error-prone work that must be undertaken every time you make a change to your code base. The easiest way to counter this is to produce repeatable automated tests that can be executed by a computer on demand. This chapter looks at a specific type of automated testing that focuses on individual components, or units, of a system. Having a suite of automated unit tests gives you the power to verify that your individual components all work as specified even after making radical changes to them.

Visual Studio 2017 has a built-in framework for authoring, executing, and reporting on test cases. This chapter focuses on creating, configuring, running, and managing a suite of unit tests as well as adding support to drive the tests from a set of data.

YOUR FIRST TEST CASE

Writing test cases is not easily automated because the test cases must mirror the functionality of the software developed. In fact, there are solid arguments against automating all but the simplest of unit tests. However, at several steps in the process, code stubs can be generated by a tool. To illustrate this, start with a straightforward snippet of code to learn to write test cases that fully exercise the code. Setting the scene is a Subscription class with a public property called CurrentStatus, which returns the status of the current subscription as an enumeration value:

VB

```
Public Class Subscription
    Public Enum Status
        Temporary
        Financial
        Unfinancial
        Suspended
    End Enum

    Public Property PaidUpTo As Nullable(Of Date)

    Public ReadOnly Property CurrentStatus As Status
        Get
            If Not Me.PaidUpTo.HasValue Then Return Status.Temporary
            If Me.PaidUpTo > Now Then
                Return Status.Financial
            Else
                If Me.PaidUpTo >= Now.AddMonths(-3) Then
                    Return Status.Unfinancial
                Else
                    Return Status.Suspended
                End If
            End If
        End Get
    End Property
End Class
```

C#

```
public class Subscription
{
    public enum Status
    {
        Temporary,
        Financial,
        Unfinancial,
        Suspended
    }
```

```
    public DateTime? PaidUpTo { get; set; }

    public Status CurrentStatus
    {
        get
        {
            if (this.PaidUpTo.HasValue == false)
                return Status.Temporary;
            if (this.PaidUpTo > DateTime.Today)
                return Status.Financial;
            else
            {
                if (this.PaidUpTo >= DateTime.Today.AddMonths(-3))
                    return Status.Unfinancial;
                else
                    return Status.Suspended;
            }
        }
    }
}
```

As you can see from the code snippet, four code paths need to be tested for the CurrentStatus property. To test this property, you create a separate SubscriptionTest test class in a new test project, into which you add a test method that contains the code necessary to instantiate a Subscription object, set the PaidUpTo property, and check that the CurrentStatus property contains the correct result. Then you keep adding test methods until all the code paths through the CurrentStatus property have been executed and tested.

Visual Studio 2017 includes a tool that can be used to help create unit tests for existing classes. It creates a test project, along with a number of methods that run your classes through some basic steps. This is described in the "IntelliTests" section later in this chapter. However, even with a tool that helps generate unit tests, you still need to know what makes a particular method a unit test. Visual Studio provides a runtime engine that can run the test cases, monitor their progress, and report on any outcome from the tests. Therefore, all you need to do is write the code to test the property in question.

To see the basic template of a test class, make sure that the test project is selected in Solution Explorer and then select Project ➪ Add Unit Test. This creates a test class and a single test method. The Unit Test template includes just a basic unit test class containing just a single method, shown in the code sample below. For this example, the test class has been changed to SubscriptionTest (as opposed to the default UnitTest1) to indicate the class being tested:

VB

```
Imports Microsoft.VisualStudio.TestTools.UnitTesting
<TestClass()>
Public Class SubscriptionTest


    <TestMethod()>
    Public Sub TestMethod1()
    End Sub
End Class
```

C#

```csharp
using System;
using Microsoft.VisualStudio.TestTools.UnitTesting;
[TestClass]
public class SubscriptionTest
{

    [TestMethod]
    public void TestMethod1()
    {
    }
}
```

Although there are a number of techniques that can be used to write your own unit tests, there are two main ideas that you should keep in mind. One is that, given a large number of unit tests in a project, it can quickly become difficult to manage them. To address this issue, it is suggested that a naming convention be used. As you might expect, there are many different conventions that can be used, but a popular one is MethodName_StateUnderTest_ExpectedBehavior. This simple naming convention ensures that test cases can easily be found and identified.

A second (and complementary) idea is to approach each test using an Arrange/Act/Assert paradigm. Start by setting up and initializing the values used in the test (the Arrange portion). Then execute the method being tested (Act). Finally, determine the outcome of the test (Assert). If you follow this approach, you end up with unit tests that look like the following:

VB

```vbnet
<TestMethod()>
Public Sub CurrentStatus_NothingPaidUpToDate_TemporaryStatus()
    ' Arrange
    Dim s as New Subscription()
    s.PaidUpTo = Nothing
    ' Act
    Dim actual as Subscription.Status = s.CurrentStatus
    ' Assert
    Assert.Inconclusive()
End Sub
```

C#

```csharp
[TestMethod]
public void CurrentStatus_NullPaidUpToDate_TemporaryStatus()
{
    // Arrange
    Subscription s = new Subscription();
    s.PaidUpTo = null;
    // Act
    Subscription.Status actual = s.CurrentStatus;
    //Assert
    Assert.Inconclusive();
}
```

Before going any further, run this test case to see what happens by right-clicking in the code window and selecting Run Tests. The result is the Test Explorer, as shown in Figure 10-1.

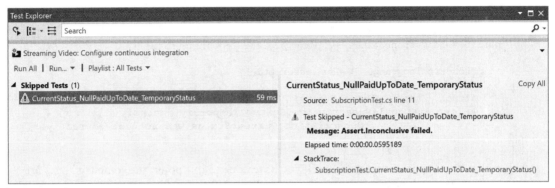

FIGURE 10-1

> **NOTE** *The context menu is just one way to select and run a test case. There is a Test menu that includes a Run submenu that allows for the execution of all or selected tests. Or you can open the Test Explorer window directly and run all or selected tests using the links (refer to Figure 10-1). In addition to each of these methods, you can also set breakpoints in your code and run test cases in the debugger by selecting one of the Debug Tests options from the main toolbar.*

Figure 10-1 shows a test case that returns an inconclusive result. The warning icon (the triangle with the exclamation) indicates that the test was skipped. In the details for the test result (on the right side of Figure 10-1), there is a message that indicates that `Assert.Inconclusive` failed. Essentially, an inconclusive assertion indicates either that a test is not complete or that the results should not be relied upon because changes may have been made that would make this test invalid. The results show basic information about the test, the result, and other useful environmental information such as the computer name and test execution duration.

In creating this unit test, the `Assert.Inconclusive` statement was inserted by hand. To complete the unit test, it is necessary to actually perform the appropriate analysis of the results to ensure that the test passed. This is accomplished by replacing the `Assert.Inconclusive` statement with `Assert.AreEqual`, as shown in the following code:

VB

```
<TestMethod()>
    Public Sub CurrentStatus_NothingPaidUpToDate_TemporaryStatus ()
        Dim target As Subscription = New Subscription
        Dim actual As Subscription.Status
        actual = target.CurrentStatus
```

```
        Assert.AreEqual(Subscription.Status.Temporary, actual, _
                   "Subscription.CurrentStatus was not set correctly.")
     End Sub
```

C#

```
[TestMethod()]
public void CurrentStatus_NullPaidUpToDate_TemporaryStatus ()
{
    Subscription target = new Subscription();
    Subscription.Status actual;
    actual = target.CurrentStatus;
    Assert.AreEqual(Subscription.Status.Temporary, actual,
                   "Subscription.CurrentStatus was not set correctly.");
}
```

Although it is not apparent from the work you have done to this point, the completed tests are grouped into one of three categories: Failed Tests, Passed Tests, and Not Run Tests. It is possible to run all the tests, only the tests from a specific category, repeat the last test run, or just the tests that you select. The Run link at the top of the Test Explorer contains a drop-down where you can select the category of tests to run. To select individual tests to run, click the desired tests (using the standard Ctrl+click or Shift+Ctrl+click to add tests after the first one), and then right-click and choose Run Selected Tests. After you fix the code that caused the tests to fail, click the Run All button to rerun these test cases and produce a successful result, as shown in Figure 10-2.

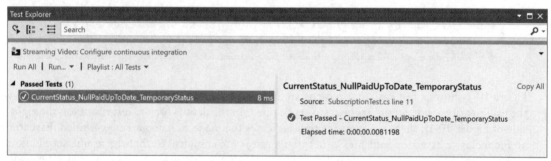

FIGURE 10-2

> **NOTE** *There is one thing to be aware of regarding unit tests. Put simply, the default behavior for a unit test method is to "pass." And the way that you change this behavior is by adding Assert statements to the method, the idea being that if one of the* Assert *statements fail, the unit test is considered to have "failed." However, when you manually create a brand new unit test, there are no assertions present, which means that the unit test doesn't start out "failing." To address this, an* Assert.Inconclusive *is automatically placed into unit tests when they are created. For any test, executing an* Assert.Inconclusive *means that the test will always fail. When you remove the* Assert.Inconclusive *statement, you are indicating that the test case is complete.*

In this example, we have exercised only one code path, and you should add further test cases that fully exercise the other categories. While you could add additional assertions to the one test method that you've created, this is not considered to be the best practice for writing unit tests. The general approach is to have each test method test one and only one thing. This means that (ideally) there is only one Assert in the method.

The reason for this is that more granular tests mean that if the test fails, the cause is usually more readily apparent. Also, keep in mind that the method does not continue executing past the first failed Assert. Multiple assertions in a method just make it a little more difficult to determine the cause of the failure. That having been said, it is common to have two or three assertions, and there is a parameter that can be passed into the Assert statement for the message that is displayed if the test fails.

Identifying Tests Using Attributes

Before going any further with this scenario, take a step back to consider how testing is carried out within Visual Studio 2017. All test cases must exist within test classes that reside in a test project. But what actually distinguishes a method, class, or project as containing test cases? Starting with the test project, if you look at the underlying XML project file, you can see that there is virtually no difference between a test project file and a normal class library project file. In fact, the only difference appears to be the project type: When this project is built, it simply outputs a standard .NET class library assembly. The key difference is that Visual Studio recognizes this as a test project and automatically analyzes it for any test cases to populate the various test windows.

Classes and methods used in the testing process are marked with an appropriate attribute. The attributes are used by the testing engine to enumerate all the test cases within a particular assembly.

TestClass

All test cases must reside within a test class that is appropriately marked with the `TestClass` attribute. Although it may appear that there is no reason for this attribute other than to align test cases with the class and member that they are testing, you later see some benefits associated with grouping test cases using a test class. For testing the `Subscription` class, a test class called `SubscriptionTest` was created and marked with the `TestClass` attribute. Because Visual Studio uses attributes to locate classes that contain test cases, the name of this class is irrelevant. However, adopting a naming convention, such as adding the Test suffix to the class being tested, makes it easier to manage a large number of test cases.

TestMethod

Individual test cases are marked with the `TestMethod` attribute, which is used by Visual Studio to enumerate the list of tests that can be executed. The `CurrentStatus_NullPaidUpToDate_TemporaryStatus` method in the `SubscriptionTest` class is marked with the `TestMethod` attribute. Again, the actual name of this method is irrelevant, because Visual Studio uses only the attributes to find tests. However, the method name is used in the various test windows when the test cases are listed, so it is useful for test methods to have meaningful names. This is especially true when reviewing test results.

Additional Test Attributes

As you have seen, the unit-testing subsystem within Visual Studio uses attributes to identify test cases. A number of additional properties can be set to provide further information about a test case. This information is then accessible either via the Properties window associated with a test case or within the other test windows. This section goes through the descriptive attributes that can be applied to a test method.

Description

Because test cases are listed by the test method name, a number of tests may have similar names, or names that are not descriptive enough to indicate what functionality they test. The Description attribute, which takes a String as its sole argument, can be applied to a test method to provide additional information about a test case.

Owner

The Owner attribute, which also takes a String argument, is useful for indicating who owns, wrote, or is currently working on a particular test case.

Priority

The Priority attribute, which takes an Integer argument, can be applied to a test case to indicate the relative importance of a test case. Though the testing framework does not use this attribute, it is useful for prioritizing test cases when you are determining the order in which failing, or incomplete, test cases are resolved.

TestCategories

The TestCategory attribute accepts a single String identifying one user-defined category for the test. Like the Priority attribute, the TestCategory attribute is essentially ignored by Visual Studio but is useful for sorting and grouping related items together. A test case may belong to many categories but must have a separate attribute for each one.

WorkItems

The WorkItem attribute can be used to link a test case to one or more work items in a work-item tracking system such as Team Foundation Server. If you apply one or more WorkItem attributes to a test case, you can review the test case when making changes to existing functionality. You can read more about Team Foundation Server in Chapter 12, "Managing Your Source Code."

Ignore

You can temporarily prevent a test method from running by applying the Ignore attribute to it. Test methods with the Ignore attribute will not be run and will not show up in the results list of a test run.

> **NOTE** *You can apply the* `Ignore` *attribute to a test class as well to switch off all the test methods within it.*

Timeout

A test case can fail for any number of reasons. A performance test, for example, might require a particular functionality to complete within a specified time frame. Instead of the tester writing complex multithreading tests that stop the test case when a particular timeout has been reached, you can apply the `Timeout` attribute to a test case with a timeout value in milliseconds, as shown in the following code. This ensures that the test case fails if that timeout is reached.

VB

```vb
<TestMethod()>
<Owner("Mike Minutillo")>
<Description("Tests the functionality of the Current Status Property")>
<Priority(3)>
<Timeout(10000)>
<TestCategory("Financial")>
Public Sub CurrentStatusTest()
    Dim target As Subscription = New Subscription
    Dim actual As Subscription.Status
    actual = target.CurrentStatus
    Assert.AreEqual(Subscription.Status.Temporary, actual, _
                "Subscription.CurrentStatus was not set correctly.")
End Sub
```

C#

```csharp
[TestMethod()]
[Owner("Mike Minutillo")]
[Description("Tests the functionality of the Current Status Method")]
[Priority(3)]
[Timeout(10000)]
[TestCategory("Financial")]
public void CurrentStatusTest()
{
    Subscription target = new Subscription();
    Subscription.Status actual;
    actual = target.CurrentStatus;
    Assert.AreEqual(Subscription.Status.Temporary, actual,
                "Subscription.CurrentStatus was not set correctly.");
}
```

This snippet augments the original `CurrentStatusTest` method with some of these attributes to illustrate their usage. In addition to providing additional information about what the test case does and who wrote it, this code assigns the test case a priority of 3 and a category of `"Financial"`.

Lastly, the code indicates that this test case should fail if it takes more than 10 seconds (10,000 milliseconds) to execute.

Unit Tests and Code Lens

Unit tests provide some additional advantage beyond the Code Lens functionality that was described in Chapter 4, "The Visual Studio Workspace." Figure 10-3 illustrates the code for a unit test as it appears in the code editor when the test class is first opened.

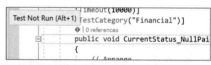

FIGURE 10-3

Immediately to the left of the References link is a little blue diamond-shaped icon. The tool tip for the icon indicates that the test has not been run. In actuality, it means that the test hasn't been run for this session. There is nothing that persists between executions of Visual Studio to indicate that the test might have been run in the past.

After the test has been executed, the icon changes. What it changes to depends on the outcome of the test. Figure 10-4 shows the icon when a test has been skipped (such as when an `Assert.Inconclusive` is executed).

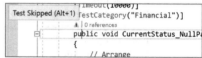

FIGURE 10-4

The icon is not just a visual representation of the test's state. When you click on the icon you see additional details about the test result, as shown in Figure 10-5. This is similar to the information displayed in the Test Explorer (refer to Figure 10-1).

> ⚠ Test Skipped - CurrentStatus_NullPaidUpToDate_TemporaryStatus
>
> **Message: Assert.Inconclusive failed.**
>
> Elapsed time: 28 ms
>
> ▲ StackTrace:
>   SubscriptionTest.CurrentStatus_NullPaidUpToDate_TemporaryStatus()
>
> Run | Debug

```
                  estCategory("Financial")]
               ⚠ | 0 references
               public void CurrentStatus_NullPaidUpToDate_TemporaryStatus()
```

FIGURE 10-5

There are two additional links at the bottom of the details pane. You can use the Run link to run the test in regular mode, or you can use the Debug link to run the test in debug mode.

When the test is successful, a green icon displays, as shown in Figure 10-6. The additional details for the test have been updated, although you can easily run or debug the test again.

> ✔ Test Passed - CurrentStatus_NullPaidUpToDate_TemporaryStatus
>
> Elapsed time: 17 ms
>
> Run | Debug

```
                  estCategory("Financial")]
               ⊘ | 0 references
               public void CurrentStatus_NullPaidUpToDate_TemporaryStatus()
```

FIGURE 10-6

The Code Lens functionality, as it pertains to unit testing, extends beyond the test class itself. Figure 10-7 contains some of the code that is being tested by the tests written as part of this chapter.

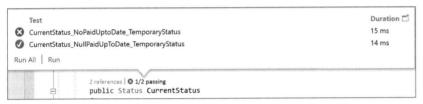

FIGURE 10-7

You can see in the code two indicators for how unit tests have performed when calling a particular property or method. The first link, above the PaidUpTo property, indicates that one unit test has invoked the PaidUpTo property and that test passed. The indicator above the CurrentStatus property says that only one of the two unit tests that use the CurrentStatus property passed. When that indicator is clicked, a list of the tests, both successful and unsuccessful, appears (as shown in Figure 10-8).

Test	Duration
❌ CurrentStatus_NoPaidUptoDate_TemporaryStatus	15 ms
✔ CurrentStatus_NullPaidUpToDate_TemporaryStatus	14 ms

Run All | Run

2 references | ❌ 1/2 passing
public Status CurrentStatus

FIGURE 10-8

ASSERTING THE FACTS

So far, this chapter has examined the structure of the test environment and how test cases are nested within test classes in a test project. What remains is to look at the body of the test case and review how test cases either pass or fail. (When a test case is generated, you saw that an Assert .Inconclusive statement is added to the end of the test to indicate that it is incomplete.)

The idea behind unit testing is that you start with the system, component, or object in a known state, and then run a method, modify a property, or trigger an event. The testing phase comes at the end, when you need to validate that the system, component, or object is in the correct state. Alternatively, you may need to validate that the correct output was returned from a method or property. You do this by attempting to assert a particular condition. If this condition is not true, the testing system reports this result and ends the test case. A condition is asserted, not surprisingly, via the Assert class. There is also a StringAssert class and a CollectionAssert class, which provide additional assertions for dealing with String objects and collections of objects, respectively.

The Assert Class

The Assert class in the UnitTesting namespace, not to be confused with the Debug.Assert or Trace.Assert method in the System.Diagnostics namespace, is the primary class used to make assertions about a test case. The basic assertion has the following format:

VB
```
Assert.IsTrue(variableToTest, "Output message if this fails")
```

C#
```
Assert.IsTrue(variableToTest, "Output message if this fails");
```

As you can imagine, the first argument is the condition to be tested. If this is true, the test case continues operation. However, if it fails, the output message is emitted and the test case exits with a failed result.

This statement has multiple overloads whereby the output message can be omitted or `String` formatting parameters supplied. Because quite often you won't be testing a single positive condition, several additional methods simplify making assertions within a test case:

➤ `IsFalse`: Tests for a negative or false condition

➤ `AreEqual`: Tests whether two arguments have the same value

➤ `AreSame`: Tests whether two arguments refer to the same object

➤ `IsInstanceOfType`: Tests whether an argument is an instance of a particular type

➤ `IsNull`: Tests whether an argument is nothing

This list is not exhaustive — several more methods exist, including negative equivalents of those listed. Also, many of these methods have overloads that allow them to be invoked in several different ways.

The StringAssert Class

The `StringAssert` class does not provide any additional functionality that cannot be achieved with one or more assertions via the `Assert` class. However, it not only simplifies the test case code by making it clear that `String` assertions are being made; it also reduces the mundane tasks associated with testing for particular conditions. The additional assertions are as follows:

➤ `Contains`: Tests whether a `String` contains another `String`

➤ `DoesNotMatch`: Tests whether a `String` does not match a regular expression

➤ `EndsWith`: Tests whether a `String` ends with a particular `String`

➤ `Matches`: Tests whether a `String` matches a regular expression

➤ `StartsWith`: Tests whether a `String` starts with a particular `String`

The CollectionAssert Class

Similar to the `StringAssert` class, `CollectionAssert` is a helper class used to make assertions about a collection of items. Some of the assertions are as follows:

➤ `AllItemsAreNotNull`: Tests that none of the items in a collection is a null reference

➤ `AllItemsAreUnique`: Tests that no duplicate items exist in a collection

➤ `Contains`: Tests whether a collection contains a particular object

➤ `IsSubsetOf`: Tests whether a collection is a subset of another collection

The ExpectedException Attribute

Sometimes test cases have to execute paths of code that can cause exceptions to be raised. Though exception coding should be avoided, conditions exist where this might be appropriate. Instead of writing a test case that includes a `Try-Catch` block with an appropriate assertion to test that an exception was raised, you can mark the test case with an `ExpectedException` attribute. For example, change the `CurrentStatus` property to throw an exception if the `PaidUp` date is prior to the date the subscription opened, which in this case is a constant:

VB

```vb
Public Const SubscriptionOpenedOn As Date = #1/1/2000#
Public ReadOnly Property CurrentStatus As Status
    Get
        If Not Me.PaidUpTo.HasValue Then Return Status.Temporary
        If Me.PaidUpTo > Now Then
            Return Status.Financial
        Else
            If Me.PaidUpTo >= Now.AddMonths(-3) Then
                Return Status.Unfinancial
            ElseIf Me.PaidUpTo > SubscriptionOpenedOn Then
                Return Status.Suspended
            Else
                Throw New ArgumentOutOfRangeException( _
        "Paid up date is not valid as it is before the subscription
opened.")
            End If
        End If
    End Get
End Property
```

C#

```csharp
public static readonly DateTime SubscriptionOpenedOn = new
DateTime(2000, 1, 1);
public Status CurrentStatus
{
    get
    {
        if (this.PaidUpTo.HasValue == false)
            return Status.Temporary;
        if (this.PaidUpTo > DateTime.Today)
            return Status.Financial;
        else
        {
            if (this.PaidUpTo >= DateTime.Today.AddMonths(-3))
                return Status.Unfinancial;
            else if (this.PaidUpTo >= SubscriptionOpenedOn)
                return Status.Suspended;
            else
                throw new ArgumentOutOfRangeException(
            "Paid up date is not valid as it is before the
subscription opened");
        }
    }
}
```

Using the same procedure as before, you can create a separate test case for testing this code path, as shown in the following example:

VB

```
<TestMethod()>
<ExpectedException(GetType(ArgumentOutOfRangeException),
    "Argument exception not raised for invalid PaidUp date.")>
Public Sub CurrentStatusExceptionTest()
    Dim target As Subscription = New Subscription

    target.PaidUpTo = Subscription.SubscriptionOpenedOn.AddMonths(-1)

    Dim expected = Subscription.Status.Temporary

    Assert.AreEqual(expected, target.CurrentStatus, _
                    "This assertion should never actually be evaluated")
End Sub
```

C#

```
[TestMethod()]
[ExpectedException(typeof(ArgumentOutOfRangeException),
    "Argument Exception not raised for invalid PaidUp date.")]
public void CurrentStatusExceptionTest()
{
    Subscription target = new Subscription();
    target.PaidUpTo = Subscription.SubscriptionOpenedOn.AddMonths(-1);

    var expected = Subscription.Status.Temporary;

    Assert.AreEqual(expected, target.CurrentStatus,
        "This assertion should never actually be evaluated");
}
```

The ExpectedException attribute not only catches any exception raised by the test case, it also ensures that the type of exception matches the type expected. If no exception is raised by the test case, this attribute causes the test to fail.

INITIALIZING AND CLEANING UP

There are occasions when you have to write a lot of setup code, code that is executed whenever you run a test case. For example, when a unit test uses a database, that database should be returned to its initial state after each test to ensure that the test cases are completely repeatable. This is also true for unit tests that modify other resources, such as the filesystem. Visual Studio provides support for writing methods that can be used to initialize and clean up around test cases. (Again, attributes are used to mark the appropriate methods that should be used to initialize and clean up the test cases.)

The attributes for initializing and cleaning up around test cases are broken down into three levels: those that apply to individual tests, those that apply to an entire test class, and those that apply to an entire test project.

TestInitialize and TestCleanup

As their names suggest, the `TestInitialize` and `TestCleanup` attributes indicate methods that should be run before and after each test case within a particular test class. These methods are useful for allocating and subsequently freeing any resources needed by all test cases in the test class.

ClassInitialize and ClassCleanup

Sometimes, instead of setting up and cleaning up after each test, it can be easier to ensure that the environment is in the correct state at the beginning and end of running an entire test class. Test classes are a useful mechanism for grouping test cases; this is where you put that knowledge to use. Test cases can be grouped into test classes that contain one method marked with the `ClassInitialize` attribute and another marked with the `ClassCleanup` attribute. These methods must both be marked as `static`, and the one marked with `ClassInitialize` must take exactly one parameter that is of type `UnitTesting.TestContext`.

AssemblyInitialize and AssemblyCleanup

The final level of initialization and cleanup attributes is at the assembly, or project, level. Methods intended to initialize the environment before running an entire test project, and cleaning up after, can be marked with the `AssemblyInitialize` and `AssemblyCleanup` attributes, respectively. Because these methods apply to any test case within the test project, only a single method can be marked with each of these attributes. Like the class-level equivalents, these methods must both be `static`, and the one marked with `AssemblyInitialize` must take a parameter of type `UnitTesting.TestContext`.

For both the assembly-level and class-level attributes, it is important to remember that even if only one test case is run, the methods marked with these attributes will also be run.

> **NOTE** *It is a good idea to put the methods marked with* `AssemblyInitialize` *and* `AssemblyCleanup` *together into their own test class to make them easy to find. If there is more than one method marked with either of these attributes, then running any tests in the project results in a runtime error. Although the error message is clear ("Cannot define more than one method with the AssemblyInitialize attribute inside an assembly"), you will need to search for the* `AssemblyInitialize` *attribute to find the different methods.*

TESTING CONTEXT

When you write test cases, the testing engine can assist you in a number of ways, including by managing sets of data so that you can run a test case with a range of data and enabling you to output additional information for the test case to aid in debugging. This functionality is available through the `TestContext` object generated within a test class and passed into the `AssemblyInitialize` and

ClassInitialize methods. The code shown below illustrates one way to capture the value of the TextContext object so that you can use it in your tests.

VB

```
Private Shared testContextInstance As TestContext
<ClassInitialize> _
Public Shared Sub MyClassInitialize(testContext As TestContext)
    testContextInstance = testContext
End Sub
```

C#

```
private static TestContext testContextInstance;
[ClassInitialize()]
public static void MyClassInitialize(TestContext testContext)
{
    testContextInstance = testContext;
}
```

Data

The CurrentStatus_NullPaidUpToDate_TemporaryStatus method written in the first section of this chapter tested only a single path through the CurrentStatus property. To fully test this property, you could have written additional methods, each with its own setup and assertions. However, this process is fairly repetitive and would need to be updated if you ever changed the structure of the CurrentStatus property. An alternative is to provide a DataSource for the CurrentStatus_NullPaidUpToDate_TemporaryStatus method whereby each row of data tests a different path through the property. To add appropriate data to this method, use the following process:

1. Create a local database file (an .MDF file) and database table to store the various test data. (The details on how to do this can be found in Chapter 26, "Visual Database Tools.") In this case, create a database called LoadTest with a table called Subscription_CurrentStatus. The table has an Identity bigint column called Id, a nullable datetime column called PaidUp, and an nvarchar(20) column called Status.

2. Add appropriate data values to the table to cover all paths through the code. Test values for the CurrentStatus property are shown in Figure 10-9.

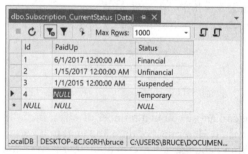

FIGURE 10-9

3. Add a `DataSource` attribute to the test case. This attribute is used by the testing engine to load the appropriate data from the specified table. This data is then exposed to the test case through the `TestContext` object.

> **NOTE** *If you are using a LocalDB database or an Excel file, you'll also want to add a* `DeploymentItem` *attribute. This ensures that the data source will be copied if the test assembly is deployed to another location.*

4. Add the following property to the `test` class. This property is used to access the current `TextContext`, which in turn gives you access to the data in the data source.

    VB

    ```
    Private testContextInstance As TestContext
    Public Property TestContext() As TestContext
       Get
           Return testContextInstance
       End Get
       Set(ByVal Value As TestContext)
           testContextInstance = Value
       End Set
    End Property
    ```

    C#

    ```
    private TestContext testContextInstance;
    public TestContext TestContext
    {
       get { return testContextInstance; }
       set { testContextInstance = value; }
    }
    ```

5. Modify the test case to access data from the `testContextInstance` object, and use the data to drive the test case, which gives you the following `CurrentStatus_NullPaidUpToDate_TemporaryStatus` method:

    VB

    ```
    <DataSource("System.Data.SqlClient", _
        "server=.\\SQLExpress;" & _
        "AttachDBFilename=|DataDirectory|\\LoadTest.mdf;" & _
        "Integrated Security=True", _
        "Subscription_CurrentStatus", DataAccessMethod.Sequential)> _
    <TestMethod()>_
    Public Sub CurrentStatus_NullPaidUpToDate_TemporaryStatus()
        Dim target As Subscription = New Subscription
        If Not IsDBNull(testContextInstance.DataRow.Item("PaidUp")) Then
            target.PaidUpTo = CType(testContextInstance.DataRow.
    Item("PaidUp"), Date)
        End If
        Dim val As Subscription.Status = _
    ```

```
        CType([Enum].Parse(GetType(Subscription.Status), _
            CStr(testContextInstance.DataRow.Item("Status"))), _
    Subscription.Status)

        Assert.AreEqual(val, target.CurrentStatus, _
            "Subscription.CurrentStatus was not set correctly.")
    End Sub
```

C#

```
    [DataSource("System.Data.SqlClient",
        "server=.\\SQLExpress;" +
        "AttachDBFilename=|DataDirectory|\\LoadTest.mdf;" +
        "Integrated Security=True",
        "Subscription_CurrentStatus", DataAccessMethod.Sequential)]
    [TestMethod()]
    public void CurrentStatus_NullPaidUpToDate_TemporaryStatus()
    {
        var target = new Subscription();
        var date = testContextInstance.DataRow["PaidUp"] as DateTime?;
        if (date != null)
        {
            target.PaidUpTo = date;
        }

        var val = Enum.Parse(typeof(Subscription.Status),
            testContextInstance.DataRow["Status"] as string);

        Assert.AreEqual(val, target.CurrentStatus,
            "Subscription.CurrentStatus was not set correctly.");

    }
```

> **NOTE** *This sample code presumes that you have a SQL Server Express instance running at* `.\SQLExpress`*. If the host name for your SQL Server instance is different, you need to use that host name as the value for the server attribute in the DataSource connection string. Also, depending on the identity used to run both SQL Server and Visual Studio, you may have some permissions issues the first time you run the test. Specifically, the identity under which SQL Server is running must have read and write permission to the* `LoadTest.mdf` *file. And the identity under which Visual Studio is running needs to have administrator rights to the SQL Server instance (so that* `LoadTest.mdf` *can be attached).*

When this test case is executed, the `CurrentStatus_NullPaidUpToDate_TemporaryStatus` method is executed four times (once for each row of data in the database table). Each time it is executed, a `DataRow` object is retrieved and exposed to the test method via the `TestContext.DataRow` property. If the logic within the `CurrentStatus` property changes, you can add a new row to the `Subscription_CurrentStatus` table to test any code paths that may have been created.

Before moving on, take one last look at the `DataSource` attribute that was applied to the `CurrentStatus_NullPaidUpToDate_TemporaryStatus` method. This attribute takes four arguments, the first three of which are used to determine which `DataTable` needs to be extracted. The remaining argument is a `DataAccessMethod` enumeration, which determines the order in which rows are returned from the `DataTable`. By default, this is `Sequential`, but it can be changed to `Random` so the order is different every time the test is run. This is particularly important when the data is representative of end user data but does not have to be processed in any particular order.

> **NOTE** *Data-driven tests are not just limited to database tables; they can be driven by Excel spreadsheets or even from Comma-Separated Values (CSV) files.*

Writing Test Output

Writing unit tests is all about automating the process of testing an application. Because of this, these test cases can be executed as part of a build process, perhaps even on a remote computer. This means that the normal output windows, such as the console, are not a suitable place for outputting test-related information. Clearly, you also don't want test-related information interspersed throughout the debugging or trace information being generated by the application. For this reason, there is a separate channel for writing test-related information so that it can be viewed alongside the test results.

The `TestContext` object exposes a `WriteLine` method that takes a `String` and a series of `String` `.Format` arguments that can be used to output information to the results for a particular test. For example, adding the following line to the `CurrentStatusDataTest` method generates additional information with the test results:

VB

```
testContextInstance.WriteLine("No exceptions thrown for test id {0}", _
    CInt(Me.TestContext.DataRow.Item(0)))
```

C#

```
testContextInstance.WriteLine("No exceptions thrown for test id {0}",
            this.TestContext.DataRow[0]);
```

> **NOTE** *Although you should use the* `TestContext.WriteLine` *method to capture details about your test executions, the Visual Studio test tools will collect anything written to the standard error and standard output streams and add that data to the test results.*

After the test run is completed, the Test Explorer window is displayed, listing all the test cases that were executed in the test run along with their results. Figure 10-10 shows this run with the completed (and passing) unit tests.

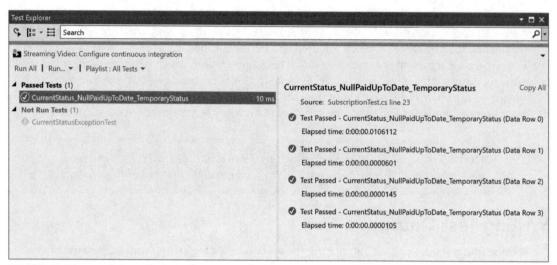

FIGURE 10-10

LIVE UNIT TESTING

Visual Studio 2017 introduces a new feature related to unit testing. Called Live Unit Testing, it allows the developer to track the impact that changes to the code is having on the success or failure of unit tests in real time. It does this within the context of the code editor. This takes the idea of catching test failures early to a new level.

> **NOTE** *Live Unit Testing is only available in the Enterprise edition of Visual Studio 2017, and only for C# and Visual Basic projects.*

Live Unit Testing must be started explicitly. Once it is started, it can be stopped or paused. The rationale behind giving the developer this control is two-fold. First, it is a separate process that is evaluating the code that you are changing, determining the unit tests that are impacted by the code change, and running the unit tests. While the performance of Live Unit Testing is pretty good, this effort does introduce additional processes running within your development environment.

The second reason for making Live Unit Testing explicit concerns significant refactoring. As you are making large changes in your code base, you will, in all probability, end up breaking a number of unit tests. Given that doing so is an expected outcome, having the Live Unit Testing process running and telling you that tests are broken is not particularly useful. So you can turn it off while the refactoring is going on and then restart it once the code base is back to a stable and working state.

Start Live Unit Testing, using the Test ➪ Live Unit Testing ➪ Start from the main menu. This launches the process that monitors your unit tests. After a few moments, your code editor window will light up with checkboxes, lines, and Xs (depending on the state of your unit test coverage). Figure 10-11 illustrates these symbols.

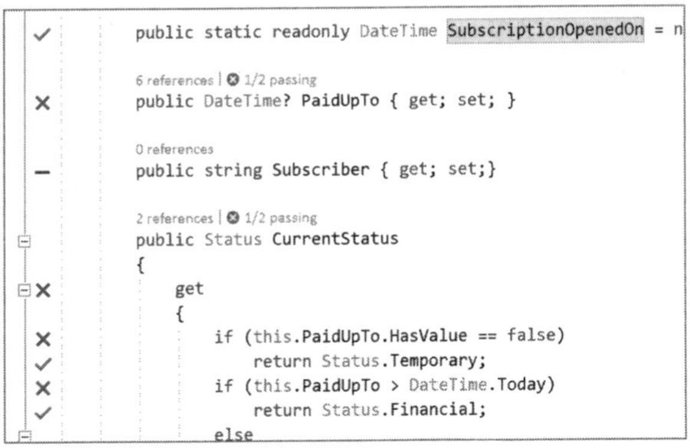

```
✓          public static readonly DateTime SubscriptionOpenedOn = n

           6 references | ❌ 1/2 passing
✗          public DateTime? PaidUpTo { get; set; }

           0 references
—          public string Subscriber { get; set;}

           2 references | ❌ 1/2 passing
           public Status CurrentStatus
           {
✗              get
               {
✗                  if (this.PaidUpTo.HasValue == false)
✓                      return Status.Temporary;
✗                  if (this.PaidUpTo > DateTime.Today)
✓                      return Status.Financial;
                   else
```

FIGURE 10-11

If you look at the first three lines in Figure 10-11, you'll see the three different symbols. The declaration for SubscriptionOpenedOn has the green checkmark. This indicates that all of the tests that use SubscriptionOpenedOn pass. The declaration for Subscriber has a blue line. This means that there are no unit tests for that line of code. And finally, the PaidUpTo declaration has a red X to the left. That means that at least one of the unit tests that use PaidUpTo is currently failing. If you're curious about how many tests are failing, the Code Lens information for PaidUpTo shows that one out of two unit tests are passing. To get even more specific information click on the red X and the list of unit tests are displayed, as shown in Figure 10-12.

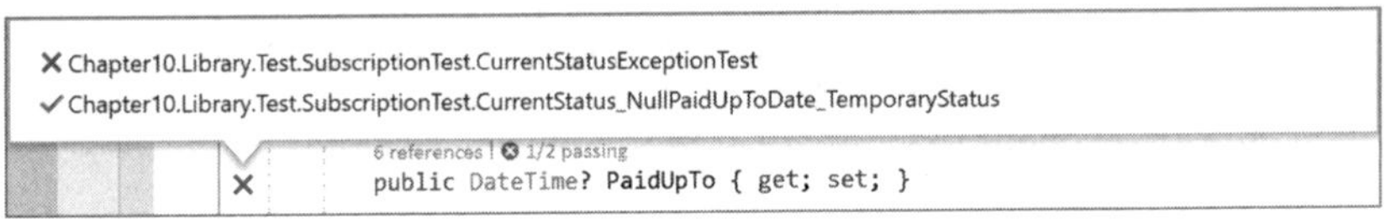

```
✗ Chapter10.Library.Test.SubscriptionTest.CurrentStatusExceptionTest
✓ Chapter10.Library.Test.SubscriptionTest.CurrentStatus_NullPaidUpToDate_TemporaryStatus

                      6 references | ❌ 1/2 passing
✗                     public DateTime? PaidUpTo { get; set; }
```

FIGURE 10-12

Clicking on the individual lines in the display will take you to the actual unit test that is referenced.

ADVANCED UNIT TESTING

Up until this point, you have seen how to write and execute unit tests. This section examines how you can add custom properties to a test case, and how you can use the same framework to test private methods and properties.

Custom Properties

The testing framework provides a number of test attributes that you can apply to a method to record additional information about a test case. This information can be edited via the Properties window and updates the appropriate attributes on the test method. At times you might want to drive your test methods by specifying your own properties, which can also be set using the Properties window. To do this, add `TestProperty` attributes to the test method. For example, the following code adds two attributes to the test method to enable you to specify an arbitrary date and an expected status. This might be convenient for ad hoc testing using the Test View and Properties window:

VB

```
<TestMethod()>
<TestProperty("SpecialDate", "1/1/2008")>
<TestProperty("SpecialStatus", "Suspended")>
Public Sub SpecialCurrentStatusTest()
    Dim target As New Subscription
    target.PaidUpTo = CType(Me.TestContext.Properties.Item("SpecialDate"), _
        Date)
    Dim val As Subscription.Status = _
        [Enum].Parse(GetType(Subscription.Status), _
        CStr(Me.TestContext.Properties.Item("SpecialStatus")))
    Assert.AreEqual(val, target.CurrentStatus, _
        "Correct status not set for Paidup date {0}", target.PaidUpTo)
End Sub
```

C#

```
[TestMethod]
[TestProperty("SpecialDate", "1/1/2008")]
[TestProperty("SpecialStatus", "Suspended")]
public void SpecialCurrentStatusTest()
{
    var target = new Subscription();

    target.PaidUpTo = this.TestContext.Properties["SpecialDate"] as DateTime?;
    var val = Enum.Parse(typeof(Subscription.Status),
        this.TestContext.Properties["SpecialStatus"] as string);

    Assert.AreEqual(val, target.CurrentStatus,
        "Correct status not set for Paidup date {0}", target.PaidUpTo);

}
```

Testing Private Members

One of the selling points of unit testing is that it is particularly effective for testing the internals of your class to ensure that they function correctly. The assumption here is that if each of your components works in isolation, there is a better chance that they will work together correctly; and in fact, you can use unit testing to test classes working together. However, you might wonder how well the unit-testing framework handles testing private methods.

One of the features of the .NET Framework is the capability to reflect over any type that has been loaded into memory and to execute any member regardless of its accessibility. This functionality does come at a performance cost because the reflection calls obviously include an additional level of redirection, which can prove costly if done frequently. Nonetheless, for testing, reflection enables you to call into the inner workings of a class and not worry about the potential performance penalties for making those calls.

The other, more significant issue with using reflection to access nonpublic members of a class is that the code to do so is somewhat messy. On the Subscription class, let's set up for the test by returning to the CurrentStatus property and changing its access from public to private.

Back in the unit test, modify the body so that it looks like the following:

VB

```
<TestMethod(), _
 DeploymentItem("Subscriptions.dll")> _
Public Sub Private CurrentStatusTest()
    ' Arrange
    Dim s = new Subscription()
    s.PaidUpTo = null
    ' Act
    Dim t = s.GetType()
    Dim result As Object
    Result = t.InvokeMember("CurrentStatus", BindingFlags.GetProperty |
        BindingFlags.Instance |BindingFlags.Public | BindingFlags.NonPublic, null,
s, null)
    ' Assert
    Assert.IsInstanceOfType(result, GetType(Subscription.Status))
    Assert.AreEqual(Subscription.Status.Temporary, Cast(result, Subscription.
Status))
End Sub
```

C#

```
[TestMethod()]
[DeploymentItem("Subscriptions.dll")]
public void Private CurrentStatusTest()
{
    // Arrange
    Subscription s = new Subscription();
    s.PaidUpTo = null;
    // Act
    Type t = s.GetType();
    object result = t.InvokeMember("CurrentStatus", BindingFlags.GetProperty |
        BindingFlags.Instance |BindingFlags.Public | BindingFlags.NonPublic, null,
s, null);
    // Assert
    Assert.IsInstanceOfType(result, typeof(Subscription.Status));
    Assert.AreEqual(Subscription.Status.Temporary, (Subscription.Status)result);
}
```

As you can see, the preceding example uses reflection, in the form of the InvokeMember method. Specifically, it retrieves the type (that would be the Subscription class) and then calls InvokeMember to retrieve (the GetProperty binding flag) the CurrentStatus property value. The result is then asserted to be of the type Subscription.Status and equal to Temporary.

INTELLITEST

Visual Studio 2017 includes a testing feature called IntelliTest. It is an outgrowth of the Pex project that has been active in Microsoft Research for a number of years. Although it can be used in a number of different situations, its strength is in filling in "holes" in unit test coverage — holes such as when legacy code has no unit tests at all, or when the unit tests that are already written don't cover the edge cases for the class under test.

To provide this functionality, IntelliTest performs an analysis of the method (or methods) that you indicate should be tested. For each method, the different paths that can be taken through the code are identified. Then a unit test is generated for each path by setting precise values for any parameters required to exercise the path. The goal is to create a set of unit tests that cover the code as completely as possible.

Create a set of IntelliTests starts by right-clicking on the class to be tested and selecting Run IntelliTest from the context menu. This examines the code in the class, generates the appropriate unit tests, and runs them. To get a sense of what the generated tests look like, consider the following method, which is added to the `Subscription` class described earlier in the chapter.

VB

```
Private subscribers = New List(Of Person)

Public Sub AddSubscriber(ByVal person As Person, paidToDate As DateTime?)

    If person.Country <> "US" And person.Country <> "CAN" Then
        Return
    End If

    Dim existingSubscriber As Person = subscribers.Where( _
        Function(p) p == person).FirstOrDefault()


    If existingSubscriber Is Nothing Then
        Subscribers.Add(person)
    End If
End Sub
```

C#

```
private List<Person> subscribers = new List<Person>();

public void AddSubscriber(Person person, DateTime? paidToDate)
{
    if (person.Country != "US" && person.Country != "CAN")
        return;

    var existingSubscriber = subscribers.Where(
        p => p == person).FirstOrDefault();

    if (existingSubscriber == null)
        subscribers.Add(person);
}
```

An example of the output can be seen in Figure 10-13.

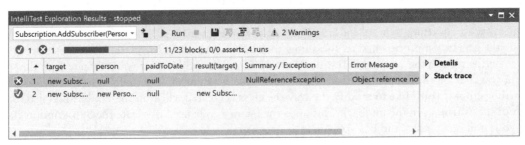

FIGURE 10-13

In Figure 10-13, there were four runs through the routine being analyzed. Since two of the runs were already covered by unit tests, only two unit tests were generated by the IntelliTest process. In the columns next to the target, you can see the values that were provided as parameters to each of the runs. It is also apparent that one of the two unit tests failed.

In the toolbar at the top, there are buttons to help you navigate through the unit tests and the results. The drop-down list contains each of the methods for which unit tests were generated. The display is only ever for a single method, so if you had selected a class declaration prior to executing IntelliTests, you would need to choose a different method from the list.

To the right of the drop-down list is a button that takes you to the unit test definition. By default, the unit tests are generated, compiled, and run from memory. There is no project added to your solution. However, if you click on the Go to Definition button, a unit test project is added, and the unit test code file is opened for you to modify. At this point, if you wish to modify the generated unit test, you are able to do so, and future executions of the IntelliTest will respect and remember your changes.

To get a sense of the level of analysis that the IntelliTest process performed to generate these tests, consider Figure 10-14, which shows the person parameter value more completely.

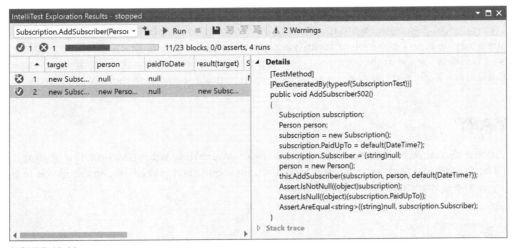

FIGURE 10-14

You can see a second view of the generated unit tests in Figure 10-15. To get to this point, the Events option was selected from the Views drop-down in the middle of the dialog. This view contains a list of events that took place when the unit tests were generated. If IntelliTest had a problem, that event appears with a warning symbol the left. The first row in Figure 10-15 contains such an event. In this case, the generation process had to guess how to create a Subscription class. When you select the row, on the right is the way IntelliTest decided to address the problem. If you're happy with the solution, you click on the Suppress button (to the left of the Warnings in the toolbar) to disable future warnings. But if you'd like to modify the way the class is created, click on the Fix button (also to the left of the Warnings in the toolbar). This adds the factory code used to create the Subscription class to your unit test project and lets you edit it as necessary.

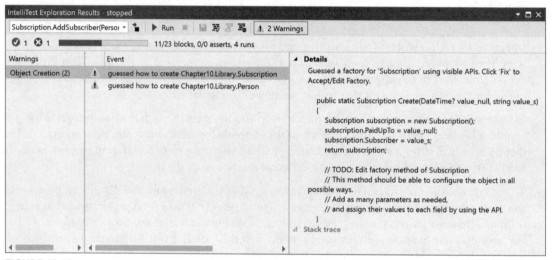

FIGURE 10-15

If you're new to writing unit tests or are working with a body of legacy code that is not currently covered by tests, the functionality of IntelliTest can be a real boon. Besides helping you generate a decently comprehensive set of unit tests, it can help you get into the mind-set of creating your own from scratch. As a minor word of warning, be careful not to depend on the generated tests. Although they do a very good job of identifying edge cases, they are not thorough. There will be pieces of business logic that the generated tests will not cover. So don't think of them as a complete set of unit tests. Rather, think of them as a good starting point for writing more of your own.

SUMMARY

This chapter described how you can use unit testing to ensure the correct functionality of your code. The unit-testing framework within Visual Studio is quite comprehensive, enabling you to both document and manage test cases.

You can fully exercise the testing framework using an appropriate data source to minimize the repetitive code you need to write. You can also extend the framework to test all the inner workings of your application. Finally, you can take advantage of IntelliTests to create unit tests against existing code, which might not already have the necessary coverage.

11

Project and Item Templates

Most development teams build a set of standards that specify how they build applications. This means that every time you start a new project or add an item to an existing project, you have to go through a process to ensure that it conforms to the standard. Visual Studio 2017 enables you to create templates that can be reused without having to modify the standard item templates that ship with Visual Studio 2017. This chapter describes how you can create simple templates and then extend them with a wizard that can change how the project is generated using the IWizard interface.

CREATING TEMPLATES

Two types of templates exist: those that create new project items and those that create entire projects. Both types of templates essentially have the same structure, as you'll see later, except that they are placed in different template folders. The project templates appear in the New Project dialog, whereas the item templates appear in the Add New Item dialog.

Item Template

Although you can build a project item template manually, it is much quicker to create one from an existing project item and make changes as required. This section begins by looking at an item template — in this case a ViewModel class that supports the INotifyPropertyChanged interface.

To begin, create a new class library application (using your language of choice) called ViewModelTemplate. Rename the Class1.cs file that is included in the project to ViewModel.cs. Then modify the code in the file so that it looks like the following.

VB

```vb
Imports System.ComponentModel

Namespace ViewModelTemplate
    ''' <summary>
    ''' The $safeitemrootname$ class.
    ''' </summary>
    Public Class ViewModel
        Implements INotifyPropertyChanged

        ''' <summary>
        ''' Raised when a property value changes.
        ''' <summary>
        Public Event PropertyChanged As PropertyChangedEventHandler _
            Implements INotifyPropertyChanged.PropertyChanged

        ''' <summary>
        ''' Raises the property changed event.
        ''' <summary>
        ''' <param name="propertyName">Name of the property.</param>
        Private Sub NotifyPropertyChanged(propertyName As String)
            RaiseEvent PropertyChanged(Me, New
                PropertyChangedEventArgs(propertyName))
        End Sub
    End Class
End Namespace
```

C#

```csharp
using System.ComponentModel;

namespace ViewModelTemplate
{
    /// <summary>
    /// The $safeitemrootname$ class.
    /// </summary>
    public class ViewModel : INotifyPropertyChanged
    {
        /// <summary>
        /// Raised when a property value changes.
        /// <summary>
        public event PropertyChangedEventHandler PropertyChanged;
```

```
        /// <summary>
        /// Raises the property changed event.
        /// <summary>
        /// <param name="propertyName">Name of the property.</param>
        private void NotifyPropertyChanged(string propertyName)
        {
            var theEvent = PropertyChanged;
            if (theEvent != null)
                theEvent(this, new
                    PropertyChangedEventArgs(propertyName));
        }
    }
}
```

There is one unusual item to note in this code. In the XML comment for the class, the name of the class has been replaced by `$safeitemrootnode$`. This is a token that will be replaced when Visual Studio generates the item to add to the project from the template. Although it's not apparent at the moment, when you export a template (which you will be doing shortly), the namespace and the class name will also be replaced with tokens.

To make a template out of the ViewModel class, select the Export Template item from the Project menu. This starts the Export Template Wizard, as shown in Figure 11-1. If you have unsaved changes in your solution, you will be prompted to save before continuing. The first step is to determine what type of template you want to create. In this case, select the Item Template radio button and make sure that the project in which the ViewModel class resides is selected in the drop-down list.

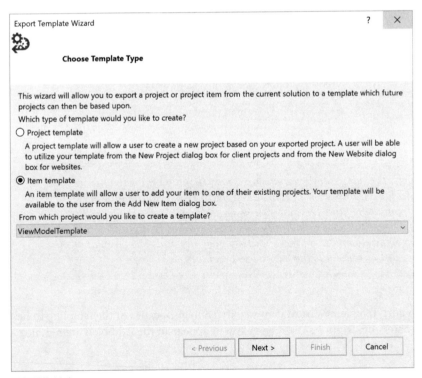

FIGURE 11-1

Click Next. You will be prompted to select the item on which you want to base the template. In this case, select the ViewModel.cs file. The use of check boxes is slightly misleading because with item templates you can select only a single item on which to base the template (selecting a second item deselects the item already selected). After you make your selection and click Next, the dialog, as shown in Figure 11-2, enables you to include any assembly references that you may require. This list is based on the list of references in the project in which that item resides.

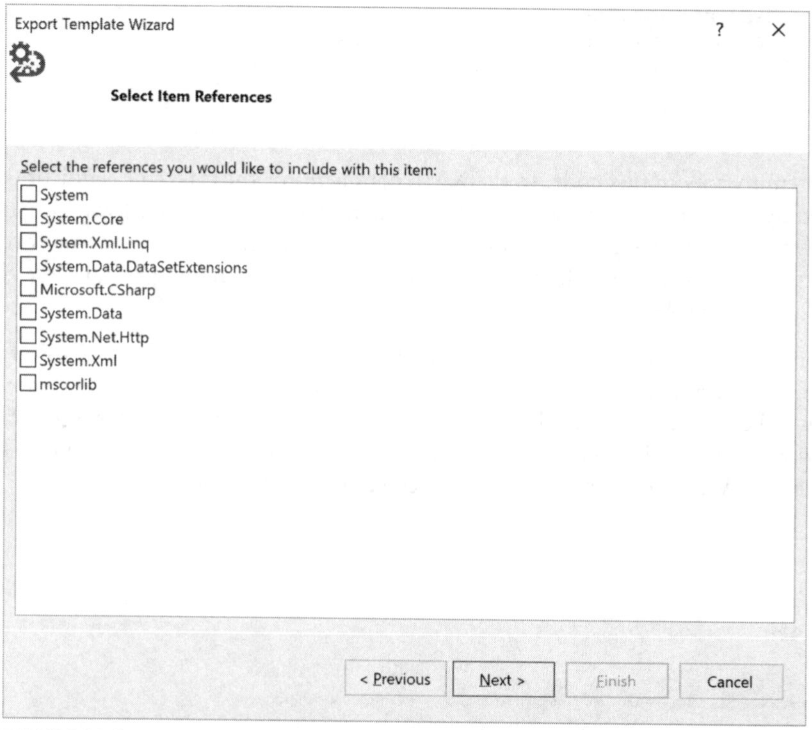

FIGURE 11-2

> **NOTE** *After selecting an assembly, a warning may display under the list stating that the selected assembly isn't preinstalled with Visual Studio and may prevent users from using your template if the assembly isn't available on their machine. Be aware of this issue, and only select assemblies that your item needs. Alternatively, you could create an installer that not only adds the template to the user's machine, but also installs the necessary assembly.*

The final step in the Export Template Wizard is to specify some properties of the template to be generated, such as the name, description, and icon that will appear in the Add New Item dialog.

Figure 11-3 shows the final dialog in the wizard. As you can see, there are two check boxes, one for displaying the output folder upon completion and one for automatically importing the new template into Visual Studio 2017.

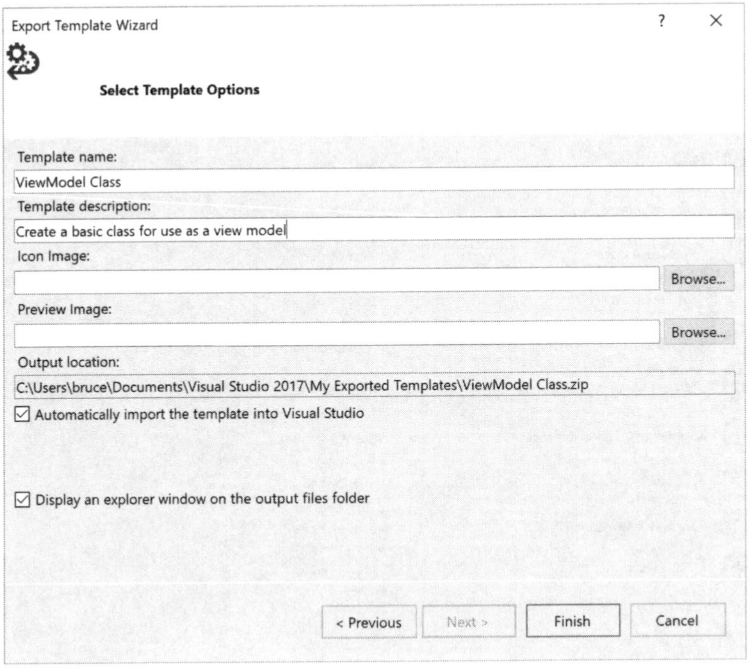

FIGURE 11-3

By default, exported templates are created in the `My Exported Templates` folder under the current user's `Documents\Visual Studio 2017` folder. Inside this root folder are a number of folders that contain user settings about Visual Studio 2017 (as shown in Figure 11-4).

You can also notice the Templates folder in Figure 11-4. Visual Studio 2017 looks in this folder for additional templates to display when you create new items. Two subfolders beneath the Templates folder hold item templates and project templates, respectively. These are divided further by language. If you check the Automatically Import the Template into Visual Studio option on the final page of the Export Template Wizard, the new template will not only be placed in the output folder but will also be copied to the relevant location (depending on language and template type) within the Templates folder. Visual Studio 2017 automatically displays this item template the next time you display the Add New Item dialog, as shown in Figure 11-5.

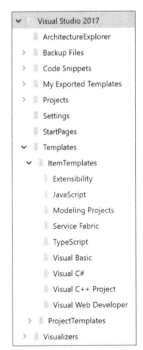

FIGURE 11-4

FIGURE 11-5

> **NOTE** *If you want an item or project template to appear under an existing cat-egory (or one of your own) in the Add New Item/New Project dialog (such as the Windows Forms category), simply create a folder with that name and put the template into it (under the relevant location as described for that template). The next time you open the Add New Item/New Project dialog, the template appears in the category with the corresponding folder name (or as a new category if a category matching the folder name doesn't exist).*

Project Template

You build a project template the same way you build an item template, but with one difference. Whereas the item template is based on an existing item, the project template needs to be based on an entire project. So, naturally, the starting point is to create a project that contains the files and refer-ences that you want in your template. Once the project is completed, a template can be generated by following the same steps you took to generate an item template, with a couple of exceptions. First, you need to select Project Template when asked what type of template to generate. And second, there is no step where you select the items to be included. All items within the project will be included in the template. After you complete the Export Template Wizard, the new project template appears in the Add New Project dialog.

Template Structure

Before examining how to build more complex templates, you need to understand what the Export Template Wizard produces. If you look in the My Exported Templates folder, you can see that each template is exported as a single compressed zip file. The zip file can contain any number of files or folders, depending on whether they are templates for single files or full projects. However, the one common element of all template zip files is that they contain a `.vstemplate` file. This file is an XML document that holds the template configuration. The following code is the `.vstemplate` file that was exported as a part of your item template earlier:

```xml
<VSTemplate Version="3.0.0"
    xmlns="http://schemas.microsoft.com/developer/vstemplate/2005"
    Type="Item">
    <TemplateData>
        <DefaultName>ViewModel Class.cs</DefaultName>
        <Name>ViewModel Class</Name>
        <Description>Create a basic class for use as a view
            model</Description>
        <ProjectType>CSharp</ProjectType>
        <SortOrder>10</SortOrder>
        <Icon>__TemplateIcon.ico</Icon>
    </TemplateData>
    <TemplateContent>
        <References />
        <ProjectItem SubType="" TargetFileName="$fileinputname$.cs"
            ReplaceParameters="true">ViewModel.cs</ProjectItem>
    </TemplateContent>
</VSTemplate>
```

At the top of the file, the `VSTemplate` node contains a `Type` attribute that specifies if this is an item template (`Item`), a project template (`Project`), or a multiple project template (`ProjectGroup`). The remainder of the file is divided into `TemplateData` and `TemplateContent`. The `TemplateData` block includes information about the template, such as its name, description, and the icon that will be used to represent it in the New Project dialog, whereas the `TemplateContent` block defines the file structure of the template.

In the preceding example, the content contains a References section, which contains a list of the assemblies that are required by this item. The files contained in this template are listed by means of the `ProjectItem` nodes. Each node contains a `TargetFileName` attribute that can be used to specify the name of the file as it will appear in the project created from this template. For a project template, the `ProjectItem` elements are contained within the `Project` node.

> **NOTE** *You can create templates for a solution that contains multiple projects. These templates contain a separate .vstemplate file for each project in the solution. They also have a global .vstemplate file, which describes the overall template and contains references to each project's individual .vstemplate files. Creating this file is a manual process, however, because Visual Studio does not currently have a function to export a solution template.*

For more information on the structure of the .vstemplate file, see the full schema at `%program-files%\Microsoft Visual Studio 15.0\Xml\Schemas\1033\vstemplate.xsd`.

Template Parameters

Both item and project templates support parameter substitution, which enables replacement of key parameters when a project or item is created from the template. In some cases these are automatically inserted. For example, when the ViewModel class was exported as an item template, the class name was removed and replaced with a template parameter, as shown here:

```
public class $safeitemname$
```

Table 11-1 lists the reserved template parameters that can be used in any project.

TABLE 11-1: Template Parameters

PARAMETER	DESCRIPTION
Clrversion	Current version of the common language run time.
GUID[1-10]	A GUID used to replace the project GUID in a project file. You can specify up to ten unique GUIDs (for example, GUID1, GUID2, and so on).
Itemname	The name provided by the user in the Add New Item dialog.
machinename	The current computer name (for example, computer01).
projectname	The name provided by the user in the New Project dialog.
Registeredorganization	The Registry key value that stores the registered organization name.
rootnamespace	The root namespace of the current project. This parameter is used to replace the namespace in an item being added to a project.
safeitemname	The name provided by the user in the Add New Item dialog, with all unsafe characters and spaces removed.
safeprojectname	The name provided by the user in the New Project dialog, with all unsafe characters and spaces removed.

PARAMETER	DESCRIPTION
Time	The current time on the local computer.
Userdomain	The current user domain.
Username	The current username.
webnamespace	The name of the current website. This is used in any web form template to guarantee unique class names.
Year	The current year in the format YYYY.

In addition to the reserved parameters, you can also create your own custom template parameters. You define these by adding a `<CustomParameters>` section to the .vstemplate file, as shown here:

```
<TemplateContent>
    ...
    <CustomParameters>
        <CustomParameter Name="$timezoneName $" Value="(GMT+8:00) Perth"/>
        <CustomParameter Name="$timezoneOffset $" Value="+8"/>
    </CustomParameters>
</TemplateContent>
```

You can refer to this custom parameter in code as follows:

```
string tzName = "$timezoneName$";
string tzOffset = "$timezoneOffset$";
```

When a new item or project containing a custom parameter is created from a template, Visual Studio automatically performs the template substitution on both custom and reserved parameters.

Template Locations

By default, custom item and project templates are stored in the user's personal `Documents\Visual Studio 2017\Templates` folder, but you can redirect this to another location (such as a shared directory on a network so you use the same custom templates as your colleagues) via the Options dialog. Go to Tools ⇨ Options, and select the Projects and Solutions node. You can then select a different location for the custom templates here.

EXTENDING TEMPLATES

Building templates based on existing items and projects limits what you can do. It assumes that every project or scenario requires exactly the same items. Instead of creating multiple templates for each different scenario (for example, one that has a main form with a black background and another that has a main form with a white background), with a bit of user interaction, you can accommodate multiple scenarios from a single template. Therefore, this section takes the project template created earlier and tweaks it so users can specify the background color for the main form.

To add user interaction to a template, you need to implement the `IWizard` interface in a class library that is then signed and placed in the Global Assembly Cache (GAC) on the machine on which the template will be executed. For this reason, to deploy a template that uses a wizard, you also need rights to deploy the wizard assembly to the GAC.

Template Project Setup

Before plunging in and implementing the `IWizard` interface, follow these steps to set up your solution:

1. Create a new WPF Application project and name it **ExtendedProjectTemplateExample**. Add a couple of additional files to the project, so that you can see that the template works. Make sure that this solution builds and runs successfully before proceeding. Any issues with this solution will be harder to detect later because the error messages that appear when a template is used are somewhat cryptic.

2. Into this solution add a Class Library project, called **WizardClassLibrary**, in which you will place the `IWizard` implementation.

3. Add to the WizardClassLibrary a new empty class file called **MyWizard**, and a blank Windows Form called **ColorPickerForm**. These will be customized later.

4. To access the `IWizard` interface, add to the Class Library project `EnvDTE.dll` and `Microsoft.VisualStudio.TemplateWizardInterface.dll` as references. `EnvDTE.dll` can be found at `%programfiles%\Common Files\Microsoft Shared\MSEnv\PublicAssemblies` while `Microsoft.VisualStudio.TemplateWizardInterface.dll` is located at `%programfiles%\Microsoft Visual Studio 2017\Enterprise\Common7\IDE\`.

IWizard

The purpose of the WizardClassLibrary, and indeed the reason for the IWizard interface, is to give you programming hooks into the template creation process. In your project, you have a form (ColorPickerForm) and a class (MyWizard). The former is a simple form that you can use to specify the color of the background of the main form. To this form you need to add a Color Dialog control, called ColorDialog1, a Panel called ColorPanel, a Button called PickColorButton (with the text Pick Color), and a Button called AcceptColorButton (with the text Accept Color). When completed, the ColorPickerForm should look similar to the one shown in Figure 11-6.

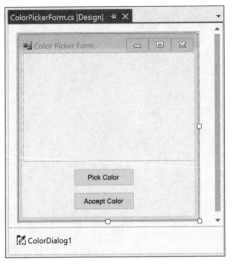

FIGURE 11-6

The following code can be added to this form. The main logic of this form is in the event handler for the Pick Color button, which opens the ColorDialog that is used to select a color:

VB

```
Public Class ColorPickerForm
    Public ReadOnly Property SelectedColor() As Drawing.Color
        Get
            Return ColorPanel.BackColor
        End Get
    End Property

    Private Sub PickColorButton_Click(ByVal sender As System.Object, _
                        ByVal e As System.EventArgs) Handles_
                        PickColorButton.Click
        ColorDialog1.Color = ColorPanel.BackColor
        If ColorDialog1.ShowDialog() = Windows.Forms.DialogResult.OK Then
            ColorPanel.BackColor = ColorDialog1.Color
        End If
    End Sub

    Private Sub AcceptColorButton_Click(ByVal sender As System.Object, _
                        ByVal e As System.EventArgs) Handles _
                        AcceptColorButton.Click
        Me.DialogResult = Windows.Forms.DialogResult.OK
        Me.Close()
    End Sub
End Class
```

C#

```csharp
using System;
using System.Drawing;
using System.Windows.Forms;

namespace WizardClassLibrary
{
    public partial class ColorPickerForm : Form
    {
        public ColorPickerForm()
        {
            InitializeComponent();

            PickColorButton.Click += PickColorButton_Click;
            AcceptColorButton.Click += AcceptColorButton_Click;
        }

        public Color SelectedColor
        {
            get { return ColorPanel.BackColor; }
        }

        private void PickColorButton_Click(object sender, EventArgs e)
        {
            ColorDialog1.Color = ColorPanel.BackColor;

            if (ColorDialog1.ShowDialog() == DialogResult.OK)
            {
                ColorPanel.BackColor = ColorDialog1.Color;
            }
        }

        private void AcceptColorButton_Click(object sender, EventArgs e)
        {
            this.DialogResult = DialogResult.OK;
            this.Close();
        }
    }
}
```

The MyWizard class implements the IWizard interface, which provides a number of opportunities for user interaction throughout the template process. Add some code to the RunStarted method, which is called just after the project-creation process starts. This provides the perfect opportunity to select and apply a new background color for the main form:

VB

```vb
Imports Microsoft.VisualStudio.TemplateWizard
Imports System.Windows.Forms

Public Class MyWizard
    Implements IWizard
```

```vb
        Public Sub BeforeOpeningFile(ByVal projectItem As EnvDTE.ProjectItem) _
                                            Implements IWizard.BeforeOpeningFile
        End Sub

        Public Sub ProjectFinishedGenerating(ByVal project As EnvDTE.Project) _
                                    Implements IWizard.ProjectFinishedGenerating
        End Sub

        Public Sub ProjectItemFinishedGenerating _
                            (ByVal projectItem As EnvDTE.ProjectItem) _
                            Implements IWizard.ProjectItemFinishedGenerating
        End Sub

        Public Sub RunFinished() Implements IWizard.RunFinished

        End Sub

        Public Sub RunStarted(ByVal automationObject As Object, _
                        ByVal replacementsDictionary As _
        Dictionary(Of String, String), _
                        ByVal runKind As WizardRunKind, _
                        ByVal customParams() As Object) _
        Implements IWizard.RunStarted
            Dim selector As New ColorPickerForm
            If selector.ShowDialog = DialogResult.OK Then
                Dim c As Drawing.Color = selector.SelectedColor
                Dim colorString As String = "System.Drawing.Color.FromArgb(" & _
        c.R.ToString & "," & _
        c.G.ToString & "," & _
        c.B.ToString & ")"
                replacementsDictionary.Add _
                                ("Background=""Silver""", _
                                 "Background=""" & colorString & """")
            End If
        End Sub

        Public Function ShouldAddProjectItem(ByVal filePath As String) As Boolean _
                                        Implements IWizard.ShouldAddProjectItem
            Return True
        End Function
    End Class
```

C#

```csharp
using System;
using System.Drawing;
using System.Windows.Forms;
using Microsoft.VisualStudio.TemplateWizard;

namespace WizardClassLibrary
{
    public class MyWizard : IWizard
    {
        public void BeforeOpeningFile(EnvDTE.ProjectItem projectItem)
        {
        }
```

```
public void ProjectFinishedGenerating(EnvDTE.Project project)
{
}

public void ProjectItemFinishedGenerating(EnvDTE.ProjectItem projectItem)
{
}

public void RunFinished()
{
}

public void RunStarted(object automationObject, Dictionary<string, string>
    replacementsDictionary, WizardRunKind runKind, object[] customParams)
{
    ColorPickerForm selector = new ColorPickerForm();

    if (selector.ShowDialog() == DialogResult.OK)
    {
        Color c = selector.SelectedColor;
        string colorString = "Color.FromArgb(" +
            c.R.ToString() + "," +
            c.G.ToString() + "," +
            c.B.ToString() + ")";
        replacementsDictionary.Add
                        ("Background=""Silver""",
                         "Background=""" + colorString + """");
    }
}

public bool ShouldAddProjectItem(string filePath)
{
    return true;
}
    }
}
```

In the `RunStarted` method, you prompt the user to select a new color and then use that response to add a new entry into the replacements dictionary. In this case, you replace `Background="Silver"` with a concatenated string made up of the RGB values of the color specified by the user. The replacements dictionary is used when the files are created for the new project because they will be searched for the replacement keys. Upon any instances of these keys being found, they will be replaced by the appropriate replacement values. In this case, look for the line specifying that the `BackColor` is `Silver`, and replace it with the new color supplied by the user.

The class library containing the implementation of the `IWizard` interface must be a strongly named assembly capable of being placed into the GAC. To ensure this, use the Signing tab of the Project Properties dialog to generate a new signing key, as shown in Figure 11-7.

After you check the Sign the Assembly check box, there will be no default value for the key file. To create a new key, select <New . . .> from the drop-down list. Alternatively, you can use an existing key file using the <Browse . . .> item in the drop-down list.

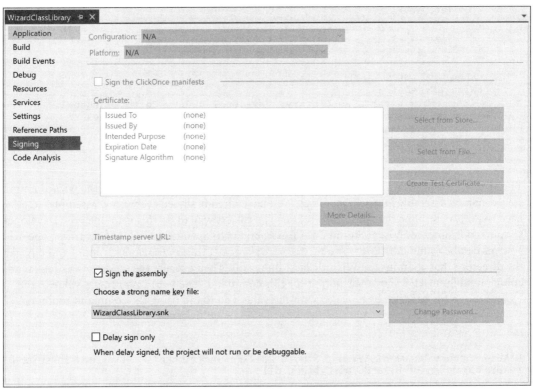

FIGURE 11-7

Generating the Extended Project Template

You're basing the template for this example on the ExtendedProjectTemplateExample project, and you need to make minor changes for the wizard you just built to work correctly. In the previous section you added an entry in the replacements dictionary, which searches for instances in which the `Background` is set to `Silver`. If you want the `MainWindow` to have the `Background` specified while using the wizard, you need to ensure that the replacement value is found. To do this, simply set the `Background` property of the `MainWindow` to `Silver`. This adds the attribute `'Background="Silver"'` to the `Grid` element in the `MainWindow.xaml` file so that it is found during the replacement phase.

Now you need to associate the wizard with the project template so that it is called when creating a new project from this template. Unfortunately, this is a manual process, but you can automate it after you make these manual changes upon subsequent rebuilds of the project. Start by exporting the ExtendedProjectTemplateExample as a new project template as per the previous instructions. Find the `.zip` file for this template in Windows Explorer. Inside the `.zip` file, locate the `.vstemplate` file and edit it. Specifically, add some additional lines (shown in bold) to the `.vstemplate` file:

```
<VSTemplate Version="2.0.0"
  xmlns="http://schemas.microsoft.com/developer/vstemplate/2005" Type="Project">
```

```
    <TemplateData>
    ...
    </TemplateData>
    <TemplateContent>
    ...
    </TemplateContent>
    <WizardExtension>
      <Assembly>WizardClassLibrary, Version=1.0.0.0, Culture=neutral,
          PublicKeyToken=022e960e5582ca43, Custom=null</Assembly>
      <FullClassName>WizardClassLibrary.MyWizard</FullClassName>
    </WizardExtension>
  </VSTemplate>
```

The `<WizardExtension>` node added in the sample indicates the class name of the wizard and the strong-named assembly in which it resides. You have already signed the wizard assembly, so all you need to do is determine the `PublicKeyToken`. The easiest way to do this is to open the Developer Command Prompt for Visual Studio 2017 (instructions to open this window for various operating systems can be found at `https://msdn.microsoft.com/library/ms229859.aspx`) and navigate to the directory that contains the WizardClassLibrary.dll. Then execute the `sn -T  <assemblyName>` command. Figure 11-8 shows the output for this command. The `PublicKeyToken` value in the `.vstemplate` file needs to be replaced with the value you found using the command prompt.

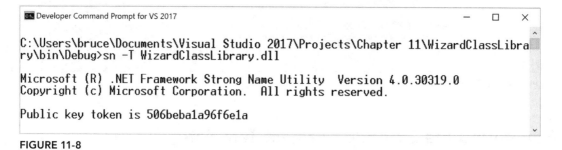

FIGURE 11-8

At this point, you have a `.zip` file containing the project template, along with an assembly that can be used to extend the project creation process. The biggest challenge comes when you try to give these pieces to someone else. Unlike the templates from the beginning of the chapter, which can be deployed by placing a `.zip` file in the appropriate directory, this extended template cannot. It needs to have the WizardLibrary.dll file placed into the GAC, and that requires an installer. Details about how to create an installer can be found in Chapter 35, "Packaging and Deployment."

STARTER KITS

A Starter Kit is essentially the same as a template but differs somewhat in terms of intent. Whereas project templates create the basic shell of an application, Starter Kits create an entire sample application with documentation on how to customize it. Starter Kits appear in the New Project window in the same way project templates do. Starter Kits can give you a big head start on a project (if you can find one focused toward your project type), and you can create your own to share with others in the same way that you created the project template previously.

ONLINE TEMPLATES

Visual Studio 2017 integrates nicely with the online Visual Studio Gallery (http://www .visualstudiogallery.com) enabling you to search for templates created by other developers that they uploaded to the gallery for other developers to download and use. You can browse the gallery and install selected templates from within Visual Studio in two ways: via the Open Project window and from the Extension Manager.

When you open the New Project window in Visual Studio, you are looking at the templates installed on your machine; however, you can browse and search the templates available online by selecting Online from the sidebar. Visual Studio then enables you to browse the templates online. When you select a template it will be downloaded and installed on your machine, and a new project will be created using it.

Visual Studio 2017 includes the Extensions and Updates window (as shown in Figure 11-9), which you can get to from Tools ⇨ Extensions and Updates. The Extensions and Updates window integrates the online Visual Studio Gallery into Visual Studio. It also allows you to browse the Visual Studio Gallery and download and install templates, as well as controls and tools.

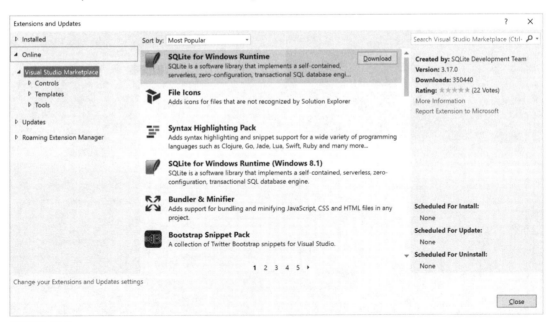

FIGURE 11-9

SUMMARY

This chapter provided an overview of how to create both item and project templates with Visual Studio 2017. Existing projects or items can be exported into templates that you can deploy to your colleagues. Alternatively, you can build a template manually and add a user interface using the IWizard interface. From what you learned in this chapter, you can now build a template solution to create a project template, and build and integrate a wizard interface.

12

Managing Your Source Code

WHAT'S IN THIS CHAPTER?

➤ Working with source control

➤ Creating, adding, and updating code in a source repository

WROX.COM CODE DOWNLOADS FOR THIS CHAPTER

The wrox.com code downloads for this chapter can be found at www.wrox.com by searching for this book's ISBN number (978-1-119-40458-3). The code and any related support files are located in their own folder for this chapter.

If you are building a small application by yourself, it's easy to understand how all the pieces fit together and to make changes to accommodate new or changed requirements. Unfortunately, even on such a small project, the codebase can easily go from being well structured and organized to being a mess of variables, methods, and classes. This problem is amplified if the application is large and complex, and if it has multiple developers working on it concurrently.

In this chapter, you'll learn about how you and your team can use features of Visual Studio 2017 to write and maintain consistent code. The first part of this chapter is dedicated to the use of source control to assist you in tracking changes to your codebase over time. Use of source control facilitates sharing of code and changes among team members, but more important, gives you a history of changes made to an application over time.

SOURCE CONTROL

Many different methodologies for building software applications exist, and though the theories about team structure, work allocation, design, and testing often differ, one point that the theories agree on is that there should be a repository for all source code for an application. Source control is the process of storing source code (referred to as checking code in) and accessing it again (referred to as checking code out) for editing. When we refer to source code, we mean any resources, configuration files, code files, or even documentation that is required to build and deploy an application.

Source code repositories vary in structure and interface. A source control repository not only provides a storage mechanism for your source code, it also provides versioning of files, branching, and remote access. And more sophisticated repositories assist with file merging and conflict resolution. More importantly, a couple of these sophisticated repositories can be used from within Visual Studio.

Version tracking, including a full history of what changes were made and by whom, is one of the biggest benefits of using a source control repository. Although most developers would like to think that they write perfect code, the reality is that quite often a change might break something else. Reviewing the history of changes made to a project makes it possible to identify which change caused the breakage. Tracking changes to a project can also be used for reporting and reviewing purposes because each change is date stamped and its author indicated.

Selecting a Source Control Repository

Visual Studio 2017 does not ship with a source control repository, but it does include rich support for checking files in and out, as well as merging and reviewing changes. To make use of a repository from within Visual Studio 2017, it is necessary to specify which repository to use. Visual Studio 2017 supports deep integration with Team Foundation Server (TFS), Microsoft's premier source control and project tracking system, along with Git, a leading open source control system. In addition, Visual Studio supports any source control client that uses the Source Code Control (SCC) API. Products that use the SCC API include Microsoft Visual SourceSafe and the free, open source source-control repositories Subversion and CVS.

To get Visual Studio 2017 to work with a particular source control provider, you must configure the appropriate information under the Options item on the Tools menu. The Options window, with the Source Control tab selected, is shown in Figure 12-1.

Initially, few settings for source control appear. However, after a provider has been selected, additional nodes are added to the tree to control how source control behaves. These options are specific to the source control provider that has been selected.

Chapter 40, "Visual Studio Team Services," covers the use of Team Foundation, which also offers rich integration and functionality as a source control repository. The remainder of this chapter focuses on the use of Git, an open-source source control repository, which can be integrated with Visual Studio 2017.

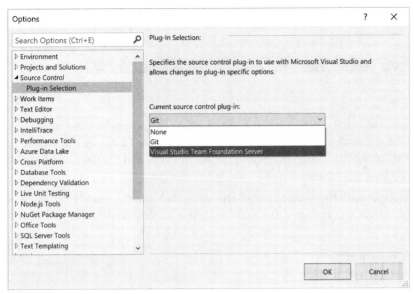

FIGURE 12-1

Environment Settings

After a source control repository has been selected from the plug-in menu, it is necessary to configure the repository for that machine. Many source control repositories need some additional settings to integrate with Visual Studio 2017. These would be found in additional panes that are part of the Settings form. However, these values are specific to the plug-in, so making generalized statements about the details is not feasible. Suffice it to say that the plug-in can provide the information necessary for you to properly configure it. And, more important, for integration with Git, there are no additional settings that need to be provided.

Accessing Source Control

This section walks through the process to add a solution to a Git repository; however, the same principles apply regardless of the repository chosen. This process can be applied to any new or existing solution that is not already under source control. We assume here that you have access to a Git repository and that it has been selected as the source control repository within Visual Studio 2017.

Adding the Solution

To begin the process (after you have selected the repository) of adding a solution to source control, use the Add to Source Control option at the very bottom right of Visual Studio, as shown in the left image in Figure 12-2. Alternatively, if you create a new solution, select the Add To Source Control check box on the New Project dialog to immediately add your new solution to a source control repository.

FIGURE 12-2

Once the solution has been added, the status bar in Visual Studio changes to show the status of your project with respect to the repository. In the image on the right of Figure 12-2, you can see the root branch (master), the name of the repository, the number of changes (3), and the number of unpublished commits (currently 0).

Most of the time, you interact with the source control repository through the Team Explorer window. There are a number of options available to you, as is apparent from the default view shown in Figure 12-3.

FIGURE 12-3

> **NOTE** *The Source Code Control (SCC) API assumes that the* `.sln` *solution file is located in the same folder or a direct parent folder as the project files. If you place the* `.sln` *solution file in a different folder hierarchy than the project files, then you should expect some "interesting" source control maintenance issues.*

Solution Explorer

The first difference that you see after adding your solution to source control is that Visual Studio 2017 adjusts the icons within the Solution Explorer to indicate their source control status.

Figure 12-4 illustrates three file states. When the solution is initially added to the source control repository, the files all appear with a little lock icon next to the file type icon. This indicates that the file has been checked in and is not currently checked out by anyone. For example, `Order.cs` and Properties have this icon.

When a solution is under source control, all changes are recorded, including the addition and removal of files. Figure 12-4 illustrates the addition of `Product.cs` to the solution. The plus sign next to `Product.cs` indicates that this is a new file. The red check mark next to the CSClassLibrary project signifies that the file has been edited since it was last checked in.

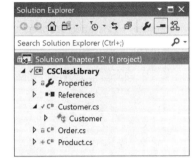

FIGURE 12-4

Changes

In a large application, it can often be difficult to see at a glance which files have been modified, recently added, or removed from a project. The Changes window, as shown in Figure 12-5, is useful for seeing which files are waiting to be committed. If there were files that were not being tracked by Git, they would be listed at the bottom of the windows.

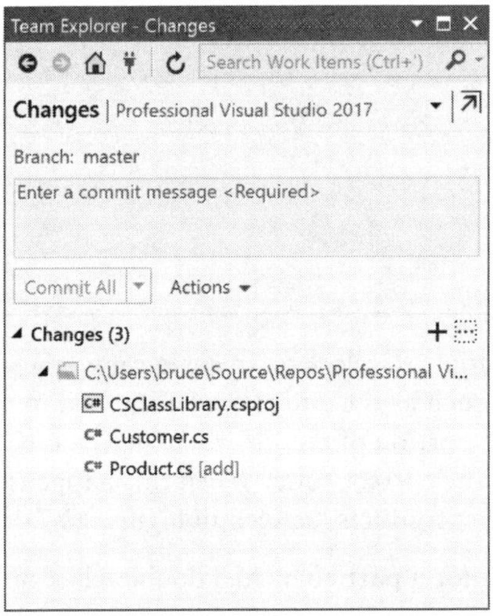

FIGURE 12-5

To initiate a commit, fill in the Commit message textbox at the top of the window and click on the Commit All button. This commits the files to your local repository. By clicking on the drop-down on the right side of the Commit All button, you can also commit and push (which pushes your repository to a remote repository) or commit and sync (which pulls from a remote repository and pushes your repository to the same remote repository).

It's also possible to stage your commits. In Git, a staged commit allows you to add files to a larger commit in small pieces. And each time you stage a commit, you can add a different message. As an example, while in the middle of a refactoring of your code, you notice that there is a typo in one of the messages. So you fix the typo and stage that single change (with the appropriate message) and continue on with your main work. When all of your work is finished, you can bundle it into a larger commit, but the individual message will be retained.

To stage files, right-click on the desired files and select Stage from the context menu. This will add the files to a staged section, as seen in Figure 12-6. Then clicking the Commit Staged button will complete the staging process.

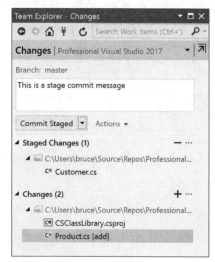

FIGURE 12-6

Merging Changes

Occasionally, changes might be made to the same file by multiple developers. In some cases, these changes can be automatically resolved if they are unrelated, such as the addition of a method to an existing class. However, when changes are made to the same portion of the file, there needs to be a process by which the changes can be mediated to determine the correct code. When this happens, the Resolve Conflicts screen is used to identify and resolve any conflicts, as seen in Figure 12-7.

The files that are in conflict are listed. To resolve the conflict for a particular file, double-click on it to reveal the additional options visible in Figure 12-8.

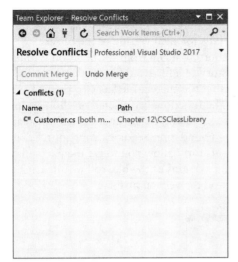

FIGURE 12-7

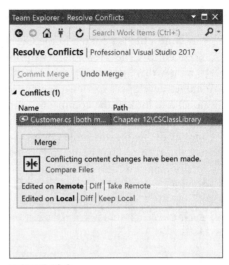

FIGURE 12-8

From here, you have a number of options available for the resolution. You can take the remote or keep the local version as is. Or you can click on the Compare Files link to display the differences between the two files, as seen in Figure 12-9.

FIGURE 12-9

Once the conflict is resolved, the file is moved to the Resolved list at the bottom of the window.

History

Any time a file is updated in the Git repository, history details for each version of the file are recorded. Use the View History option on the right-click shortcut menu from the Solution Explorer to review this history. Figure 12-10 shows what a brief history of a file would look like. This dialog enables developers to view previous versions (you can see that the current file has two previous versions) and look at the comments related to each commit. The functionality offered on this screen is dependent on the source control plug-in that is being used. For Git, these functions are the main ones available on this screen. However, if you utilize Team Foundation Server as your source control plug-in, then toolbar items and context menu options on this form allow you to get the particular version, mark a file as being checked out, compare different versions of the file, roll the file back to a previous version (which erases newer versions), and report on the version history.

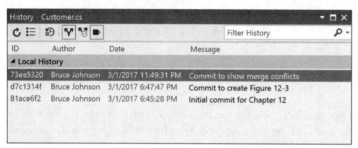

FIGURE 12-10

SUMMARY

This chapter demonstrated the rich interface of Visual Studio 2017 when using a source control repository to manage files associated with an application. Checking files in and out can be done using the Solution Explorer window, and more advanced functionality is available via the Changes window.

PART IV
Desktop Applications

- ▶ **CHAPTER 13:** Windows Forms Applications

- ▶ **CHAPTER 14:** Windows Presentation Foundation (WPF)

- ▶ **CHAPTER 15:** Universal Windows Platform Apps

13

Windows Forms Applications

WHAT'S IN THIS CHAPTER?

➤ Creating a new Windows Forms application

➤ Designing the layout of forms and controls using the Visual Studio designers and control properties

➤ Using container controls and control properties to ensure that your controls automatically resize when the application resizes

WROX.COM CODE DOWNLOADS FOR THIS CHAPTER

The wrox.com code downloads for this chapter can be found at www.wrox.com by searching for this book's ISBN number (978-1-119-40458-3). The code and any related support files are located in their own folder for this chapter.

Since its earliest days, Visual Studio has excelled at providing a rich visual environment for rapidly developing Windows applications. From simple drag-and-drop procedures to place graphical controls onto the form, to setting properties that control advanced layout and behavior of controls, the designer built into Visual Studio 2017 provides you with immense power without having to manually create the UI from code.

This chapter walks you through the rich designer support and comprehensive set of controls available for you to maximize your efficiency when creating Windows Forms applications.

GETTING STARTED

The first thing you need to start is to create a new Windows Forms project. Select the File ➪ New ➪ Project menu to create the project in a new solution. If you have an existing solution to which you want to add a new Windows Forms project, select File ➪ Add ➪ New Project.

Windows Forms applications can be created with either VB or C#. In both cases, the Windows Forms Application project template is available when you open the New Project dialog box and select the Windows Desktop category within your language of choice, as shown in Figure 13-1.

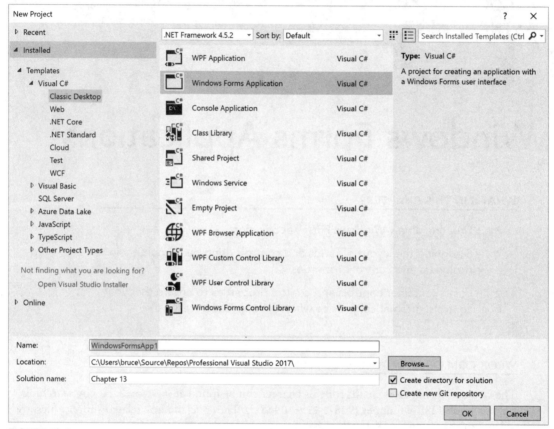

FIGURE 13-1

The New Project dialog allows you to select the .NET Framework version you are targeting. Unlike WPF applications, Windows Forms projects have been available since version 1.0 of the .NET Framework and will stay in the list of available projects regardless of which version of the .NET Framework you select. After entering an appropriate name for the project, click OK to create the new Windows Forms Application project.

THE WINDOWS FORM

When you create a Windows application project, Visual Studio 2017 automatically creates a single blank form ready for your user interface design (see Figure 13-2). You can modify the visual design of a Windows Form in two common ways: by using the mouse to change the size or position of the form or a control or by changing the value of the control's properties in the Properties window.

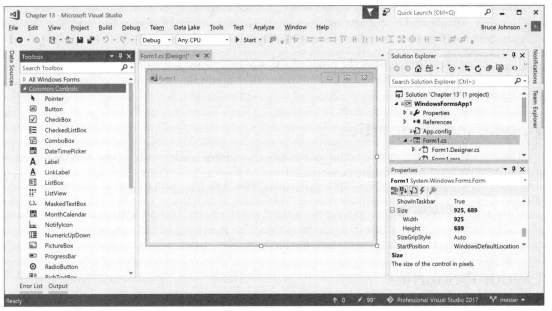

FIGURE 13-2

Almost every visual control, including the Windows Form, can be resized using the mouse. Resize grippers appear when the form or control has focus in the Design view. For a Windows Form, these are visible only on the bottom, the right side, and the bottom-right corner. Use the mouse to grab the gripper, and drag it to the size you want. As you resize, the dimensions of the form are displayed on the bottom right of the status bar.

There is a corresponding property for the dimensions and position of Windows Forms and controls. The Properties window, as shown on the right side of Figure 13-2, shows the current value of many of the attributes of the form. This includes the `Size` property, a compound property made up of the `Height` and `Width`. Click the expand icon to display the individual properties for any compound properties. You can set the dimensions of the form in pixels by entering either an individual value in both the `Height` and `Width` properties or a compound `Size` value in the format width, height.

The Properties window, as shown in Figure 13-3, displays some of the available properties for customizing the form's appearance and behavior.

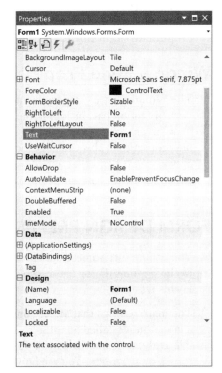

FIGURE 13-3

Properties display in one of two views: either grouped together in categories or in alphabetical order. The view is controlled by the first two icons in the toolbar of the Properties window. The following two icons toggle the attribute list between displaying Properties and Events.

Three categories cover most of the properties that affect the overall look and feel of a form: Appearance, Layout, and Window Style. Many of the properties in these categories are also available on Windows controls.

Appearance Properties

The Appearance category covers the colors, fonts, and form border style. Many Windows Forms applications leave most of these properties at their default values. The `Text` property is one that you typically change because it controls what displays in the form's caption bar.

If the form's purpose differs from the normal behavior, you may need a fixed-size window or a special border, as is commonly seen in tool windows. The `FormBorderStyle` property controls how this aspect of your form's appearance is handled.

Layout Properties

In addition to the `Size` properties discussed earlier, the Layout category contains the `MaximumSize` and `MinimumSize` properties, which control how small or large a window can be resized to. The `StartPosition` and `Location` properties can be used to control where the form displays on the screen. You can use the `WindowState` property to initially display the form minimized, maximized, or normally according to its default size.

Window Style Properties

The Window Style category includes properties that determine what is shown in the Windows Form's caption bar, including the maximize and minimize boxes, help button, and form icon. The `ShowInTaskbar` property determines whether the form is listed in the Windows taskbar. Other notable properties in this category include the `TopMost` property, which ensures that the form always appears on top of other windows, even when it does not have focus, and the `Opacity` property, which makes a form semi-transparent.

FORM DESIGN PREFERENCES

You can modify some Visual Studio IDE settings that simplify your user interface design phase. In the Options dialog (as shown in Figure 13-4), two pages of preferences deal with the Windows Forms Designer.

The main settings that affect your design are the layout settings. By default, Visual Studio 2017 uses a layout mode called SnapLines. Rather than position visible components on the form via an invisible grid, SnapLines helps you position them based on the context of surrounding controls and the form's own borders. You see how to use this mode in a moment, but if you prefer the older style of form design that originated in Visual Basic 6 and was used in the first two versions of Visual Studio .NET, you can change the `LayoutMode` property to `SnapToGrid`.

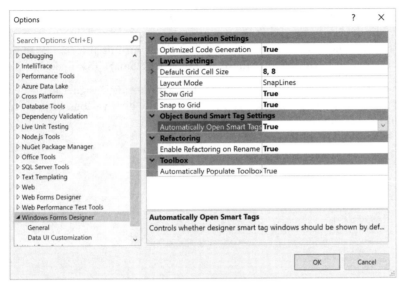

FIGURE 13-4

> **NOTE** *The SnapToGrid layout mode is still used even if the LayoutMode is set to SnapLines. SnapLines becomes active only when you are positioning a control relative to another control. At other times, SnapToGrid will be active and allow you to position the control on the grid vertex.*

You can use the `GridSize` property when positioning and sizing controls on the form. As you move controls around the form, they snap to specific points based on the values you enter here. Most of the time, you can find a grid of 8 × 8 (the default) too large for fine-tuning, so changing this to something such as 4 × 4 might be more appropriate.

> **NOTE** *Both SnapToGrid and SnapLines are aids for designing user interfaces using the mouse. After the control has been roughly positioned, you can use the keyboard to fine-tune control positions by "nudging" the control with the arrow keys.*

`ShowGrid` displays a network of dots on your form's design surface when you're in SnapToGrid mode, so you can more easily see where the controls will be positioned when you move them. You need to close the designer and reopen it to see any changes to this setting. Finally, setting the `SnapToGrid` property to False deactivates the layout aids while in SnapToGrid mode and results in pure free-form form design.

While you're looking at this page of options, you may want to change the Automatically Open Smart Tags value to False. The default setting of True pops open the smart tag task list associated with any control you add to the form, which can be distracting during your initial form design phase. Smart tags are discussed later in this chapter in the section titled "Smart Tag Tasks."

The other page of preferences that you can customize for the Windows Forms Designer is the Data UI Customization section (see Figure 13-5). This is used to automatically bind various controls to data types when connecting to a database.

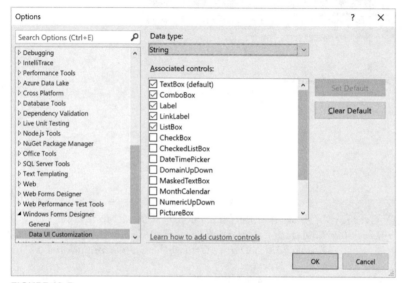

FIGURE 13-5

As you can see in the screenshot, the String data type is associated with five commonly used controls, with the TextBox control set as the default. Whenever a database field that is defined as a String data type is added to your form, Visual Studio automatically generates a TextBox control to contain the value.

The other controls marked as associated with the data type (ComboBox, Label, LinkLabel, and ListBox) can be optionally used when editing the data source and style.

> **NOTE** *It's worth reviewing the default controls associated with each data type at this time to make sure you're happy with the types chosen. For instance, all* DateTime *data type variables will automatically be represented with a DateTime Picker control, but you may want it to be bound to a MonthCalendar.*

Working with data-bound controls is discussed further in Chapter 53, "Datasets and Data Binding" in the online archive.

ADDING AND POSITIONING CONTROLS

You can add two types of controls to a Windows Form: graphical components that actually reside on the form, and components that do not have a specific visual interface displaying on the form.

You can add graphical controls to your form in one of two ways. The first method is to locate the control you want to add in the Toolbox and double-click its entry. Visual Studio 2017 places it in a default location on the form — the first control will be placed adjacent to the top and left borders of the form, with subsequent controls placed down and to the right.

> **NOTE** *If the Toolbox is closed when you end your Visual Studio session, it won't be automatically displayed next time the Windows Forms designer is opened. You can display it again by selecting View ⇨ Toolbox from the menu.*

The second method is to click and drag the entry in the Toolbox onto the form. As you drag the control over available space on the form, the mouse cursor changes to show you where the control will be positioned. This enables you to directly position the control where you want it, rather than first adding it to the form and then moving it to the desired location. Either way, when the control is on the form, you can move it as many times as you like, so it doesn't matter how you get the control onto the form's design surface.

> **NOTE** *There is actually a third method to add controls to a form: Copy and paste a control or set of controls from another form. If you paste multiple controls at once, the relative positioning and layout of the controls to each other will be preserved. Any property settings will also be preserved; although the control names may be changed because they must be unique on each form.*

When you design your form layouts in SnapLines mode (see the previous section), a variety of guidelines display as you move controls around in the form layout. These guidelines are recommended best practice for positioning and sizing markers, so you can easily position controls in context to each other and the edge of the form.

Figure 13-6 shows a Button control being moved toward the top-left corner of the form. As it gets near the recommended position, the control snaps to the exact recommended distance from the top and left borders, and small blue guidelines display.

FIGURE 13-6

These guidelines work for both positioning and sizing a control, enabling you to snap to any of the four borders of the form — but they're just the tip of the SnapLines iceberg. When additional components are present on the form, many more guidelines begin to appear as you move a control around.

In Figure 13-7, you can see a second Button control being moved. The guideline on the left is the same as previously discussed, indicating the ideal distance from the left border of the form. However, now additional guidelines display. The blue vertical line on the left side of the control confirms that the control is aligned with the left side of the other Button control already on the form. The other vertical line indicates the ideal gap between two buttons.

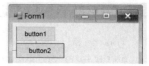

FIGURE 13-7

Vertically Aligning Text Controls

One problem with alignment of controls is that the vertical alignment of the text displayed within a TextBox is different compared to a Label. The problem is that the text within each control is at a different vertical distance from the top border of the control.

If you simply align these different controls according to their borders, the text contained within these controls would not be aligned.

As shown in Figure 13-8, an additional guideline is available when lining up controls that have text aspects to them. In this example, the Cell Phone label is lined up with the textbox containing the actual Cell Phone value. A line appears and snaps the control in place. You can still align the label to the top or bottom borders of the textbox by shifting it slightly and snapping it to their guidelines, but this guideline takes the often painful guesswork out of lining up text.

FIGURE 13-8

The other guidelines show how the label is horizontally aligned with the Label controls above it, and it is positioned the recommended distance from the textbox.

Automatic Positioning of Multiple Controls

Visual Studio 2017 gives you additional tools to automatically format the appearance of your controls after they are positioned approximately where you want them. The Format menu, as shown in Figure 13-9, is normally only accessible when you're in the Design view of a form. From here you can have the IDE automatically align, resize, and position groups of controls, as well as set the order of the controls in the event that they overlap each other. These commands are also available via the design toolbar and keyboard shortcuts.

The form displayed in Figure 13-9 contains several TextBox controls that originally had differing widths. In most situations, that looks messy and should be cleaned up by setting them all to the same width as the widest control. The Format menu provides you with the capability to automatically resize the controls to the same width, using the Make Same Size ➪ Width command.

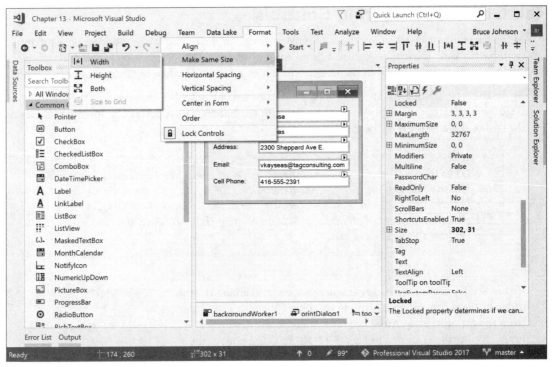

FIGURE 13-9

> **NOTE** *The commands in the Make Same Size menu use the first control selected as the template for the dimensions. You can first select the control to use as the template and then add other controls to the selection by holding down the Ctrl key and clicking them. Alternatively, when all controls are the same size, you can simply ensure they are still selected and resize the group at the same time with the mouse.*

You can perform automatic alignment of multiple controls in the same way. First, select the item whose border should be used as a base, and then select all the other elements that should be aligned with it. Next, select Format ⇨ Align, and choose which alignment should be performed. In this example, the Label controls have all been positioned with their right edges aligned. This could have been done using the guidelines, but often it's easier to use this mass alignment option.

Two other handy functions are the horizontal and vertical spacing commands. These automatically adjust the spacing between a set of controls according to the particular option you have selected.

Tab Order and Layering Controls

Many users find it faster to use the keyboard rather than the mouse when working with an application, particularly those that require a large amount of data entry. Therefore it is essential that the cursor moves from one field to the next in the expected manner when the user presses the Tab key.

By default, the tab order is the same as the order in which controls were added to the form. Beginning at zero, each control is given a value in the TabIndex property. The lower the TabIndex, the earlier the control is in the tab order.

> **NOTE** *If you set the* TabStop *property to False, the control will be skipped over when the Tab key is pressed, and there will be no way for a user to set its focus without using the mouse. Some controls can never be given the focus, such as a Label. These controls still have a* TabIndex *property; however, they are skipped when the Tab key is pressed.*

Visual Studio provides a handy feature to view and adjust the tab order of every control on a form. If you select View ➪ Tab Order from the menu, the TabIndex values display in the designer for each control, as shown in Figure 13-10. In this example the TabIndex values assigned to the controls are not in order, which would cause the focus to jump all over the form as the Tab key is pressed.

FIGURE 13-10

You can click each control to establish a new tab order. When you finish, press the Esc key to hide the tab order from the designer.

If more than one control on a form has the same TabIndex, the *z-order* is used to determine which control is next in the tab order. The z-order is the layering of controls on a form along the form's z-axis (depth) and is generally only relevant if controls must be layered on top of each other. The z-order of a control can be modified using the Bring to Front and Send to Back commands under the Format ➪ Order menu.

Locking Control Design

When you're happy with your form design, you will want to start applying changes to the various controls and their properties. However, in the process of selecting controls on the form, you may inadvertently move a control from its desired position, particularly if you're not using either of the snap layout methods or if you have many controls that are being aligned with each other.

Fortunately, Visual Studio 2017 provides a solution in the form of the Lock Controls command, available in the Format menu. When controls are locked, you can select them to change their properties, but you cannot use the mouse to move or resize them, or the form itself. The location of the controls can still be changed via the Properties grid.

Figure 13-11 shows how small padlock icons display on controls that are selected while the Lock Controls feature is active.

FIGURE 13-11

> **NOTE** *You can also lock controls on an individual basis by setting the* `Locked`
> *property of the control to True in the Properties window.*

Setting Control Properties

You set the properties on controls using the Properties window, just as you would for a form's settings. In addition to simple text value properties, Visual Studio 2017 has a number of property editor types, which aid you in setting the values efficiently by restricting them to a particular subset appropriate to the type of property.

Many advanced properties have a set of subordinate properties that can be individually accessed by expanding the entry in the Properties window. Figure 13-12 (left) displays the Properties window for a Label, with the `Font` property expanded to show the individual properties available.

Many properties also provide extended editors, as is the case for Font properties. In Figure 13-12 (right), the extended editor button in the `Font` property has been selected, causing the Font dialog to appear.

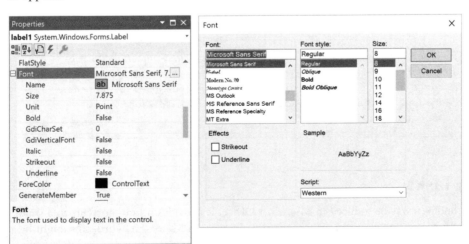

FIGURE 13-12

Some of these extended editors invoke full-blown wizards, such as the Data Connection property on some data-bound components, whereas others have custom-built inline property editors. An example of this is the `Dock` property, for which you can choose a visual representation of how you want the property docked to the containing component or form.

Service-Based Components

Two kinds of components can be added to a Windows Form — those with visual aspects to them and those without. Service-based components such as timers and dialogs, or extender controls such as tooltip and error provider components, can all be used to enhance your application.

Rather than place these components on the form, when you double-click one in the Toolbox, or drag and drop it onto the design surface, Visual Studio 2017 creates a tray area below the Design view of the form and puts the new instance of the component type there, as shown in Figure 13-13.

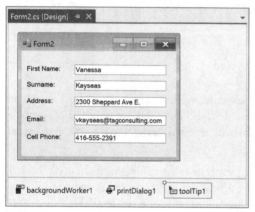

FIGURE 13-13

To edit the properties of one of these controls, locate its entry in the tray area and open the Properties window.

> **NOTE** *In the same way that you can create your own custom visual controls by inheriting from* `System.Windows.Forms.Control`, *you can create nonvisual service components by inheriting from* `System.ComponentModel.Component`. *In fact,* `System ComponentModel.Component` *is the base class for* `System .Windows.Forms.Control`.

Smart Tag Tasks

Smart tag technology was introduced in Microsoft Office. It provides inline shortcuts to a small selection of actions you can perform on a particular element. In Microsoft Word, this might be a word or phrase, and in Microsoft Excel it could be a spreadsheet cell. Visual Studio 2017 supports the concept of design-time smart tags for a number of the controls available to you as a developer.

Whenever a selected control has a smart tag available, a small right-pointing arrow displays on the top-right corner of the control. Clicking this smart tag indicator opens up a Tasks menu associated with that particular control.

Figure 13-14 shows the tasks for a newly added DataGridView control. The various actions that can be taken usually mirror properties available to you in the Properties window (such as the `Multiline` option for a TextBox control), but sometimes they provide quick access to more advanced settings for the component.

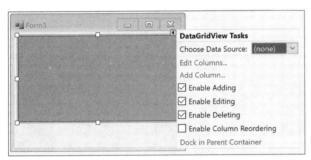

FIGURE 13-14

The Edit Columns and Add Column commands shown in Figure 13-14 are not listed in the DataGridView's Properties list, and the Data Source and Enable settings directly correlate to individual properties. (For example, Enable Adding is equivalent to the `AllowUserToAddRows` property.)

CONTAINER CONTROLS

Several controls, known as *container controls*, are designed specifically to help you with your form's layout and appearance. Rather than have their own appearance, they hold other controls within their bounds. When a container houses a set of controls, you no longer need to move the child controls individually, but instead just move the container. Using a combination of `Dock` and `Anchor` values, you can have whole sections of your form's layout automatically redesign themselves at run time in response to the resizing of the form and the container controls that hold them.

Panel and SplitContainer

The Panel control is used to group components that are associated with each other. When placed on a form, it can be sized and positioned anywhere within the form's design surface. Because it's a container control, clicking within its boundaries selects anything inside it. To move it, Visual Studio 2017 places a move icon at the top-left corner of the control. Clicking and dragging this icon enables you to reposition the Panel.

The SplitContainer control (as shown in Figure 13-15) automatically creates two Panel controls when added to a form (or another container control). It divides the space into two sections, each of which you can control individually. At run time, users can resize the two spaces by dragging the splitter bar that divides them. SplitContainers can be either vertical (refer to Figure 13-15) or horizontal, and they can be contained with other SplitContainer controls to form a complex layout that can then be easily customized by the end user without you needing to write any code.

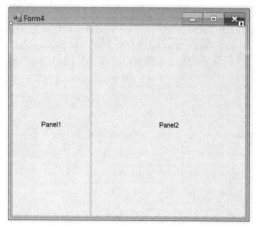

FIGURE 13-15

> **NOTE** *Sometimes it's hard to select the actual container control when it contains other components, such as in the case of the SplitContainer housing the two Panel controls. To gain direct access to the SplitContainer control, you can either locate it in the dropdown list in the Properties window, or right-click one of the Panel controls and choose the Select command that corresponds to the SplitContainer. This context menu contains a Select command for every container control in the hierarchy of containers, right up to the form.*

FlowLayoutPanel

The FlowLayoutPanel control enables you to create form designs with a behavior similar to web browsers. Rather than explicitly position each control within this particular container control, Visual Studio simply sets each component you add to the next available space. By default, the controls flow left to right, and then top to bottom, but you can use the FlowDirection property to reverse this order in any configuration depending on the requirements of your application.

Figure 13-16 displays the same form with six button controls housed within a FlowLayoutPanel container. The FlowLayoutPanel's Dock property was set to fill the entire form's design surface, so as the form is resized, the container is also automatically sized. As the form gets wider and there is available space, the controls begin to realign to flow left to right before descending down the form.

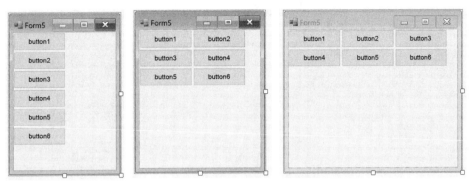

FIGURE 13-16

TableLayoutPanel

An alternative to the previously discussed container controls is the TableLayoutPanel container. This control works much like a table in Microsoft Word or in a typical web browser, with each cell acting as an individual container for a single control.

> **NOTE** *You cannot add multiple controls within a single cell directly. You can, however, place another container control, such as a Panel, within the cell, and then place the required components within that child container.*

Placing a control directly into a cell automatically positions the control in the top-left corner of the table cell. You can use the `Dock` property to override this behavior and position it as required. This property is discussed further in the section "Docking and Anchoring Controls."

The TableLayoutPanel container enables you to easily create a structured, formal layout in your form with advanced features, such as the capability to automatically grow by adding more rows as additional child controls are added.

Figure 13-17 shows a form with a TableLayoutPanel added to the design surface. The smart tag tasks were then opened and the Edit Rows and Columns command executed. As a result, the Column and Row Styles dialog displays, so you can adjust the individual formatting options for each column and row. The dialog displays several tips for designing table layouts in your forms, including spanning multiple rows and columns and how to align controls within a cell. You can change the way the cells are sized here as well as add or remove additional columns and rows.

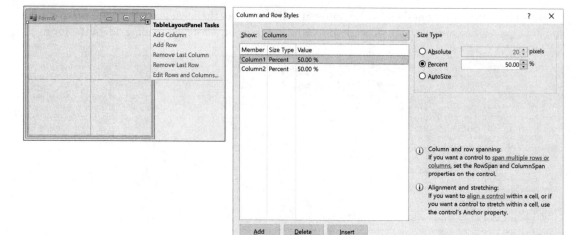

FIGURE 13-17

DOCKING AND ANCHORING CONTROLS

It's not enough to design layouts that are nicely aligned according to the design-time dimensions. At run time, a user will likely resize the form, and ideally the controls on your form will resize automatically to fill the modified space. The control properties that have the most impact on this are Dock and Anchor. Figure 13-18 shows how the controls on a Windows Form properly resize after you set the correct Dock and Anchor property values.

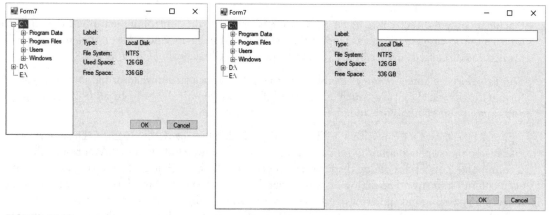

FIGURE 13-18

The Dock property controls which borders of the control are bound to the container. For example, in Figure 13-18 (left), the TreeView control Dock property has been set to Fill to fill the left panel of a SplitContainer, effectively docking it to all four borders. Therefore, no matter how large or small the left side of the SplitContainer is made, the TreeView control always resizes itself to fill the available space.

The Anchor property defines the edges of the container to which the control is bound. In Figure 13-18 (left), the two button controls have been anchored to the bottom-right of the form. When the form is resized, as shown in Figure 13-18 (right), the button controls maintain the same distance to the bottom-right of the form. Similarly, the TextBox control has been anchored to the top, left and right, which means that it can auto-grow or auto-shrink as the form is resized.

SUMMARY

In this chapter you received a good understanding of how Visual Studio can help you to quickly design the layout of Windows Forms applications. The various controls and their properties enable you to quickly and easily create complex layouts that can respond to user interaction in a large variety of ways. The techniques you learned in this chapter are user interface technology independent. So whether you are creating websites, WPF applications, Windows Store applications, Windows Phone apps, or Silverlight, the basics are the same as covered in this chapter.

14

Windows Presentation Foundation (WPF)

- ➤ Learning the basics of XAML
- ➤ Creating a WPF application
- ➤ Styling your WPF application
- ➤ Hosting WPF content in a Windows Forms project
- ➤ Hosting Windows Forms content in a WPF project
- ➤ Using the WPF Visualizer

WROX.COM CODE DOWNLOADS FOR THIS CHAPTER

The wrox.com code downloads for this chapter can be found at www.wrox.com by searching for this book's ISBN number (978-1-119-40458-3). The code and any related support files are located in their own folder for this chapter.

When starting a new Windows client application in Visual Studio, you have two major technologies to choose from — a standard Windows Forms–based application, or a Windows Presentation Foundation (WPF)–based application. Both are essentially a different API for managing the presentation layer for your application. WPF is extremely powerful and flexible, and was designed to overcome many of the shortcomings and limitations of Windows Forms. In many ways you could consider WPF a successor to Windows Forms. However, WPF's power and flexibility comes with a price in the form of a rather steep learning curve because it does things quite differently than Windows Forms.

This chapter guides you through the process to create a basic WPF application in Visual Studio 2017. It's beyond the scope of this book to cover the WPF framework in any great detail — it would take an entire book to do so. Instead, what you see is an overview of Visual Studio 2017's capabilities to help you rapidly build user interfaces using XAML.

WHAT IS WPF?

Windows Presentation Foundation is a presentation framework for Windows. But what makes WPF unique, and why should you consider using it over Windows Forms? Whereas Windows Forms uses the raster-based GDI/GDI+ as its rendering engine, WPF instead contains its own vector-based rendering engine, so it essentially isn't creating windows and controls in the standard Windows manner and look. WPF takes a radical departure from the way things are done in Windows Forms. In Windows Forms you generally define the user interface using the visual designer, and in doing so it automatically creates the code (in the language your project targets) in a .designer file to define that user interface — so essentially your user interface is defined and driven in C# or VB code. However, user interfaces in WPF are actually defined in an XML-based markup language called Extensible Application Markup Language (generally referred to as XAML, pronounced "zammel") specifically designed for this purpose by Microsoft. XAML is the underlying technology to WPF that gives it its power and flexibility, enabling the design of much richer user experiences and more unique user interfaces than was possible in Windows Forms. Regardless of which language your project targets, the XAML defining the user interface will be the same. Consequently, along with the capabilities of the user interface controls there are a number of supporting concepts on the code side of things, such as the introduction of dependency properties (properties that can accept an expression that must be resolved as their value — which is required in many binding scenarios to support XAML's advanced binding capabilities). However, you can find that the code-behind in a WPF application is much the same as a standard Windows Forms application — the XAML side of things is where you need to do most of your learning.

When developing WPF applications, you need to think differently than the way you think when developing Windows Forms applications. A core part of your thought processes should be to take full advantage of XAML's advanced binding capabilities, with the code-behind no longer acting as the controller for the user interface but serving it instead. Instead of the code "pushing" data into the user interface and telling it what to do, the user interface should ask the code what it should do, and request (that is, "pull") data from it. It's a subtle difference, but it greatly changes the way in which the presentation layer of your application will be defined. Think of it as having a user interface that is in charge. The code can (and should) act as a decision manager, but no longer provides the muscle.

There are also specific design patterns for how the code and the user interface elements interact, such as the popular Model-View-ViewModel (MVVM) pattern, which enables much better unit testing of the code serving the user interface and maintains a clean separation between the designer and developer elements of the project. This results in changing the way you write the code-behind, and ultimately changes the way you design your application. This clear separation supports the designer/developer workflow, enabling a designer to work in Expression Blend on the same part of the project as the developer (working in Visual Studio) without clashing.

By taking advantage of the flexibility of XAML, WPF enables you to design unique user interfaces and user experiences. At the heart of this is WPF's styling and templating functionality that separates the look of controls from their behavior. This enables you to alter the appearance of controls easily by simply defining an alternative "style" on that particular use without having to modify the control.

Ultimately, you could say that WPF uses a much better way of defining user interfaces than Windows Forms does, through its use of XAML to define user interfaces, along with a number of additional supporting concepts thrown in. The bad news is that the flexibility and power of XAML comes with a corresponding steep learning curve that takes some time to climb, even for the experienced developer. If you are a productive developer in Windows Forms, WPF will no doubt create considerable frustration for you while you get your head around its concepts, and it actually requires a change in your developer mindset to truly get a grasp on it and how things hold together. Many simple tasks will initially seem a whole lot harder than they should be, and would have been were you to implement the same functionality or feature in Windows Forms. However, if you can make it through this period, you will start to see the benefits and appreciate the possibilities that WPF and XAML provide. Because Silverlight shares a lot conceptually with WPF (both being XAML-based, with Silverlight not quite a subset of WPF, but close), by learning and understanding WPF you are also learning and understanding how to develop Silverlight applications.

GETTING STARTED WITH WPF

When you open the New Project dialog, you see WPF Application, and WPF Browser Application and a number of other built-in project templates that ship with Visual Studio 2017, as shown in Figure 14-1.

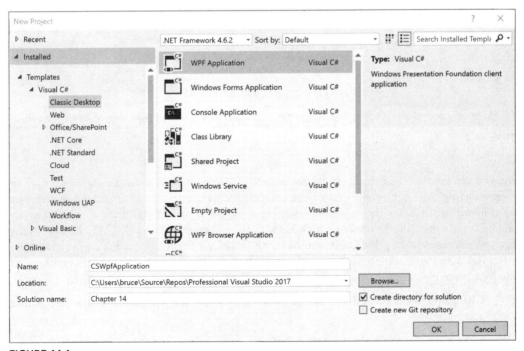

FIGURE 14-1

You can notice that these projects are for the most part a direct parallel to the Windows Forms equivalent. The exception is the WPF Browser Application, which generates an XBAP file that uses the browser as the container for your rich client application (in much the same way as Silverlight does, except an XBAP application targets the full .NET Framework, which must be installed on the client machine).

For this example you create a project using the WPF Application template, but most of the features of Visual Studio 2017 discussed herein apply equally to the other project types. The project structure generated should look similar to Figure 14-2.

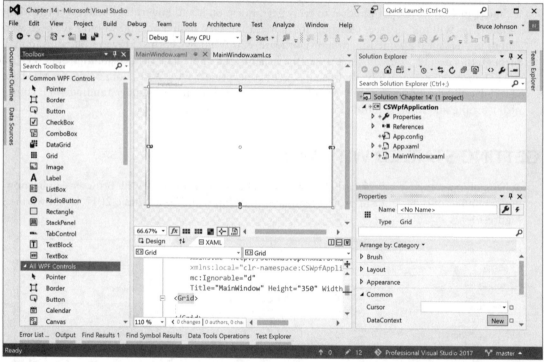

FIGURE 14-2

Here, you can see that the project structure consists of `App.xaml` and `MainWindow.xaml`, each with a corresponding code-behind file (`.cs` or `.vb`), which you can view if you expand out the relevant project items. At this stage the `App.xaml` contains an Application XAML element, which has a `StartupUri` attribute used to define which XAML file will be your initial XAML file to load (by default `MainWindow.xaml`). For those familiar with Windows Forms, this is the equivalent of the startup form. So if you were to change the name of `MainWindow.xaml` and its corresponding class to something more meaningful, you would need to make the following changes:

➤ Change the filename of the `.xaml` file. The code-behind file will automatically be renamed accordingly.

➤ Change the class name in the code-behind file, along with its constructor, and change the value of the `x:Class` attribute of the `Window` element in the `.xaml` file to reference the new name of the class (fully qualified with its namespace). Note that the last two steps are automatically performed if you change the class name in the code-behind file first and use the smart tag that appears after doing so to rename the object in all the locations that reference it.

➤ Finally, change the `StartupUri` attribute of the `Application` element in `App.xaml` to point toward the new name of the `.xaml` file (because it is your startup object).

As you can see, a few more changes need to be made when renaming a file in a WPF project than you would have to do in a standard Windows Forms project; however, it's reasonably straightforward when you know what you are doing. (And using the smart tag reduces the number of steps required.)

Working around the Visual Studio layout of Figure 14-2, you can see that the familiar Toolbox tool window attached to the left side of the screen has been populated with WPF controls that are similar to what you would be used to when building a Windows Forms application. On the right side of Figure 14-2 is the Properties tool window. You may note that it has a similar layout and behavior to the Windows Forms designer Properties tool window. However, this window in the WPF designer has additional features for editing WPF windows and controls. Finally, in the middle of the screen is the main editor/preview space, which is currently split to show both the visual layout of the window (above) and the XAML code that defines it (below).

XAML Fundamentals

If you have some familiarity working with XML (or to some extent HTML), you should find the syntax of XAML relatively straightforward because it is XML-based. XAML can have only a single root-level node, and elements are nested within each other to define the layout and content of the user interface. Every XAML element maps to a .NET class, and the attribute names map to properties/events on that class. Note that element and attribute names are case-sensitive.

Take a look at the default XAML file created for the `MainWindow` class:

```
<Window x:Class="CSWpfApplication.MainWindow"
    xmlns="http://schemas.microsoft.com/winfx/2006/xaml/presentation"
    xmlns:x="http://schemas.microsoft.com/winfx/2006/xaml"
    Title="MainWindow" Height="300" Width="300">
    <Grid>

    </Grid>
</Window>
```

Here you have `Window` as your root node and a `Grid` element within it. To make sense of it, think of it in terms of "your window contains a grid." The root node maps to its corresponding code-behind class via the `x:Class` attribute, and also contains some namespace prefix declarations (discussed shortly) and some attributes used to set the value of properties (`Title`, `Height`, and `Width`) of the `Window` class. The value of all attributes (regardless of type) should be enclosed within quotes.

Two namespace prefixes are defined on the root node, both declared using `xmlns` (the XML attribute used for declaring namespaces). You could consider XAML namespace prefix declarations to be somewhat like the `using`/`Imports` statements at the top of a class in C#/VB, but not quite. These declarations assign a unique prefix to the namespaces used within the XAML file, with the prefix used to qualify that namespace when referring to a class within it (that is, specify the location of the class). Prefixes reduce the verbosity of XAML by letting you use that prefix rather than including the whole namespace when referring to a class within it in your XAML file. The prefix is defined immediately following the colon after `xmlns`. The first definition actually doesn't specify a prefix because it defines your default namespace (the WPF namespace). However, the second namespace defines *x* as its prefix (the XAML namespace). Both definitions map to URIs rather than specific namespaces — these are consolidated namespaces (that is, they cover multiple namespaces) and hence reference the unique URI used to define that consolidation. However, you don't need to worry about this concept — leave these definitions as they are, and simply add your own definitions following them. When adding your own namespace definitions, they almost always begin with `clr-namespace` and reference a CLR namespace and the assembly that contains it, for example:

```
xmlns:wpf="clr-namespace:Microsoft.Windows.Controls;assembly=WPFToolkit"
```

Prefixes can be anything of your choosing, but it is best to make them short yet meaningful. Namespaces are generally defined on the root node in the XAML file. This is not necessary because a namespace prefix can be defined at any level in a XAML file, but it is generally a standard practice to keep them together on the root node for maintainability purposes.

If you want to refer to a control in the code-behind or by binding it to another control in the XAML file (such as `ElementName` binding) you need to give your control a name. Many controls implement the `Name` property for this purpose, but you may also find that controls are assigned a name using the `x:Name` attribute. This is defined in the XAML namespace (hence the `x:` prefix) and can be applied to any control. If the `Name` property is implemented (which it will be in most cases because it is defined on the base classes that most controls inherit from), it simply maps to this property anyway, and they serve the same purpose, for example:

```
<Button x:Name="OKButton" Content="OK" />
```

is the same as

```
<Button Name="OKButton" Content="OK" />
```

Either way is technically valid. After one of these properties is set, a field is generated (in the automatically generated code that you won't see) that you can use to refer to that control.

The WPF Controls

WPF contains a rich set of controls to use in your user interfaces, roughly comparable to the standard controls for Windows Forms. However, depending on which version of WPF you're using, you may have noticed a number of controls (such as the `Calendar`, `DatePicker`, `DataGrid`, and so on), which are included in the standard controls for Windows Forms but were not included in the standard controls for WPF. Instead, you had to turn to the free WPF Toolkit, available on NuGet, to obtain these controls. Use the Nuget Package Manager (described in Chapter 6, "Solutions, Projects, and Items"), and search for `WPF Toolkit` to install the controls into your project. This toolkit was developed by Microsoft (and enhanced over time) to help fill this gap in the original WPF release by providing some of the missing controls. The goal is to provide a reasonably complete set of controls out-of-the-box. Of course, you can still use third-party controls where the standard set doesn't suffice, but you have a reasonable base to work from.

Although the controls set for WPF are somewhat comparable to that of Windows Forms, their properties are quite different from their counterparts. For example, there is no longer a `Text` property on many controls; although you can find a `Content` property instead. The `Content` property is used to assign content to the control (hence its name). You can for the most part treat this as you would the `Text` property for a Windows Forms control and simply assign some text to this property to be rendered. However, the `Content` property can accept any WPF element, allowing almost limitless ability to customize the layout of a control without necessarily having to create your own custom control — a powerful feature for designing complex user interfaces. You may note that many controls don't have properties to accomplish what was straightforward in Windows Forms, and you may find this somewhat confusing. For example, there is no `Image` property on the WPF Button control to assign an image to a button as there is in Windows Forms. This may initially make you think WPF is limited in its capabilities, but you would be mistaken because this is where the `Content` property comes into its own. Because the `Content` property can have any WPF control assigned to it to define the content of its control, you can assign a `StackPanel` (discussed in the next section) containing both an `Image` control and a `TextBlock` control to achieve the same effect. Though this may initially appear to be more work than it would be to achieve the same outcome in Windows Forms, it does enable you to easily lay out the content of the button in whatever form you choose (rather than how the control chooses to implement the layout), and demonstrates the incredible flexibility of WPF and XAML. The XAML for the button in Figure 14-3 is as follows:

```
<Button HorizontalAlignment="Left" VerticalAlignment="Top" Width="100" Height="30">
    <Button.Content>
        <StackPanel Orientation="Horizontal">
            <Image Source="Resources/FloppyDisk.png" Width="16" Height="16" />
            <TextBlock Margin="5,0,0,0" Text="Save" VerticalAlignment="Center" />
        </StackPanel>
    </Button.Content>
</Button>
```

Other notable property name changes from Windows Forms include the `IsEnabled` property (which was simply `Enabled` in Windows Forms) and the `Visibility` property (which was `Visible` in Windows Forms). Like `IsEnabled`, you can notice that most Boolean properties are prefixed with `Is` (for example, `IsTabStop`, `IsHitTestVisible`, and so on), conforming to a standard naming scheme. The `Visibility` property, however, is no longer a boolean value — instead it is an enumeration that can have the value `Visible`, `Hidden`, or `Collapsed`.

FIGURE 14-3

The WPF Layout Controls

Windows Forms development used absolute placement for controls on its surface (that is, each control had its *x* and *y* coordinates explicitly set); although over time the `TableLayoutPanel` and `FlowLayoutPanel` controls were added, in which you could place controls to provide a more advanced means of laying out the controls on your form. However, the concepts around positioning controls in WPF are slightly different than how controls are positioned in Windows Forms. Along with controls that provide a specific function (for example, buttons, TextBoxes, and so on), WPF also has a number of controls used specifically for defining the layout of your user interface.

Layout controls are invisible controls that handle the positioning of controls upon their surface. In WPF there isn't a default surface for positioning controls as such — the surface you work with is determined by the layout controls further up the hierarchy, with a layout control generally used as the element directly below the root node of each XAML file to define the default layout method for that XAML file. The most important layout controls in WPF are the `Grid`, the `Canvas`, and the `StackPanel`, so this section takes a look at each of those. For example, in the default XAML file created for the `MainWindow` class provided earlier, the `Grid` element was the element directly below the `Window` root node, and thus would act as the default layout surface for that window. Of course, you could change this to any layout control to suit your requirements, and use additional layout controls within it if necessary to create additional surfaces that change the way their containing controls are positioned.

The next section looks at how to lay out your forms using the designer surface, but look at the XAML to use these controls first.

In WPF, if you want to place controls in your form using absolute coordinates (similar to the default in Windows Forms) you would use the `Canvas` control as a "surface" to place the controls on. Defining a `Canvas` control in XAML is straightforward:

```
<Canvas>

</Canvas>
```

To place a control (for example, a `TextBox` control) within this surface using given x and y coordinates (relative to the location of the top-left corner of the canvas) you need to introduce the concept of *attached properties* within XAML. The `TextBox` control doesn't actually have properties to define its location because its positioning within the layout control it is contained within is totally dependent on the type of control. So correspondingly, the properties that the `TextBox` control requires to specify its position within the layout control must come from the layout control itself. (Because it will be handling the positioning of the controls within it.) This is where attached properties come in. In a nutshell, attached properties are properties assigned a value on a control, but the property is actually defined on and belongs to another control higher up in the hierarchy. When using the property, the name of the property is qualified by the name of the control that the property is actually defined on, followed by a period, and then the name of the property on that control you are using (for example, `Canvas.Left`). By setting that value on another control that is hosted within it (such as your TextBox), the `Canvas` control is actually storing that value and will manage that TextBox's position using that value. For example, this is the XAML required to place the TextBox at coordinates 15, 10 using the `Left` and `Top` properties defined on the `Canvas` control:

```
<Canvas>
    <TextBox Text="Hello" Canvas.Left="15" Canvas.Top="10" />
</Canvas>
```

Although absolute placement is the default for controls in Windows Forms, best practice in WPF is to actually use the `Grid` control for laying out controls. The `Canvas` control should be used only sparsely and where necessary, because the `Grid` control is actually far more powerful for defining form layouts and is a better choice in most scenarios. One of the big benefits of the `Grid` control is that its contents can automatically resize when its own size is changed. So you can easily design a form that automatically sizes to fill all the area available to it — that is, the size and location of the controls within it are determined dynamically.

> **NOTE** *One of the controls available in the WPF Toolkit is a layout control called a* ViewBox. *When a* Canvas *element is placed inside a* ViewBox, *the positioning of the elements on the* Canvas *will be dynamically changed based on the size of the* ViewBox *container. This is a big deal for people who want absolute positioning but still want the benefit of dynamic positioning.*

The Grid control allows you to divide its area into regions (cells) into which you can place controls. These cells are created by defining a set of rows and columns on the grid, and are defined as values on the RowDefinitions and ColumnDefinitions properties on the grid. The intersections between rows and columns become the cells that you can place controls within.

To support defining rows and columns, you need to know how to define complex values in XAML. Up until now you have been assigning simple values to controls, which map to either .NET primitive data types, the name of an enumeration value, or have a type converter to convert the string value to its corresponding object. These simple properties had their values applied as attributes within the control definition element. However, complex values cannot be assigned this way because they map to objects (which require the value of multiple properties on the object to be assigned), and must be defined using *property element syntax* instead. Because the RowDefinitions and ColumnDefinitions properties of the Grid control are collections, they take complex values that need to be defined with property element syntax. For example, here is a grid that has two rows and three columns defined using property element syntax:

```
<Grid>
    <Grid.RowDefinitions>
        <RowDefinition />
        <RowDefinition />
    </Grid.RowDefinitions>
    <Grid.ColumnDefinitions>
        <ColumnDefinition Width="100" />
        <ColumnDefinition Width="150" />
        <ColumnDefinition />
    </Grid.ColumnDefinitions>
</Grid>
```

To set the RowDefinitions property using property element syntax, you need to create a child element of the Grid to define it. Qualifying it by adding Grid before the property name indicates that the property belongs to a control higher in the hierarchy (as with attached properties), and making the property an element in XAML indicates you are assigning a complex value to the specified property on the Grid control.

The RowDefinitions property accepts a collection of RowDefinitions, so you are instantiating a number of RowDefinition objects that are then populating that collection. Correspondingly, the ColumnDefinitions property is assigned a collection of ColumnDefinition objects. To demonstrate that `ColumnDefinition` (like `RowDefinition`) is actually an object, the `Width` property of the `ColumnDefinition` object has been set on the first two column definitions.

To place a control within a given cell, you again make use of attached properties, this time telling the container grid which column and row it should be placed in:

```
<CheckBox Grid.Column="0" Grid.Row="1" Content="A check box" IsChecked="True" />
```

The `StackPanel` is another important container control for laying out controls. It stacks the controls contained within it either horizontally or vertically (depending on the value of its `Orientation` property). For example, if you had two buttons defined within the same grid cell (without a `StackPanel`) the grid would position the second button directly over the first. However, if you put the buttons within a `StackPanel` control, it would control the position of the two buttons within the cell and lay them out next to one another.

```
<StackPanel Orientation="Horizontal">
    <Button Content="OK" Height="23" Width="75" />
    <Button Content="Cancel" Height="23" Width="75" Margin="10,0,0,0" />
</StackPanel>
```

THE WPF DESIGNER AND XAML EDITOR

The WPF designer is similar in layout to Windows Form's designer, but supports a number of unique features. To take a closer look at some of these, Figure 14-4 isolates this window, so you can see in more detail the various components.

First, you can notice that the window is split into a visual designer at the top and a code window at the bottom. If you prefer the other way around, you can simply click the up/down arrows between the Design and XAML tabs. In Figure 14-4 the second icon on the right side is highlighted to indicate that the screen is split horizontally. Selecting the icon to its left instead splits the screen vertically.

> **NOTE** *You will probably find that working in split mode is the best option when working with the WPF designer because you are likely to find yourself directly modifying the XAML regularly but want the ease of use of the designer for general tasks.*

If you prefer not to work in split-screen mode, you can double-click either the Design or XAML tab. This makes the relevant tab fill the entire editor window, as shown in Figure 14-5, and you can click the tabs to switch between each view. To return to split-screen mode, you just need to click the Expand Pane icon, which is the rightmost icon on the splitter bar.

```
<Window x:Class="CSWpfApplication.MainWindow"
        xmlns="http://schemas.microsoft.com/winfx/2006/xaml/presentation"
        xmlns:x="http://schemas.microsoft.com/winfx/2006/xaml"
        xmlns:d="http://schemas.microsoft.com/expression/blend/2008"
        xmlns:mc="http://schemas.openxmlformats.org/markup-compatibility/2006"
        xmlns:local="clr-namespace:CSWpfApplication"
        mc:Ignorable="d"
        Title="MainWindow" Height="350" Width="525">
    <Grid>
    </Grid>
</Window>
```

FIGURE 14-4

The only way to zoom in or out of the design surface is through a combo box at the bottom left of the designer. Along with having a number of fixed percentages, there is also the ability to fill all and fit the selection. The first zooms the designer out far enough so that all the controls are visible. The second zooms the designer in so that all the selected item is visible. This can be extremely handy when making small fiddly adjustments to the layout.

Working with the XAML Editor

Working with the XAML editor is somewhat similar to working with the HTML editor in Visual Studio. Writing XAML directly is quick and easy. One neat feature with the XAML editor is the ability to easily navigate to an event handler after it has been assigned to a control. Simply right-click the event handler assignment in XAML, and select the Go To Definition item from the pop-up menu, as shown in Figure 14-6.

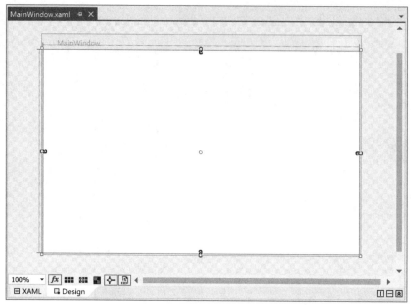

FIGURE 14-5

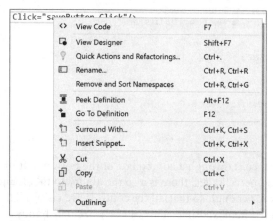

FIGURE 14-6

Working with the WPF Designer

Although it is important to familiarize yourself with writing XAML in the XAML editor, Visual Studio 2017 also has a good designer for WPF, comparable to the Windows Forms designer, and in some respects even better. This section takes a look at some of the features of the WPF designer.

Figure 14-7 shows some of the snap regions, guides, and glyphs added when you select, move, and resize a control.

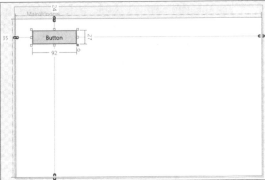

FIGURE 14-7

The left image in Figure 14-7 demonstrates the snap regions that appear when you move a control around the form (or resize it). These snap regions are similar to snap lines in the Windows Forms designer, and help you align controls to a standard margin within their container control, or easily align a control to other controls. Hold down ALT while you move a control if you don't want these snap regions to appear and your control to snap to them.

The right image in Figure 14-7 demonstrates the rulers that appear when you resize a control. This feature allows you to easily see the new dimensions of a control as you resize it to help you adjust it to a particular size.

The right image in Figure 14-7 also contains some anchor points (that is, the symbols that look like a chain link on the top and left of the button, and the "broken" chain link on the bottom and right of the button). These symbols indicate that the button has a margin applied to it, dictating the placement of the button within its grid cell. Currently, these symbols indicate that the button has a top and left margin applied, effectively "anchoring" its top and left sides to the top and left of the grid containing it. However, it is easy to swap the top anchor so that the button is anchored by its bottom edge, and swap the left anchor so that the button is anchored by its right edge instead. Simply click the top anchor symbol to have the button anchored by its bottom edge, and click the left anchor symbol to have the button anchored by its right edge. The anchor symbols swap positions, and you can simply click them again to return them back to their original anchor points. You can also anchor both sides (that is, left/right or top/bottom) of a control such that it stretches as the grid cell it is hosted within is resized. For example, if the left side of the TextBox is anchored to the grid cell, you can also anchor its right side by clicking the small circle to the right of the TextBox. To remove the anchor from just one side, click the anchor symbol on that side to remove it.

The most important control for laying out your form is the Grid control. Take a look at some of the special support that the WPF designer has for working with this control. By default your MainWindow.xaml file was created with a single grid element without any rows or columns defined. Before you commence adding elements, you might want to define some rows and columns, which can be used to control the layout of the controls within the form. To do this, start by selecting the grid by clicking in the blank area in the middle of the window, selecting the relevant node from the Document Outline tool window, or placing the cursor within the corresponding grid element in the XAML file itself (when in split view).

When the grid element is selected, a border appears around the top and left edges of the grid, highlighting both the actual area occupied by the grid and the relative sizing of each of the rows and columns, as shown in Figure 14-8. This figure currently shows a grid with two rows and two columns.

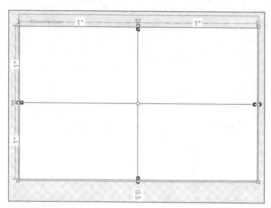

FIGURE 14-8

You can add additional rows or columns by simply clicking at a location within the border. When added, the row or column markers can be selected and dragged to get the correct sizing. You will notice when you are initially placing the markers that there is no information about the size of the new row/column displayed, which is unfortunate; however, these will appear after the marker has been created.

When you move the cursor over the size display for a row or column, a small indicator appears above or to the left of the label. In Figure 14-9, it's a lock symbol with a drop-down arrow. By selecting the drop-down, you can specify whether the row/column should be fixed (Pixel), a weighted proportion (Star), or determined by its contents (Auto). Alternatively, there is a drop-down menu that lets you specify this information, as well as performing some common grid operations.

> **NOTE** *Weighted proportion is a similar concept to specifying a percentage of the space available (compared to other columns). After fixed and auto-sized columns/rows have been allocated space, columns/rows with weighted proportions will divide up the remaining available space. This division will be equal, unless you prefix the asterisk with a numeric multiplier. For example, say you have a grid with a width of 1000 (pixels) and two columns. If both have * as their specified width, they each will have a width of 500 pixels. However, if one has a width of *, and the other has a width of 3*, then the 1000 pixels will divide into 250 pixel "chunks," with one chunk allocated to the first column (thus having a width of 250 pixels), and three chunks allocated to the second column (thus having a width of 750 pixels).*

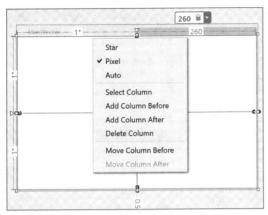

FIGURE 14-9

To delete a row or column, click the row or column, and drag it outside of the grid area. It will be removed, and the controls in the surrounding cells will be updated accordingly.

> **NOTE** *When you create a control by dragging and dropping it on a grid cell, remember to "dock" it to the left and top edges of the grid cell (by dragging it until it snaps into that position). Otherwise a margin will be defined on the control to position it within the grid cell, which is probably not the behavior you want.*

For developers the idea of Edit and Continue is that you can make changes to code while the application is being debugged and those changes will immediately be incorporated into the current execution. When that idea is applied to XAML, you have the ability to make changes to the XAML code for a page while the application is running and to have those changes immediately appear on the page.

When your application is running, a small toolbar, known as the Runtime Visual Tools, appears at the middle top, as shown in Figure 14-10.

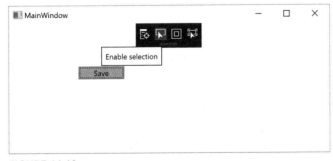

FIGURE 14-10

To modify a particular element, click on the Enable Selection icon (the second from the left) and then select to the element to be modified. At this point, changes you make to the XAML will be reflected in the application in real-time. If you want to find the element in question, you can click on the Go To Live Visual Tree icon (the left-most icon). That will open the Live Visual Tree window (Figure 14-11). From there, if you right-click on the element, you can select View Source to get to the actual XAML markup.

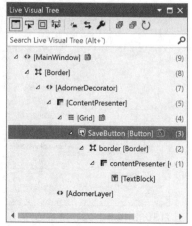

FIGURE 14-11

The Properties Tool Window

When you've placed a control on your form, you don't have to return to the XAML editor to set its property values and assign event handlers. Like Windows Forms, WPF has a Properties window; although there are quite a few differences in WPF's implementation, as shown in Figure 14-12.

The Properties tool window for Windows Forms development allows you to select a control to set the properties via a drop-down control selector above the properties/events list. However, this drop-down is missing in WPF's Properties window. Instead, you must select the control on the designer, via the Document Outline tool window, or by placing the cursor within the definition of a control in XAML view.

> **NOTE** *The Properties window can be used while working in both the XAML editor and the designer. However, if you want to use it from the XAML editor, the designer must have been loaded (you may need to switch to designer view and back if you have opened the file straight into the XAML editor), and if you have invalid XAML you may find you need to fix the errors first.*

The Name property for the control is not within the property list but has a dedicated TextBox above the property list. If the control doesn't already have a name, it assigns the value to its Name property (rather than x:Name). However, if the x:Name attribute is defined on the control element and you update its name from the Properties window, it continues to use and update that attribute.

Controls can have many properties or events, and navigating through the properties/events lists in Windows Forms to find the one you are after can be a chore. To make finding a specific property easier for developers, the WPF Properties window has a search function that dynamically filters the properties list based on what you type into the TextBox. Your search string doesn't need to be the start of the property/event name, but retains the property/event in the list if any part of its name contains the search string. Unfortunately, this search function doesn't support camel-case searching.

The property list in the WPF designer (like for Windows Forms) can be displayed in either a Category or alphabetical (Name) order. None of the properties that are objects (such as Margin) can be expanded to show/edit their properties (which they do for Windows Forms). However, if the list displays in the Category order, you can observe a unique feature of WPF's property window: category editors. For example, if you select a Button control and browse down to the Text category, you find that it has a special editor for the properties in the Text category to make setting these values a better experience, as shown in Figure 14-13.

FIGURE 14-12

FIGURE 14-13

You may have noticed that each property name has a small square to its right. This is a feature called *property markers*. A property marker indicates what the source for that property's value is. Placing your mouse cursor over a square shows a tooltip describing what it means. The icon changes based on where the value is to be sourced from. Figure 14-14 demonstrates some of these various icons, which are described here:

➤ A gray square indicates that the property has no value assigned to it and will use its default value.

➤ A black square indicates that the property has a local value assigned to it (that is, has been given a specific value).

➤ A yellow square indicates that the property has a data binding expression assigned to it. (Data binding is discussed later in the section "Data Binding Features.")

➤ A green square indicates that the property has a resource assigned to it.

➤ A purple square indicates that the property is inheriting its value from another control further up the hierarchy.

Clicking a property marker icon displays a pop-up menu providing some advanced options for assigning the value of that property, as shown in Figure 14-14.

The Create Data Binding option provides a pop-up editor to select various binding options to create a data binding expression for that value. WPF supports numerous binding options, and these and this window are described further in the next section.

The Custom Expression allows you to directly edit the binding expression that you would like to use for the property.

The Reset option is available if there is a specific value provided for a property through data binding, resource assignment, or local values. When Reset is clicked, all of the binding for this property is removed and the value reverts to its default.

The Convert to Local Value takes the current value of the property and assigns it in the control's attribute directly. It is not set up as a reusable resource, nor is the value changeable through any data. It is just a static value defined through an attribute.

The first two Resource options, Local Resource and System Resource, enable you to select a resource that you've created (or is defined by WPF) and assign it as the value of the selected property. Selecting one of the options causes the available choices to appear in a fly-away menu.

FIGURE 14-14

Resources are essentially reusable objects and values, similar in concept to constants in code. The resources are all the resources available to this property (that is, within scope and of the same type), grouped by their resource dictionary. Along with the menus, you can see the resources grouped at the bottom of the category. Figure 14-15 shows a resource of the same type as this property (RedBrushKey) that is defined within the current XAML file (under the Local grouping) along with the system-defined resources that meet the same criteria. (That is, they have the same type.) Because this is a property of type SolidColorBrush, the window displays all the color brush resources predefined in WPF for you to choose from.

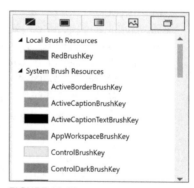

FIGURE 14-15

Returning to the other options in the menu shown in Figure 14-14, the Edit Resource option is used to edit a resource that has previously been assigned to the property's value. The dialog that gets displayed depends on the type of property. For instance, a brush property, such as the one in the example, will display a color picker dialog. Any values that are edited through this editor will affect any other property that is bound to the edited resource.

The Convert to New Resource option takes the value of the current property and turns it into a resource, with options to place the resource at one of a number of different levels. When selected, a dialog similar to the one shown in Figure 14-16 appears.

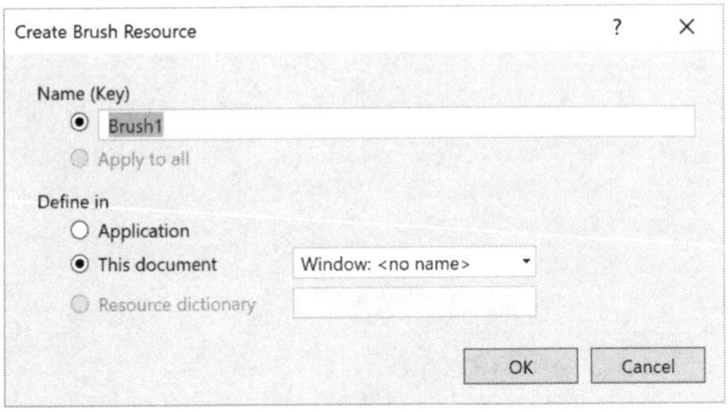

FIGURE 14-16

When a new resource is created, a XAML element is added to some part of the XAML file (or another XAML file). Along with specifying the name of the resource, you can also specify the level where it will be placed. At the bottom of Figure 14-16, you see radio buttons for Application, This Document, and Resource Dictionary. If Application is selected, the resource will be added to the `App.xaml` file. If you specify This Document, the resource will be created in the current XAML file. And if you select Resource Dictionary, the resource will be added to a separate XAML file created specifically to hold resources. Within this document, you can also select a more detailed level, starting from the top-level Window element down to the element whose property you are currently modifying. Regardless of where you put the resource, it can be reused in other places by referencing the unique key you give it.

When the resource has been created, the value of the property is automatically updated to use this resource. For example, using this option on the `Background` property of a control that has a value of `#FF8888B7` defines the following resource in `Window.Resources` with the name `BlueVioletBrushKey`:

```
<SolidColorBrush x:Key="BlueVioletBrushKey">#FF8888B7</SolidColorBrush>
```

The control will reference this resource as such:

```
Background="{StaticResource BlueVioletBrushKey}"
```

You can then apply this resource to other controls using the same means in XAML, or you can apply it by selecting the control and the property to apply it to, and using the Apply Resource option on the property marker menu described previously.

In the designer you can find that (as with Windows Forms) double-clicking a control automatically creates an event handler for that control's default event in the code-behind. You can also create event handlers for any of the control's events using the Properties window as you would in Windows

Forms. Clicking the lightning icon in the Properties window takes you to the Events view, as shown in Figure 14-17. This shows a list of events that the control can raise, and you can double-click the event to automatically create the appropriate event handler in the code-behind.

FIGURE 14-17

> **NOTE** *For VB.NET developers, double-clicking the Button control or creating the event via the Properties window wires up the event using the Handles syntax. Therefore, the event handler is not assigned to the event as an attribute. If you use this method to handle the event, you won't see the event handler defined in the XAML for the control, and thus you can't use the Go To Definition menu (from Figure 14-6) when in the XAML editor to navigate to it.*

Data Binding Features

Data binding is an important concept in WPF, and is one of its core strengths. Data binding syntax can be a bit confusing initially, but Visual Studio 2017 makes creating data bound forms easy in the designer. Visual Studio 2017 helps with data binding in two ways: with the Create Data Binding option on a property in the Properties tool window, and the drag-and-drop data binding support from the Data Sources window. This section looks at these two options in turn.

In WPF you can bind to objects (which also include datasets, ADO.NET Entity Framework entities, and so on), resources, and even properties on other controls. So there are rich binding capabilities in WPF, and you can bind a property to almost anything you want. Hand-coding these complex binding expressions in XAML can be quite daunting, but the Data Binding editor enables you to build these expressions via a point-and-click interface.

To bind a property on a control, first select the control in the designer, and find the property you want to bind in the Properties window. Click the property marker icon, and select the Create Data Binding option. Figure 14-18 shows the window that appears.

FIGURE 14-18

This window contains a number of options that help you create a binding: Binding Type, Data Source, Converter, and More Settings.

Generally the first step is to define the Binding Type. This is a drop-down list that allows you to specify the type of binding that you want to create. The choices are as follows:

➤ **Data Context:** Uses the current data context for the element

➤ **Data Source:** Allows you use an existing data source in your project

➤ **Element Name:** Uses a property on an element elsewhere in your XAML

➤ **Relative Source – Find Ancestor:** Navigates up the hierarchy of XAML elements looking for a specific element

➤ **Relative Source – Previous data:** In a list or items controls, references the data context used by the previous element in the list

➤ **Relative Source – Self:** Uses a property on the current element

➤ **Relative Source – Templated Parent:** Uses a property defined on the template for the element

➤ **Static Resource:** Uses a statically defined resource in the XAML file

Depending on the option selected in the Binding Type, the area immediately below the combo box changes. For example, if you select Data Context, you will be presented with a list of the properties visible on the data context for the element. If you select Element Name, you see a list of the elements that are in your current XAML page (as shown in Figure 14-19). The details about what these and the other binding types do are specific to XAML and therefore not within the scope of the book. But ultimately, the purpose of the binding type and the other controls is to allow you to specify not only the type of binding to use but also the path to the data.

FIGURE 14-19

The Converter section is where any value converter can be specified. The *value converter* is a class (one that implements the IValueConverter interface) that converts data as it moves back and forth from the data source and the bound property.

Finally, there is the More Settings option. These settings allow you to configure properties related to the binding that are not directly related to where the property value is coming from. Figure 14-20 illustrates these configuration settings.

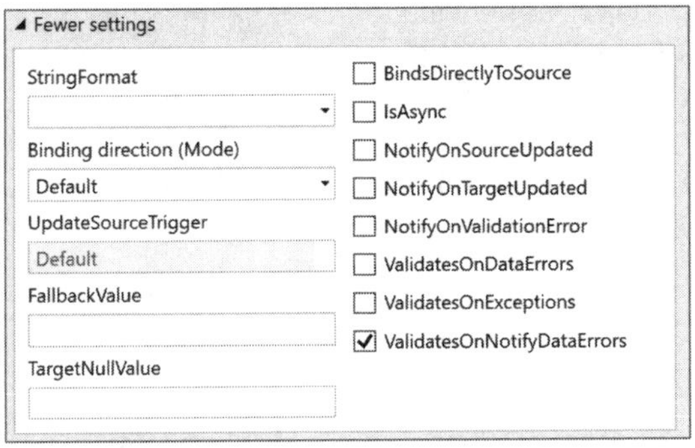

▲ Fewer settings

StringFormat

☐ BindsDirectlyToSource

☐ IsAsync

Binding direction (Mode)

Default

☐ NotifyOnSourceUpdated

☐ NotifyOnTargetUpdated

UpdateSourceTrigger

Default

☐ NotifyOnValidationError

☐ ValidatesOnDataErrors

FallbackValue

☐ ValidatesOnExceptions

☑ ValidatesOnNotifyDataErrors

TargetNullValue

FIGURE 14-20

As you can see, this binding expression builder makes creating the binding expression much easier, without requiring you to learn the data binding syntax. This is a good way to learn the data binding syntax because you can then see the expression produced in the XAML.

Now you will look at the drag-and-drop data binding features of Visual Studio 2017. The first step is to create something to bind to. This can be an object, a dataset, or an ADO.NET Entity Framework entity, among many other binding targets. For this example, you create an object to bind to. Create a new class in your project called `ContactViewModel`, and create a number of properties on it such as `FirstName`, `LastName`, `Company`, `Phone`, `Fax`, `Mobile`, and `Email` (all strings).

> **NOTE** *The name of your object is called* `ContactViewModel` *because it is acting as your* `ViewModel` *object, which pertains to the Model-View-ViewModel (MVVM) design pattern mentioned earlier. This design pattern will not be fully fleshed out in this example, however, to reduce its complexity and save potential confusion.*

Now compile your project. (This is important or otherwise the class won't appear in the next step.) Return to the designer of your form, and select Add New Data Source from the Data Sources window (available through the View ➪ Other Windows menu item). Select Object as your data source type, click Next, and select the `ContactViewModel` class from the tree. (You need to expand the nodes to find it within the namespace hierarchy.) Click the Finish button, and the Data Sources tool window appears with the `ContactViewModel` object listed and its properties below, as shown in Figure 14-21.

FIGURE 14-21

Now you are set to drag and drop either the whole object or individual properties onto the form, which creates one or more controls to display its data. By default a DataGrid control is created to display the data, but if you select the ContactViewModel item, it shows a button that, when clicked, displays a drop-down menu (as shown in Figure 14-22) allowing you to select between DataGrid, List, and Details.

➤ The DataGrid option creates a DataGrid control, which has a column for each property of the object.

➤ The List option creates a List control with a data template containing fields for each of the properties.

FIGURE 14-22

➤ The Details option creates a Grid control with two columns: one for labels and one for fields. A row will be created for each property on the object, with a Label control displaying the field name (with spaces intelligently inserted before capital letters) in the first column, and a field (whose type depends on the data type of the property) in the second column.

A resource is created in the Resources property of the window, which points to the ContactViewModel object that can then be used as the data context or items source of the controls binding to the object. This can be deleted at a later stage if you want to set the data source from the code-behind. The controls also have the required data binding expressions assigned. The type of controls created on the form to display the data depend on your selection on the ContactViewModel item.

The type of control created for each property has a default based upon the data type of the property, but like the ContactViewModel item, you can select the property to show a button that, when clicked, displays a drop-down menu allowing you to select a different control type (as shown in Figure 14-23). If the type of control isn't in the list (such as if you want to use a third-party control), you can use the Customize option to add it to the list for the corresponding data type. If you don't want a field created for that property, select None from the menu.

FIGURE 14-23

For this example, you create a details form, so select Details on the ContactViewModel item in the Data Sources window. You can change the control generated for each property if you want, but for now leave each as a TextBox and have each property generated in the details form. Now select the ContactViewModel item from the Data Sources window, and drop it onto your form. A grid will be created along with a field for each property, as shown in Figure 14-24.

Unfortunately, there is no way in the Data Sources window to define the order of the fields in the form, so you need to reorder the controls in the grid manually (either via the designer or by modifying the XAML directly).

When you look at the XAML generated, you see that this drag-and-drop data binding feature can save you a lot of work and make the process of generating forms a lot faster and easier.

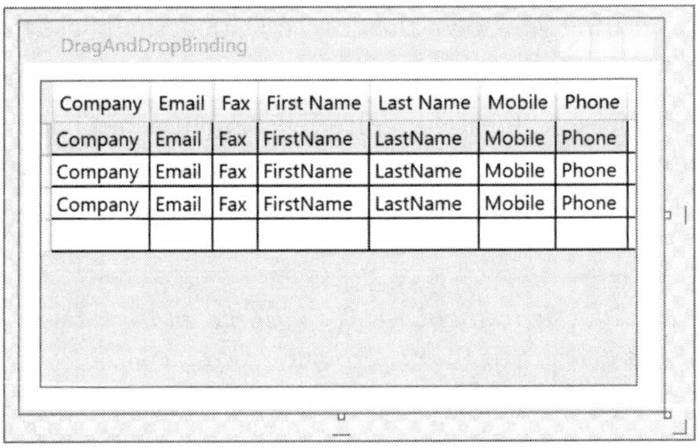

FIGURE 14-24

> **NOTE** *If you write user/custom controls that expose properties that may be assigned a data binding expression, you need to make these dependency properties. Dependency properties are a special WPF/Silverlight concept whose values can accept an expression that needs to be resolved (such as data binding expression). Dependency properties need to be defined differently than standard properties. The discussion of these is beyond the scope of this chapter, but essentially only properties that have been defined as dependency properties can be assigned a data binding expression.*

STYLING YOUR APPLICATION

Up until now, your application has looked plain — it couldn't be considered much plainer if you had designed it in Windows Forms. The great thing about WPF, however, is that the visual appearance of the controls is easy to modify, allowing you to completely change the way they look. You can store commonly used changes to specific controls as *styles* (a collection of property values for a control stored as a resource that can be defined once and applied to multiple controls), or you can completely redefine the XAML for a control by creating a *control template* for it. These resources can be defined in the Resources property of any control in your layout along with a key, which can then be used by any controls further down the hierarchy that refer to it by that key. For example, if you want to define a resource available for use by any control within your MainWindow XAML file, you can define it in Window.Resources. Or if you want to use it throughout the entire application, you can define it in the Application.Resources property on the Application element in App.xaml.

Taking it one step further, you can define multiple control templates/styles in a resource dictionary and use this as a *theme*. This theme could be applied across your application to automatically style the controls in your user interface and provide a unique and consistent look for your application.

This is what this section looks at. Rather than creating your own themes, you can actually use the themes available from the WPF Themes project on CodePlex: `http://wpfthemes.codeplex.com`.

These themes were initially designed (most by Microsoft) for use in Silverlight applications but have been converted (where it was necessary) so they can be used in WPF applications. Use one of these themes to create a completely different look for your application.

> **NOTE** *If you want to convert your own Silverlight theme to WPF, some additional information can be found at* `https://geonet.esri.com/thread/12098`.

Start by creating a new application and adding some different controls on the form, as shown in Figure 14-25.

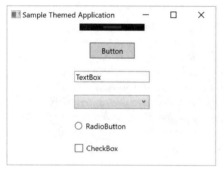

FIGURE 14-25

As you can see this looks fairly bland, so try applying a theme and seeing how you can easily change its look completely. When you download the WPF Themes project, you see that it contains a solution with two projects: one providing the themes and a demonstration project that uses them. You can use the themes slightly differently, however. Run the sample application and find a theme that you like. For the purposes of demonstration, choose the Shiny Blue theme. In the `WPF.Themes` project under the `ShinyBlue` folder, find a `Theme.xaml` file. Copy this into the root of your own project (making sure to include it in your project in Visual Studio).

Open up `App.xaml` and add the following XAML code to `Application.Resources`. You might already see it there, having been added when you included the `Theme.xaml` file in your project.

```
<ResourceDictionary>
    <ResourceDictionary.MergedDictionaries>
        <ResourceDictionary Source="Theme.xaml" />
    </ResourceDictionary.MergedDictionaries>
</ResourceDictionary>
```

This XAML code simply merges the resources from the theme file into your application resources, which applies the resources application-wide and overrides the default styling of the controls in your project with the corresponding ones defined in the theme file.

One last change to make is to set the background style for your windows to use the style from the theme file (because this isn't automatically assigned). In your `Window` element add the following attribute:

```
Background="{StaticResource WindowBackgroundBrush}"
```

Now run your project, and you can find the controls in your form look completely different, as shown in Figure 14-26.

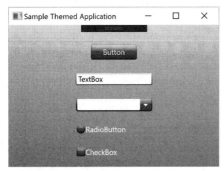

FIGURE 14-26

To change the theme to a different one, you can simply replace the `Theme.xaml` file with another one from the `WPF.Themes` project and recompile your project.

> **NOTE** *If you plan to extensively modify the styles and control templates for your application, you may find it much easier to do so in Blend for Visual Studio — a tool specifically designed for graphics designers who work with XAML. Blend for Visual Studio is much better suited to designing graphics and animations in XAML and provides a much better designer for doing so than Visual Studio (which is focused more toward developers). Blend for Visual Studio can open up Visual Studio solutions and can also view/edit code and compile projects, although it is best suited to design-related tasks. This integration of Visual Studio and Blend helps to support the designer/developer workflow. Both of these tools can have the same solution/project open at the same time (even on the same machine), enabling you to quickly switch between them when necessary. If a file is open in one when you save a change to a file in the other, a notification dialog appears asking if you want to reload the file.*

WINDOWS FORMS INTEROPERABILITY

Up until now you have seen how you can build a WPF application; however, the likelihood is that you already have a significant code base in Windows Forms and are unlikely to immediately migrate it all to WPF. You may have a significant investment in that code base and not want to rewrite it all for technology's sake. To ease this migration path, Microsoft has enabled WPF and Windows Forms to work together within the same application. Bidirectional interoperability is supported by both WPF and Windows Forms applications, with WPF controls hosted in a Windows Forms application, and Windows Forms controls hosted in a WPF application. This section looks at how to implement each of these scenarios.

Hosting a WPF Control in Windows Forms

To begin with, create a new project in your solution to create the WPF control in. This control (for the purpose of demonstration) is a simple username and password entry control. From the Add New Project dialog (see Figure 14-27), select the WPF User Control Library project template. This already includes the XAML and code-behind files necessary for a WPF user control. If you examine the XAML of the control, you can see that it is essentially the same as the original XAML for the window you started with at the beginning of the chapter except that the root XAML element is `UserControl` instead of `Window`.

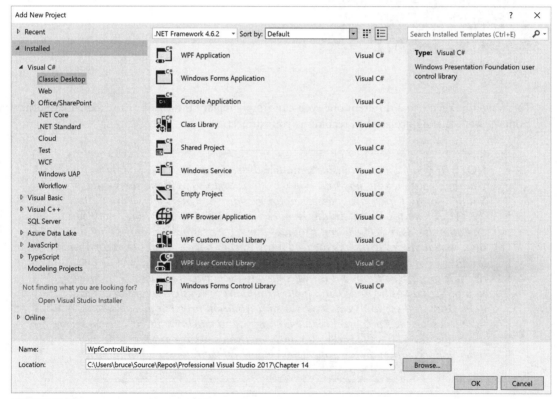

FIGURE 14-27

Rename the control to `UserLoginControl`, and add a grid, two text blocks, and two TextBoxes (actually, one TextBox and one PasswordBox) to it, as demonstrated in Figure 14-28.

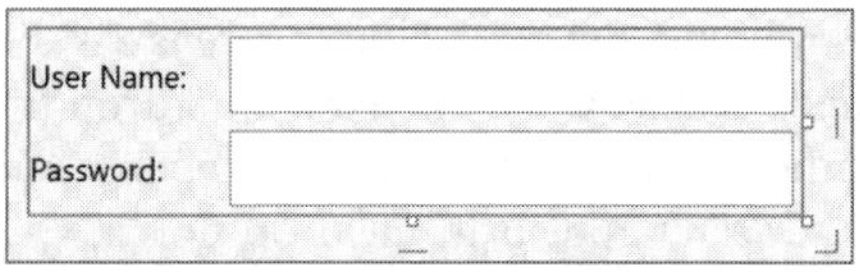

FIGURE 14-28

In the code-behind add some simple properties to expose the contents of the TextBoxes publicly (getters and setters):

VB

```
Public Property UserName As String
    Get
        Return txtUserName.Text
    End Get
    Set(ByVal value As String)
        txtUserName.Text = value
    End Set
End Property

Public Property Password As String
    Get
        Return txtPassword.Password
    End Get
    Set(ByVal value As String)
        txtPassword.Password = value
    End Set
End Property
```

C#

```
public string Username
{
    get { return txtUserName.Text; }
    set { txtUserName.Text = value; }
}

public string Password
{
    get { return txtPassword.Password; }
    set { txtPassword.Password = value; }
}
```

Now that you have your WPF control, build the project and create a new Windows Forms project to host it in. Create the project and add a reference to your WPF project that contains the control (using the Add Reference menu item when right-clicking the References in the project).

Open the form that will host the WPF control in the designer. Because the WPF control library you built is in the same solution, your `UserLoginControl` control appears in the Toolbox and can simply be dragged and dropped onto the form to be used. This automatically adds an `ElementHost` control (which can host WPF controls) and references the control as its content.

However, if you need to do this manually, the process is as follows. In the Toolbox there is a WPF Interoperability tab, under which there is a single item called the ElementHost. Drag and drop this onto the form, as shown in Figure 14-29, and you see that there is a smart tag that prompts you to select the WPF control that you want to host. If the control doesn't appear in the drop-down, you may need to build your solution.

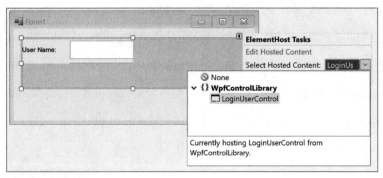

FIGURE 14-29

The control loads into the ElementHost control and is automatically given a name to refer to it in code (which you can change via the `HostedContentName` property).

Hosting a Windows Forms Control in WPF

Now take a look at the opposite scenario — hosting a Windows Forms control in a WPF application. Create a new project using the Windows Forms Control Library project template called `WinFormsControlLibrary`. Change the name of the User Control item that is part of the template to `UserLoginControl`.

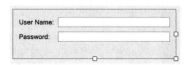

FIGURE 14-30

Open this item in the designer, and add two Labels and two TextBoxes to it, as demonstrated in Figure 14-30.

In the code-behind add some simple properties to expose the contents of the TextBoxes publicly (getters and setters):

VB

```vb
Public Property UserName As String
    Get
        Return txtUserName.Text
    End Get
    Set(ByVal value As String)
        txtUserName.Text = value
    End Set
End Property
```

```vb
Public Property Password As String
    Get
        Return txtPassword.Text
    End Get
    Set(ByVal value As String)
        txtPassword.Text = value
    End Set
End Property
```

C#

```csharp
public string Username
{
    get { return txtUserName.Text; }
    set { txtUserName.Text = value; }
}

public string Password
{
    get { return txtPassword.Text; }
    set { txtPassword.Text = value; }
}
```

Now that you have your Windows Forms control, build the project and create a new WPF project to host it in. Create the project and add a reference to your Windows Forms project that contains the control (using the Add Reference menu item when right-clicking the References in the project).

Open the form that will host the Windows Forms control in the designer. Select the WindowsFormsHost control from the Toolbox, and drag and drop it onto your form. Then modify the WindowsFormsHost element to host your control by setting the Child property to refer to the Windows Forms control, which when run renders the control, as shown in Figure 14-31.

FIGURE 14-31

DEBUGGING WITH THE WPF VISUALIZER

Identifying problems in your XAML/visual tree at run time can be difficult, but fortunately a feature called the WPF Visualizer is available in Visual Studio 2017 to help you debug your WPF application's visual tree. For example, an element may not be visible when it should be, may not appear where it should, or may not be styled correctly. The WPF Visualizer can help you track these sorts of problems by enabling you to view the visual tree, view the values of the properties for a selected element, and view where properties get their styling from.

To open the WPF Visualizer, you must first be in break mode. Using the Autos, Locals, or Watch tool window, find a variable that contains a reference to an element in the XAML document to debug. You can then click the little magnifying glass icon next to a WPF user interface element listed in the tool window to open the visualizer (as shown in Figure 14-32). Alternatively, you can place your mouse cursor over a variable that references a WPF user interface element (to display the DataTip popup) and click the magnifying glass icon there.

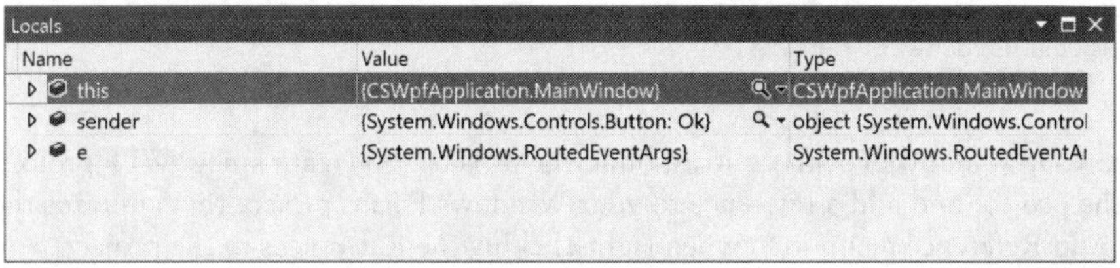

FIGURE 14-32

The WPF Visualizer is shown in Figure 14-33. On the left side of the window you can see the visual tree for the current XAML document and the rendering of the selected element in this tree below it. On the right side is a list of all the properties of the selected element in the tree, their current values, and other information associated with each property.

Because a visual tree can contain thousands of items, finding the one you are after by traversing the tree can be difficult. If you know the name or type of the element you are looking for, you can enter this into the search textbox above the tree and navigate through the matching entries using the Next and Prev buttons. You can also filter the property list by entering a part of the property name, value, style, or type that you are searching for.

If you want to edit the property of a XAML document while you are debugging the application, you have a couple of choices. First, as previously mentioned, Visual Studio 2017 supports XAML Edit and Continue functionality. So you can go straight into the XAML markup, make the changes, and have them reflected in the runtime immediately.

Alternately, Visual Studio 2017 includes a Live Property Editor. This window (shown in Figure 14-34) is available through the Debug menu. When you select a XAML element (using either the Runtime Tools or the Live Visual Tree), the current property values of the selected element appear in this window. While not all of the properties can be modified (such as properties that are bound to variables or defined in a resource dictionary), some of the more common ones can.

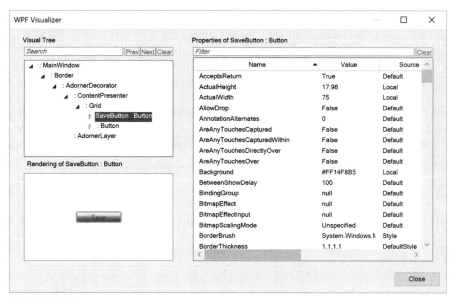

FIGURE 14-33

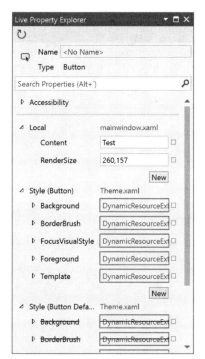

FIGURE 14-34

The result, for a XAML developer, is that the options available to help you tweak your user experience interactively have been greatly enhanced with Visual Studio 2017.

SUMMARY

In this chapter you have seen how you can work with Visual Studio 2017 to build applications with WPF. You've learned some of the most important concepts of XAML, how to use the unique features of the WPF designer, looked at styling an application, and used the interoperability capabilities between WPF and Windows Forms.

15

Universal Windows Platform Apps

WHAT'S IN THIS CHAPTER?

➤ The major characteristics and considerations of a Universal Windows Platform App

➤ Understanding the different Windows Universal templates

➤ The basic structure of a data-bound Universal Windows Platform App

➤ Utilizing platform contexts

WROX.COM CODE DOWNLOADS FOR THIS CHAPTER

The wrox.com code downloads for this chapter can be found at www.wrox.com by searching for this book's ISBN number (978-1-119-40458-3). The code and any related support files are located in their own folder for this chapter.

If you have been paying attention to the Windows development world in the last few years, you would be hard pressed to avoid the topic of Windows Universal Platform Apps. Except, of course, it hasn't always been called Windows Universal Platform Apps. Depending on the year, you might recognize it as Metro Apps. Or Windows Store Apps. Or Portable Class Libraries. The technology was similar and the packaging changed a little, but under the cover, all of these technologies shared the same purpose: to allow a developer to target different platforms using as large a shared code base as possible.

But what exactly is a Windows Universal Platform App? Or, to use the shorter term, a Windows App? And more important, what tools and techniques are available in Visual Studio 2017 to enable you to create a Windows App? In this chapter you'll learn the basic components of Windows Apps, as well as how to create them using Visual Studio 2017.

WHAT IS A WINDOWS APP?

Officially, a Windows App is an application built on the Universal Windows Platform (UWP). And UWP is the app platform for Windows 10. By itself, this doesn't sound overly impressive or different. However, what it really means is that using a single API set, a single app package, and a single store, you can deliver your application to all Windows 10 devices. This includes PCs, tablets, phones, Xbox, HoloLens, and more. The development goal is to write the application logic against a single API and use different screen sizes and interaction models (touch, mouse, keyboard, game controller, and so on) to handle the separate devices. Users get an experience that is consistent across all devices, while developers can minimize their code base and still deliver on a variety of devices.

Also on the developer side is the flexibility that UWP offers in terms of code platform. You are not forced to use C# and XAML. For example, you can choose JavaScript, Unity, or C++. All of these are supported and result in an application that will run on the different devices. Happiness abounds for all.

When you look at a Windows App, the first visual impression is one of consistency and elegance. The navigation paradigms are intuitive. The applications (see Figure 15-1) fill the entire window, providing an immersive experience for the user.

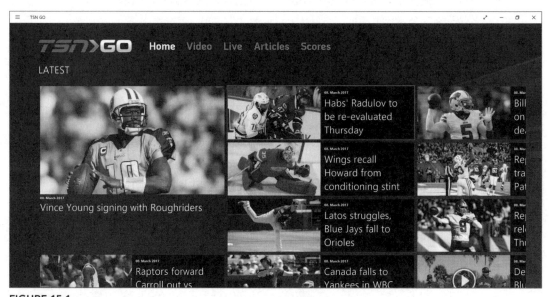

FIGURE 15-1

From a technology perspective, developers can create Windows Apps using languages with which they are already familiar. This includes C#, Visual Basic, JavaScript, and C++. But before getting into the technical side, look at the traits that make up a Windows App:

- Surfacing the content
- Snapping
- Scaling
- Semantic zoom
- Tiles
- Embracing the cloud

Content before Chrome

The purpose of your application is to surface content. It doesn't matter if that information is an RSS feed, pictures coming from your camera, or data retrieved from your corporate database; what the user cares about is the content. So when you design a Windows App, focus needs to be placed on surfacing the content.

One way to accomplish this is to use layout to improve readability. This typically involves leaving breathing space between the visual elements. Use typography to create the sense of hierarchy instead of the typical tree view commonly found in non–Windows Apps. In general, this is done by arranging the visual elements into a graduated series. It takes advantage of how the human mind organizes things. When you look at a screen, you generally notice the big and bold things first. As a result, the most important visual elements in your design should also be the biggest and boldest. You also mentally group elements together if they are visually segregated from other elements. So if you want to create a two-level hierarchy, you can create a number of large areas spaced to be obviously independent. Then within the large area, you can place smaller areas. And if you want, you can add more levels by embedding additional elements in the already existing areas.

Snap and Scale

A Windows App is designed to be used in a number of different configurations. The desktop or laptop configuration that you're used to is fine. But it is instructive to consider how your application can appear in other form factors. For example, Windows App could be available on a number of tablet devices, including the Surface. While running on a tablet, your application is going to be moved from landscape to portrait and back again. Although not every application needs to be this flexible (games, for example, are typically oriented in one direction), many can benefit from flowing between the different orientations.

Along with orientation, you also need to consider screen resolution. One of the benefits of Windows 10 is that the low end of screen resolution is 1024 × 768, and you have no more concerns about needing to support 800 × 640. However, there is still a decent range of resolutions that you need to consider: Two displays with the same resolution may not have the same pixel density (that is, pixels per square centimeters).

Even more important is how the user interface works at lower resolutions. Windows 10 is designed for touch. On low-resolution screens, you need to ensure that your touchable controls are still easily touchable — that is to say, not too small and not too close to other controls.

One further consideration is the Snap mode. In this mode, the Windows App is placed (snapped) to the left side of the display. While in this mode, the application still runs. (And the user can receive input, see messages, and so on.) However, in the rest of the screen, a separate application can run, which is conceptually not complicated, but your application must take advantage of this mode to participate well with the Windows 10 ecosystem.

Semantic Zoom

One of the common gestures in a touch interface is called the pinch. You use your thumb and forefinger to make a pinching motion on the screen to shrink the interface viewed. The opposite gesture (pushing your thumb and forefinger out) causes the interface to grow in size. Users of most smartphones are probably quite comfortable with the gesture and the expected outcome.

When your interface shows a large amount of data, even if it is pictorial, you can use this gesture to implement a semantic zoom. Conceptually, this is like a drill down into a report. Start at a high level of the information displayed. Then as you pinch, the more detailed view of the information displays. To be fair, it is not necessary that there be a more/less detailed relationship between the two views — only that there is a semantic relationship. Although more or less detail certainly fits into this category, so would a list of locations in a city and a map showing them as pushpins.

Tiles

Although it might seem trite, even in the world of applications, first impressions are important. And when you create a Windows App, the first impression that a user gets comes from your tile. Your tile is the doorway through which users access your app. Spend the time to make sure that it is nicely designed. As much as you can in the space allowed, make your tile attractive and lovable.

But beyond simple appearance, the tiles in Windows 10 are alive. When pinned to the main menu, your tile can provide information to users before they go through the front door. For some applications, this is critical. Would you want to open a weather application to see what the current temperature is? So think about the information that your application provides to your users, and decide if some of the more useful data can be put into a more immediately accessible location: your tile.

Embracing the Cloud

The cloud is significant because of the way users interact with both their applications and their data. Specifically, look at some of the demonstrations of the technology. One of the key selling points is the ubiquitous nature of the data. Start watching a video on Xbox, pause it, and then launch the video on your desktop. It remembers where you were when you paused and continues the video from that point. Create a document on your Surface tablet while on the commute home. Save the document, and then when you get home, launch your laptop, and your document is there, ready to be used. It even remembers where in the document you were.

All this functionality is made possible by using the cloud as your backing storage. Windows App interact well with Windows Azure. Make sure you take advantage of this as you consider the different storage modes and locations that your application might find useful.

CREATING A WINDOWS APP

It is a good idea to create your Windows App using a language with which you are already familiar. Fortunately, you can write Windows Apps in most .NET languages, including Visual Basic and C#. Also, Visual Studio provides the ability to create Windows Apps using HTML and JavaScript.

That last combination is aimed at making it easy for web developers to create Windows Apps. The form of JavaScript used is syntactically the same as regular JavaScript, but it uses the Windows Runtime (WinRT) libraries to perform its tasks. This requirement has the unfortunate side effect of making Windows Apps incompatible with browsers.

There are a number of requirements that must be met in order for you to create and test a Windows app. The easiest option is to be running your Visual Studio 2017 environment on Windows 10. This gives you access to the greatest number of options, including using the simulator that is described later in this chapter. If you are running on Windows 8.1, then in order to debug your Windows App, you'll need to deploy it to a remote machine running Windows 10 or be able to use an emulator (that is, run Client Hyper-V, the virtualization technology that was introduced in Windows 8). The simulator is not available in Windows 8.1.

To create your Windows App, start by creating a new project. Use the File ⇨ New ⇨ Project menu option to launch the New Project dialog. In the Installed Templates selection, under the language of your choice, you'll see a section named Windows Universal (see Figure 15-2).

There are several Windows App project templates available to you. The Class Library and Windows Runtime Component templates create assemblies used by Windows Apps. The Unit Test App and Coded UI Test Project templates create projects that can unit test Windows App libraries. The final template, Blank, provides a basic structure upon which you can build your Windows App. It consists of a single page with no predefined navigation.

As part of creating a Windows App, you need to specify the Windows 10 version that you want to target and the minimum version that you support. This information is collected in a dialog (see Figure 15-3) that appears once you have started to create the project.

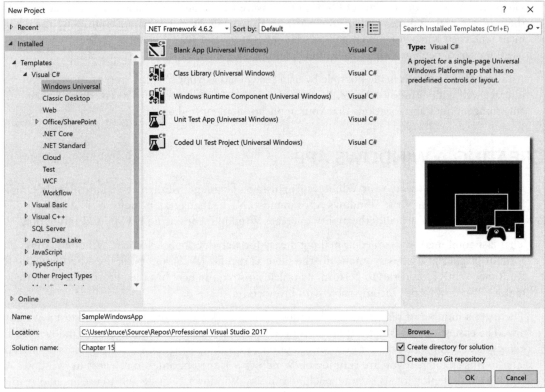

FIGURE 15-2

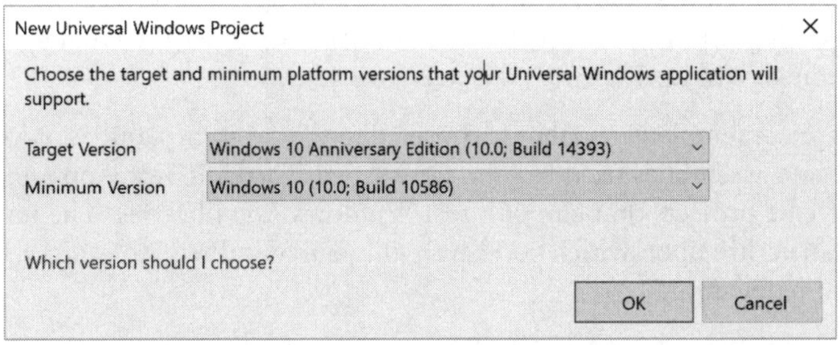

FIGURE 15-3

Once you have chosen the target and minimum version, the project can be created normally. As with most other project templates, a number of files are created, as shown in Figure 15-4.

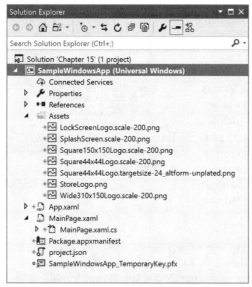

FIGURE 15-4

The starting point for the application is the MainPage. You can see this if you examine the code behind for the **App.xaml** file. The files included in the project template are:

➤ **App.xaml:** Contains the resources (or links to other resource dictionary files) used by the application. Here you can find fonts, brushes, control styles, control templates, and the application name.

➤ **MainPage.xaml:** Contains the initial page for the application.

➤ **Package.appxmanifest:** Defines the attributes of the application that will display in the marketplace.

➤ **appname_TemporaryKey.pfx:** The key pair used to provide hashing or encryption for your application.

And you might notice that in Figure 15-4 there is an Assets folder. If you examine the contents, you'll see images that are part of the application. By default, these images are used at various stages of the application running or when the application is published to the Windows Store.

But before running the application, a couple of options are available. You are probably familiar with the Run button that appears on the Visual Studio toolbar. The Windows Apps are no different; however, the options available to you do vary slightly.

The Windows Simulator

To the right of the Run button, there is a caption that reads Local Machine (see Figure 15-5). With this setting, if you run the Windows App, it is deployed onto the local machine. From a debugging perspective, this is just fine. All the Visual Studio debugging functionality is available for you to use in this mode. However, depending on the machine on which you work, using the local machine might not be sufficient. If you develop on a desktop or laptop, it might be difficult to rotate your screen 90 degrees to convert from landscape to portrait mode. It also might be challenging to perform a pinch-zoom maneuver using a mouse. To accommodate this situation, Visual Studio includes a Windows Simulator.

FIGURE 15-5

> **NOTE** *Along with using the Windows Simulator, you also have the ability to launch your application on a remote machine or a separate device. Visual Studio has the ability to handle debugging scenarios (like breakpoints and watches) in these situations. As well, if you need a different emulator, the Download New Emulators option takes you to a web page where you can choose from any of the provided emulators.*

When you start the simulator, it appears to load your operating system. And, just to be clear, the term "appears" is appropriate in the last sentence. It does not actually load up a clean or new version of Windows 10. Instead, the simulator establishes a remote desktop connection to your Windows 10 machine. As a result, you have access to your current operating system, complete with all the background services, defaults, and customizations that you have made. When the desktop is ready to be used, your Windows App is deployed onto the virtual machine, resulting in a screen similar to the one in Figure 15-6.

> **NOTE** *A word of warning regarding logging in to the remote desktop. In order to do so as part of starting up the simulator, you need to have logged into your Windows using a user ID and password combination. If you logged in using a PIN or Microsoft Hello (that is, facial recognition), you will see a message similar to Figure 15-7. What's worse, the suggested fix (locking your machine and logging in with a user ID and password) doesn't work, at least as of this writing. Instead, you need to restart your machine and log in using your user ID.*

FIGURE 15-6

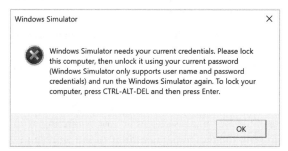

FIGURE 15-7

On the right side of the simulator, there are a number of icons. These icons enable you to act on the simulator as if it were a mobile device. Now consider some of the functionality provided through these icons, starting at the top.

The top icon on the right (the pushpin) is used to keep the simulator on top of the other windows on your computer. When pinned, the simulator will not be covered up by other applications you might have running. When unpinned, the simulator behaves like any other window. The remaining icons shown on the right side of the simulator (as shown in Figure 15-8) are described in the following sections.

Interaction Mode

The simulator provides for four different interaction modes. This is set with the first through fourth icons under the pushpin. The purpose of the interaction mode is to enable you to emulate different gestures with the use of a mouse.

The top icon (the arrow) sets the interaction mode to mouse mode. With mouse mode, your interactions with the simulator are what you would consider "typical." You click the mouse, and the click is picked up by the Windows App. The same applies to double-clicks and drags. However, when the interaction mode is set to one of the touch modes, the mouse is used to generate touch interactions. When you click on the finger pointer (the icon under the arrow), a mouse click is translated into a single touch.

FIGURE 15-8

Two-Finger Gestures

The other two touch modes (the two icons under the finger pointer icon) initiate two-finger gestures. The third icon is sets the interaction mode to pinch and zoom. This is used, as an example, when performing a semantic zoom from within your application. And as you might expect, this would be a difficult gesture to emulate using just a mouse.

However, if you click the pinch/zoom touch mode icon (the icon that looks like two diagonal arrows pointing to a dot between them), you can use the combination of mouse button and mouse wheel to perform the zoom. Start by clicking the left mouse button at the desired location. Then rotate the mouse button backward to zoom in and forward to zoom out.

Another touch gesture requiring two fingers is the rotate. Two fingers are placed on the surface and then moved in a circular motion. In the simulator, the icon that resembles an arrow circling around a dot is used to activate rotate mode. Using the mouse, the technique is similar to the pinch and zoom. Move the cursor over the desired location (the center point) and then use the mouse wheel to rotate left or right.

Device Characteristics

Another touch interaction that is difficult to emulate using a laptop is the orientation. If you try to spin your laptop around, it seems that the screen's orientation just won't change. But the simulator offers two icons to rotate the simulator. The icons are visually similar. (One is an arrow that circles in a clockwise direction, and the other is an arrow that circles in a counter-clockwise direction, as shown in the middle of Figure 15-8.) They rotate the simulator clockwise and counterclockwise by 90 degrees. Along with rotating the image of the application, it also rotates the simulator.

> **NOTE** *The simulator does not respect the* `AutoRotationPreferences` *property of a project. This property can be used to lock the application so that it displays only in a particular orientation (like landscape for certain games). However, if your project has that restriction, it cannot prevent the simulator from rotating and resizing the image. If you want to test out this functionality, you need to use an actual device.*

Along with orientation, the simulator enables you to change the resolution of the virtual device. The icon looks like a square (actually like a flat-screen desktop monitor), and when it is clicked you are presented with a list of valid screen sizes and resolutions. If you do change the resolution, it is only a simulated change. The coordinates of the points of interaction (like a touch) are converted to the coordinates that would be found if the device had the selected resolution.

Screenshots

There are two icons related to the capturing of screenshots from within the simulator. This functionality is useful because capturing images is part of the submission process to the Windows Store.

The Gear icon is used to change the settings for the screenshot. This includes whether the screenshot will be captured to both a clipboard and a file or just to the clipboard. As well, the location of the saved files can be specified.

After the settings have been set, you can capture a screenshot as required by clicking the icon (it looks like a small camera in Figure 15-8). This takes the current image from within the simulator and stores it in the clipboard and file. The resolution of the image is dependent on the resolution set for the simulator, so be aware that your image might not be as crisp and clear as you'd like, depending on the resolution that has been set.

Network Simulation

One of the more important limitations that a developer needs to take into consideration is how a Windows App works under different and changing networking conditions. By using the Network Simulation capabilities of the Simulator, it is possible to test your application under various networking constraints.

To set the state of the network, click on the Network Simulation icon. The dialog shown in Figure 15-9 appears.

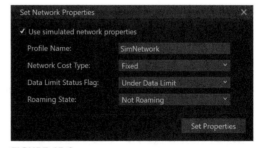

FIGURE 15-9

The options available in the dialog allow you to specify the network cost type (unknown, unlimited, fixed, or variable), the data limit status (under, approaching, or over the data limit), and the roaming state (roaming or not roaming). When you click on the Set Properties button, the NetworkStatusChanged event is raised and you can see what happens to your application.

The code you write to implement a Windows App is pretty much the same as the code you would write for any other type of project. The caveat is that, in projects that target a specific platform, you will write code specific to those platforms. And in the projects that are shared between different platforms, you will write code that is common across the platforms.

Keep in mind, however, that the delineation between platform-specific and shared code is not always so clean cut. It may be necessary for you to include some platform-specific considerations within your shared project. To accommodate that, there are a couple of conditional compilation constants that are available for use. By wrapping the platform-specific code in the appropriate compilation block (shown next), you can place the code into a common project that will only be active when it's built into the corresponding platform package.

```
public string SayHello()
{
    var greeting = "Hello from {0}!";

#if WINDOWS_APP
    greeting = string.Format(greeting, "Windows");
#endif

#if WINDOWS_PHONE_APP
    greeting = string.Format(greeting, "Windows Phone");
#endif

    return greeting;
}
```

WINDOWS RUNTIME COMPONENTS

One of the templates available when you create a Windows App is a Windows Runtime Component. This template is used to create a DLL that can export Windows Runtime (WinRT) types. The resulting assembly can be consumed by any Windows App, regardless of the language.

At first glance, it would seem that a Class Library and a Windows Runtime Component are the same thing, or close to it. So why use a Windows Runtime Component instead of a Class Library? As it turns out, the difference is relatively subtle and worth a bit more examination. While both projects produce a DLL, the Class Library is limited in terms of its potential audience of consumers. A Class Library DLL requires that the consuming project be .NET, which eliminates C++ and JavaScript projects as potential users of the functionality. The Windows Runtime Component doesn't have this limitation.

The Windows Runtime Component exports WinRT types that are consumable by any Windows App project, regardless of the target device. However, the requirement that the exposed types be WinRT-compliant restricts some use. For instance, WinRT types must be sealed and can only inherit from classes in the `Windows.UI.Xaml` namespace (classes like `Control` and `UserControl`). Public fields are not allowed, which can make using the component in an MVVM (Model-View-ViewModel) implementation difficult. For example, the following code does not compile in a Windows Runtime Component project:

```
public abstract class ObservableObject : INotifyPropertyChanged {
    public event PropertyChangedEventHandler PropertyChanged;

    protected void OnPropertyChanged([CallerMemberName] string name = null) {
        var pc = PropertyChanged;
        if (pc != null)
            pc(this, new PropertyChangedEventArgs(name));
    }
}
```

The compilation fails because abstract classes cannot be exported from a Windows Runtime Component. This is because of the restriction that published classes must be sealed. You can address this problem by removing the public keyword from the class declaration. However, when you do so, the class is no longer useable by any application that could benefit from the Windows Runtime Component library. And when you consider that the example is a typical one of a base class in an MVVM implementation, you can see where the limitations might become onerous. On the other hand, this code compiles with no problem in a Class Library project, and it can easily be used by any application that references the class library DLL.

> **NOTE** *The reference to a Model-View-ViewModel (MVVM) style application might seem slightly out of place in a discussion about Visual Studio and Universal Apps. After all, there is no requirement that an MVVM pattern be used when creating a Universal App. Although that's true, the use of the MVVM pattern is considered a best practice when it comes to applications that have XAML as the foundation for their visual appearance. So not being able to use a Windows Runtime Component library as the ViewModel is a limitation for many Universal App developers.*

.NET NATIVE COMPILATION

The compilers used in Visual Studio, whether Roslyn or the older version, generate intermediate language (IL). When the application runs, the just-in-time (JIT) compiler translates the IL to native code. This is how .NET has worked for years, and there are both positives and negatives to the approach. Included in the .NET Framework (both past and current) is a tool (NGEN) that can be used to precompile the IL for your application. This can help to decrease the start-up time for your application. (The JIT compiler does some work when a .NET application starts.)

.NET Native is also a precompilation technology, and in that regard it is similar to NGEN. However, the details make for a different user experience and might be enticing for developers of Windows Apps.

The biggest difference is the source that is used for the precompilation. NGEN uses the IL code generated by the .NET compilers. .NET Native compiles the source code (C# only, at the moment) directly to native code. As a result, you get the benefit of continuing to work with C# and take advantage of .NET (including class libraries, garbage collection, and exception handling). And you can produce applications that have the superior performance of native code. It's a win for all involved.

Part of the source for the improved performance comes from how the natively compiled application interacts with .NET. During the precompilation process, the parts of the .NET Framework used by the application are statically linked into the app. This allows the app to utilize app-local libraries of the .NET Framework. The output from the precompilation process is a single executable. There are no assemblies that need to be included in the deployment directory.

For the most part, the development of application for .NET Native is the same as for an application using JIT and NGEN. However, not every .NET application can be compiled using the .NET Native tools. Most of the differences relate to the ability to perform reflection (which is sometimes used in unexpected places, like serialization) and complete support for the dynamic keyword.

One of the things that .NET Native compilation does is to minimize the size of the resulting executable file. To accomplish this, classes and methods in the .NET Framework that are not invoked by the application are not included in the executable. All of that is fine and good until you try to reflect on a method that has been removed or use the dynamic keyword to access a method that is not accessed any other way. Fortunately, there is an option in the context menu for the project that performs a static analysis of the application to determine if it is capable of being compiled using .NET Native.

Compiling Using .NET Native Tools

The process of compiling your application into .NET Native is relatively straightforward. To begin with, develop your application normally. The .NET Native compilation doesn't take place until your application is ready to be deployed or published to the Windows Store.

Once your application is ready to go, you need to change two settings. First, you need to change the target CPU to a specific platform. You can do this through the Properties for the project or from the toolbar, as illustrated in Figure 15-10.

FIGURE 15-10

By default, projects are defined to target any CPU. To compile using .NET Native, you need to specify a particular CPU, whether it's ARM, x86, or x64.

Once the application is targeting a CPU, go to the Properties for the project, as shown in Figure 15-11.

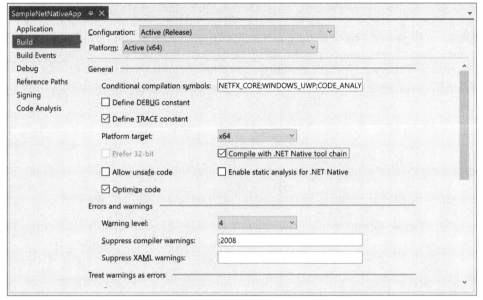

FIGURE 15-11

In the Build tab on the Properties page, there is a checkbox labeled Compile with the .NET Native tool chain. Ensure that the checkbox is checked. Once this is done, the next time you build the application, it will be compiled into .NET Native.

The resulting application produced by the .NET Native tool chain is written to a directory named `ilc.out` in the Debug or Release directory for your project. The files contained in the directory follow:

➤ **appName.exe:** A stub executable that does nothing but transfer control to a Main entry point in appName.dll

➤ **appName.dll:** A Windows DLL that contains your application code, any third-party libraries, and the code from the .NET Framework that your application uses

➤ **mrt100_app.dll:** A runtime that provides .NET services such as garbage collection

SUMMARY

The idea of creating an environment that makes it easier for developers to share functionality between different platforms has been gathering steam in Microsoft. Whether it's working toward an operating system kernel that is common across the different platforms or through Visual Studio functionality, there has been a significant push toward tooling support for all the Windows platforms (and even some non-Windows platforms).

In this chapter you learned how to create a Universal Windows App that takes advantage of this direction using Visual Studio 2017. To start, you covered the fundamental elements of style that make up a Windows App and looked at the components that make up the Universal Windows App project template. Then, you examined the simulator, considering how you can use it to test some aspects of Windows 10 that are typically confined to a tablet or phone form factor.

PART V
Web Applications

16

ASP.NET Web Forms

When Microsoft released the first version of ASP.NET, one of the most talked-about features was the capability to create a full-blown web application in the same way as you would create a Windows application. The abstractions provided by ASP.NET, coupled with the rich tooling support in Visual Studio, allowed programmers to quickly develop feature-rich applications that ran over the web in a wholly integrated way.

ASP.NET version 2.0, which was released in 2005, was a major upgrade that included new features such as a provider model for everything from menu navigation to user authentication, more than 50 new server controls, a web portal framework, and built-in website administration, to name but a few. These enhancements made it even easier to build complex web applications in less time.

The last few versions of ASP.NET and Visual Studio have focused on improving the client-side development experience. These include enhancements to the HTML Designer and CSS editing tools; better IntelliSense and debugging support for JavaScript, HTML, and JavaScript snippets; and new project templates.

In this chapter you'll learn how to create ASP.NET web applications in Visual Studio 2017, as well as look at many of the features and components that Microsoft has included to make your web development life a little (and in some cases a lot) easier.

WEB APPLICATION VERSUS WEB SITE PROJECTS

Microsoft provides two basic project types: the Web Site project type and the Web Application project type. The major differences between the two project types are fairly significant. The most fundamental change is that a Web Site project does not contain a Visual Studio project file (.csproj or .vbproj), whereas a Web Application project does. As a result, there is no central file that contains a list of all the files in a Web Site project. Instead, the Visual Studio solution file contains a reference to the root folder of the Web Site project, and the content and layout are directly inferred from its files and subfolders. If you copy a new file into a subfolder of a Web Site project using Windows Explorer, then that file, by definition, belongs to the project. In a Web Application project, you must explicitly add all files to the project from within Visual Studio.

The other major difference is in the way the projects are compiled. Web Application projects are compiled in much the same way as any other project under Visual Studio. The code is compiled into a single assembly that is stored in the \bin directory of the web application. As with all other Visual Studio projects, you can control the build through the property pages, name the output assembly, and add pre- and post-build action rules.

On the other hand, in a Web Site project all the classes that aren't code behind or user controls are compiled into one common assembly. Pages and user controls are then compiled dynamically as needed into a set of separate assemblies.

The big advantage of more granular assemblies is that the entire website does not need to be rebuilt every time a page is changed. Instead, only those assemblies that have changes (or have a down-level dependency) are recompiled, which can save a significant amount of time, depending on your preferred method of development.

Microsoft has pledged that it will continue to support both the Web Site and Web Application project types in all future versions of Visual Studio.

So which project type should you use? The official position from Microsoft is "it depends," which is certainly a pragmatic, although not particularly useful, position to take. All scenarios are different, and you should always carefully weigh each alternative in the context of your requirements and environment. However, the anecdotal evidence that has emerged from the .NET developer community over the past few years, and the experience of the authors, is that in most cases the Web Application project type is the best choice.

> **NOTE** *Unless you are developing a large web project with hundreds of pages, it is actually not too difficult to migrate from a Web Site project to a Web Application project and vice versa. So don't get too hung up on this decision. Pick one project type and migrate it later if you run into difficulties.*

CREATING WEB PROJECTS

Visual Studio 2017 gives you the ability to create ASP.NET Web Application and Web Site projects. There are a variety of templates and more functionality that you can access in doing so. This section explores what you need to know to be able to create both types of projects.

Creating a Web Site Project

As mentioned previously, creating a Web Site project in Visual Studio 2017 is slightly different from creating a regular Windows-type project. With normal Windows applications and services, you pick the type of project, name the solution, and click OK. Each language has its own set of project templates, and you have no real options when you create the project. Web Site project development is different because you can create the development project in different locations, from the local file-system to a variety of FTP and HTTP locations that are defined in your system setup, including the local Internet Information Services (IIS) server.

Because of this major difference in creating these projects, Microsoft has created separate commands and dialogs for Web Site project templates. Selecting New Web Site from the File ➪ New submenu displays the New Web Site dialog, where you can choose the type of project template you want to use (see Figure 16-1).

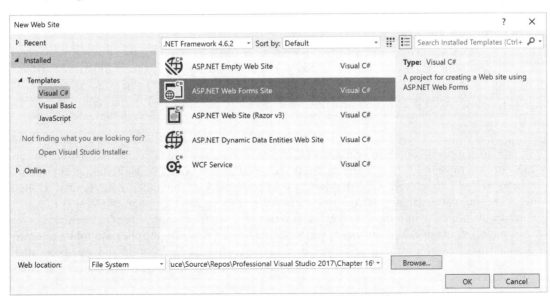

FIGURE 16-1

Most likely, you'll select the ASP.NET Web Forms Site project template. This creates a website populated with a starter web application that ensures that your initial application is structured in a logical manner. The template creates a project that demonstrates how to use a master page, menus, the account management controls, CSS, and the jQuery JavaScript library.

In addition to the ASP.NET Web Forms Site project template, there is an ASP.NET Empty Web Site project template that creates nothing more than an empty folder and a reference in a solution file. The remaining templates, which are for the most part variations on the Web Site template, are discussed later in this chapter. Regardless of which type of web project you're creating, the lower section of the dialog enables you to choose where to create the project.

By default, Visual Studio expects you to develop the website or service locally, using the normal filesystem. The default location is under the `Documents/Visual Studio 2017/WebSites` folder for the current user, but you can change this by overtyping the value, selecting an alternative location from the drop-down list, or clicking the Browse button. You can also create the web site on a UNC share, if that is your desire and you have the necessary permissions (such as read and write) on that share.

The Web Location drop-down list also contains HTTP and FTP as options. Selecting HTTP or FTP changes the value in the filename textbox to a blank `http://` or `ftp://` prefix ready for you to type in the destination URL. You can either type in a valid location or click the Browse button to change the intended location of the project.

The Choose Location dialog (shown in Figure 16-2) is shown when you click the Browse button and enables you to specify where the project should be stored. Note that this isn't necessarily where the project will be deployed because you can specify a different destination for that when you're ready to ship, so don't expect that you are specifying the ultimate destination here.

The File System option enables you to browse through the folder structure known to the system, including the My Network Places folders, and gives you the option to create subfolders where you need them. This is the easiest way to specify where you want the web project files, and the way that makes the files easiest to locate later.

> **NOTE** *Although you can specify where to create the project files, by default the solution file is created in a new folder under the* `Documents/Visual Studio 2017/Projects` *folder for the current user. You can move the solution file to a folder of your choice without affecting the projects.*

If you use a local IIS server to debug your Web Site project, you can select the File System option and browse to your `wwwroot` folder to create the website. However, a much better option is to use the local IIS location type and drill down to your preferred location under the Default Web Site folders. This interface enables you to browse virtual directory entries that point to websites that are not physically located within the `wwwroot` folder structure but are actually aliases to elsewhere in the filesystem or network. You can create your application in a new Web Application folder or create a new virtual directory entry in which you browse to the physical file location and specify an alias to appear in the website list. Also, there is a check box at the bottom of the list of servers and virtual directories labelled Use Secure Sockets Layer that, when checked, creates your web site on a server that supports HTTPS connections.

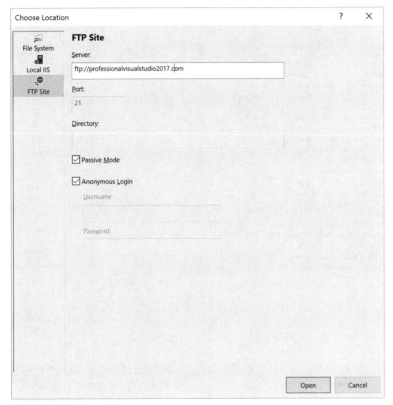

FIGURE 16-2

The FTP site location type (refer to Figure 16-2) gives you the option to log in to a remote FTP site anonymously or with a specified user. When you click Open, Visual Studio saves the FTP settings for when you create the project, so be aware that it won't test whether or not the settings are correct until it attempts to create the project files and send them to the specified destination.

> **NOTE** *You can save your project files to any FTP server to which you have access, even if that FTP site doesn't have .NET installed. However, you cannot run the files without .NET, so you can only use such a site as a file store.*

After you choose the intended location for your project, clicking OK tells Visual Studio 2017 to create the project files and store them in the desired location. After the web application has finished initializing, Visual Studio opens the Default.aspx page and populates the Toolbox with the components available to you for web development.

The Web Site project has only a small subset of the project configuration options available under the property pages of other project types, as shown in Figure 16-3. To access these options, right-click the project and select Property Pages.

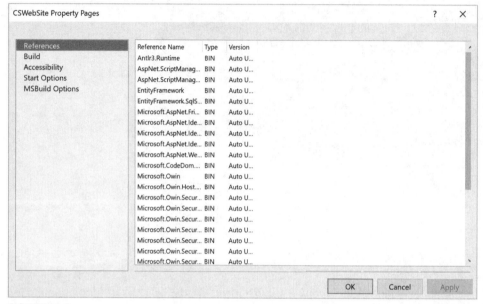

FIGURE 16-3

The References property page (refer to Figure 16-3) enables you to define references to external assemblies or web services. If you add a binary reference to an assembly that is not in the Global Assembly Cache (GAC), the assembly is copied to the \bin folder of your web project along with a .refresh file, which is a small text file that contains the path to the original location of the assembly. Every time the website is built, Visual Studio compares the current version of the assembly in the \bin folder with the version in the original location and, if necessary, updates it. If you have a large number of external references, this can slow the compile time considerably. Therefore, it is recommended that you delete the associated .refresh file for any assembly references that are unlikely to change frequently.

The Build, Accessibility, and Start Options property pages provide some control over how the website is built and launched during debugging. The accessibility validation options are discussed later in this chapter, and the rest of the settings on those property pages are reasonably self-explanatory.

The MSBuild Options property page provides a couple of interesting advanced options for web applications. If you uncheck the Allow This Precompiled Site to be Updatable option, all the content of the .aspx and .ascx pages is compiled into the assembly along with the code behind. This can be useful if you want to protect the user interface of a website from being modified. Finally, the Use Fixed Naming and Single Page Assemblies option specifies that each page be compiled into a separate assembly rather than the default, which is an assembly per folder.

Creating a Web Application Project

Creating a Web Application project with Visual Studio 2017 is a little more complex than creating a Web Site project. The number and variety of projects that are available is definitely higher. As a result, Microsoft has taken the position that a dialog box provides better clarity and control for the developer who is creating the application.

To start the process, select File ➪ New ➪ Project. When you navigate to the Web node in the Templates tree on the left, you see the dialog that appears in Figure 16-4.

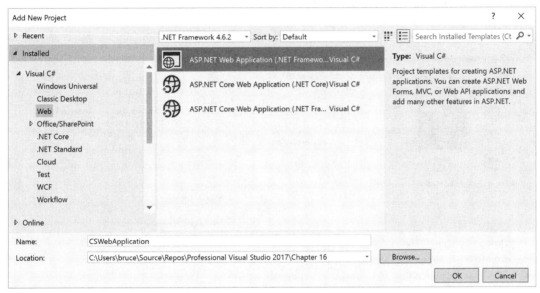

FIGURE 16-4

The number of templates in this list might be less than you expected. However, every type of Web Application project can be created from the ASP.NET Web Application template. The two additional templates, ASP.NET Core Web Application (.NET Core) and ASP.NET Core Web Application (.NET Framework), are covered in the Chapter 18, ".NET Core."

After selecting the ASP.NET Web Application, providing the necessary details about the project name and location, and clicking OK, the New ASP.NET Application dialog appears (Figure 16-5).

There are several templates from which you can choose. While the correspondence is not exact, the ASP.NET 4.6.2 templates are similar to templates found in Visual Studio 2015. They are:

➤ **Empty:** A completely empty template that allows you to add whichever items and functionality you want.

➤ **Web Forms:** Used to create the traditional ASP.NET Web Forms applications.

➤ **MVC:** Creates an application that uses the Model-View-Controller (MVC) pattern.

➤ **Web API:** Used to build a REST-based application programming interface (API) that uses HTTP as the underlying protocol. The difference between this template and MVC is that a Web API project presumes that there will be no user interface defined.

➤ **Single Page Application:** Used to create web pages with rich functionality implemented using HTML5, CSS3, and JavaScript running on the client side (in the browser).

➤ **Azure API App:** Creates an application that supports a REST-based API and will be hosted in Azure and potentially shared from within the Azure Marketplace.

➤ **Azure Mobile App:** Used to build an application that acts as the backend for a mobile application, hosted in Azure.

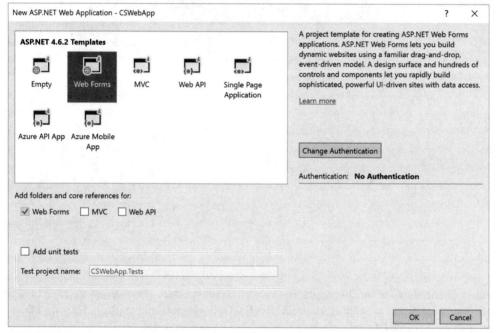

FIGURE 16-5

There are a number of other interesting options to the web application creation process in Visual Studio 2017, as shown in Figure 16-5. There are several check boxes that control functionality over and above that provided in the template. For example, you can create a Web Forms project that includes Web API references. This increase in flexibility makes it easier to create just the project you need without having to figure out which references need to be added later on.

Also, there is the option to create a unit test project that operates in conjunction with your web application. The unit test project will be created with the appropriate project references added.

Finally, there is an option in the dialog to allow you to specify the authentication mechanism that should be used. The default is to use individual user accounts, but if you click on the Change Authentication button, the dialog shown in Figure 16-6 appears.

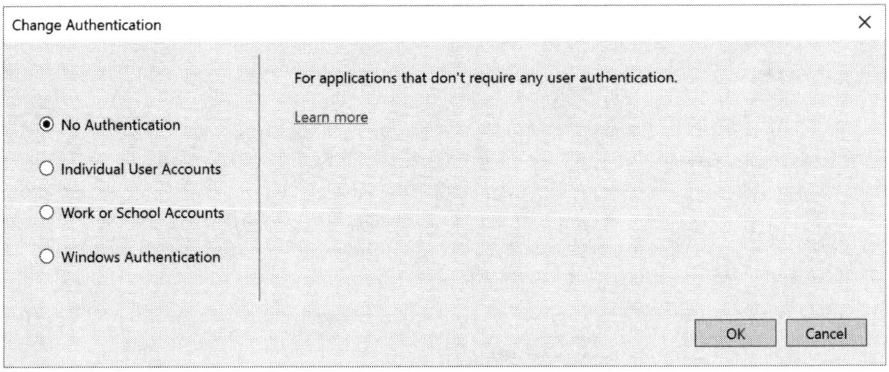

FIGURE 16-6

Here, you can specify whether you want no authentication, Windows authentication, the Active Directory membership provider (the Work or School Accounts option), or a custom membership provider (the Individual User Accounts option). If you're familiar with SqlMembershipProvider, it falls into this last category.

> **NOTE** *Not every project template supports changing the authentication method. As of this writing, Web Forms, MVC, and Web API are the only ones that do.*

When you have set the values to your desired choices, click on OK to create the project. For the following screens, the text presumes that you are working with a Web Forms project with the default authentication scheme.

After you click OK your new Web Application project will be created with a few more items than the Web Site projects. It includes an `AssemblyInfo` file, a References folder, and a My Project item under the Visual Basic or Properties node under C#.

You can view the project properties pages for a Web Application project by double-clicking the Properties or My Project item. The property pages include an additional web tab, as shown in Figure 16-7.

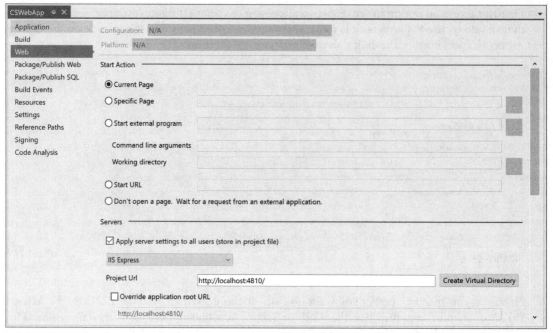

FIGURE 16-7

The options on the web page are all related to debugging an ASP.NET web application and are covered in Chapter 58, "Debugging Web Applications," and Chapter 59, "Advanced Debugging Techniques," both of which are in the online archives.

DESIGNING WEB FORMS

One of the strongest features in Visual Studio 2017 for web developers is the visual design of web applications. The HTML Designer allows you to change the positioning, padding, and margins in Design view, using visual layout tools. It also provides a split view that enables you to simultaneously work on the design and markup of a web form. Finally, Visual Studio 2017 supports rich CSS editing tools for designing the layout and styling of web content.

The HTML Designer

The HTML Designer in Visual Studio is one of the main reasons it's so easy to develop ASP.NET applications. Because it understands how to render HTML elements as well as server-side ASP.NET controls, you can simply drag and drop components from the Toolbox onto the HTML Designer surface to quickly build up a web user interface. You can also quickly toggle between viewing the HTML markup and the visual design of a web page or user control.

The modifications made to the View menu of the IDE are a great example of what Visual Studio does to contextually provide you with useful features depending on what you're doing. When you edit a web page in Design view, additional menu commands become available for adjusting how the design surface appears (see Figure 16-8).

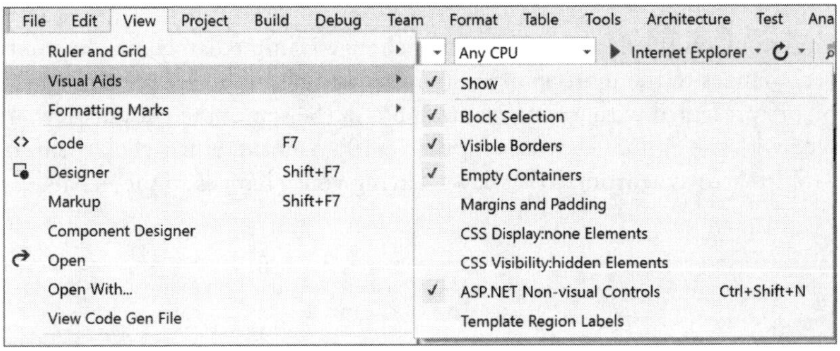

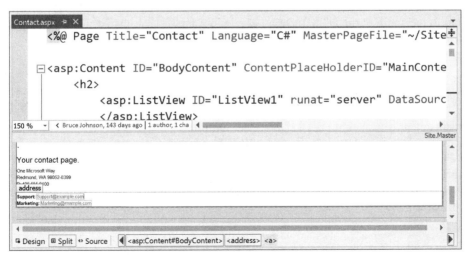

FIGURE 16-8

The three submenus at the top of the View menu — Ruler and Grid, Visual Aids, and Formatting Marks — provide you with a lot of useful tools to assist with the overall layout of controls and HTML elements on a web page.

For example, when the Show option is toggled on the Visual Aids submenu, it draws gray borders around all container controls and HTML tags such as `<table>` and `<div>` so that you can easily see where each component resides on the form. It also provides color-coded shading to indicate the margins and padding around HTML elements and server controls. Likewise, on the Formatting Marks submenu, you can toggle options to display HTML tag names, line breaks, spaces, and much more.

The HTML Designer also supports a split view, as shown in Figure 16-9, which shows your HTML markup and visual design at the same time. You activate this view by opening a page in design mode and clicking the Split button on the bottom left of the HTML Designer window.

FIGURE 16-9

When you select a control or HTML element on the design surface, the HTML Designer highlights it in the HTML markup. Likewise, if you move the cursor to a new location in the markup, it highlights the corresponding element or control on the design surface.

If you make a change to anything on the design surface, that change is immediately reflected in the HTML markup. However, changes to the markup are not always shown in the HTML Designer immediately. Instead, you are presented with an information bar at the top of the Design view stating that it is out of sync with the Source view (see Figure 16-10). You can either click the information bar or press Ctrl+Shift+Y to synchronize the views. Saving your changes to the file also synchronizes it.

> Design view is out of sync with Source view. Click here to synchronize views.

FIGURE 16-10

> **NOTE** *If you have a wide-screen monitor, you can orient the split view vertically to take advantage of your screen resolution. Select Tools ⇨ Options, and then click the HTML Designer node in the tree view. You can use a number of settings here to configure how the HTML Designer behaves, including an option called Split Views Vertically.*

Another feature worth pointing out in the HTML Designer is the tag navigator breadcrumb that appears at the bottom of the design window. This feature, which is also in the XAML Designer, displays the hierarchy of the current element or control and all its ancestors. The breadcrumb displays the type of the control or element and the ID or CSS class if it has been defined. If the tag path is too long to fit in the width of the HTML Designer window, the list is truncated, and a couple of arrow buttons display, so you can scroll through the tag path.

The tag navigator breadcrumb displays the path only from the current element to its top-level parent. It does not list any elements outside that path. If you want to see the hierarchy of all the elements in the current document, you should use the Document Outline window, as shown in Figure 16-11. Select View ⇨ Other Windows ⇨ Document Outline to display the window. When you select an element or control in the Document Outline, it is highlighted in the Design and Source views of the HTML Designer. However, selecting an element in the HTML Designer does not highlight it in the Document Outline window.

FIGURE 16-11

> **NOTE** *In some cases, you might need to reopen a form in order to populate the Document Outline Window.*

Positioning Controls and HTML Elements

One of the trickier parts of building web pages is the positioning of HTML elements. Several attributes can be set that control how an element is positioned, including whether or not it uses a relative or absolute position, the float setting, the z-index, and the padding and margin widths.

Fortunately, you don't need to learn the exact syntax and names of all these attributes and manually type them into the markup. As with most things in Visual Studio, the IDE is there to assist with the specifics. Begin by selecting the control or element that you want to position in Design view. Then choose Format ⇨ Position from the menu to bring up the Position window, as shown in Figure 16-12.

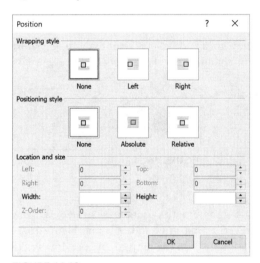

FIGURE 16-12

After you click OK, the wrapping and positioning style you have chosen and any values you have entered for location and size are saved to a style attribute on the HTML element.

If an element has relative or absolute positioning, you can reposition it in the Design view. Beware, though, of how you drag elements around the HTML Designer because you may be doing something you didn't intend! Whenever you select an element or control in Design view, a white tag appears at the top-left corner of the element. This displays the type of element, as well as the ID and class name if they are defined.

If you want to reposition an element with relative or absolute positioning, drag it to the new position using the white control tag. If you drag the element using the control itself, it does not modify the HTML positioning but instead moves it to a new line of code in the source.

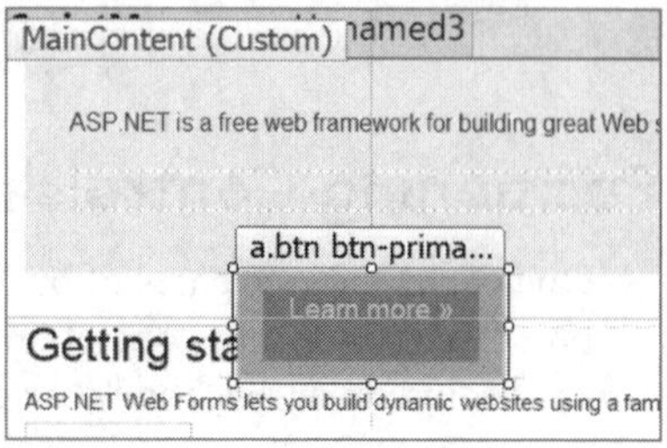

Figure 16-13 shows a button that has absolute positioning and has been repositioned 230 px down and 159 px to the right of its original position. The actual control is shown in its new position, and blue horizontal and vertical guidelines are displayed, which indicate that the control is absolutely positioned. The guidelines are shown only while the element is selected.

FIGURE 16-13

The final layout technique discussed here is setting the padding and margins of an HTML element. Many web developers are initially confused about the difference between these display attributes — which is not helped by the fact that different browsers render elements with these attributes differently. Though not all HTML elements display a border, you can generally think of padding as the space inside the border and margins as the space outside.

If you look closely within the HTML Designer, you may notice some gray lines extending a short way horizontally and vertically from all four corners of a control (see Figure 16-14). These are only visible when the element is selected in the Design view. These are called *margin handles* and allow you to set the width of the margins. Hover the mouse over the handle until it changes to a resize cursor, and then drag it to increase or decrease the margin width (see Figure 16-14).

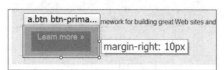

FIGURE 16-14

Finally, within the HTML Designer you can set the padding around an element. If you select an element and then hold down the Shift key, the margin handles become padding handles. Keeping the Shift key pressed, you can drag the handles to increase or decrease the padding width. When you release the Shift key, they revert to margin handles again. Figure 16-14 shows how an HTML element looks in the HTML Designer when the margin and padding widths have been set on all four sides.

At first, this means of setting the margins and padding can feel counterintuitive because it does not behave consistently. To increase the top and left margins, you must drag the handlers into the element, and to increase the top and left padding, you must drag the handlers away. However, just to confuse things, dragging the bottom and right handlers away from the element increases both margin and padding widths.

When you have your HTML layout and positioning the way you want them, you can follow good practices by using the CSS tools to move the layout off the page and into an external style sheet. These tools are discussed in the "CSS Tools" section later in this chapter.

Formatting Controls and HTML Elements

In addition to the Position dialog window discussed in the previous section, Visual Studio 2017 provides a toolbar and a range of additional dialog windows that enable you to edit the formatting of controls and HTML elements on a web page.

The Formatting toolbar, as shown in Figure 16-15, provides easy access to most of the formatting options. The leftmost drop-down list lets you control how the formatting options are applied and includes options for inline styling or CSS rules. The next drop-down list includes all the common HTML elements that can be applied to text, including the `<h1>` through `<h6>` headers, `<ul>`, `<ol>`, and `<blockquote>`.

FIGURE 16-15

Most of the other formatting dialog options are also available as entries on the Format menu. These include options for setting the foreground and background colors, font, alignment, bullets, and numbering. These options and any dialogs associated with them are similar to those available in any word processor or WYSIWYG interface, and their uses are immediately obvious.

The Insert Table dialog window, as shown in Figure 16-16, provides a way for you to easily define the layout and design of a new HTML table. Open it by positioning the cursor on the design surface where you want the new table to be placed and selecting Table ⇨ Insert Table.

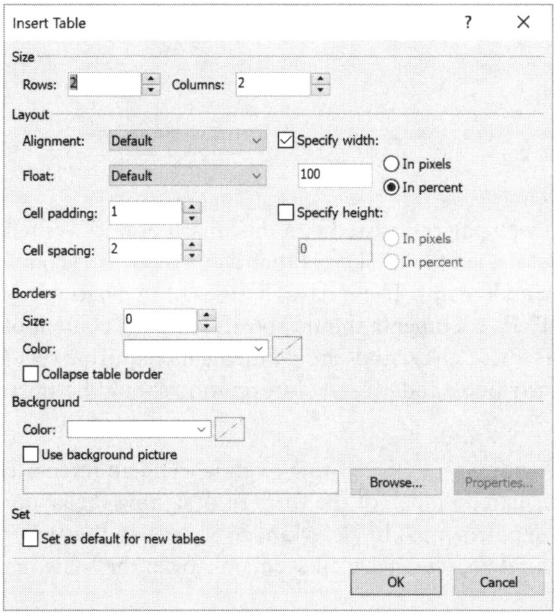

Insert Table	? ✕
Size	
Rows: 2 Columns: 2	
Layout	
Alignment: Default	☑ Specify width:
Float: Default	100 ○ In pixels ● In percent
Cell padding: 1	☐ Specify height:
Cell spacing: 2	0 ○ In pixels ○ In percent
Borders	
Size: 0	
Color:	
☐ Collapse table border	
Background	
Color:	
☐ Use background picture	
	Browse... Properties...
Set	
☐ Set as default for new tables	
	OK Cancel

FIGURE 16-16

A quite useful feature on the Insert Table dialog window is under the color selector. In addition to the list of Standard Colors, there is also the Document Colors list, as shown in Figure 16-17. This lists all the colors that have been applied in some way or another to the current page, for example as foreground, background, or border colors. This saves you from having to remember custom RGB values for the color scheme that you have chosen to apply to a page.

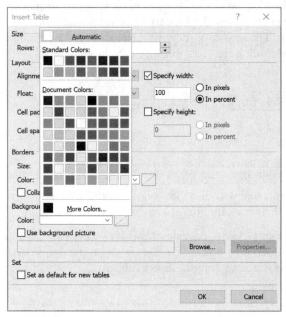

FIGURE 16-17

CSS Tools

Once upon a time, the HTML within a typical web page consisted of a mishmash of both content and presentation markup. Web pages made liberal use of HTML tags that defined how the content should be rendered, such as `<font>`, `<center>`, and `<big>`. These days, designs of this nature are frowned upon — best practice dictates that HTML documents should specify only the content of the web page, wrapped in semantic tags such as `<h1>`, `<ul>`, and `<div>`. Elements requiring special presentation rules should be assigned a `class` attribute, and all style information should be stored in external CSS.

Visual Studio 2017 has several features that provide a rich CSS editing experience in an integrated fashion. As you saw in the previous section, you can do much of the work of designing the layout and styling the content in Design view. This is supplemented by the Manage Styles window, the Apply Styles window, and the CSS Properties window, which are all accessible from the View menu when the HTML Designer is open.

The Manage Styles window lists all the CSS styles that are internal, inline, or in an external CSS file linked through to the current page. The objective of this tool window is to provide you with an overall view of the CSS rules for a particular page, and to enable you to edit and manage those CSS classes.

All the styles are listed in a tree view with the style sheet forming the top-level nodes, as shown in Figure 16-18. The styles are listed in the order in which they appear in the style sheet file, and you can drag and drop to rearrange the styles, or even move styles from one style sheet to another.

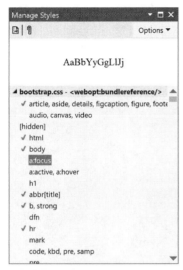

FIGURE 16-18

When you hover over a style, the tooltip shows the CSS properties in that style. The Options menu drop-down enables you to filter the list of styles to show only those that are applicable to elements on the current page or, if you have an element selected in the HTML Designer, only those that are relevant to the selected element.

> **NOTE** *The selected style preview, which is at the top of the Manage Styles window, is generally not what will actually be displayed in the web browser. This is because the preview does not take into account any CSS inheritance rules that might cause the properties of the style to be overridden.*

Rather than a complex set of icons, the Manage Styles window shows a check mark if the style is used in the current page. If a style is not used, then no check box appears.

When you right-click a style in the Manage Styles window, you are given the option to create a new style from scratch, create a new style based on the selected style, or modify the selected style. Any of these three options launch the Modify Style dialog box, as shown in Figure 16-19. This dialog provides an intuitive way to define or modify a CSS style. Style properties are grouped into familiar categories, such as Font, Border, and Position, and a useful preview displays toward the bottom of the window.

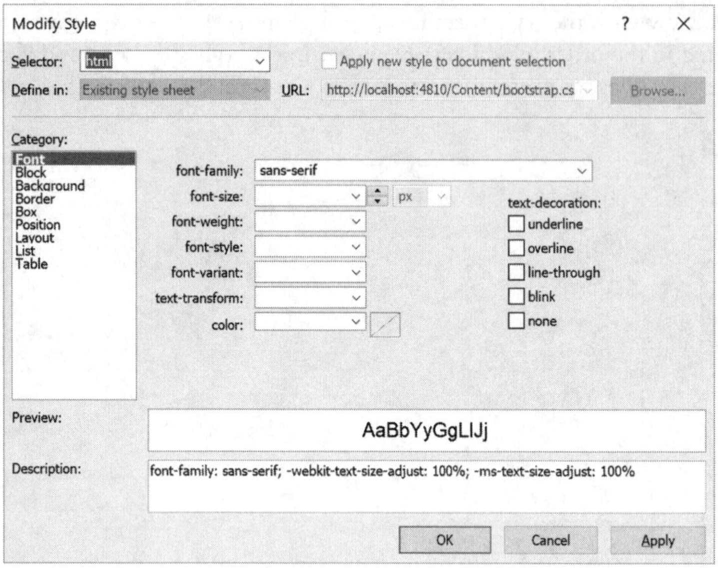

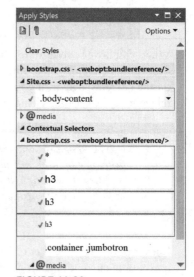

FIGURE 16-19

The second of the CSS windows is the Apply Styles window. Though this has a fair degree of overlap with the Manage Styles window, its purpose is to enable you to easily apply styles to elements on the web page. Select View ⇨ Apply Styles to open the window, which is shown in Figure 16-20. As in the Manage Styles window, all the available styles are listed in the window, and you can filter the list to show only the styles that are applicable to the current page or the currently selected element. The window uses the same check mark icon to indicate whether or not the style is being used. You can also hover over a style to display all the properties in the CSS rule.

However, the Apply Styles window displays a much more visually accurate representation of the style than the Manage Styles window. It includes the font color and weight, background colors or images, borders, and even text alignment.

When you select an HTML element in the Designer, a blue border in the Apply Styles window surrounds the styles applied to that element. Refer to Figure 16-20, where the style is active for the selected element. When you hover the mouse over any of

FIGURE 16-20

the styles, a drop-down button appears over it, providing access to a context menu. This menu has options for applying that style to the selected element or, if the style has already been applied, for removing it. Simply clicking the style also applies it to the current HTML element.

The third of the CSS windows in Visual Studio 2017 is the CSS Properties window, as shown in Figure 16-21. This displays a property grid with all the styles used by the HTML element that is currently selected in the HTML Designer. In addition, the window gives you a comprehensive list of all the available CSS properties. This enables you to add properties to an existing style, modify properties that you have already set, and create new inline styles.

Rather than display the details of an individual style, as was the case with the Apply Styles and Manage Styles windows, the CSS Properties window instead shows a cumulative view of all the styles applicable to the current element, taking into account the order of precedence for the styles. At the top of the CSS Properties window is the Applied Rules section, which lists the CSS styles in the order in which they are applied. Styles that are lower on this list override the styles above them.

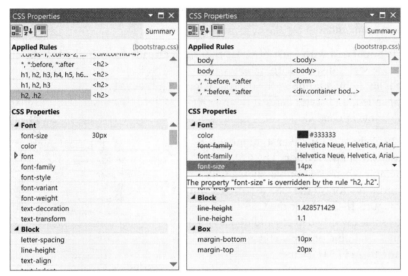

FIGURE 16-21

Selecting a style in the Applied Rules section shows all the CSS properties for that style in the lower property grid. In Figure 16-21 (left) the h2 CSS rule has been selected, which has a definition for the font-size CSS property. You can edit these properties or define new ones directly in this property grid.

The CSS Properties window also has a Summary button, which displays all the CSS properties applicable to the current element. This is shown in Figure 16-21 (right). CSS properties that have been overridden are shown with a strikethrough, and hovering the mouse over the property displays a tooltip with the reason for the override.

Visual Studio 2017 also includes a Target Rule selector on the Formatting toolbar, as shown in Figure 16-22, which enables you to control where style changes you made using the formatting toolbars and dialog windows are saved. These include the Formatting toolbar and the dialog windows under the Format menu, such as Font, Paragraph, Bullets and Numbering, Borders and Shading, and Position.

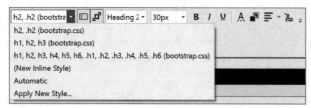

FIGURE 16-22

The Target Rule selector has two modes: Automatic and Manual. In Automatic mode Visual Studio automatically chooses where the new style is applied. In Manual mode you have full control over where the resulting CSS properties are created. Visual Studio 2017 defaults to Manual mode, and any changes to this mode are remembered for the current user.

The Target Rule selector is populated with a list of styles that have already been applied to the currently selected element. Inline styles display with an entry that reads `<inline style>`. Styles defined inline in the current page have `(Current Page)` appended, and styles defined in an external style sheet have the filename appended.

Finally, in Visual Studio 2017 there is IntelliSense support for CSS in both the CSS editor and HTML editor. The CSS editor, which is opened by default when you double-click a CSS file, provides IntelliSense prompts for all the CSS attributes and valid values, as shown in Figure 16-23. After the CSS styles are defined, the HTML editor subsequently detects and displays a list of valid CSS class names available on the web page when you add the `class` attribute to a HTML element.

FIGURE 16-23

Validation Tools

Web browsers are remarkably good at hiding badly formed HTML code from end users. Invalid syntax that would cause a fatal error if it were in an XML document, such as out-of-order or missing closing tags, often renders fine in your favorite web browser. However, if you view that same malformed HTML code in a different browser, it may look totally different. This is one good reason to ensure that your HTML code is standards-compliant.

The first step to validating your standards compliance is to set the target schema for validation. You can do this from the HTML Source Editing toolbar, as shown in Figure 16-24.

FIGURE 16-24

Your HTML markup will be validated against the selected schema. Validation works like a background spell-checker, examining the markup as it is entered and adding wavy green lines under the elements or attributes that are not valid based on the current schema.

As shown in Figure 16-25, when you hover over an element marked as invalid, a tooltip appears showing the reason for the validation failure. A warning entry is also created in the Error List window.

<img />
Validation (HTML5): Element 'img' is missing required attribute 'src'.

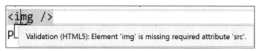

FIGURE 16-25

Schema validation will go a long way toward helping your web pages render the same across different browsers. However, it does not ensure that your site is accessible to everyone. There may be a fairly large group of people with some sort of physical impairment who find it extremely difficult to access your site due to the way the HTML markup has been coded.

The World Health Organization has estimated that approximately 285 million people worldwide are visually impaired (World Health Organization, 2014). In the United States, around 14 million people have reported experiencing vision impairment (National Center for Health Statistics, 2010). That's a large body of people by anyone's estimate, especially given that it doesn't include those with other physical impairments.

In addition to reducing the size of your potential user base, if you do not take accessibilities into account, you may run the risk of being on the wrong side of a lawsuit. A number of countries have introduced legislation that requires websites and other forms of communication to be accessible to people with disabilities.

Fortunately, Visual Studio 2017 includes an accessibility-validation tool that checks HTML markups for compliance with accessibility guidelines. The Web Content Accessibility Checker, launched from Tools ➪ Check Accessibility, enables you to check an individual page for compliance against several accessibility guidelines, including Web Content Accessibility Guidelines (WCAG) version 1.0 and the Americans with Disabilities Act Section 508 Guidelines, commonly referred to as Section 508.

Select the guidelines to check for compliance and click Validate to begin. After the web page has been checked, any issues display as errors or warnings in the Error List window, as shown in Figure 16-26.

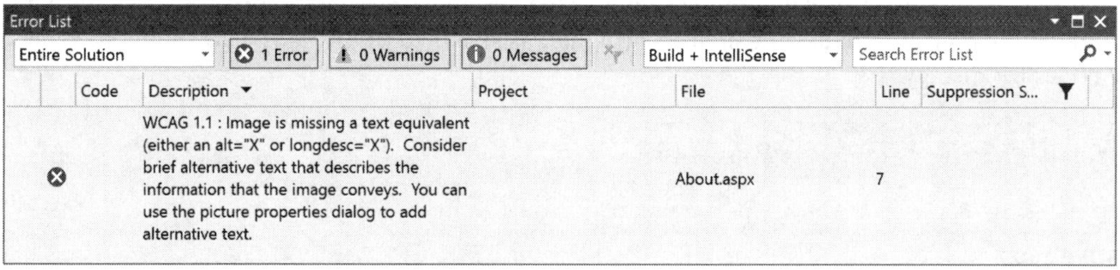
Error List
Entire Solution
1 Error
0 Warnings
0 Messages
Build + IntelliSense
Search Error List
Code
Description
Project
File
Line
Suppression S...
WCAG 1.1 : Image is missing a text equivalent (either an alt="X" or longdesc="X"). Consider brief alternative text that describes the information that the image conveys. You can use the picture properties dialog to add alternative text.
About.aspx
7

FIGURE 16-26

WEB CONTROLS

When ASP.NET version 1.0 was first released, a whole new way to build web applications was enabled for Microsoft developers. Instead of using HTML elements mingled with a server-side scripting language, as was the case with languages such as classic ASP, JSP, and Perl, ASP.NET introduced the concept of feature-rich controls for web pages that acted in ways similar to their Windows counterparts.

Web controls such as button and textbox components have familiar properties such as Text, Left, and Width, along with just as recognizable methods and events such as Click and TextChanged. In addition to these, ASP.NET 1.0 provided a limited set of web-specific components, some dealing with data-based information, such as the DataGrid control, and others providing common web tasks, such as ErrorProvider to give feedback to users about problems with information they entered into a web form.

Subsequent versions of ASP.NET introduced more than 50 web server controls including navigation components, user authentication, and improved data controls. Third-party vendors have also released numerous server controls and components that provide even more advanced functionality.

Unfortunately, there isn't room in this book to explore all the server controls available to web applications in much detail. In fact, many of the components, such as TextBox, Button, and Checkbox, are simply the web equivalents of the basic user interface controls that you may well be familiar with already. However, it can be useful to provide an overview of some of the more specialized and functional server controls that reside in the ASP.NET web developers' toolkit.

Navigation Components

ASP.NET includes a simple way to add sitewide navigation to your web applications with the sitemap provider and associated controls. To implement sitemap functionality into your projects, you must manually create the site data by default in a file called Web.sitemap, and keep it up to date as you add or remove web pages from the site. Sitemap files can be used as a data source for a number of web controls, including SiteMapPath, which automatically keeps track of where you are in the site hierarchy, as well as the Menu and TreeView controls, which can present a custom subset of the sitemap information.

After you have your site hierarchy defined in a Web.sitemap file, the easiest way to use it is to drag and drop a SiteMapPath control onto your web page design surface (see Figure 16-27). This control automatically binds to the default sitemap provider, as specified in the Web.config file, to generate the nodes for display.

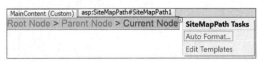

FIGURE 16-27

Though the SiteMapPath control displays only the breadcrumb trail leading directly to the currently viewed page, at times you will want to display a list of pages in your site. The ASP.NET Menu control can be used to do this and has modes for both horizontal and vertical viewing of the information. Likewise, the TreeView control can be bound to a sitemap and used to render a hierarchical menu of pages in a website.

User Authentication

Perhaps the most significant additions to the web components in ASP.NET version 2.0 were the new user authentication and login components. Using these components, you can quickly and easily create the user-based parts of your web application without having to worry about how to format them or what controls are necessary.

Every web application has a default data source added to its ASP.NET configuration when it is first created. The data source is a SQL Server Express database with a default name pointing to a local filesystem location. This data source is used as the default location for your user authentication processing, storing information about users and their current settings.

The benefit of having this automated data store generated for each website is that Visual Studio can have an array of user-bound web components that can automatically save user information without your needing to write any code.

Before you can sign in as a user on a particular site, you first need to create a user account. Initially, you can do that in the administration and configuration of ASP.NET, but you may also want to allow visitors to the site to create their own user accounts. The CreateUserWizard component does just that. It consists of two wizard pages with information about creating an account and indicates when account creation is successful.

After users have created their accounts, they need to log in to the site, and the Login control fills this need. Adding the Login component to your page creates a small form containing User Name and Password fields, along with the option to remember the login credentials, and a Log In button (see Figure 16-28).

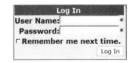

FIGURE 16-28

The trick to getting this to work correctly is to edit your `Web.config` file and change the authentication to Forms. The default authentication type is Windows, and without the change the website authenticates you as a Windows user because that's how you are currently logged in. Obviously, some web applications require Windows authentication, but for a simple website that you plan to deploy on the Internet, this is the only change you need to make for the Login control to work properly.

You can also use several controls that will detect whether or not the user has logged on, and display different information to an authenticated user as opposed to an anonymous user. The LoginStatus control is a simple bi-state component that displays one set of content when the site detects that a user is currently logged in, and a different set of content when there is no logged-in user. The LoginName component is also simple; it just returns the name of the logged-in user.

There are also controls that allow end users to manage their own passwords. The ChangePassword component works with the other automatic user-based components to enable users to change their passwords. However, sometimes users forget their passwords, which is where the PasswordRecovery control comes into play. This component, shown in Figure 16-29, has three views: UserName, Question, and Success. The idea is that users first enter their username so the application can determine and display the security question, and then wait for an answer. If the answer is correct, the component moves to the Success page and sends an email to the registered email address.

FIGURE 16-29

The last component in the Login group on the Toolbox is the LoginView object. LoginView enables you to create whole sections on your web page that are visible only under certain conditions related to who is (or isn't) logged in. By default, you have two views: the AnonymousTemplate, which is used when no user is logged in, and the LoggedInTemplate, used when any user is logged in. Both templates have an editable area that is initially completely empty.

However, because you can define specialized roles and assign users to these roles, you can also create templates for each role you have defined in your site (see Figure 16-30). The Edit RoleGroups command on the smart-tag Tasks list associated with LoginView displays the typical collection editor and enables you to build role groups that can contain one or multiple roles. When the site detects that the user logs in with a certain role, the display area of the LoginView component is populated with that particular template's content.

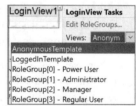

FIGURE 16-30

What's amazing about all these controls is that with only a couple of manual property changes and a few extra entries in the Web.config file, you can build a complete user-authentication system into your web application.

Data Components

Data components were introduced to Microsoft web developers with the first version of Visual Studio .NET and have evolved to be even more powerful with each subsequent release of Visual Studio. Each data control has a smart-tag Tasks list associated with it that enables you to edit the individual templates for each part of the displayable area. For example, the DataList has several templates, each of which can be individually customized (see Figure 16-31).

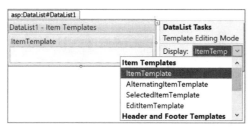

FIGURE 16-31

Data Source Controls

The data source control architecture in ASP.NET provides a simple way for UI controls to bind to data. The data source controls that were released with ASP.NET 2.0 include SqlDataSource and AccessDataSource for binding to SQL Server or Access databases, ObjectDataSource for binding to a generic class, XmlDataSource for binding to XML files, and SiteMapDataSource for the site navigation tree for the web application.

ASP.NET 3.5 shipped with a LinqDataSource control that enables you to directly bind UI controls to data sources using Language Integrated Query (LINQ). The EntityDataSource control, released with ASP.NET 3.5 SP1, supports data binding using the ADO.NET Entity Framework. These controls provide you with a designer-driven approach that automatically generates most of the code necessary for interacting with the data.

All data source controls operate in a similar way. For the purposes of this discussion, the remainder of this section uses ObjectDataSource as an example.

Before you can use ObjectDataSource, you must already have a class that acts as a repository manager created. This class is used to expose the methods that perform CRUD (Create, Read, Update, Delete) functions on the objects. Once this class is defined, you can then create an ObjectDataSource control instance by dragging it from the Toolbox onto the design surface. To configure the control, launch the Configure Data Source wizard under the smart tag for the control. Select the data context class (that would be your repository manager class), and then choose the methods in the repository manager class that implement the CRUD functionality (although only the Read method is required). Figure 16-32 shows the screen within the Configure Data Source wizard that enables you to choose the data context class. It is then a simple matter to bind this data source to a UI server control, such as the ListView control, to provide read-only access to your data.

Data View Controls

After you specify a data source, it is a simple matter to use one of the data view controls to display this data. ASP.NET ships with built-in web controls that render data in different ways, including Chart, DataList, DetailsView, FormView, GridView, ListView, and Repeater. The Chart control is used to render data graphically using visualizations such as a bar chart or line chart and is discussed in Chapter 50, "Reporting," in the online archive.

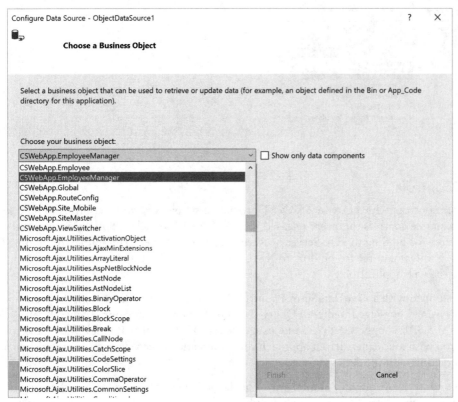

FIGURE 16-32

A common complaint about the ASP.NET server controls is that developers have little control over the HTML markup they generate. This is especially true of many of the data view controls such as GridView, which always uses an HTML table to format the data it outputs, even though in some situations an ordered list would be more suitable.

The ListView control provides a good solution to the shortcomings of other data controls in this area. Instead of surrounding the rendered markup with superfluous `<table>` or `<span>` elements, it enables you to specify the exact HTML output that is rendered. The HTML markup is defined in the templates that ListView supports:

- ➤ AlternatingItemTemplate
- ➤ EditItemTemplate
- ➤ EmptyDataTemplate
- ➤ EmptyItemTemplate
- ➤ GroupSeparatorTemplate
- ➤ GroupTemplate

➤ InsertItemTemplate

➤ ItemSeparatorTemplate

➤ ItemTemplate

➤ LayoutTemplate

➤ SelectedItemTemplate

The two most useful templates are LayoutTemplate and ItemTemplate. LayoutTemplate specifies the HTML markup that surrounds the output, and ItemTemplate specifies the HTML used to format each record that is bound to the ListView.

When you add a ListView control to the design surface, you can bind it to a data source and then open the Configure ListView dialog box, as shown in Figure 16-33, via smart-tag actions. This provides a code-generation tool that automatically produces HTML code based on a small number of predefined layouts and styles.

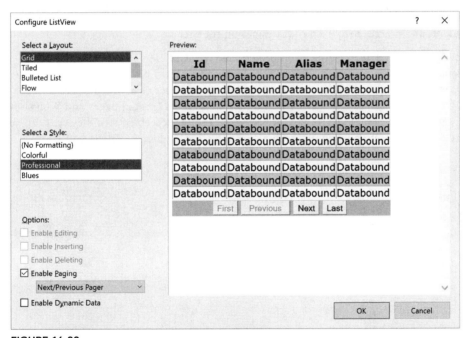

FIGURE 16-33

> **NOTE** *Because you have total control over the HTML markup, the Configure ListView dialog box does not even attempt to parse any existing markup. Instead, if you reopen the window, it simply shows the default layout settings.*

Data Helper Controls

The DataPager control is used to split the data that is displayed by a UI control into multiple pages, which is necessary when you work with large data sets. It natively supports paging via either a NumericPagerField object, which lets users select a page number, or a NextPreviousPagerField object, which lets users navigate to the next or previous page. As with the ListView control, you can also write your own custom HTML markup for paging by using the TemplatePagerField object.

Finally, the QueryExtender control, introduced in ASP.NET version 4.0, provides a way to filter data from an EntityDataSource or LinqDataSource in a declarative manner. It is particularly useful for searching scenarios.

MASTER PAGES

A useful feature of web development in Visual Studio is the ability to create *master pages* that define sections that can be customized. This enables you to define a single page design that contains the common elements that should be shared across your entire site, specify areas that can house individualized content, and inherit it for each of the pages on the site.

To add a master page to your Web Application project, use the Add New Item command from the website menu or from the context menu in the Solution Explorer. This displays the Add New Item dialog, as shown in Figure 16-34, which contains a large number of item templates that can be added to a web application. You'll notice that besides Web Forms (.aspx) pages and Web User Controls, you can also add plain HTML files, style sheets, and other web-related file types. To add a master page, select the Master Page template, choose a name for the file, and click Add.

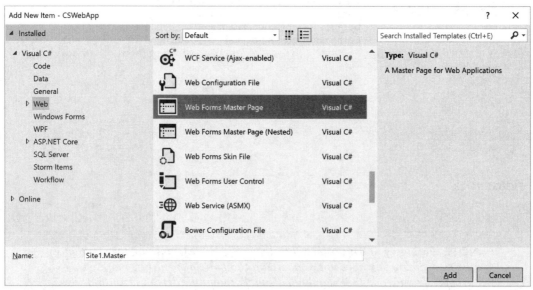

FIGURE 16-34

When a master page is added to your website, it starts out as a minimal web page template with two empty ContentPlaceHolder components — one in the body of the web page and one in the head. This is where the detail information can be placed for each individual page. You can create the master page as you would any other web form page, complete with ASP.NET and HTML elements, CSSs, and theming.

If your design requires additional areas for detail information, you can either drag a new ContentPlaceHolder control from the Toolbox onto the page, or switch to Source view and add the following tags where you need the additional area:

```
<asp:ContentPlaceHolder id="aUniqueid" runat="server">
</asp:ContentPlaceHolder>
```

After the design of your master page has been finalized, you can use it for the detail pages for new web forms in your project.

Unfortunately, the process to add a form that uses a master page is slightly different depending on whether you use a Web Application or a Web Site project. For a Web Application project, rather than adding a new Web Form, you should add a new Web Form using Master Page. This displays the Select a Master Page dialog box, as shown in Figure 16-35. In a Web Site project, the Add New Item window contains a check box titled Select Master Page. If you check this, the Select a Master Page dialog displays.

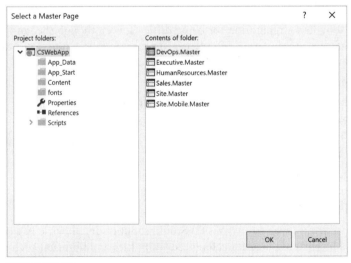

FIGURE 16-35

Select the master page to be applied to the detail page, and click OK. The new web form page that is added to the project includes one or more Content controls, which map to the ContentPlaceHolder controls on the master page.

It doesn't take long to see the benefits of master pages and understand why they have become a popular feature. However, it is even more useful to create nested master pages.

Working with nested master pages is not much different from working with normal master pages. To add one, select Nested Master Page from the Add New Item window. You are prompted to select the parent master page via the Select a Master Page window (refer to Figure 16-35). When you subsequently add a new content web page, any nested master pages are also shown in the Select a Master Page window.

RICH CLIENT-SIDE DEVELOPMENT

In the past couple of years the software industry has seen a fundamental shift toward emphasizing the importance of the end user experience in application development. Nowhere has that been more apparent than in the development of web applications. Fueled by technologies such as AJAX and an increased appreciation of JavaScript, you are expected to provide web applications that approach the richness of their desktop equivalents.

Microsoft has certainly recognized this and includes a range of tools and functionality in Visual Studio 2017 that support the creation of rich client-side interactions. There is integrated debugging and IntelliSense support for JavaScript and ASP.NET AJAX is shipped with Visual Studio 2017. These tools make it much easier for you to design, build, and debug client-side code that provides a much richer user experience.

Developing with JavaScript

Writing JavaScript client code has long had a reputation for being difficult, even though the language is quite simple. Because JavaScript is a dynamic, loosely typed programming language — different from the strong typing enforced by Visual Basic and C# — JavaScript's reputation is even worse in some .NET developer circles.

Thus, one of the most useful features of Visual Studio for web developers is IntelliSense support for JavaScript. The IntelliSense begins immediately as you start typing, with prompts for native JavaScript functions and keywords such as `var`, `alert`, and `eval`.

Furthermore, the JavaScript IntelliSense in Visual Studio 2017 automatically evaluates and infers variable types to provide more accurate IntelliSense prompts. For example, in Figure 16-36 you can see that IntelliSense has determined that `optSelected` is an HTML object because a call to the `document.getElementByID` function returns that type.

In addition to displaying IntelliSense within web forms, Visual Studio supports IntelliSense in external JavaScript files. It also provides IntelliSense help for referenced script files and libraries, such as the Microsoft AJAX library.

Microsoft has extended the XML commenting system in Visual Studio to recognize comments on JavaScript functions. IntelliSense detects these XML code comments and displays the summary, parameters, and return type information for the function.

Although Visual Studio constantly monitors changes to files in the project and updates the IntelliSense as they happen, a couple of limitations could prevent the JavaScript IntelliSense from displaying information in certain circumstances, including:

➤ A syntax or other error in an external referenced script file.

➤ Invoking a browser-specific function or object. Most web browsers provide a set of objects that is proprietary to that browser. You can still use these objects, and many popular JavaScript frameworks do; however, you won't get IntelliSense support for them.

➤ Referencing files outside the current project.

```html
<html xmlns="http://www.w3.org/1999/xhtml">
<head runat="server">
    <title>Intellisense Test Page</title>
    <script type="text/javascript">
        function showOptions() {
            var optSelected = document.getElementById("myElementId");
            optSelected.ha
        }
    </script>                  hasAttribute
</head>                        hasAttributeNS
<body>                         hasAttributes
    <form id-"form1" runat-"server">   hasChildNodes
```

FIGURE 16-36

One feature of ASP.NET that is a boon to JavaScript developers is the ClientIDMode property that is available for web server controls. In earlier versions, the value that was generated for the id attribute on generated HTML controls made it difficult to reference these controls in JavaScript. The ClientIDMode property fixes this by defining two modes (Static and Predictable) for generating these IDs in a simpler and more predictable way.

The JavaScript IntelliSense support, combined with the client-side debugging and control over client IDs, significantly enhances the ability to develop JavaScript code with Visual Studio 2017.

Working with ASP.NET AJAX

The ASP.NET AJAX framework provides web developers with a familiar server-control programming approach for building rich client-side AJAX interactions.

ASP.NET AJAX includes both server-side and client-side components. A set of server controls, including the popular UpdatePanel and UpdateProgess controls, can be added to web forms to enable asynchronous partial-page updates without your needing to make changes to any existing code on the page. The client-side Microsoft AJAX Library is a JavaScript framework that can be used in any web application, such as PHP on Apache, and not just ASP.NET or IIS.

The following walkthrough demonstrates how to enhance an existing web page by adding the ASP .NET AJAX UpdatePanel control to perform a partial-page update. In this scenario you have a simple web form with a DropDownList server control, which has an AutoPostBack to the server enabled. The web form handles the `DropDownList.SelectedIndexChanged` event and saves the value that was selected in the DropDownList to a TextBox server control on the page. The code for this page follows:

AJAXSAMPLEFORM.ASPX

```
<%@ Page Language="vb" AutoEventWireup="false"
    CodeBehind="AjaxSampleForm.aspx.vb"
    Inherits="ASPNetWebApp.AjaxSampleForm" %>
<!DOCTYPE html PUBLIC "-//W3C//DTD XHTML 1.0 Transitional//EN"
    "http://www.w3.org/TR/xhtml1/DTD/xhtml1-transitional.dtd">
<html xmlns="http://www.w3.org/1999/xhtml" >
<head runat="server">
    <title>ASP.NET AJAX Sample</title>
</head>
<body>
    <form id="form1" runat="server">
        <div>
        Select an option:
        <asp:DropDownList ID="DropDownList1" runat="server" AutoPostBack="True">
            <asp:ListItem Text="Option 1" Value="Option 1" />
            <asp:ListItem Text="Option 2" Value="Option 2" />
            <asp:ListItem Text="Option 3" Value="Option 3" />
        </asp:DropDownList>
        <br />
        Option selected:
        <asp:TextBox ID="TextBox1" runat="server"></asp:TextBox>
        </div>
        </form>
</body>
</html>
```

AJAXSAMPLEFORM.ASPX.VB

```
Public Partial Class AjaxSampleForm
    Inherits System.Web.UI.Page
    Protected Sub DropDownList1_SelectedIndexChanged(ByVal sender As Object, _
                                        ByVal e As EventArgs) _
                                Handles
DropDownList1.SelectedIndexChanged
        System.Threading.Thread.Sleep(2000)
        Me.TextBox1.Text = Me.DropDownList1.SelectedValue
    End Sub
End Class
```

Notice that in the `DropDownList1_SelectedIndexChanged` method you added a statement to sleep for 2 seconds. This exaggerates the server processing time, thereby making it easier to see the effect of the changes you will make. When you run this page and change an option in the drop-down list, the whole page will be refreshed in the browser.

The first AJAX control that you need to add to your web page is a ScriptManager. This is a non-visual control that's central to ASP.NET AJAX and is responsible for tasks such as sending script libraries and files to the client and generating any required client proxy classes. You can have only one ScriptManager control per ASP.NET web page, which can pose a problem when you use master pages and user controls. In that case, you should add the ScriptManager to the topmost parent page and a ScriptManagerProxy control to all child pages.

After you add the ScriptManager control, you can add any other ASP.NET AJAX controls. In this case, add an UpdatePanel control to the web page, as shown in the following code. Notice that TextBox1 is now contained within the UpdatePanel control.

```
<%@ Page Language="vb" AutoEventWireup="false"
    CodeBehind="AjaxSampleForm.aspx.vb"
    Inherits="ASPNetWebApp.AjaxSampleForm" %>
<!DOCTYPE html PUBLIC "-//W3C//DTD XHTML 1.0 Transitional//EN"
    "http://www.w3.org/TR/xhtml1/DTD/xhtml1-transitional.dtd">
<html xmlns="http://www.w3.org/1999/xhtml" >
<head runat="server">
    <title>ASP.NET AJAX Sample</title>
</head>
<body>
    <form id="form1" runat="server">
    <asp:ScriptManager ID="ScriptManager1" runat="server"></asp:ScriptManager>
    <div>
        Select an option:
        <asp:DropDownList ID="DropDownList1" runat="server" AutoPostBack="True">
            <asp:ListItem Text="Option 1" Value="Option 1" />
            <asp:ListItem Text="Option 2" Value="Option 2" />
            <asp:ListItem Text="Option 3" Value="Option 3" />
        </asp:DropDownList>
        <br />
        Option selected:
        <asp:UpdatePanel ID="UpdatePanel1" runat="server">
            <ContentTemplate>
                <asp:TextBox ID="TextBox1" runat="server"></asp:TextBox>
            </ContentTemplate>
            <Triggers>
                <asp:AsyncPostBackTrigger ControlID="DropDownList1"
                                          EventName="SelectedIndexChanged" />
            </Triggers>
        </asp:UpdatePanel>
    </div>
    </form>
</body>
</html>
```

The web page now uses AJAX to provide a partial-page update. When you run this page and change an option in the drop-down list, the whole page is no longer refreshed. Instead, just the text within the textbox is updated. In fact, if you run this page you can notice that AJAX is too good at just updating part of the page. There is no feedback, and if you didn't know any better, you would think that nothing is happening. This is where the UpdateProgress control becomes useful. You can place an UpdateProgress control on the page, and when an AJAX request is invoked, the HTML within the ProgressTemplate section of the control is rendered. The following code shows an example of an UpdateProgress control for your web form:

```
<asp:UpdateProgress ID="UpdateProgress1" runat="server">
    <ProgressTemplate>
        Loading.
    </ProgressTemplate>
</asp:UpdateProgress>
```

The final server control in ASP.NET AJAX that hasn't been mentioned is the Timer control, which enables you to perform asynchronous or synchronous client-side postbacks at a defined interval. This can be useful for scenarios such as checking with the server to see if a value has changed.

SUMMARY

In this chapter you learned how to create ASP.NET applications using the Web Site and Web Application projects. The power of the HTML Designer and the CSS tools in Visual Studio 2017 provide you with great power over the layout and visual design of web pages. The vast number of web controls included in ASP.NET enables you to quickly put together highly functional web pages. Through the judicious use of JavaScript and ASP.NET AJAX, you can provide a rich user experience in your web applications.

Of course, there's much more to web development than what is covered here. Chapters 17 and 18 continue the discussion on building rich web applications by exploring web technologies from Microsoft: ASP.NET MVC and .NET Core. Chapter 58 in the online archive provides detailed information about the tools and techniques available for effective debugging of web applications. Finally, Chapter 36, "Web Application Deployment," walks you through the deployment options for web applications. If you want more information after this, you should check out *Professional ASP.NET 4.5 in C# and VB* (Wrox). Weighing in at more than 1,400 pages, this is the best and most comprehensive resource available to web developers who are building applications on the most recent version of ASP.NET.

17

ASP.NET MVC

WROX.COM CODE DOWNLOADS FOR THIS CHAPTER

The wrox.com code downloads for this chapter can be found at www.wrox.com by searching for this book's ISBN number (978-1-119-40458-3). The code and any related support files are located in their own folder for this chapter.

Although ASP.NET Web Forms has been and continues to be successful, it is not without criticism. Without strong discipline it is easy for business logic and data-access concerns to creep into the user interface, making it hard to test without sitting in front of a browser. It heavily abstracts away the stateless request/response nature of the web, which can make it frustrating to debug. It relies heavily on controls rendering their own HTML markup, which can make it difficult to precisely control the final output of each page.

As an alternative, the architectural pattern called Model-View-Controller (MVC) divides the parts of a user interface into three classifications with well-defined roles. This makes applications easier to test, evolve, and maintain.

The ASP.NET Framework enables you to build applications based on the MVC architecture while taking advantage of the .NET Framework's extensive set of libraries and language options. ASP.NET MVC has been developed in an open manner with many of its features shaped by community feedback. The entire source code for the framework is available as open source. You can find the repository for it at https://github.com/aspnet.

> **NOTE** *Microsoft has been careful to state that ASP.NET MVC is not a replacement for Web Forms. It is simply an alternative way to build web applications that some people will find preferable. Microsoft has made it clear that it will continue to support both ASP.NET Web Forms and ASP.NET MVC.*

MODEL VIEW CONTROLLER

In the MVC architecture, applications are separated into the following components:

➤ **Model:** The model consists of classes that implement domain-specific logic for the application. Although the MVC architecture does not concern itself with the specifics of the data access layer, it is understood that the model should encapsulate any data access code. Generally, the model calls separate data access classes responsible for retrieving and storing information in a database.

➤ **View:** The views are classes that take the model and render it into a format where the user can interact with it.

➤ **Controller:** The controller is responsible for bringing everything together. A controller processes and responds to events, such as a user clicking a button. The controller maps these events onto the model and invokes the appropriate view.

> **NOTE** *You might be surprised to learn that the Model-View-Controller architectural pattern was first described in 1979 by Trygve Reenskaug, a researcher working on an implementation of SmallTalk. You can find the slides and notes to a 2003 presentation given by Professor Reenskaug at* `https://heim.ifi` `.uio.no/~trygver/2003/javazone-jaoo/MVC_pattern.pdf`*.*

These descriptions aren't actually helpful until you understand how they interact together. The request life cycle of an ASP.NET MVC application normally consists of the following:

1. The user performs an action that triggers an event, such as entering a URL or clicking a button. This generates a request to the controller.

2. The controller receives the request and invokes the relevant action on the model. Often this can cause a change in the model's state, although not always.

3. The controller retrieves any necessary data from the model and invokes the appropriate view, passing it the data from the model.

4. The view renders the data and sends it back to the user.

The most important thing to note here is that both the view and controller depend on the model. However, the model has no dependencies, which is one of the key benefits of the architecture. This separation is what provides better testability and makes it easier to manage complexity.

> **NOTE** *Different MVC framework implementations have minor variations in the preceding life cycle. For example, in some cases the view queries the model for the current state, instead of receiving it from the controller.*

Now that you understand the Model-View-Controller architectural pattern, you can begin to apply this knowledge to build your first ASP.NET MVC application.

GETTING STARTED WITH ASP.NET MVC

This section details the creation of a new ASP.NET MVC application and describes some of the standard components. In Visual Studio 2015, there were two different flavors of MVC, each identified by their version number. That is no longer the case, at least not while going through the project creation process described in this section. In Visual Studio 2015, the distinction between the two MVC versions related to the tools that are used to build the project and to deliver client-side resources to the browser. The MVC concepts were (and still are) the same for each of them. But what was ASP.NET MVC in Visual Studio 2015 eventually became .NET Core, which is described in Chapter 18, ".NET Core." As a result, ASP.NET MVC as covered in this chapter is the "older," more familiar, slightly less cutting-edge version.

To create a new MVC application, go to File ⇨ New Project, and select ASP.NET Web Application from the Web section. After you give a name to the project and select OK, Visual Studio asks for a number of setup parameters, such as the project template, the type of project (Web Forms, MVC, or Web API), and whether or not a unit test project for the application should be created (shown in Figure 17-1).

Your first option in defining the MVC project is to select a project template, such as Empty, MVC, Single Page Application, Web API, or Azure API App. The choice you make impacts some of the files that are downloaded. So consider this choice to be just a further refinement of the project template options available from the New Project dialog.

One of the design elements for ASP.NET projects in Visual Studio 2017 was to eliminate (at least as much as possible) the distinction between Web Forms, Web API, and MVC development styles. While that relatively utopian goal has not yet been fully realized, a significant step has been taken with the inclusion of a number of check boxes immediately below the list of templates. Where possible, if you can have different development styles within the same project template, you will be able to choose which styles to include. Again, limited by the particular template, more than one style may be included in a single project.

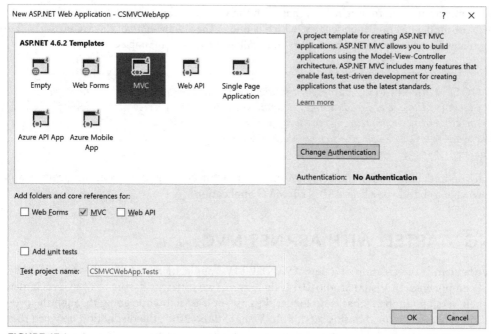

FIGURE 17-1

To add a development style to your template, ensure that the desired box (or boxes) have been checked prior to clicking on the OK button. Then, when the project is created, the files that you have chosen to include in your project will be added automatically. For this example, ensure that the MVC box has been checked before continuing.

You also have the option to create a unit test project for the application. Although this is not required, it is highly recommended because improved testability is one of the key advantages of using the MVC framework. You can always add a test project later if you want.

> **NOTE** *Visual Studio 2017 can create test projects for MVC applications using a number of unit testing frameworks. The default choice, however, is to use the built-in unit testing tools in Visual Studio.*

When an ASP.NET MVC application is first created, it generates a number of files and folders. The MVC application generated from the project template is a complete application that can be run immediately.

Figure 17-2 shows the folder structure automatically generated by Visual Studio and includes the following folders:

➤ **Content:** A location to store static content files such as themes and CSS files.

➤ **Controllers:** Contains the Controller files. Two sample controllers called `HomeController` and `AccountController` are created by the project template.

➤ **Fonts:** A location to store font files.

➤ **Models:** Contains model files. This is also a good place to store any data access classes that are encapsulated by the model. The MVC project template does not create an example model.

➤ **Scripts:** Contains JavaScript files. By default, this folder contains script files for JQuery and Microsoft AJAX along with some helper scripts to integrate with MVC.

➤ **Views:** Contains the view files. The MVC project template creates a number of folders and files in the Views folder. The Home subfolder contains two example view files invoked by the `HomeController`. The Shared subfolder contains a master page used by these views.

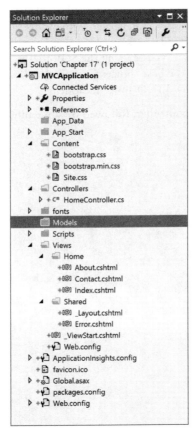

FIGURE 17-2

Visual Studio also creates a `Global.asax` file, which is used to configure the routing rules (more on that later).

Finally, if you elected to create a test project, this is created with a Controllers folder that contains a unit test stub for the `HomeController`.

Although it doesn't do much yet, you can run the MVC application by pressing F5. Exactly what it does depends on the template that you select.

CHOOSING A MODEL

The MVC project template does not create a sample model for you. Actually, the application can run without a model altogether. While in practice your applications are likely to have a full model, MVC provides no guidance as to which technology you should use. This gives you a great deal of flexibility.

The model part of your application is an abstraction of the business capabilities that the application provides. If you build an application to process orders or organize a leave schedule, your model should express these concepts. This is not always easy. It is frequently tempting to allow some of these details to creep in the View-controller part of your application.

The examples in this chapter use a simple LINQ-to-SQL model based on a subset of the AdventureWorksDB sample database as shown in Figure 17-3. You can download this sample database from `http://msftdbprodsamples.codeplex.com/`. The version of the database that you need depends on the version of SQL Server you have access to. If you're using the SQL that is included with Visual Studio 2017, then Adventure Works 2014 is the best choice. Chapter 46, "Language Integrated Queries (LINQ)," explains how to create a new LINQ-to-SQL model.

The next section explains how you can build your own controller, followed by some interesting views that render a dynamic user interface.

FIGURE 17-3

CONTROLLERS AND ACTION METHODS

A controller is a class that responds to some user action. Usually, this response involves updating the model in some way, and then organizing for a view to present content back to the user. Each controller can listen for and respond to a number of user actions. Each of these is represented in the code by a normal method referred to as an action method.

Begin by right-clicking the Controllers folder in the Solution Explorer and selecting Add ➪ Controller to display the Add Scaffold dialog, as shown in Figure 17-4. This dialog allows you to select the scaffolding option for the controller. Once you have selected the scaffold, you are prompted to select a name for your new controller. By convention, the MVC framework requires that all controller classes have names that end in "Controller," so this part is already filled in for you.

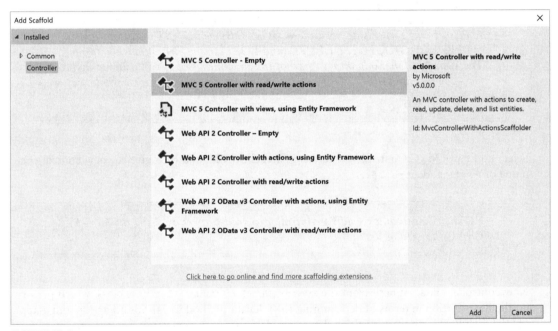

FIGURE 17-4

MVC Scaffolding

Scaffolding is a mechanism that is used in a couple of different technologies throughout .NET. For ASP.NET MVC, scaffolding is used to create a collection of pages that relate to the type of controller that you're adding. If you think of the scaffolding as a template, you're close. Typically a template is used to generate a single file from a given set of parameters. In this particular case, adding a controller using scaffolding results in a number of different files being added. The specific files and the functionality that are found therein depend on the type of scaffolding that is selected.

In Figure 17-4, you'll notice that the choices fall into three basic categories. Several of them relate to an MVC 5 controller. The others relate to a controller based on the ASP.NET Web API 2, both with and without OData 3. Within each of the groups, there are up to three different options: an empty controller, a controller that uses the Entity Framework to perform CRUD (Create/Read/Update/Delete) operations, and a controller that has the methods to perform CRUD, but no implementation. The selection of the template should be based on whether or not you plan on using MVC or the Web API (with or without OData) and secondarily on how much of the CRUD functions you would like to be automatically generated.

> **NOTE** *The ASP.NET Web API is a framework that allows a broad range of clients, from browsers to mobile devices, that consume HTTP services. On the server side, the Web API assists in the construction of easily consumable HTTP services. In terms of how it differs from MVC, in general, the answer can be given in terms of how it utilizes HTTP. MVC using a REST-based notation to identify the server-side resources that are retrieved. REST notations utilize HTTP verbs (GET, PUT, DELETE, and POST) to perform their operations. The Web API takes advantage of all of the capabilities of HTTP (including headers, the body, and full URI addressing) to create a rich and interoperable way to access resources.*

Select an Empty MVC Controller as the template, click Add, and then give the new controller a name of `ProductsController`.

> **NOTE** *You can quickly add a controller to your project by using the Ctrl+M, Ctrl+C shortcut as well.*

New controller classes inherit from the `System.Web.Mvc.Controller` base class, which performs all the heavy lifting in terms of determining the relevant method to call for an action and mapping of URL and POST parameter values. This means that you can concentrate on the implementation details of your actions, which typically involve invoking a method on a model class, and then selecting a view to render.

A newly created controller class will be populated with a default action method called `Index`. You can add a new action simply by adding a public method to the class. If a method is public, it will be visible as an action on the controller. You can stop a public method from being exposed as an action by adding the `System.Web.Mvc.NonAction` attribute to the method. The following code contains the controller class with the default action that simply renders the `Index` view, and a public method that is not visible as an action:

C#

```
public class ProductsController : Controller
{
    //
```

```
  // GET: /Products/

  public ActionResult Index()
  {
    return View();
  }

  [NonAction]
  public void NotAnAction()
  {
    // This method is not exposed as an action.
  }
}
```

VB

```
Public Class ProductsController
    Inherits System.Web.Mvc.Controller

    '
    ' GET: /Products/

    Function Index() As ActionResult
        Return View()
    End Function

    <NonAction()>
    Sub NotAnAction()
        ' This method is not exposed as an action.
    End Sub

End Class
```

> **NOTE** *The comment that appears above the Index method is a convention that indicates how the action is triggered. Each action method is placed at a URL that is a combination of the controller name and the action method name formatted like /controller/action. The comment has no control over this convention but is used to indicate where you can expect to find this action method. In this case it is saying that the index action is triggered by executing an HTTP GET request against the URL /Products/. This is just the name of the controller because an action named Index is assumed if one is not explicitly stated by the URL. This convention is revisited in the "Routing" section.*

The result of the Index method is an object that derives from the System.Web.Mvc.ActionResult abstract class. This object is responsible for determining what happens after the action method returns. A number of standard classes inherit from ActionResult that allow you to perform a number of standard tasks, including redirection to another URL, generating some simple content in a number of different formats, or in this case, rendering a view.

> **NOTE** *The* `View` *method on the* `Controller` *base class is a simple method that creates and configures a* `System.Web.Mvc.ViewResult` *object. This object is responsible for selecting a view and passing it any information that it needs to render its contents.*

It is important to note that `Index` is just a normal .NET method and `ProductsController` is just a normal .NET class. There is nothing special about either of them. This means that you can easily instantiate a `ProductsController` in a test harness, call its `Index` method, and then make assertions about the `ActionResult` object it returns.

Before moving on, update the `Index` method to retrieve a list of Products, and pass them on to the view, as shown in the following code:

C#

```csharp
public ActionResult Index()
{
    List<Product> products;

    using (var db = new AdventureWorks2014Entities())
    {
        products = db.Products.ToList();
    }

    return View(products);
}
```

VB

```vb
Function Index() As ActionResult
  Dim products As New List(Of Product)

  Using db As New AdventureWorks2014Entities
    products = db.Products.ToList()
  End Using

  Return View(products)
End Function
```

Now that you have created a model and a controller, all that is needed is to create the view to display the UI.

RENDERING A UI WITH VIEWS

In the previous section you created an action method that gathers the complete list of products and passes that list to a view. Each view belongs to a single controller and is stored in a subfolder in the Views folder, which is named after the controller that owns it. In addition, there is a Shared folder, which contains a number of shared views that are accessible from a number of controllers. When the view engine looks for a view, it checks the controller-specific area first and then checks in the shared area.

> **NOTE** *You can specify the full path to a view as the view name if you need to refer to a view that is not in the normal view engine search areas.*

The look that a particular view has depends greatly on the view engine that is used. An ASPX view looks similar to a standard ASP.NET Web Forms `Page` or `Control` having either an `.aspx` or `.ascx` extension. A Razor view has some superficial resemblance to an ASPX page, but syntactically there are significant differences. However, in general, views contain some mix of HTML markup and code blocks. They can even have master pages and render some standard controls. However, a number of important differences exist that need to be highlighted.

First, a view doesn't have a code behind page. As such, there is nowhere to add event handlers for any controls that the view renders, including those that normally happen behind the scenes. Instead, it is expected that the view will expose ways for the user to trigger action methods and a controller will respond to those events. Second, instead of inheriting from `System.Web.Page`, a view inherits from `System.Web.Mvc.ViewPage`. This base class exposes a number of useful properties and methods that can be used to help render the HTML output. One of these properties contains a dictionary of objects that were passed into the view from the controller. Finally, in the markup you can notice that there is no form control with a `runat="server"` attribute. No server form means that there is no View State emitted with the page. The majority of the ASP.NET server controls must be placed inside a server-rendered form control. Some controls such as a Literal or Repeater control work fine outside a form; however, if you try to use a Button or DropDownList control, your page throws an exception at run time.

You can create a View in a number of ways, but the easiest is to right-click the title of the action method and select Add View, which brings up the Add View dialog, as shown in Figure 17-5.

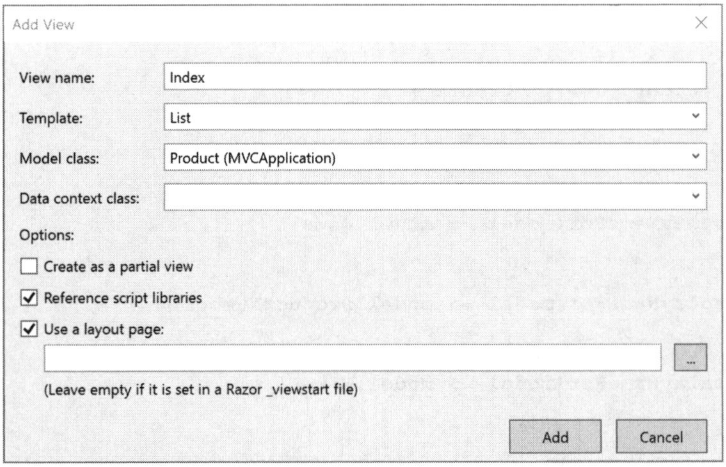

FIGURE 17-5

> **NOTE** *You can use the shortcut Ctrl+M, Ctrl+V when the cursor is inside an action method to open the Add View dialog as well.*

This dialog contains a number of options. By default, the name is set to match the name of the action method. If you change this, you need to change the constructor of the `View` to include the view name as a parameter. There are a number of templates available as well. If you select an option other than empty, you have the ability to strongly type the view by choosing the model class from the dropdown. For this example, select the List template and then choose `Product` (`MVCApplication`) from the Model Class dropdown. If you don't see the Product class straight away, you might need to build the application before adding the view. This tells Visual Studio to generate a list page for Product objects.

> **NOTE** *If you do not opt to create a strongly typed view, it will contain a dictionary of objects that need to be converted back into their real types before you can use them. It is recommended to always use strongly typed views. If you require your views to be weakly typed and you use C#, you should create a strongly typed view of the dynamic type and pass it* ExpandoObject *instances.*

When you click Add, the view should be generated and opened in the main editor window. It will look like this:

HTML

```
@model IEnumerable<MVCApplication.Product>
@{
    ViewBag.Title = "Index";
    Layout = "~/Views/_ViewStart.cshtml";
}

<h2>Index</h2>
<p>
    @Html.ActionLink("Create New", "Create")
</p>
<table class="table">
    <tr>
        <th>
            @Html.DisplayNameFor(model => model.Name)
        </th>
        <th>
            @Html.DisplayNameFor(model => model.ProductNumber)
        </th>
        <th>
            @Html.DisplayNameFor(model => model.MakeFlag)
        </th>
        <th>
```

```
        @Html.DisplayNameFor(model => model.FinishedGoodsFlag)
    </th>
    <th>
        @Html.DisplayNameFor(model => model.Color)
    </th>
    <th>
        @Html.DisplayNameFor(model => model.SafetyStockLevel)
    </th>
    <th>
        @Html.DisplayNameFor(model => model.ReorderPoint)
    </th>
    <th>
        @Html.DisplayNameFor(model => model.StandardCost)
    </th>
    <th>
        @Html.DisplayNameFor(model => model.ListPrice)
    </th>
    <th>
        @Html.DisplayNameFor(model => model.Size)
    </th>
    <th>
        @Html.DisplayNameFor(model => model.SizeUnitMeasureCode)
    </th>
    <th>
        @Html.DisplayNameFor(model => model.WeightUnitMeasureCode)
    </th>
    <th>
        @Html.DisplayNameFor(model => model.Weight)
    </th>
    <th>
        @Html.DisplayNameFor(model => model.DaysToManufacture)
    </th>
    <th>
        @Html.DisplayNameFor(model => model.ProductLine)
    </th>
    <th>
        @Html.DisplayNameFor(model => model.Class)
    </th>
    <th>
        @Html.DisplayNameFor(model => model.Style)
    </th>
    <th>
        @Html.DisplayNameFor(model => model.ProductSubcategoryID)
    </th>
    <th>
        @Html.DisplayNameFor(model => model.ProductModelID)
    </th>
    <th>
        @Html.DisplayNameFor(model => model.SellStartDate)
    </th>
    <th>
        @Html.DisplayNameFor(model => model.SellEndDate)
    </th>
```

```
            <th>
                @Html.DisplayNameFor(model => model.DiscontinuedDate)
            </th>
            <th>
                @Html.DisplayNameFor(model => model.rowguid)
            </th>
            <th>
                @Html.DisplayNameFor(model => model.ModifiedDate)
            </th>
            <th></th>
        </tr>

    @foreach (var item in Model) {
        <tr>
            <td>
                @Html.DisplayFor(modelItem => item.Name)
            </td>
            <td>
                @Html.DisplayFor(modelItem => item.ProductNumber)
            </td>
            <td>
                @Html.DisplayFor(modelItem => item.MakeFlag)
            </td>
            <td>
                @Html.DisplayFor(modelItem => item.FinishedGoodsFlag)
            </td>
            <td>
                @Html.DisplayFor(modelItem => item.Color)
            </td>
            <td>
                @Html.DisplayFor(modelItem => item.SafetyStockLevel)
            </td>
            <td>
                @Html.DisplayFor(modelItem => item.ReorderPoint)
            </td>
            <td>
                @Html.DisplayFor(modelItem => item.StandardCost)
            </td>
            <td>
                @Html.DisplayFor(modelItem => item.ListPrice)
            </td>
            <td>
                @Html.DisplayFor(modelItem => item.Size)
            </td>
            <td>
                @Html.DisplayFor(modelItem => item.SizeUnitMeasureCode)
            </td>
            <td>
                @Html.DisplayFor(modelItem => item.WeightUnitMeasureCode)
            </td>
            <td>
                @Html.DisplayFor(modelItem => item.Weight)
            </td>
            <td>
                @Html.DisplayFor(modelItem => item.DaysToManufacture)
            </td>
            <td>
```

```
            @Html.DisplayFor(modelItem => item.ProductLine)
        </td>
        <td>
            @Html.DisplayFor(modelItem => item.Class)
        </td>
        <td>
            @Html.DisplayFor(modelItem => item.Style)
        </td>
        <td>
            @Html.DisplayFor(modelItem => item.ProductSubcategoryID)
        </td>
        <td>
            @Html.DisplayFor(modelItem => item.ProductModelID)
        </td>
        <td>
            @Html.DisplayFor(modelItem => item.SellStartDate)
        </td>
        <td>
            @Html.DisplayFor(modelItem => item.SellEndDate)
        </td>
        <td>
            @Html.DisplayFor(modelItem => item.DiscontinuedDate)
        </td>
        <td>
            @Html.DisplayFor(modelItem => item.rowguid)
        </td>
        <td>
            @Html.DisplayFor(modelItem => item.ModifiedDate)
        </td>
        <td>
            @Html.ActionLink("Edit", "Edit", new { id=item.ProductID })

            @Html.ActionLink("Details", "Details", new { id=item.ProductID })

            @Html.ActionLink("Delete", "Delete", new { id=item.ProductID })
        </td>
    </tr>
}
</table>
```

This view presents the list of Products in a simple table. The bulk of the work is done in a loop, which iterates over the list of products and renders an HTML table row for each one.

HTML

```
<% foreach (var item in Model) { %>

    <tr>
      <!-- ... -->
      <td><%= Html.Encode(item.ProductID) %></td>
      <td><%= Html.Encode(item.Name) %></td>
      <!-- ... -->
    </tr>

<% } %>
```

> **NOTE** *Visual Studio can infer the type of model because you created a strongly typed view. In the page directive you can see that this view doesn't inherit from* `System.Web.Mvc.Page`. *Instead, it inherits from the generic version, which states that the model will be an* `IEnumerable` *collection of* `Product` *objects. This in turn exposes a* `Model` *property with that type. You can still pass the wrong type of item to the view from the controller. In the case of a strongly typed view, this results in a run-time exception.*

Each of the properties of the products is HTML encoded before it is rendered using the `Encode` method on the `Html` helper property. This prevents common issues with malicious code injected into the application masquerading as valid user data. ASP.NET MVC can take advantage of the `<%: ... %>` markup, which uses a colon in the place of the equals sign in ASP.NET 4 to more easily perform this encoding. Here is the same snippet again taking advantage of this technique:

HTML

```
<% foreach (var item in Model) { %>

    <tr>
        <!-- ... -->
        <td><%: item.ProductID %></td>
        <td><%: item.Name %></td>
        <!-- ... -->
    </tr>

<% } %>
```

In addition to the `Encode` method, one other `Html` helper method is used by this view: the `ActionLink` helper. This method emits a standard HTML anchor tag designed to trigger the specified action. Two forms are in use here. The simplest of these is the one designed to create a new Product record:

HTML

```
<p>
  <%= Html.ActionLink("Create New", "Create") %>
</p>
```

The first parameter is the text that will be rendered inside the anchor tag. This is the text that will be presented to the user. The second parameter is the name of the action to trigger. Because no controller has been specified, the current controller is assumed.

The more complex use of `ActionLink` is used to render the edit and details links for each product.

HTML

```
<td>
  <%= Html.ActionLink("Edit", "Edit", new { id=item.ProductID }) %> |
  <%= Html.ActionLink("Details", "Details", new { id=item.ProductID })%>
</td>
```

The first two parameters are the same as before and represent the link text and the action name, respectively. The third parameter is an anonymous object that contains data to be passed to the action method when it is called.

When you run the application and enter /products/ in your address bar, you will be presented with the page displayed in Figure 17-6. Trying to click any of the links causes a run-time exception because the target action does not yet exist.

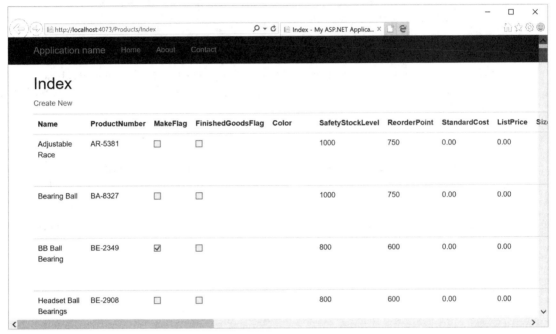

FIGURE 17-6

> **NOTE** *After you have a view and a controller, you can use the shortcut Ctrl+M, Ctrl+G to toggle between the two.*

ADVANCED MVC

This section provides an overview for some of the more advanced features of ASP.NET MVC.

Routing

As you were navigating around the MVC site in your web browser, you might have noticed that the URLs are quite different from a normal ASP.NET website. They do not contain file extensions and do not match up with the underlying folder structure. These URLs are mapped to action methods and controllers with a set of classes that belong to the routing engine, which is located in the `System.Web.Routing` assembly.

> **NOTE** *The routing engine was originally developed as a part of the ASP.NET MVC project but was released as a standalone library before MVC shipped. Although it is not described in this book, it is possible to use the routing engine with ASP.NET Web Forms projects.*

In the previous example you created a simple list view for products. This list view was based on the standard List template, which renders the following snippet for each Product in the database being displayed:

HTML

```html
<td>
  <%= Html.ActionLink("Edit", "Edit", new { id=item.ProductID }) %> |
  <%= Html.ActionLink("Details", "Details", new { id=item.ProductID })%>
</td>
```

If you examine the generated HTML markup of the final page, you should see that this becomes the following:

HTML

```html
<td>
  <a href="/Products/Edit/2">Edit</a> |
  <a href="/Products/Details/2">Details</a>
</td>
```

These URLs are made up of three parts:

➤ Products is the name of the controller. There is a corresponding `ProductsController` in the project.

➤ Edit and Details are the names of action methods on the controller. The `ProductsController` will have methods called `Edit` and `Details`.

➤ The 2 is a parameter that represents the id of the product.

Each of these components is defined in a *route*, which is set up in the `Global.asax.cs` file (or the `Global.asax.vb` file for VB) in a method called `RegisterRoutes`. When the application first starts, it calls this method and passes in the `System.Web.Routing.RouteTable.Routes` static collection. This collection contains all the routes for the entire application.

C#

```csharp
public static void RegisterRoutes(RouteCollection routes)
{
    routes.IgnoreRoute("{resource}.axd/{*pathInfo}");
```

```
        routes.MapHttpRoute(
            name: "DefaultApi",
            routeTemplate: "api/{controller}/{id}",
            defaults: new { id = RouteParameter.Optional }
        );

        routes.MapRoute(
            name: "Default",
            routeTemplate: "{controller}/{action}/{id}",
            defaults: new { controller = "Home", action = "Index", id =
                UrlParameter.Optional }
        );

    }
```

VB

```
    Shared Sub RegisterRoutes(ByVal routes As RouteCollection)
        routes.IgnoreRoute("{resource}.axd/{*pathInfo}")
        routes.MapHttpRoute( _
            "DefaultApi", _
            "api/{controller}/{id}", _
            New { .id = RouteParameter.Optional } _
        )

        routes.MapRoute( _
            "Default", _
            "{controller}/{action}/{id}", _
            New With {.controller = "Home", .action = "Index", .id = _
                UrlParameter.Optional } _
        )

    End Sub
```

The first method call tells the routing engine that it should ignore all requests for .axd files. When an incoming URL matches this route, the engine will completely ignore it and allow other parts of the application to handle it. This method can be handy if you want to integrate Web Forms and MVC into a single application. All you need to do is ask the routing engine to ignore .aspx and .asmx files.

The second method call defines a new Route and adds it to the collection. This overload of MapRoute method takes three parameters. The first parameter is a name, which can be used as a handle to this route later on. The second parameter is a URL template. This parameter can have normal text along with special tokens inside of braces. These tokens will be used as placeholders that are filled in when the route matches a URL. Some tokens are reserved and will be used by the MVC routing engine to select a controller and execute the correct action. The final parameter is a dictionary of default values. You can see that this "Default" route matches any URL in the form /controller/action/id where the default controller is Home, the default action is Index, and the id parameter defaults to an empty string.

When a new HTTP request comes in, each route in the RouteCollection tries to match the URL against its URL template in the order that they are added. The first route that can do so fills in any default values that haven't been supplied. When these values have all been collected, a Controller is created and an action method is called.

Routes are also used to generate URLs inside of views. When a helper needs a URL, it consults each route (in order again) to see if it can build a URL for the specified controller, action, and parameter values. The first route to match generates the correct URL. If a route encounters a parameter value that it doesn't know about, it becomes a query string parameter in the generated URL.

The following snippet declares a new route for an online store that allows for two parameters: a category and a subcategory. Assuming that this MVC application has been deployed to the root of a web server, requests for the URL `http://servername/Shop/Accessories/Helmets` will go to the List action on the Products controller with the parameters Category set to Accessories and Subcategory set to Helmets:

C#
```
public static void RegisterRoutes(RouteCollection routes)
{
  routes.IgnoreRoute("{resource}.axd/{*pathInfo}");

  routes.MapRoute(
    "ProductsDisplay",
    "Shop/{category}/{subcategory}",
    new {
      controller = "Products",
      action = "List",
      category = "",
      subcategory = ""
    }
  );

  routes.MapRoute(
    "Default",
    "{controller}/{action}/{id}",
    new { controller = "Home", action = "Index", id = "" }
  );
}
```

VB
```
Shared Sub RegisterRoutes(ByVal routes As RouteCollection)
  routes.IgnoreRoute("{resource}.axd/{*pathInfo}")

  routes.MapRoute( _
    "ProductsDisplay", _
    "Shop/{category}/{subcategory}", _
    New With { _
    .controller = "Products", .action = "List", _
    .category = "", .subcategory = "" _
    })

  routes.MapRoute( _
    "Default", _
    "{controller}/{action}/{id}", _
    New With {.controller = "Home", .action = "Index", .id = ""} _
  )

End Sub
```

> **NOTE** *When a* `Route` *in a* `RouteCollection` *matches the URL, no other* `Route`
> *gets the opportunity. Because of this, the order in which* `Routes` *are added*
> *to the* `RouteCollection` *can be quite important. If the previous snippet had*
> *placed the new route after the Default one, it would never get to match an*
> *incoming request because a request for* `/Shop/Accessories/Helmets` *would be*
> *looking for an* `Accessories` *action method on a* `ShopController` *with an id*
> *of Helmets. Because there isn't a* `ShopController`, *the whole request will fail.*
> *If your application is not going to the expected controller action method for a*
> *URL, you might want to add a more specific* `Route` *to the* `RouteCollection`
> *before the more general ones or remove the more general ones altogether while*
> *you figure out the problem.*

Finally, you can also add constraints to the Route to prevent it from matching a URL unless some other condition is met. This can be a good idea if your parameters are going to be converted into complex data types, such as date times later, and require a specific format. The most basic kind of restraint is a string, which is interpreted as a regular expression that a parameter must match for the route to take effect. The following route definition uses this technique to ensure that the `zipCode` parameter is exactly five digits:

C#

```
routes.MapRoute(
  "StoreFinder",
  "Stores/Find/{zipCode}",
  new { controller = "StoreFinder", action = "list" },
  new { zipCode = @"^\d{5}$" }
);
```

VB

```
routes.MapRoute( _
  "StoreFinder", _
  "Stores/Find/{zipCode}", _
  New With {.controller = "StoreFinder", .action = "list"}, _
  New With {.zipCode = "^\d{5}$"} _
)
```

The other type of constraint is a class that implements `IRouteConstraint`. This interface defines a single method `Match` that returns a Boolean value indicating whether or not the incoming request satisfies the constraint. There is one out-of-the-box implementation of `IRouteConstraint` called `HttpMethodConstraint`. This constraint can be used to ensure that the correct HTTP method, such as GET, POST, HEAD, or DELETE, is used. The following route accepts only HTTP POST requests:

C#

```
routes.MapRoute(
  "PostOnlyRoute",
  "Post/{action}",
```

```
    new { controller = "Post" },
    new { post = new HttpMethodConstraint("POST") }
);
```

VB

```
routes.MapRoute(
  "PostOnlyRoute", _
  "Post/{action}", _
  New With {.controller = "Post"}, _
  New With {.post = New HttpMethodConstraint("POST")} _
)
```

The URL routing classes are powerful and flexible and allow you to easily create "pretty" URLs. This can aid users navigating around your site and even improve your site's ranking with search engines.

Action Method Parameters

All the action methods in previous examples do not accept any input from outside of the application to perform their tasks; they rely entirely on the state of the model. In real-world applications this is an unlikely scenario. The ASP.NET MVC framework makes it easy to parameterize action methods from a variety of sources.

As mentioned in the previous section, the Default route exposes an id parameter, which defaults to an empty string. To access the value of the id parameter from within the action method, you can just add it to the signature of the method as the following snippet shows:

C#

```
public ActionResult Details(int id)
{
  using (var db = new ProductsDataContext())
  {
    var product = db.Products.SingleOrDefault(x => x.ProductID == id);

    if (product == null)
      return View("NotFound");

    return View(product);
  }
}
```

VB

```
Public Function Details(ByVal id As Integer) As ActionResult
  Using db As New ProductsDataContext
    Dim product = db.Products.FirstOrDefault(Function(p As Product)
    p.ProductID = id)

    Return View(product)
  End Using
End Function
```

When the MVC framework executes the Details action method, it searches through the parameters that have been extracted from the URL by the matching route. These parameters are matched up with the parameters on the action method by name, and then passed in when the method is called. As the details method shows, the framework can convert the type of the parameter on the fly. Action methods can also retrieve parameters from the query string portion of the URL and from HTTP POST data using the same technique.

> **NOTE** *If the conversion cannot be made for any reason, an exception is thrown.*

In addition, an action method can accept a parameter of the FormValues type that aggregates all the HTTP POST data into a single parameter. If the data in the FormValues collection represents the properties of an object, you can simply add a parameter of that type, and a new instance will be created when the action method is called. The Create action, shown in the following snippet, uses this to construct a new instance of the Product class, and then saves it:

C#
```csharp
public ActionResult Create()
{
  return View();
}

[HttpPost]
public ActionResult Create([Bind(Exclude="ProductId")]Product product)
{
  if (!ModelState.IsValid)
    return View();

  using (var db = new ProductsDataContext())
  {
    db.Products.InsertOnSubmit(product);
    db.SubmitChanges();
  }
  return RedirectToAction("List");
}
```

VB
```vb
<HttpPost()>
Function Create(<Bind(Exclude:="id")> ByVal product As Product)

  If (Not ModelState.IsValid) Then
    Return View()
  End If

  Using db As New ProductsDataContext
    db.Products.InsertOnSubmit(product)
    db.SubmitChanges()
  End Using
  Return RedirectToAction("List")
End Function
```

> **NOTE** *There are two Create action methods here. The first one simply renders the Create view. The second one is marked up with an* HttpPostAttribute, *which means that it can be selected only if the HTTP request uses the POST verb. This is a common practice in designing ASP.NET MVC websites. In addition to* HttpPostAttribute *there are also corresponding attributes for the* GET, PUT, *and* DELETE *verbs.*

Model Binders

The process to create the new Product instance is the responsibility of a *model binder.* The model binder matches properties in the HTTP POST data with properties on the type that it is attempting to create. This works in this example because the template that was used to generate the Create view renders the HTML INPUT fields with the correct name as this snippet of the rendered HTML shows:

HTML
```html
<p>
  <label for="ProductID">ProductID:</label>
  <input id="ProductID" name="ProductID" type="text" value="" />
</p>
<p>
  <label for="Name">Name:</label>
  <input id="Name" name="Name" type="text" value="" />
</p>
```

A number of ways exist to control the behavior of a model binder including the BindAttribute, which is used in the Create method shown previously. This attribute is used to include or exclude certain properties and to specify a prefix for the HTTP POST values. This can be useful if multiple objects in the POST collection need to be bound.

Model binders can also be used from within the action method to update existing instances of your model classes using the UpdateModel and TryUpdateModel methods. The chief difference is that TryUpdateModel returns a boolean value indicating whether or not it built a successful model, and UpdateModel just throws an exception if it can't. The Edit action method shows this technique:

C#
```csharp
[HttpPost]
public ActionResult Edit(int id, FormCollection formValues)
{
  using (var db = new ProductsDataContext())
  {
```

```
        var product = db.Products.SingleOrDefault(x => x.ProductID == id);

        if (TryUpdateModel(product))
        {
          db.SubmitChanges();
          return RedirectToAction("Index");
        }
        return View(product);
      }
    }
```

VB

```
    <HttpPost()>
    Function Edit(ByVal id As Integer, ByVal formValues As FormCollection)
      Using db As New ProductsDataContext
        Dim product = db.Products.FirstOrDefault(Function(p As Product)
        p.ProductID = id)

        If TryUpdateModel(product) Then
          db.SubmitChanges()
          Return RedirectToAction("Index")
        End If
        Return View(product)
      End Using
    End Function
```

Areas

An *area* is a self-contained part of an MVC application that manages its own models, controllers, and views. You can even define routes specific to an area. To create a new area, select Add ➪ Area from the project context menu in the Solution Explorer. The Add Area dialog, as in Figure 17-7, prompts you to provide a name for your area.

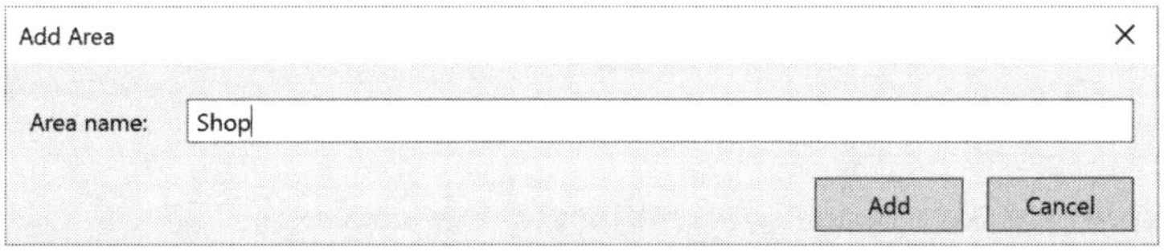

FIGURE 17-7

After you click Add, many new files are added to your project to support the area. Figure 17-8 shows a project with an area added to it named Shop.

FIGURE 17-8

In addition to having its own controllers and views, each area has a class called
*AreaName*AreaRegistration that inherits from the abstract base class AreaRegistration. This
class contains an abstract property for the name of your area and an abstract method for integrating
your area with the rest of the application. The default implementation registers the standard routes.

C#

```csharp
public class ShopAreaRegistration : AreaRegistration
{
  public override string AreaName
  {
    get
    {
      return "Shop";
    }
  }

  public override void RegisterArea(AreaRegistrationContext context)
  {
    context.MapRoute(
      "Shop_default",
      "Shop/{controller}/{action}/{id}",
      new { action = "Index", id = "" }
    );
  }
}
```

VB

```vb
Public Class ShopAreaRegistration
  Inherits AreaRegistration

  Public Overrides ReadOnly Property AreaName() As String
    Get
      Return "Shop"
```

```
      End Get
    End Property

    Public Overrides Sub RegisterArea(ByVal context As AreaRegistrationContext)
      context.MapRoute( _
        "Shop_default", _
        "Shop/{controller}/{action}/{id}", _
        New With {.action = "Index", .id = ""} _
      )
    End Sub
End Class
```

> **NOTE** *The* RegisterArea *method of the* ShopAreaRegistration *class defines a route in which every URL is prefixed with* /Shop/ *by convention. This can be useful while debugging routes but is not necessary as long as area routes do not clash with any other routes.*

To link to a controller that is inside another area, you need to use an overload of Html.ActionLink that accepts a routeValues parameter. The object you provide for this parameter must include an area property set to the name of the area that contains the controller you link to.

C#

```
<%= Html.ActionLink("Shop", "Index", new { area = "Shop" }) %>
```

VB

```
<%= Html.ActionLink("Shop", "Index", New With {.area = "Shop"})%>
```

One issue frequently encountered when adding area support to a project is that the controller factory becomes confused when multiple controllers have the same name. To avoid this issue you can limit the namespaces that a route uses to search for a controller to satisfy any request. The following code snippet limits the namespaces for the global routes to MvcApplication.Controllers, which do not match any of the area controllers.

C#

```
routes.MapRoute(
  "Default",
  "{controller}/{action}/{id}",
  new { controller = "Home", action = "Index", id = "" },
  null,
  new[] { "MvcApplication.Controllers" }
);
```

VB

```
routes.MapRoute( _
  "Default", _
  "{controller}/{action}/{id}", _
  New With {.controller = "Home", .action = "Index", .id = ""}, _
  Nothing, _
  New String() {"MvcApplication.Controllers"} _
)
```

> **NOTE** *The* `AreaRegistrationContext` *automatically includes the area namespace when you use it to specify routes, so you should need to supply only namespaces to the global routes.*

Validation

In addition to just creating or updating it, a model binder can decide whether or not the model instance that it operates on is valid. The results of this decision are found in the `ModelState` property. Model binders can pick up some simple validation errors by default, usually for incorrect types. Figure 17-9 shows the result of attempting to save a Product when the form is empty. Most of these validation errors are based on the fact that these properties are non-nullable value types and require a value.

FIGURE 17-9

The user interface for this error report is provided by the `Html.ValidationSummary` call, which is made on the view. This helper method examines the `ModelState`, and if it finds any errors, it renders them as a list along with a header message.

You can add additional validation hints to the properties of the model class by marking them up using the attributes in the `System.ComponentModel.DataAnnotations` assembly. Because the `Product` class is created by LINQ to SQL you should not update it directly. The LINQ to SQL generated classes are defined as partial, so you can extend them, but there is no easy way to attach meta data to the generated properties this way. Instead, you need to create a *meta data proxy* class with the properties you want to mark up, provide them with the correct data annotation attributes, and then mark up the partial class with a `MetadataTypeAttribute` identifying the proxy class. The following code snippet shows this technique used to provide some validation meta data to the `Product` class:

C#

```csharp
[MetadataType(typeof(ProductValidationMetadata))]
public partial class Product
{
}

public class ProductValidationMetadata
{
    [Required, StringLength(256)]
    public string Name { get; set; }

    [Range(0, 100)]
    public int DaysToManufacture { get; set; }
}
```

VB

```vb
Imports System.ComponentModel.DataAnnotations

<MetadataType(GetType(ProductMetaData))>
Partial Public Class Product

End Class

Public Class ProductMetaData
    <Required(), StringLength(256)>
    Property Name As String

    <Range(0, 100)>
    Property DaysToManufacture As Integer
End Class
```

Now, attempting to create a new Product with no name and a negative Days to Manufacture produces the errors shown in Figure 17-10.

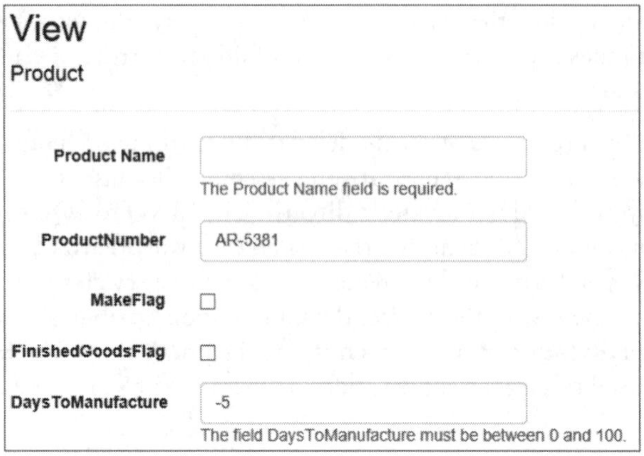

FIGURE 17-10

> **NOTE** *You might notice that along with the error report at the top of the page, for each field that has a validation error, the textbox is colored red and has an error message after it. The first effect is caused by the* Html.TextBox *helper, which accepts the value of the property that it is attached to. If it encounters an error in the model state for its attached property, it adds an* input-valida-tion-error *CSS class to the rendered* INPUT *control. The default style sheet defines the red background. The second effect is caused by the* Html .ValidationMessage *helper. This helper is also associated with a property and renders the contents of its second parameter if it detects that its attached property has an error associated with it.*

Partial Views

At times you have large areas of user interface markup that you would like to reuse. In the ASP.NET MVC framework a reusable section of view is called a partial view. Partial views act similar to views except that they have an .ascx extension and inherit from System.Web.Mvc.ViewUserControl. To create a partial view, check the Create a Partial View check box on the same Add View dialog that you use to create other views.

To render a partial view, you can use the Html.RenderPartial method. The most common over-load of this method accepts a view name and a model object. Just as with a normal view, a partial view can be either controller-specific or shared. After the partial view has been rendered, its HTML markup is inserted into the main view. This code snippet renders a "Form" partial for the current model:

C#

```
<% Html.RenderPartial("Form", Model); %>
```

VB

```
<% Html.RenderPartial("Form", Model) %>
```

> **NOTE** *You can call a partial view directly from an action using the normal View method. If you do this, only the HTML rendered by the partial view will be included in the HTTP response. This can be useful if you return data to jQuery.*

Dynamic Data Templates

Dynamic Data is a feature of ASP.NET Web Forms that enables you to render UI based on meta data associated with the model. Although ASP.NET MVC does not integrate directly with Dynamic Data, a number of features in ASP.NET MVC 4 are similar in spirit. Templates in ASP.NET MVC 4 can render parts of your model in different ways, whether they are small and simple such as a single string property or large and complex like the whole product class. The templates are exposed by Html helper methods. There are templates for display and templates for editing purposes.

Display Templates

The Details view created by the Add View dialog contains code to render each property. Here is the markup for just two of these properties:

HTML

```
<p>
  <%= Html.LabelFor(x => x.ProductID) %>
  <%= Html.DisplayFor(x => x.ProductID) %>
</p>
<p>
  <%= Html.LabelFor(x => x.Name) %>
  <%= Html.DisplayFor(x => x.Name) %>
</p>
```

Notice that the name of the property is not coded into the HTML, but it's referenced through a lambda function. This has a number of immediate advantages. First, the label is now strongly typed. It updates if you refactor your model class. In addition to this you can apply a `System.ComponentModel.DisplayName` attribute to your model (or to a model meta data proxy) to change the text that displays to the user. This helps to ensure consistency across the entire application. The following code snippet shows the Product meta data proxy with a couple of `DisplayNameAttributes`, and Figure 17-11 shows the rendered result:

FIGURE 17-11

C#

```
public class ProductValidationMetadata
{
    [DisplayName("ID")]
```

```csharp
    public int ProductID { get; set; }

    [Required, StringLength(256)]
    [DisplayName("Product Name")]
    public string Name { get; set; }

    [Range(0, 100)]
    public int DaysToManufacture { get; set; }
}
```

VB

```vb
Public Class ProductMetaData
    <DisplayName("ID")>
    Property ProductID As Integer

    <Required(), StringLength(256)> _
    <DisplayName("Product Name")>
    Property Name As String

    <Range(0, 100)>
    Property DaysToManufacture As Integer
End Class
```

The `DisplayFor` helper also provides a lot of hidden flexibility. It selects a template based on the type of the property that it displays. You can override each of these type-specific views by creating a partial view named after the type in the `Shared\DisplayTemplates` folder. You can also create controller-specific templates by putting them inside a `DisplayTemplates` subfolder within the controller-specific Views folder.

Although the display template is selected based on the type of the property by default, you can override this by either supplying the name of the template to the `DisplayFor` helper or applying a `System.ComponentModel.DataAnnotations.UIHintAttribute` to the property. This attribute takes a string that identifies the type of template to use. When the framework needs to render the display for the property, it tries to find the display template described by the UI Hint. If one is not found, it looks for a type-specific template. If a template still hasn't been found, the default behavior is executed.

If you simply apply `LabelFor` and `DisplayFor` for every property on your model, you can use the `Html.DisplayForModel` helper method. This method renders a label and a display template for each property on the model class. You can prevent a property from displaying by this helper by annotating it with a `System.ComponentModel.DataAnnotations.ScaffoldColumnAttribute` passing it the value `false`.

> **NOTE** *If you want to change the way the `DisplayForModel` renders, you can create a type-specific template for it. If you want to change the way it renders generally, create an `Object` display template.*

A number of built-in display templates are available that you can use out of the box. Be aware that if you want to customize the behavior of one of these, you need to re-create it from scratch:

➤ **String:** No real surprises, just renders the string contents itself. This template does HTML encode the property value, though.

➤ **Html:** The same as string but without the HTML encoding. This is the rawest form of display that you can have. Be careful using this template because it is a vector for malicious code injection such as Cross Site Scripting Attacks (XSS).

➤ **Email Address:** Renders an e-mail address as a mailto: link.

➤ **Url:** Renders a URL as an HTML anchor.

➤ **HiddenInput:** Does not render the property at all unless the `ViewData.ModelMetaData` `.HideSurroundingHtml` property is `false`.

➤ **Decimal:** Renders the property to two decimal places.

➤ **Boolean:** Renders a read-only check box for non-nullable values and a read-only drop-down list with True, False, and Not Set options for nullable properties.

➤ **Object:** Renders complex objects and null values.

Edit Templates

It probably comes as no surprise that there are corresponding `EditorFor` and `EditorForModel` Html helpers that handle the way properties and objects are rendered for edit purposes. Editor templates can be overridden by supplying partial views in the EditTemplates folder. Edit Templates can use the same UI hint system that display templates use. Just as with display templates, you can use a number of built-in editor templates out of the box:

➤ **String:** Renders a standard textbox, initially populated with the value if provided and named after the property. This ensures that it will be used correctly by the model binder to rebuild the object on the other side.

➤ **Password:** The same as string but renders an HTML PASSWORD input instead of a textbox.

➤ **MultilineText:** Creates a multiline textbox. There is no way to specify the number of rows and columns for this textbox here. It is assumed that you will use CSS to do that.

➤ **HiddenInput:** Similar to the display template, renders an HTML HIDDEN input.

➤ **Decimal:** Similar to the display template but renders a textbox to edit the value.

➤ **Boolean:** If the property type is non-nullable, this renders a check box control. If this template is applied to a nullable property, it renders a drop-down list containing the same three items as the display template.

➤ **Object:** Renders complex editors.

jQuery

jQuery is an open-source JavaScript framework included by default with the ASP.NET MVC framework. The basic element of jQuery is the function $(). This function can be passed a JavaScript DOM element or a string describing elements via a CSS selector. The $() function returns a jQuery object that exposes a number of functions that affect the elements contained. Most of these functions also return the same jQuery object, so these function calls can be chained together. As an example, the following snippet selects all the H2 tags and adds the word "section" to the end of each one:

JAVASCRIPT

```
$("h2").append("section");
```

To make use of jQuery, you need to create a reference to the jQuery library found in the /Scripts folder by adding the following to the head section of your page:

HTML

```
<script type="text/javascript" src="/Scripts/jquery-1.3.2.js"></script>
```

You can use jQuery to make an HTTP request by using the $.get and $.post methods (or the more flexible $.ajax method that takes a verb as one of its parameters). These methods accept a URL and can optionally have a callback function to provide the results to. The following view renders the time inside two div tags called server and client, respectively. There is also a button called update, which when clicked makes a GET request to the /time URL. When it receives the results, it updates the value displayed in the client div but not the server one. In addition to this it uses the slideUp and slideDown functions to animate the client time in the UI.

C#

```
<%@ Page Language="C#" Inherits="System.Web.Mvc.ViewPage<System.String>" %>
<!DOCTYPE html PUBLIC "-//W3C//DTD XHTML 1.0 Transitional//EN"
"http://www.w3.org/TR/xhtml1/DTD/xhtml1-transitional.dtd">
<html xmlns="http://www.w3.org/1999/xhtml">
<head runat="server">
  <title>Index</title>
  <script type="text/javascript" src="/Scripts/jquery-1.3.2.js"></script>
  <script type="text/javascript">
    $(document).ready(function () {
      $('#updater').click(UpdateNow);
    });
    function UpdateNow() {
      $.get('/time', function (data) {
        $('#clientTime').slideUp('fast', function () {
          $('#clientTime').empty().append(data).slideDown();
        });
      });
    }
  </script>
</head>
<body>
```

```
<div>
    <h2>
        Server</h2>
    <div id="serverTime">
        <%:Model %></div>
    <h2>
        Client</h2>
    <div id="clientTime">
        <%:Model %></div>
    <input type="button" value="Update" id="updater"  />
</div>
</body>
</html>
```

Here is the action method that controls the previous view. It uses the `IsAjaxRequest` extension method to determine if the request has come from jQuery. If it has, it returns just the time as a string; otherwise it returns the full view.

C#

```
public ActionResult Index()
{
  var now = DateTime.Now.ToLongTimeString();
  if (Request.IsAjaxRequest())
    return Content(now);
  return View(now as object);
}
```

VB

```
Function Index() As ActionResult
  Dim timeNow = Now.ToString()
  If Request.IsAjaxRequest() Then
    Return Content(timeNow)
  End If
  Return View(CType(timeNow, Object))
End Function
```

jQuery is a rich client-side programming tool with an extremely active community and a large number of plug-ins. For more information about jQuery, including a comprehensive set of tutorials and demos, see `http://jquery.com`.

SUMMARY

The ASP.NET MVC framework makes it easy to build highly testable, loosely coupled web applications that embrace the nature of HTTP. For many developers, it is the standard for creating new ASP.NET applications. The framework provides a flexible platform from which you can take advantage of not only the power of ASP.NET MVC, but also the tools in the wider web development ecosystem. For more information about ASP.NET MVC, see `http://asp.net/mvc`.

18

.NET Core

WHAT'S IN THIS CHAPTER?

➤ Understanding .NET Core and ASP.NET Core

➤ Using the ASP.NET Core Templates

➤ Taking advantage of the NuGet Package Manager

➤ Delivering static files using the Bower Package Manager

WROX.COM CODE DOWNLOADS FOR THIS CHAPTER

The wrox.com code downloads for this chapter can be found at www.wrox.com by searching for this book's ISBN number (978-1-119-40458-3). The code and any related support files are located in their own folder for this chapter.

The ASP.NET Framework, while still quite solid, has been getting a little long of tooth recently. Keep in mind that the basic pipeline found in ASP.NET Web Forms has remained more or less unchanged since ASP.NET 1.0. Even the ASP.NET MVC framework is over seven years old (which is 75 years old in Internet years). Much has changed in that period, and it was becoming difficult to innovate on that platform.

Even beyond innovation opportunities, some of the tools that were commonly being used in the web world were not easily integrated into the Microsoft stack. Open-source tools are the big players in the web sites of today, and that usually means that a platform needs to be compatible with them. And, as the final impetus for change, Microsoft Azure strategy is to be platform agnostic. The support for Linux platforms is equal to the ability to spin up Microsoft servers. And the functionality offered through the various services is accessible through common protocols, whether it be a REST-based API or shell scripting.

So from this situation, Microsoft created .NET Core. What it is and why developers should care are common questions, followed closely by what tooling is available in Visual Studio to help. All of those questions are addressed in this chapter.

WHAT IS .NET CORE?

This is probably at the heart of the most pressing questions on the minds of developers. Is it a replacement for the .NET Framework? Does this mean that .NET is going away? The answers aren't nearly as dire as the casual developer might think.

The goal of .NET Core is to provide an execution platform that is capable of running on multiple operating systems. Applications that have been written against .NET Core can be executed on Windows (naturally) but also on macOS and Linux. It is also intended to be used in embedded scenarios, including the ever present IoT (Internet of Things). Yes, this might seem like a laundry list of targets, but the idea is to help developers minimize the changes that need to be made to their application as they migrate from platform to platform.

Now don't get to thinking that .NET Core is a full implementation of the .NET Framework on these other platforms. It's not. It is an implementation of the .NET Standard Library on multiple platforms. The .NET Standard Library defines the set of .NET APIs that are to be implemented on every platform that supports .NET. It is a subset of the .NET Framework. As a result, it's not possible to run every .NET application on each of those platforms. However, application compatibility exists for Xamarin (`https://xamarin.com`) and Mono (`http://www.mono-project.com`) on the appropriate platforms.

From a development perspective, .NET Core applications can be developed in C# and F#, and plans are in the works to support Visual Basic as well. The SDK and compilers are provided for the different platforms, so it's possible to develop applications on the platform for which they are targeted. For instance, you can create applications for the Mac on the Mac using Visual Studio Code.

In Visual Studio 2017, there are a number of different templates that are available to create .NET Core applications. They are:

➤ **Console Application:** Creates a command-line application

➤ **Class Library:** Creates a library that will be used in other .NET Core applications

➤ **Unit Test Project:** Allows for unit testing of your projects using MSTest

➤ **xUnit Test Project:** Allows for unit testing of your projects using xUnit

➤ **ASP.NET Core Empty:** Creates an empty .NET Core application that is suitable for serving up a web site

➤ **ASP.NET Core Web App:** Creates an ASP.NET MVC application

➤ **ASP.NET Core Web API:** Creates an ASP.NET Web API application

➤ **Solution File:** Creates an empty solution

As a brief interlude before getting into the ASP.NET Core application, you should be aware that much of what can be done with .NET Core can be done using command-line tools. For example, the following command line will create a new .NET Core Console application in the traditional Hello World style:

```
dotnet new console -n HelloWorld -o src/HelloWorld
```

The result, as seen when executed in the Developer Command Prompt for VS 2017, is as follows.

```
Content generation time: 99.6688 ms
The template "Console Application" created successfully.
```

Let's finish up this Hello World example. Use the following commands to change the directory to the location of the generated source and see what it looks like.

```
cd src/HelloWorld
dir
03/25/2017  11:14 AM    <DIR>          .
03/25/2017  11:14 AM    <DIR>          ..
03/25/2017  11:13 AM                170 HelloWorld.csproj
03/25/2017  11:13 AM                180 Program.cs
               2 File(s)            350 bytes
               2 Dir(s)  229,216,518,144 bytes free
```

The last two steps are to restore the packages necessary to run the application and to run the application itself. The dotnet restore command retrieves the needed packages, while dotnet run executes the code. The result is as follows.

```
C:\Demo\HelloWorld\src\HelloWorld dotnet restore
  Restoring packages for C:\Demo\HelloWorld\src\HelloWorld\HelloWorld.csproj...
  Generating MSBuild file C:\Demo\HelloWorld\src\HelloWorld \obj\
    HelloWorld.csproj.nuget.g.props.
  Generating MSBuild file C:\Demo\HelloWorld\src\HelloWorld \obj\
    HelloWorld.csproj.nuget.g.targets.
  Writing lock file to disk. Path: C:\Demo\HelloWorld\src\HelloWorld \src\
    HelloWorld\obj\project.assets.json
  Restore completed in 2.41 sec for C:\Demo\HelloWorld\src\HelloWorld \src\
    HelloWorld\HelloWorld.csproj.

  NuGet Config files used:
      C:\Users\bruce\AppData\Roaming\NuGet\NuGet.Config
      C:\Program Files (x86)\NuGet\Config\Microsoft.VisualStudio.Offline.config

  Feeds used:
      https://api.nuget.org/v3/index.json
      C:\Program Files (x86)\Microsoft SDKs\NuGetPackages\

C:\Demo\HelloWorld\src\HelloWorld \src\HelloWorld>dotnet run
Hello World!
```

WORKING WITH ASP.NET CORE

As much as it might pain you to acknowledge, ASP.NET is old. Really old. It was first released with .NET 1.0 in 2002. Friendster had 3 million users in 2002 and Facebook didn't exist. Blockbuster turned down an opportunity to purchase Netflix. The iPod was a year old and the iPhone was but an idea. So much has changed, and not just in the consumer marketplace. The tools and techniques used to build web applications now are a far cry from .NET 1.0. And even ASP.NET MVC, a much more flexible development platform, is getting on in years.

But change for change's sake is not a good enough reason to consider a different development and deployment pattern. So let's consider what makes an ASP.NET Core application both different and worthwhile.

Architecturally, ASP.NET Core is a more modular framework than ASP.NET. ASP.NET is based on the System.Web library. And while there is a lot that is good in System.Web (everything from membership to cookies to Web Form controls), over time that particular assembly has become heavy. If you use one of these features, then the entire System.Web assembly must be included in your project. And in a world of lightweight and agile options, that is a potential problem.

The idea of modularity in ASP.NET Core applications is accomplished through packages. .NET Core includes, as the name suggests, just the core functionality that is likely to be used across different classes of applications. If you need functionality beyond that core, it can be made available to your application through the addition of packages that contain only that functionality. Need access to membership? No problem. Just add the membership package to your projects. And that's all you'll get. Your application is as small as you need for the functionality you use and no larger.

project.json versus csproj

ASP.NET Core is not completely new for Visual Studio 2017. Although only preview tooling was available when Visual Studio 2015 was released, enhancements were made to the .NET Core tools through a number of additional releases. This tooling used `project.json` as the container for project-related information.

In the abstract, there was nothing wrong with `project.json`. It was actually quite easy to understand and was supported within Visual Studio with IntelliSense capabilities. If you were creating .NET Core applications from scratch, then there were a lot of benefits that accrued from using `project.json`.

However, there were a couple of fatal flaws that eventually resulted in retiring `project.json` as the project format of choice. Probably the most influential was that MSBuild didn't support it. As well, the migration of existing, monolithic projects to `project.json` would require a large amount of effort and would be fraught with the potential for errors. Both of these concerns resulted in the `csproj` format being selected as the format for future development efforts.

This isn't a complete loss for people who fell in love with `project.json`. Microsoft has made some changes to the `csproj` format to help with some of the things that people loved about `project.json`. Probably the most useful is the fact that not every single file that is part of the project needs to be enumerated within the `csproj` file. Instead, wildcarding can be used to include files. This greatly helps reduce the number of merge conflicts that might otherwise occur when you are working with large teams.

Creating an ASP.NET Core Application

The basic mechanics of creating an ASP.NET Core application will be familiar to Visual Studio users. Start by selecting the File ⇨ New ⇨ Project menu option. The New Project dialog (shown in Figure 18-1) appears.

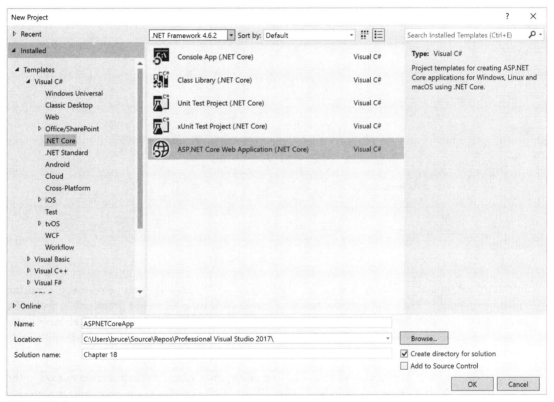

FIGURE 18-1

From the navigation list on the left, select the language of your choice (so long as your choice is Visual C #), and then select the .NET Core option to show the list of templates. Choose ASP.NET Core Web Application (.NET Core).

Alternatively, you can select the Web option from the navigation list and a list of Web templates. This includes the same ASP.NET Core Web Application (.NET Core) template, along with an ASP .NET Core Web Application (.NET Framework) template. The only difference is the runtime libraries supported by the project. The former uses the .NET Core runtime, allowing it to be deployed onto Linux or MacOS machines. The later can only be used on machines that support the .NET Framework (that is, Windows-based servers).

Regardless of the template that you decide to use, once you have provided a project name, the dialog shown in Figure 18-2 appears.

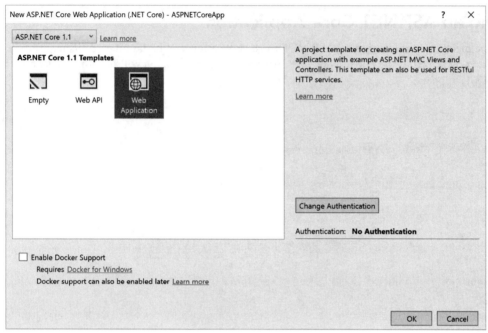

FIGURE 18-2

In this dialog, you are selecting from a list of ASP.NET Core templates that provide slightly different starting points. The Empty project template creates just that: an empty project. You will need to add all of the files, both supporting and otherwise, yourself. The Web API and Web Application project templates provide a reasonable starting point for creating a Web API or a Web application, respectively.

If you select the Web Application as your starting point, the Change Authentication button in the lower right of the dialog becomes enabled. This allows you to configure the new project with the authentication method that you would like to use. The Change Authentication dialog (Figure 18-3) appears when you click the button.

The authentication options that are available are:

➤ **No authentication:** The project will be created with no authentication configured and no files related to configuration included.

➤ **Individual User Accounts:** The project will be created with the assumption that you're using user accounts specific to your project. This includes the traditional membership provider that ASP.NET developers have been using for years, as well as third-party authentication services like Facebook or Microsoft Live.

➤ **Work or School Accounts:** The project is created assuming that you're authenticating against a claims-based authentication service like Active Directory (either locally hosted or in Azure).

➤ **Windows Authentication:** The project is created so the current Windows user will be used to provide authentication and authorization details. This option should only be used if you are creating a web application for use on an intranet.

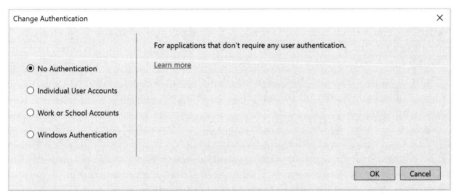

FIGURE 18-3

Once you have finished identifying the specific template you want to use, with any of the additional information that is required, the project that is created will look similar to what you see in Figure 18-4.

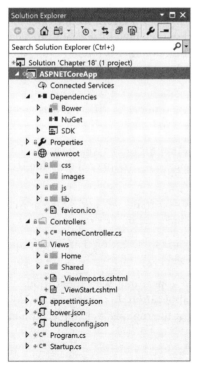

FIGURE 18-4

If this is your first time with an ASP.NET Core application, then there are a number of differences between this and an ASP.NET MVC application. And yet, there are also a couple of similarities to make sure you feel comfortable.

Let's start with the similarities. You'll notice that there is a Controllers folder that contains the controller classes. And the Views folder contains Razor (that is, the .CSHTML) files for the controllers. The files in this folder structure include the views that are shared across the different controllers.

Although the Controllers and Views folders do make up a large portion of any web application, that is pretty much the end of the similarities to an ASP.NET MVC application. To start, there is a wwwroot folder. This folder is actually the directory from which the content of the web application gets served up, at least during the development process. By default, there are subfolders called css, images, js, and lib. These folders contain the files that make up the default web application that is part of your chosen template.

> **NOTE** *There is no need for you to use the contents of these folders. Nor do you have to use the folders as they are named. You are free to modify them as you wish. This is just the default layout that was part of the template.*

There is a Dependencies node that is visible in the Solution Explorer. This node contains the different dependencies that are required by the application. With the template, there are three child nodes, one for each source of the dependency. The Bower node contains a list of the dependencies served by Bower. A more detailed description appears in the "Bower Package Manager" section later in this chapter. The NuGet node contains the list of packages that use the NuGet Package Manager to be delivered to the build process. More details on the NuGet functionality is found in the NuGet Package Manager section later in this chapter. And finally the SDK node contains the SDK files that are referenced by the application.

Beyond the wwwroot folder and the Dependencies node, there are a number of different files related to the application:

➤ **Appsettings.json:** This contains the configuration information for the web application. To a certain extent, it replaces the connection string, AppSettings and custom configuration settings that were previously found in the web.config file.

➤ **Bower.json:** The ASP.NET Core project templates uses Bower to deliver static content to the client. This file is used to configure the packages that are included in the project.

➤ **Bundleconfig.json:** This is used to configure the bundling and minification that is performed by the build process.

➤ **Program.cs:** While this might seem like a surprising file to appear in a Web application, it is used (as it always has been) as the starting point for the application. In the case of an ASP .NET Core application, it defines the process that will host the running web application and then starts it.

➤ **Startup.cs:** This contains a class that runs at startup. In general, the purpose of the class is to pull configuration information from various sources, but it also has the ability to set up a number of different pipeline functions.

Also, under the Properties node, there is another configuration file called launchSettings.json. This file contains information that is used to set up the running web application. It includes, for example, the URL (including the port number), the type of authentication that is being used, and whether a browser should be launched at start.

So you can get a sense of what the Program and Startup classes do, the following is the code from the default template:

```
public static void Main(string[] args)
{
    var host = new WebHostBuilder()
        .UseKestrel()
        .UseContentRoot(Directory.GetCurrentDirectory())
        .UseIISIntegration()
        .UseStartup<Startup>()
        .UseApplicationInsights()
        .Build();

    host.Run();
}
```

As you can see, the code itself is relatively straightforward. It creates an instance of the WebHostBuilder and then uses a number of its methods to define the behavior of the host. This includes where to find the content, which startup class to call, and whether Application Insights should be included. Once the instance has been configured, it is launched with a call to the Run method.

The Startup class is a little more wordy, but it also provides functionality to the web application at runtime, as well as at startup. The constructor for Startup (shown below) builds the configuration information.

```
public Startup(IHostingEnvironment env)
{
    var builder = new ConfigurationBuilder()
        .SetBasePath(env.ContentRootPath)
        .AddJsonFile("appsettings.json", optional: false,
          reloadOnChange: true)
        .AddJsonFile($"appsettings.{env.EnvironmentName}.json",
          optional: true)
        .AddEnvironmentVariables();
    Configuration = builder.Build();
}
```

Here, you can see that the appsettings.json file that was mentioned earlier is being loaded, along with any environment-specific configuration. But alongside building the configuration information, the Startup class included logging capabilities, features based on development versus release settings, and MVC routes.

NUGET PACKAGE MANAGER

The ability to include third-party packages in your project is taken as a given. Without such capabilities, the development effort for practically any application would be gargantuan. However, including external assemblies is not without issues. Once you have downloaded the assembly to your machine, your application works. No problem. However, what about your colleagues? Do they need to download the application as well, and make sure that it's in the same location relative to the project source code? And what happens when you check your project in? Do you include the foreign assembly? And how does the central build engine know where to find the referenced assembly?

As you can see, there are lots of questions, and none of the answers are very good. Into this maelstrom rides the NuGet Package Manager, known by most as just NuGet. NuGet is a tool that can be used from within Visual Studio, from a command line or through a build process. Its fundamental purpose is to retrieve the packages needed by your application from a central repository. To put that into the basic developer workflow, when you build your application, one of the tasks that takes place is that your machine checks to see if all of the required assemblies are available. If not, then NuGet goes to the NuGet package gallery and downloads the missing assemblies to the appropriate place and continues on with the build. If you go back and look at the list of questions in the first paragraph, you'll notice that this process addresses most of them. This is why NuGet has become so incredibly popular.

So how do you take advantage of this goodness? Well, the starting point is found in the Solution Explorer. If you right-click on a project, you can find a Manage NuGet Packages option. Or if you right-click on the solution, the context menu contains a Manage NuGet Packages for Solution option. In both cases, you are taking to the page found in Figure 18-5.

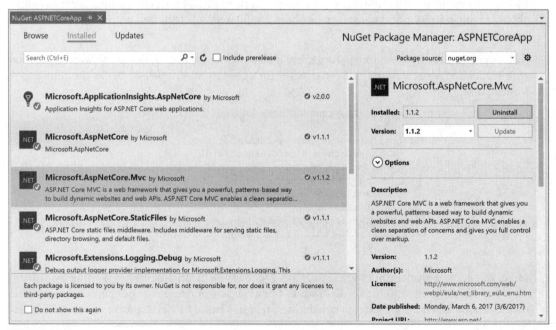

FIGURE 18-5

The starting point is to show all of the currently installed packages. They appear in the list on the left. If you select any one of them, the details about the package appear on the right. On the right side, you have the ability to uninstall a package by clicking on the Uninstall button. You can also update a package, presuming that the current version is different than the installed version. If you're just interested in updating all of your packages, there is an Updates link at the top that changes the list of installed packages to a list of those packages that actually have updates available.

If you want to install a package, click on the Browse link at the top and enter the name of the package. Packages that match the entered name (it is a wildcard search) appear in the list on the left. As before, when you select a package on the left, the details for the package, including a list of versions you can install, appear on the right.

One of the nice functions of NuGet is that installing a package makes sure that the dependencies of the package have already been installed on your machine. And, if they are not already available, then the dependencies are installed along with the package. So one way or another, at the end of the process, the package has everything it needs to run successfully. For any of the packages that you select, the list of dependencies is visible on the right. Well, it's visible if you scroll down. It's at the bottom of the details for the selected package (see Figure 18-6).

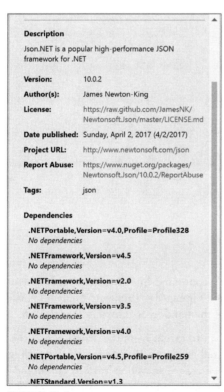

FIGURE 18-6

At the beginning of this process, there were two entry points into the NuGet page: from the project context menu and from the solution context menu. The difference is a behavior when you select a package to install or update. Figure 18-7 shows the left side of the NuGet page when you have chosen the Manage NuGet Packages for Solution option. At the top of the page, there is a list of the projects that are part of the solution. You can select one or more projects into which you want to install the package. Beyond that, the installation, uninstallation or update flow is the same.

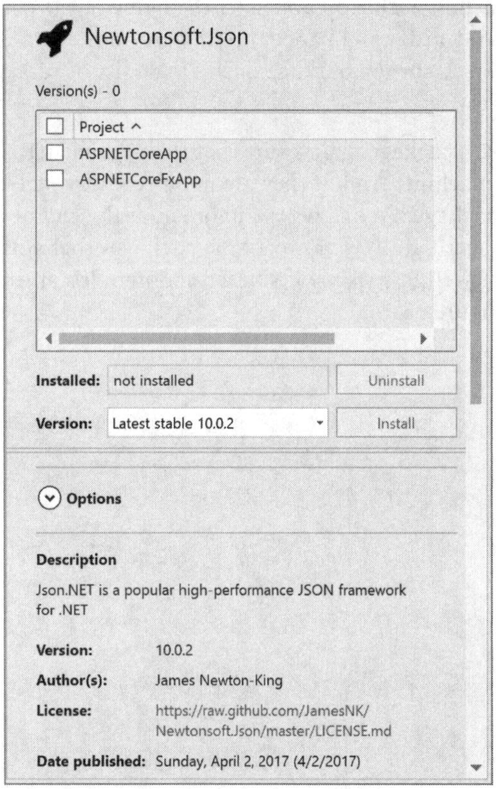

FIGURE 18-7

If a fancy graphical interface is not your style, then there is a command-line interface that can be used to manage NuGet packages. Use the Tools ➪ NuGet Package Manager ➪ Package Manager Console option to launch the command-line window. An example of the window is shown in Figure 18-8.

To install a package, choose the project into which you want to target from the dropdown at the top. Then use the Install-Package command, as illustrated in Figure 18-8 to install the package. There are other commands available, such as Uninstall-Package, as well as various command-line options to perform updates to packages. Use the Get-Help command to see the available options for a command (for example, Get-Help Install-Package shows all of the options available for Get-Help).

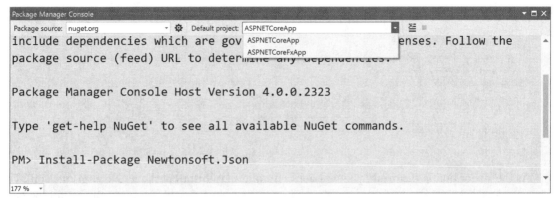

FIGURE 18-8

There is one final hidden gem about Visual Studio 2017 and NuGet. Visual Studio 2017 provides the ability to have Intellisense recommend the installation of a package based on the syntax of the code you're typing. This option is turned off by default (it does take up a decent amount of memory), so to enable it go to Tools ⇨ Options to get to the Options Dialog. Then navigate to Text Editor ⇨ C# ⇨ Advanced (shown in Figure 18-9). There are two choices that control this feature. Make sure that Suggest usings for types in reference assemblies and Suggest usings for types in NuGet packages are checked.

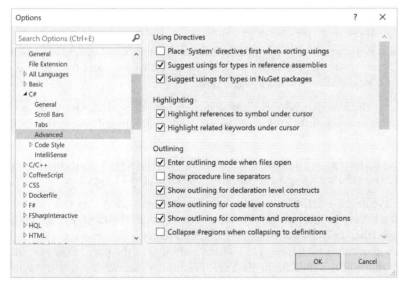

FIGURE 18-9

Once these options have been selected, then a couple of new options are available in certain Quick Action context menus. Consider Figure 18-10, which illustrates the context menu when you enter JObject, the name of a class that is a part of the common library JSON.Net.

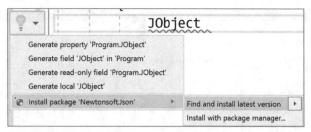

FIGURE 18-10

As the last option in the menu, you will notice an option to Install package 'Newtonsoft.Json'. This option includes two additional choices. The first, when selected, will automatically install the most recent stable version of JSON.NET. The second choice opens the NuGet Package Manager, giving you the flexibility to install the version of your choice.

BOWER PACKAGE MANAGER

Since the previous section talked about a different package manager (NuGet), a reasonable question could be why we need another. Well, the reason has got to do with the target for NuGet, which is packages that are used with .NET. What NuGet doesn't deliver is packages that contain only web content, which includes HTML, CSS and JavaScript files. That is the space into which Bower fits.

Functionally, Bower takes many of the same steps that NuGet does. When you build your application, Bower checks to make sure that all of the web files that you need to have are downloaded onto your machine. It also manages the dependency graph to minimize the number of times the same file might be used within the different packages. For instance, if you have two packages that depend on jQuery, Bower ensures that it is only downloaded a single time.

There are two ways to specify the files that Bower needs to include in your project. One is to use a graphical user interface, and the other is to edit the bower.json file to manually indicate which packages you want to include.

The graphical interface is quite similar to NuGet. To get started, right-click on a project in Solution Explorer and select Manage Bower Packages. A screen similar to Figure 18-11 appears.

Initially (but not shown in Figure 18-11), the Installed tab is displayed and the dialog shows a list of the packages that have already been registered with Bower on the left side. If you have used one of the ASP.NET Core templates, this includes Bootstrap, jQuery, and jQuery Validation. If you select one of the packages, details about that package appear on the right side of the page. There are also buttons that enable you to uninstall or upgrade the package, presuming that a more recent version is available. A dropdown list shows all of the available versions.

To add a package to your project, click on the Browse header and enter the name (or part of the name) of the package you're interested in. A list of the matching packages appears. In Figure 18-11, a search for *moment* has been performed and the base moment package has been selected for installation. On the right side, details about moment are visible, including a dropdown showing the versions and a button that will install the package. There is also a checkbox that, when selected, will update the bower.json file. More on this file momentarily (pun intended).

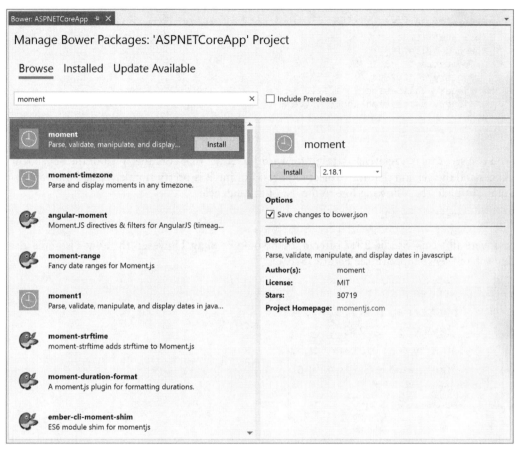

FIGURE 18-11

You can also update packages that have already been installed in your project to more current versions. To do this, click on the Update Available header. Now the left side contains those installed packages where updates are available and, when you select a package, the details and the button that can be used to update the package appear.

Also, next to the search text box is a checkbox used to indicate that you are interested in seeing prerelease versions as well as stable or released versions. By default, only stable versions are displayed. However, if this checkbox is checked, then the list of available versions includes both beta and alpha version of the package.

Besides the graphical interface, there is also a manual way to indicate the packages that you would like to include with your project. This involves directly editing the bower.json file. The file contains a list of the dependencies and, as was described earlier, can be updated through the graphic Bower

Package Manager. Following are the contents of the bower.json file as included in the ASP.NET Core templates.

```
{
  "name": "asp.net",
  "private": true,
  "dependencies": {
    "bootstrap": "3.3.7",
    "jquery": "2.2.0",
    "jquery-validation": "1.14.0",
    "jquery-validation-unobtrusive": "3.2.6"
  }
}
```

As you can see, this is a relatively straightforward JSON file that contains a list of the dependent packages and the version that the project requires. Editing it is pretty simple. To add moment, for example, just add the following line to the list of dependencies.

```
"moment": "2.18.1"
```

If that were all Visual Studio 2017 offered, that would be okay. However, the bower.json file also includes Intellisense support (see Figure 18-12).

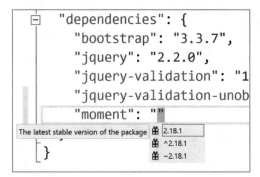

FIGURE 18-12

When you start typing the name of the package, a list of the packages that match what you type appears. Once you have selected a package, the second component shows a list of the matching versions.

One thing to notice in Figure 18-12 is that the contents of the value after the package name is not just limited to a specific version. If the version number is prefixed with a caret (^), then any version that matches the major version is considered acceptable. For example, if the value is "^2.18.2", then the latest version with a major version of 2 will be downloaded. If the version number is prefixed with a tilde (~), then the most recent minor version will be downloaded. For example, with a value of "~2.18.2", the latest version that starts with 2.18 will be downloaded.

SUMMARY

ASP.NET Core provides a platform that allows you to develop web applications that can be deployed onto a wider variety of machines than ever before. To help with that deployment, the ASP.NET Core project templates provide built-in support for some of the more commonly used web development tools. Visual Studio 2017 has integrated a number of features to provide an interesting and productive step forward for those people who are currently taking advantage of the ecosystem that has built up around the modern web.

19

Node.js Development

WHAT'S IN THIS CHAPTER?

- ➤ Understanding what Node.js is
- ➤ Creating a Node.js application
- ➤ Installing packages using Node Package Manager
- ➤ Working with task runners

WROX.COM CODE DOWNLOADS FOR THIS CHAPTER

The wrox.com code downloads for this chapter can be found at www.wrox.com by searching for this book's ISBN number (978-1-119-40458-3). The code and any related support files are located in their own folder for this chapter.

For many web developers, what is about to be suggested might seem, well, bizarre. But what if you could take the client-side programming language that you know and love (JavaScript) and use it to develop the server side of your web application? That is exactly what node.js (also known as just Node) enables you to do. What's more, Visual Studio 2017 includes a number of features that are aimed at increasing the productivity of Node developers. Those features are covered in this chapter.

GETTING STARTED WITH NODE.JS

Node.js (Node) is server-side JavaScript. To people who are used to seeing JavaScript running in a browser, this might seem a little odd. But when you get right down to it, JavaScript is just a language. There is nothing inherent in the language specification to suggest that it couldn't be used in a web server.

What makes Node something worth looking at is that it's light-weight and performs very well. The performance is the result of, among other things, some design decisions that distinguish it from other web servers. Probably the biggest choice was to make the server single-threaded. Instead of spinning up a new thread for each incoming request, the requests are handled by one thread, using events to launch the various parts of the web application as required. This reduces the memory footprint (every thread, and thus every request, takes up memory) and allows for an event-driven environment that takes advantage of non-blocking (otherwise known as asynchronous) processing. Every connection request fires an event. Data received when a form is submitted fires an event.

Practically speaking, this means that Node is designed to excel in web applications where there are a large number of requests that don't perform massive amounts of calculations and return small bundles of data as a result. It never locks up. It can support thousands of concurrent users. While a "regular" web server that has these characteristics is nice, Node really shines when it comes to supporting a RESTful API. And RESTfulness is at the heart of the modern web.

Integration between Node and Visual Studio comes through an open-source project known as Node.js Tools for Visual Studio (NTVS). It has been available for a number of years, but with the introduction of workloads in the installation and update process, you can now include NTVS in Visual Studio without a separate installation.

Assuming that you have included the Node workload, creating and executing a Node project is fairly simple. First, launch the New Project dialog using the File ⇨ New ⇨ Project menu option (see Figure 19-1). Then navigate to the Node project templates through the JavaScript and Node.js nodes in the treeview.

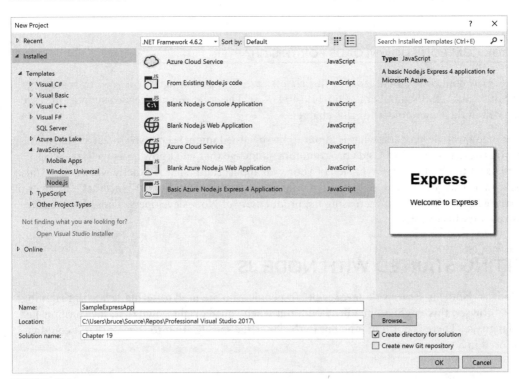

FIGURE 19-1

There are several project templates that are available. However, they are just variations on a couple of different themes. First, you can create either a Node web application or a Node console application. The difference between the two is pretty much what you'd expect: the web application services HTTP requests, while the console application is a command-line application which responds to commands entered through the keyboard. Or you can create a blank Node application, which supports minimal "Hello World" functionality, or an Express Node.js application, which provides a very nice starting point for a Node web application. Finally, you can choose a template that will run on your local Node instance or can be published to Azure and run (on Node, naturally) in an Azure Web Application. There is also a template that allows you to create a project that uses existing Node files. For this template, you will be prompted for the location of the existing files and then be able to select which files you wish to include in the new project.

For the purposes of this discussion, create a Basic Azure Node.js Express 4 Application. Once you have provided a name and click OK, the project is created. There is one additional (and, for most project templates, relatively unusual) step that needs to be performed. Node provides the functionality of a web server and listens on port 80 for incoming requests. For security reasons, Windows doesn't allow incoming requests on port 80 without requiring administrator approval. Therefore, you need to approve that functionality before it will work. So you will see a warning dialog similar to that shown in Figure 19-2. Click the Allow access button to allow Node to do its web request processing thing.

FIGURE 19-2

Now that you have created a Node project (using Express 4), you will be presented with a project that contains various components. The Solution Explorer for the project can be seen in Figure 19-3.

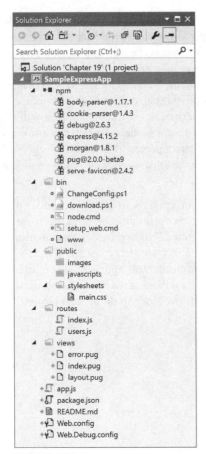

FIGURE 19-3

There are a number of folders in the Solution Explorer, most of which are named in a way that should be fairly familiar to ASP.NET MVC developers. The contents and purpose of the different folders and nodes are as follows:

➤ **npm:** Contains the packages that have been downloaded using Node Package Manager (otherwise known as npm). Along with the name of the package is the current version being used. More information about npm and how is it controlled from within your project are found in the "Node Package Manager" section later in this chapter.

➤ **bin:** Contains the startup scripts for your application. In the project template, there are both PowerShell scripts and command files. But the real example of what typically goes into this directory is found in the www file. Here is the content of the www file from the project template:

```
#!/usr/bin/env node
var debug = require('debug')('SampleExpressApp');
var app = require('../app');
```

```
app.set('port', process.env.PORT || 3000);

var server = app.listen(app.get('port'), function() {
    debug('Express server listening on port ' + server.address().port);
});
```

This is the JavaScript code that will be executed by Node when you launch your web application, whether through Visual Studio or from a command line (the command would be node www).

➤ **public:** This folder contains the static content for your application. This includes all of the JavaScript, CSS, and images as well as anything else you need that isn't dynamically generated. As you can see in Figure 19-3, there are three folders (images, javascripts, and stylesheets) that are included, but you are welcome to add more as you add different types of files to your project.

➤ **routes:** This folder contains the code for the default routes (or endpoints) that are supported by your web application and the actions that are taken when each endpoint is requested. Here is the index.js file that defines the default route for your application:

```
'use strict';
var express = require('express');
var router = express.Router();

/* GET home page. */
router.get('/', function (req, res) {
    res.render('index', { title: 'Express' });
});

module.exports = router;
```

The code here grabs the router object that is currently defined in the Express application. It then defines the following rule: for a GET request on the / path, respond by rendering the index view, using a title of Express.

➤ **views:** Contains the views used by your web application. These files are actually template files that are processed by a template engine to produce the desired HTML output. The Express 4 project template in Visual Studio 2017 uses the Pug template, but it's quite easy to use a different templating engine that is supported by Express. Just so you can get started, the following code is the index.pug file from the project template:

```
extends layout

block content
  h1= title
  p Welcome to #{title}
```

First, it includes the layout.pug template, which contains the basic structure of the HTML page (that is, the HEAD and BODY elements and the inclusion of the main.css file). Then it injects into the layout an H1 element consisting of the title variable and a paragraph that includes the value of the title variable. The value for the title is defined in the render function shown in the routes section. The result, when the application is executed, is the web page shown in Figure 19-4.

FIGURE 19-4

There are a number of additional files that are included in the project template but are not in a particular folder.

➤ **app.js:** This is the main file for the Express application. When the application is launched, this file is executed and within it, it defines all of the components that make up Express. This includes, for example, which routing files to use, the templating engine, the logging engine, how cookies are parsed, how the body of any request is parsed (URL-encoded JSON is the default), and how to handle errors (errors are handled differently in the development and production environments).

➤ **package.json:** This is, more or less, the configuration file for the application. It includes basic information, such as the name, description, version, and author of the application. It also contains a list of the dependencies, which is used by npm to retrieve the packages when required.

➤ **Web.config/Web.debug.config:** These files are not specifically required by the Node application. However, they are required to publish your Node application to Azure. They exist in the project as a result of the fact that the template for Express 4 is set up specifically to be able to publish to Azure. If you have no plans to publish to Azure, then these two files can be removed with no ill effects. The difference between the two config files is that the debug version allows for remote debugging of the Node application while is it deployed on Azure. Just think about that magic for just a moment. You are able to publish your application to Azure, connect to it from within a debugging session in Visual Studio, set breakpoints, and step through the server-side code as if it were running locally. Technology can indeed be a wonderful thing, on occasion.

When you run your application from within Visual Studio 2017, the Node web server is launched. You can see the console for Node as a separate console window, as shown in Figure 19-5.

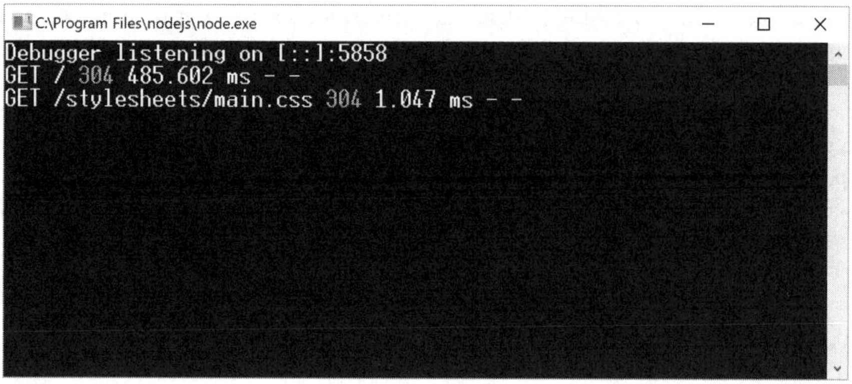

FIGURE 19-5

The initialization for the Node server is to start listening on port 1337 (not mentioned in the console, but this is the port used for the "typical" web requests in the example application) and on port 5858 for the debugging requests. It then processes a GET request on the default page (indicated by the backslash) and a GET request on the main.css stylesheet. As you continue working with your application, additional messages will appear in the window.

The ports used by the Node server are completely configurable. This is done through the project properties, shown in Figure 19-6.

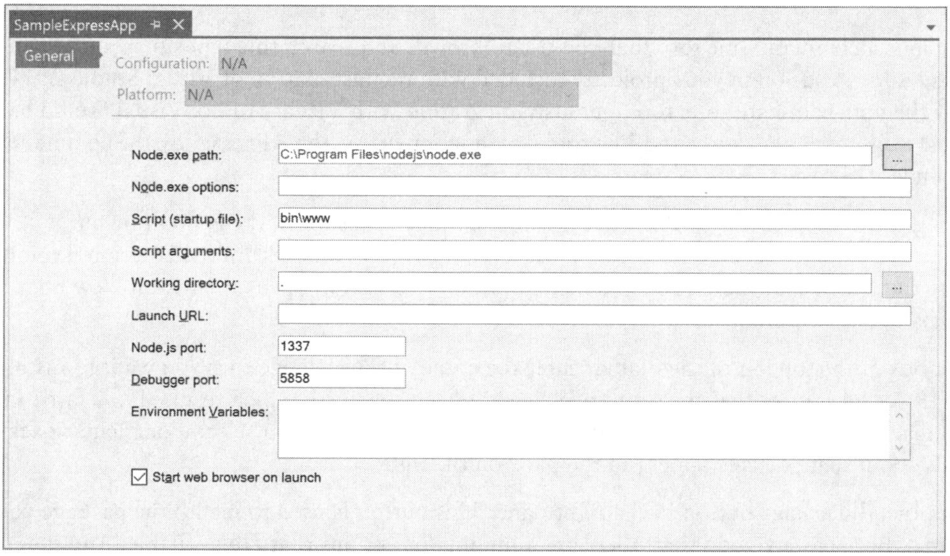

FIGURE 19-6

The project properties are accessible by right-clicking on the project in the Solution Explorer and selecting the Properties option. There are many fewer options than ASP.NET Web developers might expect. There is only one sheet and even the number of fields is relatively small. You can specify the path to the Node executable on your machine (it defaults to the value specified in your machine-level Node configuration), along with any command-line options for Node. You can specify the startup script (by default, it's the www file found in the bin folder) along with any arguments for the script. You can define the working directory (it defaults to the current directory for the project). The URL used when launching the browser can be defined, as well as whether a web browser will even be started when the application is run through Visual Studio. The two ports (the typical one and the debugging port) used by Node can be specified. Finally, any environment variables that Node will require can be defined.

NODE PACKAGE MANAGER

One of the features of Node.js is that dependencies for the web application are automatically downloaded when needed. In the case of Visual Studio 2017, "when needed" turns out to be "when the project is opened." Behind the scenes, the list of dependencies and the required version are compared to the current version of the dependent package that is on your local machine. If there are any differences, they are downloaded and made available to your application.

The technology behind this is Node Package Manager (npm). There are two elements to npm. First, there is an on-line repository of over 450,000 different packages. Each package consists of a collection of files that are required in order to make the package useful to another application. For example, jQuery is available in the npm repository. If you install jQuery using npm, then you get the JavaScript files necessary to utilize jQuery in your application. As well, you get a minimized version of the same files.

Second, npm is a command-line tool that you use to browse and search this repository and download packages for inclusion in your projects. Included with the installation of Visual Studio 2017 is not only the npm command-line tool, but also integration with Visual Studio. Visual Studio has options that will utilize the command-line tool (or, more precisely, the API used by the command-line tool) under the covers.

The starting point for accessing NPM is, as it is for so many other tools, the context menu. Specifically, you can right-click on the npm node in your project from within the Solution Explorer and choose the Install New npm Packages menu option. That action opens the Install New npm Packages dialog, shown in Figure 19-7.

In the text box at the top left of the dialog, enter the name of the package that you want to install. In Figure 19-7, you can see that the grunt package has been specified, which resulted in a fairly large number of packages that match "grunt" appearing on the left. When you select a particular package, details about that package appear in the pane on the right.

There is an Install Package button in the right pane. This button is used to install the package you have selected. But before you do that, there are a number of options that are available. And the options can have an impact on how and when the package is available.

The most important of these options is the Dependency type. There are three choices available in the dropdown, which are Standard, Developmental, and Optional. There is also a fourth type, Global, which is only available if you install the package using the command line.

FIGURE 19-7

The distinction between Standard, Developmental, and Optional relates to when the package needs to be available. For instance, the Developmental packages are expected to only be available while the application is under development. An example of a package that fits into this category would be one that is required to help you run your unit tests. Once the unit tests have passed, there is no longer any need for this package, so it won't be included once the project goes into production. A Standard package is one that is expected to be available both during development and once the application is in production. And an Optional package is one that your application will take advantage of if it's available, but if it's not, then your application will continue to function.

Each of these options installs a package locally for your project. Packages installed locally are not automatically available to other projects running on your machine. Conversely, packages that are installed globally are available to other Node projects without needing to be reinstalled. Installing packages globally will be discussed later in this section.

Below the Development type combo box is a checkbox indicating whether this package should be included in the `package.json` file. While it's not a requirement to leave this checked, if you don't, then the package will be installed as a Standard package. There is no concept of Developmental or Optional packages without a `package.json` file.

The Options section also provies two additional capabilities. You can specify the version of the package you want to install, either a particular version or the latest. In addition, there is a textbox where arguments to the npm command can be included. Once you have installed the npm package, then the `package.json` file will be updated to include your new package (assuming you chose the package.json option, which you should have).

> **NOTE** *A detailed description of what JSON is falls outside the scope of this book. If you are unfamiliar with JSON formatted strings or want to learn more about it, sites such as Tutorials Point (*`https://www.tutorialspoint.com/json`*) are useful.*

There are other ways to install new npm packages. One of the easiest is to directly modify the `package.json` file. Here is the `dependencies` section of a `package.json` file:

```
"dependencies": {
    "body-parser": "^1.15.0",
    "cookie-parser": "^1.4.0",
    "debug": "^2.2.0",
    "express": "^4.14.0",
    "morgan": "^1.7.0",
    "pug": "^2.0.0-beta6",
    "serve-favicon": "^2.3.0
}
```

> **NOTE** *There can be two other dependency properties in the* `package.json` *file. Any Developmental dependencies are included in a* `devDependencies` *property. And if you specify any Optional dependencies, then there will be an* `optional-Dependencies` *property containing those packages.*

You can see that each of the dependencies under the npm node is listed, along with the version that is used within the project. To add a new package, you can simply add to this list. The `package.json` file includes Intellisense support, so as you type both the package name and the version, you can see the options that are available, as shown in Figure 19-8.

FIGURE 19-8

When the `package.json` file is saved, the contents of the npm node in your project are updated accordingly. The biggest difference between the previously existing packages and the new packages is that the new package name doesn't have a version number. Instead, there is a `(missing)` to indicate that the package has not yet been downloaded.

In fact, there are actually three types of nodes in the npm section of your project, as shown in Figure 19-9. When the package is downloaded, the name of the package followed by the version number appears. When a new package is added, the name of the package indicates that it is missing. And when a package that had previously been downloaded but is no longer in the list of dependencies in package.json, the package name includes (not listed in package.json).

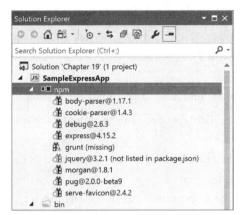

FIGURE 19-9

These two latter cases can be corrected through the context menu. If you right-click on a missing package (or on the npm node itself), then an option to Install Missing npm Package(s) is available. Selecting that option will download the package and the version will appear to the right of the package name. If the package is no longer in the package.json file, a right-click on the package will show an Uninstall npm Package(s) option in the context menu. Choosing that option will uninstall the package, removing it from the npm node.

There is a third way to install npm packages, which is to use the command-line interface. Along with supporting all of the dependency types, the command-line interface also allows you to install a package globally. To start, right-click on the project or solution in the Solution Explorer and select the Open Node.js Interactive Window option. This can also be done through the View ➪ Other Windows ➪ Node.js Interactive Window menu option. Figure 19-10 shows what the initial window looks like.

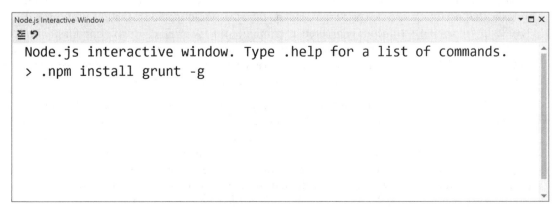

FIGURE 19-10

As you can see, this looks like a typical command-line shell, and, for the most part, it is, with the exception that the commands it understands are Node command. You can see a complete list of the available commands by using `.help`, but for our purposes, the command of interest is `.npm`.

In order to install a particular package, the command takes the form as follows:

```
.npm install [projectName] packageName <option>
```

The `projectName` option is used if your solution has more than one project in it. You provide the name of the project into which the package will be installed. The `option` is used to determine the dependency mode. The choices are:

➤ `--save`: Saves the package information in the `dependencies` section of `package.json`.

➤ `--save-dev`: Saves the package information in the `devDependencies` section of `package.json`.

➤ `--save-opt`: Saves the package information in the `optionalDependencies` section of `package.json`.

➤ `--g`: Saves the package information in a local cache where it is available for any project to use.

It's that last option that fulfills the global capability described earlier in this section, which was the fourth option that was otherwise unavailable in the Install New npm Packages dialog.

TASK RUNNER EXPLORER

As you have seen throughout this chapter, Visual Studio 2017 has a lot of relatively new features aimed at improving the life of front-end web developers. Support for tools like Node and npm help increase the productivity of development environments that are commonly used in other platforms. To extend this a little further, Visual Studio 2017 also includes support for Task Runners, like grunt and gulp.

It might not be completely clear from the name what a Task Runner is used for. When you are creating a web-based application (or even other kinds of applications, but the Task Runner Explorer is mostly focused on web applications with a heavy front-end component), there are a large number of tasks that need to take place prior to deployment. This would include tasks like minifying the JavaScript (removing extraneous characters to minimize the file size), concatenating files, *linting* the JavaScript code (which checks the JavaScript for errors), and compiling various extensions (such as the SASS or LESS extensions for CSS). These are repetitive tasks that, once the proper commands have been determined, need to be run with each compilation and deployment.

The goal of a Task Runner is to automate the execution of these repetitive tasks. In the web front-end world, two of the leading task runners are known as grunt and gulp. Both of those tools are supported by the Task Runner Explorer. In this case, support means that if your project is configured to have either grunt tasks or gulp tasks, those tasks will be visible through the Task Runner Explorer and you can manipulate or execute them as described in this section. The examples in this chapter use grunt, but everything you see done using grunt could be done using gulp.

In the previous section, you used npm to install grunt into your projects. In this section, we will use grunt to demonstrate the functionality of the Task Runner Explorer window.

So that you can follow along, there are a couple of changes that need to be made to the `package.json` file, as well as the addition of a file named `gruntfile.js`.

To start with, add a `devDependencies` section to the `package.json` file. It should look like the following:

```
"devDependencies": {
  "grunt-contrib-uglify": "~2.3.0",
  "grunt-contrib-jshint": "~1.1.0"
}
```

Save the changes, then right-click on the npm node in Solution Explorer, and choose the Install Missing npm Packages option. This will install the two packages into your project. Just so you know what you're getting, the grunt-contrib-uglify package is used to minimize (uglify is the commonly used term) JavaScript files, and the grunt-contrib-jshint package is used to perform static code analysis on your JavaScript files. Once these packages have been installed, you can move on to the next step.

In the Solution Explorer, right-click on the project and select the Add ⇨ New Item context menu option. Then choose JavaScript File from the list of item templates and give it a name of `gruntfile.js`. Click Add to add the file to the project.

The `gruntfile.js` file is used to define the tasks that grunt is able to perform. A complete explanation of grunt is beyond the scope of this book, but a brief overview will help to put the Task Runner into context. Start by adding the following contents to the newly created file.

```
module.exports = function (grunt) {
    grunt.initConfig({
        pkg: grunt.file.readJSON('package.json'),
        uglify: {
            options: {
                banner: '/*! <%= pkg.name %> <%=
                grunt.template.today("yyyy-mm-dd") %> */\n'
            },
            build: {
                src: 'src/<%= pkg.name %>.js',
                dest: 'build/<%= pkg.name %>.min.js'
            }
        },
        jshint: {
            all: ['gruntfile.js', 'public/javascripts/*.js']
        }
    });

    // Load the plugins.
    grunt.loadNpmTasks('grunt-contrib-uglify');
    grunt.loadNpmTasks('grunt-contrib-jshint');

    // Default task(s).
    grunt.registerTask('default', ['uglify', 'jshint']);
};
```

`InitConfig` initializes the grunt tasks. The parameter to that method is a JSON object that references the `package.json` file (so that grunt knows which packages are available), and a number of different tasks (`uglify` and `jshint`). Within those tasks are subtasks (`build` and `all`) that define parameter values that are specific to what those packages do. At the bottom of the `gruntfile` are a couple of statements that load the tasks that are defined internally in each of the two packages, followed by defining a default task that is actually a composite of two other tasks: `uglify` and `jshint`.

Once you have created the contents of the file, save it and open the Task Runner Explorer using the View ➪ Other Windows ➪ Task Runner Explorer menu option. Figure 19-11 shows what the Task Runner looks like with the defined grunt tasks.

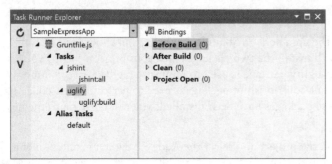

FIGURE 19-11

On the left side is a tree containing the various tasks and subtasks. They have been divided into Tasks and Alias Tasks. The Alias Tasks are those tasks that have been defined as composites of other tasks (the *default* task that is defined in the gruntfile is an alias task). These tasks can be run in a couple of ways. First, you can double-click on any task, and it will be executed. The output from the task will appear in the pane on the right side. You can also right-click on a task and select Run from the context menu.

Each of these techniques requires the developer to take a positive step to run the task. That is fine for tasks that are not commonly used, but for tasks that need to run more frequently, the Task Runner offers one additional choice: bindings.

A binding allows a particular task to be associated with a particular function within your project development cycle. There are four binding types available:

➤ **Before Build:** Runs tasks prior to the build starting.

➤ **After Build:** Runs tasks after a successful build.

➤ **Clean:** Runs tasks after a clean has been performed on the project.

➤ **Project Open:** Runs tasks when the project is initially opened.

To add a task to one of these bindings, right-click on the task. There is a Bindings option, with a fly-out that includes each of the binding types. Once the type has been selected, the task appears under the appropriate binding on the right pane (see Figure 19-12).

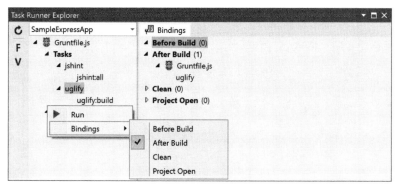

FIGURE 19-12

Now that a task is associated with a binding, it will automatically be invoked when the function within the project is initiated.

There are a couple of other features in the Task Runner Explorer that might be of interest. First, at the top of the left-hand pane, there is a dropdown of the projects in the solution. It is possible for different projects to have different grunt files. You can choose the project (and therefore the grunt file) that you wish to work with. Also, on the very left of the window, there are three icons. The top icon is used to refresh the list of tasks. This is used after you have modified the grunt file so that the Task Runner becomes aware of any changes. The other two icons are toggles that specify that a Force (the "F") or a Verbose (the "V") option be used when the task is executed.

SUMMARY

Visual Studio 2017 has included a number of features aimed at making sure that modern web developers and, in particular, front-end developers, can become more productive. This is part of the initiative toward ensuring that Visual Studio supports the needs of all developers, not just .NET developers. Its embrace of some of the more common open-source tools might seem unusual for those with a long-standing distrust of anything Microsoft. The reality is that this is just one more of the many efforts Microsoft has made to embrace the web standards that are being globally used.

20

Python Development

WHAT'S IN THIS CHAPTER?

➤ Understanding the basic structure of a Python project

➤ Managing Python environments within Visual Studio

➤ Using Cookiecutter templates to create new projects

WROX.COM CODE DOWNLOADS FOR THIS CHAPTER

The wrox.com code downloads for this chapter can be found at www.wrox.com by searching for this book's ISBN number (978-1-119-40458-3). The code and any related support files are located in their own folder for this chapter.

For some developers, the inclusion of Python tooling into Visual Studio is a non-event. People ask why they should bother with Python when there's already support for all of the .NET languages (C#, VB, F#, C++), along with JavaScript. The answer to this question is slightly philosophical. Every development language has niches in which it shines. You wouldn't want to create a web application in C++, but how about an operating system? You wouldn't want to create a photo editor in C#, what about a customer relationship management application? Each of these languages has areas of specialization where they are quite appropriate and areas where they are not. For Python, one of those areas of specialty is in scripting. Python can be used to quickly create simple applications, the language is able to express complex concepts concisely, and it can be ported to almost every platform that is available. As well, Python is frequently used by data scientists in data analytics applications as an alternative to R.

While .NET has supported Python in various forms for a number of years, Visual Studio introduces a set of tools to help Python developers as an out-of-the-box experience for the first time. In this chapter, we look at the tooling that is available as part of the Python development workload.

GETTING STARTED WITH PYTHON

Python tools are included in two different workloads within Visual Studio. If you launch the Visual Studio Installer, you can include Python tools directly through the Web & Cloud ⇨ Python development workload. They are also included in the Data science and analytical applications workload. By default, this workload includes Cookiecutter template support and Python 3 support for 64-bit systems. Through the Individual component tab available in the currently selected workload, you can also include IoT (Internet of Things) support, Azure support, Anaconda support (version 2 or 3 on 32- and 64-bit systems), and future Python support (also version 2 or 3 on 32- and 64-bit systems).

The tools that are included are part of an open-source project known as Python Tools for Visual Studio (PTVS). It has been available for a number of years for earlier versions of Visual Studio, but with the new installation and update process, it's now possible to include PTVS in Visual Studio without a separate installation.

Assuming that you have included the Python workload, the creation and execution of a Python project is relatively straightforward. To begin, launch the New Project dialog using the File ⇨ New ⇨ Project menu option (see Figure 20-1). Then navigate to the Python project templates in the treeview.

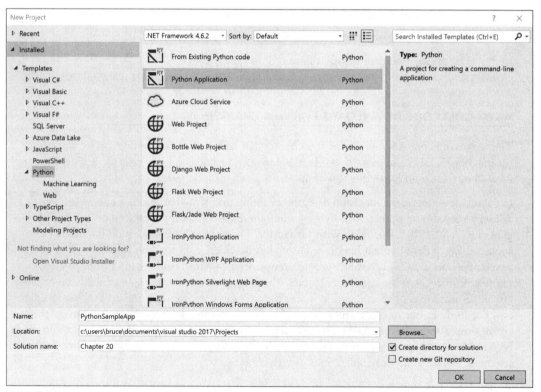

FIGURE 20-1

You will find that there are a number of different project templates available to choose from. For example, there are several different Python Web projects. One of them creates a generic web application, while the others install a particular Python framework that aims to make web development easier. Bottle, Djangos, and Flask are the frameworks that are supported.

➤ **Bottle:** A simple framework that provides a minimal set of functionality (request routing, templating, and a simple abstraction over the Web Services Gateway Interface [WSGI]). Everything else must be added as part of the development effort. The design goal for Bottle was to provide a foundation for creating a Web API.

> **NOTE** *The Web Service Gateway Interface (WSGI), is a specification that allows Web servers and application frameworks to interact using a common API. Mostly, it defines how a server or gateway will take an incoming HTTP request and invoke a framework. If that sounds simple to you, that's because it is. Fundamentally, this workflow is the basis for every web site everywhere. In WSGI, it has been reduced to just a couple of interactions.*

➤ **Django:** This framework is known as a "batteries included" framework. It includes all of the functionality that you'll need to create a web application. This includes components such as an Object-Relational Mapping (ORM) manager that is used to provide data access. You don't need to include other components into Django to get a fully functional web application.

➤ **Flask:** As opposed to Django (and like Bottle), Flask is a microframework. It includes just the basic functionality and little else. However, there are a number of extensions available to provide web server features. For instance, you'll notice that there are two Flask templates in Figure 20-1. The second, Flask/Jade, includes the Jade template engine.

> **NOTE** *There have already been a couple of mentions of templates in the description of the project types. Put simply, a template is a mechanism for creating web pages from a simple structure, like the results from a database query or an object graph. They are described in more detail in the "Cookiecutter Extension" section later in this chapter.*

Along with the Web Project templates, there are a number of other Python templates to choose from. For example, there are a number of IronPython templates. IronPython is an open source Python variant that was developed mostly in C# and targets the .NET Framework and Mono. The IronPython templates you can choose from include the ability to create a WPF application, a Windows Forms application, and a Silverlight application.

For the purposes of this discussion, create a project using the Bottle Web Project template. Since the template requires additional components, you might be prompted to add them as part of the creation process. Figure 20-2 illustrates the dialog that appears if you haven't previously installed the needed components.

PythonProject - Visual Studio - Python support   ✕

This project requires external packages

We can download and install these packages for you automatically, but we need to know whether you want to install them for just this project or for all your projects.

→ Install into a virtual environment...
Packages will only be available for this project (recommended)

→ Install into Python 3.6 (64-bit)
Packages will be shared by all projects

→ I will install them myself

⌄ Show required packages

FIGURE 20-2

Also be aware that you might be prompted to execute the installation command using elevated permissions.

The contents of the project depend very much on the template that you choose. In Figure 20-3 you can see the Solution Explorer for two Python projects: the Bottle Web Project and the generic Python Application.

As you can see, beyond a few nodes (Python Environments, References, and Search Paths), the two projects look very different. That is to be expected. Depending on the purpose of the project, the files and directories will be different. Let's take a closer look at a couple of the nodes that are in common.

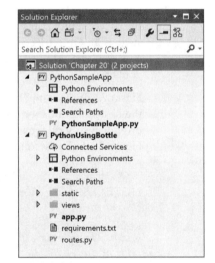

Solution Explorer   ▾ ☐ ✕

Search Solution Explorer (Ctrl+;)   🔎 ▾

Solution 'Chapter 20' (2 projects)
  ◢ PY PythonSampleApp
    ▷ 🗔 Python Environments
       ▪️ References
       ▪️ Search Paths
       PY **PythonSampleApp.py**
  ◢ PY **PythonUsingBottle**
       ☁ Connected Services
    ▷ 🗔 Python Environments
       ▪️ References
       ▪️ Search Paths
    ▷ 🗀 static
    ▷ 🗀 views
       PY **app.py**
       📄 requirements.txt
       PY routes.py

FIGURE 20-3

Python Environments

In Python, an environment is a collection of tools in which you run your code. It consists of an interpreter, a library (most frequently the Python Standard Library), and a set of installed packages. These three components then determine which language constructs and syntax are valid, the operating system functionality to which you have access, and the packages that can be made available to you. As well, within Visual Studio, an environment consists of an Intellisense database appropriate for the libraries.

As part of the installation of the Python workload, you had a number of different environments available to install. The ones you chose to install will impact some of the forms illustrated in the next few figures. The environments installed through the workload were created as *global environments*. These are environments that are available to every project. It is also possible to install an environment specifically for a project.

To see the environments that you can choose from, right-click on Python Environments in the Solution Explorer and select View Python Environments. The form shown in Figure 20-4 appears.

At the top, there is a list of all of the installed environments. For each environment, there is an icon on the right that allows you to open an interactive window for that environment. The interactive environment allows you to type and execute Python commands against that environment. Also, in some cases, there will be an icon that allows you to refresh the Completion DB. This is the database that is used to provide Intellisense information.

When you select an environment, the information at the bottom of the form changes. In Figure 20-4, you are looking at the available options for the default environment, Python 3.6 64-bit. For other environments, the specific choices might be different, but the basic ideas remain the same. You are given links to tools that would be of use to you, including the interactive window and PowerShell.

FIGURE 20-4

If you select Packages from the dropdown list, you can see the installed packages for the environment. This is the same list that appears in the environment node in the Solution Explorer. If you select IntelliSense from the dropdown list, then you can see the libraries that are included in the Completion DB and you have the option to be able to refresh it.

It is possible that two different projects installed as a global environment can have incompatible libraries. That means that you won't be able to use them in a project. To address this problem, Visual Studio provides the ability to create a *virtual environment*. In a virtual environment, there are the same components as in a regular Python environment. The difference is that the packages that are part of the environment are isolated from both the global environment and any other virtual environments.

To create a virtual environment, right-click on the Python Environments node in the Solution Explorer and select Add Virtual Environment. The dialog shown in Figure 20-5 appears.

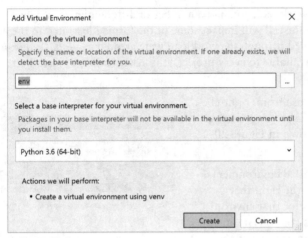

FIGURE 20-5

Here, you can provide the name and location of the environment and specify the base interpreter to be used. Once you provide the information and click Create, the environment is added to your project.

At this point, your new environment doesn't have any packages. This is addressed (and can be done for any other environment) through the Solution Explorer. Right-click on the environment and select Install Python Package. You will be taken to the pane in Figure 20-6.

Immediately above the list of installed packages, there is a text box that can be used to search the Python Package Index (PyPI) for packages. Figure 20-7 shows the results from a search for the Jade template engine. Clicking on the appropriate link will install the package in your environment.

FIGURE 20-6   **FIGURE 20-7**

Search Paths

In a typical Python environment, there is a variable named PYTHONPATH that provides the default search path for modules files. For example, if the Python command looks like IMPORT <name>, there are a number of directories that Python searches to find a match. First, the built-in modules are searched. Then the current folder for the executing code is checked. Finally, the path defined in PYTHONPATH is scanned.

Visual Studio 2017, however, ignores this environment variable. It does this specifically because the value is set for the environment system. This has the potential to raise questions that cannot be answered automatically. For example, are the reference modules intended to be used by Python 3.6 or Python 2.7? Are they intended to override the standard library modules? Is the developer aware that there actually is a match found in the path? Any of these can cause problems that are challenging to diagnose.

In Visual Studio, you can define the search paths that are to be used by your project. This means that you are adding the paths intentionally. This eliminates a lot of the challenges, because Visual Studio can assume that you're aware of whether the references are appropriate for your project.

To add a search path to your project, right-click on the Search Paths item in the Solution Explorer and select Add Folder to Search Path. The standard Open File dialog appears. You choose a directory and it appears underneath the Search Paths node. Or you can add a .zip file by choosing the Add Zip Archive to Search Path option from the context menu.

COOKIECUTTER EXTENSION

The idea behind a template in the Python world is to provide a mechanism to automatically generate code that is reused frequently within or across projects. To help support this productivity, Visual Studio 2017 includes support for the Cookiecutter template extension.

To get started with this workflow, launch the Cookiecutter window with the View ⇨ Cookiecutter Explorer option. The pane shown in Figure 20-8 appears.

There is a text box at the top that allows you to search for the template you desire to install. The search results are divided into these groups:

➤ **Installed:** Templates that have already been installed on your local machine. Once you use a template from any of the other groups, it is installed and will appear in this group in the future.

➤ **Recommended:** A curated (by Microsoft) list of templates, although it is possible to customize this feed.

➤ **GitHub:** The results of the search using the provided term on GitHub. If there are too many results, then there is a Load Mode link at the bottom of this section to load more results.

➤ **Custom:** A path to a GitHub repository or a local folder containing the template.

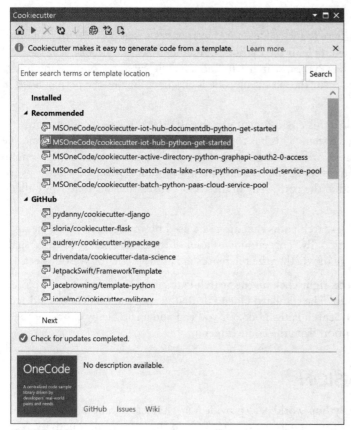

FIGURE 20-8

When you select a template and click Next, the template is cloned to your local machine and it is ready to go. Once installed locally, you are presented with a dialog that contains the options for the template. Figure 20-9 illustrates an example.

The specific options depend entirely on the template that you choose. At a minimum you'll be able to specify the location for the project to be placed. Click on Create and the template will be used to generate a Python project.

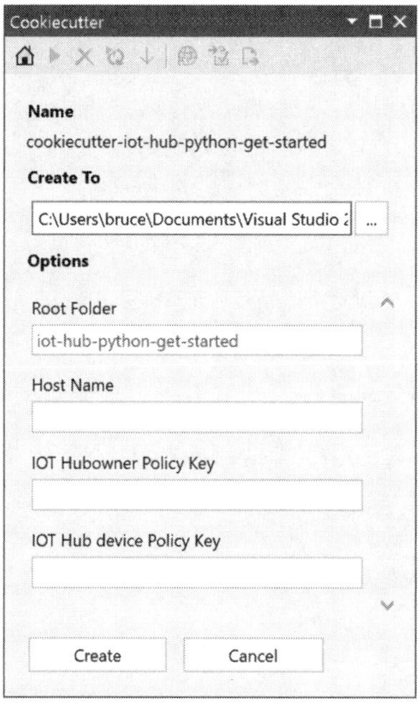

FIGURE 20-9

SUMMARY

Visual Studio 2017 includes a number of features aimed at making sure that Python developers can be productive. You can manage your Python environments, manage templates, and develop and debug your applications. This is part of Microsoft's push to embrace all types of developers and to find ways to make Visual Studio a productive environment for more and diverse groups.

PART VI
Mobile Applications

21

Mobile Applications Using .NET

WHAT'S IN THIS CHAPTER?

➤ Creating a Xamarin project for cross-platform applications

➤ Segregating UI and business logic concerns

➤ Debugging your app in Android and iOS

WROX.COM CODE DOWNLOADS FOR THIS CHAPTER

The wrox.com code downloads for this chapter can be found at www.wrox.com by searching for this book's ISBN number (978-1-119-40458-3). The code and any related support files are located in their own folder for this chapter.

Developing cross-platform applications is a tricky business. It might sound like a cliché, but there's a reason why there is no single, universal way to create applications that run on the iPhone, iPad, Android, and Windows platforms. In every case, there are trade-offs that have to be made, choices that will either limit the functionality that your application has or increase the complexity of the development effort.

Having painted that rosy picture, Visual Studio 2017 offers a couple of different approaches to creating mobile applications. In this chapter, we look at how the cross-platform development environment of Xamarin is integrated into Visual Studio. In Chapter 22, "Mobile Applications Using JavaScript," we look at how HTML, JavaScript, and Apache Cordova can be used for cross-platform development.

USING XAMARIN

Xamarin is a tool that is used to create cross-platform applications, which is to say that it strives to provide the kind of "write-once, run anywhere" productivity that is the holy grail of mobile development. Naturally, that goal is not particularly realistic. There are numerous differences between the platforms that need to be taken into account when creating applications. But Xamarin tries to minimize the differences so as to maximize code reuse.

To accomplish this, Xamarin brings several components to the table.

> ➤ **C# compiler:** Depending on the platform that you target, the output from a Xamarin project is native code (for iOS devices) or a .NET application that can then be integrated with a platform-specific runtime (Android, Universal Platforms). The result is that you can write C# code, complete with familiar syntax and libraries (such as Generics and the Parallel Task Library), and have it compile to the target platform of your choice.

> ➤ **Mono:** For years, Mono has been **the** cross-platform implementation of the .NET Framework. Xamarin takes advantage of Mono to provide the runtime needed for your application on non-iOS devices.

> ➤ **Integration with Visual Studio:** Now that Xamarin is part of Microsoft, the integration with Visual Studio has become quite deep. You can add Xamarin as a separate workload. Then, once it has been installed, you can develop and debug applications using Android and iPhone emulators. or even on a physical device.

If you're the type of developer who wants to know all of the nitty, gritty details, you should be aware that the implementation of your application will vary significantly between the different platforms. So while your code will look the same, what happens to it at build, deploy, and runtime is very different. For iOS devices, your C# code is compiled to ARM assembly language modules. The .NET Framework classes that you use are included in your application directly. For Android, the C# is compiled to Intermediate Language (IL) code and packaged with Mono. This is similar to what happens when Xamarin is used to create Windows Phone applications, with the exception of the Mono part as the .NET runtime is already available.

When it comes to allowing access to the native capabilities of the individual platforms, Xamarin takes a multi-tiered approach. First, there are SDKs for each of the platforms that are exposed as namespaces that can be referenced from C#. For iOS, there are the CocoaTouch SDK and the UIKit. For Android, Google's Android SDK is exposed. For Windows, Windows Forms, WPF, WinRT, and the Universal Windows Platform (UWP) are available.

But the real power of Xamarin is that, despite all of the differences, your business logic can be written once and reused, along with access to services, common functionality, and almost anything that doesn't relate to platform-specific features. That's not quite the holy grail that developers would hope for, but it's not bad for practical purposes.

CREATING A XAMARIN FORMS PROJECT

The initial steps for creating a Xamarin project are similar to the steps used to create any other type of project in Visual Studio. Start by clicking on the File ⇨ New ⇨ Project menu item. Or, if you have an existing solution, right-click on the solution in the Solution Explorer and select Add New Project from the context menu. Either one of these actions takes you to the New Project dialog, where you navigate to Visual C# ⇨ Cross-Platform. A list of templates appears in the center of the dialog, as shown in Figure 21-1.

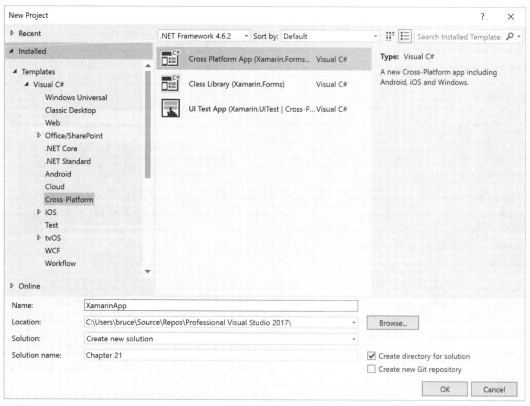

FIGURE 21-1

There are three Xamarin templates available out of the box. The Cross Platform App is the one that we'll choose and is the basis for most applications that you'll create. The Class Library creates a sharable assembly suitable for use in cross-platform applications. The UI Test App creates a project that allows you to test the user interface for your applications. Select Cross Platform App, provide the appropriate name, and click OK to start the project creation process.

When creating a Cross Platform App, there are a number of choices that you have to make. You'll find the options in the New Cross Platform App dialog, shown in Figure 21-2.

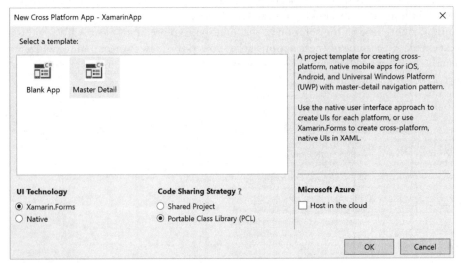

FIGURE 21-2

The first choice is between a Blank App and a Master Detail app. The difference here has to do with the number and functionality of the pages that are automatically created. The blank app is just that—a Xamarin application with a minimum number of pages available. The Master Detail application includes a page that display a list of items, a page that shows details about a particular item, and navigation functionality between the pages.

You have to decide which UI Technology you would like your application to use. The choice is between Xamarin.Forms and Native. If you select Xamarin.Forms, then your pages are constructed using Xamarin controls that are designed to more easily work across the different platforms. So, for the most part, you will only be creating a single view. If you choose Native, then the UI for each platform will be developed independently. Generally, the reason to choose Native is if your application has user interface requirements that are not met by Xamarin.Forms. Otherwise, you'll find that using Xamarin.Forms reduces the amount of code you need to create.

Finally, there is a Code Sharing Strategy. The choice deals with how you want to share code between different cross-platform projects. If you select Shared Project, then you will be using a project that is shared between the different platform projects and use `#if` compiler directives if you need to handle platform-specific requirements. The Portable Class Library (PCL) option creates a portable class library that targets the different platforms. You will have access to functionality that is available on all of the platforms, and if you need to access platform-specific functionality, you will need to use an interface to a separate, platform-specific assembly.

When you have finished making your choices, click OK to create the project. The next dialog that you see (shown in Figure 21-3) is an optional one. It allows you to connect your development machine to a Mac for the purposes of deploying and debugging your application. There is a three-screen wizard describing what you need to do on your Mac in order to allow for the connection. Once the connection has been made, you will be able to deploy your application to the Mac and launch a debugging session that includes the typical Visual Studio debugging experience. However, if you plan on using the iPhone emulator that is available within Visual Studio, this connection isn't required. The dialog will appear every time you open the project, unless and until you click the Don't show this again checkbox in the lower left of the dialog.

FIGURE 21-3

There is a second dialog that appears, although in this case it only appears when you're creating the project and not every time you open the solution. This dialog (Figure 21-4) is used to specify the target version and the minimum version of the Universal Windows project that is part of the solution. There is a dropdown for each choice containing the options that are available on your machine. Select the versions that you want and click OK to continue.

New Universal Windows Project		✕

Choose the target and minimum platform versions that your Universal Windows application will support.

Target Version	Windows 10 Creators Update (10.0; Build 15063)	⌄	ⓘ
Minimum Version	Windows 10 November Update (10.0; Build 10586)	⌄	

Which version should I choose?

		OK	Cancel

FIGURE 21-4

Now that you have done all this work, you have successfully created a cross-platform solution. The contents of the solution can be seen in the Solution Explorer that is found in Figure 21-5.

There are four projects that are part of the solution. The project called XamarinApp is the common project between the platform specific projects. The other projects each relate to a different platform, as you can see from the names. (XamarinApp.Android, XamarinApp.iOS, and XamarinApp .UWP are for the Android, iOS, and Universal Windows platforms respectively.)

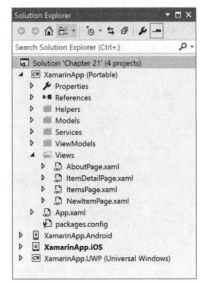

FIGURE 21-5

DEBUGGING YOUR APPLICATION

To run the application on a specific platform, set the startup project to be the project associated with the desired platform. The next step in debugging depends on which platform you're targeting.

Universal Windows Platform

For UWP, you have two choices. The first option is to deploy the application to your local machine. Right-click on the project in Solution Explorer and select Deploy from the context menu. This builds the application and installs it on your local machine. Now when you go to debug your application, make sure that the dropdown to the right of the Run button on the toolbar has Local Machine selected. With that option selected, when the Run button is pushed, the deployed instance of your application is launched and the Visual Studio debugger is attached to that process. In other words, you run your application locally and debug it normally through Visual Studio.

The second option is to debug your application through the simulator. Now, instead of actually deploying your application to your machine, you run your application within a simulator. In the dropdown to the right of the Run button on the tool bar, select Simulator. Then start the debug session for your application. See "The Windows Simulator" section in Chapter 15, "Universal Windows Platform Apps," for details on the debugging experience for the Universal Windows Platform.

Android

The debugging experience for the Android version of your application involves an emulator. You actually have a variety of emulators available to you. When you select the Android app in the dropdown on the toolbar, the dropdown immediately to the right is changed to include the list of available emulators for your machine (see Figure 21-6).

FIGURE 21-6

Select the emulator you wish to use. The default set includes x86 and ARM chipsets that target tablets and phones for several emulators. See the "Managing the Emulator" section later in this chapter for details on how you can add support for different emulators.

Once you have selected the emulator and clicked the Run button (or started a debug session through the Solution Explorer), a number of things start happening. First, your application is built locally. Then the emulator is started. If your machine has a camera, then you are given the option to have the emulator capture the camera input as its own. Figure 21-7 shows the dialog that appears. Choose the source that you want to use and click OK to continue.

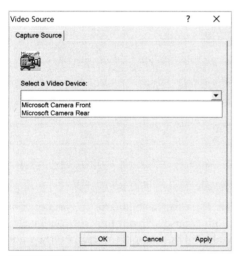

FIGURE 21-7

After a short delay, the emulator will start up. It loads up the Android apps (according to the message—yours is pretty much the only app) and then launches your application. Figure 21-8 shows the emulator running with the application from the project template.

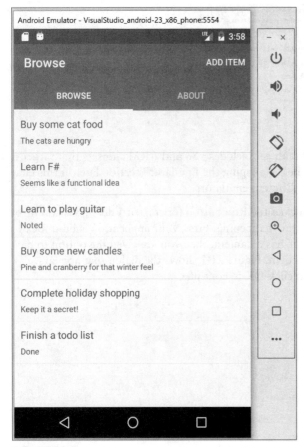

FIGURE 21-8

As you can see from Figure 21-8, the bulk of the visual interface for the emulator consists of your application. You can interact with the application using your mouse (or your finger if you have a touch screen). In this way, you can test the basic functionality of your app. However, on the right side of the emulator, several icons provide additional functionality, such as emulating different network states, geographic locations, and device rotation.

Starting from the top, there are the following icons available:

➤ **Power button:** Turns the phone off or on. It does not stop the emulator from running.

➤ **Volume Up:** Turns the volume on the phone higher.

➤ **Volume Down:** Turns the volume on the phone lower.

➤ **Rotate Left:** Rotates the emulator 90 degrees to the left.

➤ **Rotate Right:** Rotates the emulator 90 degrees to the right.

➤ **Take Screenshot:** Takes a screenshot of what is current on the emulator and saves it to a local directory. The actual directory that is used can be configured through the settings for the emulator.

➤ **Zoom:** Allows you to zoom in and out.

➤ **Back:** Emulates the clicking of the Back button.

➤ **Home:** Emulates the clicking of the Home button.

➤ **Overview:** Emulates the clicking of the Overview button.

➤ **Settings:** The ellipsis takes you to a separate dialog that is used to configure a relatively large body of settings. This dialog is discussed in the next section.

Settings Dialog

The Android emulator has a number of settings that allow you to test your application's response to real-world scenarios that would be difficult or impossible (or prohibitively costly in the case of geo-location) to duplicate in the real world. This section covers the different options that are available and how they can be used to improve the quality of your application.

The Location tab of the Extended Controls dialog shown in Figure 21-9 illustrates the options available to you to configure where the emulator thinks that it is.

FIGURE 21-9

The top half of the dialog is used to set the current location of the phone. There are two coordinate systems that are available. With the decimal system, you specify the longitude and latitude as a positive or negative number of degrees between 180 and –180 with the decimal portion of the number indicating positions between degree points. With the sexigesimal system (yes, that's a real word—look it up), you specify the latitude and longitude in degrees/minutes/seconds. In both cases, the altitude can be specified as a decimal number representing the number of meters above sea level. When you have provided all of the details, click on the Send button to pass the information along to the phone.

The lower half of the dialog allows you to use files with a GPX (GPS Exchange) format (for routes) or a KML (Keyhole Markup Language) format (for multiple placemarks) to provide location information over time.

> **NOTE** *The choice between GPX and KML depends on what source of data you have and how you plan on using it. KML is generally used to annotate maps. GPX is information that is extracted from a GPS device. Typically, the GPX format contains more information (times, routes, waypoints) and can be converted into KML. The reverse conversion is not possible.*

The lower right of the dialog has a Load Options button that launches a File Open dialog where you can pick the file you wish to you. Once you open a file, the contents are loaded into the list of waypoints. To help make this clearer, the following is an example of the contents of a GPX file.

```
<?xml version="1.0"?>
<gpx version="1.1" creator="gpxgenerator.com">
<wpt lat="43.43786397458495" lon="-79.76182408296154">
    <ele>151.00</ele>
    <time>2017-04-22T16:49:11Z</time>
</wpt>
<wpt lat="43.43459190666763" lon="-79.76482815705822">
    <ele>148.00</ele>
    <time>2017-04-22T16:52:50Z</time>
</wpt>
<wpt lat="43.434178990286796" lon="-79.76192064248607">
    <ele>145.00</ele>
    <time>2017-04-22T16:55:08Z</time>
</wpt>
<wpt lat="43.43269375344166" lon="-79.75939486008428">
    <ele>144.34</ele>
    <time>2017-04-22T16:57:23Z</time>
</wpt>
<wpt lat="43.43277166432048" lon="-79.75805375574055">
    <ele>143.07</ele>
    <time>2017-04-22T16:58:27Z</time>
</wpt>
<wpt lat="43.43789408450277" lon="-79.7617391107633">
    <ele>151.04</ele>
    <time>2017-04-22T17:05:41Z</time>
</wpt>
</gpx>
```

You can see from this data that each waypoint consists of a GPS location (latitude and longitude), an elevation, and a time. This information, once loaded into the dialog, can be played back into the emulator so that it thinks that the phone is moving around.

Another scenario that is difficult to test on a physical device is the differences in cellular networks and coverages. The Cellular tab in the Extended Controls dialog (Figure 21-10) shows the options that are available.

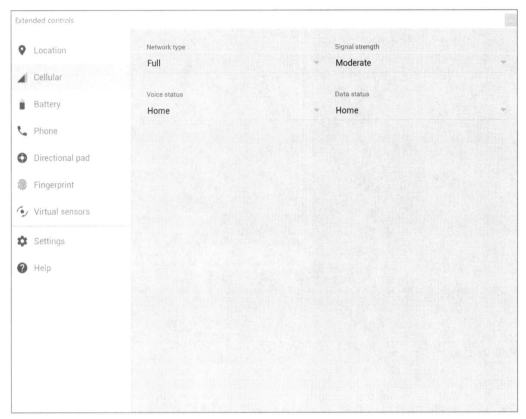

FIGURE 21-10

There are four different attributes of cellular service that can be configured through this dialog.

➤ **Network type:** The type of cellular network that the emulator is connected to. Options include GSM, HSCSD, GPRS, EDGE, UMTS, HSDPA, LTE, and Full.

➤ **Signal strength:** Emulates the level of the cellular signal that the emulator has access to. The dropdown contains a range of values from None and Poor to Great.

➤ **Voice status:** Specifies the type of voice access that the phone has. Options include Home, Roaming, Searching, Denied (emergency calls only), and Unregistered (off).

➤ **Data status:** Identifies the type of data access that the phone has. Choices are Home, Roaming, Searching, Denied, and Unregistered (off).

The Battery tab in the Extended Controls dialog allows you to simulate different conditions related to the battery. Figure 21-11 illustrates some of the choices.

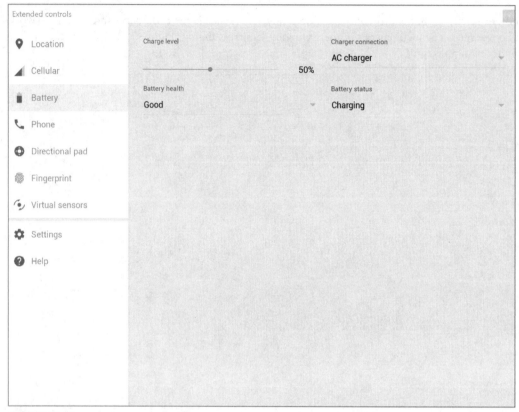

FIGURE 21-11

Through the slider bar in the top left of the pane, you can emulate different battery levels, from 0 to 100% charged. The dropdown in the top right controls whether there is an AC adapter connected to the phone. The battery health dropdown provides an array of choices that indicate the state of the battery itself. The options include Good, Failed, Dead, Overvoltage, Overheated, and Unknown. Finally, you can set the Battery status to a variety of different values: Charging, Discharging, Full, Not charging, and Unknown.

The Phone tab of the dialog (see Figure 21-12) allows you to interact with the phone through text messages or phone calls.

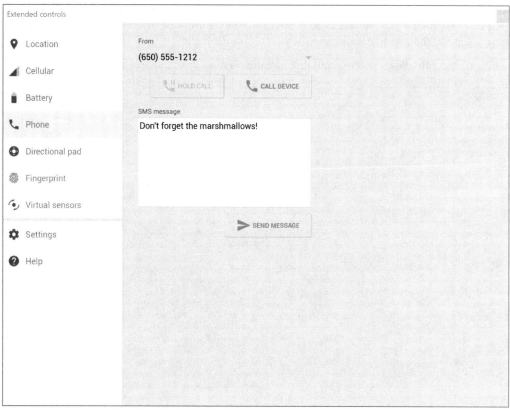

FIGURE 21-12

At the top of the pane, you can enter a phone number. If you click on the Call Device button, you initiate a phone call to the emulator. The emulator reacts as if a phone call is coming in. Once the phone call has been answered, the Hold Call button is enabled, allowing you to place the incoming call on hold. Also, the Call Device button's label is changed to End Call. Clicking on the button while it is in that state ends the current call.

To send an SMS message to the phone, enter the text of the message into the text box on the pane and click on the Send Message button. The emulator will show the text notification window, just as you would expect.

There is a Directional Pad tab that displays a directional pad in the pane on the right. Not every device supports such a pad, so this pane is not available on every device. However, if it is supported, then you can use the pad to manipulate the pointer on the device.

The Fingerprint tab allows you to emulate touching the fingerprint sensor (see Figure 21-13).

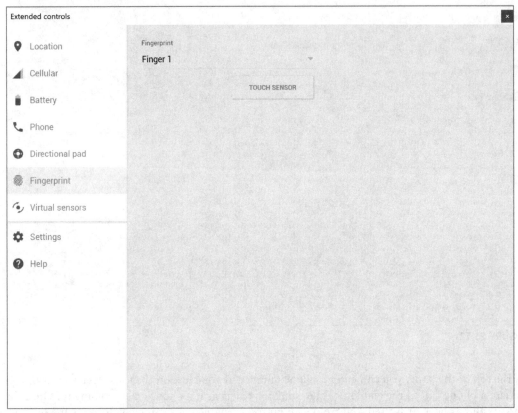

FIGURE 21-13

There is a dropdown list containing 10 different fingers. Select the finger than you want and click on the Touch Sensor button to have the emulator "touched" by the selected finger.

The Virtual sensors tab of the Extended Controls dialog provides a useful mechanism for testing your application under various physical positions of the emulator. Yes, the idea of the emulator having physical positions is strange. But Figure 21-14 illustrates the control that you have.

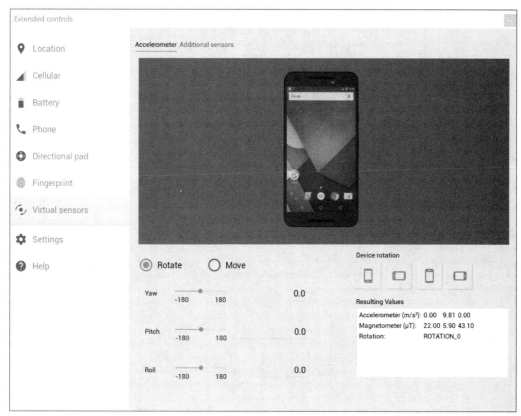

FIGURE 21-14

On the right side of the pane, there are several buttons that can be used to flip the emulator into different orientations. Below the buttons, you can see the values associated with the two sensors (the accelerometer and the magnetometer), along with the detected position.

On the left side of the pane, there are two modes for controlling the physical position. When the Rotate option is selected, you can control the yaw, pitch, and roll of the device. A visual representation of the position of the device appears in the top half of the pane. When the Move option is selected, you can control the X and Y position of the device. Again, the top portion represents the device's position in the X-Y plane. Also, the Resulting Values section of the pane displays the information that is provided by the virtual sensors to the emulator (and to your app).

Finally, the Settings tab (Figure 21-15) gives you a place to configure some elements of the emulator.

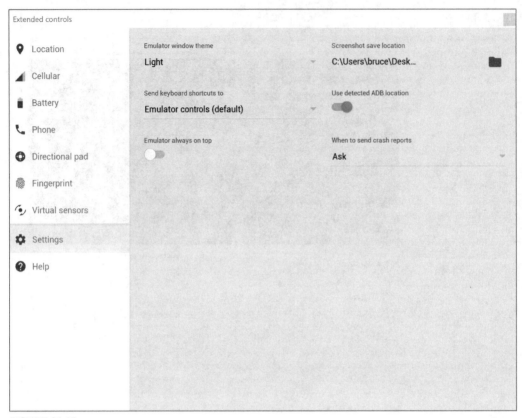

FIGURE 21-15

As mentioned earlier, this is where you can specify the directory into which the screenshots will be placed.

Managing the Emulator

There are a variety of tools available in Visual Studio 2017 to help you manage the different Android emulators. The tools range from capturing logging information from the emulator to allowing you to create new emulators or change the specifications of existing emulators.

When you were going through the debugging process, the dropdown list associated with the Run button contained a list of the supported devices. You can manage that list through the Android Virtual Device (AVD) Manager. By default, it is available as a toolbar button immediately to the right of the run button (the tooltip on the button is actually Open Android Emulator Manager [AVD]) or through the Tools ⇨ Android ⇨ Android Emulator Manager menu option. Figure 21-16 shows the device manager for the default Visual Studio 2017 installation.

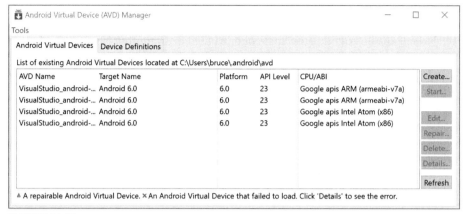

FIGURE 21-16

Down the right side, there are several buttons that allow you to create new emulator images, as well as modify those that already exist. If you select the first entry and click on Edit, you will get a screen that looks like Figure 21-17.

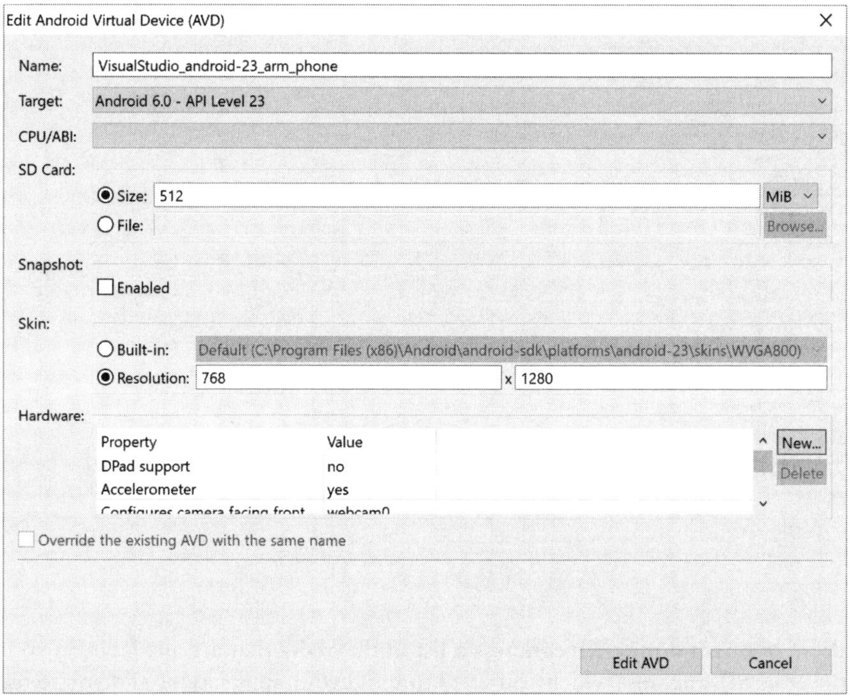

FIGURE 21-17

At the top, you can specify some basic details about the machine being emulated. This includes the APIs implemented on the default machine, the type of CPU being used, and the size of any SD card on the machine. Toward the bottom is a grid that contains the hardware that is supported by the emulator. This includes support for a directional pad, accelerometers, GPS, battery, and temperature. You can easily create different devices with different capabilities to thoroughly test your application under different hardware scenarios.

Managing the SDK

When you are building your Android application, one of the choices that you have to make is which SDK to target. This might initially seem like an abstract consideration. What is really being asked is which version of Android you would like to support. If you right-click on your Android project from within Solution Explorer and choose Properties, you will get to the Properties pages for the project (see Figure 21-18).

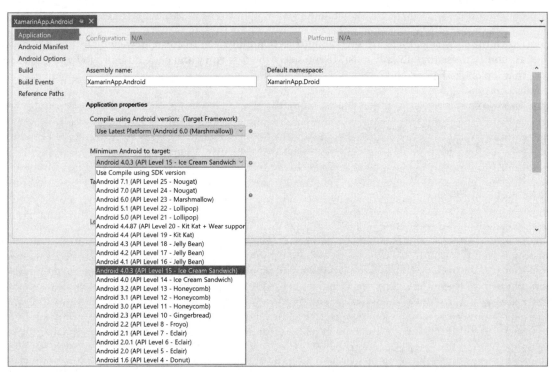

FIGURE 21-18

The Minimum Android to target dropdown contains a list of the SDKs that are available on your current device. Choose the SDK against which you want to build your application, and you're ready to go.

As time goes on, however, Android is bound to introduce additional SDKs. Visual Studio 2017 provides a mechanism to manage the SDKs that are available to you through the Android SDK Manager (Figure 21-19).

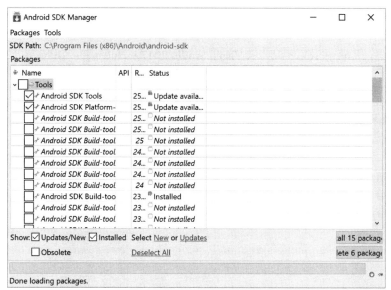

FIGURE 21-19

This dialog is accessible through the Tools ⇨ Android ⇨ Android SDK Manager menu option. Here, a complete list of the available packages is displayed. The list itself is updated as soon as the dialog is opened. And you have the ability to add or remove packages by checking or unchecking them. Below the list are a few checkboxes that are used to filter the packages that are displayed so that they only contain packages that are not installed on your machine or have updates (Updates/New), ones that are already installed (Installed), and ones that have been marked as being obsolete (Obsolete). Once you have made the desired changes, click on the Install packages or Delete packages button in the bottom right of the dialog to complete your changes.

Device Log

While you are running your application, in fact while you are running almost any application, there comes a time when you want to be able to send messages to some sort of a log. Although that is quite reasonable while you are running your Windows Forms application on your local machine, imagine the challenges associated with doing so while running your mobile application remote on a smartphone.

Fortunately, Android offers a solution and Visual Studio 2017 integrates that solution in the IDE. The solution is something called `logcat` (so called because that is the command line that displays the log file).

From a coding perspective, sending a message to `logcat` is quite straightforward. The following code does exactly that:

```
Android.Util.Log.Info("My App", "An interesting message");
```

The `Log` class also has Warn and Error methods to do the same thing, with different levels of severity.

In order to view the messages coming from a device, Visual Studio 2017 includes the Android Device Log. This dialog is available through the Tools ⇨ Android ⇨ Device Log menu option. Figure 21-20 illustrates the device log for a running emulator.

Device Log					
VisualStudio_android-23_x86_phone (Android 6.0 - API 23) ▾				Search	
Time ▾	Device Name	Type	PID	Tag	Message
04-16 16:05:10.9...	VisualStudio_an...	Debug	3562	Mono	[0x9b3bf930] hill climbing, change max number
04-16 16:05:00.0...	VisualStudio_an...	Debug	1223	hwcomposer	hw_composer sent 5 syncs in 60s
04-16 16:04:56.6...	VisualStudio_an...	Debug	3562	Mono	[0x999ef930] hill climbing, change max number ·
04-16 16:04:27.5...	VisualStudio_an...	Debug	3562	Mono	[0x999ef930] hill climbing, change max number ·
04-16 16:04:13.0...	VisualStudio_an...	Debug	3562	Mono	[0x9b3bf930] hill climbing, change max number
04-16 16:04:00.0...	VisualStudio_an...	Debug	1223	hwcomposer	hw_composer sent 4 syncs in 60s
04-16 16:03:44.2...	VisualStudio_an...	Debug	3562	Mono	[0x999ef930] hill climbing, change max number ·
04-16 16:03:28.9...	VisualStudio_an...	Debug	3562	Mono	[0x9b59e930] hill climbing, change max number
04-16 16:03:00.0...	VisualStudio_an...	Debug	1223	hwcomposer	hw_composer sent 5 syncs in 60s
04-16 16:02:58.8...	VisualStudio_an...	Debug	3562	Mono	[0x9b59e930] hill climbing, change max number
04-16 16:02:44.4...	VisualStudio_an...	Debug	3562	Mono	[0x9b59e930] hill climbing, change max number
04-16 16:02:16.0...	VisualStudio_an...	Debug	3562	Mono	[0x9b3bf930] hill climbing, change max number
04-16 16:02:01.3...	VisualStudio_an...	Debug	3562	Mono	[0x9b3bf930] hill climbing, change max number
04-16 16:02:00.0...	VisualStudio_an...	Debug	1223	hwcomposer	hw_composer sent 4 syncs in 60s
04-16 16:01:32.3...	VisualStudio_an...	Debug	3562	Mono	[0x9b59e930] hill climbing, change max number
04-16 16:01:17.3...	VisualStudio_an...	Debug	3562	Mono	[0x9b3bf930] hill climbing, change max number
04-16 16:01:00.0...	VisualStudio_an...	Debug	1223	hwcomposer	hw_composer sent 18 syncs in 60s
04-16 16:00:58.0...	VisualStudio_an...	Debug	3562	Mono	[0x9b5bf930] hill climbing, change max number
04-16 16:00:54.9...	VisualStudio_an...	Debug	3562	Mono	[0x999ef930] hill climbing, change max number ·
04-16 16:00:35.3...	VisualStudio_an...	Debug	3562	Mono	[0x9b5bf930] hill climbing, change max number
04-16 16:00:26.9...	VisualStudio_an...	Debug	3562	Mono	[0x9b5bf930] hill climbing, change max number
04-16 16:00:25.9	VisualStudio_an...	Debug	3562	Mono	[0x9b5bf930] hill climbing, change max number

FIGURE 21-20

In a dropdown at the top, you can select the specific device to retrieve the `logcat` from. If you are running an emulator (or more than one), it appears in the dropdown, as do any attached Android devices.

As you can see, the log itself is relatively simple. There is a list of messages, the ability to search through them, and the ability to pause or stop the logging process if you need to.

iOS

The debugging experience for iOS is relatively similar to the Android experience. Probably the biggest difference is that you can't build the iOS project locally on your Windows machine. You need to have a Mac device that has both Xamarin Studio and XCode installed on it in order to build the code. You can download and install XCode from `https://developer.apple.com/xcode` (be warned that you need to have an Apple ID to do so), or you can install it from the Mac App Store. As well, your Mac device needs to be connected remotely to your computer in order to initiate the build process.

The starting point occurs when the iOS project is opened. You are prompted to connect to a Mac device. Initially, there is a wizard that walks you through the steps necessary to allow remote access from your machine to the Mac. However, through a checkbox in the lower right corner, you can arrange to not be bothered with the wizard again. What is necessary, however, is to actually connect to the Mac.

When the project opens, you are presented with the dialog shown in Figure 21-21. Choose the device that you will use as your build platform and click Connect. To give credit where credit is due, I was lucky enough to have a son (Kyle) who was willing to let me borrow his Mac for this demonstration.

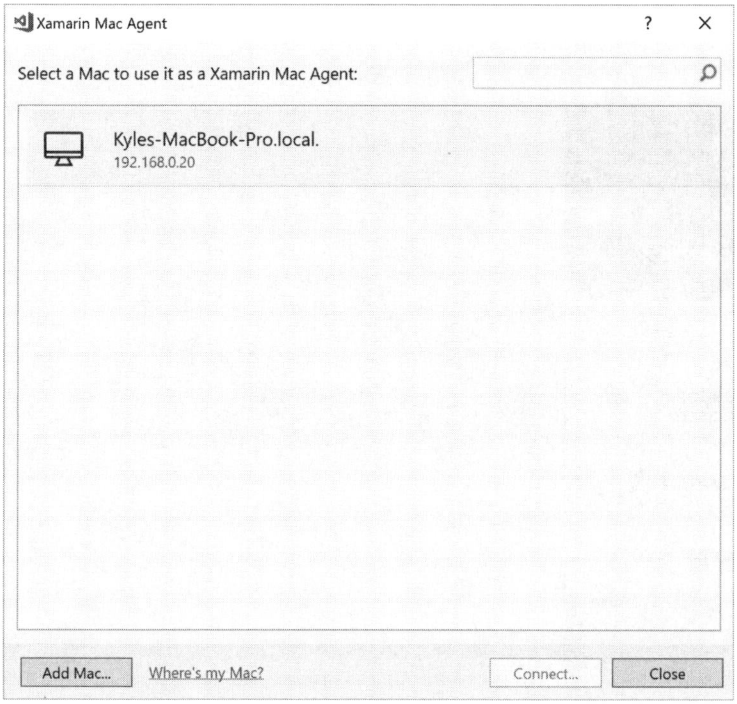

FIGURE 21-21

As part of the connection process, you will be prompted for a set of credentials. The credentials you provide need to have been given remote access permissions on the Mac. Once the permissions have been validated, the connection process then checks to make sure that you have XCode installed on the Mac. If you don't, then you'll see a message similar to that shown in Figure 21-22. As well, a dialog will appear on your Mac showing the XCode license and giving you an opportunity to install it (presuming it's not already installed).

Once you have reached the point where you've connected to the Mac machine, when you launch your application from within Visual Studio, the code is sent to the Mac system for building. The result is then deployed to either a remote device or an iOS Simulator. If you deploy to a device, you have the ability to debug your application in the manner of any other remote device. If you choose to use a simulator, then the Simulator window, similar to what you see in Figure 21-23, appears.

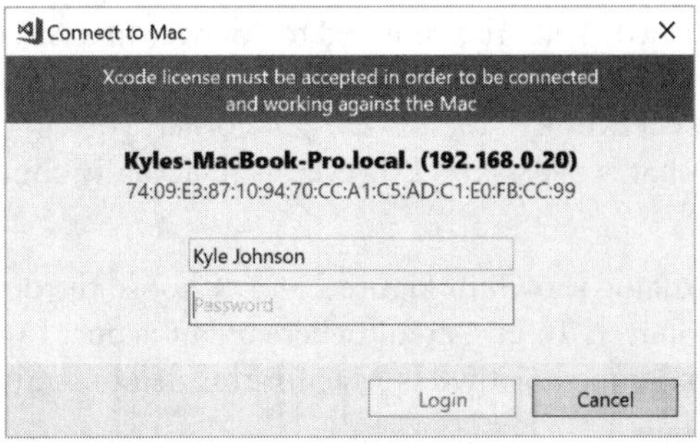

FIGURE 21-22

FIGURE 21-23

The buttons that you use to provide additional input to your application (aside from using the mouse on the central portion of the simulator itself) appear along the top. The purposes of the buttons are as follows:

➤ **Home:** Simulates clicking on the Home button on the device.

➤ **Lock:** Locks the screen on the emulator. The lock can be cleared by swiping the screen.

➤ **Screenshot:** Saves an image of the current screen to disk.

➤ **Rotate Left:** Rotates the simulator 90 degrees to the left.

➤ **Settings:** Displays a screen that is used to configure the keyboard and location for the device. You can see the Settings screen in Figure 21-24.

FIGURE 21-24

There are additional options available by right-clicking on the simulator. Figure 21-25 illustrates these options.

FIGURE 21-25

The first four options are the same as the first four items in the bar at the top of the simulator. The other options are as follows:

➤ **Rotate Right:** Rotates the simulator 90 degrees to the right.

➤ **Shake Gesture:** Emulates the shake gesture on the device.

➤ **Toggle In-Call Status Bar:** Turns the status bar that appears while you are in a call on and off.

➤ **Simulate Memory Warning:** Raises a memory warning on the device that will be interpreted by the application.

➤ **Toggle Keyboard:** Either exposes or hides the soft keyboard on the simulator.

➤ **Reboot:** Powers the simulator off and then on again.

➤ **Settings:** Displays the Settings screen seen in Figure 21-24.

SUMMARY

There is no question that one of the lures of Xamarin is to allow C# developers to create applications that work on Windows, Android, and iOS with a single body of code. While the reality is that some platform-specific development is required, Xamarin definitely help to increase the possibility of code reuse. In this chapter, we skimmed the surface of Xamarin's capabilities while examining the debugging experience of these projects as you move from platform to platform.

22

Mobile Applications Using JavaScript

WHAT'S IN THIS CHAPTER?

➤ The major characteristics of Apache Cordova

➤ Understanding the structure of an Apache Cordova project

➤ Configuring and debugging Apache Cordova applications

WROX.COM CODE DOWNLOADS FOR THIS CHAPTER

The wrox.com code downloads for this chapter can be found at www.wrox.com by searching for this book's ISBN number (978-1-119-40458-3). The code and any related support files are located in their own folder for this chapter.

In Chapter 21, "Mobile Applications Using .NET," you learned about how to use Visual Studio 2017 to create mobile applications using .NET languages. But not every developer wants to use C# to create mobile applications, not to mention the fact that many developers are much more comfortable in the web front-end world of HTML, CSS, and JavaScript. Restricting mobile development to the .NET platform would block these developers from taking part.

For developers who fit into that last category, Apache Cordova is one of the most commonly used frameworks to jump the gap between web development and mobile development. In this chapter, we examine the support that Visual Studio 2017 has for programmers working in the Cordova development space.

WHAT IS APACHE CORDOVA?

While Apache Cordova doesn't have an exceptionally long history, it has quickly become a mainstay in the world of mobile development. It was originally conceived as a way to eliminate the vast and disparate number of ways there were to create smartphone apps in the late 2000s. Depending on your platform, you might need to know C#, Objective-C, or Java, and you needed to be aware of the different UI paradigms that were also platform-specific. As an idea that arose out of a Code Camp, PhoneGap became a single unified platform that enabled developers to target all of the major phone operating systems while developing applications in a common environment, that being HTML, CSS, and JavaScript. The company that originally created PhoneGap (Nitobi Inc.) was acquired by Apache in 2011, and the source code was contributed to the Apache Software Foundation, a non-profit community of open source developers and the project renamed Apache Cordova.

Architecturally, Cordova uses HTML5 and CSS to render views and JavaScript for logic. Native device functionality, such as the camera, GPS, or accelerometer, are exposed through HTML5, pre-suming, of course, that the device's browser supports the necessary HTML5 elements. Fortunately, for the vast majority of modern phones, this is not a significant issue. Android devices, iPhones, Windows Phones, and BlackBerrys support all of the major feature categories.

Visual Studio 2017 supports Apache Cordova through a workload known as Tools for Apache Cordova or TACO. This workload is available through the main installation pane, or it can be added after the fact through the New/Add Project dialog, seen in Figure 22-1. If you click on the Open Visual Studio Installer link, the installer opens and you can select the Mobile Development with JavaScript workload.

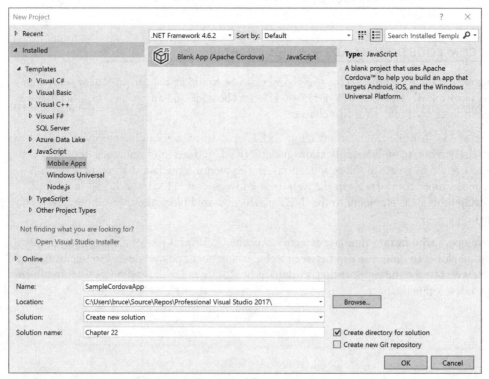

FIGURE 22-1

Upon installation, a number of tools and components are added to your system. First, both Node .js and the Node Package Manager (npm) are installed. More details about Node can be found in Chapter 19, "Node.js Development." Git for Windows is installed on the assumption that Cordova developers are familiar with using Git as a source control repository. On the Android side, a number of SDKs and build tools are included to facilitate the building and testing of your project on an Android device. Along the same lines, a number of Android device definitions can be optionally included. When they are available, you can launch your application in one of these emulators.

CREATING AN APACHE CORDOVA PROJECT

The steps in creating an Apache Cordova project starts with the New Project dialog (seen in Figure 22-1). It can be accessed through the File ⇨ New ⇨ Project menu option. Finding the Cordova template is not easy if you just navigate through the tree views on the left. It is found in the JavaScript node and then the Mobile Apps node. The only option is the Blank App (Apache Cordova) that is used to create a basic, simple web site using Cordova. Select the template, provide a name and a solution, and click OK.

If you have not created a Node.js application on your machine before, then you will be prompted to unblock a port so that Node can listen for requests. The prompt will look like the one shown in Figure 22-2. Click Allow Access so that Node will work for your application.

FIGURE 22-2

After a few moments, your project will be ready to go. The layout of the project can be seen in the Solution Explorer that is found in Figure 22-3. The next few sections talk about the main components of the Cordova project.

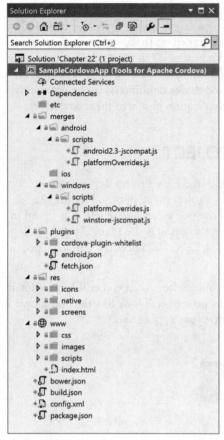

FIGURE 22-3

Merges Folder

As you can see in Figure 22-3, the merges folder contains subfolders for each of the target mobile platforms (Android, iOS, and Windows. Each of these folders contains content that is specific to the corresponding platform. That is what the merges folder is for—to provide a location where you can put assets that are dependent on the platform on which the application is executing.

Any content found in the folders is copied during the pre-build or *prepare* process. As a specific example, any content that is found in the merges/android folder is copied to the web application folder used by the Android project. This copying takes place after the base web application has been copied. The same flow takes place for both the iOS and Windows folders.

You'll notice that both the Android and Windows folders contain a platformOverrides.js file. There is also a jscompat.js file. The purpose of platformOverrides is to load the jscompat file into a `<script>` tag on the page. The jscompat file is intended to provide consistent support for newer features on older browsers. This functionality is known generically as a polyfill. For Android devices, the `bind()` functionality is added. For Windows, it adds a polyfill library known as safeHTML.

Plugins Folder

Plugins are used to access the capabilities of a native device from within Cordova that aren't already available to simple web applications. Basically, a plugin is a library that is developed to work across the different platforms and that exposes the desired native functionality to JavaScript. If necessary, the plugin will update the platform manifest (the file that lets the platform know that what functions need to be turned on for the app).

While you are certainly free to add plugins manually, you are more likely to use the interface that is provided through the `config.xml` file. This interface is described in the "Additional Files and Folders" section later in this chapter.

www Folder

As the name suggests, the www folder contains the web application content that will (eventually) be packaged into the native mobile application. It is expected that developers will spend most of their effort working with the assets in this folder.

The default entry point for the application is the index.html file. It is loaded automatically when the Cordova application is launched.

There are a number of subfolders underneath www. They are:

➤   **css:** Contains the CSS files associated with the application. There is a file in the folder as part of the project template. It is the standard CSS file for the default application.

➤   **images:** Contains any image files used by the application. There is already a file (`cordova .png`) in the folder. It is the Cordova logo that displays in the center of the initial screen in the application template.

➤   **scripts:** Contains the JavaScript files used by the web application. The folder contains an index.js file, which is bootstrap code that initializes the Cordova application. This includes registering handlers for the deviceReady, onPause, and onResume events. Also in the folder is an empty platformOverrides.js file. This file will be replaced by the file found in the merges directory, based on the target platform.

Additional Files and Folders

There are a number of other folders and files that are part of the Cordova project template.

➤   **res Folder:** Contains static files that are not part of the web application. These are files that are used with the native part of the application, such as the icon that will appear on the device, certificates used for deployment and signing, and screenshots that are part of the store package.

➤   **bower.json:** The configuration file for the Bower Package Manager. Information about Bower and the format of this file can be found in the "Bower Package Manager" section of Chapter 18, ".NET Core."

➤ **build.json:** The configuration file used by both the Android and iOS build processes. The project template includes a properly formatted file with the necessary values left black. The important portion of the file is as follows.

```
"android": {
    "release": {
        "keystore": "",
        "storePassword": "",
        "alias": "",
        "password" : "",
        "keystoreType": ""
    }
}
```

Values must be provided for the empty strings that are in the file. One of the more common ways to produce these values is to use a Java command-line tool called `keytool`. This tool creates a `keystore` file, along with information about you and your organization. The `keystore` file is then used to sign your package. The information about this file is also placed into the `ant.package` file found underneath the `android` subfolder of the `res` folder.

➤ **package.json:** The configuration file for the Node Package Manager (npm). This file isn't used by Cordova projects at the moment. However, it is expected that it will eventually replace the config.xml file in a future version of Apache Cordova.

➤ **config.xml:** The current project configuration file for Cordova. It contains information that is used for the native portion of the application, including attributes such as the application name, the included plugins, and the security settings.

While it might appear from the name that config.xml file is just an XML file, Visual Studio 2017 includes an editor so that changes are more easily made. When you double click on config.xml in Solution Explorer, you are presented with the editor pane shown in Figure 22-4.

The Common tab includes the basic information about your application. This includes the name, the author, the description, the version number, and the name of the package. The start page for your application (by default it's `index.html`) is defined here. As well, you can limit the domains to which the application has access. By default, your application can access any domain (as indicated by the asterisk), but from a security perspective, that is not a good idea. The preferred approach is to block everything and then define a list of domains that can be accessed (known as a *whitelist*). As a result, it is considered good practice to come up with a list of domains that you need to access before publishing your application.

The Toolset tab (see Figure 22-5) is used to configure the version of Cordova that you plan on using.

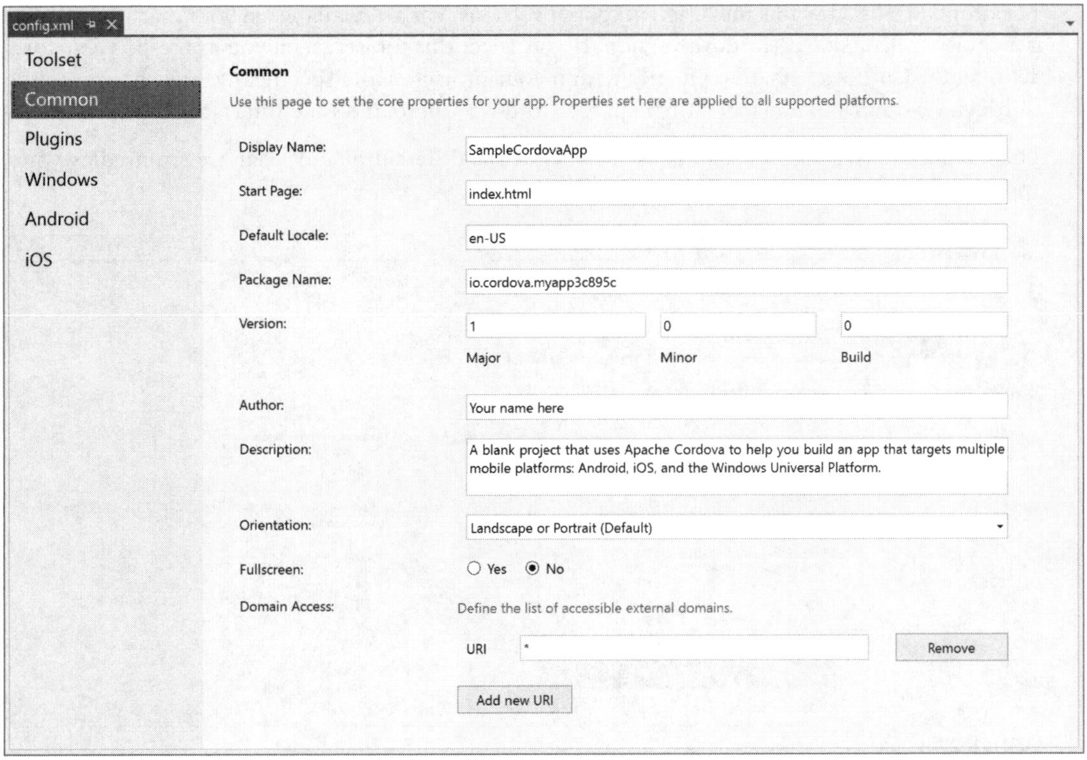

FIGURE 22-4

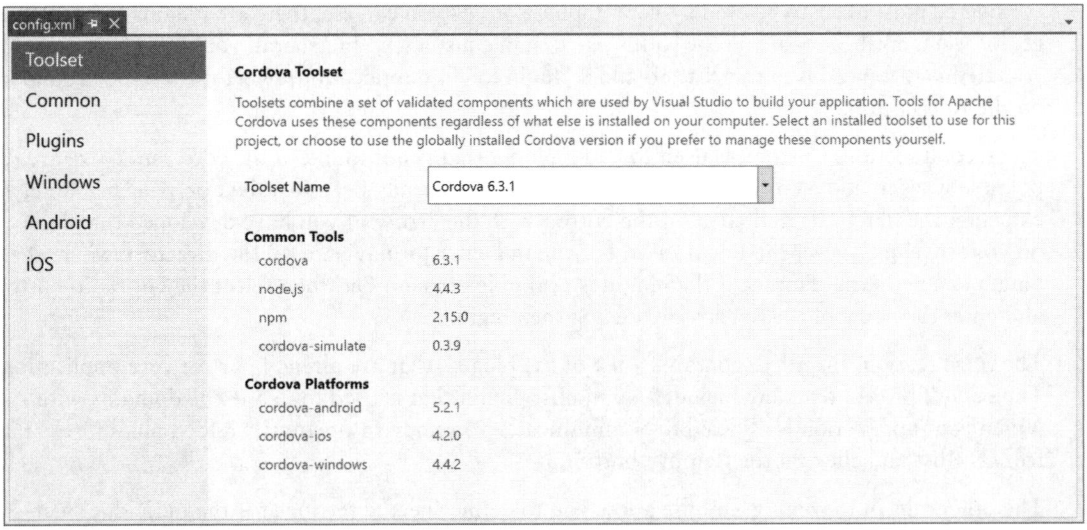

FIGURE 22-5

The dropdown list contains the different toolset versions that are available on your machine. Also, there is a choice called Global Cordova version. If you select this toolset, then you are responsible for defining the Cordova version manually within your project. More specifically, any changes to the Cordova version would be made through the Cordova Command Line Interface.

The Plugins tab (see Figure 22-6) is used to define the different plugins that are required by your application.

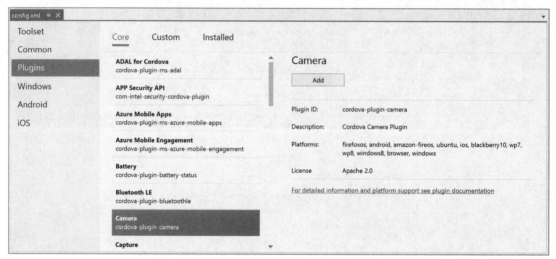

FIGURE 22-6

When the tab is first viewed, the Core section is displayed. This list contains all of the plugins that are considered most likely to be used by your application. As you can see, there are plugins for the camera, geolocation, notifications, and the status bar to name just a few. In general, you'll find that any plugin you are likely to need is in this list. To add a plugin to your application, select it from the list and click on the Add button.

The second section, Custom, is used to add a plugin that is not found in the core list. There are three possible ways to add a custom plugin. If the plugin has already been installed on your machine, you can enter the Plugin ID and click on the button with the arrow. If you have developed the plugin on your machine, select the Local radio button and enter (or navigate to) the directory where the plugin can be found. Finally, if the plugin is available through Git, then select the Git radio button and enter the name of the repository hosting the plugin.

The third section, Installed, contains a list of the plugins that are already part of your application. The default project template includes a whitelist plugin that is used to define the domains with which your application is allowed to communicate. To remove a previously added plugin, select it from the list and click on the Remove button.

The other tabs in the config.xml file allow you to define specific settings for the individual platforms. Figure 22-7 illustrates the options for the Windows platform.

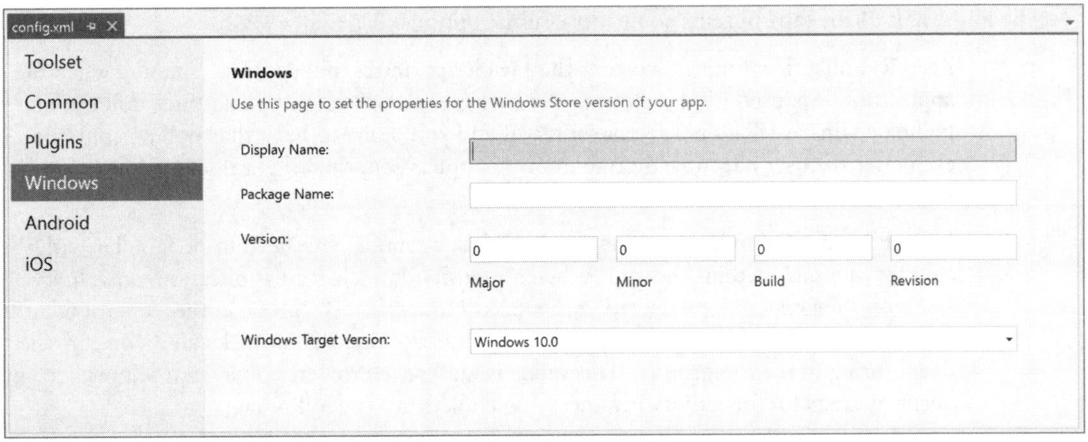

FIGURE 22-7

The values that are available to be entered in this form are quite simple: the display name, the package name, the version, and the version of Windows that is being targeted.

The Android tab (Figure 22-8) has a few more values that can be provided.

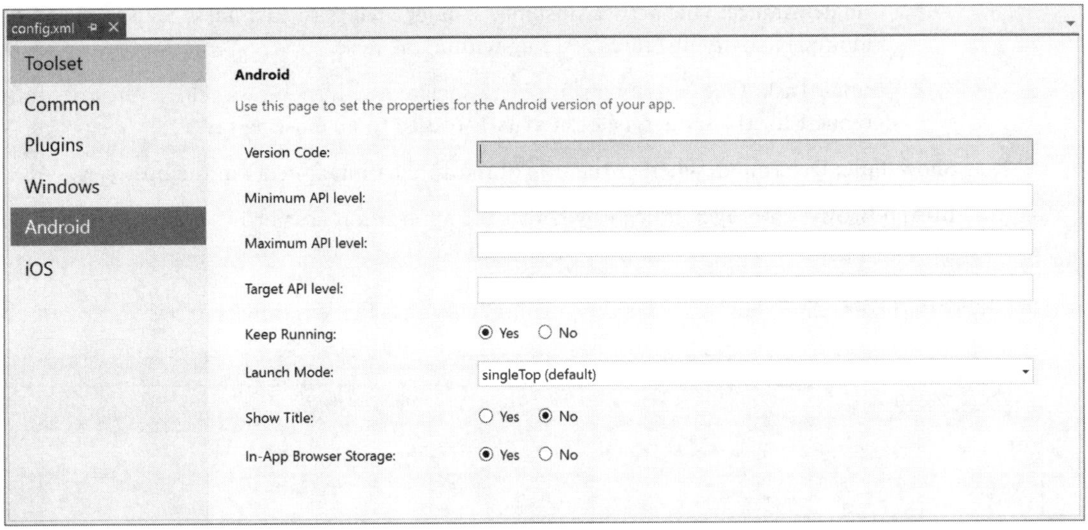

FIGURE 22-8

The top half of the tab is used to define the API that the application requires. This includes the minimum and maximum API version, along with the target (that is, the ideal) version. There is also a version number for your application. And there is no requirement that the Android version be the same as the Windows or iOS versions.

The lower half of the tab contains some more subtle options:

➤ **Keep Running:** Determines whether the JavaScript timers will continue running when the application is paused (that is, sent to the background). If your application is doing some polling against a URL on a regular interval and you'd like to have that polling continue even after the user has moved on to another application, then this value would need to be set to Yes.

➤ **Launch Mode:** To understand the details of launch mode, you need to be familiar with the concept of a *task* within Android. When a user first launches an application, an *activity instance* is created and associated with a task. Only one task can be in the foreground at a time. A long press of the Home button shows a list of the current tasks, and you can select one to bring to the foreground. This mode is really used to determine what happens to subsequent requests for an activity instance. The choices are the following:

➤ **standard:** Multiple activity instances can be created, and they all run in the same task.

➤ **singleTop:** Multiple activity instances can be created and they all run in the same task. However, if a particular type of activity instance is currently at the top of a task (that is, is currently running in the foreground), then a request for the same type of activity will not create a new instance.

➤ **singleInstance:** One activity instance is associated with each task. So you can't have multiple activity instances residing within one task.

➤ **singleTask:** One activity instance is associated with each task. However, a second request for the same type of activity is routed to an existing task.

➤ **Show Title:** Determines whether the title of the application appears in the browser.

➤ **In-App Browser Storage:** Indicates whether the application uses browser storage as part of its functionality.

The iOS tab (Figure 22-9) has the same type of simplicity that the Windows tab has.

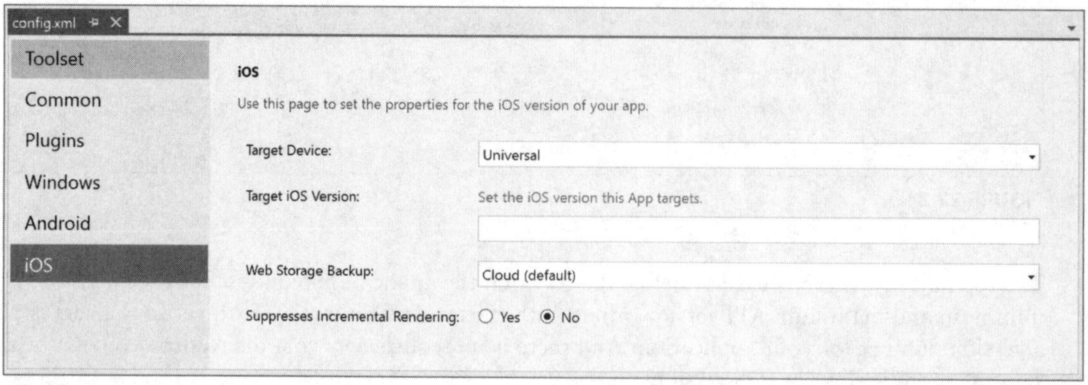

FIGURE 22-9

The Target Device can be iPhone, iPad, or Universal, where Universal means that the application is expected to be on both iPhone and iPad devices. The Target iOS Version is the version of the operating system that the application is targeting. You can specify whether the Web Storage Backup is in the cloud, is local, or doesn't occur at all. Finally, the incremental rendering of the application can be suppressed. This means that the web content will not be rendered as it arrives. Instead, the current content remains in place until all of the new content has been received.

DEBUGGING IN APACHE CORDOVA

The debugging experience associated with Apache Cordova is similar to most web applications. You can set breakpoints, see intermediate values, and change the values of variables at run time. From within Visual Studio, you have a number of options available to launch and debug your application. If you have a local device handy, then Visual Studio 2017 allows you to connect the device to your development environment and deploy and debug your application directly. There are also a number of Android emulators available. They can be installed through the Visual Studio Installer. For more details about the Android emulator, see the "Android" section of Chapter 21. The final choice involves using a simulator. It is this third option that is discussed in the rest of the chapter. To use a simulator, start by choosing the target platform from the dropdown, as shown in Figure 22-10.

FIGURE 22-10

Now for each of these options, you have a number of different choices available to you. Figure 22-11 shows three of the sets.

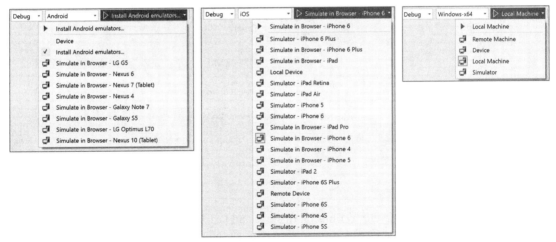

FIGURE 22-11

In general, you'll find the choices divided into two broad categories. First, there are a group of options allowing you to Simulate your application in a browser. These options include the device that is being simulated. When this choice is selected, your application is launched within Cordova

Simulate. For the uninitiated, Cordova Simulate is an open-source replacement for the Ripple simulator. If you used Cordova Tools in Visual Studio 2015, the Ripple simulator was used.

When you launch your application, a Chrome browser is started and your application is displayed within a web page. You can interact with the user interface for your application through the browser.

Along with running the application through Chrome, Visual Studio 2017 also includes a couple of pages used to change the target device while you are running. Figure 22-12 shows the Cordova Plugin Simulation page.

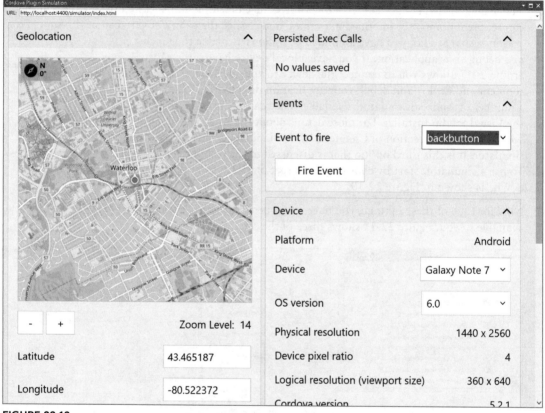

FIGURE 22-12

There are a number of different sections on this page and each of them can be expanded and collapsed as needed. There is a Geolocation section that is used to provide GPS information to your device. You can set the current location by setting a point on a map or by entering the latitude and longitude directly. You can also define the altitude of the device, as well as the accuracy for both the location and the altitude. There is also an option to load a GPX file so that navigation through a number of different locations and times can be simulated.

There is an Events section that can be used to emulate device buttons. The simulator in Chrome doesn't include any framing that shows the device buttons. So instead, you choose the desired function from the Events to File dropdown. Then click the Fire Event button to send the event to the simulator.

The is also a Device section where you can view details about your device. As you add plugins to your project, those plugins may or may not implement a custom interface that can be used during simulation. If they do, you'll see that interface in this page.

Along with the Plugins Simulation page, there is a DOM Explorer page (Figure 22-13).

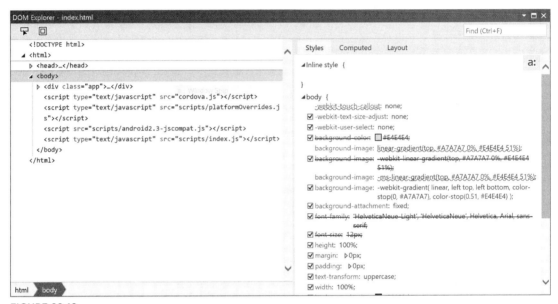

FIGURE 22-13

If you have used the Developer tools inside of the Edge browser, this page might look familiar to you. On the left is the HTML that is currently rendered within the simulator. On the right are the attributes associated with the currently selected element. The Styles and Computed tabs are used to see not only the current values for different style attributes, but also to help you figure out why they are what they are. And if you have ever worked with CSS, you'll understand that the "why" is sometimes the most challenging part. Along with style information, the Layout tab shows the current dimensions of the element's box model.

There are two ways to identify the element that you're working with. In the toolbar at the top, there are two icons. The leftmost icon turns on Select Element mode. The elements in your application (as rendered in Chrome) can be selected with a mouse, and the DOM in the left pane will change so that the selected item is visible. The second icon on the toolbar turns on element highlighting. Now, when you select an element in the DOM tree, the corresponding visual element becomes highlighted in Chrome.

SUMMARY

The ability to create mobile, cross-platform applications using Web technologies is a compelling one. Apache Cordova has gone a long way toward making that a reality. The Apache Cordova Tools for Visual Studio are a very productive addition to Visual Studio and will go a long way to help developers take advantage of Cordova.

In this chapter you learned not only how to create an Apache Cordova application, but also how to configure and debug it. This focuses on using Cordova Simulate to test your application on different platforms.

PART VII
Cloud Services

23

Windows Azure

WHAT'S IN THIS CHAPTER?

➤ Understanding Windows Azure

➤ Building, testing, and deploying applications using Windows Azure

➤ Storing data in Windows Azure tables, blobs, and queues

➤ Using SQL Azure from your application

➤ Understanding the Service Fabric

WROX.COM CODE DOWNLOADS FOR THIS CHAPTER

The wrox.com code downloads for this chapter can be found at www.wrox.com by searching for this book's ISBN number (978-1-119-40458-3). The code and any related support files are located in their own folder for this chapter.

Originally, Microsoft's approach to cloud computing was the same as its approach to desktop, mobile, and server computing, offering a development platform on top of which both ISVs and Microsoft could build great software. But the release of Azure added a number of features to the platform, features that moved it from being "just" a development platform to an environment that enables it to become an important part of any company's cloud computing strategy.

A formal definition of cloud computing is challenging to give. More precisely, it's challenging to reach an agreement on a definition. It seems as if there are as many different definitions as there are vendors. For the purpose of this book, consider "the cloud" to be any service or server accessible through the Internet that can provide functionality to devices running both on-premises (within a typical corporate infrastructure) and in the cloud. This covers almost any scenario from a single, standalone web server to a completely virtualized infrastructure.

This chapter covers the Windows Azure Platform, SQL Azure, and the Azure Service Fabric (a newer version of the product formerly known as AppFabric). The Windows Azure Platform hosts your web application, enabling you to dynamically vary the number of concurrent instances running. It also provides storage services in the form of tables, blobs, and queues. SQL Azure provides a true database service hosted in the cloud. Finally, you can use the Service Fabric to simplify the process of exposing services within your organization. This chapter also discusses some of the features of Windows Azure that might impact some of the choices that you make for development and deployment.

THE WINDOWS AZURE PLATFORM

As with most Microsoft technologies, starting with the Windows Azure platform is as easy as creating a new application, building it, and then running it. You notice that there is a node in the New Project dialog titled Cloud, which has a project template called Azure Cloud Service, as shown in Figure 23-1. If you don't see the Cloud node, it is likely because you haven't installed the Azure workload. Click on the Open Visual Studio Installer link found at the bottom of the treeview on the left to launch the Visual Studio Installer and add the workload before continuing.

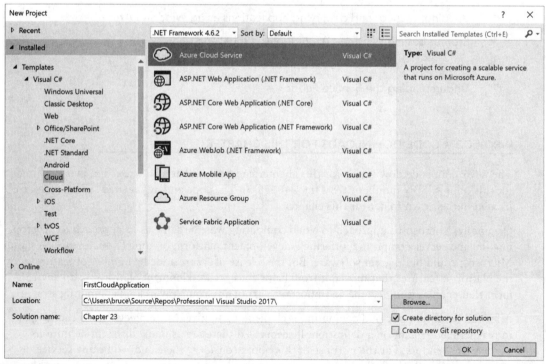

FIGURE 23-1

After selecting the Cloud Service project template, you are prompted to add one or more roles to your application. An Azure project can be broken into different roles based on the type of work they are going to do and whether they accept user input. Simply put, web roles can accept user input via an inbound connection (for example, HTTPS on port 443), whereas worker roles cannot. A typical scenario would consist of a web role used to accept data. This may be a website or a web service of some description. The web role would hand off the data, for example, via a queue, to a worker role, which would then carry out any processing to be done. This separation means that the two tiers can be scaled out independently, improving the elasticity of the application.

In Figure 23-2, both an ASP.NET web role and a worker role have been added to the cloud services solution by selecting the role and clicking the right arrow button. Notice that, new to Visual Studio 2017, there are a number of Node.js roles that are available for your selection. Selecting a role and clicking the edit symbol (which becomes visible once the role has been selected) allows you to rename the role before clicking OK to complete the creation of your application.

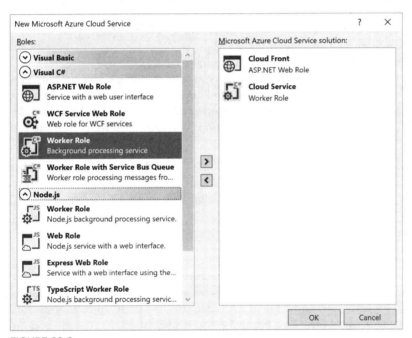

FIGURE 23-2

Because the web role you create is ultimately an ASP.NET project, the next dialog allows you to select the type of project. This dialog is discussed in detail in the "Creating a Web Application Project" section of Chapter 16, "ASP.NET Web Forms."

As you can see in Figure 23-3, the application created consists of a project for each role selected (Cloud Front and Cloud Service, respectively) and an additional project, FirstCloudApplication, that defines the list of roles and other information about your Azure application.

The Cloud Front project is essentially just an ASP.NET MVC project. If you right-click this project and select Set as Startup Project, you can run this project as with any normal ASP.NET project. On the other hand, the Cloud Service project is simply a class library with a single class, WorkerRole, which contains the entry point for the worker.

To run your Azure application, make sure the FirstCloudApplication project is set as the Startup Project, and then press F5 to start debugging. If this is your first time running an Azure application, you can notice a dialog appears that initializes the Development Storage. This process takes 1–2 minutes to complete; when done you can see that two icons have

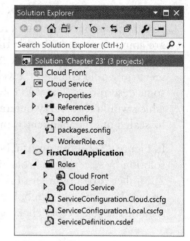

FIGURE 23-3

been added to the Windows taskbar. The first icon enables you to control the Compute and Storage Emulator services. These services mirror the table, blob, and queue storage (the Storage Emulator), and the computational functionality (the Compute Emulator) available in the Azure platform. The second icon is the IIS Express instance that provides a hosting environment in which you can run, debug, and test your application.

After the Development Storage has been initialized, you should notice that the default page of the Cloud Front project launches within the browser. Although you see only a single browser instance; multiple instances of the web role are all running in the Compute Emulator.

The Compute Emulator

In the FirstCloudApplication project are three files that define attributes about your Azure application. The first, ServiceDefinition.csdef, defines the structure and attributes of the roles that make up your application. For example, if one of your roles needs to write to the file system, you can stipulate a LocalStorage property, giving the role restricted access to a small amount of disk space in which to read and write temporary files. This file also defines any settings that the roles require at run time. Defining settings is a great way to make your roles more adaptable at run time without needing to rebuild and publish them.

The second and third files relate to the run-time configuration of the roles. The names of the files have the same basic structure (ServiceConfiguration.*location*.cscfg file) and define the run-time configuration of the roles. The *location* component of the filename determines when a particular configuration file should be used. Use the *local* instance when you debug your application. Use the *cloud* instance when you publish your application to Windows Azure. If you consider these to be similar to the debug and release versions of the web.config file, you are correct.

If you right-click the Emulator icon on the Windows taskbar and select Show Compute Emulator UI, you can see a hierarchical representation of the running applications within the emulator, as shown in Figure 23-4. As you drill-down into the deployments, you can see the FirstCloudApplication and then the two roles, Cloud Front and Cloud Service.

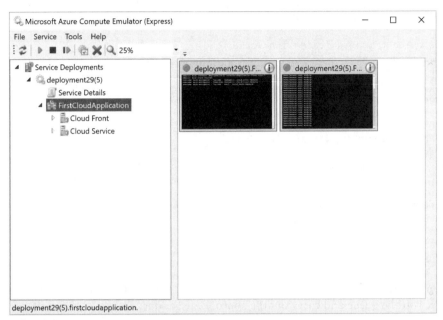

FIGURE 23-4

Within each of the roles, you can see the running (green dot) instances. In the right pane you can see the log output for each of the running instances. Clicking the title bar on any of the instances toggles that instance to display in the full pane. The icon in the top-right corner of each instance indicates the logging level. You can adjust this by right-clicking the title and selecting the wanted value from the Logging Level menu item.

Communicating between Roles

So far you have a web role with no content and a worker role that doesn't do anything. You can add content to the web role by creating an MVC application as you would for any non-Azure application.

You can pass data between web and worker roles by writing to table (structured data), blob (single binary objects), or queue (messages) storage. You work with this storage within the Azure platform via its REST interface. However, as .NET developers, this is not a pleasant or efficient coding experience. Luckily, the Azure team has put together a wrapper for this functionality that makes it easy for your application to use Windows Azure storage. If you look at the references for both the web and worker role projects, you can see a reference for `Microsoft.WindowsAzure.StorageClient` `.dll`, which contains the wrapper classes and methods that you can use from your application.

For example, consider the following code, which places a simple string into a queue:

C#

```
var storageAccountSetting =
   CloudConfigurationManager.GetSetting("DataConnectionString");
var storageAccount = CloudStorageAccount.Parse(storageAccountSetting);

// create queue to communicate with worker role
var queueStorage = storageAccount.CreateCloudQueueClient();
var queue = queueStorage.GetQueueReference("sample");
queue.CreateIfNotExists();
queue.AddMessage(new CloudQueueMessage("Message to worker"));
```

VB

```
' read account configuration settings
Dim StorageAccountSetting = _
   CloudConfigurationManager.GetSetting("DataConnectionString")
Dim StorageAccount = CloudStorageAccount.Parse(StorageAccountSetting)

' create queue to communicate with worker role
Dim queueStorage = storageAccount.CreateCloudQueueClient()
Dim queue = queueStorage.GetQueueReference("sample)
queue.CreateIfNotExists()
queue.AddMessage(New CloudQueueMessage("Message to worker"))
```

Now, to process this message after it has been added to the queue, you need to update the worker role to pop messages off the queue and carry out the appropriate actions. The following code retrieves the next message on the queue, and simply writes the response out to the log, before deleting the message off the queue. If you don't delete the message from the queue, it is pushed back onto the queue after a configurable timeout to ensure all messages are handled at least once, even if a worker role dies mid-processing. This code replaces all the code in the WorkerRole file in the Cloud Service application.

C#

```
public override void Run(){
    DiagnosticMonitor.Start("DiagnosticsConnectionString");

    Microsoft.WindowsAzure.CloudStorageAccount.
            SetConfigurationSettingPublisher((configName, configSetter) =>{
        configSetter(Microsoft.WindowsAzure.ServiceRuntime.RoleEnvironment.
           GetConfigurationSettingValue(configName));
            });

    Trace.TraceInformation("Worker entry point called");

    // read account configuration settings
    var storageAccount = CloudStorageAccount.
                   FromConfigurationSetting("DataConnectionString");

    // create queue to communicate with web role
    var queueStorage = storageAccount.CreateCloudQueueClient();
```

```
            var queue = queueStorage.GetQueueReference("sample");
            queue.CreateIfNotExist();
            Trace.TraceInformation("Cloud Service entry point called");
            while (true){
                try{
                    // Pop the next message off the queue
                    CloudQueueMessage msg = queue.GetMessage();
                    if (msg != null){
                        // Parse the message contents as a job detail
                        string jd = msg.AsString;
                        Trace.TraceInformation("Processed {0}", jd);
                        // Delete the message from the queue
                        queue.DeleteMessage(msg);
                    }
                    else{
                        Thread.Sleep(10000);
                    }
                    Trace.TraceInformation("Working");
                }
                catch (Exception ex){
                    Trace.TraceError(ex.Message);
                }
            }
        }
    }
```

VB

```
    Public Overrides Sub Run()
        DiagnosticMonitor.Start("Diagnostics.ConnectionString")

        CloudStorageAccount.SetConfigurationSettingPublisher(
                Function(configName, configSetter)
                    configSetter(RoleEnvironment.
                        GetConfigurationSettingValue(configName)))
        Trace.TraceInformation("Worker entry point called")

        ' read account configuration settings
        Dim storageAccount = CloudStorageAccount.
                    FromConfigurationSetting("DataConnectionString")
        ' create queue to communicate with web role
        Dim queueStorage = storageAccount.CreateCloudQueueClient()
        queue = queueStorage.GetQueueReference("sample")
        queue.CreateIfNotExist()
        Trace.TraceInformation("Cloud Service entry point called.")
        Do While (True)
            Try
                ' Pop the next message off the queue
                Dim msg As CloudQueueMessage = queue.GetMessage()
                If (msg IsNot Nothing) Then
                    ' Parse the message contents as a job detail
                    Dim jd As String = msg.AsString
                    Trace.TraceInformation("Processed {0}", jd)
                    ' Delete the message from the queue
                    queue.DeleteMessage(msg)
                Else
```

```
                Thread.Sleep(10000)
            End If
            Trace.TraceInformation("Working")
        Catch ex As StorageClientException
            Trace.TraceError(ex.Message)
        End Try
    Loop
End Function
```

This code overrides the Run method. This method loads configuration values and sets up local variables for working with Windows Azure storage. It then starts an infinite while loop that processes messages off the queue.

Naturally, this is just one way to move information between the web and worker roles. It has been provided just to give you an idea of the concepts that need to go into your application design. There are many other choices, and it will be up to you to choose the one most appropriate for your situation.

Application Deployment

After you build your Azure application using the Emulators, you must deploy it to the Windows Azure Platform. Before doing so you need to provision your Windows Azure account with both a hosting and a storage service. In Visual Studio 2017, you can do this through the Server Explorer. Access the Server Explorer through the View ➪ Server Explorer menu options. At the top of the Server Explorer window (see Figure 23-5), the second button from the right is used to connect to your Azure subscription. Click on the button and provide the appropriate credentials to connect to Azure.

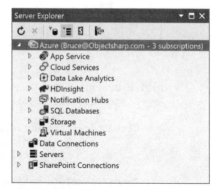

FIGURE 23-5

The FirstCloudApplication requires both web and storage roles, so right-click on the Cloud Service node and select Create Cloud Service. You see the dialog shown in Figure 23-6. Specify the name for the service (it will become the header for the URL), the data center in which your application will run, and, if you have more than one available, the subscription used to pay for any charges you accrue. Click on Create to complete the creation of the new service.

In the Solution Explorer, right-click the FirstCloudApplication project, and select Publish. This process starts by building your application and generates a deployment package and a configuration file. It also publishes those elements directly to Azure. The initial dialog in this process is shown in Figure 23-7.

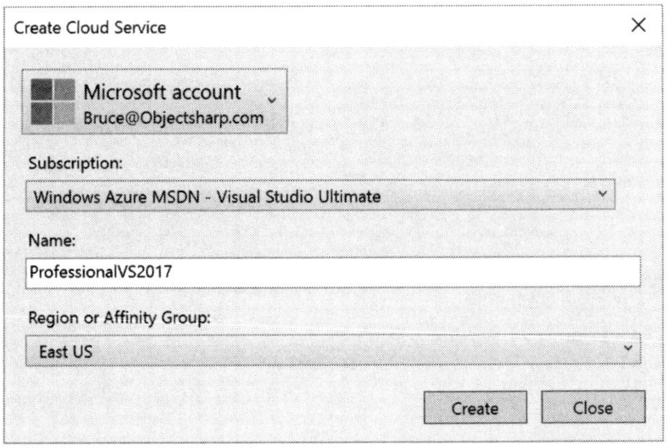

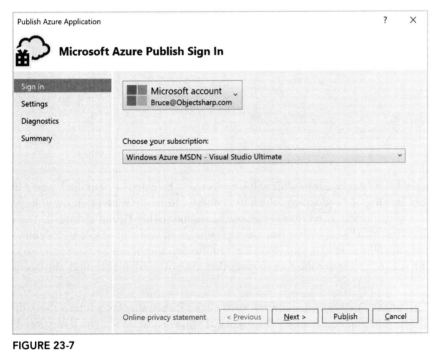

FIGURE 23-6

FIGURE 23-7

The next step in publishing your application involves specifying the settings. Click Next in the Publish dialog to display Figure 23-8.

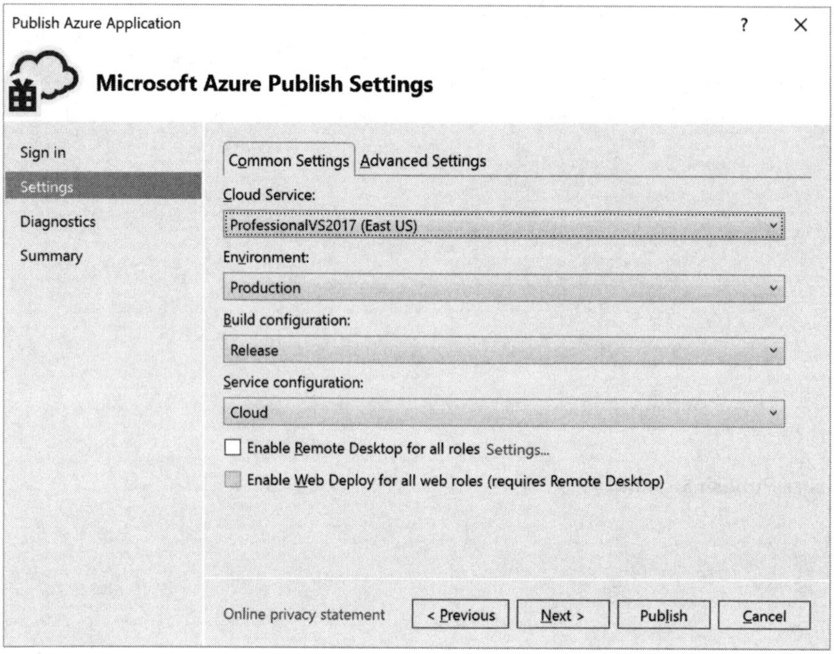

FIGURE 23-8

Through this dialog, the Cloud Service into which this project will be placed is specified, along with the environment (either Staging or Production), the build configuration (dependent on the configurations you have set up in your project), and the service configuration (either Cloud or Local). You can also enable Remote Desktop for the roles that you are deploying, and you can enable web deployment. Remote Desktop capabilities enable you to connect to the desktop of one of your roles so that you can troubleshoot issues or configure the role in ways that are not available through the configuration files.

After you specify the settings to match your requirements, click Next to display a screen that allows you to send diagnostic information to Application Insights. If you wish to do so, you'll also need to identify the Application Insights resource that is the target of the information. Once you finish with Application Insights, you are presented with a summary screen. Click the Publish button to begin the deployment. After the project is built, the Microsoft Azure Activity Log window (Figure 23-9) appears. Through the windows, which are automatically refreshed on a frequent basis, you can track the status of the deployment. After a period of time (which might span 10–15 minutes), you see that your application is deployed.

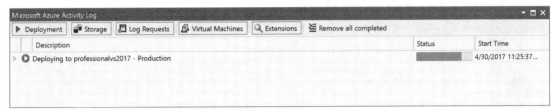

FIGURE 23-9

SQL AZURE

In addition to Azure table, blob, and queue storage, the Windows Azure Platform offers true relational data hosting in the form of SQL Azure. You can think of each SQL Azure database as being a hosted instance of a SQL Server database running in high-availability mode. This means that at any point in time there are three synchronized instances of your database. If one of these instances fails, a new instance is immediately brought online, and the data is synchronized to ensure the availability of your data.

Although the Server Explorer allows you to see the databases that have been created in Azure and you can define the elements in the database through the SQL Server Object Explorer, there is no mechanism that allows you to create a SQL Azure database directly from within Visual Studio 2017. So sign into the Windows Azure portal (`http://manage.windowsazure.com`).

> **NOTE** *This section's instructions assume that you're working with the newest version of the Azure Portal. If you're using the old Azure Portal, all of the described features are available, but the steps you follow will be different.*

Click the New icon at the top left of the page. Then click the Database node and notice that SQL Database is one of the options. When you select it, the resulting pane gives you the options to specify the name and location of the database. (Figure 23-10 illustrates a set of options.) After creating a database, you can retrieve the connection string that you need to connect to the database by selecting the database and clicking the Show database connection strings link, as shown in Figure 23-11.

FIGURE 23-10

You have a number of ways to interact with a SQL Azure database. Because SQL Azure is based on SQL Server, graphical tools, such as SQL Server Management Studio and the Server Explorer in Visual Studio 2017, are the obvious choices.

From your application you can connect to SQL Azure using the connection string retrieved from the Windows Azure portal page. The list of connection strings includes versions for not only ADO .NET, but also JDBC and PHP.

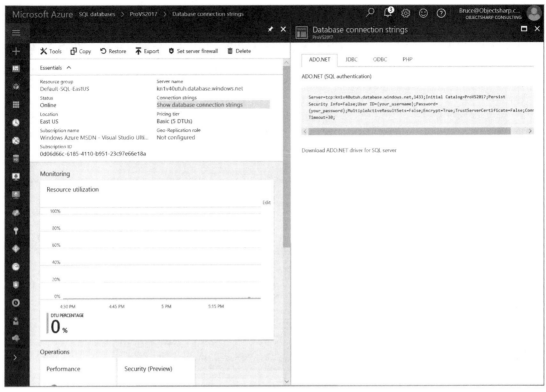

FIGURE 23-11

SERVICE FABRIC

One of the leading trends in developing enterprise-level applications is the use of microservices. The general idea behind microservices is to divide application functionality into small, independent pieces and then use different tools to stitch the services together into larger applications.

Yes, this brief description sounds like a number of other application decomposition approaches used over the past decade or longer. And there is a similarity, at least at a conceptual level, between microservices and a service-oriented architecture (SOA). Probably the main difference is that the underlying technology is much lighter weight (JSON vs XML/WSDL) and more capable of scaling easily. In other words, microservices are actually able to deliver on some of the promise of SOA.

The purpose of Service Fabric is to allow you to deploy and manage microservices across a cluster of machines. These microservices can be independently scaled up or down as your application demands. And updates to one microservice don't require any of the other microservices to change.

While it's possible to roll your own microservice environment, by using the Service Fabric programming model, you can get to a deployed application much more quickly. And there are a number of different project templates that are available in Visual Studio 2017 to help. To start, use the File ⇨ New ⇨ Project menu option to display the New Project dialog. Then choose the Cloud node on the left and Service Fabric Application from the list of templates in the center pane (Figure 23-12).

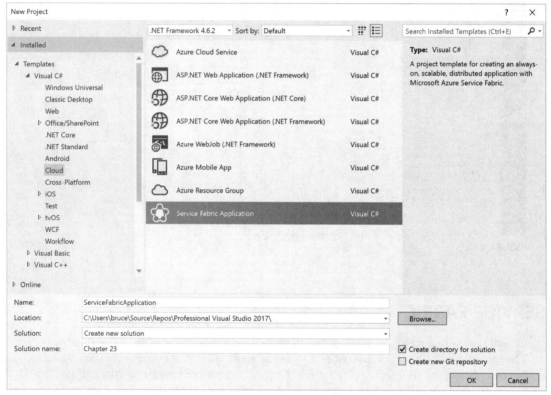

FIGURE 23-12

When you provide a name for your project and click on OK, a second dialog appears allowing you to choose from a number of different service applications (see Figure 23-13):

➤ **Stateless Service:** A service where there is no state maintained between calls. Any state that is present during the call is entirely disposed of before the next call.

➤ **Stateful Service:** A service where some portion of the state of the service is maintained between different calls.

➤ **Actor Service:** An actor, in this context, is an independent unit of computation functionality that operates within a single-threaded environment. An actor service implements an actor.

➤ **Stateless Web API:** A service that implements a Web API endpoint that doesn't maintain state.

➤ **Guest Executable:** A service that runs a single executable. Unlike the other services mentioned up to this point, it is not necessary that the service exposes an endpoint.

➤ **Guest Container (Preview):** A service that runs a single executable within a container.

➤ **ASP.NET Core:** A service that hosts an ASP.NET Core application.

FIGURE 23-13

AZURE MOBILE APP

Windows Azure Mobile App is an interesting combination of functionality. When you create a mobile app from scratch, it is a prebuilt, pre-configured website and database that exposes a REST-based API against which data can be created, updated, and retrieved.

Beyond that basic set of functionality, there are some additional features that make a compelling use case for mobile applications (phone and tablets), which require a centralized data store. This includes a client-side library supported on iOS, Android and Windows Phone/Store, simple server-side validation (coded using node.js), full customized API support (using a Visual Studio MVC project template), and integrated authentication support. In other words, a lot of functionality is easily integrated into your application, regardless of the platform on which it is running.

AZURE VIRTUAL MACHINES

The Windows Azure websites and Cloud Services that have already been covered fall into the Platform as a Service (PaaS) model of development. If you are just starting to build your application, these are very useful alternatives that are available to you. And although you can convert existing applications into this model, the level of effort involved can vary from almost zero to significant re-architecting. Not only that, there are many examples of applications that cannot be migrated into a PaaS environment.

To address this latter category, Windows Azure provides support for an Infrastructure as a Service (IaaS) model. One of the main components of this model is Windows Azure Virtual Machines. This is, as you might expect, a virtual machine that can support a wide variety of applications. This includes not only Windows-based applications, but also applications hosted in Linux. Access to the virtual machine is through a remote connection, and you are the administrator, configuring or installing as you want.

Along with providing a bare machine and operating system, the Windows Azure Portal also provides a gallery of Visual Machine types. For example, there are a number of different Linux distributions and SQL Server boxes, and it is anticipated that, over time, additional server offerings such as SharePoint will appear on the portal. And Microsoft has enabled other companies such as RightScale and SUSE to provide Virtual Machine configuration and management services simplifying the deployment of different Virtual Machine instances.

Connectivity

To support the IaaS model, Windows Azure enables a number of different forms of connectivity. When thinking about the types of connectivity that are being defined, it's useful to think about what needs to be connected within a computing infrastructure (which, ultimately, is what Azure is implementing). Connectivity can take the form of publicly and privately available endpoints. As well, the endpoints can expose different types of functionality, including load balancing and port forwarding (and the more typical serving of web pages).

Endpoints

Windows Azure endpoints are conceptually the same as the endpoints that have been available in WCF. They are IP addresses and ports exposed to other services or even to the public Internet. In the Windows Azure world, a Load Balancer can be associated with each endpoint so that the service behind the endpoint becomes scalable.

Cloud Services defines two types of public input endpoints: a simple input endpoint and an instance input endpoint. As well, there is an internal endpoint available only to Windows Azure services.

The difference between the simple input and the instance input endpoints relates to how the load balancer handles traffic. For simple input endpoints, a round-robin algorithm is used to ensure an evenly shared flow of requests. An instance input endpoint has traffic directed to a specific instance (such as a single Worker role). Typically, instance input endpoints are used to allow intraservice traffic within a cloud service.

For Virtual Machines, there are also two types of public endpoints (and they serve a different purpose than the Cloud Service endpoints). Load-balanced endpoints use a round-robin load balancing algorithm to direct traffic. Port forwarded endpoints use a mapping algorithm to redirect traffic from one port or endpoint to another.

Virtual Network

The inclusion of Virtual Machines into the Windows Azure world introduced the need to include those machines into a corporate network. With Virtual Network technology, it is possible to seamlessly extend a corporate network to include a Virtual Machine without increasing the security surface.

Windows Azure supports two types of VPN connectivity. The Virtual Network solution is a hardware-based, site-to-site VPN capability. This enables you to create a hybrid infrastructure that supports both on-premise services and Windows Azure–hosted services. To set up a Virtual Network within your environment, hardware within the corporate network might need to be modified.

The second option is named Windows Azure Connect. Unlike Virtual Network, this is a software-based VPN enabling developers to create connections between on-premise machines and Azure-based services. The software agent required to establish this connection is available only for Windows, which might limit the environments in which it can be used.

Along with the connectivity options, Windows Azure includes a number of other services designed to include the types of workloads that can be supported.

➤ **Windows Azure Traffic Manager:** Provides load-balancing capability for public HTTP endpoints exposed by Azure services. There is support for three different types of traffic distribution: geographical (traffic is directed to the server with the minimum latency from the current location); active-passive failover (traffic is sent to a backup service when the active service fails); and round-robin load balancing.

➤ **Windows Azure Service Bus:** Provides a mechanism that enables Azure services to communicate with one another. There are two different styles of service bus communication that are supported. With Relayed Messaging, the service and client both connect to a service bus endpoint. The Service Bus links these connections together, enabling two-way communication between the components. In Brokered Messaging, communication is enabled through a publish/subscribe model with durable message store. This is probably better recognized as a message queue model.

SUMMARY

In this chapter you learned about the Windows Azure Platform and how it represents Microsoft's entry into the cloud computing space. Using Visual Studio 2017, you can adapt an existing, or create a new, application or service for hosting in the cloud. The local Compute and Storage Emulators provide a great local testing solution, which means when you publish your application to Windows Azure, you can be confident that it will work without major issues.

Even if you don't want to migrate your entire application into the cloud, you can use SQL Azure and the Service Fabric offerings to host your data, address connectivity challenges, or handle scalability and reliability issues.

24

Synchronization Services

WHAT'S IN THIS CHAPTER?

> ➤ What an occasionally connected application is and why you would build an application that way

> ➤ Wiring up Synchronization Services to build an occasionally connected application

> ➤ Separating Synchronization Services across multiple tiers

> ➤ Performing both single and bidirectional synchronization

WROX.COM CODE DOWNLOADS FOR THIS CHAPTER

The wrox.com code downloads for this chapter can be found at www.wrox.com by searching for this book's ISBN number (978-1-119-40458-3). The code and any related support files are located in their own folder for this chapter.

Application design includes many extremes, ranging from standalone applications that don't share data to public web applications in which everyone connects to the same data store. A variety of peer-to-peer applications exist in which information is shared between nodes but no central data store exists. In the enterprise space, terms such as Software as a Service (SaaS) and Software and Services (S+S) reflect a hybrid model where data and services are combined within a rich application.

For the majority of business applications, the web model has become the default choice. It provides user interface functionality that is close to what you get in a rich client application with a deployment model that is easier to provide updates through. And it becomes possible to rationalize the data into a single central repository. Still, there is a drawback . . . the need to be connected to a network.

Of course, this is a problem that rich client applications can have as well. And it's one that even a cloud-based strategy is not sufficient to address. An alternative strategy is to synchronize a portion of the data repository to the client machine and to make local data requests. This not only improves performance (because all the data requests happen locally), but it also reduces the load on the server. In this chapter, you discover how building applications that are occasionally connected can help you deliver rich and responsive applications using the various synchronization services offered by Microsoft.

OCCASIONALLY CONNECTED APPLICATIONS

An occasionally connected application is one that can continue to operate regardless of connectivity status. You have a number of different ways to access data when the application is offline. Passive systems simply cache data that is accessed from the server so that when the connection is lost at least a subset of the information is available. Unfortunately, this strategy means that a limited set of data is available and is only suitable for scenarios in which there is an unstable or unreliable connection, rather than completely disconnected applications. In the latter case, an active system that synchronizes data to the local system is required. The Microsoft Synchronization Services for ADO.NET (Sync Services) is a synchronization framework that dramatically simplifies the problem of synchronizing data from any server to the local system.

SERVER DIRECT

To become familiar with the Sync Services, you can use a simple database that consists of a single table that tracks customers. You can create this using the Server Explorer within Visual Studio 2017. Right-click the Data Connections node, and from the shortcut menu, select Create New SQL Server Database. Figure 24-1 shows the Create New SQL Server Database dialog in which you can specify a server and a name for the new database.

When you enter CRM into the name field and click OK, a database with the name CRM is added to the local SQL Server instance, and a data connection is added to the Data Connections node in the Server Explorer. From the Tables node, under the newly created data connection, select Add New Table from the right-click shortcut menu, and create columns for CustomerId (primary key), Name, Email, and Phone so that the table matches what is shown in Figure 24-2.

FIGURE 24-1

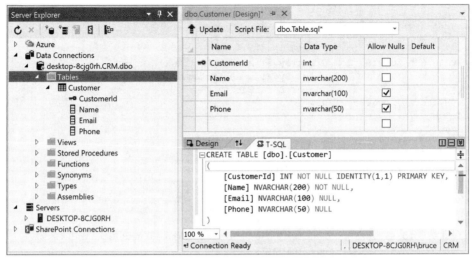

FIGURE 24-2

Now that you have a simple database to work with, it's time to create a new WPF Application. In this case the application is titled QuickCRM, and in the Solution Explorer tool window of Figure 24-3, you can see the MainWindow and two additional forms, ServerForm and LocalForm, have been added.

FIGURE 24-3

MainWindow has two buttons (refer to the editor area of Figure 24-3) and has the following code to launch the appropriate forms:

VB

```
Public Class MainWindow
    Private Sub ServerButton_Click(ByVal sender As System.Object,
                             ByVal e As System.RoutedEventArgs) _
```

```
                             Handles ServerButton.Click
            My.Forms.ServerForm.Show()
        End Sub

        Private Sub LocalButton_Click(ByVal sender As System.Object,
                              ByVal e As System.RoutedEventArgs) _
                        Handles LocalButton.Click
            My.Forms.LocalForm.Show()
        End Sub
    End Class
```

C#

```
    public partial class MainWindow : Window {
        public MainWindow(){
            InitializeComponent();
        }

        private void ServerButton_Click(object sender, RoutedEventArgs e){
            (new ServerForm()).ShowDialog();
        }
        private void LocalButton_Click(object sender, RoutedEventArgs e){
            (new LocalForm()).ShowDialog();
        }
    }
```

Before looking at how you can use Sync Services to work with local data, take a look at how you might have built an always-connected, or server-bound, version. Open the Data Sources window, click on the Add New Data Source button, and step through the Data Source Configuration Wizard, selecting the DataSet option, followed by the CRM database created earlier, saving the connection string to the application configuration file, and adding the Customer table to the CRMDataSet.

Open the ServerForm designer by double-clicking it in the Solution Explorer tool window. In the Data Sources tool window, use the drop-down on the Customer node to select Details. Then from the CustomerId node, select None. Dragging the Customer node across onto the design surface of the ServerForm adds the appropriate controls so that you can bind data to the Customer table of the dataset. It also contains the code to populate that dataset, so that you can navigate backward and forward through the database. To actually perform the navigation, a couple of buttons need to be added to the page, so that it appears as shown in Figure 24-4.

The functionality of the Next and Previous buttons is implemented in the Click event handler for those buttons. Add the following code to the code-behind file and make sure that the Click event is connected to it from within XAML.

VB

```
    Private Sub Previous_Click(ByVal sender As Object,
        ByVal e As RoutedEventArgs) _
        Dim customerViewSource As System.Windows.Data.CollectionViewSource = _
```

```vb
        CType(Me.FindResource("customerViewSource"), _
            System.Windows.Data.CollectionViewSource)
    If (customerViewSource.View.CurrentPosition > 0) Then
        customerViewSource.View.MoveCurrentToPrevious()
    End If

End Sub

Private Sub Previous_Click(ByVal sender As Object,
    ByVal e As RoutedEventArgs) _
    Dim cRMDataSet As Quick_CRM.CRMDataSet = _
        CType(Me.FindResource("cRMDataSet"), Quick_CRM.CRMDataSet)
    Dim customerViewSource As System.Windows.Data.CollectionViewSource = _
        CType(Me.FindResource("customerViewSource"), _
            System.Windows.Data.CollectionViewSource)
    If (customerViewSource.View.CurrentPosition <
        cRMDataSet.Customer.Count - 1) Then
        customerViewSource.View.MoveCurrentToNext()
    End If

End Sub
```

C#

```csharp
    private void Previous_Click(object sender, RoutedEventArgs e)
        System.Windows.Data.CollectionViewSource customerViewSource =
            ((System.Windows.Data.CollectionViewSource)
             (this.FindResource("customerViewSource")));
        if (customerViewSource.View.CurrentPosition > 0)
            customerViewSource.View.MoveCurrentToPrevious();
    }

    private void Next_Click(object sender, RoutedEventArgs e)
    {
        Quick_CRM.CRMDataSet cRMDataSet =
            ((Quick_CRM.CRMDataSet)(this.FindResource("cRMDataSet")));
        System.Windows.Data.CollectionViewSource customerViewSource =
            ((System.Windows.Data.CollectionViewSource)
             (this.FindResource("customerViewSource")));
        if (customerViewSource.View.CurrentPosition < cRMDataSet.Customer.Count - 1)
            customerViewSource.View.MoveCurrentToNext();
    }
```

This completes the part of the application that connects directly to the database to access the data. You can run the application and verify that you can access data while the database is online. If the database goes offline or the connection is lost, an exception is raised by the application when you attempt to retrieve from the database.

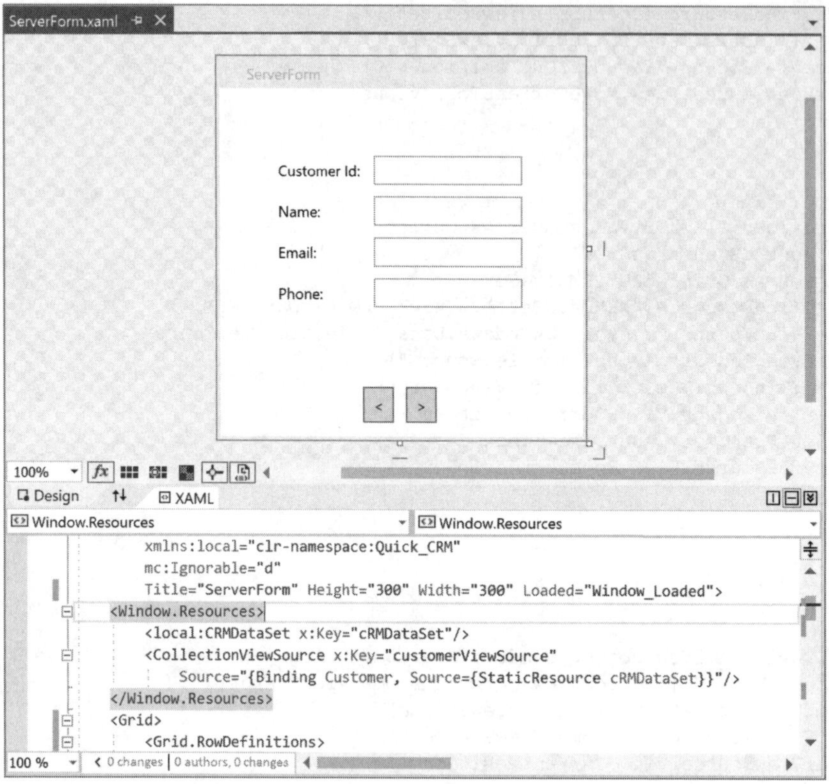

FIGURE 24-4

GETTING STARTED WITH SYNCHRONIZATION SERVICES

Underlying the ability to synchronize data between a local and remote database is the Sync Framework. For Visual Studio 2017, version 2.1 of the Sync Framework is the one to work with, and to use the synchronization functionality that we're discussing in this chapter, you need to make sure that it has been installed. It is available through NuGet.

To start, add a LocalDB to your project. Use the Add New Item dialog (right-click the project in Solution Explorer, and select Add ⇨ New Item). In the dialog, navigate to the Data folder, and select the Service-Based Database template. For this example, give it the name LocalCRM.mdf. Then, in the Data Sources window, add a new Data Source. The Data Source Configuration Wizard is launched. Choose a Database, then select Dataset, set the data connection to point to LocalCRM.mdf, accept the default connection string (which should be called LocalCRMConnectionString), and save the string in the configuration file. On the final screen of the wizard, a message indicates that the database doesn't contain any objects. Have no fear. You'll be adding objects soon enough.

For this example, you need to add a form that displays the data that is stored on the client. While the LocalForm form is in design mode, drag the Customer node from the CRMDataSet data source onto the form. This action creates a connection to the server database, which is addressed momentarily.

Part of the process of a synchronized application is to get the data in sync. To do this, the databases need to be provisioned with a number of different elements. These elements enable change tracking to be managed on the tables, making it easier to keep the data on the two sides synchronized. This provisioning is done programmatically. And conveniently, it enables the database schemas to be kept in sync as well. Start by opening the MainWindow and adding a Load event handler to the form. In the Load event, you need to perform three steps. First, provision the server. Second, provision the client. And finally synchronize the data.

One of the key concepts with the Sync Framework is scope. By adding one or more tables to the scope, you can arrange for all the updates for the tables to be included in a single transaction. This sounds simple and straightforward, but there is a bit of a wrinkle. If you are performing a large number of updates, keeping them all in one transaction can have a negative impact on performance. So there is a setting (`BatchSize` on the synchronization provider object) that controls how many updates are kept in each transaction. If you want to batch your updates, set the `BatchSize` property to a nonzero value.

Start by provisioning the server. Add the following code to the Load event handler for the MainWindow form.

VB

```
Dim scopeName = "CRMScope"
Dim serverConn = New SqlConnection(Settings.Default.CRMConnectionString)
Dim clientConn = New SqlConnection(Settings.Default.LocalCRMConnectionString)
Dim serverProvision = New SqlSyncScopeProvisioning(serverConn)
If Not serverProvision.ScopeExists(scopeName) Then
    Dim serverScopeDesc = New DbSyncScopeDescription(scopeName)
    Dim serverTableDesc =
        SqlSyncDescriptionBuilder.GetDescriptionForTable("Customer", _
        serverConn)
    serverScopeDesc.Tables.Add(serverTableDesc)
    serverProvision.PopulateFromScopeDescription(serverScopeDesc)
    serverProvision.Apply()
End If
```

C#

```
var scopeName = "CRMScope";
var serverConn = new SqlConnection(Settings.Default.CRMConnectionString);
var clientConn = new SqlConnection(Settings.Default.LocalCRMConnectionString);
var serverProvision = new SqlSyncScopeProvisioning(serverConn);
if (!serverProvision.ScopeExists(scopeName))
{
    var serverScopeDesc = new DbSyncScopeDescription(scopeName);
    var serverTableDesc =
        SqlSyncDescriptionBuilder.GetDescriptionForTable("Customer",
        serverConn);
    serverScopeDesc.Tables.Add(serverTableDesc);
    serverProvision.PopulateFromScopeDescription(serverScopeDesc);
    serverProvision.Apply();
}
```

In this code, you can see the basic provisioning steps. The first step is to create the scope-provisioning object using a connection to the server database. Then, if the named scope has not already been added, create a new instance of the scope, add the wanted tables to the scope, and then apply the provisioning functionality.

The scope information is maintained beyond the running of the application. In other words, if you create a scope the first time the application runs, that scope still exists the next time the application runs. This has two side effects. First, it means that you should uniquely name your scopes so that there is no inadvertent collision with other applications. Second, you can't add a new table to a scope and have that table be provisioned properly (at least not without performing additional configuration).

For the second step, do the same thing with the client provisioning:

VB

```
Dim clientProvision = New SqlSyncScopeProvisioning(clientConn)
If Not clientProvision.ScopeExists(scopeName) Then
    Dim serverScopeDesc = New DbSyncScopeDescription(scopeName)
    Dim serverTableDesc =
        SqlSyncDescriptionBuilder.GetDescriptionForTable("Customer", _
        clientConn)
    clientScopeDesc.Tables.Add(clientTableDesc)
    clientProvision.PopulateFromScopeDescription(slientScopeDesc)
    clientProvision.Apply()
End If
```

C#

```
var clientProvision = new SqlSyncScopeProvisioning(clientConn);
if (!clientProvision.ScopeExists(scopeName))
{
    var clientScopeDesc = new DbSyncScopeDescription(scopeName);
    var clientTableDesc =
        SqlSyncDescriptionBuilder.GetDescriptionForTable("Customer",
        clientConn);
    clientScopeDesc.Tables.Add(clientTableDesc);
    clientProvision.PopulateFromScopeDescription(clientScopeDesc);
    clientProvision.Apply();
}
```

The third step is to perform the synchronization. The Sync Framework 2.1 includes a SyncOrchestrator (as opposed to the SyncAgent in the previous versions) to manage the synchronization process. Add the following code below the two provisioning blocks:

VB

```
Dim syncOrchestrator = New SyncOrchestrator()
Dim localProvider = New SqlSyncProvider(scopeName, clientConn)
Dim remoteProvider = New SqlSyncProvider(scopeName, serverConn)
syncOrchestrator.LocalProvider = localProvider
syncOrchestrator.RemoteProvider = remoteProvider
syncOrchestrator.Direction = SyncDirectionOrder.Download

Dim syncStats = syncOrchestrator.Synchronize()
```

C#

```csharp
var syncOrchestrator = new SyncOrchestrator();
var localProvider = new SqlSyncProvider(scopeName, clientConn);
var remoteProvider = new SqlSyncProvider(scopeName, serverConn);
syncOrchestrator.LocalProvider = localProvider;
syncOrchestrator.RemoteProvider = remoteProvider;
syncOrchestrator.Direction = SyncDirectionOrder.Download;

var syncStats = syncOrchestrator.Synchronize();
```

This is the data and schema synchronization step. There is a provider object created for each end of the synchronization. One of the additions with Sync Framework 2.1 is support for SQL Azure as being one of the endpoints.

The final addition is a small piece of code added to the Load method for the LocalForm. If you recall, you dragged the Customer node from the CRMDataSet data source, which is linked to the CRM database. You need to change that to link to the local CRM storage. So in the Load method, prior to the fill, the connection string for the table adapter is changed to point to the local CRM. When finished, the Load method should look like the following:

VB

```vb
Private Sub LocalForm_Load(ByVal sender As System.Object, _
                           ByVal e As System.Windows.RoutedEventArgs) _
                           Handles LocalForm.Load
    Me.customerTableAdapter.Connection.ConnectionString = _
        QuickCRM.Properties.Settings.Default.LocalCRMConnectionString
    Me.customerTableAdapter.Fill(this.cRMDataSet.Customer)
End Sub
```

C#

```csharp
private void LocalForm_Load(object sender, RoutedEventArgs e)
{
    this.customerTableAdapter.Connection.ConnectionString =
        QuickCRM.Properties.Settings.Default.LocalCRMConnectionString;
    this.customerTableAdapter.Fill(this.cRMDataSet.Customer);
}
```

At this point, you can run the application. After a brief pause (while the provisioning is taking place), the MainWindow displays. Click the Server Data button to display the Server form. Modify a number of records in the database. Close the form and click the Local Data button. The modified data is visible.

Close the Local form and click the Server Data button again. In the Server form, change the existing ones. When you finish, close the form and reopen the Local form. Your changes are not there; however, when you click the button that you added to the toolbar (which basically performs a refresh), the new and changed data becomes visible.

> **NOTE** *If you receive a SyncException indicating that a COM class was not registered when the Synchronize method is executed, there can be a couple of causes. First, if you're running on a 64-bit platform, make sure that the 64-bit version of the Sync Framework has been installed. Also, if you attempt to create an application for a 32-bit machine while running on a 64-bit platform, make sure that the 32-bit version of the Sync Framework has been installed.*

SYNCHRONIZATION SERVICES OVER N-TIERS

So far, the entire synchronization process is conducted within the client application with a direct connection to the server. One of the objectives of an occasionally connected application is to synchronize data over any connection, regardless of whether it is a corporate intranet or the public Internet. Unfortunately, with the current application you need to expose your SQL Server so that the application can connect to it. This is clearly a security vulnerability, which you can solve by taking a more distributed approach. Sync Services has been designed with this in mind, enabling the server components to be isolated into a service that can be called during synchronization.

Sync Services supports separating the synchronization process so that the communication to either of the endpoints can be implemented in a custom provider. From the perspective of an N-Tier application, the actual implementation of the provider could be done through a WCF service (for example) instead of a direct database connection. To do this, you need to create a WCF service that implements the four methods that makes up Sync Service, as shown in the following `IServiceCRMCacheSyncContract` interface:

VB

```vb
<ServiceContractAttribute()> _
Public Interface IServiceCRMCacheSyncContract
    <OperationContract()> _
    Function ApplyChanges(ByVal groupMetadata As SyncKnowledge, _
                         ByVal dataSet As DataSet, _
                         ByVal syncSession As SyncSession) As SyncContext
    <OperationContract()> _
    Function GetChanges(ByVal groupMetadata As SyncKnowledge, _
                         ByVal syncSession As SyncSession) As SyncContext
    <OperationContract()> _
    Function GetSchema(ByVal tableNames As Collection(Of String), _
                         ByVal syncSession As SyncSession) As SyncSchema
    <OperationContract()> _
    Function GetServerInfo(ByVal syncSession As SyncSession) As SyncServerInfo
End Interface
```

Now, create a custom provider class derived from the `SyncProvider` base class. In your custom class, you override some of the methods from the base class and call the corresponding methods through the WCF service proxy.

After the class has been constructed, you can set the Remote Provider on the Sync Orchestrator to be a new instance of the custom `SyncProvider` class. Now, when you call `Synchronize`, Sync Services uses the Remote Provider to call the methods on the WCF Service. The WCF Service in turn communicates with the server database carrying out the synchronization logic.

SUMMARY

In this chapter you have seen how to use the Microsoft Sync Framework to build an occasionally connected application. Although you have other considerations when building such an application, such as how to detect network connectivity, you have seen how to perform synchronization of both the data and the schema, and how to separate the client and server components into different application tiers. With this knowledge, you can begin to work with this technology to build richer applications that can continue to work regardless of where they are used.

25

SharePoint

SharePoint, one of Microsoft's strongest product lines, is a collection of related products and technologies that broadly service the areas of document and content management, web-based collaboration, and search. SharePoint is also a flexible application hosting platform, which enables you to develop and deploy everything from individual Web Parts to full-blown web applications. This chapter discusses some of the great features that you can expect.

From a development perspective, SharePoint supports two different application models. The legacy model involves directly working with the basic building blocks of SharePoint, which makes it possible to create and manipulate lists and items programmatically. But there is a second model, the App Model, that increases the choices available to developers. You can access the same building blocks of SharePoint (albeit through a different interface), but your application can be hosted outside of SharePoint.

Before you get into what's available in Visual Studio 2017 to support SharePoint development, the chapter spends a little time looking at the options. Then the choices you have to make within Visual Studio will be placed into the appropriate context.

SHAREPOINT EXECUTION MODELS

When it comes to creating a SharePoint application, there is one fundamental question that needs to be addressed: Where will my code run? There are three possible answers, and the requirements of your application determine the correct choice and the version of SharePoint that you wish to target.

Farm Solution

Also known as a managed solution, a farm solution is deployed on the server side of your SharePoint environment. In other words, the compiled assemblies and other resources are installed onto the SharePoint server. When the application runs, it executes in the SharePoint worker process itself (w3wp.exe). This gives your application access to the complete SharePoint application programming interface (API).

The deployment itself can take one of two forms. With the full-trust execution model, the assembly is installed into the global assembly cache (GAC) on the SharePoint server. For a partial-trust execution model, the assembly is placed into the `bin` folder within the SharePoint server's IIS file structure. In both cases, installation is performed on the server itself.

A number of administrators are uneasy about the fact that the assembly is deployed on the server and your application runs within SharePoint. As a result of the tight integration with SharePoint, it is possible for a poorly developed application to seriously (and negatively) affect the entire SharePoint farm. As a result, some companies ban farm solutions.

Sandbox Solution

The sandbox solution was introduced as an answer to the concerns that administrators had with the farm solution. Its biggest benefit is that, rather than deploying into the GAC or the `bin` folder on the server, it is deployed into a specialized library inside SharePoint. As a starting point, this means that no executable code needs to be deployed onto the SharePoint server. This also means that you no longer need to have administrator rights to SharePoint in order to deploy an application. The solution is deployed into a site collection, and therefore administrative rights on the site collection are sufficient.

However, this mode of application development was deprecated as of SharePoint 2016. The reason is that the introduction of the third mode, the App Model, provided the benefits of the Sandbox Solution (no deployment into the GAC, the application doesn't have to be executed on the SharePoint Server itself) while avoiding the limitations (only a subset of SharePoint functionality is available). So while Visual Studio does include sandbox solution templates for SharePoint 2013, the recommendation is to utilize the third mode, the App Model, in place of the sandbox solution.

App Model

SharePoint 2016 (and SharePoint 2013, for that matter) includes the App Model. As an execution model, it is significantly different from the models supported in earlier versions of SharePoint. The biggest change is that none of the code in the application is deployed onto the SharePoint server. Instead, you create a separate Web application, hosted on its own server. That application is then incorporated into the SharePoint server pages so that it appears to be part of the SharePoint site.

At the heart of the App Model are a couple of object models that are used by SharePoint Apps to communicate with SharePoint. There is a JavaScript version (known as the Client Side Object Model or CSOM) and a server-side version (that would run on the server that hosts your web application, not on the SparePoint server). Both of these models use a REST-based API that is exposed by SharePoint to access any SharePoint data or functionality.

But if the application doesn't run inside of the SharePoint server, where does it run? The choice belongs to the developer, and there are two hosting scenarios from which you can select:

➤ **SharePoint-Hosted:** The application is hosted in its own site collection on the SharePoint server. Although it might seem that this violates the idea that code is not installed on the server, this type of hosting comes with a limit on what the app can do. Any business logic must run in the context of the browser client. As a rule, this means that the business logic is written in JavaScript. The application can create and use SharePoint lists and libraries, but access to those elements must be initiated from the client.

➤ **Provider-Hosted:** The application is hosted on a separate web server — separate from the SharePoint server, that is. As a matter of fact, a provider-hosted app can be run on any web server technology that is available. There is no requirement that the application be written in ASP.NET or even in .NET. A PHP application works just as well. The reason is that the business logic can be implemented either in JavaScript or in the server-side code of the application. Access to SharePoint data is achieved through CSOM code in JavaScript or by using the REST-based API.

The rest of this chapter runs through the SharePoint development tools in Visual Studio 2017 and demonstrates how to build and deploy SharePoint solutions for the different execution models.

PREPARING THE DEVELOPMENT ENVIRONMENT

If you plan to develop for SharePoint 2016, you need access to SharePoint running either on a Windows server or in the cloud (that is, SharePoint Online). If you are developing for SharePoint 2013, you have the option of using SharePoint Foundation, a free, reasonably functionally complete version of SharePoint that runs on a non-Windows Server. This option is not available with SharePoint 2016.

> ## SHAREPOINT SERVER VERSUS SHAREPOINT FOUNDATION
>
> SharePoint 2013 comes in two editions: SharePoint Server and SharePoint Foundation. SharePoint Foundation is the free version of SharePoint targeted at smaller organizations or deployments. It includes support for Web Parts and web-based applications, document management, and web collaboration functionality such as blogs, wikis, calendars, and discussions.
>
> SharePoint Server, on the other hand, is aimed at large enterprises and advanced deployment scenarios. It has a cost for the server product as well as requiring a client access license (CAL) for each user. SharePoint Server includes all the features of SharePoint Foundation as well as providing multiple SharePoint sites, enhanced navigation, indexed search, access to back-end data, personalization, and Single Sign-On.

As of SharePoint 2016, there is no longer a Foundation version of SharePoint available. Instead, Microsoft recommends one of two different approaches to setting up a development environment:

➤ For farm solutions, you need to be working on the same platform as a working SharePoint server. This means you need a Windows Server environment. This can be a virtual machine created in Windows Azure or running on Hyper-V on your local machine. But you need to have the appropriate version of SharePoint Server installed and working, along with Visual Studio.

➤ For App Model solutions, you need to have access to a running instance of SharePoint. This can be a server running somewhere within your network or a SharePoint Online site.

Since many developers have access to a SharePoint Online site through an MSDN Subscription or an Office 365 Developer license, the rest of this chapter will focus on SharePoint development using the App Model.

There are a number of different ways to create a SharePoint Online site suitable for development. In general, you can do one of the following:

➤ Sign up for a free, one-year Office 365 Developer license through the Office 365 Developer Program (`http://dev.office.com/devprogram`).

➤ Get a 30-day free trial (`https://portal.microsoftonline.com/Signup/MainSignUp .aspx?OfferId=6881A1CB-F4EB-4db3-9F18-388898DAF510&DL=DEVELOPERPACK`).

➤ Buy an Office 365 subscription (`https://portal.microsoftonline.com/Signup/ MainSignUp.aspx?OfferId=C69E7747-2566-4897-8CBA-B998ED3BAB88&DL= DEVELOPERPACK`).

Once you have your subscription, you need to assign the SharePoint Online license to yourself and create a site. You will be adding a link to your application under development to this site, so it's a good idea to make this site exclusive for your development efforts. It is considered a best practice to only install applications from the SharePoint Store onto production SharePoint Online instances.

Once you have the SharePoint site created, there is one additional step that needs to be performed. The previously noted best practice is actually the default setting for SharePoint Online. There is no mechanism in the Administrative interface that allows you to set up *sideloading*. Sideloading is the process by which external applications can be added to a SharePoint Online site. So in order to test your application from within SharePoint Online, you need to run the following PowerShell script:

```
$programFiles = [environment]::getfolderpath("programfiles")
add-type -Path $programFiles'\SharePoint Online Management
Shell\Microsoft.Online.SharePoint.PowerShell\Microsoft.SharePoint.Client.dll'
Write-Host 'To enable SharePoint app sideLoading, enter Site Url, username and
password'

$siteurl = Read-Host 'Site Url'
$username = Read-Host "User Name"
$password = Read-Host -AsSecureString 'Password'

if ($siteurl -eq '')
{
    $siteurl = 'https://mysite.sharepoint.com/sites/SiteName'
    $username = 'myuserid@mysite.onmicrosoft.com'
    $password = ConvertTo-SecureString -String 'MyPassword1'
        -AsPlainText -Force
}
$outfilepath = $siteurl -replace ':', '_' -replace '/', '_'

try
{
    [Microsoft.SharePoint.Client.ClientContext]$cc = New-Object
Microsoft.SharePoint.Client.ClientContext($siteurl)
    [Microsoft.SharePoint.Client.SharePointOnlineCredentials]$spocreds = New-Object
Microsoft.SharePoint.Client.SharePointOnlineCredentials($username, $password)

    $cc.Credentials = $spocreds
    Write-Host -ForegroundColor Yellow 'SideLoading feature is not enabled on the
site:' $siteurl
    $site = $cc.Site;

    $sideLoadingGuid = new-object System.Guid "AE3A1339-61F5-4f8f-81A7-ABD2DA956A7D"
    $site.Features.Add($sideLoadingGuid, $true,
[Microsoft.SharePoint.Client.FeatureDefinitionScope]::None);
    $cc.ExecuteQuery();
    Write-Host -ForegroundColor Green 'SideLoading feature enabled on site' $siteurl

    #Activate the Developer Site feature
}
catch
{
    Write-Host -ForegroundColor Red 'Error encountered when trying to enable
SideLoading feature' $siteurl, ':' $Error[0].ToString();
}
```

Credit belongs to Microsoft MVP Colin Phillips for posting this script on his blog.

Note that one of the requirements is for the Microsoft.SharePoint.Client DLL. If you already have it on your device, you can change the script (specifically at line 2) to reference your path. Otherwise, you can install the SharePoint Online Management Shell (`http://www.microsoft.com/en-ca/download/details.aspx?id=35588`), which will place the DLL in the location indicated by the script. Once the script has run successfully, then you are ready to use your SharePoint Online site as a development target.

CREATING A SHAREPOINT PROJECT

To create a SharePoint solution in Visual Studio 2017, select File ⇨ New ⇨ Project. Filter the project types by selecting Visual C# or Visual Basic followed by Office/SharePoint. Now you need to make a choice regarding the execution model for your application. Templates for both farm solutions and SharePoint Add-Ins are available (see Figure 25-1).

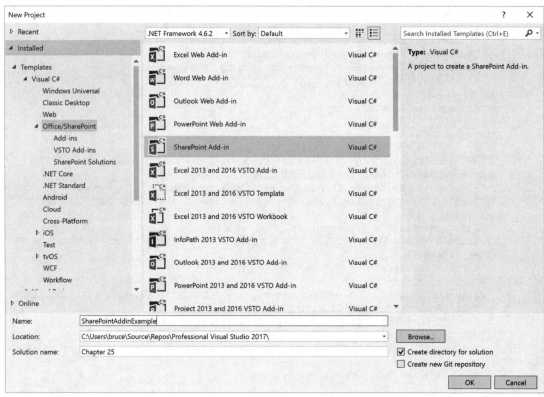

FIGURE 25-1

From the farm solutions perspective, a number of SharePoint project templates for SharePoint 2010, 2013, and 2016 ship with Visual Studio 2017. While the decision of the execution model is important, beyond that, it doesn't really matter which template you select. Most of the SharePoint components that can be created with these project templates can also be created as individual items in an existing SharePoint solution.

For the App Model, there is really only a single project template to use, that being SharePoint Add-In. For this reason, select it, provide a project and solution name, and click OK to start the creation process.

The first step in the creation process is to specify the target SharePoint site and where you'd like to host your application. Figure 25-2 shows the dialog in question.

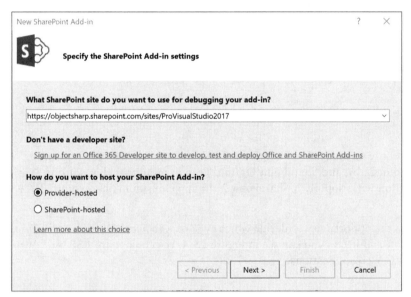

FIGURE 25-2

The first text box is the URL for the SharePoint site that is used for debugging your add-in. There is also a link that takes you to a URL that describes different options that help you deploy and test a SharePoint add-in (or an Office add-in for that matter). Below that link you get to choose the hosting model that you will use for your add-in. The two choices, Provider-hosted and SharePoint-hosted, are described in the "App Model" section earlier in this chapter.

Once you provide that information and click the Next button, you can choose the SharePoint version that you wish to target (Figure 25-3).

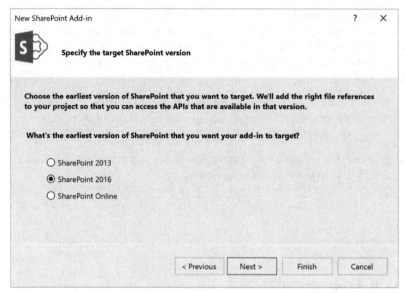

FIGURE 25-3

Since the App Model was only introduced in SharePoint 2013, the only choices you have are SharePoint 2013, SharePoint 2016, and SharePoint Online. Keep in mind that this is just the earliest version that your application will support. A SharePoint 2013 app can run in SharePoint 2016 with no issues.

The next dialog gives you the opportunity to decide which type of web application you will use to implement your SharePoint add-in. As you can see in Figure 25-4, the choices are ASP.NET Web Forms and ASP.NET MVC Web applications.

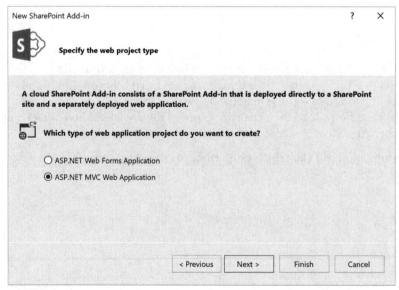

FIGURE 25-4

A SharePoint Add-In solution contains two projects. The larger of the two is a web application that is your implementation of the add-in. It can be any web application, although the project template has just the two choices. It is also possible to remove the web project that is part of the initial solution and replace it with a different one after the solution is created.

The second project is used to connect your web application with SharePoint. It contains a configuration file, an image that will be used in the SharePoint site to represent your application, and a manifest file. More details about the contents of the manifest file are found later in this section.

The next step in the solution creation process involves configuring authentication (see Figure 25-5).

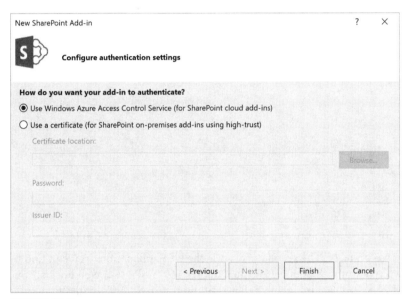

FIGURE 25-5

Here your choice depends on the target for your deployment. For the first option, you will be using Azure Access Control Service. This means that you will be expected to log into your SharePoint site and your application with the same credentials. Once you have logged into your SharePoint site, your credentials will automatically be available to your application for further authorization functionality (such as assigning roles).

The second choice is to use a certificate. This option is used if your SharePoint server is on-premises. You will be required to provide the location of the certification and any password necessary to install it.

Once you finish configuring authentication, the SharePoint Add-in solution is created. Figure 25-6 illustrates what the solution looks like with an ASP.NET MVC application as the implementation project.

FIGURE 25-6

As you can see, there are two projects. The second project is the web application. You can find more details about the two types of web applications in Chapter 16, "ASP.NET Web Forms," and Chapter 17, "ASP.NET MVC." It is the first project that is of interest to SharePoint developers.

The first project is the SharePoint Add-in project. It is used to connect the web application to a SharePoint site by providing information that is used when the Add-in is added to SharePoint. There are three files in the project. The app.config file is a standard configuration file. If you look at the details, you'll find that it contains minimal information about WebGrease and Newtonsoft.Json dependencies.

There is also an AppIcon.png file. This is an image file that is associated with your application in the SharePoint site once it has been deployed.

The final file, AppManifest.xml, contains most of the information that connects your web application to SharePoint. It also has a designer to help you organize the information. If you double-click on the file, you'll see a designer similar to the one that appears in Figure 25-7.

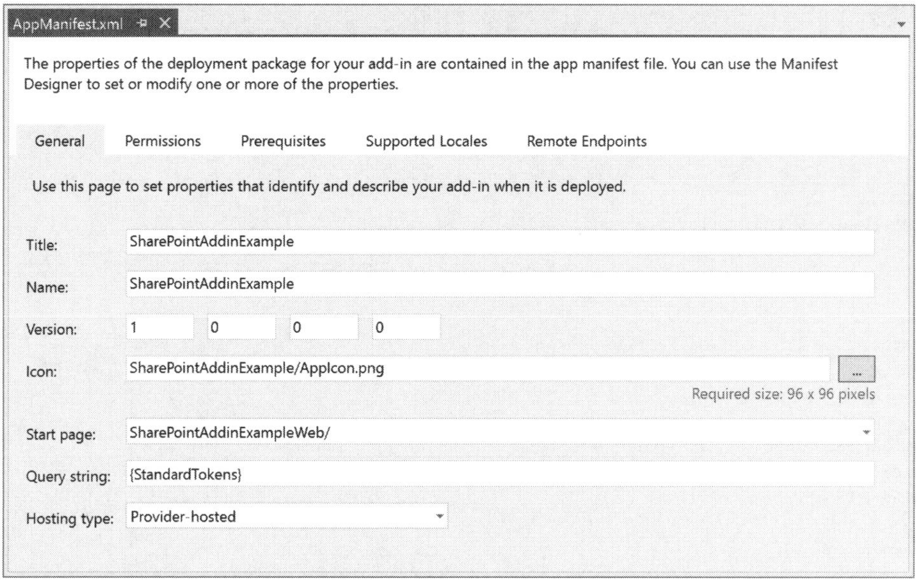

FIGURE 25-7

This first tab contains general information about the SharePoint Add-in. This includes the title, name, and version number. The difference between the name and title relates to where the information appears. The title appears at the top of the browser window for the application. The name appears within SharePoint to indicate the application to the user.

The icon property defines the image that is displayed, along with the name, in SharePoint. The Start page is the URL to the first page displayed to the user when the application is launched. There is a query string property allowing you to specify additional parameters to the page. At a minimum, you should include the {StandardTokens} value that is visible in Figure 25-7. This ensures that sufficient information is provided for your application to communicate with the SharePoint server. Finally, you can specify the hosting type. This is a dropdown value that allows you to change between Provider-hosted and SharePoint-hosted.

The second tab, labelled Permissions and shown in Figure 25-8, is used to identify the permissions that are required by your application with respect to the SharePoint site.

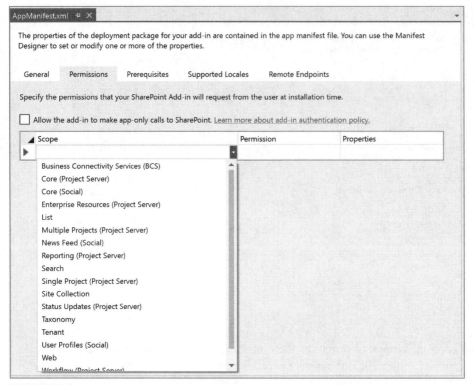

FIGURE 25-8

A SharePoint add-in has the ability to interact with SharePoint's functionality and elements. In this dialog, you can specify the different permissions that are required by your application. Each permission has three components. First is the scope. This is one of the different SharePoint entities seen in Figure 25-8. Once you have selected the scope, you can add the other two pieces. The Permission is chosen from a list, and the choices that appear in the list are based on the selected scope. For instance, if you choose List as the scope, then you can select from Read, Write, Manage, and FullControl. If you select Workflow, then the only permission is Elevate. Finally, there is the properties component. This is a collection of name/value pairs, and again, the set of values is dependent on the context of the scope. For instance, the List scope would expect to have the name of the list as one of the properties.

You can define more than one permission for your application. When your application is loaded into SharePoint, the user who is installing it will be asked to give these permissions to the application. If they choose to not give permissions to your app, then the app won't be installed. That is, the permission list is an all or nothing condition for installation.

The Prerequisites tab (Figure 25-9) is used to define the set of services that your application requires in the SharePoint environment in order to function.

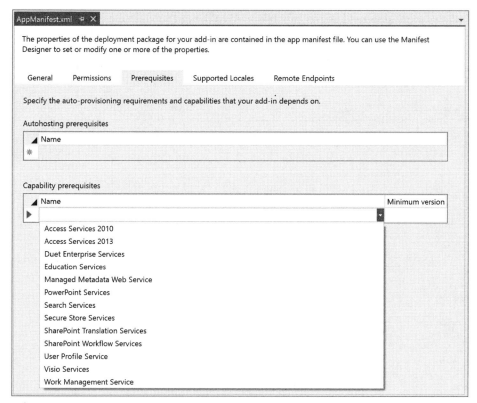

FIGURE 25-9

There are two sets of prerequisites. The Autohosting prerequisites are needed if you have selected SharePoint-hosted as the deployment option. You can ensure that your application has access to a database and a web site through these prerequisites. If you chose Provider-hosted, then you are responsible for setting any requirements on your own.

> **NOTE** *To avoid confusion, there is a difference between the SharePoint-hosted deployment option and an option that was available in SharePoint 2013 called* Autohosted. *An Autohosted deployment would automatically create an Azure Web site, deploy your web application into it, and link it up with your SharePoint environment. For a number of reasons, this deployment model never made it out of preview. However, this is* not *the same as the Autohosting prerequisites for the SharePoint-hosted deployment that is discussed in this section.*

The second set of prerequisites is used to define the services that must be available on the SharePoint server. The list of possible choices is visible in Figure 25-9. You can identify more than one capability, and for each, you can provide the minimum version that is needed.

Figure 25-10 shows the Supported Locales tab. It is used to define the localizations that are supported and to map a particular resource file to each one. On the left, you choose the locale from the dropdown. Then you can create the resource file that is associated with that locale on the right. When you select a locale, it will automatically create the resource file named using the standard locale code by default, but you can change it if you'd like.

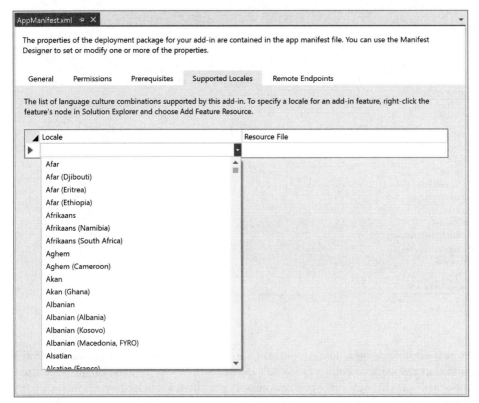

FIGURE 25-10

The last tab, Remote Endpoints (Figure 25-11), is used to define any remote endpoints that need to be accessed by your application. By default, when your application runs within the context of SharePoint, it can only communicate with the server. In other words, you can't make an AJAX call to a completely different URL. This tab lets you define the endpoints that your application will be allowed to communicate with. Specify the URL in the top text box and click Add. This places the URL into the second box and, when deployed, your app will be able to make requests to it.

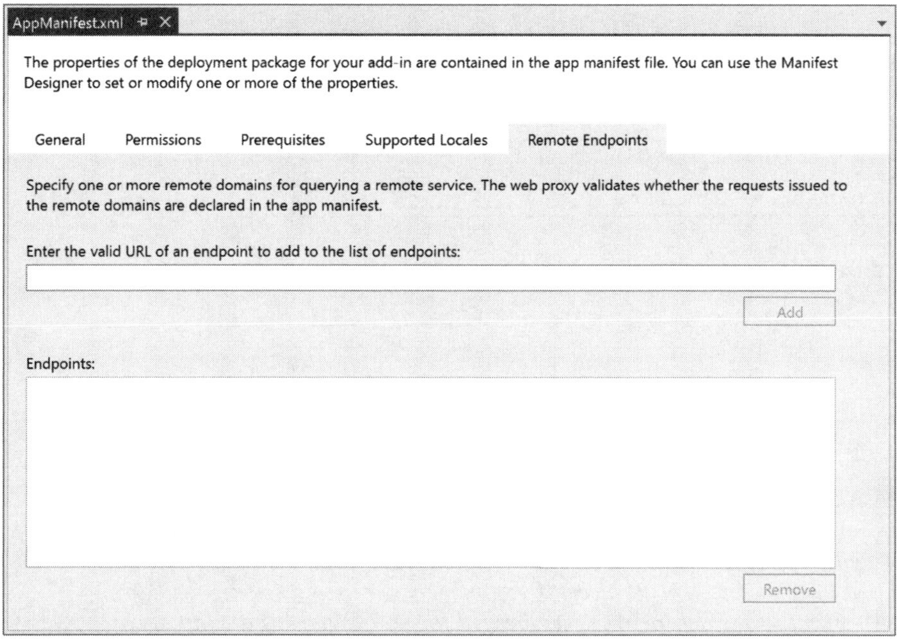

FIGURE 25-11

RUNNING YOUR APPLICATION

When it comes to being able to run and debug your SharePoint Add-in, it's important to be aware that, ultimately, the Add-in is just a Web application. As such, you are able to execute, test, and debug it as you would any other Web application. The only thing to remember is that in order to run within the context of SharePoint, you actually need to run both the Web application and the SharePoint application. In the Solution Explorer, right-click on the solution and choose Set StartUp Projects. In the dialog that appears, you should see that both of the projects in your solution have been set to start when you run the application. Setting the Action for the Web application to `Start` is necessary to debug your application. Setting the Action for the SharePoint application (the one with the `AppManfect.xml` file) to `Start` is necessary to load your application in to SharePoint.

When you run your application, you will be presented with a number of different warning dialogs. First, you will be asked to install a self-signed Localhost certificate (see Figure 25-12). This certificate is required to run your web site in HTTPS, something that SharePoint demands.

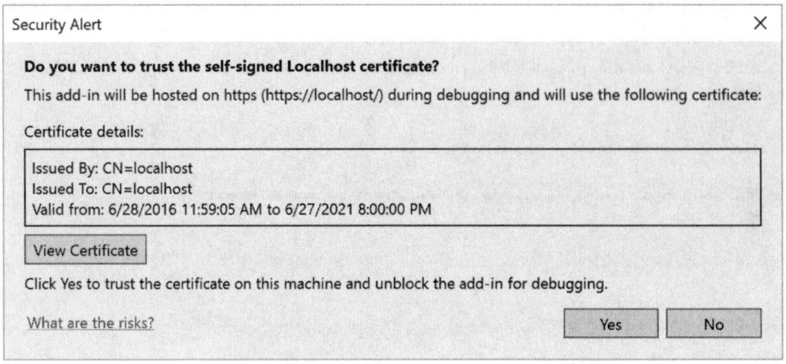

Security Alert   ✕

Do you want to trust the self-signed Localhost certificate?

This add-in will be hosted on https (https://localhost/) during debugging and will use the following certificate:

Certificate details:

Issued By: CN=localhost
Issued To: CN=localhost
Valid from: 6/28/2016 11:59:05 AM to 6/27/2021 8:00:00 PM

[View Certificate]

Click Yes to trust the certificate on this machine and unblock the add-in for debugging.

What are the risks?   [Yes]   [No]

FIGURE 25-12

> **NOTE** *You might notice that the certificate shown in Figure 25-12 has a valid date from 2016. You may or may not see something similar on your machine. If you have used a self-signed certificate associated with localhost in the past, then it will just be reused for this project. If you have never used a self-signed certificate on your machine before, one gets created for you as part of the initial running of the application.*

Then you get a warning confirming that what you just selected is really what you want to do. An example is found in Figure 25-13.

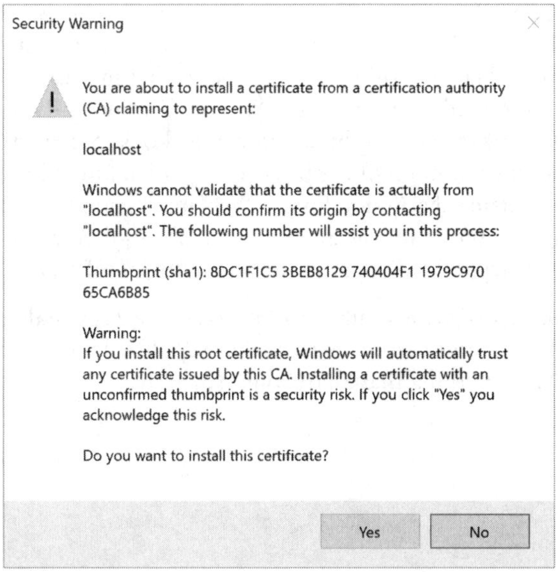

Security Warning   ✕

⚠ You are about to install a certificate from a certification authority
    (CA) claiming to represent:

    localhost

    Windows cannot validate that the certificate is actually from
    "localhost". You should confirm its origin by contacting
    "localhost". The following number will assist you in this process:

    Thumbprint (sha1): 8DC1F1C5 3BEB8129 740404F1 1979C970
    65CA6B85

    Warning:
    If you install this root certificate, Windows will automatically trust
    any certificate issued by this CA. Installing a certificate with an
    unconfirmed thumbprint is a security risk. If you click "Yes" you
    acknowledge this risk.

    Do you want to install this certificate?

                                              [Yes]   [No]

FIGURE 25-13

Next up is your credentials for the SharePoint site. Once they have been successfully entered, you will be taken to the SharePoint site and be prompted to allow your application to have access to SharePoint (Figure 25-14).

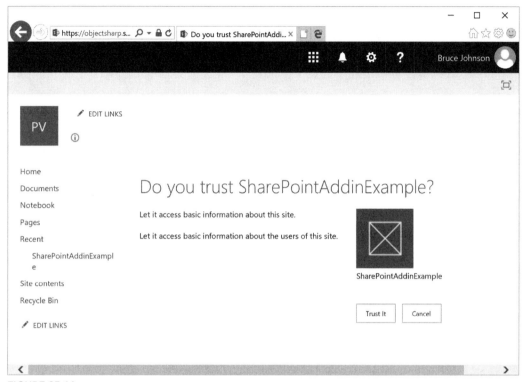

FIGURE 25-14

This is the point where you are installing your application into SharePoint. It has already confirmed that the SharePoint site has all of the required capabilities. This dialog will also include a list of the permissions that your application demands. If you click on Trust It, then the application is installed and ready to go.

SUMMARY

In this chapter you learned how to build solutions for Microsoft SharePoint 2016 and SharePoint Online. The development tools in Visual Studio 2017 enable you to easily develop SharePoint Add-ins. Through the web application that is the implementation of the add-in, you have access to the components and functionality that SharePoint provides.

This chapter just scratched the surface of what is possible with SharePoint development. If you are interested in diving deeper into this topic, visit the SharePoint Developer Center at `https://msdn` `.microsoft.com/en-us/library/office/jj162979.aspx`.

PART VIII
Data

26

Visual Database Tools

WHAT'S IN THIS CHAPTER?

- ➤ Understanding the data-oriented tool windows within Visual Studio 2017

- ➤ Creating and designing databases

- ➤ Managing database changes using ReadyRoll

- ➤ Searching through your SQL databases

WROX.COM CODE DOWNLOADS FOR THIS CHAPTER

The wrox.com code downloads for this chapter can be found at www.wrox.com by searching for this book's ISBN number (978-1-119-40458-3). The code and any related support files are located in their own folder for this chapter.

Database connectivity is essential in almost every application you create, regardless of whether it's a Windows-based program or a website or service. When Visual Studio .NET was first introduced, it provided developers with a great set of options to navigate to the database files on their filesystems and local servers, with the Server Explorer, data controls, and data-bound components. The underlying .NET Framework included ADO.NET, a retooled database engine more suited to the way applications are built today.

Visual Studio includes tools and functionality to give you more direct access to the data in your application. One way it does this is by providing tools to assist with designing tables and managing your SQL Server objects. This chapter looks at how you can create, manage, and consume data using the various tool windows provided in Visual Studio 2017, which can be collectively referred to as the Visual Database Tools.

DATABASE WINDOWS IN VISUAL STUDIO 2017

A number of windows specifically deal with databases and their components. From the Data Sources window that shows project-related data files and the Data Connections node in the Server Explorer, to the Database Diagram Editor and the visual designer for database schemas, you can find most of what you need directly within the IDE. It's unlikely that you need to venture outside of Visual Studio to work with your data.

Figure 26-1 shows Visual Studio 2017 in the process of a database-editing session. Notice how the windows, toolbars, and menus all update to match the particular context of editing a database table. In the main area is the list of columns belonging to the table. Below the column list is the SQL statement that can be used to create the table. The normal Properties tool window contains the properties for the current table. The next few pages take a look at each of these windows and describe their purposes so that you can use them effectively.

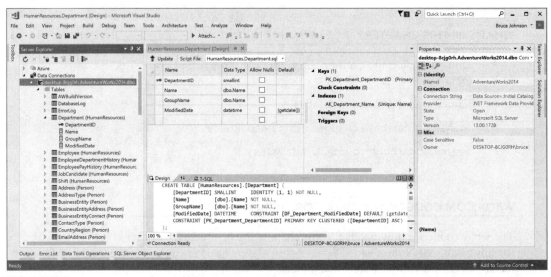

FIGURE 26-1

Server Explorer

You can use the Server Explorer to navigate the components that make up your system (or indeed the components of any server to which you can connect). One useful component of this tool window is the Data Connections node. Through this node, Visual Studio 2017 provides a significant subset of the functionality available through other products, such as SQL Server Management Studio, for creating and modifying databases.

Figure 26-1 shows the Server Explorer window with an active database connection (AdventureWorks2014.dbo). The database icon displays whether you are actively connected to the database and contains a number of child nodes dealing with the typical components of a modern database, such as Tables, Views, and Stored Procedures. Expanding these nodes lists the specific database components along with their details. For example, the Tables node contains a node for the `Department` table, which in turn has nodes for each of the columns, such as `DepartmentID`, `Name`, and `GroupName`. Selecting any of these nodes enables you to quickly view the properties within the Properties tool window. This is the default database view; you can switch to either Object Type or Schema view by selecting Change View, followed by the view to change to, from the right-click context menu off the database node. Each of these views simply groups the information about the database into a different hierarchy. The Schemas view groups the elements into Schemas, Assemblies and System-supplied objects.

To add a new database connection to the Server Explorer window, click the Connect to Database button at the top of the Server Explorer or right-click the Data Connections root node, and select the Add Connection command from the context menu.

If this is the first time you have added a connection, Visual Studio asks you what type of data source you are connecting to. Visual Studio 2017 comes packaged with a number of Data Source connectors, including Access, SQL Server, and Oracle, as well as a generic ODBC driver. It also includes a data source connector for a Microsoft SQL Server Database.

The Database File option borrows from the easy deployment model of its lesser cousin, Microsoft Access. With SQL Server Database File, you can create a flat file for an individual database. This means you don't need to attach it to a SQL Server instance. This flexibility makes it highly portable; you simply deliver the `.mdf` file containing the database along with your application.

After you choose the data source type to use, the Add Connection dialog appears. Figure 26-2 shows this dialog for a SQL Server Database File connection with the settings appropriate to that data source type.

FIGURE 26-2

> **NOTE** *If you have previously defined a data connection in Visual Studio and chosen the Always Use This Selection check box in the Change Data Source dialog, then you are taken directly to the Add Connection dialog. In that case, Figure 26-2 is the dialog that appears when you click the Change button.*

The Change button takes you to the Data Sources page, enabling you to select a different type of database connection for your Visual Studio session. Creating a SQL Server Database File is very straightforward. Just type or browse to the location where you want the file and specify the database name for a new database. If you want to connect to an existing database, use the Browse button to locate it on the filesystem.

Generally, the only other task you need to perform is to specify whether your SQL Server configuration uses Windows or SQL Server Authentication. As part of theinstallation of Visual Studio 2017, you have an option to install SQL Server 2016 Express, which uses Windows Authentication as its base authentication model.

> **NOTE** *The Test Connection button displays an error message if you try to connect to a new database file. This is because it doesn't exist until you click OK, so there's nothing to connect to!*

This dialog will be slightly different for different connection types. But regardless of the type, when you click OK, Visual Studio attempts to connect to the database. If successful, it adds it to the Data Connections node, including the child nodes for the main data types in the database. Alternatively, if the database doesn't exist, Visual Studio prompts you by asking if it should go ahead and create it. You can also create a new database by selecting Create New SQL Server Database from the right-click menu off the Data Connections node in the Server Explorer.

Table Editing

The easiest way to edit a table in the database is to double-click its entry in the Server Explorer. An editing window (Figure 26-3) then displays in the main workspace, consisting of three components. The left side of the top section is where you specify each field name, data type, and important information such as length of text fields, the default value for new rows, and whether the field is nullable. On the right side of the top section are additional table attributes. These include the keys, the indices, any constraints or foreign keys that are defined, and any triggers.

The lower half of the table editing workspace contains the SQL statement that, when executed, will create the table.

Right-clicking on one of the elements on the right gives you access to a set of commands that you can perform against the table (shown in Figure 26-3). Depending on which heading you right-click, the context menu allows you to add keys, indices, constraints, foreign keys, and triggers.

For any of the columns in the table, the Properties window contains additional information beyond what is shown in the workspace. The column properties area enables you to specify all the available properties for the particular Data Source type. For example, Figure 26-4 shows the Properties window for a field, DepartmentID, which has been defined with an identity clause automatically increased by 1 for each new record added to the table.

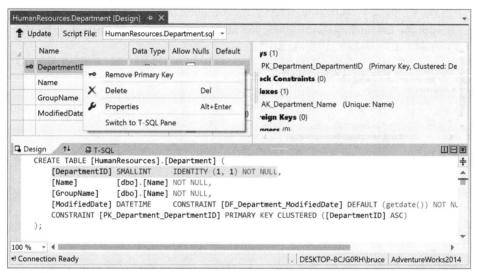

FIGURE 26-3

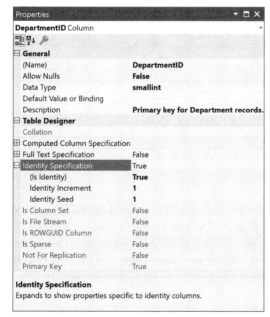

FIGURE 26-4

Relationship Editing

Most databases likely to be used by your .NET solutions are relational in nature, which means you connect tables together by defining relationships. To create a relationship, open one of the tables that will be part of the relationship, and right-click the Foreign Keys header at the right of the workspace. This creates a new entry in the list, along with a new fragment in the SQL statement (found at the bottom of the workspace). Unfortunately, this information is just a placeholder. In order to specify the details of the foreign key relationship, you need to modify the properties for the SQL fragment that was added, as shown in Figure 26-5.

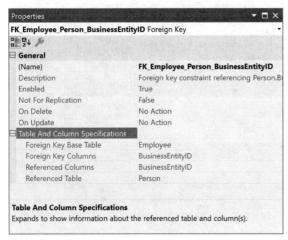

FIGURE 26-5

Views, Stored Procedures, and Functions

To create and modify views, stored procedures, and functions, Visual Studio 2017 uses a text editor, as shown in Figure 26-6. Because there is no IntelliSense to help you create your procedure and function definitions, Visual Studio doesn't allow you to save your code if it detects an error.

To help you write and debug your stored procedures and functions, there are snippets available to be placed in your SQL statements. The right-click context menu includes an Insert Snippet option that has snippets for creating a stored procedure, a view, a user-defined type, and a wide variety of other SQL artifacts. The context menu also includes options to execute the entire stored procedure or function.

A word of warning about executing the SQL for existing artifacts: When you double-click to look at the definition, the SQL that is displayed is the SQL that would be used to create the artifact. That is to say that double-clicking on a view will display the CREATE VIEW SQL statement. If you execute that statement, you will attempt to create a view that already exists, resulting in a number of error statements. If you're attempting to modify the artifact, you need to change the statement to the ALTER version.

```
dbo.uspLogError.sql ⋈ ×
↥ Update
⊟-- uspLogError logs error information in the ErrorLog table about the
 ¦ -- error that caused execution to jump to the CATCH block of a
 ¦ -- TRY...CATCH construct. This should be executed from within the scope
 ¦ -- of a CATCH block otherwise it will return without inserting error
 ¦ -- information.
⊟CREATE PROCEDURE [dbo].[uspLogError]
 ¦     @ErrorLogID [int] = 0 OUTPUT -- contains the ErrorLogID of the row inserted
 ¦ AS                                   -- by uspLogError in the ErrorLog table
⊟BEGIN
 ¦     SET NOCOUNT ON;
 ¦
⊟ ¦     -- Output parameter value of 0 indicates that error
 ¦     -- information was not logged
 ¦     SET @ErrorLogID = 0;
 ¦
⊟ ¦     BEGIN TRY
 ¦         -- Return if there is no error information to log
⊟ ¦         IF ERROR_NUMBER() IS NULL
 ¦             RETURN;
 ¦
⊟ ¦         -- Return if inside an uncommittable transaction.
 ¦         -- Data insertion/modification is not allowed when
100 %  ▾  ◂                                                                      ▸
⌁ Connection Ready          (local)  DESKTOP-8CJG0RH\bruce  AdventureWorks2014  00:00:00  0 rows
```

FIGURE 26-6

The Data Sources Window

The Data Sources window contains any active data sources known to the project, such as data sets (as opposed to the Data Connections in the Server Explorer, which are known to Visual Studio overall). To display the Data Sources tool window, use the View ➪ Other Windows ➪ Show Data Sources menu command.

The Data Sources window has two main views, depending on the active document in the workspace area of the IDE. When you edit code, the Data Sources window displays tables and fields with icons representing their types. This aids you as you write code because you can quickly reference the type without looking at the table definition.

When you edit a form in Design view, however, the Data Sources view changes to display the tables and fields with icons representing their current default control types (initially set in the Data UI Customization page of Options). Figure 26-7 shows that the text fields use TextBox controls, whereas the ModifiedDate field uses a DateTimePicker control. The icons for the tables indicate that all tables will be inserted as DataGridView components by default as shown in the drop-down list.

FIGURE 26-7

SQL Server Object Explorer

If you are a regular developer of database applications in Visual Studio, odds are good that you're familiar with the SQL Server Management Studio (SSMS). The reason for the familiarity is that there are tasks that need to be performed that don't fit into the Server Explorer functionality. To alleviate some of the need to utilize SQL Server Management Studio, Visual Studio 2017 includes the SQL Server Object Explorer. Through this information, some of the functionality not found in the Server Explorer can be found in an interface that is somewhat reminiscent of SSMS. To launch the SQL Server Object Explorer, use the View ➪ SQL Server Object Explorer option.

To start working against an existing SQL Server instance, you need to add it to the Explorer. Right-click the SQL Server node, or click the Add SQL Server button (second from the left). The dialog that appears is the standard one that appears when connecting to SSMS. You need to provide the server name and instance, along with the authentication method that you want to use. Clicking the Connect button establishes the connection.

When the connection has been made, three nodes underneath the server appear. These are the Databases, Security items, and Server Objects that are part of that instance (see Figure 26-8).

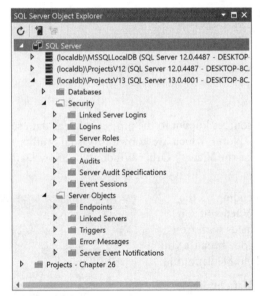

FIGURE 26-8

Under the Security and Server Objects nodes, a number of subfolders are available. These subfolders contain various server-level artifacts. These include logins, server roles, linked servers, triggers, and so on that are defined on the server. For each of the subfolders, you can add or modify the entities that are presented. For example, if you right-click the EndPoints node, the context menu provides the option to add either a TCP- or HTTP-based endpoint. When the Add option is selected, T-SQL code is generated and placed into a freshly opened designer tab. The T-SQL code, when executed, creates the artifact. Of course, you must modify the T-SQL so that when it is executed the results will be as wanted.

The Databases node also contains subfolders. The difference is that here each subfolder represents a database on the SQL Server instance. As you expand a database node, additional folders containing Tables, Views, Synonyms, Programmability items, Server Broker storage elements, and Security appear. For most of these items, the process to create or edit is commonplace. Right-clicking the subfolder and selecting the Add New option generates the SQL statement needed to create the selected item. (Naturally, you need to change a couple of values.) Or you could right-click on an existing item and select the View Properties or other similarly named menu options. This displays the T-SQL code that would alter the selected item. You can then change the appropriate values and execute the statement by clicking the Update button (see Figure 26-9).

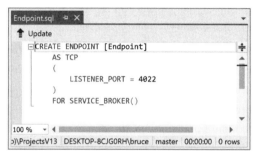

FIGURE 26-9

EDITING DATA

Visual Studio 2017 also has the capability to view and edit the data contained in your database tables. To edit the information, right-click on the table you want to view in the Server Explorer and select the Show Table Data option from the context menu. You see a tabular representation of the data in the table, as shown in Figure 26-10, enabling you to edit it to contain whatever default or test data you need to include. As you edit information, the table editor displays indicators next to fields that have changed.

You can also show the diagram, criteria, and SQL panes associated with the table data you're editing by right-clicking anywhere in the table and choosing the appropriate command from the Pane submenu. This can be useful for customizing the SQL statement used to retrieve the data, for example, to filter the table for specific values or just to retrieve the first 50 rows.

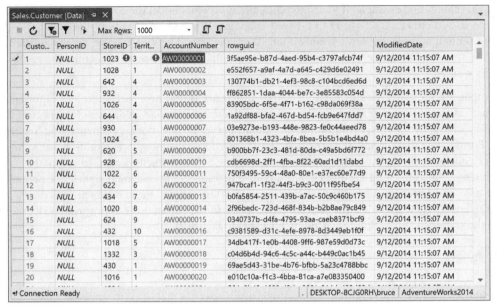

FIGURE 26-10

REDGATE DATA TOOLS

As part of an attempt to improve the integration between Visual Studio and database artifacts, Microsoft partnered with Redgate to include three different tools in Visual Studio 2017.

➤ **ReadyRoll Core:** Provides source control and deployment assistance to SQL Server artifacts.

➤ **SQL Prompt Core:** Provides code completion for SQL. Think of it as IntelliSense for SQL statements and you're pretty close.

➤ **SQL Search:** Allows you to search for SQL objects within and across databases.

Each of these is covered in more detail in the subsequent sections.

ReadyRoll Core

One of the most common tasks for developers is making changes to a database. That's a task that is fraught with challenges. Some developers make the changes directly against the database. This makes it challenging to track which changes have been made and to propagate those changes to QA or production systems. Other developers spend a great deal of effort maintaining migration scripts, for both data and schema, to handle the changes that are made to the database during development.

The purpose of ReadyRoll Core is to make the lives of both of these types of developers easier. It provides a mechanism for generating and maintaining the scripts necessary to deploy, migrate, and update databases, both at the data and the schema level.

The starting point is a new SQL Server project. Use File ⇨ New ⇨ Project to open the New Project dialog. On the left, navigate to the SQL Server node. You should see two project templates, as shown in Figure 26-11.

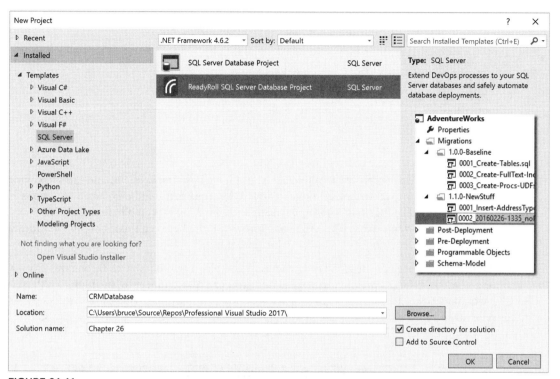

FIGURE 26-11

The first template, SQL Server Database Project, is the legacy template. There is also a ReadyRoll SQL Server Database Project available. Provide an appropriate project and solution name and click OK to create the project.

> **NOTE** *If you don't see the ReadyRoll project in the list, then use the Visual Studio Installer to install the ReadyRoll components. You can find them in the list of Individual Components in the Visual Studio Installer. See Chapter 1, "A Quick Tour," for more details.*

The project that is created can be seen in the Solution Explorer in Figure 26-12.

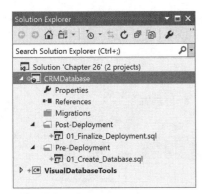

FIGURE 26-12

The project itself consists mostly of three folders: Migrations, Post-Deployment, and Pre-Deployment. Into each of these folders you will place (or generate) SQL scripts that will be executed at various points in the process. The Pre- and Post-Deployment scripts will be executed before and after the database deployment, respectively. The Migration scripts are run between those two, as they form the actual deployment.

Once the project has been created, the next step is to connect it to a database. To be fair, if you are creating a new database as part of your application, you can also connect to an empty database. But for this example, open the ReadyRoll pane by using View ➪ ReadyRoll. There are three steps that need to be taken to get started, and the pane indicates where you are. The pane shown in Figure 26-13 is what the pane looks like after you have created a project and connected to a database.

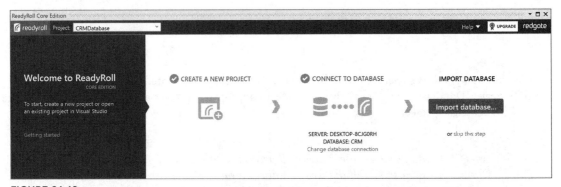

FIGURE 26-13

When you connect your project to a database, you get a dialog that allows you to create a connection. You can select a recently used connection (and that is recently used across all of the projects that you have opened, not just the database project). Or you can work with databases that have been defined in any of three different zones. Figure 26-14 shows the dialog that is used to choose databases in the different zones: local (on your machine), network (within your current network), or Azure.

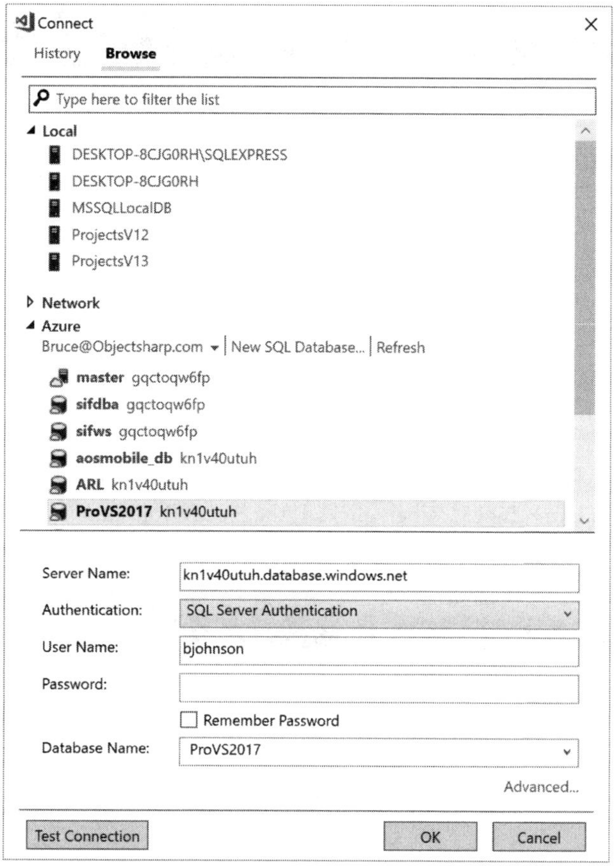

FIGURE 26-14

In this dialog, you are presented with a list of database servers. Once you select the desired server, the fields in the lower half of the form are used to define the connection. This includes the specific database, the authentication mode, and any required credentials. There is a button that allows you to test the connection to make sure your information is correct. When you are finished, clicking on OK links the selected database to the database project.

Once you have connected to an existing database, you can use the Import Database button (as seen in Figure 26-13) to create the initial scripts. After a few minutes (the actual time depends on the number of objects in the database), the ReadyRoll pane looks similar to Figure 26-15.

You can see from the messages in the body of the pane that a single table (Customer) was created. It also indicates that a migration script was placed into the project. You can double-click on the script to see what was actually created.

Across the top of the ReadyRoll pane, there are a number of controls aimed at giving you access to commonly needed functionality. On the left is a dropdown list containing the database projects that are in your current solution. Changing the project allows you to target your commands at different projects.

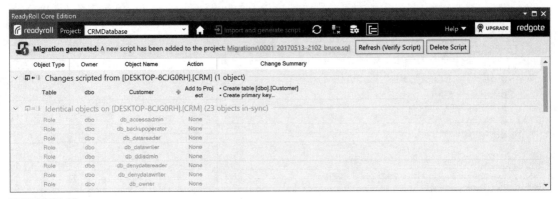

FIGURE 26-15

Depending on exactly what is displayed on the pane, you might see a Home icon to the right of the list of database projects. It can be seen in Figure 26-15. When clicked, the ReadyRoll pane looks like to Figure 26-16.

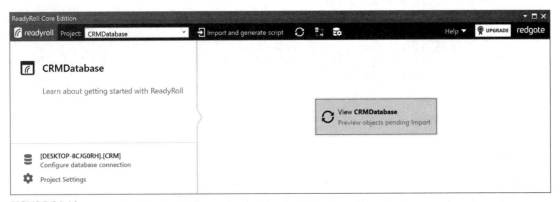

FIGURE 26-16

The next two controls will be covered in a few moments. They are used to import changes made to the database into the database project. The last two icons are used to open the target database in SQL Server Management Studio (SSMS) and to modify the connection for the target database.

Now that the connection to the database has been made, you are free to modify the database as you need to. You can use the SQL Object Explorer built into Visual Studio. You can also use SSMS. How you change the database is not important. When you are finished making the changes (for this example, an address column was added to the Customer table), come back to the ReadyRoll pane and click on the icon that refreshes the list of database object changes (the circular arrows in Figure 26-16). The result is shown in Figure 26-17.

FIGURE 26-17

You can see that the change that you made is included in the pane. When you click on the Import and generate script link, a SQL script is created and placed in the project in the Migration folder. You can repeat this process as often as you need to modify the database.

When it comes time to publish your database project, at the moment, the process is a little clunky. If you right-click on the database project, you'll notice a Publish option. However, when you click on it, you see a message box saying that the database can't be published through Visual Studio. Instead, there is a command line that can be used to publish the database, and one of the buttons on the dialog generates that command for the current project and puts it on the clipboard.

SQL Prompt Core

The goal of SQL Prompt Core is to introduce some of the productivity of IntelliSense into writing SQL commands. To start, open up a new SQL query window using Tools ⇨ SQL Server ⇨ New Query. The window opens and you are prompted for a connection against which you will be writing the query. Once you have the connection, you are ready to start writing.

Presuming that you are working against the CRM database, type SELECT * FROM. Add a space after the FROM and you will see something like Figure 26-18.

Here you can choose any one of the available objects. This is precisely the kind of help that you expect when editing code files.

Beyond this basic functionality, there are other options available. In Figure 26-19, there is a relatively normal SQL query.

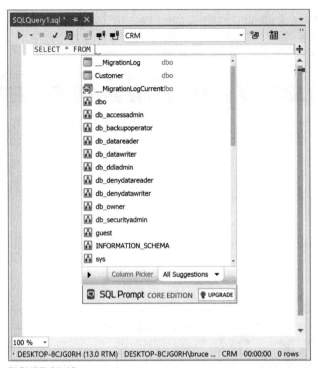

FIGURE 26-18

FIGURE 26-19

When the cursor is just to the right of the asterisk, using the Tab key will automatically replace the asterisk with the list of fields for the current table. If you don't want to choose all of the columns, use Ctrl+Space to open the list of items and click on the Column Selector tab. What you see resembles Figure 26-20.

One final feature in SQL Prompt Core is the ability to suggest (and autocomplete) JOIN statements in your query. As you start to type the ON clause, the foreign key relationships in the tables are evaluated and the possible JOINs are presented to you.

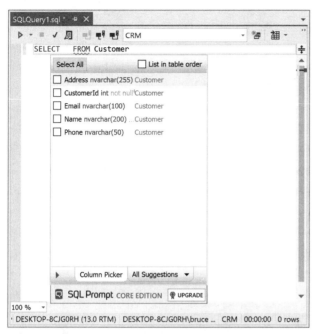

FIGURE 26-20

SQL Search

When you are making changes to your database, it is frequently useful to be able to search either within a database or even across multiple databases for particular elements. In Visual Studio 2017, this functionality is available through the Tools ⇨ SQL Search option. Figure 26-21 shows this window.

In the bar along the top of the window, you can select the databases that are to be scanned through a dropdown. Place a checkmark beside the database to include and click on OK. Then enter a value into the search box on the right and all of the selected databases are searched. Figure 26-22 illustrates a set of results.

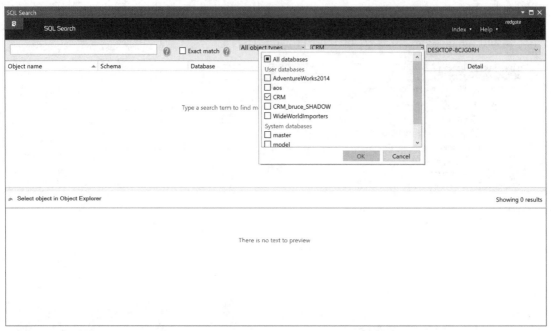

FIGURE 26-21

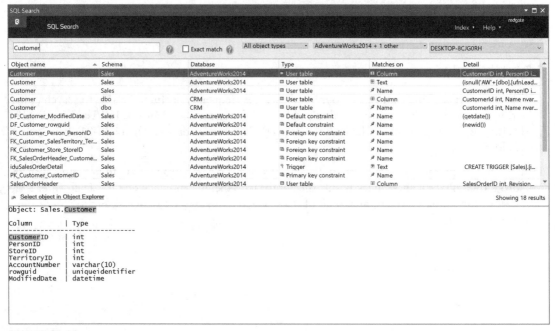

FIGURE 26-22

In some cases, there is contextual information available about the result. If that's the case (and there is a column in the results called Detail that contains the context), then selecting the item causes the context to be displayed in the lower half of the pane.

SUMMARY

With the variety of tools and windows available in Visual Studio 2017, you can easily create and maintain databases without leaving the IDE. You can manipulate data and define database schemas visually using the Properties tool window with the Schema Designer view.

More importantly for developers who are frequently manipulating databases, Visual Studio 2017 includes a number of tools aimed at helping manage and deploy databases in a real-world production environment.

27

The ADO.NET Entity Framework

WHAT'S IN THIS CHAPTER?

- ➤ Understanding the Entity Framework
- ➤ Creating an Entity Framework model
- ➤ Querying Entity Framework models

WROX.COM CODE DOWNLOADS FOR THIS CHAPTER

The wrox.com code downloads for this chapter can be found at www.wrox.com by searching for this book's ISBN number (978-1-119-40458-3). The code and any related support files are located in their own folder for this chapter.

One of the core requirements in business applications (and many other types of applications) is the ability to store and retrieve data in a database. However, that's easier said than done because the relational schema of a database does not blend well with the object hierarchies that you prefer to work with in code. To create and populate these object hierarchies required a lot of code to be written to transfer data from a data reader into a developer-friendly object model, which was then usually difficult to maintain. It was such a source of constant frustration that many developers turned to writing code generators or various other tools that automatically created the code to access a database based on its structure. However, code generators usually created a 1:1 mapping between the database structure and the object model, which was hardly ideal either, leading to a problem called "object relational impedance mismatch," where how data was stored in the database did not necessarily have a direct relationship with how developers wanted to model the data as objects. This led to the concept of Object Relational Mapping (ORM), where an ideal object model could be designed for working with data in code, which could then be mapped to the schema of a database. When the mapping is complete, an ORM framework should take over the burden of translating between the object model and the database, leaving developers to focus on actually solving the business problem (rather than focusing on the technological issues of working with data).

To many developers, ORM frameworks are the Holy Grail for working with data in a database as objects, and there's no shortage of debate over the strengths and pitfalls of the various ORM frameworks that are available. You won't delve into these arguments in this chapter, but simply look at how to use the ADO.NET Entity Framework — Microsoft's ORM framework.

This chapter takes you through the process of creating an Entity Framework model of a database, and how to use it to query and update the database. The Entity Framework is a huge topic, with entire books devoted to its use. Therefore, it would be impossible to go through all its features, so this chapter focuses on discussing some of its core features and how to start and create a basic entity model.

The Entity Framework model you create in this chapter will be used in a number of subsequent chapters where database access is required in the samples.

WHAT IS THE ENTITY FRAMEWORK?

Essentially, the Entity Framework is an ORM framework. Object Relational Mapping enables you to create a conceptual object model, map it to the database, and the ORM framework can take care of translating your queries over the object model to queries against the database, returning the data as the objects that you've defined in your model.

Here are some of the important concepts involved in the Entity Framework and some of the terms used throughout this chapter:

➤   **Entity Model:** The entity model you create using the Entity Framework consists of three parts:

   ➤   **Conceptual model:** Represents the object model, including the entities, their properties, and the associations between them

   ➤   **Store model:** Represents the database structure, including the tables/views/stored procedures, columns, foreign keys, and so on

   ➤   **Mapping:** Provides the glue between the store model and the conceptual model (that is, between the database and the object model), by mapping one to the other

   Each of these parts is maintained by the Entity Framework as XML using a domain-specific language (DSL).

➤   **Entity:** Entities are essentially just objects (with properties) to which a database model is mapped.

➤   **Entity Set:** An entity set is a collection of a given entity. You can think of it as an entity being a row in a database, and an entity set being the table.

➤ **Association:** Associations define relationships between entities in your entity model and are conceptually the same as relationships in a database. Associations are used to traverse the data in your entity model between entities.

➤ **Mapping:** Mapping is the core concept of ORM. It's essentially the translation layer from a relational schema in a database to objects in code.

GETTING STARTED

To demonstrate some of the various features in the Entity Framework, the example in this section uses the AdventureWorks2014 sample database developed by Microsoft as one of the sample databases for SQL Server.

The AdventureWorks2014 database is available for download from `https://github.com/ Microsoft/sql-server-samples/releases/tag/adventureworks2014`.

Adventure Works Cycles is a fictional bicycle sales chain, and the AdventureWorks2014 database is used to store and access its product sales data.

Follow the instructions from the CodePlex website detailing how to install the database from the downloaded script in a SQL Server instance (SQL Server Express Edition is sufficient) that is on or can be accessed by your development machine.

Now you will move on to create a project that contains an Entity Framework model of this database. Start by opening the New Project dialog and creating a new project. The sample project you create in this chapter uses the WPF project template. You can display data in a WPF DataGrid control defined in the `MainWindow.xaml` file named `dgEntityFrameworkData`.

Now that you have a project that can host and query an Entity Framework model, it's time to create that model.

CREATING AN ENTITY MODEL

You have two ways of going about creating an entity model. The usual means to do so is to create the model based on the structure of an existing database; however, with the Entity Framework it is also possible to start with a blank model and have the Entity Framework generate a database structure from it.

The sample project uses the first method to create an entity model based on the AdventureWorks2014 database's structure.

The Entity Data Model Wizard

Open the Add New Item dialog for your project, navigate to the Data category, and select ADO.NET Entity Data Model as the item template (as shown in Figure 27-1). Call it `AdventureWorks2014Model.edmx`.

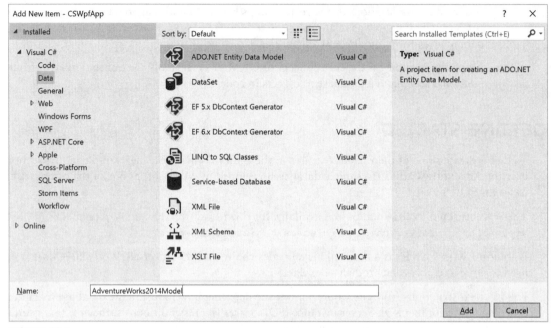

FIGURE 27-1

This starts the Entity Data Model Wizard that can help you start building an Entity Framework model.

As the first step, the dialog in Figure 27-2 enables you to select whether you want to automatically create a model from a database, start with an empty model, start with an empty model for code-first design, or create a code-first model using an existing database.

> **NOTE** *The idea behind the code-first approach to database design is to allow you to start the process by creating the classes. These classes should be focused on providing the attributes that your application requires. Then, as the classes are created, the database design is modified to match your class model (along with any necessary configuration). This approach is common when you are using a Domain Driven Design methodology.*

The empty model option is useful when you want to create your model from scratch, and either mapping it manually to a given database or letting the Entity Framework create a database based on your model.

However, you can create an entity model from the AdventureWorks2014 database, so for the purpose of this example use the EF Designer from Database option, and get the wizard to help you create the entity model from the database.

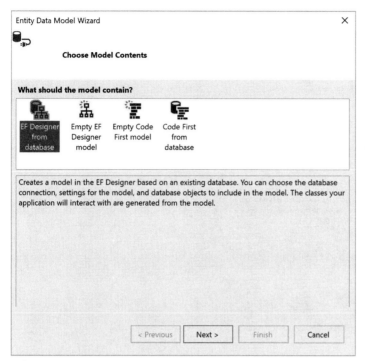

FIGURE 27-2

Moving to the next step, you now need to create a connection to the database (as shown in Figure 27-3). You can find the most recent database connection you've created in the drop-down list, but if it's not there (for example, if this is the first time you've created a connection to this database) you need to create a new connection. To do so, click the New Connection button, and go through the standard procedure to select the SQL Server instance, authentication credentials, and finally, the database.

If you use a username and password as your authentication details, you can choose not to include those in the connection string (containing the details required to connect to the database) when it is saved because this string is saved in plain text that would enable anyone who sees it to have access to the database. In this case you would have to provide these credentials to the model before querying it for it to create a connection to the database. If you don't select the check box to save the connection settings in the `App.config` file, you also need to pass the model the details on how to connect to the database before you can query it.

Next, the wizard asks you which version of Entity Framework to use. The choices presented include, by default, version 6.0 and 5.0. The reason to include version 5.0 (and to allow you to have older versions as well) is to support existing applications that have not yet upgraded to version 6.0. Keep the default of version 6.0 and click Next.

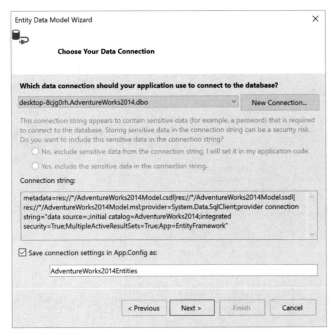

FIGURE 27-3

In the next step, the wizard connects to the database and retrieves its structure (that is, its tables, views, and stored procedures), which displays in a tree for you to select the elements to be included in your model (see Figure 27-4).

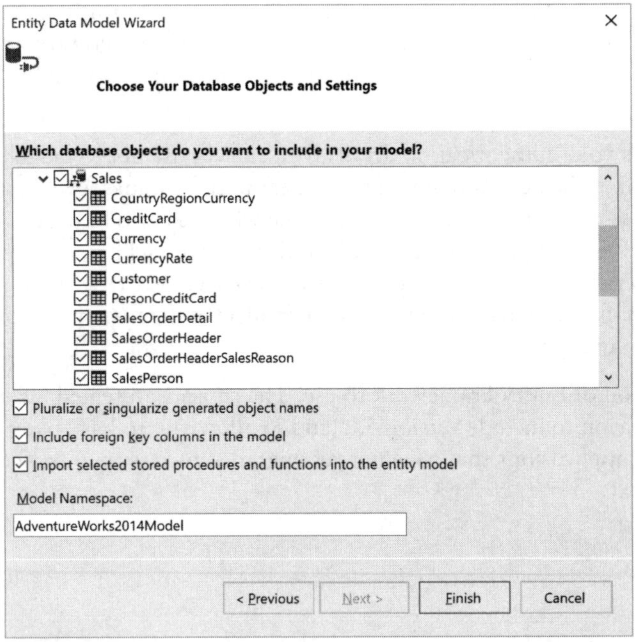

FIGURE 27-4

Other options that can be specified on this screen include:

➤ **Pluralize or singularize generated object names:** This option (when selected) intelligently takes the name of the table/view/stored procedure and pluralizes or singularizes the name based on how that name is used in the model. (Collections use the plural form, entities use the singular form, and so on.)

➤ **Include foreign key columns in the model:** The Entity Framework supports two mechanisms for indicating foreign key columns. One is to create a relationship and hide the column from the entity, instead representing it through a relationship property. The other is to explicitly define the foreign key in the entity. If you wish to use the explicit definition, select this option to include it in your entities.

➤ **Import selected stored procedures and functions into the entity model:** While the entity data store supports the inclusion of stored procedures and functions, they need to be imported as functions in order to be accessible through the model. If you select this option, the stored procedures and functions that you choose in this dialog will automatically be imported into the model.

➤ **Model Namespace:** This enables you to specify the namespace in which all the classes related to the model will be created. By default, the model exists in its own namespace (which defaults to the name of the model entered in the Add New Item dialog) rather than the default namespace of the project to avoid conflict with existing classes with the same names in the project.

Select all the tables in the database to be included in the model. Clicking the Finish button in this screen creates an Entity Framework model that maps to the database. You might get prompted with a security warning about running a text template. The reason is that the generation of the classes used by Entity Framework is accomplished through a T4 Template. Visual Studio will prompt you for confirmation before running a template unless you have previously disabled that warning. See Chapter 43, "Code Generation with T4," in the online archive for more information about T4 Templates.

Once generated, you can view the model in the Entity Framework designer, adjust it per your requirements, and tidy it up as per your tastes (or standards) to make it ideal for querying in your code.

The Entity Framework Designer

After the Entity Framework model has been generated, it opens in the Entity Framework designer, as shown in Figure 27-5.

The designer has automatically laid out the entities that were created by the wizard, showing the associations it has created between them.

You can move entities around on the designer surface, and the designer automatically moves the association lines and tries to keep them neatly laid out. Entities automatically snap to a grid, which you can view by right-clicking the designer surface and selecting Grid ➪ Show Grid from the context menu. You can disable the snapping by right-clicking the designer surface and unchecking Grid

⇨ Snap to Grid from the context menu to have finer control over the diagram layout, but entities line up better (and hence make the diagram neater) by leaving the snapping on.

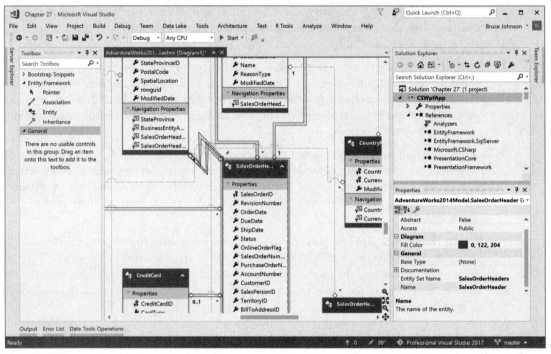

FIGURE 27-5

As you move entities around (or add additional entities to) the diagram, you may find it gets a little messy, with association lines going in all directions to avoid getting "tangled." To get the designer to automatically lay out the entities neatly again according to its own algorithms, you can right-click the designer surface and select Diagram ⇨ Layout Diagram from the context menu.

Entity Framework models can quickly become large and difficult to navigate in the Entity Framework designer. Luckily, the designer has a few tools to make navigating it a little easier. The designer enables you to zoom in and out using the zoom buttons in its bottom-right corner (below the vertical scrollbar — see Figure 27-6). The button sandwiched between these zoom in/out buttons zooms to 100% when clicked.

FIGURE 27-6

To zoom to a predefined percentage, right-click the designer surface, and select one of the options in the Zoom menu. In this menu you can also find a Zoom to Fit option (to fit the entire entity model within the visible portion of the designer), and a Custom option that pops up a dialog enabling you to type a specific zoom level.

In addition, selecting an entity in the Properties tool window (from the drop-down object selector) automatically selects that entity in the designer and brings it into view; right-clicking the entity in the Model Browser tool window (described shortly) and selecting the Show in Designer menu item does the same. These make it easy to navigate to a particular entity in the designer, so you can make any modifications as required.

You can minimize the space taken by entities by clicking the icon in the top-right corner of the entity. Alternatively, you can roll up the Properties/Navigation Properties groupings by clicking the +/– icons to their left. Figure 27-7 shows an entity in its normal expanded state, with the Properties/Navigation Properties groupings rolled up, and completely rolled up.

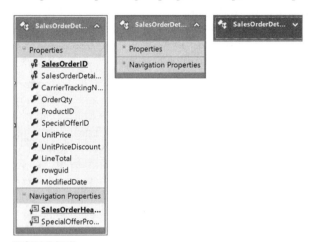

FIGURE 27-7

You can expand all the collapsed entities at one time by right-clicking the designer surface and selecting Diagram ⇨ Expand All from the context menu. Alternatively, you can collapse all the entities in the diagram by right-clicking the designer surface and selecting Diagram ⇨ Collapse All from the context menu.

A visual representation of an entity model (as provided by the Entity Framework designer) can serve a useful purpose in the design documentation for your application. The designer provides a means to save the model layout to an image file to help in this respect. Right-click anywhere on the designer surface, and select Diagram ⇨ Export as Image from the context menu. This pops up the Save As dialog for you to select where to save the image. It defaults to saving as a bitmap (.bmp); if you open the Save As Type drop-down list, you can see that it can also save to JPEG, GIF, PNG, and TIFF. PNG is probably the best choice for quality and file size.

It can often be useful (especially when saving a diagram for documentation) to display the property types against each property for an entity in the designer. You can turn this on by right-clicking the designer surface and selecting Scalar Property Format ⇨ Display Name and Type from the context menu. You can return to displaying just the property name by selecting the Scalar Property Format ⇨ Display Name item from the right-click context menu.

As with most designers in Visual Studio, the Toolbox and Properties tool windows are integral parts of working with the designer. The Toolbox (as shown in Figure 27-8) contains three controls: Entity, Association, and Inheritance. How to use these controls with the designer is covered shortly. The Properties tool window displays the properties of the selected items in the designer (an entity, association, or inheritance), enabling you to modify their values as required.

In addition to the Toolbox and Properties tool windows, the Entity Framework designer also incorporates two other tool windows specific to it — the Model Browser tool window and the Mapping Details tool window — for working with the data.

FIGURE 27-8

The Model Browser tool window (as shown in Figure 27-9) enables you to browse the hierarchy of both the conceptual entity model of the database and its storage model. Clicking an element in the Store model hierarchy shows its properties in the Properties tool window; however, these can't be modified (because this is an entity modeling tool, not a database modeling tool). The only changes you can make to the Store model is to delete tables, views, and stored procedures (which won't modify the underlying database). Clicking elements in the Conceptual model hierarchy also shows their properties in the Properties tool window (which can be modified), and its mappings display in the Mapping Details tool window. Right-clicking an entity in the hierarchy and selecting the Show in Designer menu item from the context menu brings the selected entity/association into view in the designer.

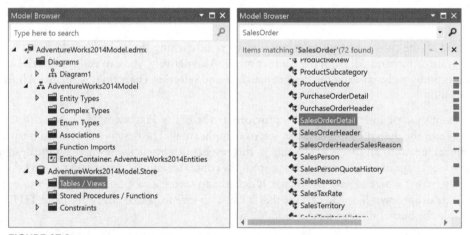

FIGURE 27-9

The second picture in Figure 27-9 demonstrates the searching functionality available in the Model Browser tool window. Because your entity model can get quite large, it can be difficult to find exactly what you are after. Therefore, a good search function is important. Type your search term in the search textbox at the top of the window, and press Enter. In this example the search term was SalesOrder, which highlighted all the names in the hierarchy (including entities, associations, properties, and so on) that contained the search term. The vertical scrollbar has the places in the hierarchy (which has been expanded) highlighted where the search terms have been found, making it easy to see where the results were found throughout the hierarchy. The number of results is shown just below the search textbox, next to which are an up arrow and a down arrow to enable you to navigate through the results. When you finish searching, you can click the cross icon next to these to return the window to normal.

The Mapping Details tool window (as shown in Figure 27-10) enables you to modify the mapping between the conceptual model and the storage model for an entity. Selecting an entity in the designer, the Model Browser tool window, or the Properties tool window shows the mappings in this tool window between the properties of the entity to columns in the database. You have two ways to map the properties of an entity to the database: either via tables and views, or via functions (that is, stored procedures). On the left side of the tool window are two icons, enabling you to swap the view between mapping to tables and views, to mapping to functions. However, focus here just on the features of mapping entity properties to tables and views.

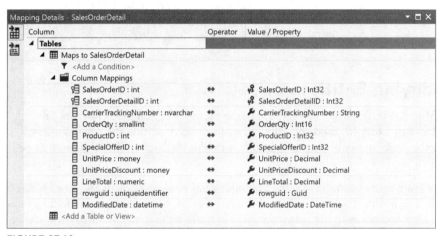

FIGURE 27-10

The table/view mapping has a hierarchy (under the Column column) showing the tables mapped to the entity, with its columns underneath it. To these columns you can map properties on your entity (under the Value/Property column) by clicking in the cell, opening the drop-down list that appears, and selecting a property from the list.

A single entity may map to more than one database table/view (bringing two or more tables/views into a single entity). To add another table/view to the hierarchy to map to your entity, click in the bottom row where it says <Add a Table or View> and select a table/view from the drop-down list. When you add a table to the Mapping Details tool window for mapping to an entity, it automatically matches columns with the same name to properties on the entities and creates a mapping between them. Delete a table from the hierarchy by selecting its row and pressing the Delete key.

Conditions are a powerful feature of the Entity Framework that enable you to selectively choose which table you want to map an entity to at run time based on one or more conditions that you specify. For example, say you have a single entity in your model called Product that maps to a table called Products in the database. However, you have additional extended properties on your entity

that map to one of two tables based on the value of the ProductType property on the entity —
if the product is of a particular type, it maps the columns to one table, if it's another type, it
maps the columns to the other table. You can do this by adding a condition to the table mapping.
In the Mapping Details window, click in the row directly below a table to selectively map where it
says <Add a Condition>. Open the drop-down list that appears, which contains all the properties
on the entity. Select the property to base your condition on (in the given example it would be the
ProductType property), select an operator, and enter a value to compare the property to. Note that
there are only two operators: Equals (=) and Is. You can add additional conditions as necessary to
determine if the table should be used as the source of the data for the given properties.

> **NOTE** *A number of advanced features are available in the Entity Framework
> but not available in the Entity Framework designer (such as working with the
> store schema, annotations, referencing other models, and so on). However, these
> actions can be performed by modifying the schema files (which are XML files)
> directly.*

Creating/Modifying Entities

The Entity Data Model Wizard gave you a good starting point by building an entity model
for you. In some cases this may be good enough, and you can start writing the code to query it, but
you can now take the opportunity to go through the created model and modify its design as per
your requirements.

Because the Entity Framework provides you with a conceptual model to design and work with, you
are no longer limited to having a 1:1 relationship between the database schema and an object model
in code, so the changes you make in the entity model won't affect the database in any way. So you
may want to delete properties from entities, change their names, and so on, and it will have no effect
on the database. In addition, because any changes you make are in the conceptual model, updating
the model from the database will not affect the conceptual model (only the storage model), so your
changes won't be lost.

Changing Property Names

Often you might work with databases that have tables and columns containing prefixes or suf-
fixes, over/under use of capitalization, or even names that no longer match their actual function.
This is where the use of an ORM like the Entity Framework can demonstrate its power because
you can change all these in the conceptual layer of the entity model to make the model nice to
work with in code (with more meaningful and standardized names for the entities and associations) without needing to modify the underlying database schema. Luckily, the tables and columns
in the AdventureWorks2014 database have reasonably friendly names, but if you wanted to change
the names, it would simply be a case of double-clicking the property in the designer (or selecting it
and pressing F2), which changes the name display to a textbox enabling you to make the change.

Alternatively, you can select the property in the designer, the Model Browser tool window, or the Properties tool window, and update the Name property in the Properties tool window.

Adding Properties to an Entity

Now look at the process of adding properties to an entity. Three types of properties exist:

➤ **Scalar properties:** Properties with a primitive type, such as string, integer, Boolean, and so on.

➤ **Complex properties:** A grouping of scalar properties in a manner similar to a structure in code. Grouping properties together in this manner can make your entity model a lot more readable and manageable.

➤ **Navigation properties:** Used to navigate across associations. For example, the SalesOrderHeader entity contains a navigation property called SalesOrderDetails that enables you to navigate to a collection of the SalesOrderDetail entities related to the current SalesOrderHeader entity. Creating an association between two entities automatically creates the required navigation properties.

The easiest way to try this is to delete a property from an existing entity and add it back again manually. Delete a property from an entity. (Select it in the designer and press the Delete key.) To add it back again, right-click the entity, and select Add ⇨ Scalar Property from the context menu. Alternatively, a much easier and less frustrating way when you are creating a lot of properties is to simply select a property or the Properties header and press the Insert key on your keyboard. A new property will be added to the entity, with the name displayed in a textbox for you to change as required.

The next step is to set the type of the property; you need to move over to the Properties tool window to set it. The default type is string, but you can change this to the required type by setting its Type property.

Properties that you want to designate as entity keys (that is, properties used to uniquely identify the entity) need their Entity Key property set to True. The property in the designer will have a picture of a little key added to its icon, making it easy to identify which properties are used to uniquely identify the entity.

You can set numerous other properties on a property, including assigning a default value, a maximum length (for strings), and whether or not it's nullable. You can also assign the scope of the getter and setter for the property (public, private, and so on), useful for, say, a property that will be mapped to a column with a calculated value in the database where you don't want the consuming application to attempt to set the value (by making the setter private).

The final task is to map the property to the store model. You do this as described earlier using the Mapping Details tool window.

Creating Complex Types

Though you can create a complex type from scratch, the easiest way to create a complex type is to refactor an entity by selecting the scalar properties on the entity to be included in the complex type and having the designer create the complex type from those properties. Follow these instructions to move the name-related properties on the Person entity to a complex type:

1. Select the name-related properties on the Person entity (FirstName, LastName, MiddleName, NameStyle, Suffix, Title) by selecting the first property, and while holding down the Ctrl key selecting the other properties (so they are all selected at the same time).

2. Right-click one of the selected properties, and select the Refactor ⇨ Move To New Complex Type menu item.

3. In the Model Browser will be the new complex type that it created, with its name displayed in a textbox for you to name to something more meaningful. For this example, simply call it PersonName.

4. The Entity Framework designer will have created a complex type, added the selected properties to it, removed the selected properties from the entity, and added the complex type that it just created as a new property on the entity in their place. However, this property will just have ComplexProperty as its name, so you need to rename it to something more meaningful. Select the property in the designer, press F2, and enter Name in the textbox.

You will now find that by grouping the properties together in this way, the entity will be easier to work with in both the designer and in code.

Creating an Entity

So far you've been modifying existing entities as they were created by the Entity Data Model Wizard. However, now take a look at the process to create an entity from scratch and then mapping it to a table/view/stored procedure in your storage model. Most of these aspects have already been covered, but walk through the required steps to get an entity configured from scratch.

You have two ways to manually create entities. The first is to right-click the designer surface and select Add New ⇨ Entity from the context menu. That pops up the dialog shown in Figure 27-11, which helps you set up the initial configuration of the entity. When you enter a name for the entity in the Entity Name field, you'll notice that the Entity Set field automatically updates to the plural form of the entity name (although you can change this entity set name to something else if required). The Base Type drop-down list enables you to select an existing entity in your entity model that this entity inherits from (discussed shortly). There is also a section enabling you to specify the name and type of a property to automatically create on the entity and set as an entity key.

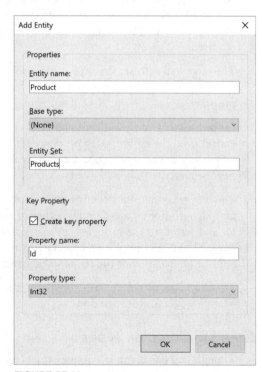

FIGURE 27-11

The other way to create an entity is to drag and drop the Entity component from the Toolbox onto the designer surface. However, it doesn't bring up the dialog from the previous method, instead opting to immediately create an entity with a default name, entity set name, and entity key property. You then have to use the designer to modify its configuration to suit your needs.

The steps needed to finish configuring the entity are as follows:

1. If required, create an inheritance relationship by specifying that the entity should inherit from a base entity.

2. Create the required properties on the entity, setting at least one as an entity key.

3. Using the Mapping Details tool window, map these properties to the storage schema.

4. Create any associations with other entities in the model.

5. Validate your model to ensure that the entity is mapped correctly.

> **NOTE** *All entities must have an entity key that can be used to uniquely identify the entity. Entity keys are conceptually the same as a primary key in a database.*

You aren't limited to mapping to a single database table/view per entity. This is one of the benefits of building a conceptual model of the database — you may have related data spread across a number of database tables, but through having a conceptual entity model layer in the Entity Framework, you can bring those different sources together into a single entity to make working with the data a lot easier in code.

> **NOTE** *Make sure you don't focus too much on the structure of the database when you create your entity model — the advantage of designing a conceptual model is that it enables you to design the model based on how you plan to use it in code. Therefore, focus on designing your entity model, and then you can look at how it maps to the database.*

Creating/Modifying Entity Associations

You have two ways of creating an association between two entities. The first is to right-click the header of one of the entities and select Add New ➪ Association from the context menu. This displays the dialog shown in Figure 27-12.

This dialog includes:

➤ **Association Name:** Give the association a name. This becomes the name of the foreign key constraint in the database if you update the database from the model.

➤ **Endpoints:** These specify the entities at each end of the association, the type of relationship (one-to-one, one-to-many, and so on), and the name of the navigation properties that it creates on both entities to navigate from one entity to the other over the association.

➤ **Add Foreign Key Properties to the Entity:** This enables you to create a property on the "foreign" entity that acts as a foreign key and map to the entity key property over the association. If you've already added the property that will form the foreign key on the associated entity, you should uncheck this check box.

FIGURE 27-12

The other way to create an association is to click the Association component in the Toolbox, click one entity to form an end on the association, and then click another entity to form the other end of the association. (If it is a one-to-many relationship, select the "one" entity first.) Using this method gives the association a default name, creates the navigation properties on both entities, and assumes a one-to-many relationship. It will not create a foreign key property on the "foreign" entity. You can then modify this association as required using the Properties tool window.

> **NOTE** *You cannot use the association component in a drag-and-drop fashion from the Toolbox.*

Despite having created the association, you aren't done yet unless you used the first method and selected the option to create a foreign key property for the association. Now you need to map the property that acts as the foreign key on one entity to the entity key property on the other. The entity whose primary key is one endpoint in the association is known, but you have to tell the Entity Framework explicitly which property to use as the foreign key property. You can do this by selecting the association in the designer and using the Mapping Details tool window to map the properties.

When this is done, you may want to define a referential constraint for the association, which you can assign by clicking the association in the designer and finding the Referential Constraint property in the Properties tool window.

Entity Inheritance

In the same way that classes can inherit from other classes (a fundamental object-oriented concept), so can entities inherit from other entities. You have a number of ways to specify that one entity should inherit from another, but the most straightforward method is to select an entity in the designer, find its Base Type property in the Properties tool window, and select the entity from the drop-down list that this entity should inherit from.

Validating an Entity Model

At times your entity model may be invalid (such as when a property on an entity has not been mapped to the storage model, or its type cannot be converted from/to the mapped column's data type in the database); however, despite having an invalid entity model your project can still compile.

You can run a check to see if your model is valid by right-clicking the designer surface and selecting the Validate menu item from the context menu. This checks for any errors in your model and displays them in the Error List tool window.

You can also set the Validate On Build property for the conceptual model to True (click an empty space on the designer surface, and then you can find the property in the Properties tool window), which automatically validates the model each time you compile the project. However, again, an invalid model will not stop the project from successfully compiling.

Updating an Entity Model with Database Changes

The structure of databases tends to be updated frequently throughout the development of projects, so you need a way to update your model based on the changes in the database. To do so, right-click the designer surface, and select the Update Model from Database menu item. This opens the Update Wizard (as shown in Figure 27-13) that obtains the schema from the database, compares it to the current storage model, and extracts the differences. These differences display in the tabs in the wizard. The Add tab contains database objects that aren't in your storage model, the Refresh tab contains database objects that are different in the database from their corresponding storage model objects, and the Delete tab contains database objects that are in the storage model but no longer in the database.

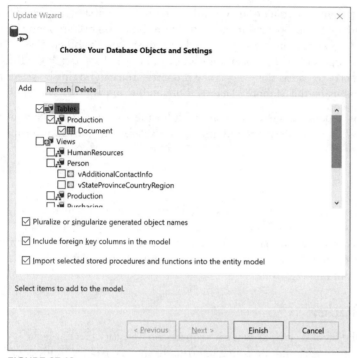

FIGURE 27-13

Select the items from these three tabs that you want to add, refresh, or delete, and click the Finish button to have your entity model updated accordingly.

QUERYING THE ENTITY MODEL

Now that you've created your entity model, you no doubt want to put it to the test by querying it, working with and modifying the data returned, and saving changes back to the database. The Entity Framework provides a number of ways to query your entity model, including LINQ to Entities, Entity SQL, and query builder methods. However, this chapter focuses specifically on querying the model with LINQ to Entities.

LINQ to Entities Overview

Details about LINQ can be found in Chapter 46, "Language Integrated Queries (LINQ)," in the online archive. That chapter specifically focuses on the use of LINQ to Objects, LINQ to SQL, and LINQ to XML; however, the Entity Framework has extended LINQ with its own implementation called LINQ to Entities. LINQ to Entities enables you to write strongly typed LINQ queries against your entity model and have it return the data as objects (entities). LINQ to Entities handles the mapping of your LINQ query against the conceptual entity model to a SQL query against the underlying database schema. This is an extraordinarily powerful feature of the Entity Framework, abstracting away the need to write SQL to work with data in a database.

Getting an Object Context

To connect to your entity model, you need to create an instance of the object context in your entity model. So that the object context is disposed of when you finish, use a using block to maintain the lifetime of the variable:

VB

```
Using context As New AdventureWorks2014Entities()
    'Queries go here
End Using
```

C#

```
using (AdventureWorks2014Entities context = new AdventureWorks2014Entities())
{
    // Queries go here
}
```

> **NOTE** *Any queries placed within the scope of the* using *block for the object context aren't necessarily executed while the object context is in scope. As detailed in the "Debugging and Execution" section of Chapter 46, "Language Integrated Queries (LINQ)," in the online archive, the execution of LINQ queries is deferred until the results are iterated. (That is, the query is not run against the database until the code needs to use its results.) This means that if the variable containing the context has gone out of scope before you are actually using the results, the query will fail. Therefore, ensure that you have requested the results of the query before letting the context variable go out of scope.*

If you need to specify the connection to the database (such as if you need to pass in user credentials or use a custom connection string rather than what's in the App.config file) you can do so by passing the connection string to the constructor of the object context (in this case AdventureWorks2014Entities).

> **NOTE** *The connection string passed into the constructor is not quite the same as a connection string passed into the typical database connection object. In the case of the Entity Framework, the connection string includes a description of where to find the meta data for the entities.*

CRUD Operations

It would be hard to argue against the most important database queries being the CRUD (Create/Read/Update/Delete) operations. Read operations return data from the database, whereas the Create/Update/Delete operations make changes to the database. Create some LINQ to Entities queries to demonstrate retrieving some data from the database (as entities), modify these entities, and then save the changes back to the database.

> **NOTE** *While you get up to speed on writing LINQ to Entities queries, you may find LINQPad to be a useful tool, providing a "scratchpad" where you can write queries against an entity model and have them executed immediately so that you can test your query. You can get LINQPad from* http://www.linqpad.net.

Data Retrieval

Just like SQL, LINQ to Entity queries consist of `selects`, `where` clauses, `order by` clauses, and `group by` clauses. Take a look at some examples of these. The results of the queries can be assigned to the `ItemsSource` property of the DataGrid control created earlier in the `MainWindow.xaml` file, enabling you to visualize the results:

VB

```
dgEntityFrameworkData.ItemsSource = qry
```

C#

```
dgEntityFrameworkData.ItemsSource = qry;
```

There are actually a number of ways to query the entity model within LINQ to Entities, but you can just focus on one method here. Assume that the query is between the using block demonstrated previously, with the variable containing the instance of the object context simply called `context`.

To return the entire collection of customers in the database, you can write a select query like so:

VB

```
Dim qry = From c In context.Customers
          Select c
```

C#

```
var qry = from c in context.Customers
          select c;
```

You can filter the results with a `where` clause, which can even include functions/properties such as `StartsWith`, `Length`, and so on. This example returns all the customers whose last name starts with A:

VB

```
Dim qry = From c In context.Customers
          Where c.Name.LastName.StartsWith("A")
          Select c
```

C#

```
var qry = from c in context.Customers
          where c.Name.LastName.StartsWith("A")
          select c;
```

You can order the results with an `order by` clause — in this example you order the results by the customer's last name:

VB

```
Dim qry = From c In context.Customers
          Order By c.Name.LastName Ascending
          Select c
```

C#

```
var qry = from c in context.Customers
          orderby c.Name.LastName ascending
          select c;
```

You can group and aggregate the results with a group by clause — in this example you group the results by the salesperson, returning the number of sales per salesperson. Note that instead of returning a Customer entity you request that LINQ to Entities returns an implicitly typed variable containing the salesperson and his sales count:

VB

```
Dim qry = From c In context.Customers
          Group c By salesperson = c.SalesPerson Into grouping = Group
          Select New With
          {
              .SalesPerson = salesperson,
              .SalesCount = grouping.Count()
          }
```

C#

```
var qry = from c in context.Customers
          group c by c.SalesPerson into grouping
          select new
          {
              SalesPerson = grouping.Key,
              SalesCount = grouping.Count()
          };
```

> **NOTE** *It can be useful to monitor the SQL queries generated and executed by the Entity Framework to ensure that the interaction between the entity model and the database is what you'd expect. For example, you may find that because an association is being lazy loaded, traversing the entity hierarchy across this association in a loop actually makes repeated and excessive trips to the database. Therefore, if you have SQL Server Standard or higher, you can use the SQL Profiler to monitor the queries being made to the database and adjust your LINQ queries if necessary.*

Saving Data

The Entity Framework employs change tracking — where you make changes to data in the model, it tracks the data that has changed, and when you request that the changes are saved back to the database, it commits the changes to the database as a batch. This commit is via the SaveChanges() method on the object context:

VB

```
context.SaveChanges()
```

C#

```
context.SaveChanges();
```

A number of ways to update data exists (for different scenarios), but for purposes of simplicity, this example takes simple straightforward approaches.

Update Operations

Assume you want to modify the name of a customer (with an ID of 1), which you've retrieved like so:

VB

```
Dim qry = From c In context.Customers
          Where c.CustomerID = 1
          Select c

Dim customer As Customer = qry.FirstOrDefault()
```

C#

```
var qry = from c in context.Customers
          where c.CustomerID == 1
          select c;

Customer customer = qry.FirstOrDefault();
```

All you need to do is modify the name properties on the customer entity you've retrieved. The Entity Framework automatically tracks that this customer has changed, and then calls the SaveChanges() method on the object context:

VB

```
customer.Name.FirstName = "Chris"
customer.Name.LastName = "Anderson"

context.SaveChanges()
```

C#

```
customer.Name.FirstName = "Chris";
customer.Name.LastName = "Anderson";

context.SaveChanges();
```

Create Operations

To add a new entity to an entity set, simply create an instance of the entity, assign values to its properties, add the new entity to the related collection on the data context, and then save the changes:

VB

```
Customer customer = new Customer()
customer.Name.FirstName = "Chris"
customer.Name.LastName = "Anderson"
customer.Name.Title = "Mr."
customer.PasswordHash = "*****"
customer.PasswordSalt = "*****"
customer.ModifiedDate = DateTime.Now
context.Customers.AddObject(customer)

context.SaveChanges()
```

C#

```
Customer customer = new Customer();
customer.Name.FirstName = "Chris";
customer.Name.LastName = "Anderson";
customer.Name.Title = "Mr.";
customer.PasswordHash = "*****";
customer.PasswordSalt = "*****";
customer.ModifiedDate = DateTime.Now;
context.Customers.AddObject(customer);

context.SaveChanges();
```

After the changes are saved back to the database your entity can now have the primary key that was automatically generated for the row by the database assigned to its `CustomerID` property.

Delete Operations

To delete an entity, simply use the `DeleteObject()` method on its containing entity set:

VB

```
context.Customers.DeleteObject(customer)
```

C#

```
context.Customers.DeleteObject(customer);
```

Navigating Entity Associations

Of course, working with data rarely involves the use of a single table/entity, which is where the navigation properties used by associations are useful indeed. A customer can have one or more addresses, which is modeled in your entity model by the Customer entity having an association with the CustomerAddress entity (a one-to-many relationship), which then has an association with the Address entity (a many-to-one relationship). The navigation properties for these associations make it easy to obtain the addresses for a customer.

Start by using the query from earlier to return a customer entity:

VB

```
Dim qry = From c In context.Customers
          Where c.CustomerID = 1
          Select c

Dim customer As Customer = qry.FirstOrDefault()
```

C#

```
var qry = from c in context.Customers
          where c.CustomerID == 1
          select c;

Customer customer = qry.FirstOrDefault();
```

You can enumerate and work with the addresses for the entity via the navigation properties like so:

VB

```
For Each customerAddress As CustomerAddress In customer.CustomerAddresses
    Dim address As Address = customerAddress.Address
    'Do something with the address entity
Next customerAddress
```

C#

```
foreach (CustomerAddress customerAddress in customer.CustomerAddresses)
{
    Address address = customerAddress.Address;
    // Do something with the address entity
}
```

Note how you navigate through the CustomerAddress entity to get to the Address entity for the customer. Because of these associations there's no need for joins in the Entity Framework.

However, there is an issue here with what you're doing. At the beginning of the loop, a database query will made to retrieve the customer addresses for the current customer. Then, for each address in the loop, an additional database query will be made to retrieve the information associated with the Address entity! This is known as *lazy loading* — where the entity model requests data only from the database when it actually needs it. This can have some advantages in certain situations; however, in this scenario it results in a lot of calls to the database, increasing the load on the database server, reducing the performance of your application, and reducing your application's scalability. If you then did this for a number of customer entities in a loop, that would add even more strain to the system. So it's definitely not an ideal scenario as is.

Instead, you can request from the entity model when querying for the customer entity that it eagerly loads its associated CustomerAddress entities and their Address entities. This requests all the data in one database query, thus removing all the aforementioned issues, because when navigating through these associations the entity model now has the entities in memory and does not have to go back to the database to retrieve them. The way to request that the model does this is to use the `Include` method, specifying the path (as a string) of the navigation properties (dot notation) to the associated entities whose data you also want to retrieve from the database at the same time as the actual entities being queried:

VB

```
Dim qry = From c In context.Customers
                        .Include("CustomerAddresses")
                        .Include("CustomerAddresses.Address")
        Where c.CustomerID = 1
        Select c

Dim customer As Customer = qry.FirstOrDefault()
```

C#

```
var qry = from c in context.Customers
                        .Include("CustomerAddresses")
                        .Include("CustomerAddresses.Address")
        where c.CustomerID == 1
        select c;

Customer customer = qry.FirstOrDefault();
```

ADVANCED FUNCTIONALITY

There's too much functionality available in the Entity Framework to discuss in detail, but here's an overview of some of the more notable advanced features available that you can investigate further if you want.

Updating a Database from an Entity Model

It's possible with the Entity Framework to create an entity model from scratch, and then have the Entity Framework create a database according to your model. Alternatively, you can start with an existing database, but then get the Entity Framework to update the structure of your database based on the new entities/properties/associations that you've added to your entity model. To update the structure of the database based on additions to your model, you can use the Generate Database Wizard by right-clicking the designer surface and selecting the Generate Database from Model menu item.

Adding Business Logic to Entities

Though you are fundamentally building a data model with the Entity Framework rather than business objects, you can add business logic to your entities. The entities generated by the Entity Framework are partial classes, enabling to you extend them and add your own code. This code may respond to various events on the entity, or it may add methods to your entity that the client application can use to perform specific tasks or actions.

For example, you might want to have the Product entity in your AdventureWorks2014 entity model automatically assign the value of the `SellEndDate` property when the `SellStartDate` property is set (only if the `SellEndDate` property does not have a value). Alternatively, you may have some validation logic or business logic that you want to execute when the entity is being saved.

Each property on the entity has two partial methods that you can extend: a `Changing` method (before the property is changed) and a `Changed` method (after the property is changed). You can extend these partial methods in your partial class to respond accordingly to the value of a property being changed.

Plain Old CLR Objects (POCO)

One of the big complaints with the first version of the Entity Framework was that your entities had to inherit from `EntityObject` (or implement a set of given interfaces), meaning that they had a dependency on the Entity Framework — which made them unfriendly for use in projects where test-driven development (TDD) and domain-driven design (DDD) practices were employed. In addition, many developers wanted their classes to be persistence ignorant — that is, contain no logic or awareness of how they were persisted.

By default, the entities generated from the Entity Model Data Wizard in the Entity Framework v6 still inherit from `EntityObject`, but you now have the ability to use your own classes that do not need to inherit from `EntityObject` or implement any Entity Framework interfaces, and whose design is completely under your control. These types of classes are often termed Plain Old CLR Objects, or POCO for short.

Entity Framework Core

A lot of work has been invested into making .NET applications (or a subset of .NET applications, actually) work across different platforms. As part of this effort, Microsoft released Entity Framework Core for use in .NET Core applications. This is a lightweight, cross-platform version of Entity Framework 6.0. There is some missing functionality, but the vast majority of features carry across.

If you are thinking about upgrading from Entity Framework Core to Entity Framework 6.0, you might want to reconsider. Although the name ("Entity Framework") and the classes are the same, the namespace is different. And, in reality, they are different products even if they fulfill the same function. In fact, it's possible to use both Entity Framework and Entity Framework Core in the same project. From that standpoint, any move from one version to the other could reasonably be considered to be a port and not an upgrade.

SUMMARY

In this chapter you learned that the Entity Framework is an Object Relational Mapper (ORM) that enables you to create a conceptual model of your database to interact with databases in a more productive and maintainable manner. You then learned how to create an entity model and how to write queries against it in code.

28

Data Warehouses and Lakes

WHAT'S IN THIS CHAPTER?

➤   Understanding the ideas behind Apache Hadoop and HDInsight

➤   Executing Hive queries and Pig job against a Hadoop cluster

➤   Examining the performance of Hadoop jobs

WROX.COM CODE DOWNLOADS FOR THIS CHAPTER

The wrox.com code downloads for this chapter can be found at www.wrox.com by searching for this book's ISBN number (978-1-119-40458-3). The code and any related support files are located in their own folder for this chapter.

In an industry where buzzwords abound, "big data" is currently sitting at the pinnacle of hype. One would think it was a cure for cancer, the eradication of poverty, and the latest cat video all rolled up into one. Even if you're skeptical about the hype, there is bound to be a nugget of potential usefulness in the technology. With Visual Studio 2017 and some recent additions to Windows Azure, now is the time to not only look at what big data really is, but also to consider the tools that are available to help with it. In this chapter, we discuss some of the basic ideas of Apache Hadoop, along with an examination of the tools that Visual Studio 2017 brings.

WHAT IS APACHE HADOOP?

You're definitely not the first person to ask that question, and you won't be the last. If you're developing in the Microsoft space, it's quite likely that you're also asking about HDInsight. Fortunately, those two questions are related. HDInsight is the cloud-based implementation of Hadoop found in Azure. So a discussion of Hadoop is also a discussion about HDInsight.

An understanding of Hadoop is rooted in an understanding of two core concepts: the Hadoop Distributed File System and MapReduce. Once you understand these, you can consider additional components, HDInsight, and Azure Data Lakes.

Hadoop Distributed File System

As you might expect from something with the word "big" in its name, big data is expected to work with large volumes of data. That data could be structured (such as containing well-defined columns of data, similar to a database or a log file) or unstructured (like a Facebook or Twitter feed). But regardless of its form, there is a large quantity of data, and that data will need to be stored.

The Hadoop Distributed File System (HDFS) is designed to accommodate this need. It is designed to allow a file or files to be placed on a number of different servers. So, if you had 10 million files that you needed to store, but each server could only store 500,000, you could use HDFS to place those files on more than 20 different servers. Alternatively, if you had a single file that was 20 terabytes in size and each server could only store 500GB, HDFS would allow you to distribute that file across more than 40 different servers.

At this level, the functionality of HDFS is not that different from any other distributed file system. However, one of HDFS's strengths is that it was designed to be fault tolerant. The reason for this design choice is that one of the architectural goals for HDFS was to be able to run on commodity hardware. When working with large clusters, the term "commodity hardware" is frequently synonymous with "unreliable," which is to say that there is a non-zero and non-trivial possibility that any node in the cluster might fail at any time. So HDFS was constructed to allow for the failure of any node to be quickly detected and automatically recovered from.

MapReduce

The idea behind MapReduce is almost breathtaking in its simplicity. If you consider what most data-driven applications look like, there is a client portion and a server portion. The server portion might also include a web server (if the application is web-based), but there will be a database server used someplace in the architecture. When the client part of the application needs some data, it makes a request to the server. The data is then transported, generally across a network, from the server to the client.

Now consider how problematic that architecture can be if you need access to large files. Even with a 10 Gigabit ethernet network, a 10TB file would take more than two hours to transfer. That does not bode well for the response time of a traditional data-driven application.

MapReduce inverts this architecture. It works on the premise that when working with a large database, it is cheaper to move computation than it is to move data. MapReduce gives developers a framework to *map* their computational functionality onto the same nodes as the data. Then, when the computation is complete, only the results are sent back to a central location (*reduced*) for further processing.

Additional Components

Hadoop doesn't just stop with these HDFS and MapReduce. To create a fully supported production environment, there are a number of other elements that need to be considered. These include the following.

➤ **YARN:** A platform that is responsible for scheduling jobs and managing resources used in the Hadoop environment.

➤ **Hive:** A data warehouse that is built on top of Hadoop. Because of the structure of Hadoop, ad hoc queries are supported particularly well. Hive helps to provide the capability to query large datasets in an interface that is similar to SQL.

➤ **HBase:** A NOSQL implementation that has been built on top of HDFS. While this is not a replacement for a classic SQL database, there is another component, Trafodion, that aims to provide an ODBC (Open DataBase Connectivity) interface to HBase.

➤ **Storm:** Allows the data in HDFS to be processed in real time, as opposed to the batch processing that is implemented within MapReduce.

Naturally, there are even more components available, depending on the kind of functionality that you need. Hadoop is a very popular open-source project with a large and active user community.

HDInsight

HDInsight is a cloud distribution of the Hadoop technology stack. Specifically, it consists of HDFS, YARN, and MapReduce. However, to make it easier to get started in Hadoop, Azure has a number of different pre-configured clusters from which you can choose:

➤ **Hadoop:** The basic combination of HDFS, YARN, and MapReduce. This is your choice if you wish to utilize the standard Hadoop platform.

➤ **HBase:** Includes the HBase component to allow for NOSQL support for the underlying data.

➤ **Hive:** Adds support for interactive querying of the underlying dataset using the Hive component.

➤ **Kafka:** Similar to Storm, in that it provides the ability to process Hadoop data as a stream, it includes message broker functionality, which allows publish and subscribe capabilities against a stream.

➤ **R Server:** Adds the R Server on each of the nodes to support R-based analytics of the data. For more information on the R language and its use, see Chapter 29, "Data Science and Analytics."

➤ **Spark:** Adds the Spark component that provides support for in-memory processing of the data to improve performance.

➤ **Storm:** Includes the Storm component to the Hadoop implementation to allow for real-time processing of the data stream.

As you can see, the choices that you have are quite varied. One of the guarantees that Azure brings is that features are added on a regular basis. New options are always emerging.

Azure Data Lakes

The Azure Data Lake offering also fits into the Hadoop picture. As a quick definition, a data lake is a repository capable of containing any type of data, regardless of its size or structure. It can handle a large file or many small files. Along with this unlimited storage capability, the Azure Data Lake is designed to handle a high volume of small writes at a low level of latency. From a practical perspective, if you have a system that is generating a large volume of data quickly (such as an Internet of Things [IoT] network of devices), then it can be written to the data lake without slowing down the rest of the system or falling behind on the ingestion.

At an implementation level, Azure Data Lake is an HDFS, which means that you can use it as the storage for a Hadoop cluster. But it can also be used to support other analytic applications, like R-Enterprise (from Revolution) or Cloudera.

DATA LAKE TOOLS FOR VISUAL STUDIO

Your HDInsight and Data Lake deployments in Azure can be managed and used through Visual Studio 2017. To do this, you can install the Data Storage and Processing workload using the Visual Studio Installer. This workload includes the SDKs needed to connect to your HDInsight and Data Lake resources. As well, it adds a number of templates to Visual Studio that help facilitate the creation of projects that utilize those resources.

In order to demonstrate some of these templates, you need to have an HDInsight deployment within your Azure account. For most people, this means creating one. Keep in mind that while the creation of an HDInsight cluster is very simple, it is not cheap to keep up and running. This is not the same as a simple web application, which can be accessed for a few dollars a month or less. A basic HDInsight cluster includes 6 servers using 40 cores, at an hourly cost that quickly adds up. So be warned. Information on how to create a generic HDInsight cluster can be found at `https://docs .microsoft.com/en-us/azure/hdinsight/hdinsight-hadoop-provision-linux-clusters`.

Details about your HDInsight clusters are available through the Server Explorer, as shown in Figure 28-1.

Underneath your Azure node in Server Explorer, you will see an HDInsight node. Expanding this node displays all of the HDInsight deployments in your subscription. Each of those deployments can be further expanded to show the database, storage, and log files associated with the cluster.

The management capabilities through Server Explorer are relatively limited. For example, you can't create an HDInsight cluster through Server Explorer, although you can connect to an existing one if you know the connection URL, storage name, key, and administrator credentials for the cluster. This process is launched by right-clicking on the HDInsight node and choosing the Add a HDInsight Cluster option from the context menu.

If you right-click on an existing cluster, you have a number of choices. From a management perspective, you can choose to manage your cluster through the Azure Portal by selecting the Manage Cluster in Azure Portal option. You can run a Hive query or view the jobs that are currently running in the cluster.

FIGURE 28-1

For an individual Hive database, you have the option to be able to create a table through Server Explorer. Right-click on the database and select the Create a table menu option. The script designer shown in Figure 28-2 appears.

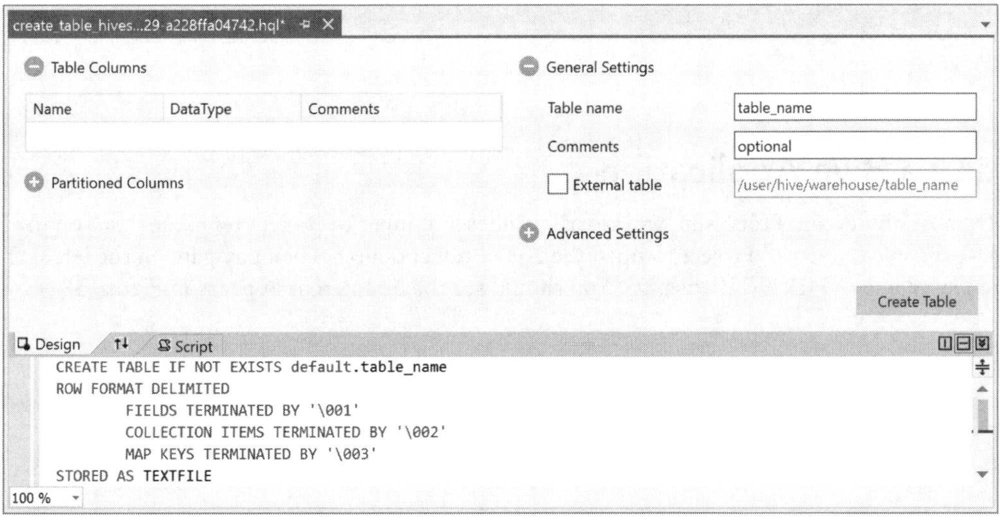

```
CREATE TABLE IF NOT EXISTS default.table_name
ROW FORMAT DELIMITED
        FIELDS TERMINATED BY '\001'
        COLLECTION ITEMS TERMINATED BY '\002'
        MAP KEYS TERMINATED BY '\003'
STORED AS TEXTFILE
```

FIGURE 28-2

This designer is used to create HQL (Hive Query Language) statements that create tables within Hive. As you can see from the lower portion of the screen, the syntax for HQL is similar to T-SQL. The top portion of the screen gives you a visual reference for some of the options, but if you have the skill set, you can always write the HQL directly. At the top, you can define the columns and data types that appear in the table, give the table a name, and indicate whether the table will be external (stored as a file in the file system) or just kept in the database. Under the advanced settings, you can choose the file format (the choice is a text file), and specify the field (or column), collection (or row), and map key delimiters.

When you create a new table, it appears in the list of tables for the database. If you right-click on any of those tables, you can view the first 100 rows of the table in a grid, as seen in Figure 28-3.

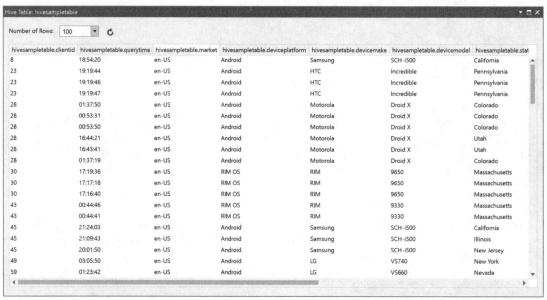

FIGURE 28-3

Creating a Hive Application

The Data Analytics and Processing workload includes a number of project templates for you to use. Use the File ⇨ New ⇨ Project to open the New Project dialog. Then navigate on the left side to Azure Data Lake ⇨ HIVE (HDInsight). You should see the dialog that appears in Figure 28-4.

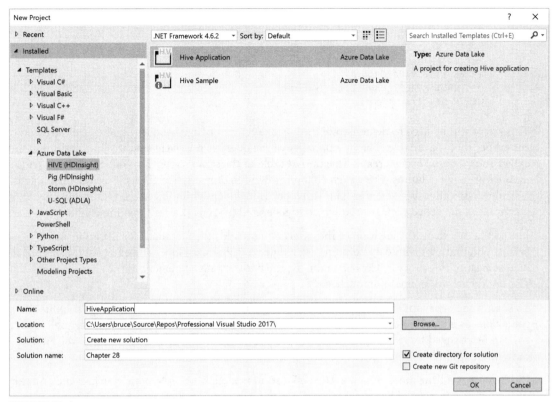

FIGURE 28-4

There is a Hive Sample template for you to play with, but for this example, choose Hive Application. Give the project a name and location and click OK.

The resulting project is quite spartan, as you can see from Figure 28-5. There is nothing more than an HQL file, which also opens by default.

The HQL file is where the work is done. For the most part, the Hive project is really a container for scripts that you wish to run against a particular HDInsight cluster. Add the following script to the Script.Hql file:

FIGURE 28-5

```
set hive.execution.engine=tez;
DROP TABLE log4jLogs;
```

```
CREATE EXTERNAL TABLE log4jLogs (t1 string, t2 string, t3 string,
    t4 string, t5 string, t6 string, t7 string)
    ROW FORMAT DELIMITED FIELDS TERMINATED BY ' '
    STORED AS TEXTFILE LOCATION '/example/data/';
SELECT t4 AS sev, COUNT(*) AS count FROM log4jLogs
    WHERE t4 = '[ERROR]' AND
        INPUT__FILE__NAME LIKE '%.log'
    GROUP BY t4;
```

This script will be used to demonstrate the basic execution of a Hive query and to see the different output that is available. The functionality of the query is relatively simple. First, it drops a table called `log4jLogs`. Next it creates an external table of the same name. This table is defined with a number of string columns where each column is delimited by a space. The source for this table is text files found in /example/data/. This directory is included with the generic HDInsight cluster, and it contains a file called `sample.log` which is generated by `log4j`, a Java logging engine.

Just so that it's clear, the creation of the external data adds the metadata for the table into HDInsight, and that metadata contains a reference to the source link. The external table is not modified as part of this process. Correspondingly, the DROP TABLE statement only deletes the metadata. The underlying files remain untouched.

To submit the query for execution, you can simply click on the Submit button. This submits the statements as a batch to HDInsight for execution. The particular cluster to which the job is submitted can be changed by selecting the desired target from the dropdown to the right of the Submit button.

If the query is a little more complex, then instead of just clicking on Submit, you can click on the dropdown to the right of Submit. This exposes the Advanced option, which gives you more choices to provide with the submission. The dialog that is shown in Figure 28-6 illustrates the available options.

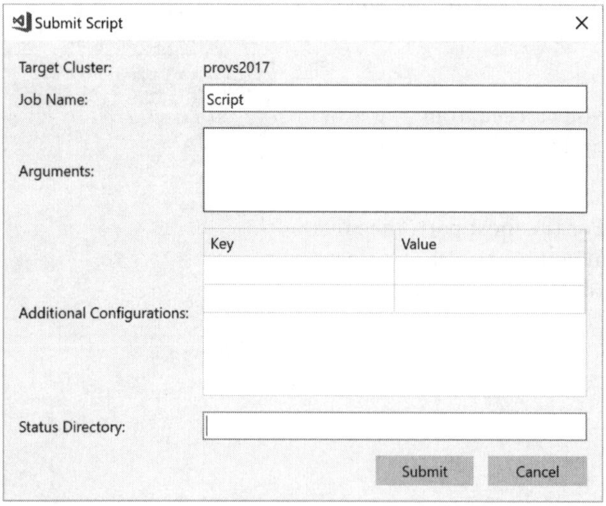

FIGURE 28-6

You can specify the name of the script that is provided to HDInsight, the command-line arguments, a set of key/value pairs that can be accessed by the script, and a directory into which status information for the job will be placed.

When the job is submitted, the Job Summary screen appears, similar to what is shown in Figure 28-7.

FIGURE 28-7

As the job is running, the state of the job will change from initializing to running to completed. Once completed, you have access to a number of different output options. First, to see the results from executing the batch, click on the Job Output link at the bottom. The results for the sample query are shown in Figure 28-8. To be clear (since the word "ERROR" appears in the output), the original query was designed to parse the log file and count the number of times the string [ERROR] appears as the fourth word in any line within any file that has an extension of .log. You can download these results by clicking on the Download File button.

FIGURE 28-8

The Job Query link in Figure 28-7 takes you to the batch of statements that were executed as part of this job. The Job Log link shows the log generated when the batch was executing. And the View Yarn Logs link will generate the YARN logs and store them in the storage account associated with your HDInsight cluster.

Creating a Pig Application

What you find as you create different HDInsight applications is that the basic flow is the same. What changes is the language that is used to define the job that is executed within HDInsight. The Apache Pig application is a good example, albeit with just enough extras to be worth looking at even if you're only writing Hive queries.

The creation of the project is pretty much the same as the Hive application. The difference is that instead of choosing Hive ⇨ Hive Application in the New Project dialog, you select Pig ⇨ Pig Application. The resulting project is just as barren, but instead of a `script.hql` file, a `script.pig` file is generated. Add the following code to the file:

```
LOGS = LOAD 'wasbs:///example/data/sample.log';
LEVELS = foreach LOGS generate
    REGEX_EXTRACT($0, '(TRACE|DEBUG|INFO|WARN|ERROR|FATAL)', 1)
        as LOGLEVEL;
FILTEREDLEVELS = FILTER LEVELS by LOGLEVEL is not null;
GROUPEDLEVELS = GROUP FILTEREDLEVELS by LOGLEVEL;
FREQUENCIES = foreach GROUPEDLEVELS generate group as LOGLEVEL,
    COUNT(FILTEREDLEVELS.LOGLEVEL) as COUNT;
RESULT = order FREQUENCIES by COUNT desc;
DUMP RESULT;
```

The language used in this application is (I kid you not) Pig Latin. The above script loads the `sample.log` file from storage. It then transforms the contents of the log file, extracting the log levels, removing levels that are null, and then grouping and counting the number of log entries for each level. When you are finished with this script, submit it to HDInsight for execution. The Job Summary screen appears. When complete, you can use the links at the bottom of the screen to view the logs and the output. However, compared to Figure 28-7, there is a significant addition to the Job Summary, as seen in Figure 28-9.

On the right side of the screen, once the job has completed, a visual representation appears of the steps that were part of the job. On the top is a flow chart with each of the stages in the job. At the bottom is the script for the job. One of the cooler features is found in the middle. There is a Job Playback section that allows you to see the steps that are being executed in real time.

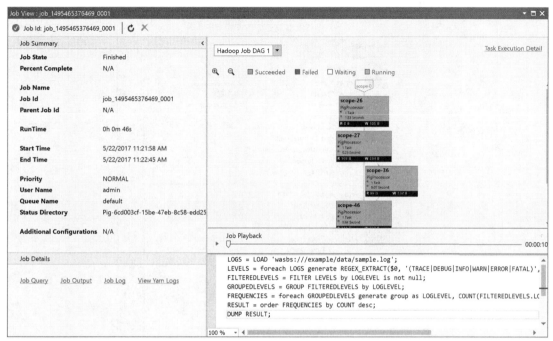

FIGURE 28-9

The fact that the Job Playback is in real time gives you a sense of how long each of the stages takes. The color of each stage changes as it is executed and then completed. The idea is that, unlike a simple sample job, actual Pig jobs can take a long time to run. Determining where the bottlenecks are is a big part of the development process. So, Visual Studio provides some tools to help with this.

By hovering over a stage, the tooltip shows details about the execution of the stage, including the name, the state, the time taken in the stage, how much memory was used, and how many records were processed (see Figure 28-10).

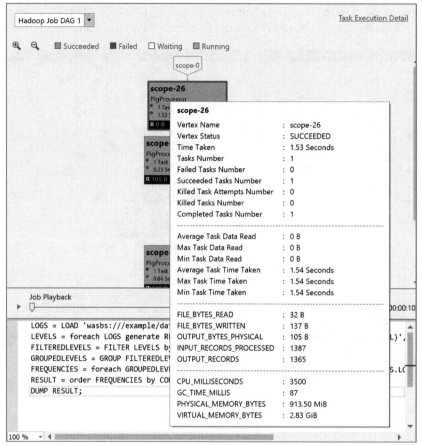

FIGURE 28-10

This goes a long way toward determining which stage is acting like a performance hog (pun intended). But you can get even more detailed information about a stage. Simply click on the Task Execution Detail link that is in the top right corner. The pane shown in Figure 28-11 appears.

In this page, you can start to see where your Pig application is being parallelized. Each of the scopes that appears in Figure 28-9 is shown in the Gantt chart view in the top right of Figure 28-11. You can filter the tasks down using the Smart Query section on the left. These options allow you to focus on failed tasks in your process, the most I/O intensive (for both reading and writing), and the tasks that had the worst throughput. Below the Gantt chart is a list of the scopes, along with information about the time, memory, and I/O used. This allows you to quickly identify the scopes that are taking the most processing time and see if there are ways to optimize your application.

Information about previously executed HDInsight jobs is available through the Server Explorer. Right-click on the HDInsight cluster and choose the View Jobs menu option. A pane similar to the one in Figure 28-12 displays.

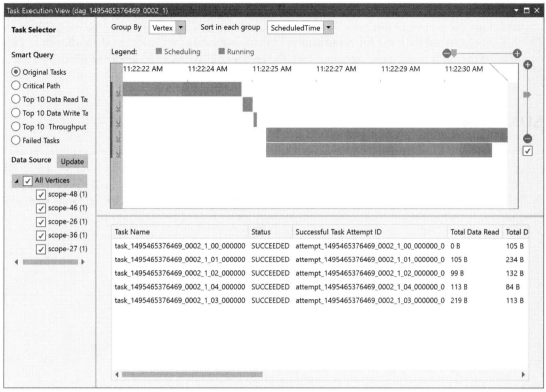

FIGURE 28-11

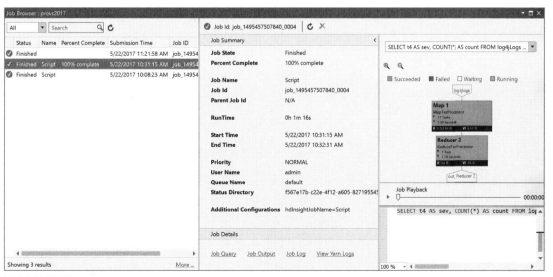

FIGURE 28-12

The screen originally contains just a list of previously executed jobs of all types. That is to say, the list is does not consist of just Hive or Pig batches, but any batch job that was submitted. When you click on any of the jobs, the Job Summary information appears on the right side of the pane. This includes the execution graph, complete with the ability to play back the job and to drill into the details of the job's execution.

SUMMARY

In this chapter you learned about Apache Hadoop and how it can be used to process large quantities of both structured and unstructured data. As well, through the Data Lake Tools for Visual Studio, you are able to create projects that create different types of applications that will run on Hadoop or HDInsight. Some of the visualizations that help developers optimize the HDInsight jobs were also covered.

29

Data Science and Analytics

WHAT'S IN THIS CHAPTER?

➤ Understanding the basic functionality of R

➤ Working with R Interactive Window to execute commands

➤ Creating and manipulating plot windows

WROX.COM CODE DOWNLOADS FOR THIS CHAPTER

The wrox.com code downloads for this chapter can be found at www.wrox.com by searching for this book's ISBN number (978-1-119-40458-3). The code and any related support files are located in their own folder for this chapter.

All developers know that applications need data, and a large number know how to manipulate data to perform the standard operations that applications require. Although that's working with data, it's not data science. The goal of data science is to analyze data, particularly the large volumes produced as "big data." To do that, data scientists need to have skills in statistical methods, data analysis, and working with data at scale.

One of the leading languages used by data analysts is R. R was specifically designed to be used to manipulate and analyze data, and it has deep and powerful integration with data visualizations. When you get right down to it, producing data visualizations helps you convert "data" to "information," which is one of the most important aspects of analyzing data.

Visual Studio 2017 includes a Data Science and Analysis workload that includes the project template and tools to help you take advantage of R. In this chapter, we have a brief overview of what R can do and then examine the tools that have been provided to help with it.

WHAT IS R?

Just because it's way too much fun to not start this way, R is a language derived from S. Created at Bell Laboratories in the 1970s, S is a language used by data scientists to perform statistical operations on datasets. (The "S" is for "Statistics.") R is a different implementation of S, but sufficiently derivative so that most S programs can be compiled and run in the R environment. And an "environment" is really the best way to describe how R is used. In general, the R environment provides the following:

➤ An effective mechanism for accessing data. R has libraries that allow you to integrate with most common database formats.

➤ A collection of operations that are used to work with arrays and matrices.

➤ The ability to generate graphical representations of data to a number of different devices, including on-screen and hardcopy.

➤ A programming language that includes the basics, such as loops, conditionals, recursive functions, and I/O.

The best way to get a sense of R in general and R Tools for Visual Studio in particular is to try it out. To do so, you need to make sure that the Data Science and Analytics workload has been installed into your instance of Visual Studio. This workload includes all of the libraries needed by R, as well as both Python and F#.

R TOOLS FOR VISUAL STUDIO

Developing in R is intended to be an interactive process. You run commands against an R engine, view the results, make adjustments, and try again. The workflow in R Tools is designed to facilitate this type of flow. To start, create an R project. Use File ➪ New ➪ Project to display the New Project dialog (Figure 29-1).

Navigate to the R node on the left side and choose the R Project template. Provide a name for your project and click OK. It takes little time to create a solution, as seen in Figure 29-2.

There are three files in the newly created project.

➤ **.Rhistory:** Contains the command history for your project. As you type commands, this file gets updated, and when you close your project, the file is saved. By doing so, you have your command history available to you the next time you open your project.

➤ *projectname*.**rproj:** The basic settings file for your project. This can be edited manually to change things like the version number, what happens to your workspaces and command history when you save the project, and some other settings related to how code is formatted within the editor window. Figure 29-3 shows the default settings when you create an R project.

➤ **script.R:** An empty file waiting for you to put R script into it.

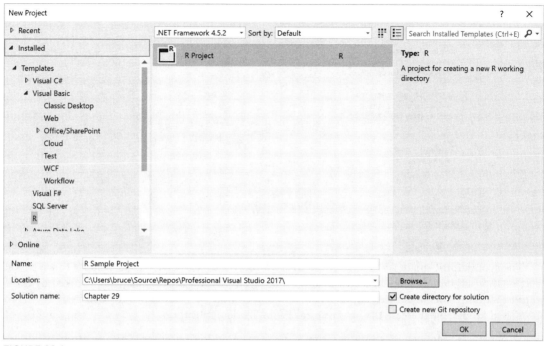

FIGURE 29-1

FIGURE 29-2

Unlike many development efforts in Visual Studio, the starting point for working with R is not the Solution Explorer. Instead, it starts with the R Interactive window (see Figure 29-4).

You activate the R-Interactive window with Ctrl+2 or by using the R Tools ➪ Windows ➪ Interactive menu option.

This window is known as a REPL (Read-Eval-Print Loop). You type commands into the window, each command is evaluated, and the results printed to the window. The commands are cumulative, so that if you use one command to create a function, that function will be available to subsequent commands.

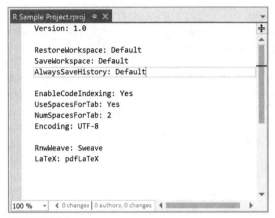

FIGURE 29-3

The syntax for R might seem a little odd to C#/VB.NET developers. This is because R is a functional programming language. Most things that you do within the language are invoked by calling a function. To demonstrate, as well as to show some of the functionality provided by R Tools for Visual Studio, we'll create the prototypical Hello World application.

To get started, double-click on the script.R file in the Solution Explorer. This opens up an editor for your R script. Type in the following lines of code:

```
say_hello <- function(name, extra) {
    print(paste("Hello ", name, "!", sep = ""))
}
```

This code creates a function and assigns it to `say_hello`. There are a number of items to take note of in this short snippet. First, the `<-` is the assignment operator. If you are used to working with C# or Visual Basic, this would typically be the equal sign. And the R editor window is nice enough to recognize that your fingers might actually type = without thinking. It will automatically convert your = into `<-` on your behalf.

The rest of the snippet is relatively straightforward. The `print` function is used to send output to the current window. The `paste` function is used to concatenate strings. You can see that not only are positional parameters allowed, but also named parameters. The `sep` parameter allows you to define the character that appears between each of the parameters passed into `paste`.

Now that the code has been written, it needs to be executed. This involves moving the code to the R Interactive window. Although you could cut and paste the code, the editor window offers a faster way. Select all three lines in the window and use Ctrl+Enter. This copies the code to the interactive window and executes it.

Now that the code has been executed, there is a `say_hello` function available to you. It is available through IntelliSense in the script editor (see Figure 29-5) or in the Interactive window.

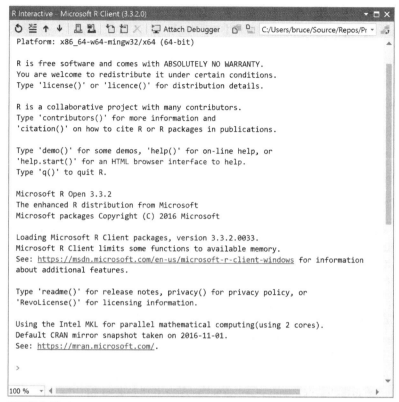

FIGURE 29-4

FIGURE 29-5

To invoke the function, enter the following into the Interactive window:

```
say_hello("gentle reader")
```

The results can be seen in Figure 29-6.

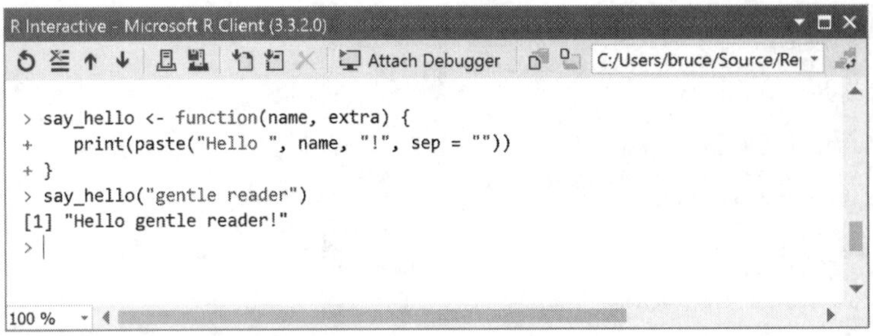

```
R Interactive - Microsoft R Client (3.3.2.0)                     ▾ ⬚ ✕
↺ ⩲ ↑ ↓   ⧉ ⧉  ⧉ ⧉ ✕   🖵 Attach Debugger   ⧉ ⧉  C:/Users/bruce/Source/Rep ▾  ⧉

> say_hello <- function(name, extra) {
+     print(paste("Hello ", name, "!", sep = ""))
+ }
> say_hello("gentle reader")
[1] "Hello gentle reader!"
> |

100 %  ▾  ◂                                                      ▸
```

FIGURE 29-6

Debugging an R Script

R Tools for Visual Studio provide many of the features that you expect from a development language in Visual Studio. Through your interactions with the editor window and the interactive window, you have already seen syntax coloration and IntelliSense support. It is also possible to debug your R application through Visual Studio.

To start, go to the script.R editor window and select the paste function. Push the F9 function button to insert a breakpoint at this location. This sets a breakpoint on this line, but you can set the breakpoint using any of the other techniques available through Visual Studio. As well, you can set Conditions or Actions on the breakpoint.

Once you have the breakpoint configured as you wish, it's a two-step process to launch the script in debug mode. First, you need to attach a debugger. Click on the Attach debugger button that is at the top of the Interactive window (visible in Figure 29-6). This initializes the debugging process for your scripts.

Next, you need to mark the script for debugging. Right-click in the editor window and select Source R Script from the context menu. This causes a debug_source command to be executed in the interactive window. You will see something resembling the following code (it will have your own path to the script.R file) appear in the interactive window.

```
rtvs::debug_source("C:/Users/bruce/Source/Repos/Professional Visual
Studio 2017/Chapter 29/R Sample Project/script.R", encoding = "Windows-1252")
```

This command marks each of the functions found in the script for debugging. After sourcing the script, you can execute the say_hello command. The function will be executed as before, but the breakpoint will be hit, as you can see in Figure 29-7.

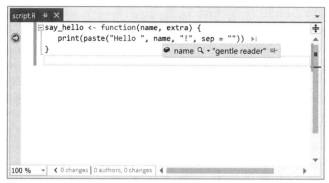

FIGURE 29-7

R Tools for Visual Studio includes many of the debugging features that you would expect, including things like tooltips that display the current value. You can see an example in Figure 29-7 where the current value of name is displayed. This is true even when the value passed into the method is a set of data. Execute the following command in the interactive window:

```
say_hello("gentle reader", mtcars)
```

The mtcars variable is a built-in data collection. It contains 1974 Motor Trend data on fuel consumption and a number of other attributes on more than 30 automobiles. When the command is executed, you will again hit the breakpoint that you previously defined. When you hover over the extra parameter, Figure 29-8 is the result.

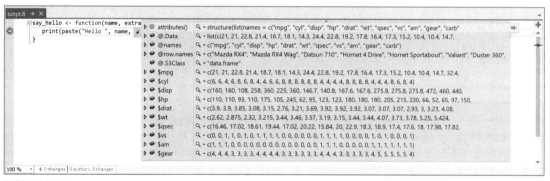

FIGURE 29-8

Tooltips are not the only way to explore a variable while debugging R scripts. You can open the Variable Explorer using Ctrl+8 or R Tools ⇨ Windows ⇨ Variable Explorer menu option. When at the breakpoint, you should see the window that appears in Figure 29-9.

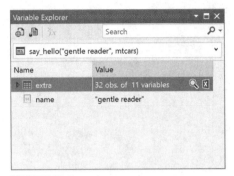

FIGURE 29-9

For simple variables, you can see the current value. For more complicated variables, like the data set, you can expand and view the hierarchy of values and objects. However, data sets also expose two additional methods for viewing the data. When you click the icon at the extreme right of the extra row, it opens Excel and loads the data into a spreadsheet. Another option is to click on the magnifying glass icon to display the details in a separate window, as shown in Figure 29-10.

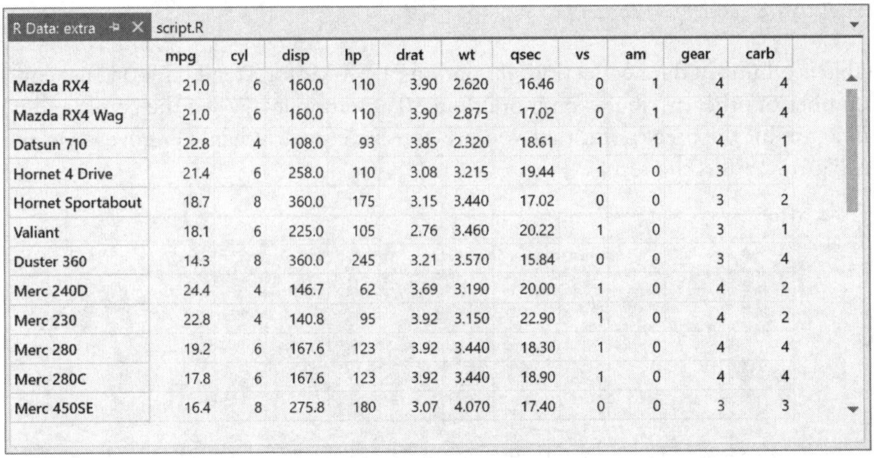

R Data: extra ⊕ ✕	script.R										
	mpg	cyl	disp	hp	drat	wt	qsec	vs	am	gear	carb
Mazda RX4	21.0	6	160.0	110	3.90	2.620	16.46	0	1	4	4
Mazda RX4 Wag	21.0	6	160.0	110	3.90	2.875	17.02	0	1	4	4
Datsun 710	22.8	4	108.0	93	3.85	2.320	18.61	1	1	4	1
Hornet 4 Drive	21.4	6	258.0	110	3.08	3.215	19.44	1	0	3	1
Hornet Sportabout	18.7	8	360.0	175	3.15	3.440	17.02	0	0	3	2
Valiant	18.1	6	225.0	105	2.76	3.460	20.22	1	0	3	1
Duster 360	14.3	8	360.0	245	3.21	3.570	15.84	0	0	3	4
Merc 240D	24.4	4	146.7	62	3.69	3.190	20.00	1	0	4	2
Merc 230	22.8	4	140.8	95	3.92	3.150	22.90	1	0	4	2
Merc 280	19.2	6	167.6	123	3.92	3.440	18.30	1	0	4	4
Merc 280C	17.8	6	167.6	123	3.92	3.440	18.90	1	0	4	4
Merc 450SE	16.4	8	275.8	180	3.07	4.070	17.40	0	0	3	3

FIGURE 29-10

When the Variable Explorer opened, the scope was set to the current method by default. You can change the scope if there are different variables you want to explore. Above the list of variables and their values, there is a dropdown list. This list contains all of the packages that have been installed as well as a scope called .GlobalEnv. This scope contains all of the variables and functions defined at the command-line level. So if you choose .GlobalEnv, you will see the say_hello function.

Workspaces

The idea behind a workspace is to allow you to change where your scripts are running, while maintaining a comparable user experience regardless of where the execution takes place. From a practical perspective, it is likely that you will be developing your R scripts against a subset of the actual data. At some point, you will need to run your script against real data. Workspaces allow you to both define and quickly switch between workspaces.

Figure 29-11 shows a Workspaces window. You can display it using Ctrl+9 or the R Tools ⇨ Windows ⇨ Workspaces menu option.

You can see three separate workspaces have been defined. The Microsoft R Client is the engine that is defined by default when the Data Science and Analytic workload is installed. On this machine, the CRAN 3.4.0 engine has been installed and a workspace has been created that points to the CRAN server. As well, a workspace has been defined against a remote instance of an R Server that is running in Azure.

To define a new workspace, click on the Add link. A section is displayed within the Workspaces window, as seen in Figure 29-12.

FIGURE 29-11

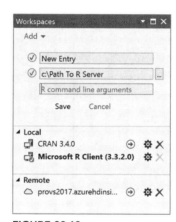

FIGURE 29-12

Provide a name for your entry and either a URL or a path to the R Server executables. For remote entries, you'll need to provide a URL. If you have installed different versions of R locally, then a path is sufficient.

The R Interactive window works against the currently active workspace. This is denoted by a green checkmark in the icon to the left of the name. Currently the Microsoft R Client is the active workspace. To change the workspace, click on the right-pointing arrow icon. This not only changes the workspace, but causes messages indicating the details about the new instance to be displayed. From that point forward, any executed commands will be run on the remote server.

Plotting Windows

One of the strengths of R is its ability to visualize data. Along with some built-in functionality, there are a number of libraries that are available to facilitate this capability. A frequently used one is called ggplot. But to get you started, let's look at the basic plotting functionality. Execute the following command in the interactive window:

```
plot(mtcars@mpg)
```

This generates a plot of the mpg column (for Miles per Gallon) in the mtcars dataset. The result can be seen in Figure 29-13.

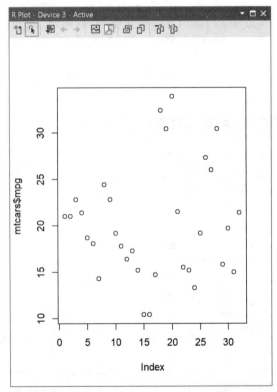

FIGURE 29-13

A second dimension can be added to this plot by executing a slightly different command:

```
plot(mtcars$mpg,mtcars@disp)
```

The result, seen in Figure 29-14, maps the miles per gallon against the engine displacement.

Naturally, there are R functions that will let you generate line graphs, add labels and legends, and change colors for the various elements. But that gets more into the realm of R and out of the realm of Visual Studio. In the plot window, you do have a number of options available to you.

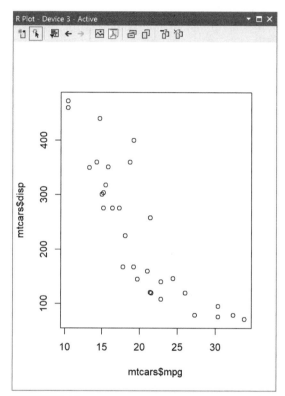

FIGURE 29-14

The first couple of icons allow you to manipulate plot windows. The first icon lets you create a new plot window. The `plot` command sends its output to the currently active plot window. Creating a plot window starts a new window and makes it the active one. The second icon is used to activate that plot window, making it the target for the interactive window's commands.

The next three icons are used to work with the plot history. The first icon launches the Plot History window (Figure 29-15).

These are the most recently created plots. You can zoom in or out on the plots or show them in the window using the Show Plot icon or by clicking the Shot Plot option in the context menu.

Back in the plot window, to the right of the Plot History icon, there are two arrows that let you navigate back and forth through the plot history.

The next four icons let you convert the plot to a different format. It can be saved as an image (.png) or an Adobe Acrobat (.pdf) file. It can also be copied to the clipboard as a bitmap (.bmp) or a Windows Metafile (.wpf).

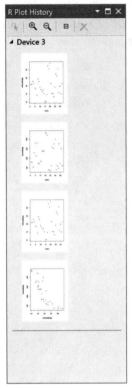

FIGURE 29-15

The last two icons let you remove the last plot that you added to the plot window or to just clear all of the plots from the window. Once the plots have been cleared, they are also removed from the Plot History window.

SUMMARY

If analyzing data is in the list of tasks you need to do regularly (or you're supporting people who do so), then the R language is an incredibly useful tool. With the extensibility provided by Visual Studio, R Tools for Visual Studio has been integrated into the development environment quite seamlessly. In this chapter, we looked at some of the ways that Visual Studio can help increase the productivity of a data analyst who is working with R, both while using the tool and while creating an R Project.

PART IX
Debugging

30

Using the Debugging Windows

WHAT'S IN THIS CHAPTER?

➤ Learning basic debugging concepts in Visual Studio, including breakpoints and DataTips

➤ Understanding the debugging windows in Visual Studio

WROX.COM CODE DOWNLOADS FOR THIS CHAPTER

The wrox.com code downloads for this chapter can be found at www.wrox.com by searching for this book's ISBN number (978-1-119-40458-3). The code and any related support files are located in their own folder for this chapter.

Debugging an application is one of the more challenging tasks developers must tackle, but correct use of the Visual Studio 2017 debugging windows can help you analyze the state of the application and determine the cause of any bugs. This chapter examines the numerous windows available in Visual Studio 2017 to support you in building and debugging applications.

THE CODE WINDOW

The most important window for debugging purposes is the code window. With the capability to set breakpoints and step through code, this window is the starting point for almost all debugging activities. Figure 30-1 shows a simple snippet of code with both a breakpoint (red dot) and the current execution point (yellow arrow) visible.

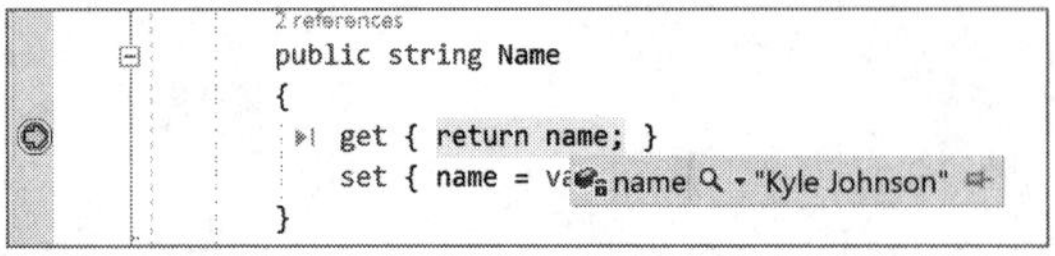

FIGURE 30-1

Breakpoints

The first stage in debugging an application is usually to identify the area causing the error by setting a breakpoint and gradually stepping through the code. Chapter 31, "Debugging with Breakpoints," covers in detail setting breakpoints and working with the current execution point. Breakpoints are marked in the code window with a red dot in the margin of the page and a colored highlighting of the code itself.

When a breakpoint is encountered within a running application, the current execution point is marked with a yellow arrow in the margin, and the actual code is also highlighted in yellow. This marker can be dragged forward and backward to control the order of execution. However, you should do this judiciously because it can impact the behavior of the application.

DataTips

After hitting a breakpoint, the application is paused, or is in Debug Mode. In this mode, you can retrieve information about current variables simply by hovering your mouse over the variable name. Figure 30-1 shows that the value of the name variable is currently "Kyle Johnson." This debugging tooltip is commonly referred to as a DataTip, and you can use it not only to view the values of simple types, such as strings and integers, but also to drill down and inspect more complex object types, such as those made up of multiple nested classes.

> **NOTE** *DataTips are used to both query and edit the value of a variable.*

In Chapter 57, "DataTips, Debug Proxies, and Visualizers," in the online archive, you'll learn how the layout of this DataTip can be customized using type proxies and type visualizers.

THE BREAKPOINTS WINDOW

When debugging a complex issue, you can set numerous breakpoints to isolate the problem. Unfortunately, this has two side effects. One, the execution of the application is hampered because you have to continually press F5 to resume execution. Two, and more significantly, the execution of the application is slowed considerably by the presence of conditional breakpoints, which enable you to specify an expression that is executed to determine if the application should be paused. The more complex the breakpoint conditions are, the slower the application will run. Because these breakpoints can be scattered through multiple source files, it becomes difficult to locate and remove breakpoints that are no longer required.

The Breakpoints window, as shown in Figure 30-2, is accessible via Debug ➪ Windows ➪ Breakpoints and provides a useful summary of all the breakpoints currently set within the application. Using this window, breakpoints can easily be navigated to, disabled, and removed.

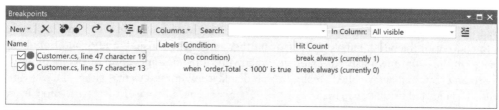

FIGURE 30-2

Two currently active breakpoints are in the `Customer.cs` file (refer to Figure 30-2). The first is a regular breakpoint with no conditions. The second breakpoint has a condition whereby the application will break only if the `order.OrderTotal` property has a value less than 1000.

The Breakpoints window, like most other debugging windows, is made up of two regions: the toolbar and the breakpoint list. Several functions are available on the toolbar in Visual Studio 2017, including search, import, and export of breakpoints. These functions are explained further in Chapter 31, "Debugging with Breakpoints."

Each item in the breakpoint list is represented by a check box that indicates whether or not the breakpoint is enabled, an icon and breakpoint descriptor, and any number of columns that show properties of the breakpoint. The columns can be adjusted using the Columns drop-down from the toolbar. You can set additional breakpoint properties by right-clicking the appropriate breakpoint and choosing the desired option from the context menu.

THE OUTPUT WINDOW

One of the first debugging windows you encounter when you run your application is the Output window. By default, the Output window appears every time you build your application and shows the build progress. Figure 30-3 shows the successful build of a sample solution. The final line of the Output window indicates a summary of the build, which in this case indicates one successfully built project. In the output there is also a summary of the warnings and errors encountered during the build. In this case there were no errors or warnings. Although the Output window can be useful if for some reason the build fails unexpectedly, most of the time the errors and warnings are reported in the Error List.

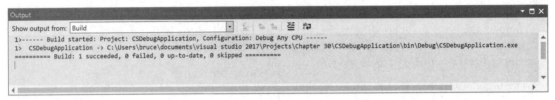

FIGURE 30-3

The Output window has a secondary role as the standard output while the application runs. You can use the drop-down on the left of the toolbar to toggle between output sources. Figure 30-3 shows the output of the build, but as you perform other activities in Visual Studio, additional entries are created in the drop-down list. For example, when you run your application in Debug mode, Visual Studio creates an entry called Debug, which displays any messages that either the run time or your code has emitted using `Debug.Write` or `Debug.WriteLine`. Likewise, a Refactor entry is created to show the results of any recent refactoring operation that was performed.

> **NOTE** *The output from external tools such as* `.bat` *and* `.com` *files that are executed through Visual Studio (as External Tools) is normally displayed in the Command window. The output from these tools can also be displayed in the Output window by setting the Use Output Window option in the Tools ⇨ External Tools dialog box.*

The other icons on the toolbar, in order from left to right, enable you to navigate to the source of a build message, go to the previous message, go to the next message, clear the window contents, and toggle word wrapping for the Output window.

THE IMMEDIATE WINDOW

Often when you write code or debug your application, you want to evaluate a simple expression either to test a bit of functionality or to remind yourself of how something works. This is where the Immediate window (Debug ⇨ Windows ⇨ Immediate) comes in handy. This window enables you to run expressions as you type them. Figure 30-4 shows a number of statements — from basic assignment and print operations to more advanced object creation and manipulation.

A `Customer` object is created in a C# project within the Immediate window (refer to Figure 30-4). Within a Visual Basic project, you can't do explicit variable declaration (for example, Dim x as Integer). Instead it is done implicitly using the assignment operator.

One of the more useful features of the Immediate window is that you can use it while you write code. When you create objects in the Immediate window at design time, it invokes the constructor and creates an instance of that object without running the rest of your application.

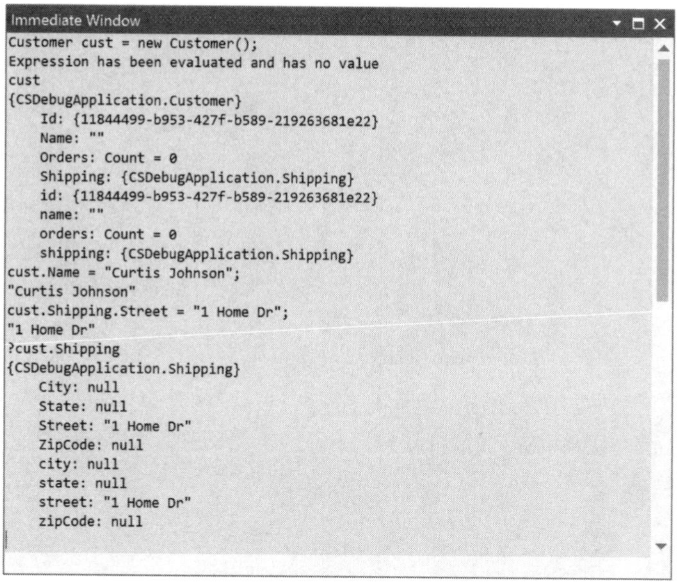

```
Immediate Window                                    ▾ □ X
Customer cust = new Customer();
Expression has been evaluated and has no value
cust
{CSDebugApplication.Customer}
    Id: {11844499-b953-427f-b589-219263681e22}
    Name: ""
    Orders: Count = 0
    Shipping: {CSDebugApplication.Shipping}
    id: {11844499-b953-427f-b589-219263681e22}
    name: ""
    orders: Count = 0
    shipping: {CSDebugApplication.Shipping}
cust.Name = "Curtis Johnson";
"Curtis Johnson"
cust.Shipping.Street = "1 Home Dr";
"1 Home Dr"
?cust.Shipping
{CSDebugApplication.Shipping}
    City: null
    State: null
    Street: "1 Home Dr"
    ZipCode: null
    city: null
    state: null
    street: "1 Home Dr"
    zipCode: null
```

FIGURE 30-4

If you invoke a method or property that contains an active breakpoint, Visual Studio changes to Debug mode and breaks at the breakpoint. This is especially useful if you work on a particular method that you want to test without running the entire application.

The Immediate window supports a limited form of IntelliSense, and you can use the arrow keys to track back through the history of previous commands executed.

> **NOTE** *IntelliSense is supported only in the Immediate window when running in Debug mode, not during design-time debugging.*

The Immediate window also enables you to execute Visual Studio commands. To submit a command, you must enter a greater than symbol (>) at the start of the line. There is an extremely large set of commands available; almost any action that can be performed within Visual Studio is accessible as a command. Fortunately, IntelliSense makes navigating this list of available commands more manageable.

There is also a set of approximately 100 predefined aliases for commands. One of the more well-known aliases is ?, which is a shortcut for the Debug.Print command that prints out the value of a variable. You can see the full list of predefined aliases by entering >alias, as shown in Figure 30-5.

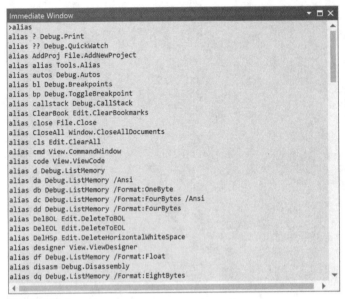

```
Immediate Window                                      ▾ □ ✕
>alias
alias ? Debug.Print
alias ?? Debug.QuickWatch
alias AddProj File.AddNewProject
alias alias Tools.Alias
alias autos Debug.Autos
alias bl Debug.Breakpoints
alias bp Debug.ToggleBreakpoint
alias callstack Debug.CallStack
alias ClearBook Edit.ClearBookmarks
alias close File.Close
alias CloseAll Window.CloseAllDocuments
alias cls Edit.ClearAll
alias cmd View.CommandWindow
alias code View.ViewCode
alias d Debug.ListMemory
alias da Debug.ListMemory /Ansi
alias db Debug.ListMemory /Format:OneByte
alias dc Debug.ListMemory /Format:FourBytes /Ansi
alias dd Debug.ListMemory /Format:FourBytes
alias DelBOL Edit.DeleteToBOL
alias DelEOL Edit.DeleteToEOL
alias DelHSp Edit.DeleteHorizontalWhiteSpace
alias designer View.ViewDesigner
alias df Debug.ListMemory /Format:Float
alias disasm Debug.Disassembly
alias dq Debug.ListMemory /Format:EightBytes
```

FIGURE 30-5

THE WATCH WINDOWS

Earlier in this chapter you saw how to use DataTips in the code window to examine the content of a variable by hovering the mouse over a variable name. When the structure of the object is more complex, it becomes difficult to navigate the values using just the DataTip. Visual Studio 2017 has a series of Watch windows that display variables, providing an easy-to-use interface for drilling down into the structure.

QuickWatch

The QuickWatch window (Debug ➪ QuickWatch) is a modal dialog that you can launch by right-clicking the code window. Whatever you select in the code window is inserted into the Expression field of the dialog, as shown in Figure 30-6, where a myCustomer object is visible. Previous expressions you have evaluated appear in the drop-down associated with the Expression field.

The layout of the Value tree in the QuickWatch window is similar to the DataTip. Each row shows the variable name, the current value, and the type of object. The value of the variable can be adjusted by typing in the Value column.

Use the Add Watch button to add the current expression to one of the Watch windows. These are variables to be continuously watched.

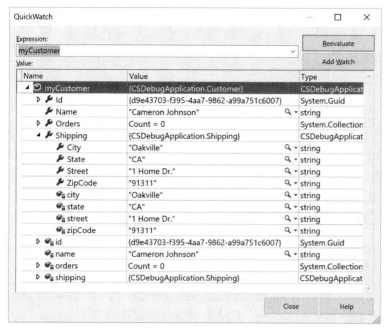

FIGURE 30-6

Watch Windows 1–4

Unlike the QuickWatch window, which is modal and shows a variable value at a particular execution point, you can use the Watch windows to monitor a variable value as you step through your code. Although there are four Watch windows, a single window is sufficient in most cases. Having four separate windows means that you can have different sets of variables in the different windows, which might be useful if you work through a more complex issue that involves multiple classes.

Figure 30-7 shows a myOrder and myCustomer class in a Watch window (Debug ➪ Windows ➪ Watch 1 to Watch 4). Similar to both the QuickWatch window and the DataTips discussed previously, you can use the user interface to drill down into more complex data types.

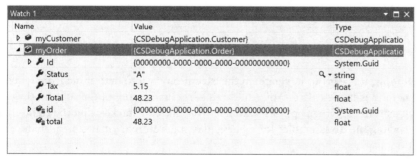

FIGURE 30-7

Additional variables to be watched can be added either by typing into the Name column on an empty line or by right-clicking the variable in the code window and selecting Add Watch from the context menu.

Autos and Locals

The Autos and Locals windows are two special Watch windows in which the variables are automatically added by the debugger. The Autos window (Debug ➪ Windows ➪ Autos) contains variables that are used in the current, preceding, and future lines of code. Similarly, the Locals window (Debug ➪ Windows ➪ Locals) shows all variables used in the current method. Other than being automatically generated, these windows behave the same as the Watch windows.

THE CODE EXECUTION WINDOWS

In addition to inspecting the contents of variables during a debugging session, it is essential that you carefully evaluate the logic of your code to ensure that everything executes in the order that you expect. Visual Studio 2017 has a group of debugger windows that show exactly what was loaded and being executed at the time you paused the program execution. This allows you to better understand the run-time behavior of your source code and quickly track down logic errors.

Call Stack

As applications grow in complexity, it is quite common for the execution path to become difficult to follow. The use of deep inheritance trees and interfaces can often obscure the execution path. This is where the call stack is useful. Each path of execution must have a finite number of entries on the stack (unless a cyclic pattern emerges, in which case a stack overflow is inevitable). The stack can be viewed using the Call Stack window (Debug ➪ Windows ➪ Call Stack), as shown in Figure 30-8.

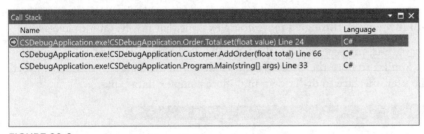

FIGURE 30-8

Using the Call Stack window, it is easy to navigate up the execution path to determine from where the current executing method is being called. You can do this by clicking any of the rows in the call stack, which are known as frames. Other options available from the call stack, using the right-click context menu, enable viewing the disassembler for a particular stack frame, setting breakpoints, and varying what information displays.

Threads

Most applications use multiple threads at some point. In particular for Windows applications, you need to run time-consuming tasks on a thread separate from the main application for the user interface to always appear responsive. Of course, concurrent execution of threads makes debugging more difficult, especially when the threads access the same classes and methods.

Figure 30-9 shows the Threads window (Debug ➪ Windows ➪ Threads), which lists all the active threads for a particular application. Notice that in addition to the threads created in the code, the debugger has created additional background threads. For simplicity, the threads used by this application, including the main user interface thread, have been given names so that they can easily be distinguished.

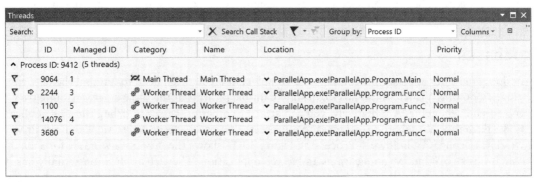

FIGURE 30-9

The Threads window shows an arrow next to the thread currently viewed in the code window. To navigate to another thread, simply double-click that thread to bring the current location of that thread into view in the code window and update the call stack to reflect the new thread.

In Break mode, all threads of an application are paused. However, when you step through your code with the debugger, the next statement to be executed may or may not be on the same thread you are interested in. If you are interested only in the execution path of a single thread, and the execution of other threads can be suspended, right-click the thread in the Threads window, and select Freeze from the context menu. To resume the suspended thread, select Thaw from the same menu.

Debugging multithreaded applications is explained further in Chapter 59, "Advanced Debugging Techniques" in the on-line archive.

Modules

The Modules window (Debug ➪ Windows ➪ Modules), as shown in Figure 30-10, displays a list of assemblies referenced by the running application. Those assemblies that make up the application can also have debugging symbols loaded, which means that they can be debugged without dropping into the disassembler. This window is particularly useful if you want to find the version of an assembly currently loaded and where it has been loaded from.

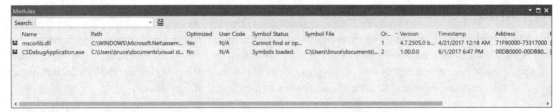

FIGURE 30-10

The symbols have been loaded for the `CSDebugApplication.exe` application (refer to Figure 30-10). The other assembly has been skipped because they contain no user code and are optimized. If an appropriate symbol file is available, you can load it for an assembly via the Load Symbols option from the right-click context menu.

Processes

Building multitier applications can be quite complex, and you often need to have all the tiers running. To do this, Visual Studio 2017 can start multiple projects at the same stage, enabling true end-to-end debugging. Alternatively, you can attach to other processes to debug running applications. Each time Visual Studio attaches to a process, that process is added to the list in the Processes window (Debug ➪ Windows ➪ Processes). Figure 30-11 shows the Processes window for a solution containing two Windows applications and a web application. The web application actually has two processes associated with it, one for the server-side code (`iisexpress.exe`) and one for the client-side code (`iexplore.exe`).

Name ▲	ID	Path	Title	State	Debugging	Connection...	Connection...
CSDebugApplic...	19900	C:\Users\bruce\...	C:\Users\bruce\documents\visual studio 20...	Running	IntelliTrace, Ma...	Default	DESKTOP-8...
ParallelApp.exe	19844	C:\Users\bruce\...	C:\Users\bruce\documents\visual studio 20...	Running	IntelliTrace, Ma...	Default	DESKTOP-8...
iexplore.exe	15316	C:\Program Files...	C:\Program Files (x86)\Internet Explorer\iex...	Running	Script	Default	DESKTOP-8...
iisexpress.exe	9316	C:\Program Files...	C:\Program Files (x86)\IIS Express\iisexpress....	Running	IntelliTrace, Ma...	Default	DESKTOP-8...

FIGURE 30-11

The toolbar at the top of the Processes window enables you to detach or terminate a process that is currently attached or attach to another process.

THE MEMORY WINDOWS

The next three windows are typically used for low-level debugging when all other alternatives have been exhausted. Stepping into memory locations, using a disassembler, or looking at Registry values requires a lot of background knowledge and patience to analyze and make use of the information presented. Only in rare cases while developing managed code would you be required to perform debugging at such a low level.

Memory Windows 1–4

You can use the four Memory windows to view the raw contents of memory at a particular address. Whereas the Watch, Autos, and Locals windows provide a way to look at the content of variables, which are stored at specific locations in memory, the Memory window shows you the big picture of what is stored in memory.

Each of the four Memory windows (Debug ➪ Windows ➪ Memory 1 to Memory 4) can examine different memory addresses to simplify debugging your application. Figure 30-12 shows an example of the information that displays when using this window. You can use the scrollbar on the right of the window to navigate forward or backward through the memory addresses to view information contained in neighboring addresses. If you're trying to find the address of a particular variable, simply type that variable into the Address section at the top of the window. The address of the variable replaces the variable name in the Address section and the body of the window shows the memory around that address.

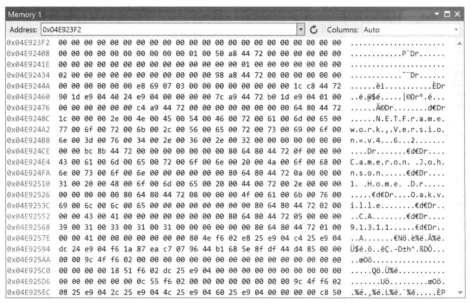

FIGURE 30-12

Disassembly

Interesting debates arise periodically over the relative performance of two different code blocks. Occasionally this discussion devolves to talking about which MSIL instructions are used, and why one code block is faster because it generates one fewer instruction. Clearly, if you call that code block millions of times, disassembly might give your application a significant benefit. However, more often than not, a bit of high-level refactoring saves more time and involves less arguing. Figure 30-13 shows the Disassembly window (Debug ➪ Windows ➪ Disassembly) where a new GUID is created and then assigned to a variable. You can see MSIL instructions that make up this action.

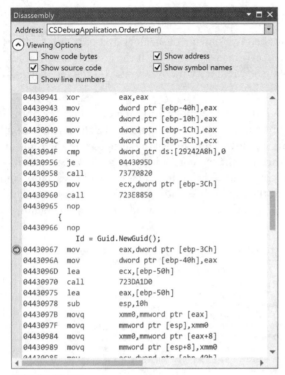

FIGURE 30-13

A breakpoint has been set on the call to the constructor, and the execution point is at this breakpoint (refer to Figure 30-13). While still in this window, you can step through the lines of MSIL and review what instructions are executed.

Registers

Using the Disassembly window to step through MSIL instructions can become difficult to follow as different information is loaded, moved, and compared using a series of registers. The Registers window (Debug ➪ Windows ➪ Registers), as shown in Figure 30-14, enables the contents of the various registers to be monitored. Changes in a register value are highlighted in red, making it easy to see what happens as each line steps through in the Disassembly window.

```
Registers                                                     ▾ ☐ ✕
EAX = 00000000 EBX = 003DF09C ECX = 046E2600 EDX = 029D37A0 ESI = 046E24D0
   EDI = 003DEFEC EIP = 04430967 ESP = 003DEF48 EBP = 003DEF98 EFL = 00000246

0x003DEF5C = 046E2600
```

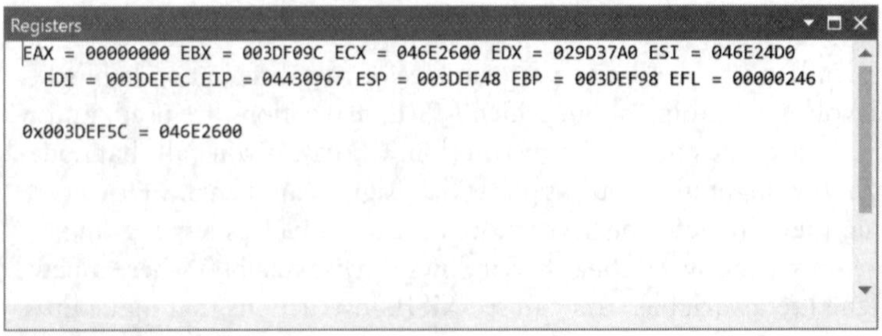

FIGURE 30-14

THE PARALLEL DEBUGGING WINDOWS

Nowadays it is almost impossible to purchase a new computer that has a single processor. The trend to include multiple CPUs, which has been necessary due to physical limitations that have been reached in CPU architecture, will certainly continue into the future as the primary way for hardware vendors to release faster computers.

Unfortunately, software that has not been written to explicitly run on multiple CPUs does not run faster on a multi-core machine. This is a problem for many users who have been conditioned over the past couple of decades to expect their applications to run faster when they upgrade to newer hardware.

The solution is to ensure that your applications can execute different code paths concurrently on multiple CPUs. The traditional approach is to develop software using multiple threads or processes. Unfortunately, writing and debugging multithreaded applications is difficult and error-prone, even for an experienced developer.

Visual Studio 2017 and .NET Framework (since version 4.6) include a number of features aimed to simplify the act of writing such software. The Task Parallel Library (TPL) is a set of extensions to the .NET Framework to provide this functionality. The TPL includes language constructs, such as the `Parallel.For` and `Parallel.ForEach` loops, and collections specifically designed for concurrent access, including `ConcurrentDictionary` and `ConcurrentQueue`.

In the `System.Threading.Tasks` namespace are several classes that greatly simplify the effort involved in writing multithreaded and asynchronous code. The `Task` class is similar to a thread; however, it is more lightweight and therefore performs much better at run time.

Writing parallel applications is only one part of the overall development life cycle — you also need effective tools for debugging parallel applications. To that end Visual Studio 2017 includes two debugging windows aimed specifically at parallel debugging — the Parallel Stacks window and the Parallel Tasks window.

Parallel Stacks

You can use the Call Stack window to view the execution path of the current line of code when debugging. One of the limitations of this window is that you can see only a single call stack at a time. To see the call stack of other threads, you must use the Threads window or Debug Location toolbar to switch the debugger to a different thread.

The Parallel Stacks window (Debug ⇨ Windows ⇨ Parallel Stacks), as shown in Figure 30-15, is one of the more useful windows for debugging multithreaded and parallelized applications. It provides not just a way to view multiple call stacks at once but also provides a graphical visualization of the code execution, including showing how multiple threads are tied together and the execution paths that they share.

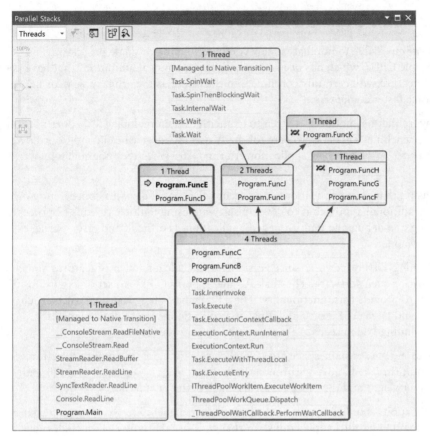

FIGURE 30-15

The Parallel Stacks window in Figure 30-15 shows an application currently executing multiple threads. The call graph is read from bottom to top. The Main thread appears in one box (bottom left), and the other threads are grouped together in different boxes. The reason for these threads being grouped is because they share the same call stack. For example, at the current break-point, there are four threads that share a call stack that starts with _ThreadPoolWaitCallback .PerformWaitCallback and ends (at the top) with FuncC. Of those four threads, one continues on to execute FuncD and FuncE. Another executes FuncF, FuncG, and FuncH. The last two threads start with executing FuncI and FuncJ before splitting their call stack into FuncK on one hand and a Task.Wait on the other. You can see how visualizing all the call stacks at once provides a much better understanding of the state of the application as a whole and what has led to this state, rather than just the history of an individual thread.

A number of other icons are used on this screen. The execution point of the current thread is shown with a yellow arrow. This is against FuncE in a box on the center left side of the diagram (refer to

Figure 30-15). Each box that the current thread has progressed through as part of its execution path is highlighted in blue. The wavy lines (also known as the cloth thread icon) shown against the calls to FuncK and FuncH in the top-right boxes indicates that these are the current execution points of a noncurrent thread.

You can hover over the thread count label at the top of each box to see the Thread IDs of the applicable threads. You can also right-click any entry in a call stack to access various functions such as navigating to the applicable line of source code in the code editor or switching the visualization to a different thread.

If you work with an application that uses numerous threads or tasks, or has a deep call stack, you may find that the Parallel Stacks call graph visualization does not fit into one window. In this case a thumbnail view appears in the bottom-right corner of the window, which enables you to easily pan around the visualization. You can see this in Figure 30-16.

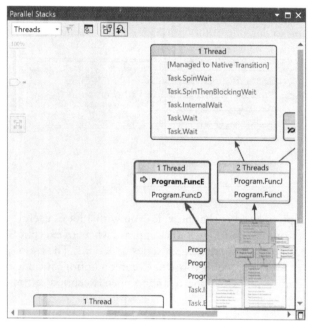

FIGURE 30-16

Parallel Tasks

At the beginning of this section, the Task Parallel Library was introduced, which includes the `Task` class found in `System.Threading.Tasks` and the `Parallel.For` loops. The Tasks window (Debug ➪ Windows ➪ Tasks), as shown in Figure 30-17, assists you in debugging applications that use these features by displaying a list with the state of all the current tasks.

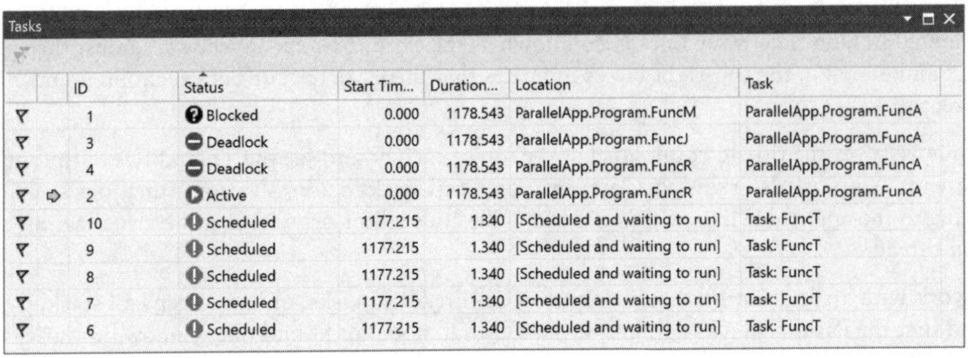

FIGURE 30-17

The application that has been paused has created a variety of tasks that are running, deadlocked, or in a waiting state. You can click the flag icon to flag one or more tasks for easier tracking.

> **NOTE** `Parallel.For`, `Parallel.ForEach`, *and the Parallel LINQ library (PLINQ) use the* `System.Threading.Tasks.Task` *class as part of their underlying implementation.*

EXCEPTIONS

Visual Studio 2017 has a sophisticated exception handler that provides you with a lot of useful information. Figure 30-18 shows the Exception Assistant screen that appears when an exception is raised. In addition to providing more information, it also displays a series of actions. The list of possible actions varies depending on the type of exception being thrown. Common options include the ability to view details of the exception, to copy it to the clipboard, and to open exception settings.

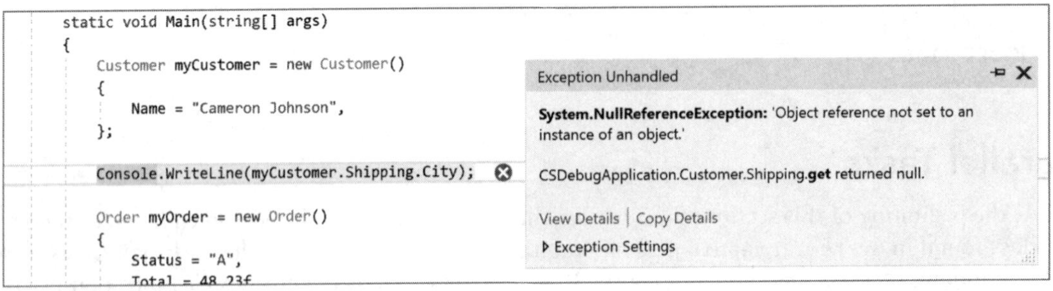

FIGURE 30-18

If you select the View Details action item from the exception, you are presented with a modal dialog that provides a breakdown of the exception that was raised. Figure 30-19 shows the attributes of the exception, including the Stack Trace, which can be viewed by using the Text Visualizer associated with the property value.

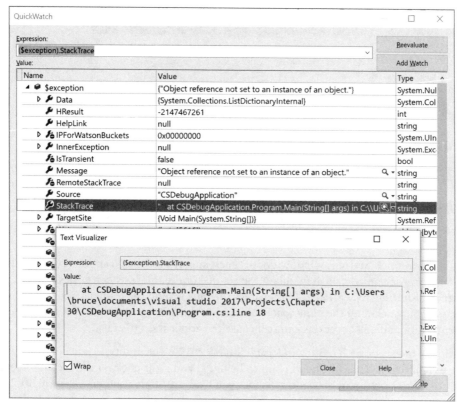

FIGURE 30-19

Of course, at times exceptions are used to control the execution path in an application. For example, some user input may not adhere to a particular formatting constraint, and instead of using a Regular Expression to determine whether or not it matches, a parse operation has been attempted on the string. When this fails, it raises an exception, which can easily be trapped without stopping the entire application.

By default, all exceptions are trapped by the debugger because they are assumed to be exceptions to the norm that shouldn't have happened. In special cases, such as invalid user input, it may be important to ignore specific types of exceptions. This can be done via the Exceptions window, accessible from the Debug menu.

Figure 30-20 shows the Exception Settings window (Debug ⇨ Exception Settings), which lists all the exception types that exist in the .NET Framework. Each exception has two debugging options. The debugger can be set to break when an exception is thrown, regardless of whether or not it is handled. If the Just My Code option has been enabled (which is defined across all of the projects in your solution in Tools ⇨ Options, then Debugging ⇨ General), checking the check box causes the debugger to break (that is, pause execution) any time that exception is not handled within a user code region. More information on Just My Code is provided in Chapter 57, "DataTips, Debug Proxies, and Visualizers," in the online archive.

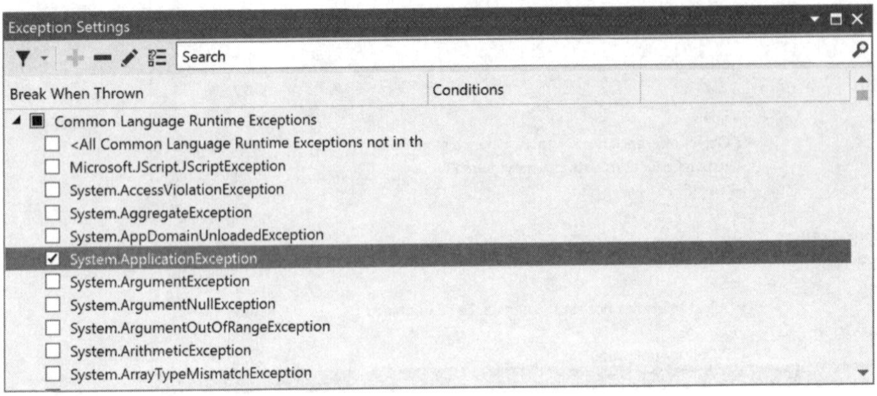

FIGURE 30-20

Unfortunately, the Exception Settings window doesn't pick up any custom exception types that you may have created, but you can add them manually. Select one of the top-level categories (such as Common Language Runtime Exceptions). This enables the plus icon in the toolbar. You need to provide the full class name, including the namespace; otherwise, the debugger cannot break on handled exceptions. Clearly, unhandled exceptions can still cause the application to crash.

One of the additions to exception handling in Visual Studio 2017 is the ability to add conditions when handling exceptions will cause a breakpoint to be hit. If you right-click on the exception and select the Edit Conditions option in the context menu, you'll see the dialog shown in Figure 30-21 appear.

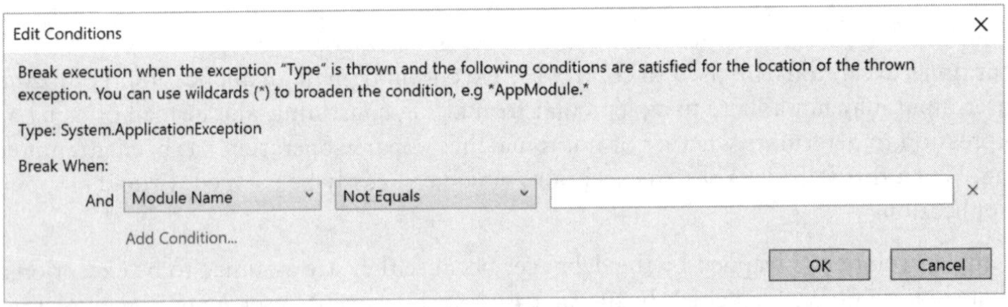

FIGURE 30-21

Here you can specify which modules the breakpoint functionality is used in. The only condition you can add is to select the module names to be considered. It is possible, however, to use an asterisk (*) as a wild card when specifying the module name in the condition.

SUMMARY

This chapter has described each of the debugging windows in detail so that you can optimize your debugging experience. Although the number of windows can seem somewhat overwhelming at first, they each perform an isolated task or provide access to a specific piece of information about the running application. You can easily learn to navigate between them, returning to those that provide the most relevant information for you.

31

Debugging with Breakpoints

WHAT'S IN THIS CHAPTER?

➤ Using breakpoints, conditional breakpoints, and tracepoints to pause code execution

➤ Controlling the program execution during debug by stepping through code

➤ Modifying your code while it runs using the Edit and Continue feature

WROX.COM CODE DOWNLOADS FOR THIS CHAPTER

The wrox.com code downloads for this chapter can be found at www.wrox.com by searching for this book's ISBN number (978-1-119-40458-3). The code and any related support files are located in their own folder for this chapter.

Long gone are the days when debugging an application involved adding superfluous output statements to track down where an application was failing. Visual Studio 2017 provides a rich, interactive debugging experience that includes breakpoints, tracepoints, and the Edit and Continue feature. This chapter covers how you can use these features to debug your application.

BREAKPOINTS

A *breakpoint* is used to pause, or break, an application at a particular point of execution. An application that has been paused is in Break mode, causing a number of the Visual Studio 2017 windows to become active. For example, you can use the Watch window to view variable values. Figure 31-1 shows a breakpoint added to the constructor of the Customer class. The application breaks on this line if the Customer class constructor is called.

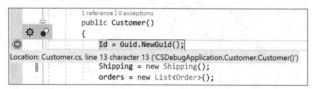

FIGURE 31-1

Setting a Breakpoint

You can set breakpoints either through the Debug menu, using the Toggle Breakpoint item from the right-click context menu, or by using the keyboard shortcut F9. The Visual Studio 2017 code editor also provides a shortcut for setting a breakpoint using a single mouse-click in the margin. An application can be paused only on a line of executing code. This means that a breakpoint set on either a comment or a variable declaration is repositioned to the next line of executable code when the application is run.

Simple Breakpoints

You can set a breakpoint on a line of code by placing the cursor on that line and enabling a breakpoint using any of the following methods:

➤ Selecting Toggle Breakpoint from the Debug menu

➤ Pressing F9

➤ Clicking once in the margin of the code window with the mouse

Once a breakpoint has been set for a line, additional details for the breakpoint can be specified through Settings. You can access Settings by right-clicking the content menu or hovering your mouse over the breakpoint icon in the margin and clicking on the gear image (see Figure 31-1). Both actions cause the Settings subwindow to appear (see Figure 31-2). In this window, you can see that the breakpoint is set at line 13 of the Customer.cs file. There is also a character number that indicates the character position in the line where the breakpoint is set. This is only really useful when multiple statements appear on a single line. Clicking on the link where that information appears changes the interface to allow for modification of the line and character position, as shown in Figure 31-3.

Function Breakpoints

Another type of breakpoint that you can set is a function breakpoint. The usual way to set a breakpoint on a function is to select the function signature and either press F9 or use the mouse to create a breakpoint. In the case of multiple overloads, this requires you to locate all the overloads and add the appropriate breakpoints (unless, of course, your intent is to set a breakpoint within one specific overload). Setting a function breakpoint enables you to set a breakpoint on one or more functions by specifying the function name.

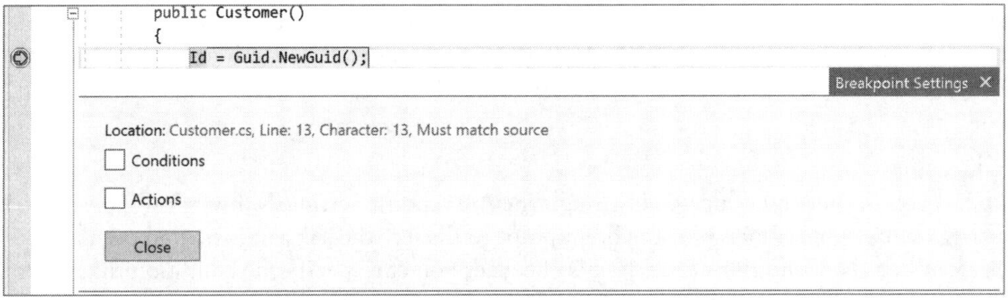

FIGURE 31-2

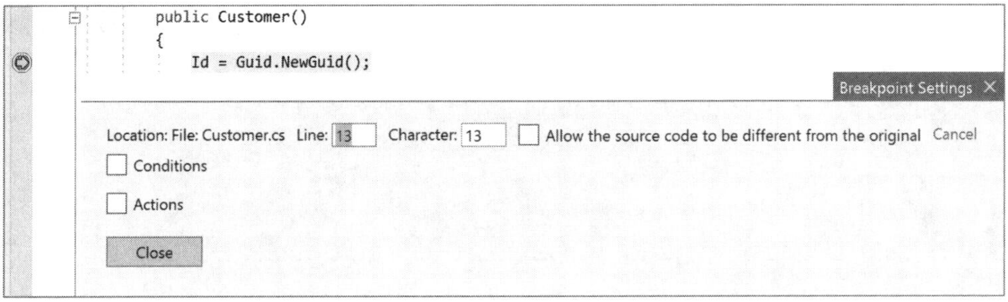

FIGURE 31-3

To set a function breakpoint, from the New Breakpoint item on the Debug menu, select Function Breakpoint. This loads the New Function Breakpoint dialog, as shown in Figure 31-4, in which you can specify the name of the function on which to break.

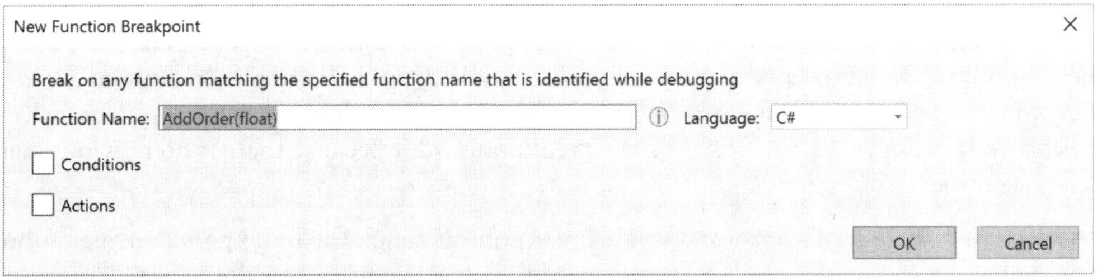

FIGURE 31-4

When setting a function breakpoint, you can specify either the exact overload you want to set the breakpoint on or just the function name. In Figure 31-4, the overload with a single float parameter has been selected. Unlike a full method signature, which requires a parameter name, to select a particular function overload, you should provide only the parameter type. If you omit the parameter information and there are multiple overloads, a breakpoint is set in every method.

Adding Break Conditions

Though breakpoints are useful for pausing an application at a given point to review variables and watch application flow, if you are looking for a particular scenario, it may be necessary to break only when certain conditions are valid. Breakpoints can be tailored to search for particular conditions, to break after a number of iterations, or even to be filtered based on process or machine name.

Condition

A breakpoint condition can be specified through the Breakpoint Settings subwindow. Select Settings from the right-click context menu for the breakpoint to display the subwindow, as shown in Figure 31-5. When the Conditions checkbox is checked, you can specify the condition that must be met before execution halts when the breakpoint is reached. If the condition evaluates to `false`, the application continues past the breakpoint without breaking.

FIGURE 31-5

In Figure 31-5, which is for a breakpoint set within the `Order` class, the condition specifies that the order total must be greater than 1,000. As with most debugging windows, the Condition field provides rich IntelliSense support to aid writing valid conditions. If an invalid condition is specified, the debugger throws an appropriate error message and the application breaks the first time the breakpoint is reached.

Sometimes it is more relevant to know when the value of this condition changes rather than when it is true. The When Changed option available in the middle drop-down in the Breakpoint Settings subwindow breaks the application when the value of the condition changes. If this option is selected, the application does not break the first time the breakpoint is hit because there is no previous status to compare against.

You can specify multiple conditions for a single breakpoint through the Breakpoint Settings subwindow. You do this by clicking on the Add condition link below the first drop-down box. However, you can only specify a condition of each type once. For example, Figure 31-6 illustrates the Breakpoint Settings subwindow with a second condition added. Note that in the visible drop-down, Conditional Expression is not a valid choice. (It was already used for the first condition.)

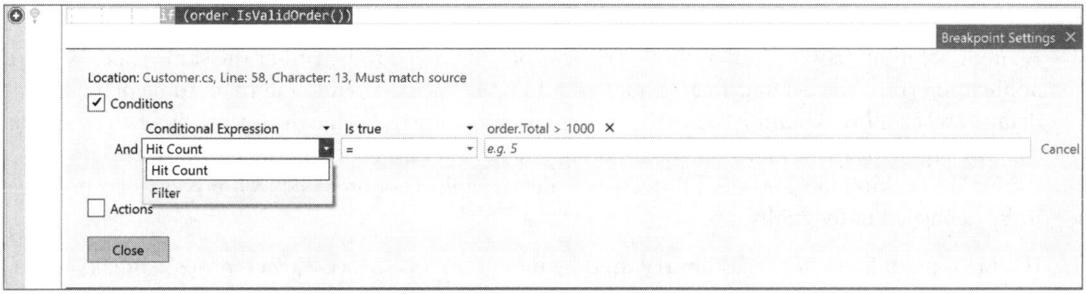

FIGURE 31-6

> **NOTE** *Using multiple breakpoints with complex conditions can significantly slow down the execution of your application, so it is recommended that you remove breakpoints that are no longer relevant in order to speed up the running of your application.*

Hit Count

Though it's perhaps not as useful as breakpoint conditions, it is also possible to break after a particular number of iterations through a breakpoint. This is defined through the Conditions in the Breakpoint Settings subwindow. Choose Hit Count from the condition type drop-down, as illustrated in Figure 31-7.

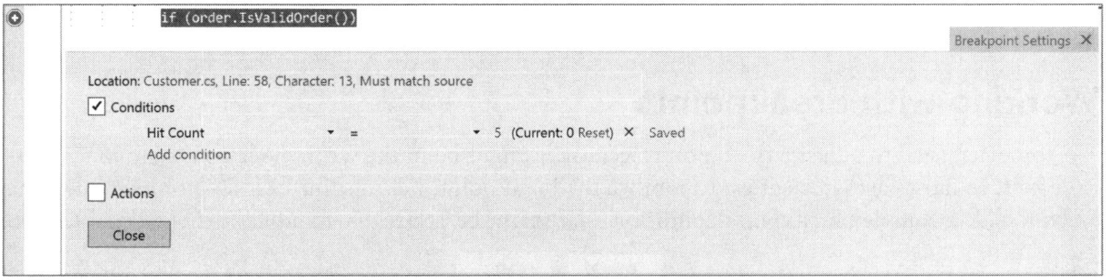

FIGURE 31-7

Every time the application runs, the hit count is reset to zero and can be manually reset using the Reset link. The hit count is unique to each breakpoint. The hit count condition (selected from the middle drop-down) can be one of three options:

➤ **Is Equal To (=):** Break if the hit count is equal to the value specified.

➤ **Multiple Of:** Break if the hit count is a multiple of the value specified.

➤ **Is Greater Than or Equal To (>=):** Break if the hit count is greater than or equal to the value specified.

Filter

A single solution may contain multiple applications that need to be run at the same time. When the application runs, the debugger can attach to all these processes, enabling them to be debugged. By default, when a breakpoint is reached, all the processes break. You can control this behavior from the Debugging (General) node in the Options window, accessible from the Options item on the Tools menu. Unchecking the Break All Processes When One Process Breaks check box enables processes to be debugged individually.

If a breakpoint is set in a class library used by more than one process, each process breaks when it reaches that breakpoint. Because you might be interested in debugging only one of these processes, you can place a filter on the breakpoint that limits it to the process you are interested in. If you debug applications on multiple machines, you also can specify a machine name filter.

Filtering can be useful for a multithreaded application for which you want to limit the breakpoints to a particular thread. Although the breakpoint is triggered only when a thread matches the filter criteria, all threads still pause. Figure 31-8 shows the Filter condition in the Breakpoint Settings sub-window, along with the possible filter conditions.

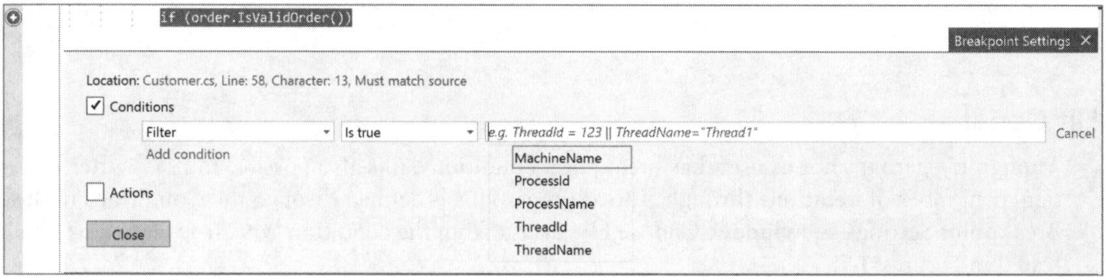

FIGURE 31-8

Working with Breakpoints

You often need to adjust a breakpoint because it might be in the wrong location or no longer relevant. In most cases it is easiest to remove the breakpoint, but in some cases — for example, when you have a complex breakpoint condition — it might be preferable to adjust the existing breakpoint.

Deleting Breakpoints

To remove a breakpoint that is no longer required, select it, either in the code editor or in the Breakpoints window (accessed through the Debug ➪ Windows ➪ Breakpoints menu option and shown in Figure 31-9), and remove it using the Toggle Breakpoint item from the Debug menu. Alternatively, the Delete Breakpoint item from the right-click context menu or the Delete Breakpoint icon from the Breakpoints window toolbar can remove the breakpoint. As you might expect, any configuration regarding the deleted breakpoint (such as conditions, filters, and so on) is lost.

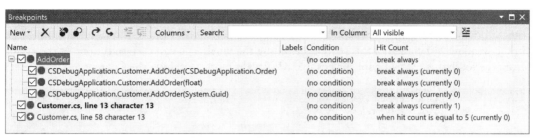

FIGURE 31-9

Disabling Breakpoints

Instead of deleting a breakpoint, simply disabling the breakpoint can be useful when you have a breakpoint condition set or you track a hit count. To disable a breakpoint, select it either in the code editor or in the Breakpoints window, and disable it using the Disable Breakpoint item from the right-click context menu. Or, from the code editor, hover over the breakpoint in the margin and then click on the Disable Breakpoint icon (the one on the right) that appears. Alternatively, you can uncheck the check box against the breakpoint in the Breakpoints window. Figure 31-10 shows how a disabled breakpoint would appear in the code window.

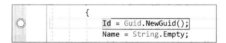

FIGURE 31-10

Labeling Breakpoints

Visual Studio 2017 includes the capability to assign a label to a breakpoint. This is particularly useful if you want to group a set of related breakpoints together. When labeled, you can search for and perform a bulk action on all breakpoints with a specific label.

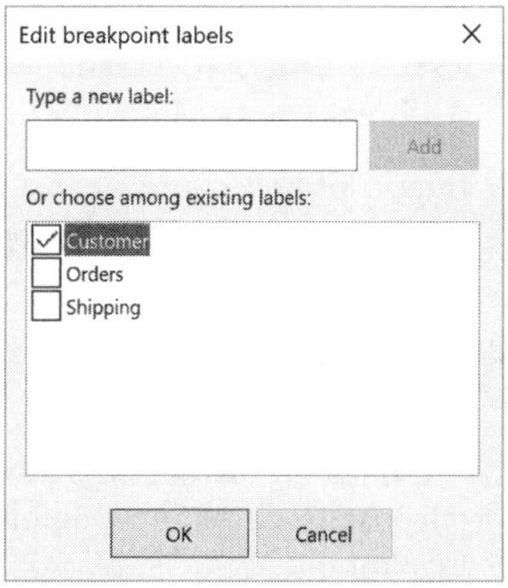

To assign a label to a breakpoint, right-click the breakpoint, and choose Edit Labels. This displays the Edit Breakpoint Labels dialog, as shown in Figure 31-11, where you can attach one or more labels to the breakpoint.

After you have labeled your breakpoints, you can perform bulk actions on them by opening the Breakpoints window (Debug ⇨ Windows ⇨ Breakpoints). This window, as shown

FIGURE 31-11

in Figure 31-12, enables you to filter the list by typing a value in the Search box and pressing Enter. Once you do so, only those breakpoints that contain the search value are displayed. Each column in the window is included in this search, including the label. You can then select one of the actions from the toolbar, such as Enable or Disable All Breakpoints Matching the Current Search Criteria.

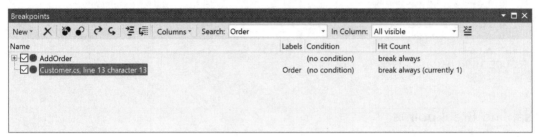

FIGURE 31-12

> **NOTE** *By default, the search will be performed across all columns shown in the Breakpoints window. You can limit the search to specific columns by changing the Columns drop-down from All Visible to a specific column.*

Import and Export of Breakpoints

Another debugging feature provided by Visual Studio 2017 is the import and export of breakpoints. This feature enables you to back up and restore breakpoints, and share them among developers.

Export of breakpoints is performed from the Breakpoints window (Debug ⇨ Windows ⇨ Breakpoints). If you want to export only a subset of your breakpoints, first filter the list by entering a search criterion. When the list of breakpoints that you want to export displays, click the Export All Breakpoints Matching the Current Search Criteria button from the toolbar.

Import of breakpoints can also be performed from the Breakpoints window by clicking the appropriate button on the toolbar.

TRACEPOINTS

A *tracepoint* differs from a breakpoint in that it triggers an additional action when it is hit. For purposes such as applying filters, conditions, and hit counts, a tracepoint can be thought of as a breakpoint.

Tracepoints can be compared to using either Debug or Trace statements in your code, but tracepoints can be dynamically set as the application is being debugged and will not affect your code.

You can create tracepoints from an existing breakpoint using the Breakpoint Settings subwindow. In the subwindow, click on the Actions checkbox to show the details, as found in Figure 31-13.

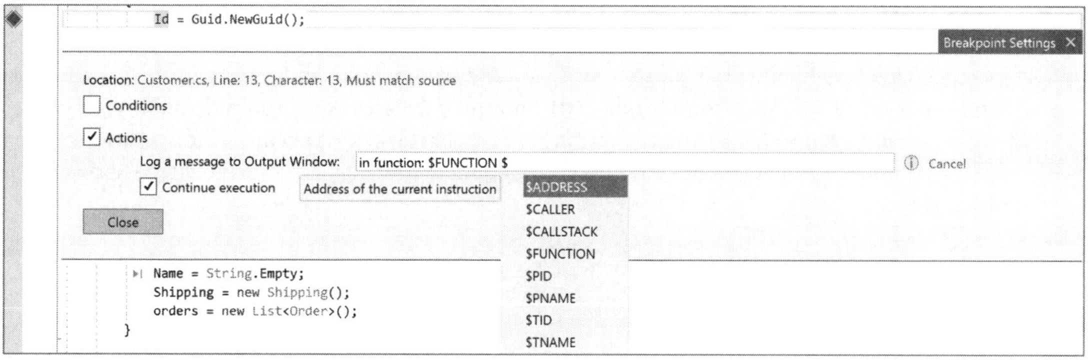

FIGURE 31-13

The result of hitting a tracepoint is to display a message in the Output window. In the text box for the tracepoint, enter the message that you want displayed. There are a number of variables that can be used to display the current state. These variables are prefixed by a dollar sign ($) and are available through IntelliSense. Figure 31-13 includes the available variables. They are:

➤ **$ADDRESS**: The current instructions

➤ **$CALLER**: The name of the function that called the current method

➤ **$CALLSTACK**: The current call stack

➤ **$FUNCTION**: The name of the current function

➤ **$PID**: The current process ID

➤ **$PNAME**: The name of the current process

➤ **$TID**: The current thread ID

➤ **$TNAME**: The name of the current thread

By default, after a tracepoint action has been defined, the Continue Execution check box will be checked, so the application will not break at this point. Unchecking this option causes the application to break at the tracepoint as if it were a breakpoint. The message will be printed prior to the application breaking.

After you set a tracepoint, the code window changes the appearance of that line of code to indicate that a tracepoint has been set. This is shown in the top left corner of Figure 31-13, where the tracepoint appears with a red diamond in the margin.

If the Continue Execution check box is unchecked, the visual appearance of the tracepoint becomes the same as that of a breakpoint. The rationale for this behavior is that the diamond-shaped visual cue indicates that the debugger will not stop at the tracepoint, rather than indicating that there are actions associated with the tracepoint.

EXECUTION CONTROL

After reaching a breakpoint, it is often useful to step through code and review both variable values and program execution. Visual Studio 2017 not only enables you to step through your code, but it also permits you to adjust the execution point to backtrack or even repeat operations. The line of code about to be executed is highlighted, and an arrow displays on the left, as shown in Figure 31-14.

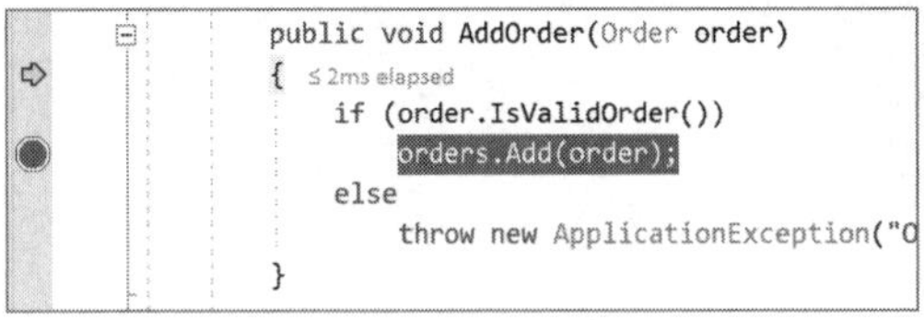

```
         public void AddOrder(Order order)
       { ≤ 2ms elapsed
           if (order.IsValidOrder())
               orders.Add(order);
           else
               throw new ApplicationException("O
       }
```

FIGURE 31-14

Stepping through Code

The first step to manipulate the execution point is simply to step through code in the expected order of execution. You can use three sizes of increments to step the debugger forward. It is important to remember that when stepping through code it is actually being run, so variable values may change as you progress through the application.

Stepping Over (F10)

Stepping Over is fully executing the line that currently has focus and progressing to the next line in the current code block. If the end of the code block has been reached, Stepping Over returns to the calling code block.

Stepping Into (F11)

Stepping Into behaves the same as Stepping Over when the line is a simple operator, such as a numeric operation or a cast. When the line is more complex, Stepping Into steps through all user code. For example, in the following code snippet, pressing F10 through the TestMethod steps through only the lines of code within TestMethod. Pressing F11 steps through TestMethod until the MethodA call is made, and then the debugger steps through MethodA before returning to TestMethod:

C#

```
public void TestMethod()
{
    int x = 5 + 5;
    MethodA();
}
```

```csharp
private void MethodA()
{
    Console.WriteLine("Method A being executed");
}
```

Stepping Out (Shift+F11)

If you step into a long method by accident, it is quite often convenient to step back out of that method without having to either step over every line in that method or set a breakpoint at the end of the method. Stepping Out moves the cursor out of the current method to where it was called. Considering the previous snippet, if you entered MethodA, pressing Shift+F11 would immediately return the cursor to the end of TestMethod.

Step Filtering

One useful feature is the ability to automatically step over properties and operators. In many cases, public properties are simply wrappers for a private member variable, and as a result there is little to be gained from stepping into them while debugging. This debugger option is especially useful if you call a method that passes a number of properties as parameters, such as the method call listed here:

C#

```csharp
printShippingLabel(cust.name, shipTo.street, shipTo.city, shipTo.state,
    shipTo.zipCode);
```

With the Step Over Properties and Operators option enabled, the debugger steps directly into the first line of the printShippingLabel method if you press F11. If you need to, you can manually step into a specific property by right-clicking the code editor window and selecting Step Into Specific. This displays a submenu with each of the available properties listed, as shown in Figure 31-15.

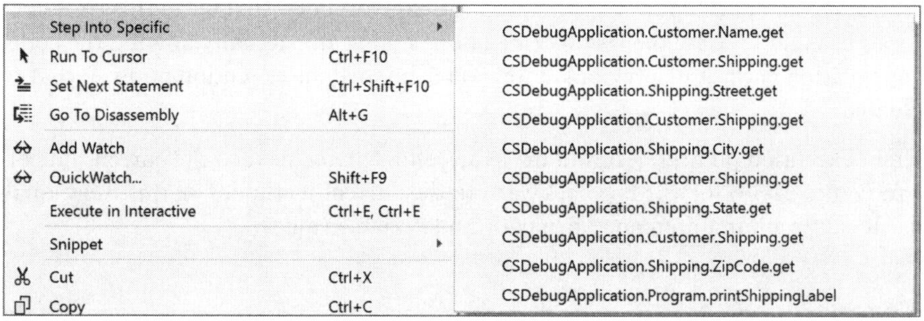

FIGURE 31-15

The Step Over Properties and Operators option is enabled by default. You can enable or disable it during debugging by right-clicking anywhere in the code editor window and selecting it from the context menu or from the Options dialog window. (Select Tools ➪ Options, and then from the tree view on the left side, select Debugging).

Run to Cursor

A frequently used mechanism to move through your code while debugging is the Run to Cursor function. While you have stopped at a breakpoint, you can place your cursor anyplace else in the code, right-click, and select Run to Cursor from the context menu. The execution of your application will then continue until it reaches the line of code that had been selected, where it will stop. Consider it to be Step In/Over on steroids.

There are a couple things to note about Run to Cursor functionality. If you click on a line of code that doesn't get hit during execution, the application will continue running, even to termination if that's how the flow of control works. If the application hits a line of code that requires user input before continuing, the breakpoint at your cursor will still be hit after the input has been provided. And if, while running to your cursor, a different breakpoint is hit, then execution will still stop at your cursor.

Visual Studio 2017 introduced an easier way to invoke the Run to Cursor functionality. Called Run to Click, it reduces the friction associated with Run to Cursor. As you can see in Figure 31-16, there is a green arrow to the left of the beginning of the code. When you click on that arrow, it runs the application, stopping on the current line as a breakpoint. In other words, it's the Run to Cursor function (complete with the same notes and caveats), but instead of needing to use the context menu, it's just a click away.

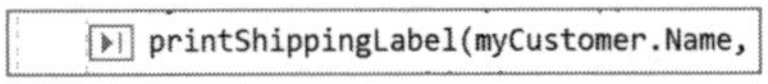

```
[▶] printShippingLabel(myCustomer.Name,
```

FIGURE 31-16

Moving the Execution Point

As you become familiar with stepping in and out of functions, you will find that you are occasionally overzealous and accidentally step over the method call you are interested in. In this case, what you need to do is go back and review the last action. Though you can't actually unwind the code and change the application back to its previous state, you can move the execution point so that the method is reevaluated.

To move the current execution point, select and drag the yellow arrow next to the current line of execution (refer to Figure 31-14) forward or backward in the current method. Use this functionality with care because it can result in unintended behavior and variable values.

EDIT AND CONTINUE

One of the most useful features of Visual Studio 2017 debugging is Edit and Continue. Both C# and Visual Basic have support for Edit and Continue, enabling you to make changes to your application on the fly. Whenever your application is paused, you can make changes to your code and then resume execution. The new or modified code is dynamically added to your application with the changes taking immediate effect.

Rude Edits

At this point, you are likely wondering whether any limitations exist on the changes that you can make. The answer is yes, and there are quite a few types of *rude edits,* which refer to any code change that requires the application to be stopped and rebuilt. A full list of rude edits is available from the Visual Studio 2017 help resource under the Edit and Continue topic, and they include the following:

➤ Making changes to the current, or active, statement

➤ Making changes to the list of global symbols — such as new types or methods — or changing the signatures of methods, events, or properties

➤ Making changes to attributes

Stop Applying Changes

When changes are made to the source code while the application is paused, Visual Studio must integrate, or apply, the changes into the running application. Depending on the type or complexity of the changes made, this could take some time. If you want to cancel this action, you can select Stop Applying Code Changes from the Debug menu.

SUMMARY

Most developers who use Visual Studio 2017 use breakpoints to track down issues with their applications. In this chapter, you learned how to optimize the use of breakpoints to reduce the amount of time spent locating the issue. You also saw how to use tracepoints to generate output (for those cases when breakpoints impact your application's flow).

Visual Studio provides other tools to ease the debugging process in the book's online archive examines how to work with data tips and utilize custom proxy types and visualizers while in a debugging session. As always, the goal is to reduce the time spent wading through unnecessary lines of code.

PART X
Build and Deployment

32

Upgrading with Visual Studio 2017

WHAT'S IN THIS CHAPTER?

➤ Taking advantage of the IDE when working on older projects

➤ Updating projects to use the latest run time and libraries

WROX.COM CODE DOWNLOADS FOR THIS CHAPTER

The wrox.com code downloads for this chapter can be found at www.wrox.com by searching for this book's ISBN number (978-1-119-40458-3). The code and any related support files are located in their own folder for this chapter.

The days of needing to migrate every developer to the latest version of Visual Studio before the first person can use it are now, more or less, behind us. There are two reasons for this. The first is multitargeting, which is a geeky way of saying that you can compile applications in Visual Studio 2017 so that they can run on a wide range of .NET Frameworks, including older versions. Also, Microsoft has stabilized on a solution and project file format, so opening a solution in Visual Studio 2017 does not (usually) keep it from being opened by earlier versions of Visual Studio. This goes as far back as even Visual Studio 2013 or 2012. As the "usually" suggests, there are exceptions to this. But now the main roadblock to upgrading is not so much about Visual Studio as it is the tooling that comes with it. Many projects upgrade just fine. But some tools, such as SQL Server Data Tools, are automatically upgraded with the installation, and compatibility with earlier versions is not guaranteed.

In this chapter, you see how easy it is to migrate existing .NET applications into Visual Studio 2017. This is done in two parts: upgrading to Visual Studio 2017 and then upgrading the .NET Framework version the application makes use of to 4.6.2.

UPGRADING FROM RECENT VISUAL STUDIO VERSIONS

The process of upgrading projects from Visual Studio 2015 to 2017 is as simple as an upgrade process can be. And in some cases, you can even upgrade your projects from Visual Studio 2013, 2012, and 2010 SP1 with little effort. For most types of projects, there is little to no upgrade process. You can simply open your project using Visual Studio 2017 and start using the IDE. And saving the project from within Visual Studio 2017 does not keep people using these older versions from being able to open and work the projects as before. In other words, by all appearances, there doesn't seem to actually be an upgrade process for many projects.

Still, as seamless as the upgrade process might seem most of the time, not every single project fits into that category. As a result, when a project from Visual Studio 2015 is opened in Visual Studio 2017, it is placed into one of three categories:

➤ **Changes required** — Some modifications of the project and assets are required to open the project in Visual Studio 2017. After the changes have been made, the project can still be opened in earlier versions of Visual Studio (that is, 2015, 2013, and 2012).

➤ **Update required** — Some modifications of the projects and assets are required. After the changes have been made, the project may not be opened from Visual Studio 2015 or earlier.

➤ **Unsupported projects** —Projects that fall into this category cannot be opened from Visual Studio 2017.

With most projects (Table 32-1 outlines the exceptions), round-trip compatibility is a reality. You can create projects in Visual Studio 2015, open the projects in Visual Studio 2017, and then open them again in Visual Studio 2015 or even Visual Studio 2013. Of course, there are some limitations to this process. For example, the changes that you make to your project can't use features specific to Visual Studio 2017, for example, changing your project to target .NET 4.6.2. But beyond that fairly reasonable sort of restriction, backward compatibility exists. And, in many cases, it's exactly the same with Visual Studio 2012 or Visual Studio 2010 SP1 — with the caveat that each of the opened projects will fall into the categories mentioned earlier.

TABLE 32-1: Compatible Project Types

PROJECT TYPE	COMPATIBILITY ISSUES
.NET Core Projects	.NET Core projects created in Visual Studio 2015 used a preview version of the tooling that included an .xproj file. Opening the project in Visual Studio 2017 creates a .csproj file (you are prompted to upgrade). While the .xproj file remains, it is not updated if you add files to your project in Visual Studio 2017. And since Visual Studio 2015 doesn't support .csproj files, you won't be able to open the updated project in that version.
ASP.NET MVC 5, ASP.NET MVC 4	If the project uses Application Insights, you will be required to authenticate once for each version of Visual Studio. But after the credentials have been provided, you won't be required to log in again. And you cannot create MVC 4 projects in Visual Studio 2017.

PROJECT TYPE	COMPATIBILITY ISSUES
ASP.NET MVC 3	Visual Studio 2017 does not support ASP.NET MVC 3. To open the project in Visual Studio 2017, you need to convert your project to ASP.NET MVC 4.
ASP.NET MVC 2	Visual Studio 2017 doesn't support ASP.NET MVC 2. To open the project in Visual Studio 2017, you need to convert your project to ASP.NET MVC 4. This is actually a two-step process that involves first converting to ASP.NET MVC 3 and then converting to ASP.NET MVC 4. By using these two steps, you can take advantage of the automatic conversion tools that are available.
ASP.NET Web Forms	None
BizTalk	BizTalk projects (either 2010 or 2013) are not supported out-of-the-box in Visual Studio 2017.
Blend	None
Coded UI Test	None
F#	None. However, to enable F# features in Visual Studio 2017, you need to upgrade your application to version 4.1 of F#.
LightSwitch	LightSwitch is not supported in Visual Studio 2017.
Modeling	None. However, there are some differences in the menus. Modeling projects are now referred to as *Dependency Validation* projects. And UML diagrams are no longer supported. When you edit the files, they are opened as XML files.
Office 2007 VSTO	This requires a one-way upgrade to Visual Studio 2017.
Office 2010 VSTO	None, as long as the project targets .NET Framework 4 or later. Otherwise, it requires a one-way upgrade.
Rich Internet Applications	None, although the templates used to create these projects have been removed. However, you can open and modify existing applications.
SharePoint 2007	The project must be upgraded to SharePoint 2013 or SharePoint 2016 before it can be opened in Visual Studio 2017.
SharePoint 2010	The project must be upgraded to SharePoint 2013 or SharePoint 2016 before it can be opened in Visual Studio 2017.
SharePoint 2013	None
SharePoint 2016	SharePoint Add-In projects created using the Office Developer Tools Preview 2 cannot be opened in Visual Studio 2017. The workaround is to open the .csproj or .vbproj files and change MinimumVisualStudioVersion from 12.0 to 12.2.

continues

TABLE 32-1 *(continued)*

PROJECT TYPE	COMPATIBILITY ISSUES
Silverlight 5, 4, or 3	Silverlight projects are not supported in Visual Studio 2017.
SQL Server Express LocalDB	The database file must be upgraded to SQL Server 2012. Database files that are not upgraded cannot be accessed through the LocalDB functionality but are still available through SQL Server Express.
SQL Server 2008 R2 Express	None
SQL Server Report Project	You need to install the Microsoft Report Projects for Visual Studio extension from the Visual Studio Gallery.
Visual C++	Projects created in Visual Studio 2015 will open with no problem, but if the project was created in earlier versions of Visual Studio, it's possible that an upgrade of the project or targeting a more recent toolset might be required.
WCF	None
Windows Azure Tools	Start by installing the Azure SDK for .NET. Then, if your project requires updating, it will be done automatically when you open it.
Windows Forms	None
Windows Phone 7.1, 8, 8.1	These projects are not supported in Visual Studio 2017.
Windows Store 8, 8.1	These projects are not supported in Visual Studio 2017.
Windows Workflow	None
WPF	None

To start with, let's go through the various project types that are backward compatible. This would be projects that fit into the first two categories previously listed. One of the assumptions made with this compatibility is that Visual Studio is allowed to automatically upgrade the project. The automatic upgrade process is initiated by simply opening the project in Visual Studio.

Naturally, you're left with a list of project types that are no longer supported by Visual Studio 2017. This includes the following project types:

➤ Front Page Websites

➤ LightSwitch

➤ MSI/Setup Projects

➤ Silverlight

➤ Visual Studio Macros

➤ Windows Mobile

➤ Windows Phone

➤ Windows Store

UPGRADING TO .NET FRAMEWORK 4.6.2

After you migrate your application across to Visual Studio 2017 and tidy up your build environment, you should consider the upgrade path to .NET Framework 4.6.2. With the last few upgrades (actually, since the base of .NET stabilized at version 2.0), there have not been many breaking changes. The same is true for .NET 4.6.2, which means that the upgrade from any version should be relatively painless.

In most cases, upgrading your application is just a matter of changing the Target Framework project property. Figure 32-1 shows the project properties dialog for a C# Console Application project. On the Application tab there is a drop-down that lists the different target frameworks available for you to select.

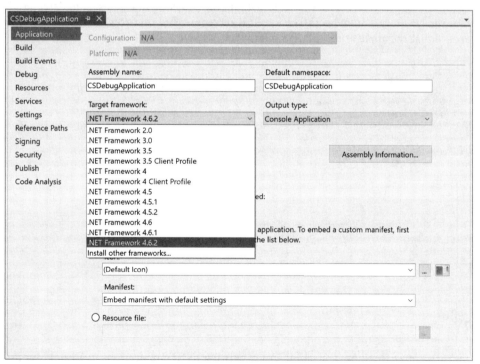

FIGURE 32-1

> **NOTE** *For VB projects, this drop-down list is in the Advanced Compile Options dialog box, which you can access from the Compile tab in the project properties designer.*

One of the additions to .NET with versions 3.5 and 4.0 was the concept of a Client Profile. If you have had the joy of downloading and installing the full version of the .NET Framework, you can appreciate the size of the code base. However, not all of the code base is valuable to every single type of project. For example, .NET includes classes related to the processing of incoming requests to generate HTML in a website. This type of class is not likely to be used if you create an application that runs on a standalone client computer. For this reason, Visual Studio 2017 enables you to target your applications to a subset of the .NET Framework known as the Client Profile. Refer to the drop-down in Figure 32-1 to see the available options.

The Client Profile was discontinued in .NET Framework 4.5. The optimization of the download package for .NET, along with additional deployment alternatives, has led to the decision that there is no need to provide both the full package and the client profile. As a result, after .NET 4.0, the only choices available in the drop-down are the full .NET versions.

As soon as you select a new framework version, the dialog in Figure 32-2 appears. If you select Yes, all pending changes to the project will be saved and the project will be closed, updated, and reopened with the new target framework version. It is recommended that you immediately attempt a rebuild to ensure that the application still compiles.

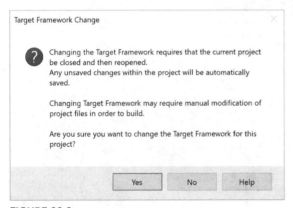

FIGURE 32-2

SUMMARY

In this chapter, you have seen how you can upgrade existing .NET applications to Visual Studio 2017 and version 4.6.2 of the framework. Using the latest toolset and framework version clearly has some advantages in performance, functionality, and usability. However, don't overlook the limitations that using the latest .NET Framework might impose. If your target market still uses old operating systems, such as Windows 2000, you may want to stay on version 2.0 of the framework because this is supported on these platforms. Visual Studio 2017 enables you to have the best of both worlds, only upgrading when you want to.

33

Build Customization

WHAT'S IN THIS CHAPTER?

➤ Customizing the build environment

➤ Performing actions at the beginning and the end of the build

➤ Creating custom MSBuild scripts

WROX.COM CODE DOWNLOADS FOR THIS CHAPTER

The wrox.com code downloads for this chapter can be found at www.wrox.com by searching for this book's ISBN number (978-1-119-40458-3). The code and any related support files are located in their own folder for this chapter.

Although you can build most of your projects using the default compilation options set up by Visual Studio 2017, occasionally you need to modify some aspect of the build process to achieve what you want. This chapter looks at the various build options available to you in both Visual Basic and C#, outlining what the different settings do so that you can customize them to suit your requirements.

In addition, you learn how Visual Studio 2017 uses the MSBuild engine to perform its compilations and how you can get under the hood of the configuration files that control the compilation of your projects.

GENERAL BUILD OPTIONS

Before you start on a project, you can modify some settings in the Options pages for Visual Studio 2017. These options apply to every project and solution that you open in the IDE and as such can be used to customize your general experience for compiling your projects.

The first port of call for professional Visual Basic developers should be the General page of the Projects and Solutions group. By default, the Visual Basic development settings of the IDE hide some of the build options from view, so the only way to show them is to activate the Show Advanced Build Configurations option.

When this is active, the IDE displays the Build Configuration options in the My Project pages, and the Build ➪ Configuration Manager menu command also becomes accessible. Other language environments don't need to do this because these options are activated on startup. (Although you can certainly turn them off if you don't want them cluttering your menus and pages.)

Two other options on this page relate to building your projects. One enables Visual Studio to automatically show the Output window when you start a build, and the other enables Visual Studio to automatically show the Error window if compilation errors occur during the build process. By default, all language configurations have both of these options turned on.

The Build and Run options page (as shown in Figure 33-1) in the Projects and Solutions group has more options available to you to customize the way your builds take place.

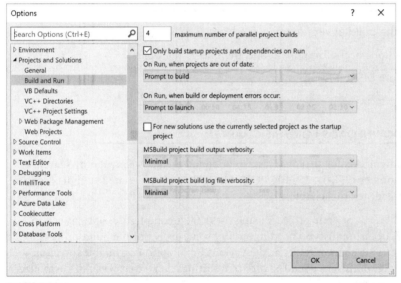

FIGURE 33-1

It's unclear from this page, but some of these options affect only C# projects, so it's worth running through each option, what it does, and what languages it affects:

➤ **Maximum Number of Parallel Project Builds:** This controls how many simultaneous build processes can be active at any one time (assuming the solution being compiled has multiple projects). This number should be set to match the number of processors on your build machine.

➤ **Only Build Startup Projects and Dependencies on Run:** This option builds only the part of the solution directly connected to the startup projects. This means that any projects that are not dependencies for the startup projects are excluded from the default build process. This option is active by default, so if you have a solution that has multiple projects called by the startup projects through late-bound calls or other similar means, they will not be built automatically. You can either deactivate this option or manually build those projects separately.

➤ **On Run, When Projects Are Out of Date:** This option gives you three choices for out-of-date projects (projects that have changed since the last build). The default is Always Build, which forces the build process to occur whenever you run the application. The Never Build option always uses the previous build of out-of-date projects, and the Prompt to Build gives you an option to build for each out-of-date project. Note that this applies only to the Run command, and if you force a build through the Build menu, projects are rebuilt according to the other settings in the build configuration and on this Options page.

➤ **On Run, When Build or Deployment Errors Occur:** This controls the action to take when errors occur during the build process. Despite official documentation to the contrary, this option does indeed affect the behavior of builds in Visual Basic and C#. Your options here are the default Prompt to Launch, which displays a dialog prompting you for which action to take; Do Not Launch, which does not start the solution and returns to design time; and Launch Old Version, which ignores compilation errors and runs the last successful build of the project.

The option to launch an old version enables you to ignore errors in subordinate projects and still run your application; but because it doesn't warn you that errors occurred, you run the risk of getting confused about what version of the project is active.

When you use the Prompt to Launch option, if you subsequently check the Do Not Show This Dialog Again option in the prompt dialog, this setting is updated to either Do Not Launch or Launch Old Version, depending on whether you choose to continue.

> **NOTE** *It is recommended that you set the On Run, When Build or Deployment Errors Occur property to Do Not Launch because this can improve the efficiency with which you write and debug code — one fewer window to dismiss!*

➤ **For New Solutions Use the Currently Selected Project as the Startup Project:** This option is useful when you build a solution with multiple projects. When the solution is being built, the Visual Studio build process assumes that the currently selected project is the startup project and determines all dependencies and the starting point for execution from there.

➤ **MSBuild Project Build Output Verbosity:** Visual Studio 2017 uses the MSBuild engine for its compilation. MSBuild produces its own set of compilation outputs, reporting on the state of each project as it's built. You have the option to control how much of this output is reported to you:

➤ By default, the MSBuild verbosity is set to Minimal, which produces only a small amount of information about each project, but you can turn it off completely by setting this option to Quiet, or expand on the information you get by choosing one of the more detailed verbosity settings.

➤ MSBuild output is sent to the Output window, which is accessible via View ➪ Other Windows ➪ Output (under some environmental setups this will be View ➪ Output). If you can't see your build output, make sure you have set the Show Output From option to Build (see Figure 33-2).

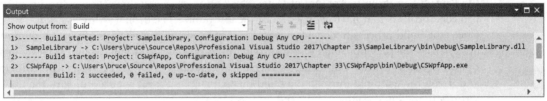

FIGURE 33-2

➤ **MSBuild Project Build Log File Verbosity:** When Visual Studio builds a C++ project, it generates a text-based log file of MSBuild activities as well as the normal information that goes to the Output window. The amount of information that goes into this text file can be controlled independently using this option. One way to take advantage of this is to have more detailed information go into the log file and leave the Output window set to Minimal, which streamlines the normal development experience but gives you access to more detailed information when things go wrong. If you do not want Visual Studio to produce this separate log file, you can turn it off using the Projects and Solutions ➪ VC++ Project Settings ➪ Build Logging setting.

It's also worth taking a look at the other Options pages in the Projects and Solutions category because they control the default Visual Basic compilation options (Option Explicit, Option Strict, Option Compare, and Option Infer), and other C++-specific options relating to build. Of note for C++ developers is the capability to specify PATH variables for the different component types of their projects, such as executables and include files, for different platform builds, and whether to log the build output (see the preceding list).

MANUAL DEPENDENCIES

Visual Studio 2017 can detect interproject dependencies between projects that reference each other. This is then used to determine the order in which projects are built. Unfortunately, in some circumstances Visual Studio can't determine these dependencies, such as when you have custom steps in the build process. Luckily, you can manually define project dependencies to indicate how projects are related to each other. You can access the dialog shown in Figure 33-3 by selecting either the Project ➪ Project Dependencies or Project ➪ Build Order menu commands.

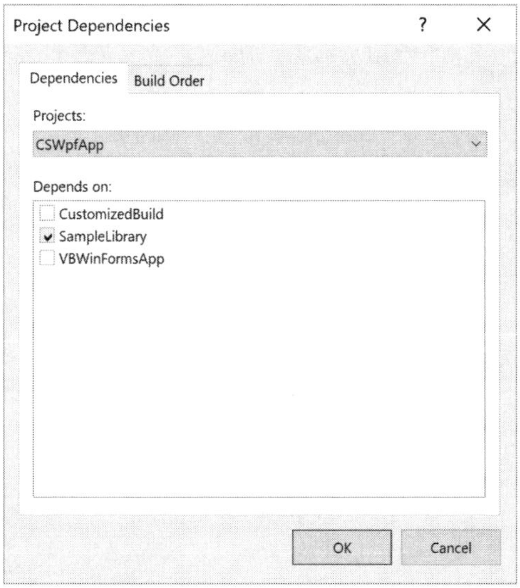

FIGURE 33-3

> **NOTE** *These menu commands are available only when you have a solution with multiple projects in the IDE.*

You first select the project that is dependent on others from the drop-down, and then check the projects it depends on in the bottom list. Any dependencies that are automatically detected by Visual Studio 2017 will already be marked in this list. You can use the Build Order tab to confirm the order in which the projects will be built.

THE VISUAL BASIC COMPILE PAGE

Visual Basic projects have an additional set of options that control how the build process occurs. To access the compile options for a specific project, open My Project by double-clicking its entry in the Solution Explorer. When the project Options page displays, navigate to the Compile page from the list on the left side (see Figure 33-4).

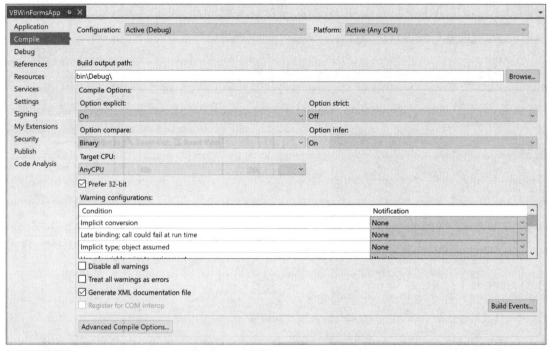

FIGURE 33-4

The Build Output Path option controls where the executable version (application or DLL) of your project is stored. For Visual Basic, the default setting is the `bin\Debug\` or `bin\Release\` directory (depending on the current configuration), but you can change this by browsing to the wanted location.

> **NOTE** *You should enable the Treat All Warnings as Errors option because this can, in most cases, encourage you to write better, less error-prone code.*

You should be aware of two additional sets of hidden options. The Build Events button at the bottom of the Compile page is available to Visual Basic developers who want to run actions or scripts before or after the build has been performed. They are discussed in a moment. The other button is labeled Advanced Compile Options.

Advanced Compiler Settings

Clicking the Advanced Compile Options button displays the Advanced Compiler Settings dialog (see Figure 33-5) in which you can fine-tune the build process for the selected project, with settings divided into two broad groups: Optimizations and Compilation Constants.

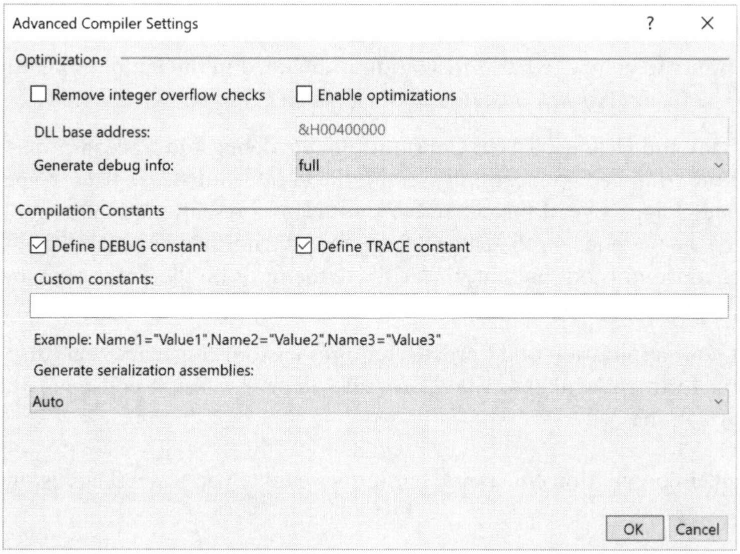

FIGURE 33-5

Optimizations

The settings in the Optimizations group control how the compilation is performed to make the build output or the build process itself faster or to minimize the output size. Normally, you can leave these options alone, but if you do require tweaks to your compilation, here's a summary of what each option does:

➤ **Remove Integer Overflow Checks:** By default, your code is checked for any instance of a possible integer overflow, which can be a potential cause for memory leaks. Deactivating this option removes those checks, resulting in a faster-running executable at the expense of safety.

➤ **Enable Optimizations:** Optimizing the build may result in faster execution and/or a smaller executable with the penalty being that it takes marginally longer to build.

➤ **DLL Base Address:** This option enables you to specify the base address of the DLL in hexadecimal format. This option is disabled when the project type will not produce a DLL.

➤ **Generate Debug Info:** This controls when debug information will be generated into your application output. By default, this option is set to full (for Debug configurations), which enables you to attach a debugger to a running application. You can also turn debugging information off completely or set the option to pdb-only (the default for Release configurations) to generate only the Program DataBase (PDB) debugging information. The latter means that you can still debug the application when it is started from within Visual Studio 2017 but you can see only the disassembler if you try to attach to a running application.

Compilation Constants

You can use compilation constants to control what information is included in the build output and even what code is compiled. The Compilation Constants options control the following:

➤ **Define DEBUG Constant and Define TRACE Constant:** Enable debug and trace information to be included in the compiled application based on the DEBUG and TRACE flags, respectively. From a functional perspective, if the DEBUG constant is not present, then the compiler excludes calls to any of the methods on the Debug class from the finished application. Similarly, if the TRACE constant is not present, then calls to methods on the Trace class are not included in the compiled application.

➤ **Custom Constants:** If your application build process requires custom constants, you can specify them here in the form ConstantName="Value". If you have multiple constants, they should be delimited by commas.

The last option doesn't fall under compilation constants, but it does enable you to further customize the way the project builds.

➤ **Generate Serialization Assemblies:** By default, this option is set to Auto, which enables the build process to determine whether serialization assemblies are needed, but you can change it to On or Off if you want to hard-code the behavior.

> **NOTE** *Serialization assemblies are created using the* Sgen.exe *command-line tool. This tool generates an assembly that contains an* XmlSerializer *for serializing (and deserializing) a specific type. Normally these assemblies are generated at run time the first time an* XmlSerializer *is used. Pre-generating them at compile time can improve the performance of the first use. Serialization assemblies are named* TypeName .XmlSerializers.dll. *See the documentation of* Sgen.exe *for more info.*

Build Events

You can perform additional actions before or after the build process by adding them to an events list. Click the Build Events button on the My Project Compile page to display the Build Events dialog. Figure 33-6 shows a post-build event that executes the project output after every successful build.

Each action you want to perform should be on a separate line, and can be added directly into either the Pre-Build Event Command Line text area or the Post-Build Event Command Line text area, or you can use the Edit Pre-Build and Edit Post-Build buttons to access the known predefined aliases that you can use in the actions.

FIGURE 33-6

> **NOTE** *If your pre- or post-build event actions are batch files, you must prefix them with a call statement. For example, if you want to call* `archive_previous_build` `.bat` *before every build, you need to enter* `call archive_previous_build.bat` *into the Pre-Build Event Command Line text box. In addition to this, encase any paths that contain spaces in double-quotes. This applies even if the path with spaces comes from one of the built-in macros.*

As shown in Figure 33-7, the Event Command Line dialog includes a list of macros you can use in the creation of your actions. The current value displays for each macro so that you know what text will be included if you use it.

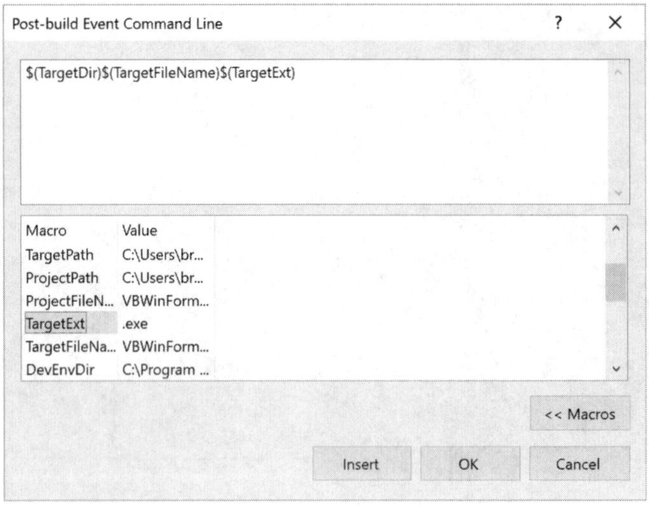

FIGURE 33-7

In this sample, the developer has created a command line of `$(TargetDir)$(TargetFileName)` `$(TargetExt)`, assuming that it would execute the built application when finished. However, analyzing the values of each of the macros, it's easy to see that the extension will be included twice, which can be amended quickly by either simply removing the `$(TargetExt)` macro or replacing the entire expression with the `$(TargetPath)` macro.

At the bottom of the Build Events dialog (see Figure 33-6), there is an option to specify the conditions under which the Post-Build Event will be executed. The valid options follow:

➤ **Always:** This option runs the Post-Build Event script even if the build fails. Remember that there is no guarantee when this event fires that Visual Studio has produced any files, so your post-build script should handle this scenario.

➤ **On Successful Build:** This is the default option. It causes the Post-Build Event script to be run whenever the build is considered to be successful. Note that this means that it will run even if your project is up to date (and therefore is not rebuilt).

➤ **When the Build Updates the Project Output:** This option is similar to On Successful Build, except that it fires only the Post-Build Event script when the project output files have changed. This is a great option for keeping a local cache of archived builds of your projects because it means you copy only a file into the archive if it has changed since the last build.

There are no filter options for determining if the Pre-Build Event will be executed.

C# BUILD PAGES

C# provides its own set of build options. In general, the options are the same as those available to a Visual Basic project, but in a different location because C# programmers are more likely to tweak the output than Visual Basic developers, who are typically more interested in rapid development than in fine-tuning performance. Or so says the common wisdom.

Instead of a single Compile page in the project property pages, C# has a Build page and a Build Events page. The Build Events page acts in exactly the same way as the Build Events dialog in Visual Basic, so refer to the previous discussion for information on that page.

As you can see in Figure 33-8, many of the options on the Build page have direct correlations to settings found in the Compile page or in the Advanced Compiler Settings area of Visual Basic. Some settings, such as Define DEBUG Constant and Define TRACE Constant, are identical to their Visual Basic counterparts.

However, some are renamed to fit in with a C++-based vocabulary; for example, Optimize Code is equivalent to Enable Optimizations. As with the Visual Basic compile settings, you can determine how warnings are treated, and you can specify a warning level.

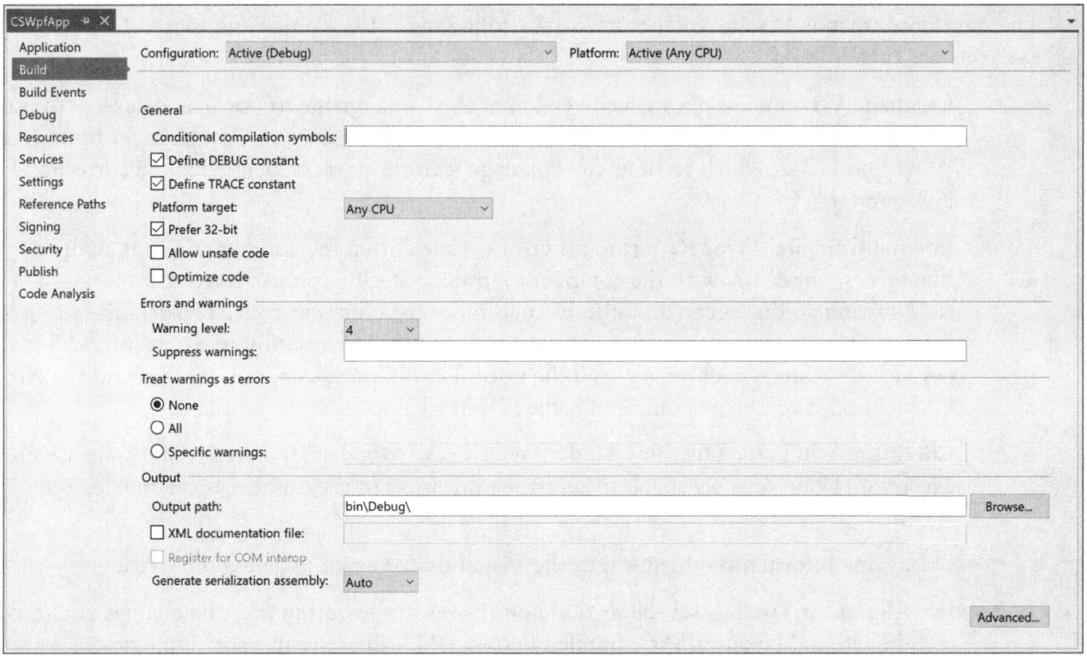

FIGURE 33-8

Clicking the Advanced button on the Build page invokes the Advanced Build Settings dialog, as shown in Figure 33-9, which includes settings that are not accessible to Visual Basic developers. These settings give you tight control over how the build will be performed, including information on the internal errors that occur during the compilation process and what debug information is to be generated.

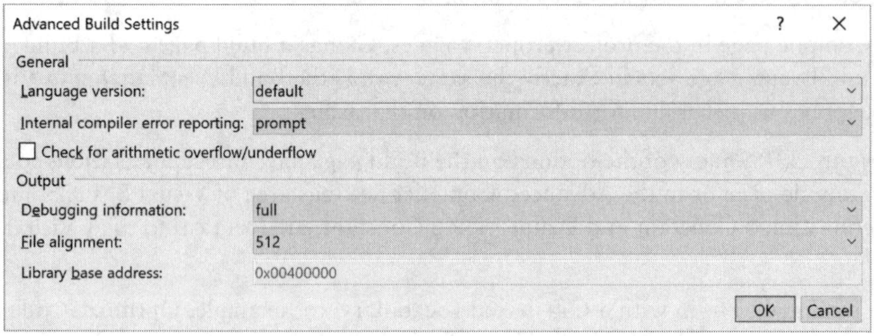

FIGURE 33-9

These settings are mostly self-explanatory, so the following list is a quick summary of what effect each one has on the build:

➤ **Language Version:** Specifies which version of the C# language to use. The default is to use the current version. In Visual Studio 2017, along with five versions of C#, the other options are ISO-1 and ISO-2, which restricts the language features to those defined in the corresponding ISO standard.

➤ **Internal Compiler Error Reporting:** If errors occur during the compilation (not compilation errors, but errors with the compilation process itself), you can have information sent to Microsoft so that it can add it to its revision of the compiler code. The default setting is Prompt, which asks you whether you want to send the information to Microsoft. Other values include None, which won't send the information; Send, to automatically send the error information; and Queue, which adds the details to a queue to be sent later.

➤ **Check for Arithmetic Overflow/Underflow:** Checks for overflow errors that can cause unsafe execution. Underflow errors occur when the precision of the number is too fine for the system.

➤ **Debugging Information:** Identical to the Visual Basic Generate debug info setting.

➤ **File Alignment:** Used to set the section boundaries in the output file, and enables you to control the internal layout of the compiled output. The values are measured in bytes.

➤ **Library Base Address:** Identical to the Visual Basic DLL Base Address setting.

Using these settings for your projects enables you to closely control how the build process performs. However, you have another option with Visual Studio 2017, which is to edit the build scripts directly. This is made possible because Visual Studio 2017 uses MSBuild for its compilations.

MSBUILD

Visual Studio 2017 uses MSBuild as its compilation engine. MSBuild uses XML-based configuration files to identify the layout of a build project, including all the settings discussed earlier in this chapter, as well as what files should be included in the actual compilation.

Visual Studio uses MSBuild configuration files as its project definition files. This enables the MSBuild engine to be used automatically when compiling your applications within the IDE because the same settings file is used for both your project definition in the IDE and the build process.

How Visual Studio Uses MSBuild

As mentioned, the contents of Visual Studio 2017 project files are based on the MSBuild XML Schema and can be edited directly in Visual Studio, so you can customize how the project is loaded and compiled.

However, to edit the project file you need to effectively remove the project's active status from the Solution Explorer. Right-click the project you want to edit in the Solution Explorer, and choose the Unload Project command from the bottom of the context menu that displays.

The project will be collapsed in the Solution Explorer and marked as unavailable. In addition, any open files that belong to the project will be closed while it is unloaded from the solution. Right-click the project entry again, and an additional menu command will be available to edit the project file (see Figure 33-10).

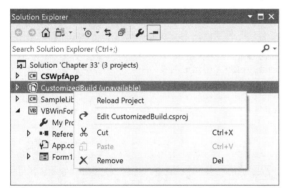

FIGURE 33-10

The XML-based project file will be correspondingly opened in the XML editor of Visual Studio 2017, enabling you to collapse and expand nodes. The following code is a sample MSBuild project file for an empty C# project:

```
<?xml version="1.0" encoding="utf-8"?>
<Project ToolsVersion="15.0" xmlns="http://schemas.microsoft.com/developer/msbuild
  /2003">
  <Import Project="$(MSBuildExtensionsPath)\$(MSBuildToolsVersion)
  \Microsoft.Common.props" Condition="Exists('$(MSBuildExtensionsPath)
  \$(MSBuildToolsVersion)\Microsoft.Common.props')" />
```

```xml
<PropertyGroup>
  <Configuration Condition=" '$(Configuration)' == '' ">Debug</Configuration>
  <Platform Condition=" '$(Platform)' == '' ">AnyCPU</Platform>
  <ProjectGuid>3f95e678-9ec2-48f0-909b-f282642f5fbe</ProjectGuid>
  <OutputType>Library</OutputType>
  <AppDesignerFolder>Properties</AppDesignerFolder>
  <RootNamespace>CustomizedBuild</RootNamespace>
  <AssemblyName>CustomizedBuild</AssemblyName>
  <TargetFrameworkVersion>v4.6.2</TargetFrameworkVersion>
  <FileAlignment>512</FileAlignment>
</PropertyGroup>
<PropertyGroup Condition=" '$(Configuration)|$(Platform)' == 'Debug|AnyCPU' ">
  <DebugSymbols>true</DebugSymbols>
  <DebugType>full</DebugType>
  <Optimize>false</Optimize>
  <OutputPath>bin\Debug\</OutputPath>
  <DefineConstants>DEBUG;TRACE</DefineConstants>
  <ErrorReport>prompt</ErrorReport>
  <WarningLevel>4</WarningLevel>
</PropertyGroup>
<PropertyGroup Condition=" '$(Configuration)|$(Platform)' == 'Release|AnyCPU' ">
  <DebugType>pdbonly</DebugType>
  <Optimize>true</Optimize>
  <OutputPath>bin\Release\</OutputPath>
  <DefineConstants>TRACE</DefineConstants>
  <ErrorReport>prompt</ErrorReport>
  <WarningLevel>4</WarningLevel>
</PropertyGroup>
<ItemGroup>
  <Reference Include="System"/>
  <Reference Include="System.Core"/>
  <Reference Include="System.Xml.Linq"/>
  <Reference Include="System.Data.DataSetExtensions"/>
  <Reference Include="Microsoft.CSharp"/>
  <Reference Include="System.Data"/>
  <Reference Include="System.Net.Http"/>
  <Reference Include="System.Xml"/>
</ItemGroup>
<ItemGroup>
  <Compile Include="Class1.cs" />
  <Compile Include="Properties\AssemblyInfo.cs" />
</ItemGroup>
<Import Project="$(MSBuildToolsPath)\Microsoft.CSharp.targets" />
</Project>
```

The XML contains the information about the build. Most of these nodes directly relate to settings you saw earlier in the Compile and Build pages but also include any Framework namespaces that are required. The first PropertyGroup element contains project properties that apply to all build configurations. This is followed by two conditional elements that define properties for each of the two build configurations, Debug and Release. The remaining elements are for project references and project-wide namespace imports.

When the project includes additional files, such as forms and user controls, each one is defined in the project file with its own set of nodes. For example, the following code shows the additional XML that is included in a standard Windows Application project, identifying the Form, its designer code file, and the additional application files required for a Windows-based application:

```
<ItemGroup>
  <Compile Include="Form1.cs">
    <SubType>Form</SubType>
  </Compile>
  <Compile Include="Form1.Designer.cs">
    <DependentUpon>Form1.cs</DependentUpon>
  </Compile>
  <Compile Include="Program.cs" />
  <Compile Include="Properties\AssemblyInfo.cs" />
  <EmbeddedResource Include="Properties\Resources.resx">
    <Generator>ResXFileCodeGenerator</Generator>
    <LastGenOutput>Resources.Designer.cs</LastGenOutput>
    <SubType>Designer</SubType>
  </EmbeddedResource>
  <Compile Include="Properties\Resources.Designer.cs">
    <AutoGen>True</AutoGen>
    <DependentUpon>Resources.resx</DependentUpon>
  </Compile>
  <None Include="Properties\Settings.settings">
    <Generator>SettingsSingleFileGenerator</Generator>
    <LastGenOutput>Settings.Designer.cs</LastGenOutput>
  </None>
  <Compile Include="Properties\Settings.Designer.cs">
    <AutoGen>True</AutoGen>
    <DependentUpon>Settings.settings</DependentUpon>
    <DesignTimeSharedInput>True</DesignTimeSharedInput>
  </Compile>
</ItemGroup>
```

You can also include additional tasks in the build process in the Target nodes for `BeforeBuild` and `AfterBuild` events. However, these actions will not appear in the Visual Studio 2017 Build Events dialog discussed earlier. The alternative is to use a `PropertyGroup` node that includes `PreBuildEvent` and `PostBuildEvent` entries. For instance, if you wanted to execute the application after it was successfully built, you could include the following XML block immediately before the closing `</Project>` tag:

```
<PropertyGroup>
  <PostBuildEvent>"$(TargetDir)$(TargetFileName)"</PostBuildEvent>
</PropertyGroup>
```

When you finish editing the project file's XML, you need to re-enable it in the solution by right-clicking the project's entry in the Solution Explorer and selecting the Reload Project command. If you still have the project file open, Visual Studio asks if you want to close it to proceed.

The MSBuild Schema

An extended discussion on the MSBuild engine is beyond the scope of this book. However, it's useful to understand the different components that make up the MSBuild project file so that you can look at and update your own projects.

Four major elements form the basis of the project file: *items*, *properties*, *targets*, and *tasks*. Brought together, you can use these four node types to create a configuration file that describes a project in full, as shown in the previous sample C# project file.

Items

Items are those elements that define inputs to the build system and project. They are defined as children of an ItemGroup node, and the most common item is the Compile node used to inform MSBuild that the specified file is to be included in the compilation. The following snippet from a project file shows an Item element defined for the Form1.cs file of a Windows Application project:

```
<ItemGroup>
  <Compile Include="Form1.cs">
    <SubType>Form</SubType>
  </Compile>
</ItemGroup>
```

Properties

PropertyGroup nodes are used to contain any properties defined to the project. Properties are typically key/value pairings. They can contain only a single value and are used to store the project settings you can access in the Build and Compile pages in the IDE.

PropertyGroup nodes can be optionally included by specifying a Condition attribute, as shown in the following sample code:

```
<PropertyGroup Condition=" '$(Configuration)|$(Platform)' == 'Release|x86' ">
  <DebugType>pdbonly</DebugType>
  <Optimize>true</Optimize>
  <OutputPath>bin\Release\</OutputPath>
  <DefineConstants>TRACE</DefineConstants>
  <ErrorReport>prompt</ErrorReport>
  <WarningLevel>4</WarningLevel>
</PropertyGroup>
```

This XML defines a PropertyGroup that will be included only in the build if the project is being built as a Release for the x86 platform. Each of the six property nodes within the PropertyGroup uses the name of the property as the name of the node.

Targets

Target elements enable you to arrange tasks (discussed more in the "Assembly Versioning via MSBuild Tasks" section) into a sequence. Each Target element should have a Name attribute to identify it, and it can be called directly, thus enabling you to provide multiple entry points into the build process. The following snippet defines a `Target` with a name of `BeforeBuild`:

```
<Target Name="BeforeBuild">
</Target>
```

Tasks

`Tasks` define actions that MSBuild can execute under certain conditions. You can define your own tasks or take advantage of the many built-in tasks, such as `Copy`. Shown in the following snippet, `Copy` can copy one or more files from one location to another:

```
<Target Name="CopyFiles">
    <Copy
        SourceFiles="@(MySourceFiles)"
        DestinationFolder="\\PDSERVER01\SourceBackup\"
    />
</Target>
```

Assembly Versioning via MSBuild Tasks

One aspect of most automated build systems is planning application versioning. In this section, you see how you can customize the build process for your project so that it can accept an external version number. This version number will be used to update the `AssemblyInfo` file, which will subsequently affect the assembly version. Start by looking at the `AssemblyInfo.cs` file, which typically contains assembly version information such as the following:

```
[Assembly: AssemblyVersion("1.0.0.0")]
```

What the build customization needs to do is replace the default version number with a number supplied as part of the build process. To do this, use an external MSBuild library entitled MSBuildTasks, which is a project on GitHub (`https://github.com/loresoft/msbuildtasks`). The specific package is available on NuGet and can be installed into your project by running the `Install-Package MSBuildTasks` command from the Package Manager Console window.

This package includes a `FileUpdate` task that you can use to match on a regular expression. Before you can use this task, you need to import the MSBuildTasks Targets file.

```
<Project ToolsVersion="15.0" DefaultTargets="Build"
xmlsn="http://schemas.microsoft.com/developer/msbuild/2003">
   <!-- Required Import to use MSBuild Community Tasks -->
   <PropertyGroup>
      <MSBuildCommunityTasksPath>$(SolutionDir)\.build</MSBuildCommunityTasksPath>
   </PropertyGroup>

   <Import Project="$(MSBuildCommunityTasksPath)\MSBuild.Community.Tasks.
   Targets" />
      . . .
```

Because you want to update the `AssemblyInfo` file before the build, you could add a call to the `FileUpdate` task in the `BeforeBuild` target. This would make it harder to maintain and debug later. A much better approach is to create a new target for the `FileUpdate` task and then make the `BeforeBuild` target depend upon it, as follows:

```
<Import Project="$(MSBuildToolsPath)\Microsoft.CSharp.targets" />
<Target Name="BeforeBuild" DependsOnTargets="UpdateAssemblyInfo">
</Target>
<Target Name="UpdateAssemblyInfo">
  <Message Text="Build Version: $(BuildVersion)" />
  <FileUpdate Files="Properties\AssemblyInfo.cs"
              Regex="\d+\.\d+\.\d+\.\d+"
              ReplacementText="$(BuildVersion)" />
</Target>
```

Here you can use a property called `$(BuildVersion)`, which doesn't yet exist. If you run MSBuild against this project now, it can replace the version numbers in your `AssemblyInfo` file with a blank string. Unfortunately, this does not compile. You could simply define this property with some default value like this:

```
<PropertyGroup>
    <BuildVersion>0.0.0.0</BuildVersion>
    <Configuration Condition=" '$(Configuration)' == '' ">Debug</Configuration>
```

This works, but it means that when building your project in Visual Studio 2017 it will always have the same version. Luckily, the MSBuildTasks library has another task called `Version`, which can generate a version number for you. Here is the code:

```
<Target Name="BeforeBuild" DependsOnTargets="GetVersion;UpdateAssemblyInfo">
</Target>
. . .
<Target Name="GetVersion" Condition=" $(BuildVersion) == ''">
  <Version BuildType="Automatic" RevisionType="Automatic" Major="1"
Minor="3" >
    <Output TaskParameter="Major" PropertyName="Major" />
    <Output TaskParameter="Minor" PropertyName="Minor" />
    <Output TaskParameter="Build" PropertyName="Build" />
    <Output TaskParameter="Revision" PropertyName="Revision" />
  </Version>
  <CreateProperty Value="$(Major).$(Minor).$(Build).$(Revision)">
    <Output TaskParameter="Value" PropertyName="BuildVersion" />
  </CreateProperty>
</Target>
```

The new `GetVersion` target will be executed only if `$(BuildVersion)` is not specified. It calls into the `Version` task from MSBuildTasks, which sets the major version number to 1 and the minor version number to 3. (You could, of course, configure these instead of hard-coding them.) The Build and Revision numbers are automatically generated according to a simple algorithm. These components of the version are then put together in a `CreateProperty` task, which comes with MSBuild, to create the full `$(BuildVersion)` that you need. Finally, this task has been added to the list of targets that `BeforeBuild` depends on.

Now when you build the project in Visual Studio 2017, you will get an automatically generated version number as per usual. In your automated build process, you can specify the version number as an argument to the MSBuild call, for example:

```
MSBuild CustomizedBuild.csproj /p:BuildVersion=2.4.3154.9001
```

SUMMARY

You can customize the default build behavior with an enormous range of options in Visual Studio 2017 because of the power and flexibility of the MSBuild engine. Within the project file you can include additional actions to perform both before and after the build has taken place, as well as include additional files in the compilation.

34

Obfuscation, Application Monitoring, and Management

WHAT'S IN THIS CHAPTER?

➤ Exploring the features of Dotfuscator and Analytics–Community Edition, a free post-build hardening tool that ships with Visual Studio

➤ Understanding how obfuscation can be used to prevent your assemblies from being easily decompiled

➤ Using tamper defense to protect your application assemblies from unauthorized modification

WROX.COM CODE DOWNLOADS FOR THIS CHAPTER

The wrox.com code downloads for this chapter can be found at www.wrox.com by searching for this book's ISBN number (978-1-119-40458-3). The code and any related support files are located in their own folder for this chapter.

If you've peeked under the covers at the details of how .NET assemblies are executed, you will have picked up on the fact that instead of compiling to machine language (and regardless of the programming language used), all .NET source code is compiled into the Microsoft Intermediary Language (MSIL, or just IL, for short). The IL is then *just-in-time* compiled when it is required for execution. This two-stage approach has a number of significant advantages, such as enabling you to dynamically query an assembly for type and method information, using reflection. However, this is a double-edged sword because this same flexibility means that once-hidden algorithms and business logic can easily be reverse-engineered and modified, legally or otherwise. This chapter introduces tools and techniques that help to protect your source code from prying eyes and monitor the execution of your applications.

THE IL DISASSEMBLER

Before looking at how you can protect your code from other people and monitor its behavior "in the wild," it is important to consider how you can build better applications in the first place. A useful tool for this is the Microsoft .NET Framework IL Disassembler, or ILDasm. You can execute ILDasm by launching the Developer command prompt. If you are running Windows 8 or 10, enter **command prompt** into the Search text box (for Windows 8, you need to use the Search charm to display the text box). In Windows 7, you can find the developer command prompt at All Programs ➪ Microsoft Visual Studio 2017 ➪ Visual Studio Tools ➪ Visual Studio Command Prompt. Once the command prompt is running, enter ILDasm to launch the Disassembler. In Figure 34-1, a small class library has been opened using this tool, and you can immediately see the namespace and class information contained within this assembly.

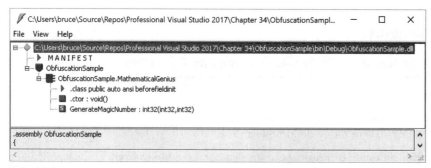

FIGURE 34-1

To compare the IL that is generated, the original source code for the MathematicalGenius class is as follows:

C#

```
namespace ObfuscationSample
{
    public class MathematicalGenius
    {
        public static Int32 GenerateMagicNumber(Int32 age, Int32 height)
        {
            return (age * height) + DateTime.Now.DayOfYear;
        }
    }
}
```

VB

```
Namespace ObfuscationSample
    Public Class MathematicalGenius
```

```
            Public Shared Function GenerateMagicNumber(ByVal age As Integer, _
                                            ByVal height As Integer) As Integer
                Return (age * height) + Today.DayOfWeek
            End Function
        End Class
    End Namespace
```

Double-clicking the `GenerateMagicNumber` method in ILDasm opens up an additional window that shows the IL for that method. Figure 34-2 shows the IL for the `GenerateMagicNumber` method, which represents your super-secret, patent-pending algorithm. In actual fact, anyone who is prepared to spend a couple of hours learning how to interpret MSIL could quickly work out that the method simply multiplies the two `int32` parameters, `age` and `height`, and then adds the current day of the year to the result.

```
ObfuscationSample.MathematicalGenius::GenerateMagicNumber : int32(int32,int32)          —    □    ×
Find   Find Next
.method public hidebysig static int32  GenerateMagicNumber(int32 age,
                                            int32 height) cil managed
{
  // Code size       23 (0x17)
  .maxstack  2
  .locals init ([0] valuetype [mscorlib]System.DateTime V_0,
           [1] int32 V_1)
  IL_0000:  nop
  IL_0001:  ldarg.0
  IL_0002:  ldarg.1
  IL_0003:  mul
  IL_0004:  call        valuetype [mscorlib]System.DateTime [mscorlib]System.DateTime::get_Now()
  IL_0009:  stloc.0
  IL_000a:  ldloca.s    V_0
  IL_000c:  call        instance int32 [mscorlib]System.DateTime::get_DayOfYear()
  IL_0011:  add
  IL_0012:  stloc.1
  IL_0013:  br.s        IL_0015
  IL_0015:  ldloc.1
  IL_0016:  ret
} // end of method MathematicalGenius::GenerateMagicNumber
```

FIGURE 34-2

If you haven't spent any time understanding how to read MSIL, a decompiler can convert this IL back into one or more .NET languages.

DECOMPILERS

One of the most widely used decompilers is JustDecompile from Telerik (available for download at `http://www.telerik.com/products/decompiler.aspx`). JustDecompile can be used to decompile any .NET assembly into C# or Visual Basic. In Figure 34-3, the same assembly that you just accessed using ILDasm is opened in JustDecompile.

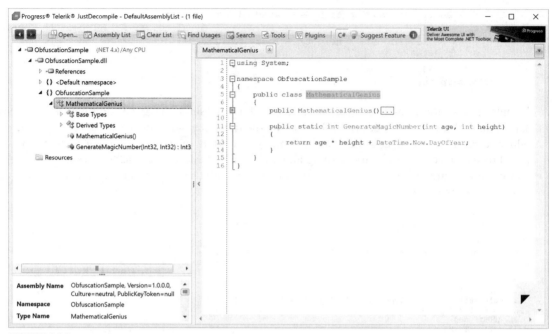

FIGURE 34-3

In the pane on the left of Figure 34-3, you can see the namespaces, type, and method information in a layout similar to ILDasm. Double-clicking a method opens the Disassembler pane on the right, which displays the contents of that method in the language specified in the toolbar. In this case, you can see the C# code that generates the magic number, which is almost identical to the original code.

> **NOTE** *When using JustDecompile, you may notice that some of the .NET Framework base class library assemblies are listed, such as System, System.Data, and System.Web. Because obfuscation has not been applied to these assemblies, they can be decompiled just as easily using JustDecompile. However, Microsoft has moved large portions of the actual .NET Framework (a subset known as the CoreCLR) into open source, which means you can browse the original source code of these assemblies including the inline comments.*

If the generation of the magic number were a real secret on which your organization depended in order to make money, the ability to decompile this application would pose a significant risk. This capability should affect not only how you deliver your code, but also how you might design your application. Obfuscation, discussed in the next section, is one possible approach to mitigating (but not completely eliminating) this risk.

OBFUSCATING YOUR CODE

So far, this chapter has highlighted the need for better protection for the logic embedded in your applications. Obfuscation is the art of renaming symbols and modifying code paths in an assembly so that the logic is unintelligible and can't be easily understood if decompiled. Numerous products can obfuscate your code, each using its own tricks to make the output less likely to be understood. Visual Studio 2017 ships with the Community Edition of Dotfuscator and Analytics from PreEmptive Solutions, which this chapter uses as an example of how you can apply obfuscation to your code.

> **NOTE** *Obfuscation does not prevent your code from being decompiled; it simply makes it more difficult for a programmer to understand the source code if it is decompiled. Using obfuscation also has some consequences that need to be considered if you need to use reflection or strong-name your application.*

Dotfuscator and Analytics

Although Dotfuscator can be launched from the Tools menu within Visual Studio 2017, it is a separate product with its own licensing. The Community Edition (CE) contains only a subset of the functionality of the commercial edition of the product, the Dotfuscator Suite. If you are serious about trying to hide the functionality embedded in your application, you should consider upgrading. You can find more information on the commercial version of Dotfuscator at `http://www.preemptive.com/products/dotfuscator/compare-editions`.

Dotfuscator CE uses its own project format to keep track of which assemblies you are obfuscating and any options that you specify. After starting Dotfuscator from the Tools menu, it opens with a new unsaved project. Select the Inputs node in the navigation tree, and then click the button with the plus sign under the Inputs listing to add the .NET assemblies that you want to obfuscate. Figure 34-4 shows a new Dotfuscator project into which has been added the assembly for the application from earlier in this chapter.

> **NOTE** *Unlike other build activities that are typically executed based on source files, obfuscation is a post-build activity that works with an already compiled set of assemblies. Dotfuscator takes an existing set of assemblies, applies the obfuscation algorithms to the IL, and generates a set of new assemblies.*

On the right side of the interface, make sure that Library mode is unchecked. Then you can select Build Project from the Build menu, or click the Build button (fourth from the left) on the toolbar, to obfuscate this application. If you have saved the Dotfuscator project, the obfuscated assemblies will be added to a Dotfuscated folder under the folder where the project was saved. If the project has not been saved, the output is written to `c:\Dotfuscated`.

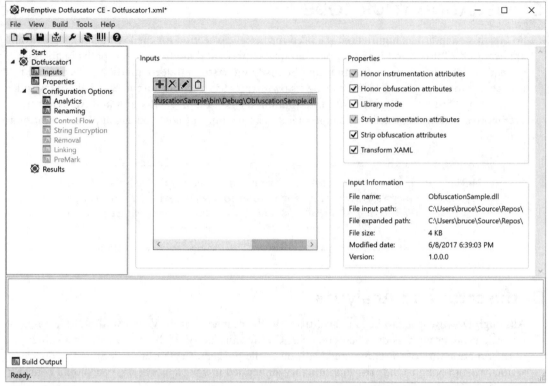

FIGURE 34-4

If you open the generated assembly using JustDecompile, as shown in Figure 34-5, you can see that the `GenerateMagicNumber` method has been renamed, along with the input parameters. In addition, the namespace hierarchy has been removed, and classes have been renamed. Although this is a rather simple example, you can see how numerous methods with similar, nonintuitive names could cause confusion and make the source code difficult to understand when decompiled.

> **NOTE** *The free version of Dotfuscator obfuscates assemblies by only renaming classes, variables, and functions. The commercial version employs several additional methods to obfuscate assemblies, such as modifying the control flow of the assembly and performing string encryption. In some cases, control flow actually triggers an unrecoverable exception inside decompilers, effectively preventing automated decompilation.*

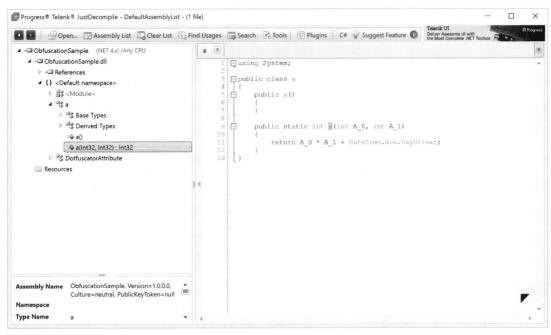

FIGURE 34-5

The previous example obfuscated the public method of a class, which is fine if the method will be called only from assemblies obfuscated along with the one containing the class definition. However, if this were a class library or API that will be referenced by other unobfuscated applications, you would see a list of classes that have no apparent structure, relationship, or even naming convention. This would make working with this assembly difficult. Luckily, Dotfuscator enables you to control what is renamed during obfuscation. Before going ahead, you need to refactor the code slightly to pull the functionality out of the public method. If you didn't do this and you excluded this method from being renamed, your secret algorithm would not be obfuscated. By separating the logic into another method, you can obfuscate that while keeping the public interface unchanged. The refactored code would look like the following:

C#

```csharp
namespace ObfuscationSample
{
    public class MathematicalGenius
    {
        public static Int32 GenerateMagicNumber(Int32 age, Int32 height)
        {
            return SecretGenerateMagicNumber(age, height);
        }
```

```
        private static Int32 SecretGenerateMagicNumber(Int32 age, Int32 height)
        {
            return (age * height) + DateTime.Now.DayOfYear;
        }
    }
}
```

VB

```
Namespace ObfuscationSample
    Public Class MathematicalGenius
        Public Shared Function GenerateMagicNumber(ByVal age As Integer, _
                                        ByVal height As Integer) As Integer
            Return SecretGenerateMagicNumber(age, height)
        End Function

        Private Shared Function SecretGenerateMagicNumber(ByVal age As Integer, _
                                        ByVal height As Integer) As Integer
            Return (age * height) + Today.DayOfWeek
        End Function
    End Class
End Namespace
```

After rebuilding the application, you need to reopen the Dotfuscator project by selecting it from the Recent Projects list. You have several different ways to selectively apply obfuscation to an assembly. First, you can enable Library mode on specific assemblies by selecting the appropriate check box on the Inputs screen (see Figure 34-4). This has the effect of keeping the namespace, class name, and all public properties and methods intact, while renaming all private methods and variables. Second, you can manually select which elements should not be renamed from within Dotfuscator. To do this, open the Renaming item from the navigation tree, as shown in Figure 34-6.

The Renaming dialog opens on the Exclusions tab where you can see the familiar tree view of your assembly with the attributes, namespaces, types, and methods listed. As the name of the tab suggests, this tree enables you to exclude certain elements from being renamed. The GenerateMagicNumber method (refer to Figure 34-6), as well as the class that it is contained in, is excluded. (Otherwise, you would have ended up with something like b.GenerateMagicNumber, where b is the renamed class.) In addition to explicitly choosing which elements will be excluded, you can also define custom rules that can include regular expressions.

After you build the Dotfuscator project, click the Results item in the navigation tree. This screen shows the actions that Dotfuscator performed during obfuscation. The new name of each class, property, and method displays as a subnode under each renamed element in the tree. You can see that the MathematicalGenius class and the GenerateMagicNumber method have not been renamed, as shown in Figure 34-7.

FIGURE 34-6

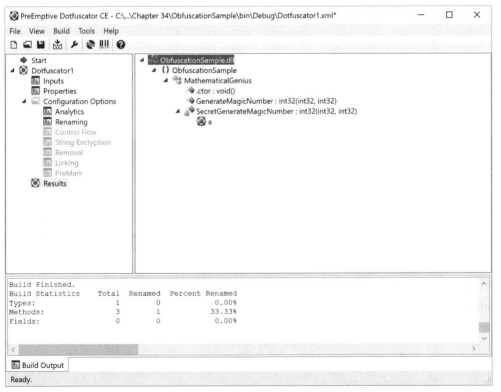

FIGURE 34-7

The `SecretGenerateMagicNumber` method has been renamed to a, as indicated by the subnode with the Dotfuscator icon.

Obfuscation Attributes

In the previous example you saw how to choose which types and methods to obfuscate within Dotfuscator. Of course, if you were to start using a different obfuscating product, you must configure it to exclude the public members. It would be more convenient to annotate your code with attributes indicating whether a symbol should be obfuscated. You can do this by using the `Obfuscation` and `ObfuscationAssemblyAttribute` attributes from the `System.Reflection` namespace.

The default behavior in Dotfuscator is to override exclusions specified in the project with the settings specified by any obfuscation attributes. Refer to Figure 34-4 to see a series of check boxes for each assembly added to the project, of which one is Honor Obfuscation Attributes. You can change the default behavior so that any exclusions set within the project take precedence by unchecking the Honor Obfuscation Attributes option on a per-assembly basis.

ObfuscationAssemblyAttribute

The `ObfuscationAssemblyAttribute` attribute can be applied to an assembly to control whether it should be treated as a class library or as a private assembly. The distinction is that with a class library it is expected that other assemblies will be referencing the public types and methods it exposes. As such, the obfuscation tool needs to ensure that these symbols are not renamed. Alternatively, as a private assembly, every symbol can be potentially renamed. The following is the syntax for `ObfuscationAssemblyAttribute`:

C#
```
[assembly: ObfuscateAssemblyAttribute(false, StripAfterObfuscation=true)]
```
VB
```
<Assembly: ObfuscateAssemblyAttribute(False, StripAfterObfuscation:=True)>
```

The two arguments that this attribute takes indicate whether it is a private assembly and whether to strip the attribute off after obfuscation. The preceding snippet indicates that this is not a private assembly and that public symbols should not be renamed. In addition, the snippet indicates that the obfuscation attribute should be stripped off after obfuscation — after all, the less information available to anyone wanting to decompile the assembly, the better.

Adding this attribute to the `AssemblyInfo.cs` or `AssemblyInfo.vb` file automatically preserves the names of all public symbols in the ObfuscationSample application. This means that you can remove the exclusion you created earlier for the `GenerateMagicNumber` method.

ObfuscationAttribute

The downside of the `ObfuscationAssemblyAttribute` attribute is that it exposes all the public types and methods regardless of whether they existed for internal use only. On the other hand, the `ObfuscationAttribute` attribute can be applied to individual types and methods, so it provides a much finer level of control over what is obfuscated. To illustrate the use of this attribute, refactor the example to include an additional public method, `EvaluatePerson`, and place the logic into another class, `HiddenGenius`:

C#

```csharp
namespace ObfuscationSample
{

    [System.Reflection.ObfuscationAttribute(ApplyToMembers=true, Exclude=true)]
    public class MathematicalGenius
    {
        public static Int32 GenerateMagicNumber(Int32 age, Int32 height)
        {
            return HiddenGenius.GenerateMagicNumber(age, height);
        }

        public static Boolean EvaluatePerson(Int32 age, Int32 height)
        {
            return HiddenGenius.EvaluatePerson(age, height);
        }
    }

    [System.Reflection.ObfuscationAttribute(ApplyToMembers=false, Exclude=true)]
    public class HiddenGenius
    {
        public static Int32 GenerateMagicNumber(Int32 age, Int32 height)
        {
            return (age * height) + DateTime.Now.DayOfYear;
        }

        [System.Reflection.ObfuscationAttribute(Exclude=true)]
        public static Boolean EvaluatePerson(Int32 age, Int32 height)
        {
            return GenerateMagicNumber(age, height) > 6000;
        }
    }
}
```

VB

```vb
Namespace ObfuscationSample
    <System.Reflection.ObfuscationAttribute(ApplyToMembers:=True,Exclude:=True)> _
    Public Class MathematicalGenius
        Public Shared Function GenerateMagicNumber(ByVal age As Integer, _
                                         ByVal height As Integer) As Integer
            Return HiddenGenius.GenerateMagicNumber(age, height)
        End Function

        Public Shared Function EvaluatePerson(ByVal age As Integer, _
                                         ByVal height As Integer) As Boolean
            Return HiddenGenius.EvaluatePerson(age, height)
        End Function
    End Class

    <System.Reflection.ObfuscationAttribute(ApplyToMembers:=False,Exclude:=True)> _
    Public Class HiddenGenius
```

```
Public Shared Function GenerateMagicNumber(ByVal age As Integer, _
                                ByVal height As Integer) As Integer
    Return (age * height) + Today.DayOfWeek
End Function

<System.Reflection.ObfuscationAttribute(Exclude:=True)> _
Public Shared Function EvaluatePerson(ByVal age As Integer, _
                                ByVal height As Integer) As Boolean
    Return GenerateMagicNumber(age, height) > 6000
End Function
End Class
End Namespace
```

In this example, the `MathematicalGenius` class is the class that you want to expose outside of this library. As such, you want to exclude this class and all its methods from being obfuscated. You do this by applying the `ObfuscationAttribute` attribute with both the `Exclude` and `ApplyToMembers` parameters set to `True`.

The second class, `HiddenGenius`, has mixed obfuscation. As a result of some squabbling among the developers who wrote this class, the `EvaluatePerson` method needs to be exposed, but all other methods in this class should be obfuscated. Again, the `ObfuscationAttribute` attribute is applied to the class so that the class does not get obfuscated. However, this time you want the default behavior to be such that symbols contained in the class are obfuscated, so the `ApplyToMembers` parameter is set to `False`. In addition, the `Obfuscation` attribute is applied to the `EvaluatePerson` method so that it will still be accessible.

Words of Caution

In a couple of places it is worth considering what can happen when obfuscation — or more precisely, renaming — occurs, and how it can affect the workings of the application.

Reflection

The .NET Framework provides a rich reflection model through which types can be queried and instantiated dynamically. Unfortunately, some of the reflection methods use string lookups for type and member names. Clearly, the use of renaming obfuscation prevents these lookups from working, and the only solution is not to mangle any symbols that may be invoked using reflection. Note that control flow obfuscation does not have this particular undesirable side-effect. Dotfuscator's *smart obfuscation* feature attempts to automatically determine a limited set of symbols to exclude based on how the application uses reflection. For example, say that you use the field names of an enum type. Smart obfuscation can detect the reflection call used to retrieve the enum's field name and then automatically exclude the enum fields from renaming.

Strongly Named Assemblies

One of the purposes behind giving an assembly a strong name is that it prevents the assembly from being tampered with. Unfortunately, obfuscating relies on taking an existing assembly and modifying the names and code flow before generating a new assembly. This would mean that the assembly no longer has a valid strong name. To allow obfuscation to occur, you need to delay signing of your assembly by checking the Delay Sign Only check box on the Signing tab of the Project Properties window, as shown in Figure 34-8.

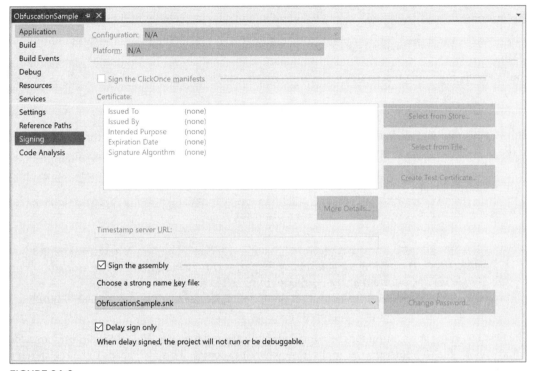

FIGURE 34-8

After building the assembly, you can then obfuscate it in the normal way. The only difference is that after obfuscating you need to sign the obfuscated assembly, which you can do manually using the Strong Name utility, as shown in this example:

```
sn -R ObfuscationSample.exe ObfuscationKey.snk
```

> **NOTE** *The Strong Name utility is not included in the default path, so you need to either run this from a Visual Studio Command Prompt (Start ⇨ All Programs ⇨ Microsoft Visual Studio 2017 ⇨ Visual Studio Tools) or enter the full path to* `sn.exe`*.*

Debugging with Delayed Signing

As displayed on the Project Properties window, checking the Delay Sign Only box prevents the application from being able to be run or debugged. This is because the assembly will fail the strong-name verification process. To enable debugging for an application with delayed signing, you can register the appropriate assemblies for verification skipping. This is also done using the Strong Name utility. For example, the following code skips verification for the `ObfuscationSample.exe` application:

```
sn -Vr ObfuscationSample.exe
```

Similarly, the following reactivates verification for this application:

```
sn -Vu ObfuscationSample.exe
```

This is a pain for you to do every time you build an application, so you can add the following lines to the post-build events for the application:

```
"$(DevEnvDir)..\..\..\Microsoft SDKs\Windows\v7.0A\bin\NETFX 4.0 Tools\sn.exe" -Vr
"$(TargetPath)"
"$(DevEnvDir)..\..\..\Microsoft SDKs\Windows\v7.0A\bin\NETFX 4.0 Tools\sn.exe" -Vr
"$(TargetDir)$(TargetName).vshost$(TargetExt)"
```

> **WARNING** *Depending on your environment, you may need to modify the post-build event to ensure that the correct path to* `sn.exe` *is specified.*

The first line skips verification for the compiled application. However, Visual Studio uses an additional `vshost` file to bootstrap the application when it executes. This also needs to be registered to skip verification when launching a debugging session.

APPLICATION MONITORING AND MANAGEMENT

The version of Dotfuscator that ships with Visual Studio 2017 has a lot of functionality for adding run-time monitoring and management functionality to your applications. As with obfuscation, these capabilities are injected into your application as a post-build step, which means you typically don't need to modify your source code in any way to take advantage of them.

The application monitoring and management capabilities include

➤ **Tamper Defense:** Exits your application and optionally notifies you if it has been modified in an unauthorized manner.

➤ **Application Expiry:** Configure an expiration date for your application, after which it will no longer run.

➤ **Application Usage Tracking:** Instrument your code to track usage, including specific features within your application.

Only the Tamper Defense functionality is discussed in this book (in the "Tamper Defense" section later in this chapter). A different technique for tracking application feature usage is discussed in the "Application Instrumentation and Analytics" section, also later in this chapter.

Although you can use the Honor Instrumentation Attributes check box to turn on and off the injection of the instrumentation code (visible in Figure 34-4), the default behavior is to have instrumentation enabled.

Specifying the functionality to be injected into your application is accomplished by adding Dotfuscator attributes — either as a custom attribute within your source code or through the Dotfuscator UI.

Tamper Defense

Tamper defense provides a way for you to detect when your applications have been modified in an unauthorized manner. Whereas obfuscation is a *preventative control* designed to reduce the risks that stem from unauthorized reverse engineering, tamper defense is a *detective control* designed to reduce the risks that stem from unauthorized modification of your managed assemblies. The pairing of preventative and detective controls is a widely accepted risk management pattern, for example, fire prevention and detection.

Tamper defense is applied on a per-method basis, and tamper detection is performed at run time when a protected method is invoked.

To add tamper defense to your application, select the Analytics node under the Configuration Options portion of the navigation menu and then select the Attributes tab. You see a tree that contains the assemblies you have added to the Dotfuscator project with a hierarchy of the classes and methods that each assembly contains. Navigate to the `HiddenGenius.GenerateMagicNumber` function, right-click it, and select Add Attribute. This displays the list of available Dotfuscator attributes, as shown in Figure 34-9.

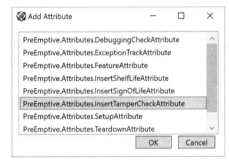

FIGURE 34-9

Select the `InsertTamperCheckAttribute` attribute, and click OK. The attribute is added to the selected method. You can now build the Dotfuscator project to inject the tamper defense functionality into your application.

To help you test the tamper defense functionality, Dotfuscator ships with a simple utility that simulates tampering of an assembly. Called TamperTester, you can find this utility in the same directory in which Dotfuscator is installed (by default at `C:\Program Files\Microsoft Visual Studio`

15.0\PreEmptive Solutions\Dotfuscator and Analytics Community Edition). This should be run from the command line with the name of the assembly and the output folder as arguments:

```
tampertester ObfuscationSample.exe c:\tamperedapps
```

> **WARNING** *Make sure you run the TamperTester utility against the assemblies that were generated by Dotfuscator and not the original assemblies built by Visual Studio.*

By default, your application immediately exits if the method has been tampered with. You can optionally configure Dotfuscator to generate a notification message to an endpoint of your choosing. The commercial edition of Dotfuscator includes two primary extensions to the CE version; it enables you to add a custom handler to be executed when tampering is detected, supporting a custom real-time tamper defense in lieu of the default exit behavior; and PreEmptive Solutions offers a notification service that accepts tamper alerts and automatically notifies your organization as an incident response.

Application Instrumentation and Analytics

As a developer, the goal is to build an application that meets your users' needs while reducing any issues that might be encountered. To meet this aim, it is important to be able to gain an understanding of what your users are experiencing, both good and bad, in your application. That's where analytics come into play. Analytics are capable of providing a full view of your application. This includes not only any exceptions or other unexpected behavior, but also which parts of the application are being used.

For analytics to be useful, there needs to be a mechanism to both capture and report on them. As part of the Azure platform, Microsoft provides the Application Insights platform. Application Insights is not new; it was part of Visual Studio Online. Now it has been integrated into Azure and is available through the Azure portal.

For your application to participate, you need to instrument your application appropriately. Fortunately, Visual Studio 2017 includes a couple of tools to make this easier.

Depending on the type of project that you created, the Application Insights SDK is automatically included in your reference list. For existing projects (and, in general, Application Insights is anticipated to be used with web or UWP applications), you can add the Application Insights SDK by selecting Add Application Insights from the context menu for the project from within Solution Explorer. Once the SDK is available, you'll need to configure Application Insights. Again, through the context menu in the project, select Configure Application Insights. This shows a screen similar to what you see in Figure 34-10.

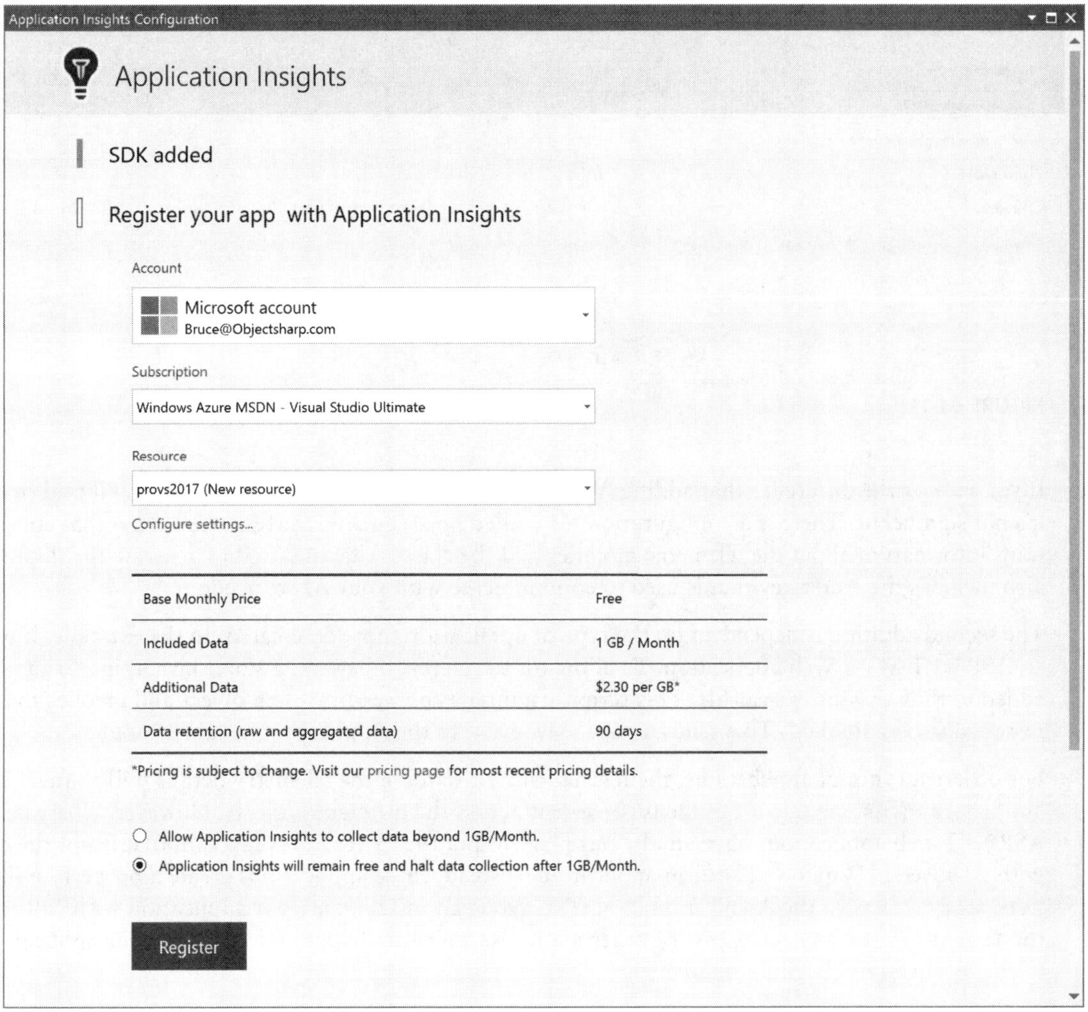

FIGURE 34-10

One you have logged in to your Azure subscription, there are two additional options available to you. If your account is associated with multiple Azure subscriptions, select the subscription you want used for this project. Also, you can specify the resource to which the Application Insights telemetry should be sent. If you are creating a new resource, clicking the Configure Settings link reveals the dialog that appears in Figure 34-11. Through this, you can specify the Resource Group (which corresponds to the region in which the telemetry will be gathered), the name of the resource, and the region in which the service will be hosted.

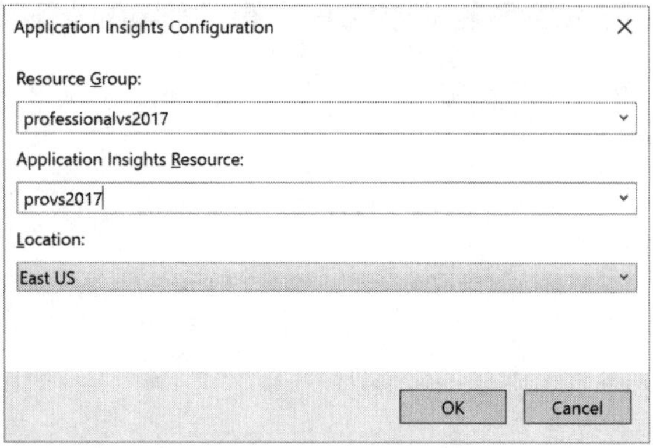

FIGURE 34-11

If you look at the difference that adding Application Insights to your project made, you'll find that it's not significant. There is a configuration file (called `ApplicationInsights.config`) that contains information about the telemetry modules and the classes that are used to generate the data. It also includes the secret key that is used to communicate with your Azure account.

The second addition is dependent on the type of application that you created. In the example, it was an ASP.NET MVC Web application. To allow for telemetry to be sent, a small JavaScript script is added to the `_Layout.cshml` file. This script instantiates an `appInsights` object and invokes the `tracePageView` method. This sends a page view event to the Application Insights resource.

For different types of applications, the mechanism for sending the telemetry details will change. The `ApplicationInsights.config` file is consistent across the different projects. However, whereas ASP.NET web applications have an obvious place to put the `tracePageView` call, that is not the case with a Universal Windows Platform application. Instead, these applications create a property named `TelemetryClient` at the Application level. Then you can instrument your application with calls to the `TrackPageView`, `TrackEvent`, or other methods to push different metrics from your application to the Application Insights resource.

SUMMARY

This chapter introduced two tools — ILDasm and JustDecompile — which demonstrated how easy it is to reverse-engineer .NET assemblies and learn their inner workings. You also learned how to use Dotfuscator and Application Insights to do the following:

➤   Protect your intellectual property using obfuscation

➤   Harden your applications against modification using tamper defense

➤   Add telemetry to your application

35

Packaging and Deployment

WROX.COM CODE DOWNLOADS FOR THIS CHAPTER

The wrox.com code downloads for this chapter can be found at www.wrox.com by searching for this book's ISBN number (978-1-119-40458-3). The code and any related support files are located in their own folder for this chapter.

One area of software development that is often overlooked is how to deploy the application. Building an installer can transform your application from an amateur utility to a professional tool. This chapter looks at how you can build a Windows Installer for just about any type of .NET application.

The installation tool discussed in this chapter is the Windows Installer XML (WiX) Toolset. This toolset, which is available through the Extensions and Updates dialog, enables you to specify the contents and functionality of the installation package through XML files. And although the idea of using XML files might initially sound daunting, it provides all the functionality that had been part of Visual Studio setup projects in earlier versions of Visual Studio. In fact, it provides even more functionality. And although the toolset is tightly integrated into Visual Studio, it is also available through a command-line interface, making it quite suitable to use in a build process.

The output from WiX is, ultimately, a Windows Installer package that can be delivered to someone who wants to install your application. Typically, this is an `.MSI` (Microsoft Installer) file, although WiX also supports patch files (`.MSP`), installation modules (`.MSM`), and transforms (`.MST`). Be aware that not every .NET application can be installed using a Windows Installer. Applications delivered through the Windows Store, for example, fit into this category, as do ClickOnce applications (covered in the ClickOnce section in this chapter). Also, you can't deploy web applications to Azure using MSI. The deployment of web application, both to Azure and using WiX, is covered in Chapter 36, "Web Application Deployment."

WINDOWS INSTALLER XML TOOLSET

WiX is a toolkit that consists of a number of different components, each with its own purpose. And because geeks like to find humor in naming, the components are named after elements related to candles. (WiX is pronounced "wicks" as in "the candle has four wicks.") The components are:

➤ **Candle:** The compiler that converts XML documents to object files that contain symbols and/or references to symbols.

➤ **Light:** The linker that takes one or more object files and resolves the symbols references. The output for Light also typically includes the packaged MSI or MSM file.

➤ **Lit:** A tool that can combine multiple object files (such as are produced by Candle) into a new object file that can then be processed by Light.

➤ **Dark:** A decompiler that examines existing MSI and MSM files and generates the XML documents that represent the installation package.

➤ **Tallow/Heat:** Tallow generates a WiX file list code by walking a directory tree. The fragment of XML produced is suitable for incorporation with other WiX source files by Candle. Heat is a more recent tool that performs a similar task, albeit in a more general manner.

➤ **Pyro:** A tool used to create Patch files (`.msp` files) without the need for the Windows Installer SDK.

➤ **Burn:** A tool that acts as a bootstrapper/installer chainer. The basic idea is to allow packages to specify dependencies, and the Burn coordinates the installation of the prerequisites prior to the installation of the main package.

To start creating a WiX package, you need to get the toolkit installed into your development environment. You can install the WiX Toolset by navigating to Tools ⇨ Extensions and Updates. Then enter WiX Toolset in the search box in the top right corner of the dialog that appears. When the WiX Toolset Visual Studio 2017 Extension appears in the central section, click on the Download button to start the installation. You'll need to restart Visual Studio to complete the process. As well as the Extension, which includes the project templates, you'll need to install the Wix Build Tools. You can find the current installation files for Wix at `http://wixtoolset.org/releases`.

Building an Installer

To build an installer with Visual Studio 2017, you need to add an additional project to the application that you want to deploy. Figure 35-1 shows the available setup and deployment project templates included with WiX. Either the setup project or the bootstrapper project can be used for most standalone applications. This includes ASP.NET applications or web services. The difference between the two is the format of the output, with the bootstrapper project producing an .EXE file, while the setup project creates an .MSI file. If you want to build an installer that will be integrated into a larger installer, you may want to build a merge module. Alternatively, you can use the Setup Library project to create an installer component—a wixlib—a piece of installation functionality that you might use in multiple installation packages, in a manner similar to the way you use assemblies in multiple applications.

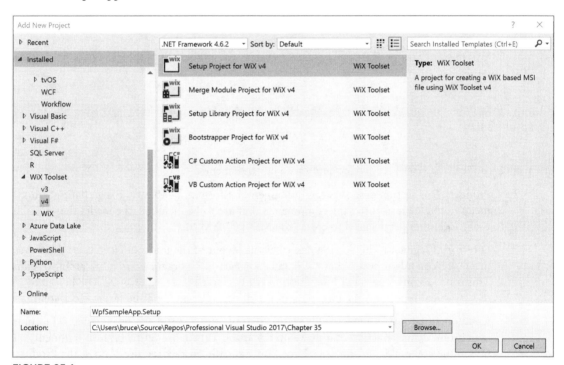

FIGURE 35-1

Upon creation of the project, a single file appears in the designer. To be fair, the setup project does contain other files, but the Product.wxs file is the starting point and the heart of the installation package. So begin by taking a look at the contents. Figure 35-2 shows the default file.

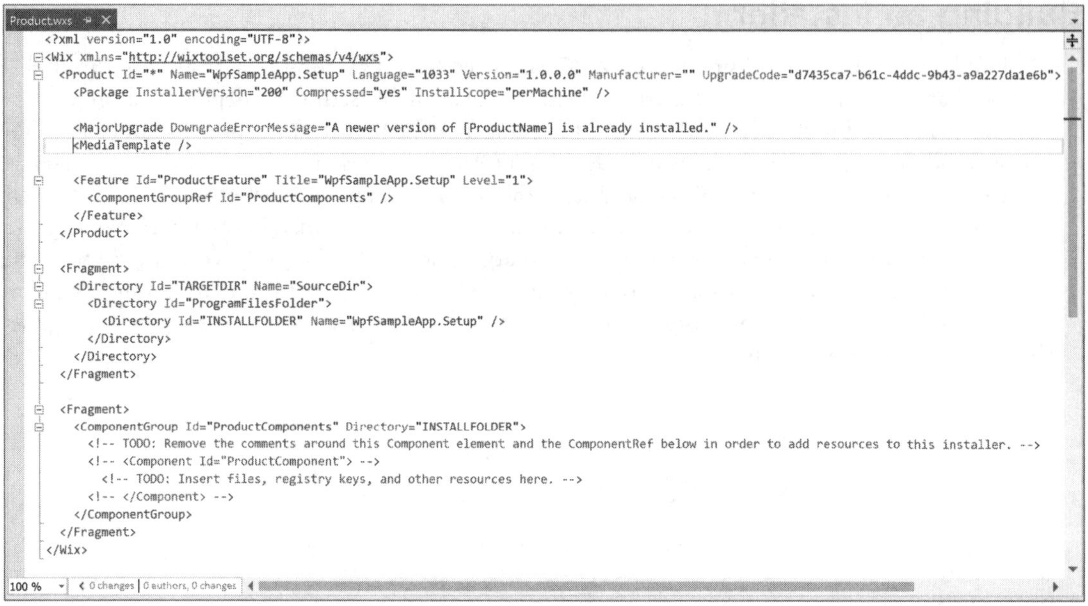

FIGURE 35-2

You can notice that the file is divided into three main elements:

➤ **Product:** This section describes the fundamental information about the installation. This includes the manufacturer, the components that are to be included, the media that is to be used, and other details used to create the MSI or MSM file.

➤ **Directory Fragment:** This section describes the layout of the folders placed onto the target machine. You might notice that the default appears to be organized in a hierarchical manner. This is not a coincidence but a function of the declarative nature of WiX. The hierarchy in this fragment represents the hierarchy of the directory created on the target file system.

➤ **Component Group Fragment:** This section describes the features to be installed. The component group defines the files that make up a feature. Through a yet-to-be-seen fragment, the files in the component group are mapped onto the directory structure. And in the Product fragment, the component groups that make up the product are identified.

To start, consider the Product element. As already mentioned, this element describes the piece of software being installed. In the Product element, there are a number of attributes that should be defined — or at least modified from the default.

There are two GUIDs related to the Products. The Id attribute is used to uniquely identify your package. The WiX product enables you to specify an asterisk as a GUID value, in which case the GUID is generated as part of the compilation process. For the Product, you should take advantage of this because each installation will be different and therefore will need a unique identifier.

The second GUID is the `UpgradeCode`. This value is used if you create an upgrade installation package — in other words, for the installation package for the second or subsequent versions of your product. Every upgrade needs to reference the upgrade code, so unlike the `Id` attribute, this value will be the same for every version of your product. As such, you should set the attribute value to a GUID that you generate.

The other four attributes that should be set relate more to the user interface and experience of the installation process. The `Name` attribute is the name of the product. This is the value that appears when you look at the Program and Features portion of Control Panel. The `Language` attribute is the culture identifier for this installation. The default value of 1033 is U.S. English. The `Version` attribute is the version of the product that is installed and is in the typical format for a version number. Finally, the `Manufacturer` attribute defines the organization producing the product.

The `Product` element has a number of subelements that provide additional details about the installation. The `MajorUpgrade` element can determine the action that should be taken when an application is upgraded to a more recent version. Possible actions include uninstalling the old version and installing the new one, replacing the files or a custom action.

The purpose of the `MediaTemplate` element indicates the size and format of the media onto which the installation package will be placed. In fact, through WiX you can specify into which media component (such as a DVD disc) that a particular file will be placed. The default `MediaTemplate`, however, is usually sufficient because it includes the values that create a single file.

The remaining element in the `Product` describes the feature (or features) included in the installation package. A *feature* in WiX parlance is a collection of deployment items intended to be installed as an atomic unit. It could be as simple as one file per feature, or there could be multiple files in a single feature. But regardless, from the user's perspective, the feature is the level at which the user has the choice to install or not to install. As such, there can be one or more `Feature` elements in the `Product`.

The example shown in Figure 35-2 has only a single feature. The attributes are, for the most part, fairly typical. The `Id` is a unique textual identifier for the feature. The `Title` is the name given to the feature. It appears in the installation user interface, so it should be user-friendly. The `Level` is used to nest `Features` one within the other.

For a given feature, you specify the `ComponentGroups` that are related to it. The `ComponentGroup` indicates a particular block of installation elements. It can be a single assembly or a configuration file; it can be a collection of files of different type. But the important aspect to the declaration is that the `Id` for the `ComponentGroup` must match a `ComponentGroup` defined in one of the subsequent fragments.

The next major component to a WiX file is the `Directory` fragment. First, notice that it's not actually a second-level XML element (that is, at the same level as the `Product`). Instead, it's a subelement of a fragment. This arrangement is done to allow `Directory` fragments to be placed in different packages and still be easily combined by the linker when the installation file is constructed.

The contents of the `Directory` fragment are intended to mimic the file system that will exist on the target system after the installation is complete. Referring to Figure 35-2, you can see that there is a three-level nesting that has been defined. Each level has an Id associated with it. The Id can be meaningful, as is the case here. But ultimately, you have the ability to map the placement of individual files into specific directories by referencing the Id. The Name attribute is optional; however if you plan to create directories where none already exist, as is the case with the INSTALLFOLDER element, it should be included. In the example, the default value for the directory created under Program Files is the name of the project.

The final fragment (refer to Figure 35-2) is a ComponentGroup, which contains a reference to the individual files that make up the group. The Id for the group is important because it must match an Id specified in the ComponentGroupRef back when the Features were being listed. The ComponentGroup element has a Directory attribute; the value of this attribute specifies the directory where the files in the group will be placed. The value must match one of the Ids of a Directory element in the Directory fragment.

Using Heat to Create Fragments

WiX provides a tool that examines various types of artifacts and creates WiX fragments based on which it finds. The tool is known as Heat. And fortunately, one of the artifact types that it understands is Visual Studio project files.

Heat is a useful tool. However, it is a command-line utility and, as such, you need to take a simple step to integrate it into Visual Studio. Specifically, it needs to be placed into your External Tools collection. To access the collection, select Tools ⇨ External Tools from the menu. The dialog shown in Figure 35-3 appears.

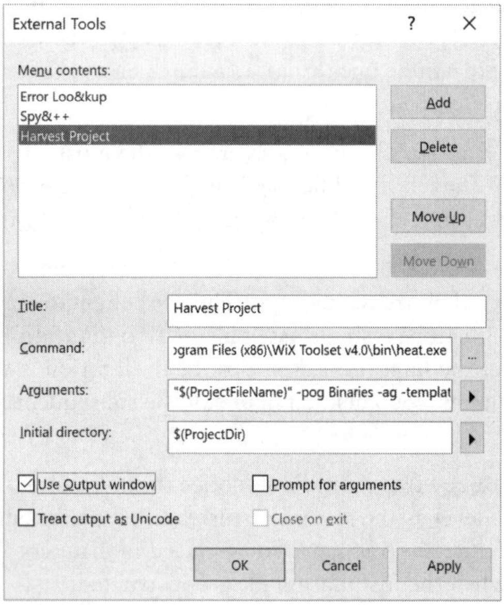

FIGURE 35-3

To add a new command, click the Add button. For the new tool, specify a name of **Harvest Project**. The command (which, not surprisingly, is implemented in heat.exe) is found in the WiX Toolset v3.11 directory underneath Program Files, or Program Files (x86) if you're running on a 64-bit machine. The Arguments value is where the magic takes place. There are a number of parameters that need to be defined. And you can use the project tokens as well. Set the Argument value to the following.

```
project "$(ProjectFileName)" -pog Binaries -ag -template fragment -out
$(TargetName).wxs
```

Finally, set the Initial Directory value to $(ProjectDir). This enables the utility to find the needed files starting at the project's root. Make sure that Use Output Window is checked; then a final click on the OK button completes the creation process.

Now that the Heat command is available, you can put it to use. First, in Solution Explorer, make sure that the file within the project being harvested is selected. Then use the Tools ⇨ Harvest Project menu option to scan the current project. If all goes well, the Output window should look something like Figure 35-4. Yes, it looks like nothing happened. But in the absence of any error messages, the scan was successful.

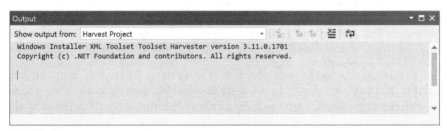

FIGURE 35-4

The result from harvesting your project in this manner is a .wxs file. More precisely, it is a .wxs file that has the same name as your project. You can locate it in the same directory as your project file. To view that file in Visual Studio, use the Show All Files button in the Solution Explorer. You'll notice that a .wxs file is now visible. Double-click it to open the file. The results should appear similar to Figure 35-5, which is generated from a simple "Hello World" style WPF application named WpfSampleApp.

The contents of these WiX fragments complete the installation packaging story. There are two fragments visible. The first contains a DirectoryRef element. The purpose of this element is to enable multiple components to be placed into the same directory in the target machine.

Inside the DirectoryRef are two Component elements. Each component represents a file. The first component is the executable for the project. The second component is the configuration file. The Source attribute indicates the components.

```
WpfSampleApp.wxs  ⌐ ×
 <?xml version="1.0" encoding="utf-8"?>
 <Wix xmlns="http://schemas.microsoft.com/wix/2006/wi">
    <Fragment>
       <DirectoryRef Id="WpfSampleApp.Binaries">
          <Component Id="cmpB68808A504FAB2F7A399B29E59C0056E" Guid="*">
             <File Id="filEA5FFF2619D646068DD5111DA51A3B86" Source="$(var.WpfSampleApp.TargetDir)\WpfSampleApp.exe" />
          </Component>
          <Component Id="cmp294B8AC259E569C58315C8738BE32B76" Guid="*">
             <File Id="filD6AD66F0B54E050CAC4F3EFB05340249" Source="$(var.WpfSampleApp.TargetDir)\WpfSampleApp.exe.config" />
          </Component>
       </DirectoryRef>
    </Fragment>
    <Fragment>
       <ComponentGroup Id="WpfSampleApp.Binaries">
          <ComponentRef Id="cmpB68808A504FAB2F7A399B29E59C0056E" />
          <ComponentRef Id="cmp294B8AC259E569C58315C8738BE32B76" />
       </ComponentGroup>
    </Fragment>
 </Wix>

100 %    ◄
```

FIGURE 35-5

The second fragment is the `ComponentGroup` previously discussed. The difference is that the `ComponentGroup` in Figure 35-2 had no files. This one does. In particular, the files contained in this `ComponentGroup` (as represented by the `ComponentRef` elements) refer to the files' identity in the `DirectoryRef` element. The `Id` attribute in the `ComponentRef` matches the `Id` in the `Component` in the `DirectoryRef`.

This constant indirection might seem quite convoluted. And to a certain extent it is. But it enables a great deal of flexibility. By defining a directory reference and including components within it, you can place files from different components into the same physical directory with a minimum of effort.

The Heat-generated fragments need to be incorporated into the setup project to be included in the installation package. To accomplish this, copy the two fragments and paste them into the `Product`.wxs file from the setup project. In doing so, delete the existing `ComponentGroup` fragment.

Now the two components need to be referenced in the `Product`.wxs file. This is done in two steps. First, in the Feature element in the `Product`, set the `ComponentGroupRef Id` to be the `Id` of the `ComponentGroup` in the Heat-generated fragments. In the example, that would be `WpfSampleApp`.Binaries. This includes the components as part of the feature being installed.

Second, in the `DirectoryRef` element in the Heat-generated fragment, set the `Id` to `INSTALLFOLDER`. This links the components (and the files) into the target directory when the installation is performed. These changes should result in a `Product`.wxs file that looks like Figure 35-6.

There is one more step that needs to be done before the setup project can be built. You might notice that in the fragment generated by Heat, there were two references to `$(var.WpfSampleApp`.TargetDir)`. This is a preprocessor variable that will be resolved when the setup project is built. However, as it currently stands, the variable is unrecognized. To change that, you need to add a reference to the WpfSampleApp project to the WiX project. Right-click on the WiX project in Solution Explorer and select Add Reference. In the Add Reference dialog that appears, select the Project tab and double-click on the WpfSampleApp. Then click OK to complete the process.

```
Product.wxs    ⏻  ✕
    <?xml version="1.0" encoding="UTF-8"?>
  <Wix xmlns="http://wixtoolset.org/schemas/v4/wxs">
    <Product Id="*" Name="WpfSampleApp.Setup" Language="1033" Version="1.0.0.0"
             Manufacturer="" UpgradeCode="d7435ca7-b61c-4ddc-9b43-a9a227da1e6b">
      <Package InstallerVersion="200" Compressed="yes" InstallScope="perMachine" />

      <MajorUpgrade DowngradeErrorMessage="A newer version of [ProductName] is already
      <MediaTemplate />

      <Feature Id="ProductFeature" Title="WpfSampleApp.Setup" Level="1">
        <ComponentGroupRef Id="WpfSampleApp.Binaries" />
      </Feature>
    </Product>

    <Fragment>
      <Directory Id="TARGETDIR" Name="SourceDir">
        <Directory Id="ProgramFilesFolder">
          <Directory Id="INSTALLFOLDER" Name="WpfSampleApp.Setup" />
        </Directory>
      </Directory>
    </Fragment>

    <Fragment>
      <DirectoryRef Id="INSTALLFOLDER">
        <Component Id="cmpB68808A504FAB2F7A399B29E59C0056E" Guid="*">
          <File Id="filEA5FFF2619D646068DD5111DA51A3B86"
                Source="$(var.WpfSampleApp.TargetDir)\WpfSampleApp.exe" />
        </Component>
        <Component Id="cmp294B8AC259E569C58315C8738BE32B76" Guid="*">
          <File Id="filD6AD66F0B54E050CAC4F3EFB05340249"
                Source="$(var.WpfSampleApp.TargetDir)\WpfSampleApp.exe.config" />
        </Component>
      </DirectoryRef>
    </Fragment>
    <Fragment>
      <ComponentGroup Id="WpfSampleApp.Binaries">
        <ComponentRef Id="cmpB68808A504FAB2F7A399B29E59C0056E" />
        <ComponentRef Id="cmp294B8AC259E569C58315C8738BE32B76" />
      </ComponentGroup>
    </Fragment>
  </Wix>
100 %    ▾   ‹ 0 changes | 0 authors, 0 changes  ◀
```

FIGURE 35-6

Now the project can be built. The output from the build process (that is, the .MSI file) can be found in the bin\Debug directory. If you execute this file (by double-clicking on it in Windows Explorer, for example), you'll see a standard set of installation screens. And the result will be a file placed into your Program Files directory named WpfSampleApp.Setup. To remove this, you need to use the Programs And Features application within Control Panel to uninstall the application. In other words, you have created a full-fledged installation of your application.

As you might expect, a large number of customizations can be done to the installation, both in terms of its functionality and its appearance. If you are interested in the details and capabilities, visit the WiX home page at http://wixtoolset.org. There, you can find not only the full documentation, but also links to tutorials and even the complete source code.

The Service Installer

You can create an installer for a Windows Service the same way you would create an installer for a Windows application. However, a Windows Service installer not only needs to install the files into the appropriate location, but it also needs to register the service so it appears in the services list.

The WiX Toolset provides a mechanism for doing this. It is the `ServiceInstall` and `ServiceControl` elements that describe what you want to happen when the service is installed. The XML related to these components can be seen next:

```
<Component Id='ServiceExeComponent'
  Guid='YOURGUID-D752-4C4F-942A-657B02AE8325'
  SharedDllRefCount='no' KeyPath='no'
  NeverOverwrite='no' Permanent='no' Transitive='no'
  Win64='no' Location='either'>
  <File Id='ServiceExeFile' Name='ServiceExe.exe' Source='ServiceExe.exe'
    ReadOnly='no' Compressed='yes' KeyPath='yes' Vital='yes'
    Hidden='no' System='no'
    Checksum='no' PatchAdded='no' />
  <ServiceInstall Id='MyServiceInstall' DisplayName='My Test Service'
    Name='MyServiceExeName' ErrorControl='normal' Start='auto'
    Account='Local System' Type='ownProcess'
    Vital='yes' Interactive='no' />
  <ServiceControl Id='MyServiceControl' Name='MyServiceExeName'
    Start='install' Stop='uninstall' Remove='uninstall' />
</Component>
```

The `File` element is similar in purpose to the WiX fragments illustrated in Figure 35-6. In this case, it identifies that file that implements the service that is being installed. The most important element is `KeyPath`. It needs to be set to yes, whereas the `KeyPath` in the `Component` needs to be set to no.

The `ServiceInstall` element contains information about the service. This includes the name that appears in the service control applet (`DisplayName`) and the "real" name of the service (the `Name` attribute). If you have created installers for services in earlier versions of Visual Studio, you might be recosting the `Account` and `Interactive` attributes as being related to the account under which the service will run and whether the service will interact with the desktop.

The `ServiceControl` element describes what should happen to the service when it is installed. The three attributes in `ServiceControl` that matter are `Start`, `Stop`, and `Remove`. The values of these attributes determine what should happen when the service in installed or removed. The values previously shown would have the service start when it is installed, and both stopped and removed when the service is uninstalled.

CLICKONCE

Using a Windows installer is a sensible approach for any application development. However, deploying an installer to thousands of machines, and then potentially having to update them, is a daunting task. Although management products help reduce the burden associated with application deployment, web applications often replace rich Windows applications because they can be dynamically updated, affecting all users of the system. *ClickOnce* enables you to build self-updating Windows applications. This section shows you how to use Visual Studio 2017 to build applications that can be deployed and updated using ClickOnce.

One Click to Deploy

To demonstrate the functionality of ClickOnce deployment, this section uses the same application used to build the Windows Installer, WpfSampleApp, which simply displays an empty form. To deploy this application using ClickOnce, select the Publish option from the right-click context menu of the project. This opens the Publish Wizard, which guides you through the initial configuration of ClickOnce for your project.

The first step in the Publish Wizard enables you to select a location to deploy to. You can choose to deploy to a local website, an FTP location, a file share, or even a local folder on your machine. Clicking Browse opens the Open Web Site dialog, which assists you in specifying the publishing location.

The next step asks you to specify where the users are expecting to install the application from. The default option is for users to install from a CD or DVD-ROM disc. More commonly, you want to install from a file share on a corporate intranet or a website on the Internet. Note that the location you publish to and the location the users install from can be different. This can be useful while testing new releases.

The contents of the final step change depending on the installation option selected. If your application is installed from a CD or DVD-ROM, this step asks if the application should automatically check for updates. If this option is enabled, you must provide a location for the application to check. In the case that your users will be installing from a file share or website, it is assumed that the application will update from the location that it was originally installed from. Instead, the final question relates to whether the application will be available offline. If the offline option is selected, an application shortcut is added to the Start menu, and the application can be removed in the Add/Remove Programs dialog in the operating system. The user can run the application even if the original installation location is no longer available. If the application is only available online, no shortcut is created, and the users must visit the install location every time they want to run the application.

The last screen in the wizard enables you to verify the configuration before publishing the application. After the application has been published, you can run the Setup.exe bootstrap file that is produced to install the application. If you install from a website, you get a publish.htm file generated as well. This file, shown in Figure 35-7, uses some JavaScript to detect a few dependencies and provides a Run button that launches the Setup.exe.

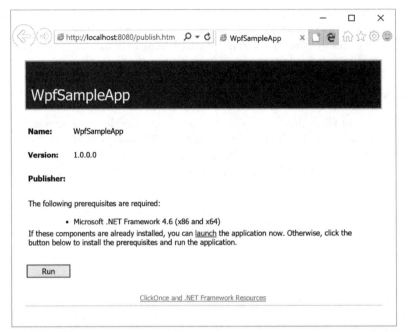

FIGURE 35-7

Clicking the Run button at this location displays a dialog prompting you to run or save `Setup.exe`. Selecting Run (or running `Setup.exe` from a different kind of install) shows the Launching Application dialog, as shown in Figure 35-8, while components of your application are retrieved from the installation location.

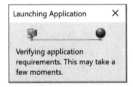

FIGURE 35-8

After information about the application has been downloaded, a security warning launches, as shown in Figure 35-9. In this case, the security warning is raised because although the deployment manifest has been signed, it has been signed with a certificate that is not known on the machine on which it is installed.

> **NOTE** *The deployment manifest of a ClickOnce application is an XML file that describes the application to be deployed along with a reference to the current version. Although it is not required, each deployment manifest can be signed by the publisher to provide the manifest with a strong name. This prevents the manifest from being tampered with after it is deployed.*

Three options are available for signing the deployment manifest. By default, Visual Studio 2017 creates a test certificate to sign the manifest, which has the format `application name_TemporaryKey .pfx` and is automatically added to the solution. (This happens when the application is first published using the Publish Now button.) Though this certificate can be used during development, it is not recommended for deployment. The other alternatives are to purchase a third-party certificate, from a company such as VeriSign, or to use the certificate server within Windows Server to create an internal certificate.

FIGURE 35-9

The advantage of getting a certificate from a well-known certificate authority is that it can automatically be verified by any machine. Using either the test certificate or an internal certificate requires installation of that certificate in the appropriate certificate store. Figure 35-10 shows the Signing tab of the Project Properties window, where you can see that the ClickOnce manifest is signed with a certificate that has been generated on the local computer. An existing certificate can be used by selecting it from the store or from a file. Alternatively, another test certificate can be created.

If you want your application to install with a known publisher, you need to add the test certificate into the root certificate store on the machine on which you install the product. Because this also happens to be the deployment machine, you can do this by clicking More Details. This opens a dialog that outlines the certificate details, including the fact that it can't be authenticated. (If you use the certificate created by default by Visual Studio 2017, you need to use the Select from File button to reselect the generated certificate and then use the More Details button. There seems to be an issue here, in that the details window does not show the Install Certificate button without this additional step.) Clicking Install Certificate enables you to specify that the certificate should be installed into the Trusted Root Certification Authorities store. This is not the default certificate store, so you need to browse for it. Because this is a test certificate, you can ignore the warning that is given, but remember that you should not use this certificate in production. Now when you publish your application and try to install it, you see that the dialog includes the publisher. You are still warned that additional security permissions need to be granted to this application for it to execute.

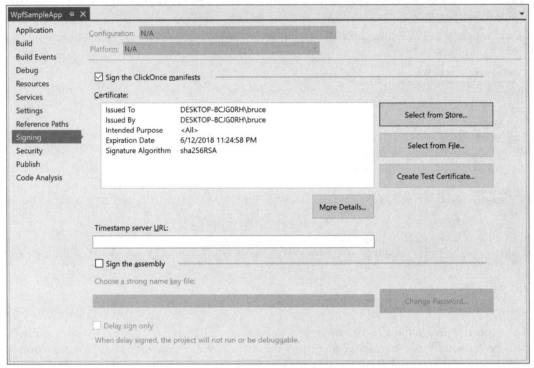

FIGURE 35-10

ClickOnce deployment manifests are rated on four security dimensions. You've just seen how you can specify a well-known publisher, critical for safe installation of an application. By default, ClickOnce publishes applications as full trust applications, giving them maximum control over the local computer. This is unusual because in most other cases Microsoft has adopted a security-first approach. To run with full trust, the application requires additional security permissions, which might be exploited. The Sample Application will be available online and offline; and though this isn't a major security risk, it does modify the local file system. Lastly, the location from which the application is installed is almost as important as the publisher in determining how dangerous the application might be. In this case, the application was published within the local network, so it is unlikely to be a security threat.

Ideally, you would like to bypass the Application Install dialog and have the application automatically be granted appropriate permissions. You can do this by adding the certificate to the Trusted Publishers store. Even for well-known certificate authorities, for the application to install automatically, the certificate needs to be added to this store. With this completed, you see only the progress dialog as the application is downloaded, rather than the security prompt.

When installed, the application can be launched either by returning to the installation URL or by selecting the shortcut from the newly created Start Menu folder with the same name as the application.

One Click to Update

At some point in the future, you might make a change to your application — for example, you might add a button to the simple form you created previously. ClickOnce supports a powerful update process that enables you to publish the new version of your application in the same way you did previously, and existing versions can be upgraded the next time they are online. As long as you are content with the current set of options, the update process is just the Publish process. When using the Publish Wizard to update an existing application, all the values previously used to publish the application are preconfigured for you.

You can check the settings in the Publish tab of the Project Properties designer (Figure 35-11). The designer shows the publish location, the installation location, and the install mode of the application. There is also a setting for the Publish Version. This value is not shown in the Publish Wizard, but by default this version starts at 1.0.0.0 and increments the right-most number every time the application is published.

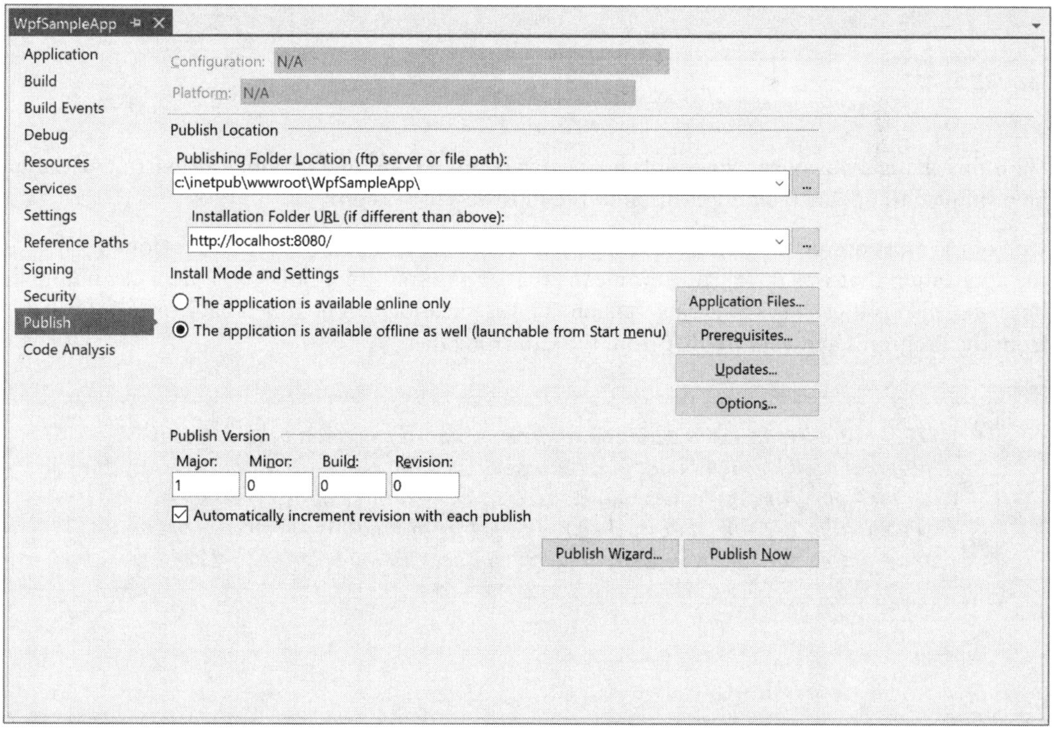

FIGURE 35-11

Along the right are a number of buttons that bring up more advanced options, most of which are not exposed by the wizard. The Application Updates dialog (Figure 35-12) enables you to configure how frequently the application updates itself. In Figure 35-12, the application checks for an update once every seven days, and that check occurs after it has started. You can also specify a minimum required version, which can prevent older clients from executing until they are updated.

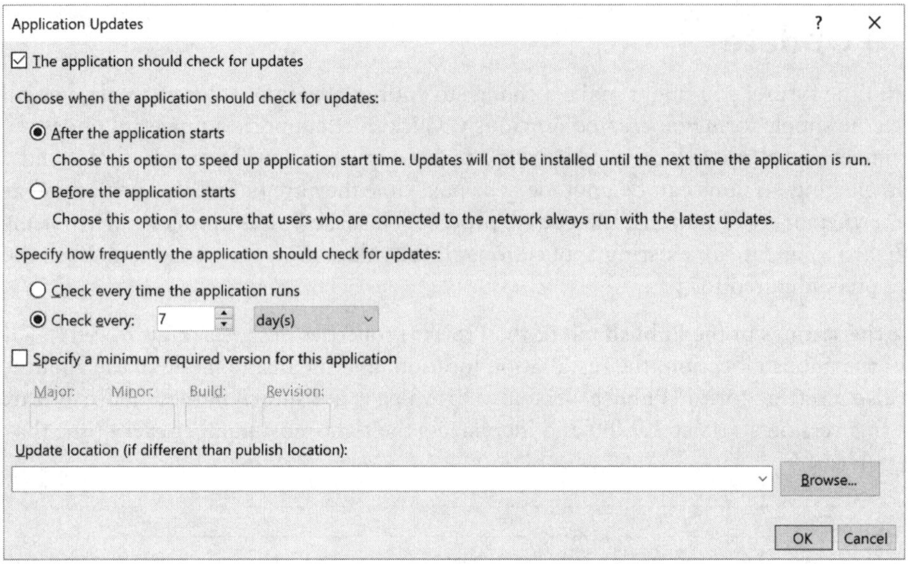

FIGURE 35-12

With this change, now when you publish a new version of your application, any existing users will be prompted to update their application to the most recent version.

One of the most powerful features of ClickOnce deployment is that it tracks a previous version of the application that was installed. This means that at any stage, not only can it do a clean uninstall, but it can also roll back to the earlier version. The application can be rolled back or uninstalled from the Programs and Features list from the Control Panel.

> **NOTE** *For users to receive an update, they do need to contact the original deployment URL when the application performs the check for a new version (for example, when the application starts). You can also force all users to upgrade to a particular version (that is, they won't get prompted) by specifying the minimum required version in the Application Updates dialog (Figure 35-12).*

SUMMARY

This chapter walked you through the details of building installers for various types of applications. Building a good-quality installer can make a significant difference in how professional your application appears. ClickOnce also offers an important alternative for those who want to deploy their application to a large audience.

36

Web Application Deployment

WHAT'S IN THIS CHAPTER?

- ➤ Publishing website and web projects

- ➤ Publishing database scripts with web applications

- ➤ Creating web application packages for deployment with the Web Deployment tool

- ➤ Keeping machines up to date with the Web Platform Installer

- ➤ Extending the Web Platform Installer to include your own applications

WROX.COM CODE DOWNLOADS FOR THIS CHAPTER

The wrox.com code downloads for this chapter can be found at www.wrox.com by searching for this book's ISBN number (978-1-119-40458-3). The code and any related support files are located in their own folder for this chapter.

In Chapter 35, "Packaging and Deployment," you saw how to deploy your Windows application using either an installer or ClickOnce. But how do you deploy web applications? This chapter walks you through deploying website and web application projects. It also covers packaging web applications for remote deployment with the Web Deployment tool and integrating with the Web Platform Installer.

One of the most important aspects of building your application is to think about how you will package it so that it can be deployed. Though a large proportion of web applications are only for internal release, where a simple copy script might be sufficient, if you do want to make your web application available for others to purchase and use, you need to focus on making the deployment process as simple as possible.

WEB DEPLOYMENT

Web application projects are quite different from Web Site projects, yet the tool used to deploy them is the same. Visual Studio 2017 includes the capability to deploy both types with the Web Deployment tool, which is used to easily import and export IIS applications along with their dependencies — such as IIS meta data and databases — from the command line, IIS management console, PowerShell cmdlets, or directly from Visual Studio. It also provides the ability to manage several versions of configuration data for different environments in a clean manner without duplication.

Even more, if you are deploying ASP.NET 5 applications, the deployment can include everything your application needs to run, up to and including the .NET Framework.

Publishing a Web Application

The quickest way to deploy a Web project is to simply publish it directly from Visual Studio. Select the Publish item from the right-click context menu in Solution Explorer to display the Publish dialog. Each time you do a deployment you do so against a particular profile, which encapsulates the target environment settings. A Web Application project maintains a collection of profiles, which enable you to deploy the one web application to a number of target environments and keep the settings for each separate.

If this is the first time you have run the Publish dialog in your project, you need to specify the publish target (see Figure 36-1).

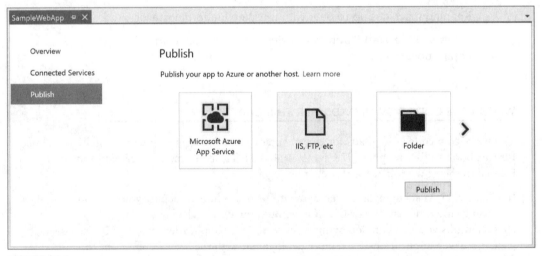

FIGURE 36-1

There are several options available to you initially. In the cloud, you can publish to either Microsoft Azure App Service or a Microsoft Azure Virtual Machine. You can import a previously created set of publishing settings (in the form of a `.publishsettings` file). Or you can publish to IIS, an FTP site, or a folder.

For the purpose of following along with this chapter, select the IIS, FTP, etc. target. You will then go to the Connection tab in the Publish dialog (shown in Figure 36-2).

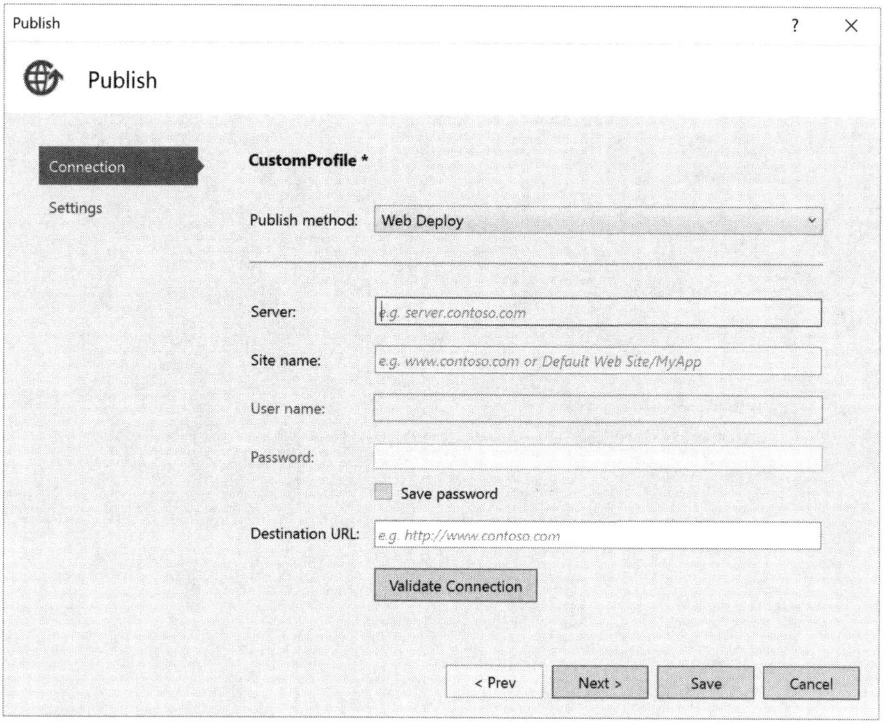

FIGURE 36-2

The Connection tab in this wizard enables you to define the connection to the deployment target. Several options for Publish Method determine what you see in the lower part of the dialog window: Web Deploy, Web Deploy Package, FTP, and File System. The File System option enables you to enter the target location (a directory in the filesystem) for the web application to be published. The FTP option offers the same but also enables you to enter FTP credentials. The Web Deploy option enables you to specify the service URL and the destination URL as well as the site/application combination that is the target of the publication. If necessary, credentials can be provided. The Web Deploy Package option takes what would normally be deployed through a Web Deploy and packages it into a Zip file. So instead of needing to identify the target system, you can just specify the path to the file that will be created.

The Settings tab enables you to configure some additional settings for the deployment. Again, the publish methods break the contents of this step into two categories. Both categories enable you to specify the configuration (by default, Debug and Release) that will be deployed. In addition, there are check boxes that can remove all the files from the target that are not deployed, precompile the application, and exclude any files in the App_Data folder. Not all options are available for all publishing methods. Finally, the Web Deploy and Web Deploy Package include a section that enables a database to be deployed with the web application (Figure 36-3).

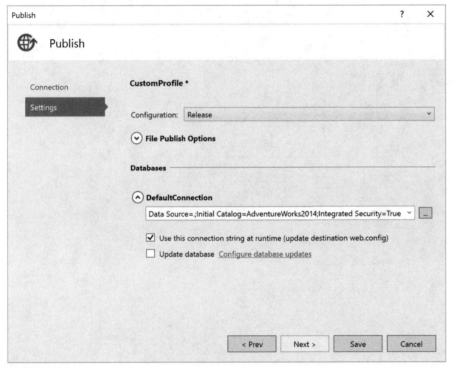

FIGURE 36-3

When you deploy a database, the Publish Wizard examines your development environment and identifies any databases that might be part of the application. These become choices that you can make in the drop-down list. Alternatively, you can specify the database connection manually. Also, there are check boxes that enable you to update the web.config file with the new connection information and to update the schema of an existing database with the deploying database.

If you use the Web Deploy Package option, it packages all the necessary files, along with all the metadata required to install and configure your application package, into a single Zip file. This Zip file can then be installed via the IIS 7.0/8.0 management interface, the command line, PowerShell cmdlets, or directly from Visual Studio.

The final step in this process is to click on the Save button. This actually performs two actions. First, it saves the publish profile in your project. Second, it performs the publication. Depending on the type of publication, you might need to log into Visual Studio with Administrator privileges. This is the case when performing a Web Deploy.

Publishing to Azure

Visual Studio 2017 has a number of features that allow you to more easily integrate your development with Microsoft Azure. The publishing process is one of those areas in which a large number of formerly manual steps have been combined into a seamless process.

To publish your web application to Azure, start by selecting Microsoft Azure App Service as your publish target. You'll also need to specify whether you're going to create a new App Service or deploy to an existing one. This is done through the radio buttons visible in Figure 36-4.

FIGURE 36-4

Whether you choose to create a new service or use an existing one, you will need to indicate your Azure account. In the top right corner of Figures 36-5 and 36-6, there is a dropdown list containing the Microsoft Accounts that Visual Studio is aware of. You can select the account associated with the Azure subscription you want to use and provide credentials (indicated by the Reenter your credentials link in Figure 36-5).

To use an existing App Service, you will need to provide the information shown in Figure 36-5.

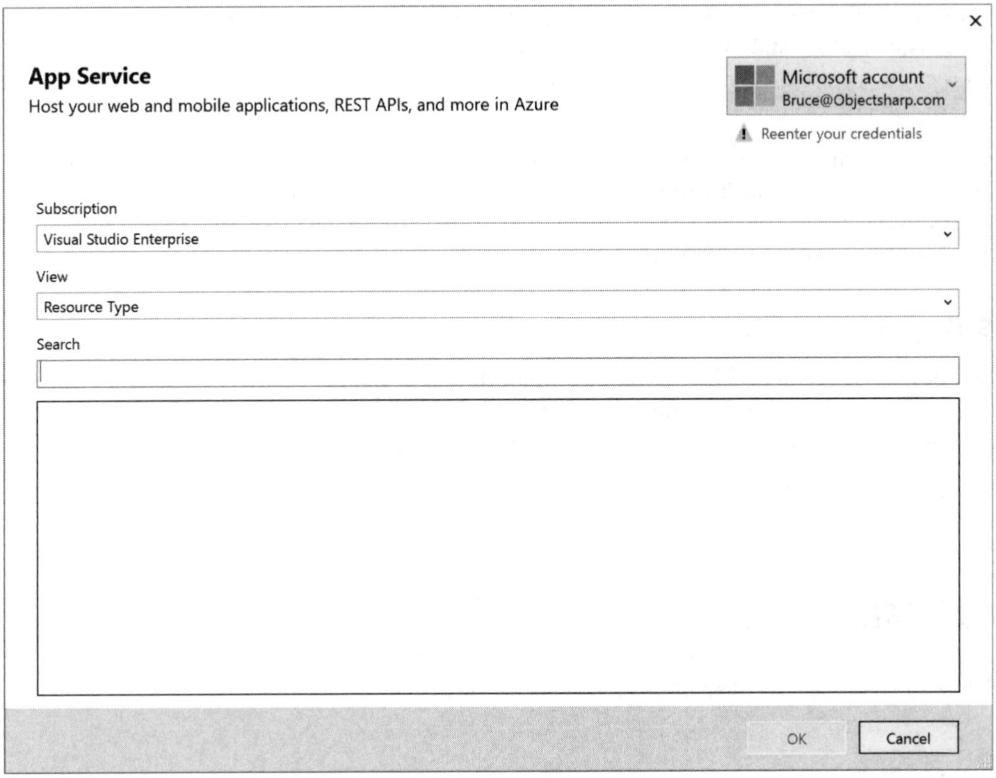

FIGURE 36-5

Select the subscription in which your existing app service is located. The list of previously defined app services appears in the box at the bottom. Select the desired app service and click OK.

When you create a new app service, additional information is required. Figure 36-6 illustrates the type of information that you must provide.

As part of the creation process, you need to select a name for your website that is unique. It is entered into the Web App Name field and immediately checked for validity. Other options in the dialog include the subscription under which the web app is created (if you have more than one subscription associated with your account), the region in which the web app will be created, and the App Service Plan. The App Service Plan value is used to specify the size of the app service that you want to create. "Size" in this case identifies the number of cores, the available RAM, and some additional features (like the number of staging areas and whether automatic scaling is supported). The best option depends on the amount of traffic you expect, the pattern of that traffic (steady vs in bursts), and the management features that you need. Clicking on the New button opens a dialog (Figure 36-7) that lets you specify the size.

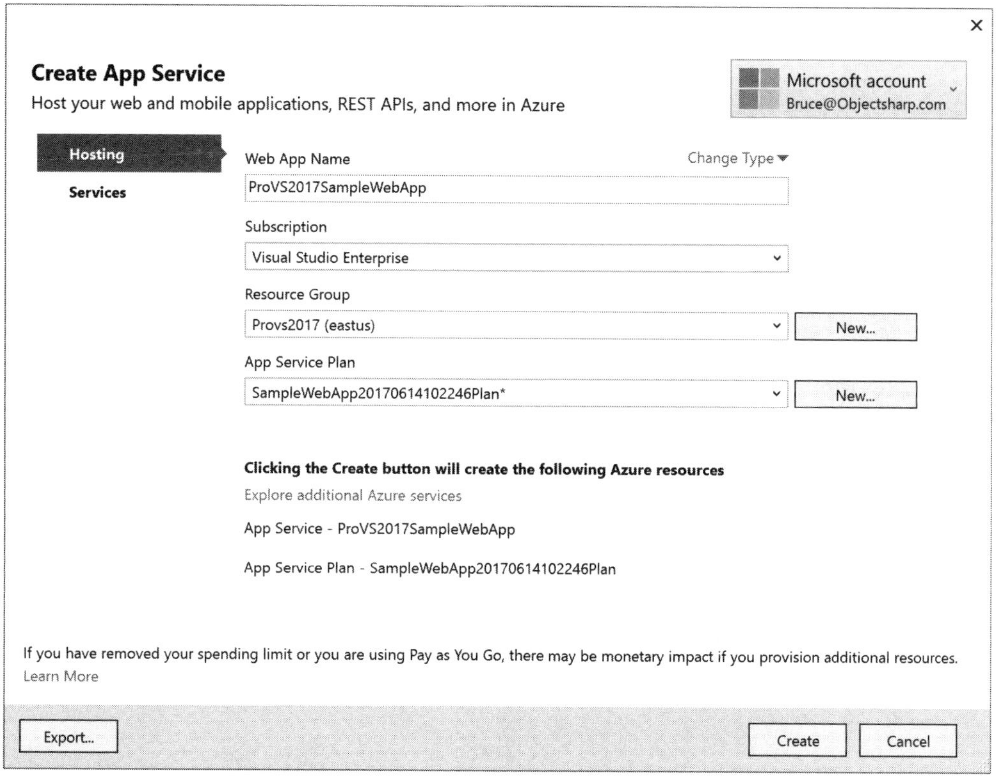

FIGURE 36-6

The Create App Service Plan dialog includes a Services tab, the contents of which appear in Figure 36-8.

This tab is used to define additional services that are part of your application and the app service. Initially, there is the App Service plan that you specified in Figure 36-6. That appears in the lower list of Figure 36-8. For this example, it is all that you need to include. However, if your application requires it, you can add more Azure resources to your deployment. The top list in Figure 36-8 shows SQL Database as an option. If you click on the plus sign to the right of that entry, you will be prompted for the information that Azure needs to create a SQL Database resource. That resource is then associated with your deployment.

FIGURE 36-7

Clicking on the Create button causes the web app to be created in Azure. When you're finished, you're returned to the Connection tab described in this chapter's "Publishing a Web Application" section. The difference is that all the details related to your new web app have been filled in and you're ready to move to the Settings tab. Once the rest of the details of the publication have been provided, clicking on the Publish button causes the output for your web application project to be promoted to Azure and your web app to be ready to accept requests.

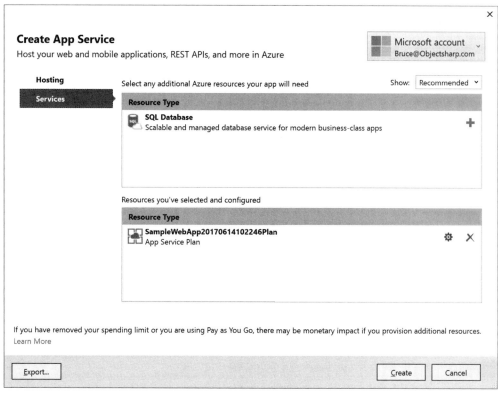

FIGURE 36-8

WEB PROJECT INSTALLERS

In addition to using the Publish Wizard tool, you can create a standard Windows Installer package to manage a web application or website deployment. You do this using the same Windows Installer Toolkit (WiX) component covered in Chapter 35, "Packaging and Deployment." But moving files onto the target machine is not sufficient for a web project. The installation needs to create a virtual directory as well. Fortunately, WiX supports this functionality. Consider the .wxs file shown here:

```
<?xml version="1.0" encoding="UTF-8"?>
<Wix xmlns="http://schemas.microsoft.com/wix/2006/wi"
     xmlns:iis="http://schemas.microsoft.com/wix/IIsExtension">
```

```xml
<Product Id="381ED4A8-90AA-49F5-9F63-CD128B33895C" Name="Sample Web App"
    Language="1033" Version="1.0.0.0" Manufacturer="Professional Visual Studio 2017"
    UpgradeCode="A8E5F094-C6B0-46E5-91A1-CC5A8C65079D">
    <Package InstallerVersion="200" Compressed="yes" />
    <Media Id="1" Cabinet="SampleWebApp.cab" EmbedCab="yes" />
    <Directory Id="TARGETDIR" Name="SourceDir">
        <Directory Id="ProgramFilesFolder">
            <Directory Id="WebApplicationFolder" Name="MyWebApp">
                <Component Id="ProductComponent" Guid="80b0ee2a-a102-46ec-a456-
33a23eb0588e">
                    <File Id="Default.aspx" Name="Default.aspx"
                        Source="..\SampleWebApp\Default.aspx" DiskId="1" />
                    <File Id="Default.aspx.cs" Name="Default.aspx.cs"
                        Source="..\SampleApp\Default.aspx.cs" DiskId="1"/>
                    <iis:WebVirtualDir Id="SampleWebApp" Alias="SampleWebApp"
                        Directory="WebApplicationFolder" WebSite="DefaultWebSite">
                        <iis:WebApplication Id="SampleWebApplication" Name="Sample" />
                    </iis:WebVirtualDir>
                </Component>
            </Directory>
        </Directory>
    </Directory>
    <iis:WebSite Id='DefaultWebSite' Description='Default Web Site'
        Directory='WebApplicationFolder'>
        <iis:WebAddress Id="AllUnassigned" Port="80" />
    </iis:WebSite>
    <Feature Id="ProductFeature" Title="Sample Web Application" Level="1">
        <ComponentRef Id="ProductComponent" />
    </Feature>
</Product>
</Wix>
```

Several elements are unique to web installation. First, notice that the WiX element contains a namespace with a prefix of iis. This namespace contains the elements processed to create the virtual directory. You also need to add a reference in your setup project to the WixIIsExtension assembly in the WiX Toolkit directory.

The second difference is in the Component placed inside the Directory hierarchy. The WebVirtualDir element is used to create a virtual directory. Specifically, the directory named WebApplicationFolder is created, with the directory added to the default website for the server. In the WebVirtualDir element, the WebApplication directs the installer to make the just-created virtual directory a web application.

Finally, notice the WebSite element. This tells the installer to utilize (or create, if necessary) the default website when accessing the WebApplicationFolder directory. The WebAddress element sets the application to listen on port 80 on all unassigned endpoints.

THE WEB PLATFORM INSTALLER

Web applications tend to rely on a large number of technologies and tools to function correctly both during development and in production. Even after your environment is correctly set up for a single application, relationships and dependencies between applications need to be understood and managed. Finally, there are always new tools, libraries, and applications available on the Internet, which you can build on when creating your own projects. As your environment becomes more complex, it can be quite a challenge to keep everything working correctly and up to date.

The Microsoft Web Platform Installer, as shown in Figure 36-9, is a simple tool designed to manage the software that you have installed on your web servers and development machine.

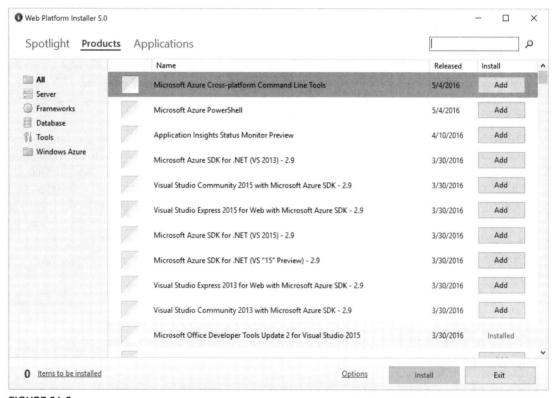

FIGURE 36-9

After you download the Web Platform Installer from `http://www.microsoft.com/web`, you can run it as many times as you like. It can detect which components you already have on your machine, and you can add and remove components with the click of a button. It can even take care of dependencies between components and install everything you need.

The Web Platform Installer can manage components beyond just the Web Platform. Also available is a collection of applications from the Microsoft Web Application Gallery at `http://www.microsoft.com/web/gallery`. These applications are filed under various categories under the Web Applications tab. Just like the components in the Web Platform, these applications can have their own prerequisites and the Web Platform Installer can ensure they are installed.

If you are already packaging your web application for deployment with the Web Deploy Package option from the Publish dialog, it is ready to be distributed using the Web Platform Installer. You can get your application added to the Web Application Gallery by filling in a simple form on the Microsoft Web portal. After your application is approved, it shows up ready to be installed on any machine with the Web Platform Installer on it.

Extending the Web Platform Installer

It is quite easy to have your application included in the Web Application Gallery to make it available to a large audience. There are some scenarios in which you would like to take advantage of the Web Platform Installer but do not want to make your application publicly available. This might be because your application is used privately within your company or because your application is not yet ready for release and you want to test the deployment procedure.

The Web Platform Installer relies on atom feeds to ensure that the list of components and products that it installs are always kept up to date. Each entry in these feeds corresponds to an application or component in the user interface of the Web Platform Installer. The Web Platform and Web Application tabs each come from different feeds at `http://www.microsoft.com/web/webpi/5.0/WebProductList.xml` and `http://www.microsoft.com/web/webpi/5.0/WebApplicationList.xml`, respectively. In addition to these two feeds, each installation of the Web Platform Installer can specify additional feeds that reference more components.

Here is a sample feed for a simple timesheets web application:

```xml
<?xml version="1.0" encoding="utf-8"?>
<feed xmlns="http://www.w3.org/2005/Atom">
  <webpiFile version="4.2.0.0"/>
  <title>Adventure Works Product WebPI Feed</title>
  <link href="http://www.professionalvisualstudio.com/SampleProductFeed.xml" />
  <updated>2015-02-10T08:29:14Z</updated>
  <author>
    <name>Adventure Works</name>
    <uri>http://www.professionalvisualstudio.com</uri>
  </author>
  <id>http://www.professionalvisualstudio.com/SampleProductFeed.xml</id>

  <entry>
    <productId>TimeSheets</productId>
    <title resourceName="Entry_AppGallerySIR_Title">Adventure Works Timesheets
</title>
    <summary resourceName="Entry_AppGallerySIR_Summary">
      The Adventure Works corporate Timesheeting system</summary>
    <longSummary resourceName="Entry_AppGallerySIR_LongSummary">
```

```
   The Adventure Works corporate Timesheeting system</longSummary>
<productFamily resourceName="TestTools">Human Resources</productFamily>
<version>1.0.0</version>
<images>
  <icon>c:\AdventureWorksIcon.png</icon>
</images>
<author>
  <name>Adventure Works IT</name>
  <uri>http://www.professionalvisualstudio.com</uri>
</author>
<published>2015-02-10T18:26:31Z</published>

<discoveryHint>
  <or>
    <discoveryHint>
      <registry>
        <keyPath>HKEY_LOCAL_MACHINE\SOFTWARE\AdventureWorks\Timesheets</keyPath>
        <valueName>Version</valueName>
        <valueValue>1.0.0</valueValue>
      </registry>
    </discoveryHint>
    <discoveryHint>
      <file>
        <filePath>%ProgramFiles%\AdventureWorks\Timesheets.exe</filePath>
      </file>
    </discoveryHint>
  </or>
</discoveryHint>
<dependency>
  <productId>IISManagementConsole</productId>
</dependency>
<installers>
  <installer>
    <id>1</id>
    <languageId>en</languageId>
    <architectures>
      <x86 />
      <x64 />
    </architectures>
    <osList>
      <os>
        <!-- the product is supported on Vista/Windows Server SP1 + -->
        <minimumVersion>
          <osMajorVersion>6</osMajorVersion>
          <osMinorVersion>0</osMinorVersion>
          <spMajorVersion>0</spMajorVersion>
        </minimumVersion>
        <osTypes>
          <Server />
          <HomePremium />
          <Ultimate />
          <Enterprise />
          <Business />
        </osTypes>
```

```
        </os>
      </osList>
      <eulaURL>http://www.professionalvisualstudio.com/eula.html</eulaURL>
      <installerFile>
        <!-- size in KBs -->
        <fileSize>1024</fileSize>
        <installerURL>http://www.professionalvisualstudio.com/Timesheets_x86.msi
        </installerURL>
        <sha1>111222FFF000BBB444555EEEAAA777888999DDDD</sha1>
      </installerFile>
      <installCommands>
        <msiInstall>
          <msi>%InstallerFile%</msi>
        </msiInstall>
      </installCommands>
    </installer>
  </installers>
</entry>
<tabs>
  <tab>
  <groupTab>
  <id>AdventureWorksHRTab</id>
  <name>Adventure Works Human Resources</name>
  <description>Adventure Works HR Apps</description>
  <groupingId>HRProductFamilyGrouping</groupingId>
  </groupTab>
  </tab>
</tabs>
<groupings>
  <grouping>
    <id>HRProductFamilyGrouping</id>
    <attribute>productFamily</attribute>
    <include>
      <item>Human Resources</item>
    </include>
  </grouping>
</groupings>
</feed>
```

The first part specifies some standard information about the feed, including the date it was last updated and author information. This is all useful if the feed is consumed using a normal feed reader. Following this is a single `entry` node containing information about the application. The Web Platform Installer can use the value of `productId` to refer to the application in other places, including being listed as a dependency for other components.

The `discoveryHint` node determines if this application is already installed. The sample application can be detected by looking for a specific Registry key value or by looking for a specific application by name. If either one of these items is found, the Web Platform Installer considers this application to be already installed. In addition to these two kinds of hints, you can use an `msiProductCode` hint to detect applications installed via Microsoft Installer (MSI).

The sample timesheets application has a dependency on the IIS Management Console. Each component that your application relies upon can be specified by its `productId`. If it is not already installed on the target machine, the Web Platform Installer installs it for you. In addition to dependencies, you can specify `incompatibilities` for your application, which can prevent both applications from installing at once.

The last component of the application entry is the `installers` element. There should be one `installer` element for each installer that you want to make available, and they should all have different identifiers. Each installer can be targeted at a specific range of languages, operating systems, and CPU architectures. If the target environment doesn't fall into this range, the installer will not be shown. Each installer should specify an installer file, which will be downloaded to a local cache before the specified `installCommands` are executed against it.

> **NOTE** *An installer file requires a size and a SHA1 hash so that the Web Platform Installer can verify that the file has been downloaded correctly. Microsoft provides a tool called File Checksum Integrity Verifier (`fciv.exe`), which can be used to generate the hash. You can download this tool from* `http://download.microsoft.com`.

The final two elements relate to what displays in the Web Platform Installer user interface. Each `tab` element adds to the list of tabs on the left. In the example, you add a tab based on a `grouping` of products, which is defined in the `groupings` element based on the `productFamily` attribute.

To add this feed to a Web Platform Installer instance, click the Options link to bring up the Options page. Enter the URL to the atom feed into the textbox, and click the Add Feed button. When you click OK the Web Platform Installer refreshes all the feeds and reloads all the applications including any custom installations that you have defined in your feed.

SUMMARY

This chapter showed you how to use a number of the features of Visual Studio 2017 to package your web applications and get them ready for deployment. The Web Deployment tool makes deployment to a number of environments and machines quick and painless. The Windows Installer Toolkit provides a mechanism to perform a typical installation of a web application. Finally, the Web Platform Installer provides you with an easy way to reach a large number of potential customers or to manage your own suite of enterprise applications.

37

Continuous Delivery

WHAT'S IN THIS CHAPTER?

➤ Understanding some of the terminology related to Continuous Delivery

➤ How to configure Continuous Delivery for your solution

➤ Take advantage of the Continuous Delivery Tools for Visual Studio

WROX.COM CODE DOWNLOADS FOR THIS CHAPTER

The wrox.com code downloads for this chapter can be found at www.wrox.com by searching for this book's ISBN number (978-1-119-40458-3). The code and any related support files are located in their own folder for this chapter.

In Chapter 36, "Web Application Deployment," you saw a number of different ways that Web applications can be deployed quickly and painlessly. Certainly, the technology involved in automating the deployment of Web applications has come a long way over the past few years. In fact, it has gotten to the point where it is quite possible to provision a server, deploy an application, run tests, and then decommission the server using nothing but scripts.

While this sounds nice, it is actually a major component of a rising practice within the software development world: Continuous Delivery (CD). In this chapter, we look at the tooling available through Visual Studio 2017 and Team Foundation Services to help support this endeavor.

NOMENCLATURE

The world of Continuous Delivery introduces a number of terms that you either might not be familiar with or might only know in a different context. So it's worthwhile to take a few minutes to define some of these terms, just to make sure that you understand their meaning in the context of continuous delivery.

Continuous Delivery

Continuous Delivery is a process that allows you to get all types of software changes (including bug fixes, new features, and experimental development) into production in a fast, safe and sustainable way.

One of the fundamental ideas is that it shouldn't take a long period of time for a piece of software to get into production. This means that instead of spending weeks designing a set of features, months developing them, and finally releasing them into production, the cycle from start to finish is greatly shortened. You might even have multiple deployments to production every single day. The time from "hey, I think this might be a good idea" to being able to deliver it to the client could be measured in hours and days instead of not weeks and months.

Exactly how this is accomplished depends on the environments involved. A common practice is to set up a *release pipeline*. This is a series of successful environments that support progressively longer and more rigorous integration, load, and user acceptance testing.

For example, you might have a development environment, a QA environment, and a production environment. Each of these environments should be identical (ideally) or at least similar enough that moving the application from one environment to the other is painless. The starting point for a release is triggered by *continuous integration* (see the next section), and there is automation that moves the release from environment to environment depending on the successful completion of a suite of tests.

A release pipeline is not the sole measure of whether you're performing continuous delivery. Depending you your needs, you might utilize techniques like features flags, deployment rings, and infrastructure as code. Each of these is aimed at solving the same problem: being able to move code to production safely and quickly.

Continuous Integration

Continuous delivery is triggered by continuous integration. And continuous integration (CI) is the process of automating the building and testing of the source code every time a team member commits a change to version control.

The idea behind CI is twofold. First, consider that development is a relatively solo occupation. You write code, fix bugs, and tweak design. Then you need to merge your results into the main code base so that others can use it or it can be deployed. However, if you want days or weeks to integrate your changes into the code base, the effort can be extraordinary, not to mention fraught with the possibility of introducing new, and as yet undiscovered, bugs.

Continuous integration is triggered the moment you commit your changes. It starts by building the entire application. Then, if successful, it runs the code through a series of tests. This not only ensures that your changes haven't accidentally clashed with someone else's changes, it also makes sure that there are no regression bugs that have been accidentally introduced.

DevOps

As a term, DevOps has grown in significance in the past five years. It is now part of the zeitgeist for thought leaders in the development world. But getting any significant agreement on exactly what is meant by DevOps is difficult. Part of the reason for this difficulty is because DevOps isn't really a "thing." It's more of a process and the tools that are used to support that process. And that process is to enable continuous delivery.

Consider for a moment the genesis of the term. It's a contraction of "Development" and "Operations." The idea is to suggest that the greatest level of success is achieved by taking two formerly independent groups and joining them for the greater glory. To be frank, developers frequently don't think about what it's going to take to deploy and monitor their applications, and operations staff is frequently seen as imposing unrealistic restrictions on what would otherwise be awesome and world-changing applications. Combining development and operations together helps ensure that development and operations staff cooperate more productively.

A common approach to the DevOps process is to take advantage of something developed to help fighter pilots—the OODA Loop. OODA stands for Observe, Orient, Decide, Act. In the world of software, this means that, as part of your development and deployment cycle, you observe the current demands, results and requirements, identify what you can do about them (the "orient" phase), decide on the best course of action to take, and then act on that decision. This loop repeats itself for every delivery.

Ultimately, DevOps is the ability to quickly deliver on business value, determine the success or failure of that delivery, and then correct or continue in that direction. The speed with which you can perform this loop is your cycle time. The goal is to find ways to shorten this cycle time. To accomplish this, you take steps like implementing smaller features, using more automation, ensuring the quality of the product produced by your release pipeline, and improving the telemetry of your application.

Two of those items (smaller features and more automation) are determined by corporate culture and choices. The use of telemetry is covered in Chapter 34, "Obfuscation, Application Monitoring, and Management," specifically in the "Application Instrumentation and Analytics" section. In this chapter, we look at some of the tools available in Visual Studio to help with the release pipeline.

CONTINUOUS DELIVERY TOOLS

In keeping with the philosophy of trying to minimize the footprint of Visual Studio (and because not every project benefits from continuous delivery), the tooling for continuous delivery is available through a separate extension. To install the Continuous Delivery Tools, open the Extensions and

Updates dialog (Tools ⇨ Extensions and Updates. Then select the Online node in the tree view on the left and enter "Continuous" into the search text box on the right (see Figure 37-1).

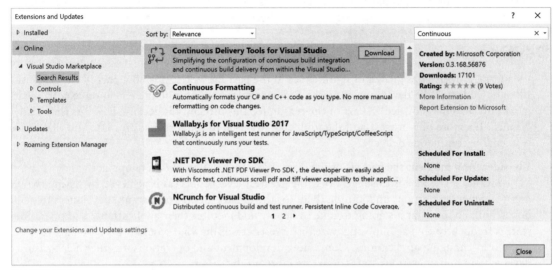

FIGURE 37-1

You should see the Continuous Delivery Tools for Visual Studio at or near the top of the results. Click on the Download button to start the installation process. Along with needing to accept the licensing conditions, you will need to restart Visual Studio for the installation to complete.

Setting Up Continuous Delivery

For each repository and branch that you want to participate in continuous delivery, you will need to set up a pipeline. For our example, we will be working with an ASP.NET Single Page Application project that has a single branch (master) and has been committed to a Git repository in Team Services. But the steps that are described in this section apply to any ASP.NET application, including ASP.NET Core.

To start, choose the Configure Continuous Delivery option from the Build menu. This launches the Configure Continuous Delivery dialog, as seen in Figure 37-2.

The top portion of the dialog is used to identify the repository and branch. The repository is provided automatically based on the current solution's repository and can't be changed. The branch is a dropdown list of all of the branches defined within that repository. The lower portion of the dialog allows you to define the Azure resource that is going to be used to manage the pipeline. The Subscription dropdown contains a list of all of the subscriptions associated with the user ID found in the top right of the dialog. Naturally, if you change that user ID, the list of subscriptions is likely to change as well. Below the subscription is a dropdown containing all of the currently defined continuous delivery services. By default, a new service is created with some default settings, but you can change those values by clicking on the Edit link, causing Figure 37-3 to be displayed.

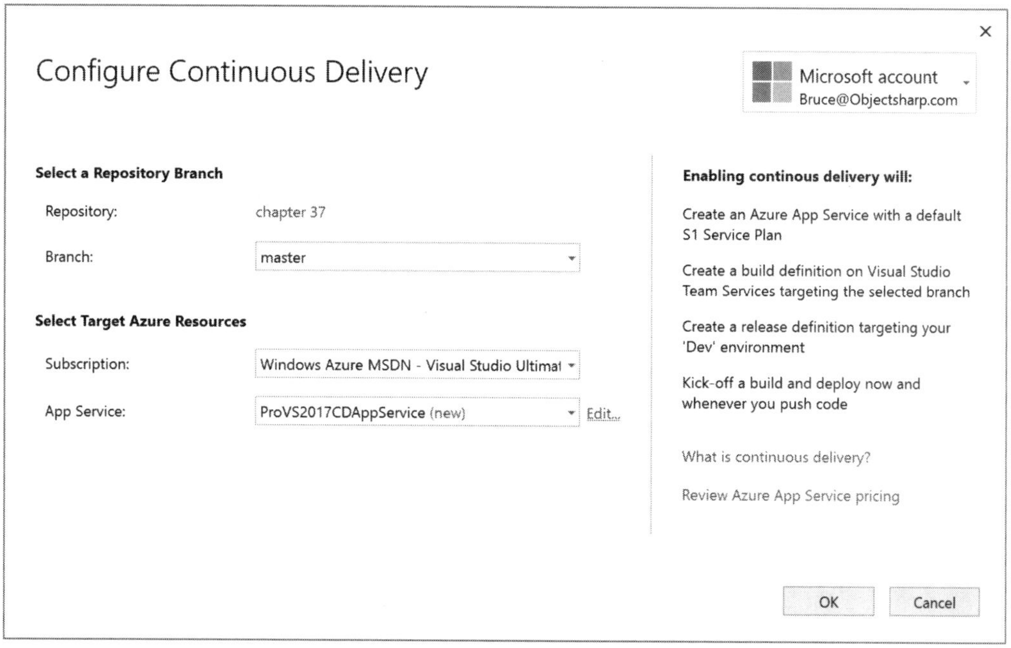

FIGURE 37-2

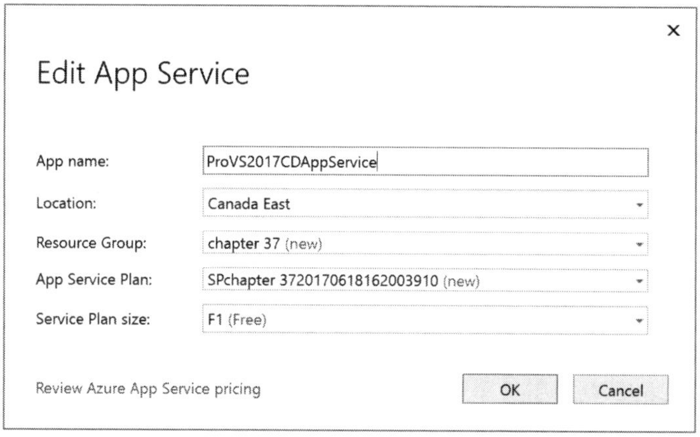

FIGURE 37-3

Here you can define the name of the service (useful for being able to know what functionality the service is related to as you manage it through the Azure portal), the location in which the service will be created, the resource group into which the service will be placed, the name of the app service plan, and the pricing tier that you will use for the service. The different tiers provide different build speeds, depending on the complexity of the projects being built.

When all of this information is configured to suit your needs, click on the OK button on the Configure Continuous Delivery dialog to start the creation of the pipeline. You will see output similar to what is shown in Figure 37-4 if your creation process is successful. The most common reason for failure, at least in my experience, is that the creation process doesn't like it if your repository contains any spaces it in. So take that into consideration as you name your repository.

```
Output
Show output from: Continuous Delivery Tools

Configuring continuous delivery. This might take several minutes...

Creating Azure resources:
    Creating App Service Plan SPprofessionalvisualstudio201720170618110920499.......done
    Creating App Service professionalvisualstudio2017........done

Creating build and release definitions............................................done

The continuous build delivery setup for Team Project professional visual studio 2017 completed successfully. Builds are now automatically generated and deployed to
Details:
    App Service:  professionalvisualstudio2017
    VSTS Team Project Name: Professional Visual Studio 2017
    VSTS Team Project: https://tag.visualstudio.com/Professional Visual Studio 2017
    Build Definition: https://tfs.app.visualstudio.com/A39930495-333a-4333-82f6-a142a1d6e03a/_permalink/_build/index?collectionId=39930495-333a-4333-82f6-a142a1d6e03a
    Release Definition: https://tag.visualstudio.com/6abe41ef-4d4b-40b2-9170-9f0f9ce5ef95/_release?definitionId=1
```

FIGURE 37-4

Heads Up Code Analysis

One of the main tenets of continuous integration and continuous delivery is to deliver information about the quality of the build and release pipeline to the appropriate people as quickly as possible. A second and even more important tenet is to take steps to ensure that the quality of the codebase is maintained with each commit. One of the tools that the Continuous Delivery Tools provides to assist with both of these is Heads Up Code Analysis.

You can find the Heads Up Code Analysis data on the Changes tab within the Team Explorer (see Figure 37-5).

You'll notice that there is a Build & Code Analysis Results section. Here you will find information related to the most recent build or code analysis run. If there are build errors or warnings, you'll see the information in the Errors and Warnings label. If the build is

FIGURE 37-5

completely clean and you have configured code analysis to run automatically, then the warnings and messages associated with that analysis will appear. Alternatively, you can run the code analysis portion manually by clicking on the Refresh Analytics link. If you click on the View Issues link, you are taken to the Error List where detailed information about the items can be found.

The rules that are used in the code analysis process are defined separately from this page. You access the configuration details through the Analyze ➪ Configure Code Analysis menu. There you can set up the code analysis properties for either the current project or the entire solution. Figure 37-6 shows the form used for the entire solution.

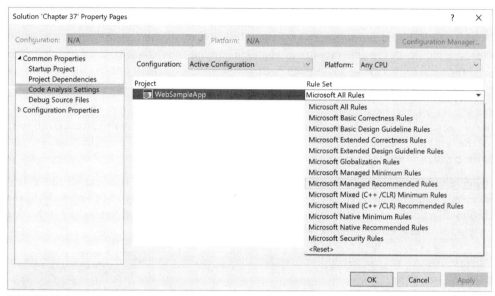

FIGURE 37-6

Each of the projects in the solution appears on the form. Next to each project you can identify the rule set that is used when code analysis is performed. Figure 37-6 shows the rules that are available out of the box. But you can install additional rule sets through the Extensions and Updates dialog, or you can create your own custom rule sets built to fit the needs of your organization.

Automatic Build Notifications

One of the things that happened when you configured Continuous Delivery is that you defined a default build for your project. The build performs a compilation of all of the projects in your solution and is automatically triggered every time you commit your code to source control. Not only does the build compile your solution, but if you have associated your project with an Azure App Service, it will automatically deploy the compiled and tested application to Azure.

When the build is completed, again believing that getting information to you quickly is important, a popup message appears at the bottom of the Visual Studio IDE (see Figure 37-7).

FIGURE 37-7

This popup contains the name of the build, who requested the build, and the ultimate state of the build (that is, whether it succeeded or failed). You'll also notice the icon that appears in the status bar at the bottom. At the moment, there is a green checkmark. This indicates that the last build for this solution was successful. If the last build had failed, then a red "X" appears. The purpose is to let you know what the state of the code in source control is at that moment. This matters because the typical rhythm for a developer is to finish coding a feature, run the unit tests locally to make sure everything passes, get the latest version of the solution from source control (performing any merges that are required), run the tests again, and then commit their changes. If the current state of the build is red (otherwise known as "broken"), then you won't be able to retrieve the latest version of the source code and successfully run your tests, and your code won't compile either.

From that same icon, you have a couple of options available to you. You can configure continuous delivery (usually used only if you haven't already configured it in the past) or you can go to the details of the last build. Choosing that second option takes you to the web page that contains the result of the build, as seen in Figure 37-8.

If you're interested in viewing or modifying the build that is performed, it is accessible through a couple of paths, but, ultimately, you need to be on the Team Services web site. In Figure 37-8, there is an Edit Build Definition link that can be used, or if you are within Visual Studio, go to the Team Explorer window and get to the Builds tab (Figure 37-9).

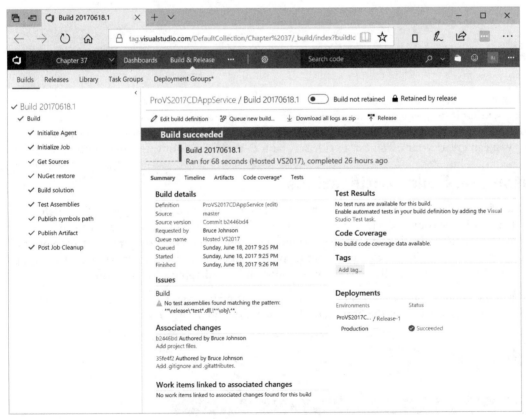

FIGURE 37-8

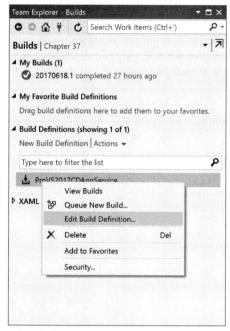

FIGURE 37-9

At the bottom of the window, there is a list of defined builds for this repository. Right-click on the desired build and select the Edit Build Definition option. This launches the Team Services web site and takes you to the build definition (Figure 37-10).

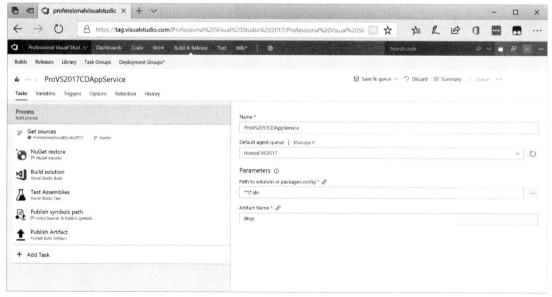

FIGURE 37-10

SUMMARY

This chapter defined some of the more common terms related to continuous integration and delivery. As well, it showed you how to configure continuous delivery for your project and described the tools that are available to you to help keep you informed of the status of your project and the build and release pipeline without needing to leave Visual Studio 2017.

PART XI
Visual Studio Editions

38

Visual Studio Enterprise: Code Quality

WHAT'S IN THIS CHAPTER?

➤ Creating models of your solution

➤ Enforcing application architecture

➤ Exploring existing architectures

WROX.COM CODE DOWNLOADS FOR THIS CHAPTER

The wrox.com code downloads for this chapter can be found at www.wrox.com by searching for this book's ISBN number (978-1-119-40458-3). The code and any related support files are located in their own folder for this chapter.

Visual Studio 2017 was released with three separate editions, given names that are by now quite familiar to developers. Visual Studio 2017 Community and Visual Studio 2017 Professional are functionally almost identical. The only significant difference is that the Professional edition supports the CodeLens feature and the Community edition doesn't. That isn't to say that you can ignore Professional and just use the "free" version. While functionally quite similar, the license for the two products is very different. Without going into details (because, honestly, Microsoft licensing is complicated enough that they offer courses in it), Community can only be used on projects related to open source, academic research, in a learning environment, or if your company doesn't cross thresholds related to a specific number of developers, a number of PCs, or annual revenue.

The third Visual Studio 2017 edition is known as the Enterprise edition. In this edition, there are a number of features that have been added to Visual Studio. In general, the features fall into two categories—measuring and managing code and application quality, and improving the unit testing and debugging experiences. In both case, the added features are aimed at scenarios that would be more likely to be found in an "enterprise" (as opposed to a smaller organization). The next two chapters will look at these different groups of features, starting with those related to code quality in this chapter.

DEPENDENCY VERIFICATION

A *model* in software terms is an abstract representation of some process or object. You create models to better understand and communicate to others the way different parts of the application are intended to work. In earlier versions of Visual Studio, you would include artifacts like UML diagrams in your modeling projects. However, in Visual Studio 2017, support for UML diagrams has been removed, due at least in part because the usage levels of that feature were low in comparison to the effort involved in keeping it in line with changes to how Visual Studio is constructed.

So while in Visual Studio 2017 there is still a modeling project, its contents and purpose have significantly changed. Now it is used to support dependency verification, including the newly added Live Dependency Verification feature. To start this process, use the New Project menu option to launch the New Project dialog (Figure 38-1).

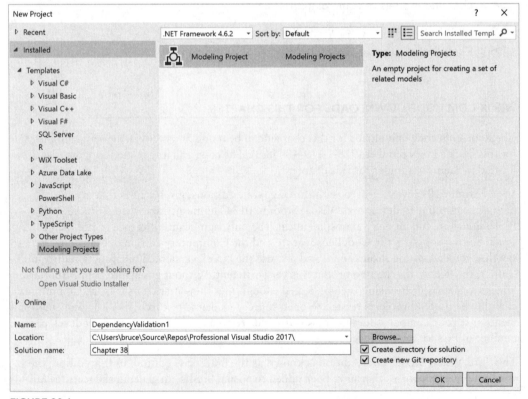

FIGURE 38-1

You can find modeling projects on their own node in the New Project dialog. Once you have created a project, you can see (Figure 38-2 shows the Solution Explorer) that there isn't much to the project.

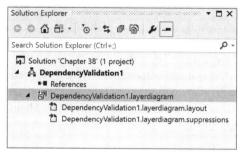

FIGURE 38-2

The element that was created with the project is the Layer Diagram, which will be used to perform the dependency validation for the entire solution. If you double-click on the artifact, you will see a designer appear, as shown in Figure 38-3.

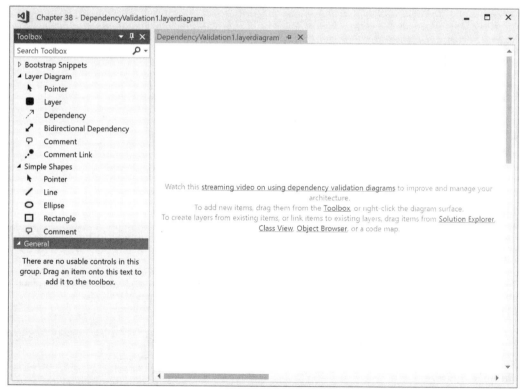

FIGURE 38-3

Figure 38-3 also includes the Toolbox for the designer. The purpose of the Layer Diagram is to allow you to specify the high-level structure of a software solution. It identifies the different areas or layers of your application and defines the relationships between them.

Each layer is a logical group of classes that commonly share a technical responsibility, such as being used for data access or presentation. From within the designer, you can drag each layer onto the design surface and configure it with a name. You can draw directed or bidirectional dependency links between layers. A layer depends on another layer if any of its components have a direct reference to any of the components in the layer it depends on. If there is not an explicit dependency, it is assumed that no components match this description. Figure 38-4 illustrates a simple Layer Diagram.

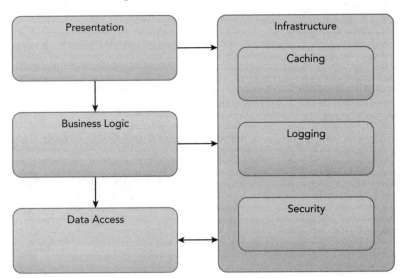

FIGURE 38-4

Layers can be nested inside one another. Specifically, the layers on the right side of Figure 38-4 have been nested in that manner. The reason for doing this is to make changes to the diagram easier. If you need to make changes in the future, the associations "follow" as you move the layers around.

After you create a Layer Diagram, you can use it to discover communications between layers in your compiled application and to verify that these links match the design. More specifically, you can associate projects with the different layers. Then, as part of the build or even as part of your coding, you will be notified if what you are doing doesn't fit within the previously defined layers.

Before you do this, you need to associate projects with each layer. And you need to add a component to the project that allows it to participate in Live Dependency Validation. As you add projects to your solution, you will see a warning appear in the Solution Explorer (see Figure 38-5).

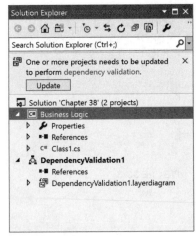

FIGURE 38-5

Projects that are part of the live validation need to have the Microsoft.DependencyValidation .Analyzers Nuget package installed. Clicking on the Update button will automatically add the package to the new project. Once the package has been added to the solution, other projects that you add will get the Nuget package.

To associate a project with a layer, drag the project from the Solution Explorer onto the layer. Or you can drag your project directly onto the surface to create a new layer. Or you can drag a folder. Or even a class. Regardless of what element you drag, entries are added to the Layer Explorer tool window (Figure 38-6), and a number inside each layer is updated to reflect the number of artifacts associated with it.

Name	Categories	Layer	Supports Validation	Identifier
Campaign Manager.exe	Assembly	Campaign Mana...	True	(Assembly="Campaign Manager")
Business Logic.dll	Assembly	Business Logic	True	(Assembly="Business Logic")
Data Access.dll	Assembly	Data Access	True	(Assembly="Data Access")

FIGURE 38-6

After the Layer Diagram has assemblies associated with it, you can fill in any missing dependencies by selecting Generate Dependencies from the design surface context menu. This analyzes the associated assemblies, builds the project if necessary, and fills in any missing dependencies. Note that the tool won't ever delete unused dependencies.

> **NOTE** *Not all artifacts that can be linked to a Layer Diagram support validation. The Layer Explorer window has a Supports Validation column, which can help you determine if you have linked artifacts for which this is true.*

When your Layer Diagram contains all the layers and only the dependencies that you would expect, you can verify that your application matches the design specified by the Layer Diagram. To do this, you can select Validate from the design surface context menu. The tool analyzes your solution structure and any violations found appear as build errors, as shown in Figure 38-7. Double-clicking one of these errors takes you to the location of the error.

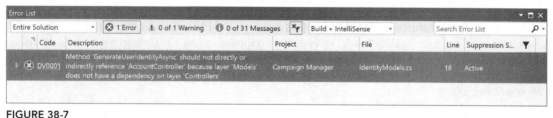

FIGURE 38-7

Beyond placing errors into the Error List dialog, Live Dependency Validation actually marks the errors in code, and the information for the error is directly available right at the source, as can be seen in Figure 38-8.

FIGURE 38-8

In order to make Dependency Validation even more useful, it is possible to specify additional constraints on the classes that are part of a layer. Select a layer in the design surface and then open the Properties window (see Figure 38-9).

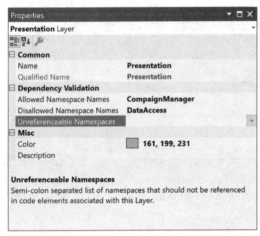

FIGURE 38-9

You will notice three properties associated with the layer that allow you to configure the namespaces which are or are not allowed within the layer. Each property is a semicolon-separated list of namespaces. The purpose of the Allowed Namespace Names and Disallowed Namespace Names is relatively self-evident. If a class is in one of those lists, it either can or can't be used within the code in that layer. The Unreferencable Namespaces item contains a list of namespaces that not only can't be used within the layer, but can't be referenced by any of the assemblies used in the namespace.

EXPLORING CODE WITH CODE MAPS

Many advanced features in Visual Studio are designed to help you understand and navigate the structure of an existing code base. Dependency Graphs give you a high-level view of the relationships between various types of components within your project. The Code Map window enables you to deep dive into different areas while still leaving a trail of breadcrumbs to help you understand where you are.

One of the hardest aspects of navigating a new code base is understanding where you are in relation to everything else. The Code Map window (Figure 38-10) enables you to navigate through the class usage relationships with single clicks, displaying a node graph that eases the process of figuring out where you are in the code base.

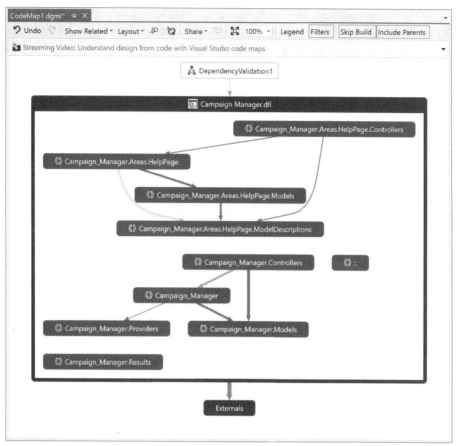

FIGURE 38-10

The Code Map shown in Figure 38-10 was generated by using the Architecture ⇨ Generate Code Map For Solution menu option. Once the application has been built, Visual Studio examines the code and diagrams the links between the top-level assemblies.

The generated diagram is actually a Dependency Graph. A Dependency Graph enables you to visualize the dependencies between items at different levels of focus.

Five basic options specify the way a Dependency Graph is arranged based on the direction of arrows: top to bottom, left to right, bottom to top, and right to left. The fifth option is the Quick Clusters layout, which attempts to arrange the items so that they are closest to the things they connect to. You can change the layout by using the Layout drop-down at the top of the diagram's design surface.

When you click on one of the nodes, it expands so that you can see contained elements. By continuing down through the hierarchy, you can view all the elements, including their accessibility.

While you are editing your code, Visual Studio makes it easy to jump into the code map. From within the text editor, right-click on a method name and select the Code Map ⇨ Show on Code Map option. This takes you to the Code Map diagram and expands the appropriate nodes so that you can see the method definition, along with both the callers (where the method is called from) and the callees (other methods that are called from within the selected method).

CODE CLONING

The goal of code cloning is to help you find sections of code that are similar, with an eye toward refactoring. There are two ways to approach code cloning. The first is to select a fragment of code and then use the Code Clone function to search for similar fragments. The other is to allow Code Clone to search through the code for you, again looking for similar fragments.

To work from a fragment, select the block of code in the text editor and then choose the Find Matching Clones in Solution option from the context menu. To search the entire solution, use the Analyze ⇨ Analyze Solution for Code Clones menu option. Regardless of which option you choose, the result will be a window similar to Figure 38-11.

Code Clone Analysis Results		
Clone Group	Clone Count	
⊿ Strong Match 1 (2 Files)	2	
ModelNameHelper:GetModelName - C:\Users\bruce\Source\Repos\Professional Visual Studio 2017\Chapter 38\Campaign Manager\Areas\HelpPage\ModelDescriptions\ModelNameHelper.cs lines 19-30		
XmlDocumentationProvider:GetTypeName - C:\Users\bruce\Source\Repos\Professional Visual Studio 2017\Chapter 38\Campaign Manager\Areas\HelpPage\XmlDocumentationProvider.cs lines 139-150		
▷ Medium Match 1 (1 File)	2	
▷ Medium Match 2 (1 File)	2	
▷ Medium Match 3 (1 File)	2	
4 Clone Groups | 8 Cloned Snippets | 107 Lines of Cloned Code		Streaming Video: Finding and managing cloned code ▾

FIGURE 38-11

In Figure 38-11, you can see that the matches have been grouped by strength. There are one strong match and three medium matches. You can expand the matches to see the files involved, and you can hover over the line to see the underlying code. Double-clicking on a line takes you to the line in the text editor.

SUMMARY

Dependency Validation provides a great way for you to communicate the design of your application clearly, unambiguously, and effectively. The ability to verify that your application meets the architecture as designed by the Layer Diagram can be a useful sanity check to ensure project quality standards remain high and architectural decisions are not abandoned after the project is underway. And with Live Dependency Validation, you can go a step further and ensure that the solution won't even build when the design is violated.

Getting up to speed with an existing code base can be hard. Using Dependency Graphs is an easy way to identify the relationships between various parts of your application. The Code Map window enables you to rapidly move through the connections between components in the system to find the items you want. Finally, the ability to navigate to the Code Map directly from an existing method enables you to quickly grasp the fundamentals of how a method interacts with other methods and classes within the application.

39

Visual Studio Enterprise: Testing and Debugging

WHAT'S IN THIS CHAPTER?

➤ Creating different tests for web and Windows applications

➤ Viewing memory usage within a .NET application

➤ Generating unit tests for legacy code

WROX.COM CODE DOWNLOADS FOR THIS CHAPTER

The wrox.com code downloads for this chapter can be found at www.wrox.com by searching for this book's ISBN number (978-1-119-40458-3). The code and any related support files are located in their own folder for this chapter.

You can test an application in many ways. Chapter 10, "Unit Testing," introduced the concept of unit tests, which are small executable pieces of code that verify a particular aspect of behavior for a single method or class. This chapter examines the advanced tools built into Visual Studio that are available for other testing tasks, including testing web applications.

> **NOTE** *Visual Studio also contains a product called Test Manager. This tool is designed for testers to interact directly with Team Foundation Servers and manage test plans, suites, and cases. Test Manager is available with the Enterprise edition of Visual Studio and as a part of a separate pack called Test Elements. If you are a tester, or spend a great deal of time working on the testing aspect of development projects, then Test Manager is worth a look. Although it is beyond the scope of this book, Test Manager's numerous tools can not only make your life easier, but it can make capturing and conveying exception conditions to the development team seamless.*

AUTOMATED TESTS

An automated test is a piece of code that verifies the behavior of your application without any user input or control. After the system has been asked to run an automated test, it can be left unattended until it completes.

The starting point for creating a new automated test is a testing project. The mechanics of creating a test project were covered in Chapter 10, but for the upcoming examples it's useful to create a Web Performance and Load Test project. To add a new test to an existing project, use the Add ➪ New Item option from the Solution's context menu. There is a Test node in the Add New Item dialog with the different test templates displayed on the right side. Alternatively (and probably more convenient), the context menu also includes options to add a Unit Test, a Load Test, a Web Performance Test, a Coded UI Test, an Ordered Test, or a Generic Test (see Figure 39-1).

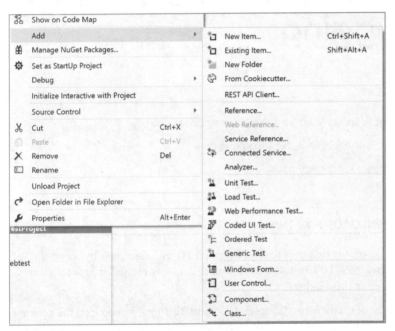

FIGURE 39-1

Web Performance Tests

This type of automated test simulates web requests and enables you to inspect the responses and evaluate different conditions to determine if the test passes. When you create a new Web Performance Test, Internet Explorer opens ready to start navigating. If this is your first performance test, you might get prompted to enable the Web Test Recorder add-on. With the Web Test Recorder enabled, as shown in Figure 39-2, navigate to and around your site as if you were a normal user. That includes entering any data that is needed. (The actual values that are used can be modified programmatically each time the web test is executed.) When done, simply click Stop. This opens the Web Test Designer, as shown in Figure 39-3. From there you can customize your test, adding validation and extraction rules, context parameters, comments, data sources, calls to other Web Performance Tests, or insert transactions. You can also specify response time goals for requests.

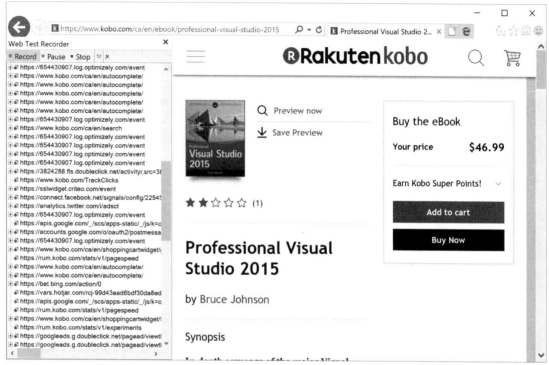

FIGURE 39-2

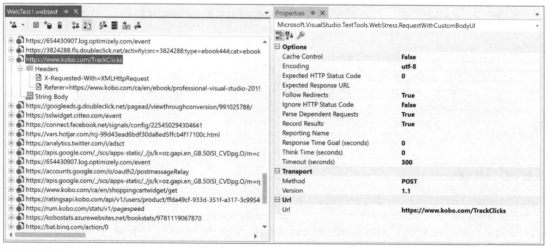

FIGURE 39-3

You often need to run the same set of tests against different web servers; to do this, configure which server the test runs against as a context parameter. From the Web Test Designer, you can right-click the main node and select Parameterize Web Servers. Visual Studio inspects the URLs in each request and determines the context parameters it needs to create.

You can link your requests using the output from one of them as input for the next; to do this, add extraction rules to a specific request. You can extract from fields, attributes, HTTP headers, hidden fields, and text, or even use regular expressions. The result of an extraction sets a context parameter, which you can then use, for example, as a form or query string parameter in further requests. You can add a product and then search for it using the ID in another request.

You can add form and query string parameters from the context menu of a request. By selecting a form or query string parameter from the properties window, you can set its value to a context parameter or bind it to a data source.

No test framework would be complete without validations. When you record a test, a Response URL Validation Rule is added asserting that the response URL is the same as the recorded response URL. This is not enough for most scenarios. From the context menu at the Web Performance Test or for an individual request, you can add validation rules. You can check that a form field or attribute has a certain value or that a particular tag is included, find some text, or ascertain that the request doesn't take more than a specified length of time.

You can run a Web Performance Test directly from the Web Test Designer. After a test is run, you can see its details by double-clicking it in the Test Results window. To open this window, from the Test Windows menu, select Test Results. There you can see each request's status, total time, and bytes. When you select a request, you'll see the details of the selected request and received response, values of the context parameters, validations and extraction rules, and a web browser–like view displaying the web page.

If you need additional flexibility, you can code the Web Performance Tests using .NET and the Web Testing Framework. The best way to learn how to use the framework and start coding your test is by generating code for a recorded Web Performance Test. You have this option (Generate Code) in the Web Test context menu.

> **NOTE** *Although Visual Studio provides support for some ASP.NET-specific features, you can use Web Performance Tests for sites built using other technologies.*

Load Tests

Whereas web and load testing are meant to test functional requirements, Load Tests can run a set of tests repeatedly, so you can see how your application performs. When you create a new Load Test, you are presented with a wizard that guides you through the necessary steps.

The first choice you face is which infrastructure to use to drive your load tests. Visual Studio Team Services provides the capability to run load tests on web sites using Azure. Alternatively, you might have the requisite servers available within your own corporate environment. Keep in mind that in order to effectively run a load test, you are going to need a number of machines available to you. These machines will generate the requests that are then sent to your web site. There are limits to how many users a single machine can effectively replicate, so if you want to run tests that simulate thousands of users, you are going to need a fairly large number of machines.

Once you have identified the infrastructure that the test will be using, you need to create a scenario. The scenario includes how long the test will last, how long you want to run the tests to warm up the target application, and whether you want to use think times. When you recorded the Web Performance Tests, the time you took between each request was also recorded and can be used as the think time. It can be edited for each web request in the properties window, or you can have the load test vary the think times based on the recorded think times.

> **NOTE** *The warm-up time for a load test allows the target application to connect to data sources, retrieve cached information, or perform other initialization steps that would impact performance when the application is starting up, but not once the application has been running for a while.*

As part of the scenario, you'll define the load pattern; for example, a constant load of 100 users or a load increasing by 10 every 10 seconds until you get to 200 users. The next steps, Test, Browser, and Network Mix, define how tests will be run by virtual users, specify which browsers will be used to run the tests, and determine the kinds of network that will be simulated. In the Test Mix step you can add Generic, Ordered, and Web Performance Tests.

In the Counter Sets step, you'll add the computers that you want to monitor and the performance counters you are interested in. For example, you can monitor your Database Server and IIS. In the last step, Run Settings, you can specify the test duration or test iterations, how often samples will be taken for performance counters, a test description, how many identical errors will be recorded, and the validation level. We defined a validation level for each Validation Rule in our Web Performance Tests. Because evaluation of these rules can be expensive, in Load Tests only rules with a level equal to or below the specified validation level will be evaluated.

When you click Finish, you are presented with the Load Test Designer, as shown in Figure 39-4. There you can add scenarios, counter sets, or new run settings.

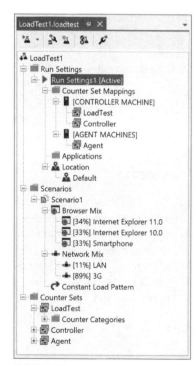

FIGURE 39-4

When you run the tests, you'll see the Load Test Monitor; by default it shows the Performance view. This shows a graph of various performance metrics over the life of the text (illustrated in Figure 39-5). At the bottom is a list of the metrics. They can be added or removed from the graph visualization by using the check box on the left of each item. Above the graph, you click on the Details link to change to a view that shows details about the performance metrics. To the right of the title, there is a link that allows you to download the report.

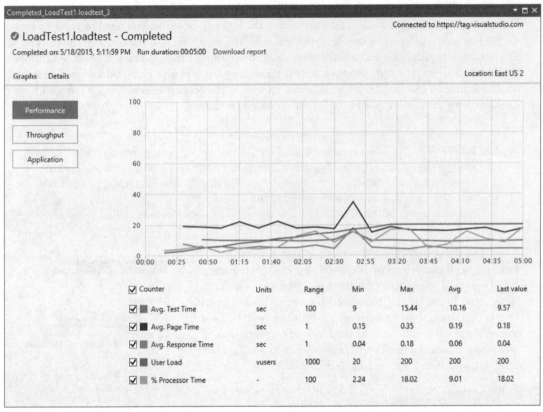

FIGURE 39-5

Once the report has been downloaded, the link changes to View Report. A click on that link displays the screen shown in Figure 39-6. Here you can use buttons on the toolbar to toggle between a Summary or Tables view, export to Excel or CSV, and add analysis notes. In the Graphs view at the bottom, you have a legends pane. There you can select/deselect the counters that you want to include in the graphs. In the Tables view, you can see the Requests, Errors, Pages, SQL Trace, Tests, Thresholds, and Transactions.

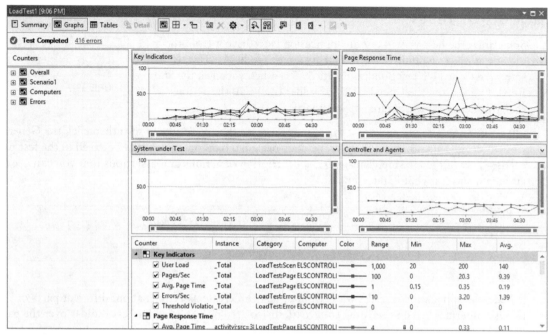

FIGURE 39-6

One thing to be aware of if you are using the Team Services infrastructure to run your load tests is the costs. Every user has a limited number of test minutes per month. That number will cover some simple usage scenarios. However for more complex scenarios or longer tests, you can purchase additional minutes. And when you compare the cost to other cloud-based services, not to mention what the alternative of purchasing the servers and running them in-house would cost, the result is quite reasonable.

It is not required that the load tests work only with HTTP or HTTPS endpoints. The cloud-based tests can run against any endpoint that is accessible over the Internet. This does mean that you might not be able to perform a load test against an internal-only website. To handle that situation, you need to turn to Test Load Agents.

Test Load Agent

For performing load testing on websites that are local to your corporate network, you can install one or more Test Load Agents. These agents allow you to distribute the work of request generation and submission across different machines. Each agent can simulate approximately 1,000 users per processor. This product requires a separate installation and requires one controller and at least one agent. To configure the environment, select the Manage Test Controllers button on the toolbar for the Load Test designer. There you can select a controller and add agents.

Coded UI Tests

Sometimes the best way to test an application is to drive it from the outside as a user would. When you create a new Coded UI Test, it starts the Coded UI Test Builder (Figure 39-7). When you click the Start Recording button, the Coded UI Test Builder tracks all the actions that you take with the mouse and keyboard.

FIGURE 39-7

Open your application, and use it to get into the state that you'd like to test; then click the Generate Code button. This prompts you to name your recorded method, which will be saved in the test project as a part of the UI Map. This map is a description of actions and assertions that you can use to automate and test your application.

> **NOTE** *Each test project contains a single UI Map, which all the Coded UI Tests share.*

When your application is in the wanted state, you can create assertions about different parts of the user interface. To do this, drag the crosshair icon from the Coded UI Test Builder over the part of the UI that you want to make an assertion about. When you release the mouse button, the Add Assertions dialog displays, as in Figure 39-8.

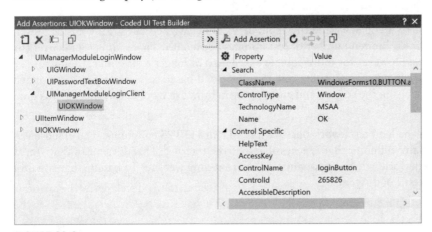

FIGURE 39-8

On the left is a collapsible panel showing the UI control map, which displays the hierarchy of all controls that have been identified so far. On the right is a list of properties that the Coded UI Test Builder has identified along with their values. To make an assertion about one of these properties, you can right-click it and select Add Assertion. Each assertion has a comparator and a comparison value to be tested against.

Generic Tests

Not every kind of test is covered in Team System. This is why Microsoft included the concept of Generic Tests, so you can easily use custom tests and also the rest of the features such as Test Results, Assign Work Items, and Publish Test Results.

To configure a Generic Test, you need to specify an existing program and optionally specify its command-line arguments, additional files to deploy, and environment variables. The external application can communicate the test result back to Team System in two ways. One is with the Error Level, where a value of 0 indicates success and anything else is considered a failure. The other is to return an XML file that conforms to the `SummaryResult.xsd` schema located in Visual Studio's installation path. In MSDN you can find information about this schema and how to report detailed errors using XML.

Ordered Tests

Use Ordered Tests when you need to group tests and run them as a whole, or if tests have dependencies on each other and need to be run in a particular order. It's a good practice to create atomic Unit Tests in order to run them in isolation with repeatable results. It isn't recommended to use Ordered Tests just to deal with dependencies between Unit Tests. A good reason for creating Ordered Tests is to create a performance session for more than one test.

In the Ordered Test Editor, you have a list of the available tests that you can add to the Ordered Test; the same test can be added more than once. You can also choose to continue after a failure. When the test is run, it executes each of the selected tests in the specified order.

INTELLITRACE

One of the banes of a professional developer's existence is the "no repro" bug. This is a bug that a tester has found while exploring the application. Yet when the bug description is passed back to the development team, the team cannot reproduce it. So the bug goes back and forth with neither side able to identify the difference between the two systems that would seem to be the root of the issue.

With IntelliTrace, the tester can capture a detailed view of exactly what was happening in the application when the bug occurred. This information is then provided to the developer, who can actually step through the application and see the values of the variables as if they had attached to the running process. From the perspective of one who has dealt with this situation many times, there is little question that IntelliTrace is a valuable tool to add to the developer's toolbox.

The default configuration for IntelliTrace is to collect information at specific, predefined points within the .NET Framework. The actual points depend on the type of application or library involved. Windows Forms apps would be focused on user interface events such as key presses and button clicks. ASP.NET applications are concerned with requests. (Note that this does not include client-side events.) ADO.NET gathers events on command executions. If the defaults are not to your liking, use the IntelliTrace Events options page (IntelliTrace ⇨ IntelliTrace Events page from the Tools ⇨ Options menu option).

When one of these points of interest is hit, the debugger collects the desired values for the event. It also gathers generally useful information such as the call stack and the current active threads. The information is saved to an IntelliTrace log.

In Visual Studio 2017, IntelliTrace is now part of the Diagnostic Tools window, which is available through the Debug ➪ Show Diagnostic Tools menu option. Figure 39-9 illustrates the Diagnostic Tools window with the Events tab selected.

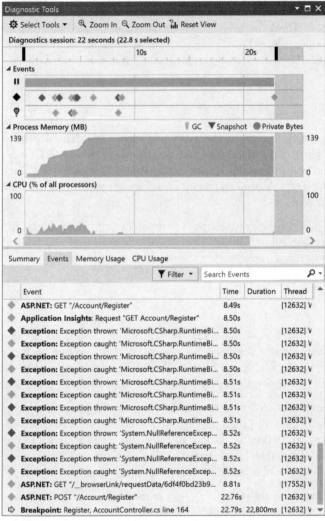

FIGURE 39-9

Each of the events tracked by IntelliTrace gets its own line at the bottom of the screen. It is also represented by a diamond in the event timeline at the top of the screen. That way you have not only information about the event, but also when it happened. From Figure 39-9 you can see that sometime after the web application started, something was clicked to trigger a request for the Account/Register page, followed (after some exceptions) by a post to Account/Register, and then the execution hit a breakpoint.

Clicking on an event reveals some additional details about it. In addition, in some cases, you will see an Activate Historical Debugging link. Clicking on that link takes you to the line of source code that generated the event. While in the source, you have access to the values of the variables as they were at the time of the event.

Visual Studio 2017 supports the ability for log files to be captured on a production server that does not have Visual Studio installed on it. A CAB file named `IntelliTraceCollection.cab` contains the necessary assemblies. The CAB file is unpacked on the production machine, and then, using a number of PowerShell commands, the IntelliTrace collector can be turned on. Now the events and calls are collected into an `.iTrace` file. When finished, the file can be sent to a development machine. Using Visual Studio to open the file causes the Diagnostic Tools window to appear.

The range of data that can be collected is quite varied. Table 39-1 lists the types of data that can be collected by IntelliTrace, along with the source for the data.

TABLE 39-1: IntelliTrace Data Collection Types

TYPE	CONTENTS	SOURCE
Performance	Function calls that exceeded a configured threshold for performance	Operations Manager for ASP.NET, System Center 2016, Microsoft Monitoring Agent
Exception Data	The full call stack for any exception raised	All sources
System Info	The specifications and settings on the system on which the log is captured	All Sources
Threads List	The threads that were used during the execution	All Sources
Test Data	The test steps and the results that were recorded for each	Test Manager
Modules	The modules that were loaded during execution, in the order in which they were loaded	All Sources

> **WARNING** *The files generated by IntelliTrace can get large. And if IntelliTrace capturing is turned on, the files are created each time you run a debugging session. In that situation, you can have multiple gigabytes of tracing information that accumulate on your development machine. So it's a good idea to keep IntelliTrace turned off until you need it.*

At the top of Figure 39-9, the Events timeline is visible. The timeline illustrates a visual history of the events recorded by IntelliTrace, including breakpoints, stepping through calls, and breaking exceptions (as opposed to those that were caught and handled). There are three rows in the timeline. The top line (with the pause icon to the left) shows the elapsed time for the debugging run. The middle line (with the diamond icon on the left) shows events that would typically appear in the Output window during the debugging process. This includes any debug messages that have been included in your application. The bottom line (with the lightbulb icon to the left) shows the IntelliTrace events that occur.

In the second row, the color of the diamonds indicates the source of the event. Red is a breakpoint being hit, yellow is when a step runs to completion, blue is for a Break All, and black is for anything that is otherwise uncategorized.

The range of time in the timeline is automatically updated as you hit breakpoints and step through your application. The intent is to keep the events filtered to a reasonably sized subset based on your current actions. In addition, the list of events below the timeline is filtered based on the timeline range at the top.

Diagnostic Tools

Visual Studio 2017 include a Diagnostic Tools window through which you can collect and view information about memory usage and CPU utilization that your application generates. The Diagnostic Tools window is activated through the Debug ⇨ Windows ⇨ Show Diagnostic Tools menu option. You can turn on or off the collection of this information through the Select Tools button in the Diagnostic Tools window, as seen in Figure 39-10.

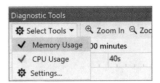

FIGURE 39-10

When Memory Usage or CPU Usage has been selected, a graph of the usage over time appears below the Debugger Events timeline, as shown in Figure 39-11.

As you change the timeline range for the diagnostics window, the view of the Memory Usage and CPU Usage graphs is modified as well. This allows you to drill into a more detailed look at the timing of your usage.

Below the timeline, the Memory Usage tab is used to access details about your memory usage. There is an icon that allows you to take a snapshot of the memory at any time you would like. Each snapshot places a row in the tab, as seen in Figure 39-12.

As Figure 39-12 shows, memory increased by more than 64MB in the 113 seconds between the snapshots. And the number of objects increased by almost 3,100. To get more details about either the change in allocated memory or the entirety of the memory being used, click on the number of bytes. This shows a list of the types that were added between the snapshots, including the number of bytes of memory allocated to each type. You can see an example in Figure 39-13.

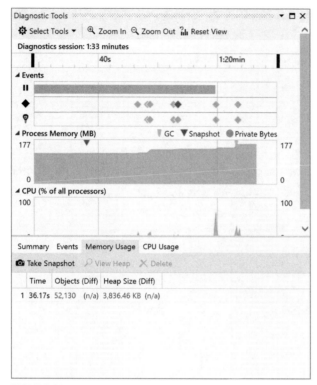

FIGURE 39-11

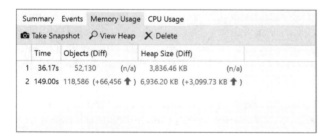

FIGURE 39-12

If desired, you can go deeper into the analysis process. By double-clicking on a type, a map of the instances of that type is displayed. You can drill down further into the line of code that actually created a particular instance. In other words, your ability to track and trace memory issues in Visual Studio has never been greater.

Snapshot #2 Heap iisexpress.exe (149.00s)						▾ ☐ ✕
Managed Memory (iisexpress.exe)			Compare to: Snapshot #1	✔ ▾	Search type names	

Object Type	Count Diff.	Size Diff. (Bytes) ▾	Inclusive Size Diff. (Bytes)	Count	Size (Bytes)	Inclusive Size (Bytes)
RuntimeType+RuntimeTypeCache	+112	+355,068	+377,520	276	739,112	793,396
SqlProviderManifest	+1	+226,400	+227,060	1	226,400	227,060
BundleResponse	+2	+179,192	+182,156	7	643,096	648,564
RuntimeType	+5,479	+154,000	+154,000	7,212	208,856	209,240
DbCompiledModel	+3	+134,404	+473,564	3	134,404	473,564
Signature	+1,122	+69,008	+69,008	2,099	129,580	129,580
CompiledRegexRunnerFactory	+9	+63,600	+79,900	30	215,316	276,040
Hashtable	+117	+41,424	+346,492	672	234,600	1,445,940
StorageMappingItemCollection	+3	+38,316	+107,380	3	38,316	107,380
List<Object>	+115	+35,620	+73,152	218	68,836	138,812
Dictionary<XmlQualifiedName, XmlSchemaObject>	+237	+34,892	+211,020	237	34,892	211,020
TdsParserStateObject	+2	+32,880	+49,424	2	32,880	49,424
ArrayList	+668	+32.540	+75.184	1.329	86.592	397,164

Paths to Root	Referenced Types			
Object Type	Reference Count Diff.	Reference Count ▾	
◢ List<Object>			
▷ CompiledRegexRunnerFactory	+27	90	
▷ Func<Object, Object>	+38	38	
▷ Func<Shaper, IEntityWrapper>	+12	12	
▷ Func<CallSite, Object, Object>	+1	7	
▷ ActionMethodDispatcher+ActionExecutor	+5	6	
▷ Func<Object>	+5	5	

FIGURE 39-13

INTELLITEST

While there is little question that creating unit tests for your code while you write it is the most effective way to generate them, the reality for most developers is that they will spend at least part of the time working on code that hasn't been written that way. As a result, there are probably large blocks of code in your application that are not covered by tests. It would take a great deal of effort, which management frequently sees as unnecessary, to go back and write the tests. To help address these problems, Visual Studio 2017 includes a tool called IntelliTest.

IntelliTest examines your source code and uses it to create a set of unit tests and test data based on the structure of your code. The goal is to ensure that every statement in your code is covered by at least one unit test.

To get started, open up one of your code files, locate a method for which you would like to generate unit tests, and then right-click to reveal the context menu. Then select IntelliTest ⇨ Run IntelliTest. After a few moments, a window similar to the one shown in Figure 39-14 appears.

In Figure 39-14, you can see that paths that were examined by IntelliTest. For each path, if you select it, the right side of the window contains the unit test that would be generated to cover the code. At the moment, this exploration hasn't been converted into an actual suite of unit tests. To do this, click on the Save button in the toolbar in Figure 39-14. The process of saving the unit test will create a unit test project if one doesn't already exist. It will then add the unit tests to a class that is named based on the class and method against which you ran the IntelliTest.

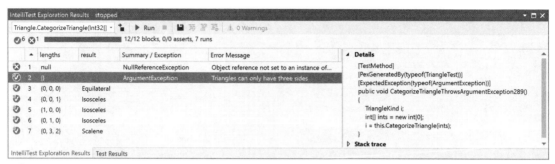

FIGURE 39-14

SUMMARY

In this chapter you saw the different features included in Visual Studio 2017 to support testing and debugging your application. You started with Web Performance Tests, which enable you to reproduce a set of requests, and then you continued with Load Tests, which help to simulate several users executing your tests simultaneously to stress your application. You also looked at automating your application with Coded UI Tests, which help to test the ways in which your user can interact with your system. Generic Tests can be used to wrap existing tests that use other mechanisms, and Ordered Tests can help you run a set of tests sequentially. You then learned how to automatically generate unit tests to cover code that didn't already test in place using IntelliTest.

40

Visual Studio Team Services

WHAT'S IN THIS CHAPTER?

➤ Visualizing source code repository changes

➤ Managing project tasks

➤ Creating and executing build configurations

WROX.COM CODE DOWNLOADS FOR THIS CHAPTER

The wrox.com code downloads for this chapter can be found at www.wrox.com by searching for this book's ISBN number (978-1-119-40458-3). The code and any related support files are located in their own folder for this chapter.

Software projects are notoriously complex; few are delivered successfully on time, within budget, and up to the wanted quality levels. As software projects increase and require larger teams, the processes involved to manage them are more complicated, and not just for the manager, but also for the developers, the testers, the architects, and the customer. Over time there have been many approaches to solving software project management problems, including quality models such as CMMI, methodologies such as RUP, or Agile Practices, Scrum, and Continuous Integration. Clearly a tool that helps support all the pieces necessary to ensure more successful software projects is (or should be) on the wish list of every development manager.

The most basic requirement for a software project, even for the smallest one-person project, is to have a source control repository. For bigger projects, more sophisticated features are needed, such as labeling, shelving, branching, and merging. Project activities need to be created, prioritized, assigned, and tracked, and at the end of the day (or better yet, even before every change is checked in to your repository) you need to ensure that everything builds and all tests pass. To make this process smoother and improve team communication, a way to report to project managers or peer developers is also required.

Microsoft provides software that enables you to do all of this in the form of Team Foundation Server (TFS). In this chapter, you'll see how version control works, how it integrates with work item tracking, and how each change can be verified to ensure it works before it is checked in. You'll also learn how project managers can see reports to get a better understanding of the project status and how they can work using Excel and Project to manage work items. The team can interact using the project's portal in SharePoint, and different stakeholders can get the information they need through the report server or configure it to get their reports directly by email.

There are two available forms of TFS. You can install TFS 2017 onto one or more servers that are under the direct control of the organization. This is the on-premise form of TFS. As well, Microsoft has a cloud-based version of TFS known as Visual Studio Team Services (VSTS, previously known as Visual Studio Online or VSO). This version has many of the same functions and features as the on-premise version. The biggest difference is that VSTS does not expose the same number of extensibility points. However, the pace of change in VSTS is quite rapid, and in many cases features that eventually will be found in TFS are implemented and available in VSTS months beforehand.

Because Visual Studio Team Services is accessible to most readers, the examples in this chapter use VSTS.

GETTING STARTED WITH GIT

Initially, TFS supported a version control system known as Team Foundation Version Control (TFVC). This is a centralized version control system where each developer has a single version of each file and historical information for the file is maintained on the server. When you branch a file, that process takes place on the server. Although this system works, it is hobbled by the fact that in order to perform relatively common version control operations (like checking history), you need to be connected to the server.

Git, on the other hand, is an open-source, distributed version control system. Each developer gets a copy of the source code on their machine and can commit changes or view history without communicating with the server. Branches in Git are much more lightweight and, again, are done without talking to the server. At some point, when the developer is ready, the local branches can be merged and published to the server.

> **NOTE** *Git as a version control system has a life outside of the Visual Studio ecosystem. It is widely used in other development environments and languages. Also, even though there is a similarity (intentionally) in names, Git is not the same thing as GitHub. Where Git is a version control system, GitHub is a service that hosts Git repositories. In other words, GitHub is a service for projects that utilize Git.*

Over time, VSTS has greatly increased its support for Git, to the point where Git repositories are the default version control system for new projects. This is not to say that TFVC is no longer available. It is. But unless you have a specific need to choose TFVC, you're better off sticking with Git, safe in the knowledge that you can always add TFVC should the need for it arise later in a project. For the examples in the rest of this chapter, we'll be using Git as the version control system, and we'll be using a Single Page Web application.

The starting point for using Git comes in two locations within Visual Studio 2017. When you are creating a project, there is an option in the New Project dialog (circled in Figure 40-1) to create a Git repository at the same time as the project.

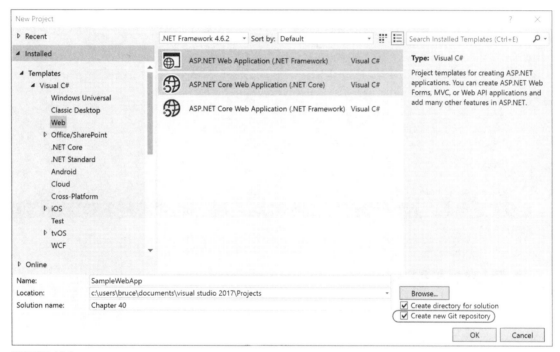

FIGURE 40-1

Alternatively, you can add an existing project to source control through a control found at the bottom right of the main IDE (circled in Figure 40-2).

In the latter case, you might get the Team Explorer presented to you with an option to push your project to Team Services, GitHub, or a remote repository. There's no need to make that choice right now unless you want to. The presumption made in this workflow is that you've been working on your project for a little while and might want to publish it to a remote repository for safekeeping.

The Team Explorer window in the heart of version control within Visual Studio 2017 is designed to allow the developer to focus on the most common tasks related to version control, but also drill into these tasks to quickly get to the functionality required. Figure 40-3 illustrates the initial view of this window.

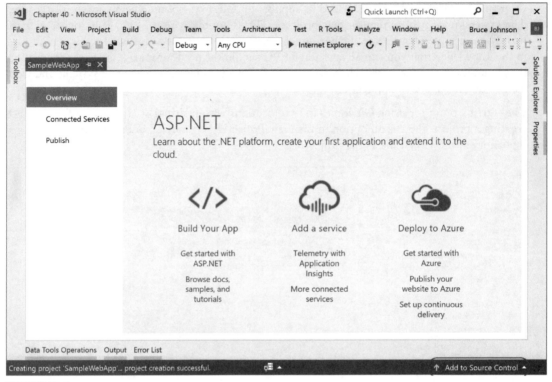

FIGURE 40-2

FIGURE 40-3

At this point, you are working solely with a local Git repository. As such, the choices you have are limited to those functions that are related to local development effort. However, to take advantage of Team Services, you need to connect to a Team Services project. To do this, click on the electrical plug icon in the tool bar. This changes the Team Explorer window to the one seen in Figure 40-4.

Here you can see your local Git repositories, along with the projects that are available in the Team Services or GitHub accounts that you've created. If you don't see your Team Services or GitHub account in the list, click on the Manage Connections link. Through that option, you can connect to Team Services or GitHub. Once you have establishing a connection to a remote repository, the number of options you have changes. Figure 40-5 shows the Team Explorer Home view after you have connected to an existing Team Services project.

FIGURE 40-4

FIGURE 40-5

VERSION CONTROL

The version control functionality associated with Team Explorer revolves around a number of very commonly used functions: committing, branching, and syncing. In this section, we look at these functions and how they are implemented through Team Explorer.

Committing

As part of its commitment to being lightweight, Git does not automatically make snapshots of your code as you edit your project. Instead, you are required to manually inform Git about the specific changes that need to be saved by committing them to your repository. A commit actually consists of the following information:

➤ A snapshot of the files saved in the commit. Git actually includes all of the files in your repository in the snapshot. This makes moving from branch to branch very fast.

➤ A reference to the parent commit. This is the commit (or commits, in the case of a merge) that immediately preceded the current commit.

➤ A comment that describes the changes in the commit. You, the person making the commit, are responsible for writing the comment.

Before files can be committed, they must first be staged. This lets Git know which updates you want to include in the next commit. Although it might seem odd that the process of staging files is manual, the benefit is that you can selectively add some files to a commit while excluding others.

Visual Studio 2017 helps make the staging process as painless as possible. If you click on the Changes option in the Home view, you will get to a screen similar to the one shown in Figure 40-6.

At the bottom of Figure 40-6, you can see that the changes (which are automatically tracked by Visual Studio) have been grouped into Staged and Unstaged collections. All of the changes start off as unstaged. You can moved them to a staged state by right-clicking on the file (or a selection of many files) and choosing the Stage option. To stage all of the files that have been changed, click on the plus sign to the right of the heading. Similarly, you can unstage files using the Unstage option in the context menu or the minus sign at the right of the heading.

FIGURE 40-6

Once all of the files have been staged or unstaged appropriately, you enter the commit message into the text box at the top of the window and click on the Commit button. This last action commits your changes to the local repository.

Branching

Technically speaking, a Git branch is just a reference that keeps track of the exact history of a set of commits. As described in the previous section, committing causes a block of changes to be snapshotted. That snapshot actually takes place within the context of a branch. There is a default branch (typically called the *master*), but you can create as many branches as you would like. When you perform a commit, you are actually adding your changes to the current branch.

To create a branch in Team Explorer, go to the Branches pane (click on Branches from the Home view). As shown in Figure 40-7, there is a list of your local repositories at the bottom of the window, along with a list of the current branches.

Right-click on branch that you wish to use as the base for the next branch and choose the New Local Branch from... option. This reveals a text box where you can specify the name of the branch (shown at the top of Figure 40-7). Provide a name for the new branch and click on the Create Branch button to create the new branch.

FIGURE 40-7

Switching between branches is a quick way to move between two different branches. In Git parlance, switching branches is performed using a *checkout* command. Right-click on the branch you wish to move to and select Checkout from the context menu. Your project is then loaded with the files from the new branch.

You see a number of other options available at the top of the Branches window. This includes the ability to merge and rebase branches. While getting into the details of what these functions do (they are relatively sophisticated Git features), be aware that should you need them, the options are available from within Team Explorer.

Syncing

All of the work done to this point has been within your local Git repository. At some point, you are likely to want to move your local commits back to the central repository. This is accomplished through the Sync option from the Team Explorer Home view.

When it comes to syncing with a remote repository, there are generally three steps that need to take place. First, you *fetch* any incoming commits. These are changes that have been made to the remote repository since the last time you synced. As part of the fetch process, you might be asked to *merge* the changes into your code. This happens if some of the remote changes impacted the same files that you have modified. The process of merging is greatly facilitated by the tooling within Visual Studio. Once the merge has been performed, it's incumbent on you to recompile and retest your application with these new updates in place. Then, finally, you *push* your changes back to the remote repository.

In the Team Explorer window, all of these actions take place within the Sync window, seen in Figure 40-8.

In the top portion of the window, a list of the incoming commits is visible. The Fetch link is available to bring those commits into your local repository. You would then need to merge them into your branch. The Pull link performs a pull, which is the equivalent of a fetch followed by a merge.

Once you are satisfied that any remote changes have been incorporated into your application, you use the Push link in the Outgoing Commits section to push your changes back to the remote repository.

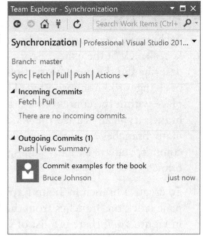

WORK ITEM TRACKING

FIGURE 40-8

Team Services enables you to manage activities using *work items*. As you see in the following sections, you can search for work items using *work item queries* and manage them using Visual Studio, Excel, or Project. Different types of work items are defined by your process template. A process template defines the building blocks of work item tracking in Team Services.

> **NOTE** *Team Services supports hierarchical work items. As a result, you can create subtasks and parent tasks. You can also create predecessor and successor links between work items, which enables you to manage task dependencies. These work item links even synchronize with Microsoft Excel and Microsoft Project, providing even greater flexibility for managing work items.*

Work Item Queries

As you can see from the list of queries shown in Figure 40-9, you can look for different work items using the work item queries from Team Explorer. The Scrum process template includes a number of different team queries, grouped into different folders. As you might expect, the number of queries available out of the box is different for the other process templates.

> **NOTE** *There is a folder of queries called Workbook Queries in the SharePoint portal, created when a new team project is added to a local TFS server. These are used to support some of the Excel workbook reports found in the Documents area.*

FIGURE 40-9

Most of the time the standard queries are sufficient, but you have the option to create new ones. If you have sufficient permissions (such as, if you're a project administrator) you can add new team queries to make them available to everyone with access to this project. If you have permission to modify the process template, you can add new team queries, so projects created with the edited templates include them. Changes in the templates don't apply to team projects already created. If you don't have permission to publish a publicly available query, you still have the ability to create a personal query that will be visible to just you.

> **NOTE** *When you create the same queries over and over from one project to another, you should add those to your process templates. Over time, there will be less need to create custom queries.*

To create a new query, click the New Query link (refer to Figure 40-9). Alternatively, you can right-click the My Queries node and select New Query.

Now you can visually design your query. In this case (as shown in Figure 40-10) you care only about the work items of the selected project, assigned to the current user and under Iteration 1. You specify this using the @Me and @Project variables. You can also specify which columns you want visible in the grid and sorting options by using the Column Options link just above the query results section. After all the criteria and columns have been set up, run the new query to see a sublist of the work items.

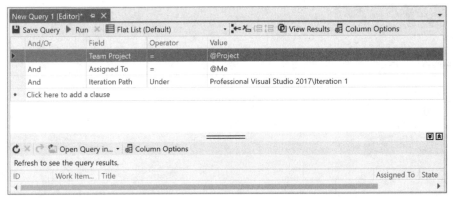

FIGURE 40-10

In Team Services, queries can take advantage of the hierarchical work item structure to show work items that are directly related, enabling you to see the impact of cutting a feature or the required tasks necessary to complete a feature. You can also show query results in a flat list, a list of work items and their direct links, or a tree of work items. Each of these is identified by a small icon that appears next to the query in the Team Explorer. And you can change the layout by using a drop-down control (refer to Figure 40-10 with the default value of Flat List). Also, you can create folder structures for your work item queries, and each query or folder can be secured separately.

> **NOTE** *Although a folder of work item queries can be secured, there is nothing stopping unauthorized users from duplicating the queries.*

Work Item Types

In the default team project template, you have seven types of work items: bug, task, user story, epic, feature, issue, and test case. Each work item has different fields depending on its type. For example, a bug has test information and a system info field, whereas a task contains effort information about estimated, remaining, and completed hours. Other project templates have different, albeit similar, work item types. All these fields are customizable at either a template or team-project level.

Adding Work Items

The basic way to add work items is via the Team ⇨ New Work Item menu option and selecting the work item type you want to add, or with the New Work Item link in the Team Explorer (refer to Figure 40-9). Regardless of how it is created, you get the Work Item entry screen (Figure 40-11). Through this screen, all the information related to the work item can be entered or modified. Along with basic description information, each work item can be related to many other TFS artifacts through links. Team Services (and TFS 2017) understands several different types of links, including

Parent, Child, Predecessor, and Successor. To add a link, click the Links tab (the third tab from the left on the right side of the window), and click the Add Link button.

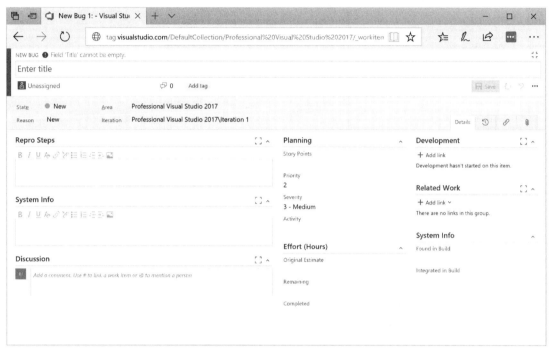

FIGURE 40-11

Work Item State

During your normal daily activity, you'll work on tasks described by work items assigned to you. Each work item is described by a simple state machine that determines the allowed next states for any given state. This state machine is a part of the work item definition and is determined by the process template. Whenever a new state is selected, you can provide a reason for the state transition. The reason field enables you to differentiate between the bugs that are active because they are new and those that are active because they have reoccurred.

BUILDS

Team Foundation Build, a part of both Team Services and TFS, has the capability to get the latest version of a solution from source Control, build the projects as configured, run tests, perform other tasks, and finally report the results and leave the output in a shared folder. When you create a repository, a default build is created as well. You can see that build, along with the results of previous builds, in the Builds window (Figure 40-12), available from the Home view of Team Explorer.

FIGURE 40-12

To create a new build definition, click the New Build Definition link. This opens a web page in Team Services (Figure 40-13) through which you can define the new build as required.

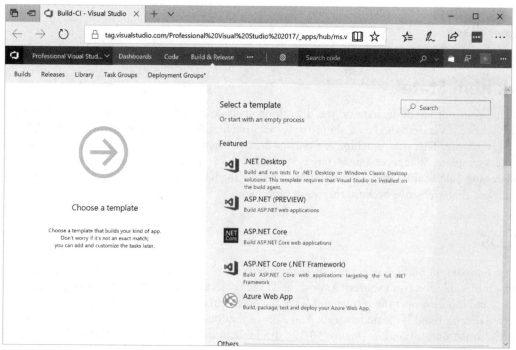

FIGURE 40-13

While it is possible to define a build so that it starts whenever a commit is performed to the remote repository, you can also start a build manually. To do so, right-click on the desired build and select Queue New Build in the context menu. After the build is queued, you can open it by double-clicking it in the My Builds list. This opens the Build Report (shown in Figure 40-14).

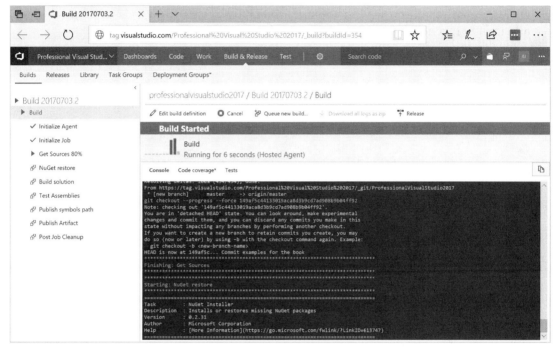

FIGURE 40-14

The screen shows the current activity in near real-time, as well as information on previous build statuses and durations. It also provides links to a number of other areas and activities related to this build.

WEB PORTAL

The last few features that have been discussed involved defining and running processes through a web site. That web site is Team Services, and the specific functionality is available through the Web Portal for your repository. This portal provides a central location for all of the artifacts associated with your project. This includes source code, work items, build definitions, build results, and test information. In other words, it's a nice, convenient, one-stop location for all of what you need to develop your application.

SUMMARY

In this chapter, you saw how Visual Studio and Visual Studio Team Services can help you get the work done by integrating version control using Git, work item tracking and management, build definitions, and build execution. All of these features can be managed either through Visual Studio 2017 or through the Team Services web site, making for a relatively seamless blending of project management functionality.

INDEX

H

I

Q

U

Y

Z